D1476790

South Asian Literature in English

South Asian Literature in English

An Encyclopedia

Edited by
Jaina C. Sanga

GREENWOOD PRESS
Westport, Connecticut • London

Library of Congress Cataloging-in-Publication Data

South Asian literature in English : an encyclopedia / edited by Jaina C.
Sanga.—1st ed.
    p. cm.
  Includes bibliographical references and index.
  ISBN 0-313-32700-9 (alk. paper)
  1. South Asian literature (English)—Encyclopedias. 2. English
literature—South Asian authors—Encyclopedias. I. Sanga, Jaina C.,
1961–
PR9570.S642S67 2004
820.9′954′03—dc22   2003025239

British Library Cataloguing in Publication Data is available.

Library of Congress Catalog Card Number: 2003025239
ISBN: 0-313-32700-9

First published in 2004

Greenwood Press, 88 Post Road West, Westport, CT 06881
An imprint of Greenwood Publishing Group, Inc.
www.greenwood.com

Printed in the United States of America

The paper used in this book complies with the
Permanent Paper Standard issued by the National
Information Standards Organization (Z39.48–1984).

10 9 8 7 6 5 4 3 2 1

For Monica

Contents

Preface

This encyclopedia covers topics related to literature written in English by authors who were either born in South Asia or who identify themselves with that region. The geographic areas that this volume focuses on are the nations of India, Pakistan, Bangladesh, and Sri Lanka.

In the global marketplace of literature, South Asian writing in English has recently received unprecedented attention. The publication of Salman Rushdie's seminal novel, *Midnight's Children* in 1981 as well as the popularity of his subsequent works, Michael Ondaatje's Booker Prize for *The English Patient* in 1992, Arundhati Roy's Booker Prize for *The God of Small Things* in 1997, Jhumpa Lahiri's Pulitzer Prize for *Interpreter of Maladies* in 2000, and V. S. Naipaul's Nobel Prize for Literature in 2003, are just a few of the notable highlights that have anchored a place for South Asian writing in English on the international literary scene.

While the novel, and to a lesser extent, the short story, are the two genres that are most widely circulated and consumed, it is important to note that there is a substantial amount of writing in English in other genres as well: poetry, drama, autobiography, and travelogues also vividly render the South Asian imagination. Contemplating the scope and limitations of each genre enables a richer, more comprehensive approach to the study of South Asian literature in English.

The South Asian experience imagined in English rehearses numerous salient characteristics. Many works call attention to the idea of Empire and interrogate the colonial moments of the subcontinents vertiginous history. The struggle for Independence, the contentious saga of the Partition of India and Pakistan in 1947, the mass migration of Hindus and Muslims on both sides of the newly created borders, and the ensuing violence, have found provocative expression in the literature of India and Pakistan. The ethnic tensions in Sri Lanka, the long-standing conflict between the Sri Lankan government and the Tamil Tiger rebels that claimed more than 60,000 lives and displaced more than 1.5 million people from their homes have found voice in Sri Lankan literature. A brutal civil war fought for independence from Pakistan has figured in the Bangladeshi literary imagination. Ideas of nationalism and attempts to define the new nations have also been important concerns. The vulgar atrocities prompted by the caste system, the rampant communalism that continues to thwart secularism, and the growing sensitivity to the rights of women and disenfranchised minorities are vital issues that are consistently and systematically represented in the literature. In some works, social and political issues and events are writ large, presented on a grand scale in generational sagas; in other works, they are miniaturized, distilled into images that depict the mundane business of everyday living.

Much of the writing focuses on the issue of identity, often juxtaposing notions of public and private, collective and individual, or local and foreign, in an attempt to expose the points of collision that mark the exegesis of hybrid constructions. Religion and politics begin to matter profoundly as discussions of progress are confronted with ancient traditions. South Asian authors writing in English tend to favor a secular humanist perspective: when religious orthodoxy is pitted against the changing social circumstances of an increasingly globalizing world, we see the emergence of a new type of identity—an identity that is built on tolerance, suspicious of undue past veneration, and embodied in the perspectives of an enlightened humanism. The notion of identity is an important focus in the poetry of the region: In the work of women poets, especially, there is a range of highly volatile emotive expression that attempts to describe women's issues in the sociopolitical construction of the nation. In the resultant complexity of some of their verse, we witness the extent to which identity is implicated in ethnic-, class-, and gender-based dissonances.

For many of the writers, particularly those who have left their native lands, the act of writing becomes a way to reclaim their homeland, and the notion of memory figures prominently in such narratives. The immigrant's story has in fact proved to be a fecund subject, and much like the Irish, Jewish, Chinese, and Polish writers, South Asians, too, have attempted to record the predicament of displacement, celebrating and/or questioning the act of straddling two cultures and coping with new worlds. These narratives are not merely stereotypical comic descriptions of immigrants, but rather realistic reflections of characters who are flawed, everyday people, and whose individual trials and triumphs help us see the complexity of the immigrant condition.

The settings of the narratives are as varied as the themes. Hari Kunzru's novel, *The Impressionist,* for instance, stretches from the Rajasthan desert, Agra, Fatehpur, and Bombay to London, Oxford, and finally to the remote West African landscape. Hanif Kureishi's work is set primarily in Britain. David Davidar's *The House of Blue Mangoes* is set in the lush, tropical spaces of southern India. Jhumpa Lahiri's short stories take place in urban American as well as Indian settings. Kamila Shamsie's *In a City by the Sea* is set in Karachi. Salman Rushdie's *Shame* is obviously set in Pakistan, but the narrator goes through great pains to tell us that the country is not Pakistan at all but an altogether fictitious place. Yet others, such as R. K. Narayan, create wholly imaginary locales for their stories.

Although this encyclopedia is clearly limited to South Asian writing in English, it is necessary to point out that the various writers use the English language in distinct ways. Many of the writers incorporate the syntax of everyday speech, or use Indianized words and phrases in their texts. Often, in an effort to authenticate place, character, or experience, writers parlay a certain subcontinental English diction that is marked by a specific cadence. Some writers prefer to use a standard, formal version of the language, while others experiment with the normative register and attempt to use the language in brave new ways.

The popularity of South Asian writing in English can be attributed to the fact that there is a definite context for this literature. The monumental rise of South Asian novelists in particular, has, appropriately enough, been compared to the burgeoning of the Latin American novelists of the 1970s and 1980s. The trinity represented by Gabriel Garcia Marquez, Carlos Fuentes, and Mario Vargas Llosa epitomized the novel tradition because they were regarded as the unofficial historians for their countries where political upheaval and military dictatorship had silenced individual voices. South Asian writers in English can be seen as the alternative interpreters of the subcontinents many histories. Their representations matter profoundly as they enable us to envision the various registers and textures of experiences of a vast and complicated region. Their narratives provide relevant commentaries on polemical cultural and political issues, provoking an assessment of the role of literature in imagining the nation.

What about the future of South Asian writing in English? Will South Asian writers be able to sustain their imaginative paradigms and persist in producing writing of high quality? And, is this a literature that will continue to influence future generations around the world? In recent years, the overwhelming literary and commercial success of the South Asian novel has meant big prizes and big advances for writers and huge profits for publishers. Literature in other genres still lags far behind, although it is gradually getting noticed in academic circles. While it may be difficult to judge the staying power of all the individual writers or to judge the long-term relevance of particular works, it is obvious, even from a cursory appraisal, given the brilliance and sophistication of this literature thus far, not to mention the sheer volume of on-going imaginative production, that South Asian literature will continue to make its mark on the world literary scene. Within South Asia, generally speaking, economic development has had a positive impact on cultural development, and especially during the past five decades, South Asia has generated more and more intellectuals who have turned their attention to artistic expression. As for diasporic South Asians, the trend some 20 years ago was to pursue professions in science and engineering; now, however, the trend has changed, howsoever marginally, and there is an increasing number of second generation immigrants who are encouraged by their parents to study the arts, and professions such as writing and filmmaking are less often considered perfunctory. Moreover, the literary audience around the world has become, generally, more globally aware, so that it is possible, for instance, to discuss a phenomenon such as "Bollywood"—as Manil Suri, Vikram Chandra, and others have done—and not be dismissed as totally incomprehensible.

The point of this volume is to provide a systematic and engaging discussion of some of the relevant literary topics so as to help beginning students as well as more advanced academic scholars gain a further understanding of South Asian literature. Since English literature in South Asia has gained prominence and momentum particularly after the end of British colonialism of the region, that is, post 1947, a majority of the entries focus on contemporary authors and literary issues. I have made a conscious effort, however, to include a few pertinent entries that describe pre-Independence subjects—"East India Company," "Minute on Indian Education," "Sir William Jones," "British Raj," "Imperial Myth," and so on—in order to provide a more contextual approach to the study of South Asian literature in English.

This encyclopedia includes entries on novelists, novels, and cinematic adaptations of novels, as well as poets, dramatists, autobiographers, short-story writers, theoreticians, theoretical terms, themes, genres, literary movements, and key historical events. All the entries are arranged alphabetically, and vary in length from 200 to 3,500 words, depending on the nature and complexity of the topic. Each entry includes a thorough discussion of the topic, and, in the case of authors, each entry includes a biographical sketch as well as an assessment of their major works and themes. All the entries conclude with a "Further Reading" section that is meant to direct the reader to additional sources about the topic. A "Selected Bibliography" at the end of the volume is divided into three sections: the first includes anthologies that feature South Asian writing; the second contains general, critical secondary works; and the third provides a list of useful journals and periodicals.

Although there are several reference books that include discussions of South Asia, they are quite different in scope and purpose from this one. For example, *The Cambridge Encyclopedia of India, Pakistan, Bangladesh, Sri Lanka, Nepal, and Bhutan,* edited by Francis Robinson (Cambridge, Eng. and New York: Cambridge UP, 1989) is a general reference volume on the region and does not have a specific literary focus. Books such as Daya De Silva's *Sri Lanka Since Independence: A Reference Guide to the Literature* (New Delhi: Navrang, 1992), although literary in focus, are area specific and do not address the South Asian region as a whole. The Sahitya Akademi (India's official academy of letters and literature) does publish excellent lists and references on South Asian literature, for instance, Amaresh Datta's *Sahitya Akademi Encyclopedia A-to-Z* (New Delhi, 1987), but again, these are quite different in scope and purpose from the current volume. This encyclopedia effectively complements *South Asian Novelists in English: An A to Z Guide* (Westport: Greenwood, 2003), which I have edited; however, this volume attempts a wider focus by incorporating poets, dramatists, films, theoreticians, and historical moments into the grand narrative.

I am acutely aware of the attendant problematics and limitations of this encyclopedia. Confining this volume to literature in English inadvertently posits the superiority of English over other indigenous languages. It is not as though South Asian literature written in the host of regional languages is less important; in fact, there is a recognizably long and sophisticated tradition of literature written in languages other than English. This volume does not intend to subvert the regional literatures, but rather attempts to recognize the prevalence of English as a modern, South Asian language. Moreover, South Asia is hardly a monolithic entity, and a volume such as this does run the risk of collapsing disparate identities and imposing an artificial sense of commonality amongst distinct agendas. However, the regions shared history of colonialism, and the fact that this literature is written in English does indeed provide a basis to explore some meaningful connections. To a large extent, the project of putting together an encyclopedia rehearses the Orientalist enterprise of cataloguing and organizing information; I am critically conscious of how such an endeavor is implicated in the process of canonization. Also, it must be emphasized that South Asian literature in English is by no means a tidy, compact category; it is rather a protean phenomenon, constantly evolving and shifting its parameters. This encyclopedia does not claim to be all-inclusive: lack of space and time has prevented the inclusion of numerous entries. Despite its limitations, I hope this volume gives the reader a sense of the fascinating trajectory of the South Asian literary tradition.

I am immensely grateful to all the contributors, scattered around the world, who have written entries for this encyclopedia. Reading and editing their entries has significantly enriched my own perspectives of South Asian literature. My sincere thanks to Dr. George Butler, senior editor at Greenwood Press for his support and guidance; to Dr. Emmanuel Nelson, series advisor, for his friendship and encouragement; and to the publication, production, and marketing staff at Greenwood Press for all their hard work with this project. Thanks to Dr. Satchit Srinivasan for his help in researching South Asian history, and to photo expert Lisa Kirchner for procuring the fabulous photographs for this encyclopedia. With humble gratitude, I acknowledge Dr. Paul Love, director of the Study Center for Indian Literature in English and Translation (SCILET) at The American College in Madurai, and Dr. Niti Sampat-Patel, professor of English and film studies at St. Xavier's College, Mumbai, for serving on the editorial board of this encyclopedia. Their advice and expertise, as well as their meticulous reading of the manuscript, has made this a better book.

Chronology

Major Historical and Political Events

Circa 2500–1800 B.C.	The Indus Valley civilization flourishes in the northwest region of India, along the Indus River, in an area roughly bounded by the modern cities of Karachi, Islamabad, Delhi, and Ahmadabad. Mohenjo-daro and Harappa are its principal sites; in addition, there are scores of other settlements.
Circa 1500 B.C.	Indo-Aryan people enter the subcontinent from the northwest and settle in Punjab and the Ganges River valley. Much of modern Indian culture and religion stems from the Sanskritic myths and literature of this era, which are still sacrosanct today. A Brahmanic civilization grows over 2,000 years; this becomes the basis of Hinduism.
Circa 900–520 B.C.	A rich outpouring of epic literature and mythology, including the Mahabharata, the Ramayana, and the Vedas and the Puranas, all of which form the core of Hinduism and its offshoots.
327–325 B.C.	Alexander the Great penetrates the northwestern frontier of India and crosses the Indus, but does not make much of an impression. His troops ultimately mutiny at the prospect of taking on the Nanda dynasty's prodigious army and force Alexander to return. The only major Greek influence in the area is in the Gandhara region (in modern Afghanistan).
325–200 B.C.	Chandragupta Maurya overthrows the Nanda dynasty and establishes the Mauryan dynasty, which will prove to have very far reaching consequences, both for India and much of Central and East Asia. The Mauryans unify most of India, with Ashoka's empire stretching from Kandahar (in modern Afghanistan) to Bengal and from the northern tip of modern Kashmir to the Nilgiri hills in southern India. Ashoka embraces Buddhism and is responsible for its spread.

Circa 200 B.C.– 300 A.D.	Imperial disintegration is accompanied by a blooming of cultural integration and artistic, scientific, and commercial innovation. Literary examples include Patanjali's *Yogasutra,* the *Manusmriti* (Manu's code of law), Vatsyana's *Kamasutra,* and Kautilya's *Arthashashtra.* Indian culture and commerce begins spreading to Southeast Asia, to the states of modern Malaysia, Indonesia, Vietnam, and Cambodia.
Circa 300– 500	The Gupta dynasty integrates much of northern and Central India into an imperium. There is a tremendous flowering of art, architecture, sculpture, and literature. Seminal advances in medicine and mathematics (including the introduction of the modern so-called Arabic numerals, the widespread use of the decimal system, and the invention of the zero) will have profound effects on the world.
Circa 650	Arab traders introduce Islam to India.
1192	The first Muslim kingdom, the Delhi Sultanate is established.
1498	Vasco de Gama, a Portuguese explorer, lands in Calicut.
1505–1510	The Portuguese arrive in Colombo, Ceylon, marking the beginning of European interest in the island.
	Portuguese invaders take over Goa, a seaport on the western coast of India. Goa remains in Portuguese control until 1961.
1526	Emperor Babur invades India from Afghanistan. The Mughal Empire is founded.
1613	British East India Company establishes a trading outpost at Surat. Subsequent trading centers open in Bombay (1661) and Calcutta (1691). The Dutch (1609) and the French (1674) also set up trading outposts in India.
1629	Mughal emperor Shah Jehan begins to build the Taj Mahal at Agra. The monument, a tomb for his wife, Mumtaz, takes 22 years to complete.
1757	British commander Robert Clive defeats the Nawab of Bengal at the decisive Battle of Plassey. The British East India Company controls Bengal, India's most populous province, as well as important areas of the Deccan, and launches the British Empire in India. The British exploit Indian labor, commercial and agricultural products, and limit India's access to world trade with tariffs.
1772	Warren Hastings is appointed first Governor-General of British India. The British rely on superior military power, as well as bribery, extortion, political manipulation of regional chieftains, and the growing disunity among smaller Indian kingdoms to subjugate the entire subcontinent.

1815   British win control over Ceylon and start bringing in Tamil laborers from southern India to work on the tea, coffee, and coconut plantations.

1830   The first Indian indentured laborers are exported to Mauritius, an island in the Indian Ocean. In 1838, following the abolition of slavery, thousands of Indians are brought to the British Caribbean to work in the sugarcane, coffee, and timber plantations. Indians settle mainly in Guyana (British Guiana), Trinidad and Tobago, Guadeloupe, Jamaica, Suriname (Dutch Guiana), and Maritinique. Today, about 50 percent of the total population of countries such as Guyana and Trinidad are the descendants of Indian indentured laborers.

From the 1870s onward, Indians are taken as indentured laborers to build the railway in eastern and southern Africa, and from 1879 onward, Indian laborers are sent to Fiji to work in the sugarcane plantations.

1835   British institute education reforms in India. English is adopted as the medium of instruction and the language of Indian law courts. The British use the educational system to create an indigenous elite of civil servants to help them administer the vast country. Indians begin to fear not only the loss of political power but the loss of their cultural identity as well.

1839   First Opium War in China: The British-owned East India Company has been shipping Indian-grown opium to China since 1637. The fertile riverbed of the Ganges has the most suitable conditions for growing opium. The effects of the opium trade on Chinese society are devastating as millions of people become addicted to the drug. In 1729, the Chinese emperor, Yung Cheng, tries to ban opium from entering China, but is unsuccessful. After the first Opium War, the Chinese are forced to pay a large indemnity when they are defeated by the British. Things come to a head again, in 1857, in the second Opium War. China incurs heavy losses again and several towns and provinces are acceded to Britain, including, ultimately, the takeover by the British of the prized Hong Kong.

1857   The Sepoy Mutiny (First War of Independence) begins near Delhi, fueled by general unrest and a large-scale conspiracy among sepoys, the native troops employed by the British. Despite its failure, the mutiny marks a symbolic moment in India's impetus for self-government.

The East India Company, which has been having many disputes with the British government, is finally dissolved and the British Crown takes direct control of India. Covertly, though, the Company's authority in India continues within several social and political arenas.

1876   Queen Victoria is declared empress of India.

1885   The Indian National Congress is founded, one of many organizations dedicated to the struggle against British rule. Several prominent Hindus and Muslims support the Indian National Congress, spreading the message of political awareness and national unification.

1906   The Muslim League is founded, with British support, diverting influential Muslims from unified support for the Indian National Congress and dividing the independence struggle.

1914–1918   World War I: India sends troops to support the British in Europe.

1919   The Treaty of Versailles ends World War I.

The Rowlatt Act is passed in India: this authorizes the British government to imprison any person without proper trial and conviction in a court of law.

Mahatma Gandhi organizes the first civil disobedience campaign. Gandhi's philosophy is based on *ahinsa,* nonviolence, and he becomes the champion of India's fight for independence.

The Jallianwalla Baag massacre at Amritsar, where General Dyer commands troops to open fire at a crowd of unarmed Indians who have gathered to peacefully demonstrate against the British presence in India, further angers Indian nationalists.

1942   Mahatma Gandhi inaugurates the Quit India movement, and his political party, the Congress Party, is outlawed.

1946   British concede self-rule to India provided the Congress Party and the Muslim League are able to compromise. The idea of partitioning India and forming a separate nation for Muslims receives considerable attention.

1947   Lord Mountbatten, the last British viceroy, transfers power to India on August 15. Jawaharlal Nehru is appointed the first prime minister of India.

A predominantly Muslim state, comprising East and West Pakistan is established with Muhammad Ali Jinnah as the president. The two regions are separated from each other by about 1,500 km of Indian territory. Hindus and Sikhs in West Pakistan migrate east into India, and some Muslims head predominantly west across the newly created borders. There is unprecedented violence on both sides of the border.

The issue of Kashmir is hotly contested and ultimately remains unresolved. Under the partition plan administered by the British, Kashmir is free to accede to India or Pakistan. Although Muslims are in majority in the region of Kashmir, the Hindu maharaja, Hari Singh, elects to accede to India and signs over allegiance to the Indian government in return for military aid. Pakistan claims that Kashmir should be a part of Pakistan since over 70 percent of the population in the state is Muslim.

1948	Ceylon gains independence.
1950	India becomes a republic on January 26, and the constitution is formally adopted.
1953–1959	There is an increasing demand to separate states along linguistic lines. Language riots erupt in Bombay. Gujarat and Maharashtra become separate states.
1956	Solomon Bandaranaike is elected leader of Ceylon on a wave of Sinhalese nationalism. Sinhala is made the official language and other measures are introduced to bolster Sinhalese and Buddhist sentiments. In 1959, Bandaranaike is assassinated by a Buddhist monk. He is succeeded by his widow, Srimavo, who continues the project of nationalization. She is overthrown in 1965 by the Opposition United National Party but returns to power in 1970. The Tamil minority is increasingly disenfranchised from the majority Sinhalese population due to an oppressive imposition of affirmative action that actively discriminates against the Tamils. This ultimately leads to a violent (and still ongoing) civil war.
1962	India goes to war with China over disputed northern territory. India is comprehensively trounced.
1965	India goes to war with Pakistan when Pakistani troops launch a covert offensive across the border into Indian-administered Jammu and Kashmir. India retaliates by crossing the international border at Lahore.
1966	Indira Gandhi, daughter of Jawaharlal Nehru, becomes prime minister of India.
1971	East Pakistan struggles for emancipation from Pakistan. After a violent civil war, in which India aids East Pakistan, the independent nation of Bangladesh is formed with Sheikh Mujibur Rahman as the leader.
	Zulfikar Ali Bhutto becomes chief martial law administrator of West Pakistan.
1972	Ceylon changes its name to Sri Lanka. Buddhism is declared the country's official religion, further antagonizing the Tamil minority. In 1976, an organization, Liberation Tigers of Tamil Eelam (LTTE), is formed as tensions increase in Tamil-dominated areas to the north and east. There is ongoing violent conflict between the LTTE and the Sri Lankan government.
1974	India tests its first nuclear device.
1975	Sheikh Mujibur Rahman becomes president of Bangladesh, but the political situation worsens and he is assassinated in a military coup. Martial law is imposed until 1979. In 1982, General Ershad assumes power, but his attempts to instate Islam as the state religion are met with serious opposition.

1975	Indian Prime Minister Indira Gandhi is found guilty of electoral malpractice. Her government declares a state of emergency that includes the arrest of opposition leaders, press censorship, and other contentious programs.
1977	General Mohammad Zia ul-Haq of Pakistan seizes power, arrests Bhutto and declares martial law. In 1979, Bhutto is hanged after disputed conviction for conspiring to commit a political murder.
1985–1990	Initial attempts at peace talks between the Sri Lankan government and the LTTE fail.
	Government forces push the LTTE back into the northern city of Jaffna and create new councils for Tamil areas in the north and east. The government agrees to admit an Indian peace-keeping force. After getting bogged down in the fighting, however, Indian troops leave. Violence between the Sri Lankan army and the separatists escalates.
1988	Pakistan's General Zia-ul-Haq and many senior military officers are killed in a plane crash. Benazir Bhutto, daughter of General Zulfikar Bhutto, and her Pakistan People's Party win the majority vote in the general elections. After several turbulent years, and after the term of Prime Minister Nawaz Sharif in 1993, Benazir Bhutto becomes prime minister for the second time when her party wins the general elections. In 1997, however, Sharif's Pakistan Muslim League party wins the elections by a landslide margin, and Sharif resumes power until he is deposed in 1999.
1989	Kashmir insurgency: Armed resistance to Indian rule breaks out in Kashmir with some separatist groups calling for an independent nation, pledging allegiance to neither India nor Pakistan, and others calling for union with Pakistan. India accuses Pakistan of supplying weapons to the militants.
1990	General Ershad of Bangladesh resigns following mass protests. The following year Ershad is convicted and jailed for corruption and illegal possession of weapons. Begum Khaleda Zia, widow of President Zia Rahman, becomes prime minister.
1992	Babri Masjid, a mosque in Ayodhya, a city in northern India, is demolished by Hindu mobsters who claim the site is sacred since it was the birthplace of one of the Hindu gods; violent Hindu-Muslim riots erupt in several cities.
1993	Sri Lankan president Premadasa is killed in a LTTE bomb attack.

President Kumaratunga comes to power in 1994, pledging to end the war. Peace talks open with LTTE, but there is little success. LTTE resumes its bombing campaign and the government launches a major offensive, driving separatists out of Jaffna. In 1996, a state of emergency is declared after the LTTE bomb Colombo, the capital city. The violence continues until 1998 when the Tamil Tigers bomb Sri Lanka's holiest Buddhist site.

1998   India conducts underground nuclear tests in the western desert state of Rajasthan near the border with Pakistan. In response, Pakistan conducts six tests in Baluchistan. The nuclear arms race has begun. Both nations also have long-range missiles. The international community heavily criticizes both nations as fears of a nuclear confrontation grow. The United States, Japan, and several European countries order economic sanctions against India and Pakistan, and billions of dollars in loans, aid, and trade are in jeopardy.

1999   Kargil War: India launches air strikes against Pakistani-backed forces that have infiltrated the mountains in Indian-administered Kashmir, north of Kargil. Pakistan insists that these are not state-sanctioned forces but rather *freedom fighters* fighting for the liberation of Indian-administered Jammu and Kashmir. Under pressure from the international community, the conflict ends, with both sides claiming victory. Pakistani prime minister Nawaz Sharif orders the infiltrating forces to withdraw.

In October, General Pervez Musharraf stages a military coup in Pakistan, deposing elected prime minister Nawaz Sharif. Although the coup is condemned by the international community, which calls for elections and a prompt return to civilian government, General Musharraf's assumption of power is sanctioned by the supreme court of Pakistan for a period of three years.

2000   There is ongoing strife between Bangladesh and Pakistan. Pakistan claims that during the 1971 war 26,000 people died, whereas Bangladesh says nearly three million were killed. Bangladesh wants Pakistan to apologize for the alleged genocide and provide monetary compensation.

2001   India, irritated by the sudden friendship between the United States and Pakistan following the September 11 attacks on the World Trade Center and the Pentagon, points out that while Pakistan might now be helping the United States fight terrorism on the Afghan front, it is simultaneously supporting terrorism on its own borders with India.

On December 13, suicide bombers attack the Indian parliament in New Delhi, killing 14 people. Indian officials blame the deadly attack on Islamic terrorists supported by Pakistan.

2002   In a peace initiative sponsored by Norway, the Sri Lankan government and Tamil Tiger rebels sign a permanent ceasefire agreement. The rebels drop their demand for a separate state and agree to share power with the government. Minority Tamils have autonomy in the mainly Tamil-speaking north and east. Despite the peace talks, there are some complex issues that remain outstanding, and the Tamil Tigers claim they are compromising their position.

2003   There is unprecedented economic growth in India. India's relations with China improve.

Pakistan struggles politically as it attempts to curb its support for the Taliban. Pakistan's president Pervez Musharraf, recognizing that an Islamic path for the nation is not sustainable, works toward dismantling fundamentalist strongholds.

Prime Minister Atal Bihar Vajpayee of India and president Musharraf agree to negotiate a compromise. For the first time, peace between the two nations seems possible.

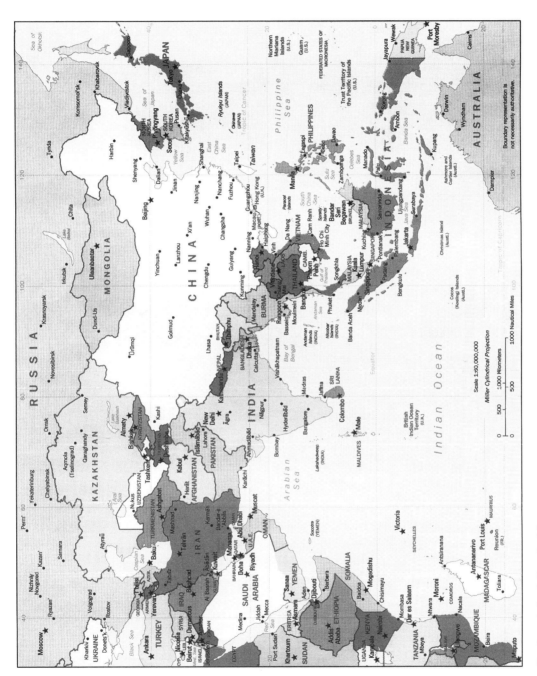

Southern Asia. © Bunche Library.

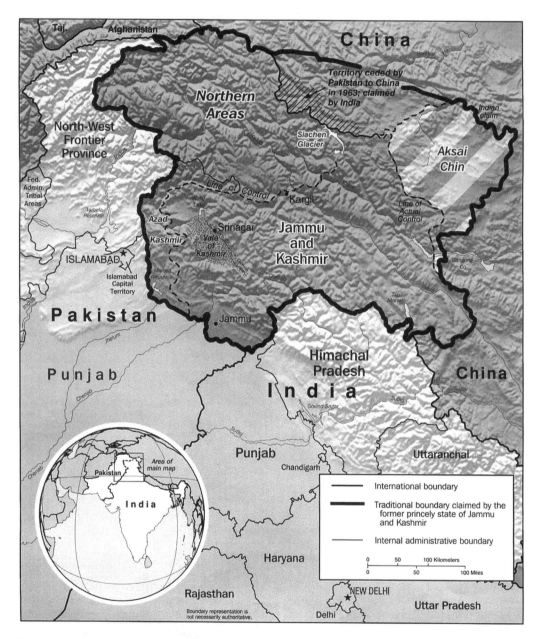

Disputed area of Kashmir. © Bunche Library.

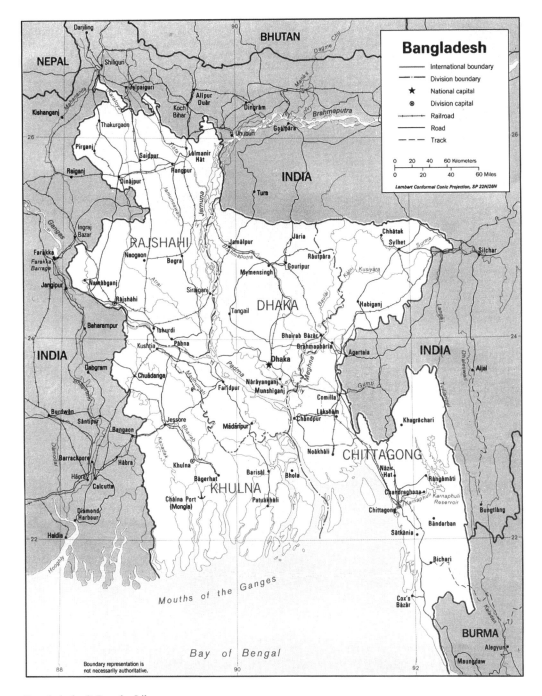

Bangladesh. © Bunche Library.

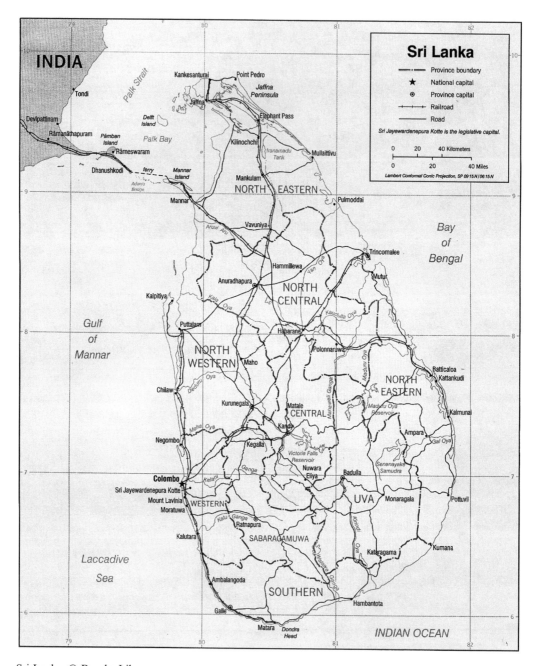

Sri Lanka. © Bunche Library.

Entries by Topic

Drama

Literary and Historical Terms and Issues

Literary Theorists

Novel/Film Adaptations

Novelists

Novels

Poetry

Short-Story Collections

A

Afternoon Raag by Amit Chaudhuri

Afternoon Raag, Amit Chaudhuri's second book, was published in 1993. Set in Oxford, Bombay, and Calcutta, it is written wholly in first person. The protagonist is an Indian student studying at Oxford. His parents live in Bombay but relocate permanently to Calcutta toward the end of the narrative. Some of the episodes set in Oxford provide desultory accounts of the student's romantic complications (he is involved with two women students). Others describe his interactions with fellow students, including another male Indian student who has a passion for the English language. There are also short sections describing the student's daily routine, the local neighborhood, his flat, and his interactions with other (presumably British) people in Oxford.

The episodes set in Bombay describe life in his parents' suburban apartment, the neighbors, the visits of his music teacher, his mother's early morning music practice sessions, and the local neighborhood. Interspersed within this are reminiscences of his parents' early lives and origins in what is now Bangladesh, and of his sessions with his music teacher (now dead) in India. In at least two chapters, the narrator muses about the nature and principles of Indian classical music and the essentially meandering, extempore, discursive nature of its core oeuvre, the Alaap, and implicitly draws comparisons with the highly structured, and predetermined nature of Western music. The book itself begins with a dedication to a musician, presumably Chaudhuri's own music teacher, in the form of a poem.

Afternoon Raag stands out from the author's other work as the only book to be written wholly in first person. In this context, and also when read in sequence after *A Strange and Sublime Address,* it comes across as drawing deeply from the author's own experiences. In contrast to an exuberant child's eye view of things in his first novel, *Afternoon Raag* adopts a rather melancholy and adult perspective. The muted theme of a mild but not uncomfortable displacement explored in the earlier book is developed in a darker fashion in the context of the protagonist's apparent homesickness in Oxford. The descriptions of Indian music serve to underscore the author's own trademark writing style, which uses seemingly desultory descriptions of quotidian life, reminiscences and observations, to draw detailed and loving pictures of his characters. *Afternoon Raag* was published to much critical acclaim and won the Southern Arts Literature prize and the Encore award for best second novel.

Born in 1962 in Calcutta, Amit Chaudhuri was raised in Bombay and graduated from University College, London. He received his doctorate from Balliol College, Oxford. Chaudhuri lives in Calcutta with his wife and daughter. Chaudhuri has published four novels and a short-story collection and has written for several well-known publications such as *The Guardian* and the *London Review of Books*. He has been the recipient of several awards for his writing, including the Betty Trask Prize, the Commonwealth Writer's Prize for Eurasia, and the LA Times award. Chaudhuri has also edited the *Picador Book of Modern Indian Literature* (2001).

Padma Chandrasekaran

Further Reading

Apte, Poornima. "Book Review." *Desi Journal: Chronicles of the Indian Diaspora.* (2002). 2 Sept. 2002 <http://www.desijournal.com/book.asp?articleid=17>.

Kakutani, Michiko. "Books of the Times." *New York Times* 26 Feb. 1999: 48–49.

Truax, Alice. "Book Review Desk: The Allure of the Everyday." *New York Times* 28 March 1999: 12–13.

Ahmad, Aijaz

Aijaz Ahmad is well known for bringing Marxism as a primary mode of analysis into the field of postcolonial and South Asian studies. In 1992, Ahmad published his controversial *In Theory: Classes, Nations, Literatures,* followed by the lesser-known *Lineages of the Present* in 1996. In addition, Ahmad has also edited *Ghazals of Ghalib* (1971) and has collaborated with Fred Pfeil and Modhumita Roy in the forthcoming collection of the writings of literary critic Michael Sprinker, entitled *A Singular Voice.*

In Theory can be described as a collection of interlinked essays, but it also seeks to bring to the forefront the importance of Marxism as a hermeneutic category, especially in the field of postcolonial studies. Ahmad views postcolonialism's dalliance with poststructuralism with profound skepticism arguing that the marginalization of Marxism in the field of colonial discourse analysis engenders a failure to adequately focus on "the determinate set of mediations which connect the cultural productions of a period with other kinds of productions and political processes" (*In Theory* 5). Ahmad then proceeds to examine key figures in postcolonial theory through the analytical schema of Marxist "cultural historiography" (*In Theory* 5).

Although Ahmad's analysis of Edward Said and Frederic Jameson has broad significance to the way colonial discourse analysis functions in South Asia, it is not immediately relevant to a South Asian context. This analysis of *In Theory*, therefore, focuses only on those aspects of the text that examine the presence/absence of Marxist thought in a specifically South Asian scenario. Two essays in *In Theory* are particularly germane to an understanding of South Asian literature and culture: "Salman Rushdie's *Shame*" and "Indian Literature: Notes Toward the Definition of a Category."

In his analysis of Salman Rushdie's 1983 novel *Shame,* Ahmad argues that Rushdie's novel elicits a favorable response from the Western world in which it is produced and by whom it is consumed because it answers to every thematic preoccupation assigned to an "authentic" Third World text: "representations of colonialism, nationhood, post-coloniality, the typology of rulers, their powers, corruptions, and so forth" (*In Theory* 124). Because these thematic preoccupations locate a certain type of text as the authentic repository of Third World literary production, Ahmad claims that in *Shame* the "experience of . . . a ruling elite . . . is presented, in the rhetorical stance of the book, as the experience of a 'country' " (140).

With the above argument in mind, Ahmad also challenges the construction of the category "Indian Literature." In this essay, Ahmad addresses his difficulty with the deployment of the arbitrary designation "Third World Literature" that erases the specificity of historical and material conditions within which this literature is produced. To demonstrate the inappropriateness of such a category, Ahmad points out that he "cannot [even] confidently speak, as a theoretically coherent category, of an *'Indian'* Literature" let alone "Third World Literature" (*In Theory* 243).

Arguing that Indian literature, as a body of work, is far too diverse to be situated as a singular unit of literary classification, Ahmad claims that Indian literature can instead only be characterized by its "multilinguality" and "polyglot fluidity" (*In Theory* 248). In order to adequately deploy the term "Indian Literature" as a theoretical and critical category of similarity as well as of difference, a new method of teaching as well as studying Indian literature is required: a method that is comparative, rather than hierarchical, in structure and application.

Lineages of the Present: Ideology and Politics in Contemporary South Asia was first published in India in 1996 and then republished in England in 2001. Like *In Theory,* this book is also "a series of interlocking essays" (Ahmad, *Lineages* ix) that ranges in its thematic and chronological contents from the Partition of India in 1947 to the destruction of the Babri Mosque in 1992. Ahmad seeks to uncover how "the lineages of historical time that went into the making of a present remain a sedimented part . . . of that present" (Ahmad, *Lineages* x). For example, in his essay on Partition entitled "Tryst with Destiny," Ahmad argues that Partition was not a historically isolated agent of cataclysm but part of a long concatenation of events that regularly disrupted the "civilities of the politics of equality" (Ahmad, *Lineages* xii). Ahmad, thus, holds the Muslim League as well as the Indian National Congress culpable for the emergence of Partition. In a later essay, Ahmad examines the career of Maulana Abdul Kalam Azad in the context of Independence and Partition and argues that however flawed a political leader Azad might have

been, he should be remembered for his commitment to secularism and for his aspirations toward "a culturally composite India" (Ahmad, *Lineages* 102).

Because a large part of *Lineages of the Present* reviews the dominance of the right in South Asia, Ahmad also examines the growth of right-wing military and religious power in Pakistan. The essay entitled "Democracy and Dictatorship in Pakistan, 1971–80" remains relevant even today in its astute observation on the central role that Pakistan inhabits in U.S. overseas strategy. Cautioning, "imperialism may develop a serious stake in the continuation of a military regime," Ahmad also forecasts the possibility of "radical-nationalist" revolutions in Afghanistan and Iran engendering similar "mass movements" within Pakistan (Ahmad, *Lineages* 59).

Although Ahmad claims *In Theory* to be the extent of his entanglement with literary criticism, some essays in *Lineages of the Present,* most notably the essay entitled "In the Mirror of Urdu: Recompositions of Nation and Community, 1947–65," take up the theme of literary writing in extensive detail. Ahmad argues that Urdu engineered an identity amongst its literary practitioners that went beyond the politics of religion, location, and communal identity. This feeling of being part of a distinct literary voice persisted well into the decades following Partition and was permanently destroyed not by Partition as much as "the accumulating processes of the succeeding years . . . culminating in war and its repercussions" (Ahmad, *Lineages,* 110).

Ahmad has a staunch core group of admirers in both India and in the West who recognize his unflinching commitment to social equality and secularism. The contents of an entire issue of the journal *Public Culture* have been devoted to debating *In Theory.* In India, a new anthology on postcolonial theory, *Contesting Postcolon-*

ialisms, contains two essays on *In Theory.* As the gradual increase in Ahmad's work indicates, critics of South Asian polity and culture are recognizing the central importance of Ahmad's arguments in both *In Theory* and *Lineages of the Present.*

Pallavi Rastogi

Further Reading

Ahmad, Aijaz. *In Theory.* New York and London: Verso, 1992.

Ahmad, Aijaz. *Lineages of the Present.* New York and London: Verso, 2002.

Jain, Jasbir, and Veena Singh, eds. *Contesting Postcolonialisms.* Jaipur: Rawat, 2000.

Alexander, Meena

Meena Alexander. Photo by Robin Holland.

Meena Alexander, who has received considerable critical attention in the past decade, has shuttled between the multiple places and spaces of India, Sudan, Britain and the United States. She knows many languages including English, Hindi, French, Malayalam, and Arabic and has written in multiple genres, from poetry to literary criticism, from memoir to fiction. Born in Allahabad, India, in 1951, Alexander grew up in Sudan making regular trips back to her grandparents' home in Kerala. Finishing her Ph.D. in Romanticism from the University of Nottingham, England, she taught in Delhi and Hyderabad for a few years before migrating to the United States after her marriage to David Lelyveld, a historian of South Asia. In an interview, Alexander says, "I'm an Indian writer; I'm also an American writer. It's all a question of multiple boundaries and affiliations" (Ali and Rasiah 79). Most of Alexander's writing explores themes of migrancy, exile, border crossing, and the multiple births, migrations, anchorages, and allegiances that form her identity. Some themes that are introduced in her early books of poetry—*The Bird's Bright Ring* (1976), *Without Place* (1978), *I Root My Name* (1977), and *Stone Roots* (1980)—

continue to appear in all her work. As the titles reveal, one of Alexander's major preoccupations in these volumes is the search for roots, whether through an evocation of local names, figures, events, and landscapes or through connection with the experiences of her family's female community. The later collections, *The Storm* (1989) and *Night-Scene, the Garden* (1989), explore issues of defining a strong female self through the recuperation of ancestral, especially matrilineal, memories, the significance of her grandfather's house and its loss, the pain of exile and dislocation, and the significance of rituals and ceremonies in finding a sense of order, wholeness, and meaning in life.

In *House of a Thousand Doors* (1988), a collection of poetry mixed with imaginary letters to her grandmother and mother, as well as short lyrical prose pieces, Alexander focuses on the figures of her grandmothers, the strict and strong paternal grandmother and the maternal grandmother, who stepped out of her home into the world, defying the dictates of conventional feminine behavior by becoming a political activist. Alexander tries to find her identity through the figures of these grandmothers. Recurring figures, places, and memories in her poetry define their formative significance in her life. Alexander's poems often focus on the personal as well as the political, as is evident in the poems of *River and Bridge* (1996). In "Art of Pariahs," she tackles the issue of racial tensions in the United States and admits that the poem was written following the racial incidents targeting South Asians in New Jersey. The poems in the collection have titles such as "Relocation," "News of the World," "The Young of Tiananmen," and "Prison Cell." They focus on various issues: censorship (a poem is dedicated to the Indian activist and street theater personality Safdar Hashmi, who was murdered for speaking against the government's apathy for the working classes); the 1947 partition of the Indian subcontinent and the communal riots in postcolonial India; experiences of childbirth and early idyllic childhood memories; evocation of figures from Indian mythology and literature; and meditations on cultural displacement. The poem, "Port Sudan," in the recently published *Illiterate Heart* (2002) is dedicated to and evokes memories of her father in Sudan, "my sweet father: who held me high above the waters," and recalls also the multiplicity of tongues that inform her being.

In addition to these several volumes of poetry, Alexander has also written two novels: *Nampally Road* (1991) and *Manhattan Music* (1997). The former is an unflinching look at the politics of 1970s India, the endemic corruption, the suspension of civil liberties, and the abuse of power by the government bureaucrats through the story of Mira, a teacher of English who returns to England. Mira finds it hard to maintain the boundaries between art, life, and politics as she abandons teaching Wordsworth in order to express a sense of solidarity with Rameeza Be, a lower-class Muslim woman who is brutally raped by the police. In a different context, *Manhattan Music* also focuses on two

women as they come together in their search for the self, home, and identity. Through trying to help Sandhya Rosenblum, an Indian immigrant woman facing an acute sense of disassociation, displacement, and disorientation, performance artist Draupadi Dinkins, who describes herself as "most part Indian, part African . . . also part Asian-American, from Japanese, Chinese, and Filipino blood . . . [and] a smattering of white— low European" (Alexander, *Manhattan* 47), comes to a deeper understanding of her hybrid self, and their friendship provides a testimony to the communities forged in the diaspora. The story takes place against the background of the communal riots in India and the Persian Gulf War.

Alexander has also written the memoir *Fault Lines* (1993) and the mixed-genre *The Shock of Arrival* (1996), both of which address a range of issues relating to displacement and fragmentation. In *Fault Lines,* Alexander relates how all the cities that she has shuttled between since her childhood—Tiruvella, Kozencheri, Allahabad, Pune, Khartoum, Nottingham, Hyderabad, Delhi, New York—constitute her past and present identity. There is no easy belonging to any of these "homelands." She recalls her upper-caste Syrian Orthodox Christian background in detail, her maternal grandfather Ilya's lessons on the violence of colonialism, the Indian national struggle, and the pressures of conforming to appropriate female behavior. Alexander also takes up the issue of language and its ramifications in postcolonial societies and writes, "Colonialism seems intrinsic to the burden of English in India, and I felt robbed of literacy of my own mother tongue" (Alexander, *Fault* 128). Additionally, she also engages with her present home where she has to live with the truth of her multiracial body that sets her thinking of what it means to be "Unwhite" in America, of the pressures of living in a "dark" and "female" body, and of being exoticized in the adopted home. *The Shock of Arrival* is a mix of fiction, criticism/theory, personal reflection, and poetry. The narrative shifts between different genres, locations, and issues as Alexander negotiates her identity in the multicultural U.S. terrain. In this memoir, Alexander is also interested in seeing herself in a tradition of Indian women writers, as well as an Asian American writer, and also forging alliances with other women writers of color in the United States. There are critical formulations on the literary foremothers, the radical poet Kamala Das and the poet-politician Sarojini Naidu whose work Alexander attempts to locate in the crucible of colonialism and nationalism, in the context of Gandhian feminism, and the nationalists' resolution of "the woman question" in the nineteenth century. As a woman writer in the diaspora, she also meditates on the issue of the double pressures facing her from patriarchy and racism.

Alexander's work has been received favorably both in India and the United States. Her writings in poetry and memoir are more successful than her fiction, which struggles to imagine situations beyond the range of her personal experiences. John Oliver Perry bestows high praise on her poetry, "Not limiting her sphere of importance to feminist poetry, one can say that, except for two or three male poets, Meena Alexander has produced the most substantial poetry yet to appear in the genre of Indo-English poetry" (125). Inderpal Grewal praises *Nampally Road* for its "complex representation of India in the Indira Gandhi era," and adds, "the range of women is impressive [and] effectively dismantles the simplistic colonial constructs of the monolithic Third World woman as victim" (228). Reviewing *Fault Lines,* Nalini Natarajan comments that Alexander's "sophisticated interweaving of many narratives, those of her grandmother, her mother, other female relatives, fe-

male servants and wanderers such as the stone-eating girl, reveals a subjectivity interpenetrated by narratives of women everywhere" (143).

Anupama Arora

Further Reading

Alexander, Meena. *Fault Lines: A Memoir.* New York: Feminist Press, 1993.

Alexander, Meena. *Manhattan Music.* San Francisco: Mercury House, 1997.

Ali, Zainab, and Dharini Rasiah. "An Interview with Meena Alexander." *Words Matter: Conversations with Asian American Writers.* Ed. King-Kok Cheung. Honolulu: U of Hawaii P (in association with UCLA Asian American Studies Center Los Angeles), 2000. 69–91.

Davé, Shilpa. "The Doors to Home and History: Post-Colonial Identities in Meena Alexander and Bharati Mukherjee." *Amerasia Journal* 19.3 (1993): 103–13.

Grewal, Inderpal. "Reading and Writing the South Asian Diaspora: Feminism and Nationalism in North America." *Our Feet Walk the Sky. The Women of South Asian Descent Collective.* San Francisco: Aunt Lute Books, 1993. 226–36.

Natarajan, Nalini, Rev. of *Fault Lines* by Meena Alexander. *MELUS* 20.1 (Spring 1995): 143–45.

Perry, John Oliver. "Exiled by a Woman's Body: Substantial Phenomena in Meena Alexander's Poetry." *Journal of South Asian Literature* 21.1 (Winter-Spring 1986): 125–32.

Shankar, Lavina Dhingra. "Postcolonial Diasporics: Writing in Search of a Homeland: Meena Alexander's *Manhattan Music, Fault Lines,* and *The Shock of Arrival.*" *LIT: Literature Interpretation Theory* 12.3 (Sept. 2001): 285–312.

Anand, Mulk Raj

Mulk Raj Anad was born in Peshawar, Pakistan, in 1905, the son of a coppersmith and soldier. He attended the Khalsa College, Amritsar, and the University of Punjab before completing his higher studies at the universities in Cambridge and London. Through the early 1930s, he worked as a lecturer, a broadcaster at the British Broadcasting Corporation, and as a contributor to T. S. Eliot's literary journal, *Criterion.* His friends in the establishment included the likes of Herbert Read, George Orwell, and Henry Miller, while he drew inspiration from the works of Maxim Gorky and James Joyce. Moreover, by this time he was strongly motivated by the writings of Karl Marx and enrolled as a member of the Communist Party. He was sufficiently outraged by the civil war in Spain (1936) and joined the fight for the republican cause. Later, he divided his time between his literary career in England and with Mahatma Gandhi in the fight for India's independence, and after 1945, he returned permanently to India. In fact, Gandhi was to exercise an enormous influence on Anand for the rest of his life and help shape his social conscience and, consequently, his writing.

In Anand's writing, one continually hears the rumblings of a suppressed voice, incessant and strong, but muffled by the stifling quilt of convention and tradition. This is really the voice of the outsider, the minority of one. It strives to make itself heard above the din of a conformity that has various manifestations—religion, the caste system, colonization, and wealth— and in doing so, produces a variety of speakers. These speakers generally occupy subordinate spaces in society, but nevertheless feel burning within them the desire to lash out against the systems that have coalesced to keep them in subordination. Anand gives a voice of these who have been denied the fundamental right to human dignity and his novels become repositories of the darkest of passions ranging from anger to hatred. Yet, refulgent beneath the reservoir of strangled feeling lies the innate goodness that Anand believes is present in his heroes: their capacity to do good, to occupy a position of subservience through necessity and still retain their humanity and live to face the challenges of a new day.

Inevitably, Anand's heroes seem estranged from their place of birth, compelled to travel thousands of miles to seek their fortunes. Often, they drift from one provincial Indian town to another before making bold journeys to the great metropolises of Bombay or Delhi, and sometimes across the oceans to Europe. Along the way they encounter a kaleidoscopic range of characters, whom Anand brings alive in a way that is possible only by someone who could have encountered them firsthand. Writing largely about pre-Independence India in the 1930s and its peoples, he was able to recreate to perfection the social, moral, and political conditions of the times.

In 1936, Anand published *Coolie,* a picaresque novel that attempts to trace the coming of age of Munoo, a poor teenage village boy. But Munoo is destined never to see adulthood as, overworked and tubercular, he dies at the age of 15. This novel closely followed his *Untouchable* published in 1935, and although lacking the intensity of the earlier work, it is nonetheless valuable as a social document of the period and notable for its lyricism as well. Here, Anand effectively weaves his pet themes of the varied natures of man, the power of money, inevitability, and death to produce a narrative that effortlessly recounts events as disparate as the Viceregal ball at Simla and the union strike in the cotton mills of Bombay.

Munoo is an orphan who grows up with a freedom borne of life in the fields with his cattle or gamboling with his friends in the local river, but he is wrenched from his pastoral idylls and forced to work as a servant in the house of a bank clerk in the dusty town of Sham Nagar. Even though he is abused and mistreated, Munoo retains his boyish wonder for life around him: the aroma of the sweetshops, the glistening leather boots of the Sahibs, the youthful beauty of his master's daughter. They all combine to course through his veins like an elixir and mitigate his abject condition. Anand weaves together the competing states of Munoo's drudgery and elation with expertise, showing how a young boy can put up with almost anything so long as he gets to partake of the wonders of life around him. For example, his first experiences with electric fans, trains, and telephones are traumatic, as he cannot understand what these machines do. But later, he is charmed by the sounds emanating from a gramophone, and finally, when he is brutally beaten by his master, it is the swift, thundering darkness of a railway carriage that propels him to new lives in huge cities that reverberate to the throb of industrial activity.

Anand also reveals that the human condition can be infinitely adapted. In *Across the Black Waters* (1940), he describes how Lalu, an Indian soldier, slowly loses his inhibitions about eating with foreigners and his fear of white people, and how even the most ingrained traditions—such as not wearing one's shoes in the kitchen—are slowly erased. Instead, he struggles to adjust to the terrors of Flanders fields in 1914. Eventually, race, religion, wealth, and caste are all leveled in the face of the monster of war. Anand's heroes are all Indians, but those anywhere around the world who belong to the same social class understand their travails. Imbued as they are with a strong socialistic vision, Anand's books, for example, *The Village* (1939) and *The Sword and the Sickle* (1942), reiterate that ultimately, it is economic factors that determine societal functions and positions. In spite of the status accorded them via the caste system, both Brahmin (priest) and Kshatriya (warrior) boys work as menials in the homes of Vaishyas (merchants), and it is servility and assiduousness at their work that decides who survives and who starves. Munoo, whose luck does not hold, is compelled to make the final descent into the world of the "coolie," the day laborer who does anything for a price, that price sometimes being no more than that of a single, coarse meal. Even to the ingenuous Munoo it becomes apparent that there are but two classes: the rich and the poor. And it is the preserve of the rich to beat and harass the poor, and the lot of the poor to meekly accept their fate.

In fact, the inevitability of fate is a recurring motif in Anand's work. The untouchables are doomed to sweep roads and wash latrines all their lives, while laborers must acquiesce to every whim of their foreman; and the soldier finds strength to venture into battle knowing that he will die since this is his destiny. Colonization is bitterly resented, even as simultaneously, the colonized look upon the colonizers with a sense of awe, race acting as a barrier preventing familiarity between the two. Anand paints the local British officials in no flattering light (as in *Two Leaves and a Bud*, 1937) but also admits that the chasm between Indians and foreigners is unbridgeable, since the former construe it as such and come to regard such a power equation as fixed and unchangeable while in reality this may not always be the case.

The fascination with the inevitable is found strongly even in Anand's short stories, which are among his finest works. In "The Shadow of Death," he chronicles the final hours of a wife forced to commit sati, even as he narrates why the act is so unnecessary. Again, in "Mother," he highlights the bizarre condition of the poor who offer prayers to a cow (since it is a holy animal) and yet allow it to starve to death. The animal is beaten mercilessly by its owners, and it is doomed to die, but no sooner is it dead than they start praying to it to ensure that they are not punished for this crime in the after world. Anand tries to show us the absurdity of inevitability, and how within the inexorable passage of time actions must beget fitting reactions. In "A Pair of Mustachios," strongly reminiscent of the writing of Anton Chekov, he tells us of a once powerful landlord who has fallen on bad days and who is smartly relieved of all his possessions by the wily moneylender. This last had dared to ape the flourishing "tiger-moustache" of the landlord and, in return for all his goods and chattels, agreed to glue his "goat-moustache" down in place for the rest of his life. The decline of powerful men, their inability to shake off traditional belief in the face of modern practicality, their slow slide to poverty, and the progress of the bourgeoisie (at the cost of the proletariat) underscore the tragic inescapability of fate.

Anand writes with a grace born of technical brilliance and remains intensely readable because of the genuineness of the experience behind his writing. To read him is to absorb in entirety the worlds he has witnessed and to inhabit them ourselves.

Devapriyo Das

Further Reading

Cowasjee, Saros, and Vasant Shahane, eds. *Modern Indian Fiction.* New Delhi: Viras, 1981.

Lindsay, Jack. *Mulk Raj Anand: A Critical Essay.* Bombay: Hind Kitabs, 1948.

Walsh, William. *Indian Literature in English.* London: Longman, 1996.

Anglophone Literature

The term *Anglo,* referring to a person of English origin, has typically been used in conjunction with other terms, such as Anglo-Saxon or Anglo-Indian. The term *anglophone* has more commonly been used to differentiate, for instance, an English-speaking Canadian from a francophone or a French-speaking one. The phrase *anglophone literature* has been used to define postcolonial literatures in English written by writers located in or originally from countries where English is not the primary or native language, or not the only language, as signified by writers from African, Caribbean, and South Asian countries that were under British colonialism. However, as a result of the continuing proliferation of literatures in English produced in the diaspora, anglophone literature now refers to all writing produced in English from the United Kingdom, the United States, Canada, Australia, and New Zealand, and indeed, from any part of the world.

The phenomenon of diasporic writing has complicated especially the categorization of writers under specific national identities. In the past, the works of writers such as Joseph Conrad, originally from Poland, and Henrik Ibsen, a Norwegian, have been classified under English literature. But now, South Asian diasporic writers such as Salman Rushdie, who have produced almost all their works in the West, make difficult the classification of literatures under conventional taxonomies. Notwithstanding the fact that diasporic writers continue to be classified under the categories of their countries of origin, as in this encyclopedia, or that hyphenated categories, such as African American or Asian American, continue to be used in anthologies and academic departments, all literatures written in English from any part of the world, are subsumed, broadly, under the category anglophone literature.

However, to fully convey its corpus in the South Asian context, we need to examine the beginnings of the South Asian anglophone literature which go back to British colonialism in India, more specifically to the creation and institution of English literary studies in British India, as excellently chronicled by Gauri Viswanathan in *The Masks of Conquest* (1989).

The British realized that the most efficient solution to their problems in governing India would be to educate Indians who would help the colonial government run the country. Consequently, the British colonial government passed the Charter Act in 1813 to make education a state responsibility, giving the British the authority to educate Indians. Also, in 1816, those Indians who wanted instruction in the language and literature of England founded the Hindu College in Calcutta. A strong incentive for Indians to learn English was that the better paying jobs required knowledge of English.

Two acts passed in 1835 that propelled the course of English learning in India. The English Education Act of 1835, proposed by Governor-General William

East Indian servants serve dinner to British officers in the mess tent. Courtesy of North Wind Picture Archives.

Bentinck made English the medium of instruction in educational institutions. And Sir Thomas Macaulay's Minute on Indian Education, in February, 1835, spelled out the English language imperative, to "form a class who may be interpreters between us and the millions whom we govern; a class of persons, Indian in blood and colour, but English in taste, in opinions, in morals, and in intellect." Though the English language was being taught in India before 1835, the acts were instrumental in leading to the creation of English literature as a discipline.

Consequently, Indians were formally introduced to the study of English literature. Attracted to English romanticism and supported by the fact that poetry was an already established tradition in Indian languages and culture, the Indian literary imagination was inspired to create Indian poetry in English, which dominated the Indian literary scene in the nineteenth century. What captured the poetic pen of Indian writers were the cadences and imagery of the English Romantic poets, as seen in the poetry of Henry Louis Vivian Derozio (1807–31), half Indian, half Portuguese, who combined romantic form with Indian content and is known as the father of Indian English poetry. Of the poets who made a mark next, Toru Dutt (1856–77), her cousin Romesh Chunder Dutt (1848–1909), and Manmohan Ghose (1870?–1924), stand out. Tarulata Datta (Toru Dutt), like Derozio was a Christian, but unlike him, he was influenced by both English and French literatures. Her father

Govin Datta converted to Christianity when she was six, taking his family to Europe in 1869. Toru Dutt lived in both France and England, and with her sister, Aru, wrote English translations of French poems collected in *A Sheaf Gleaned in French Fields* (1875). Toru, like her brother and sister, died young of consumption in 1877.

Others who later produced distinguished poetry include Rabindranath Tagore (1861–1941), who translated his poems from Bengali into English in the collection *Gitanjali* (1912), for which he was awarded the Nobel Prize in 1913. Of the several poets Tagore inspired, two that stand out are Sri Aurobindo Ghose (1872–1950), who, like Toru Dutt combined Indian theme and English poetic form, and wrote his epic *Savitri,* which took 50 years to complete, and Sarojini Naidu (1879–1949), who wrote her first book of poems *The Golden Threshold* (1905) to high acclaim in England, followed by *The Bird of Time* (1912) and *The Broken Wing* (1917). Sarojini Naidu's brother, Harindranath Chattopadhyaya, who was also a communist and a humanist, drew on the mystical tradition, too, in *The Feast of Youth* (1918) in addition to showing the influences of Aurobindo's idealism and Tagore's romanticism.

By World War II, Indian poetry showed a decided shift from the romantic strain to the modernist trend, as seen in the works produced by Nissim Ezekiel, Dom Moraes, P. Lal, and Kamala Das. As more and more Indians were writing poetry, a major publishing source, especially for new poets, was P. Lal's Writers Workshop. This Workshop published: Nissim Ezekiel's *Sixty Poems* (1953); P. Lal's *Love's the First* (1962); Kamala Das's *Summer in Calcutta* (1965); A. K. Ramanujan's *The Striders* (1966); and Agha Shahid Ali's *Bone-Sculpture* (1972) and *In Memory of Begum Akhtar* (1975).

By the end of the twentieth century and into the twenty-first century, South Asian poets have continued to experiment with and create new trends, making their mark in poetry in English.

While poets in the nineteenth century drew on the Romantic strain largely, the novel in India emulated the Victorian style. However, a look at the history of anglophone literature in South Asia in the nineteenth and twentieth centuries highlights the fact that the novel did not make a mark, like poetry, on the literary scene till the 1930s. The emergence of anglophone literature in nineteenth-century India can be seen largely as a response to the presence of the British as rulers, educators, and missionaries. Raja Rammohan Roy (1774–1833) saw the English language as a medium of literary communication that would potentially enable and promote greater understanding between Indian and British cultures. He died in Bristol in 1833 though his complete English works were not available until 1906. Among the early novels was Bankim Chandra Chatterjee's *Rajmohan's Wife* (1864), the only one he wrote in English before switching to Bengali. However, it was the 1930s that saw the emergence of three top Indian writers, Mulk Raj Anand (1905–), Raja Rao (1908–), and R. K. Narayan (1909–2000), who brought the Indian idiom and flavor into their writing.

A major theme in twentieth-century South Asian literature has been India's struggle for independence and its partition. Several novels, especially in the first half of the twentieth century, were immersed in the Gandhian philosophy of nonviolence. The swaraj (home-rule), the swadeshi (the buying of natively produced goods only), and issues of national concern—India's fight for freedom, the plight of the landless peasants, and the untouchables outside the caste system. For example, Raja Rao's *Kanthapura* (1938), Khwaja Ahmad Abbas's *Inquilab* (1955), Manohar Malgonkar's *Bend in the Ganges* (1964),

Khushwant Singh's *Train to Pakistan* (1956), Attia Hosain's *Sunlight on a Broken Column* (1961), Bapsi Sidhwa's *Cracking India: A Novel* (1991), Anita Desai's *Clear Light of Day* (1980), and Salman Rushdie's *Midnight's Children* (1980) have all drawn on the independence movement and the subsequent partition of the subcontinent.

While novelists such as Anita Desai, Attia Hosain, and Kamala Markandaya explored the individual in relation to family, culture, and society. An earlier writer, Govind V. Desani in his novel, *All About H. Hatterr* (1948) foreshadowed Salman Rushdie's *Midnight's Children* (1980), especially in his sense of the comic and his innovative use of language. *Midnight's Children,* which won the Booker Prize, opened up possibilities for the literary expression of English by South Asian writers. Rushdie, among other things, legitimized the use of Indianisms in literature, drawing on the hybridization of English and Hindustani, by showing the ways in which, for example, Indian words are given English suffixes. He paved the way for other innovations by myriad South Asian writers, such as Arundhati Roy, whose novel *The God of Small Things* (1997) also won the Booker Prize, the first by an Indian writing in English in India.

Hena Ahmad

Further Reading

Datta, Amaresh. *Encyclopedia of Indian Literature.* New Delhi: Sahitya Akademi, 1987–1994. 5 vols.

Hawley, John C., ed. *Encyclopedia of Postcolonial Studies.* Westport: Greenwood, 2001.

Sanga, Jaina C., ed. *South Asian Novelists in English: An A-to-Z Guide.* Westport: Greenwood, 2003.

Viswanathan, Gauri. *Masks of Conquest: Literary Study and British Rule in India.* Delhi: Oxford UP, 1998.

Williams, H. M. *Indo-Anglian Literature 1800–1970: A Survey.* Bombay: Orient Longman, 1977.

Appachana, Anjana

Anjana Appachana, who has enjoyed increasing literary success in India, England, the United States, and Europe, was born May 10, 1956 in Mercara, India. After completing an undergraduate degree at Delhi University, Appachana received an M.A. in sociology at Jawaharlal Nehru University in 1978. Upon graduating, she worked for the World Wildlife Fund in New Delhi and then for DCM Data Products in New Delhi. In 1982, she married Rajiv Krishna Sinha, a professor of business, and in 1985, they moved to the United States, where her husband taught and she enrolled in and received an M.F.A. from Pennsylvania State University. Although Appachana returns regularly to India, she now lives with her husband and daughter in Tempe, Arizona, where she writes and teaches creative writing at Arizona State University.

Appachana began writing fiction, some of which was published in journals such as *Illustrated Weekly of India* and *Imprint,* before she moved to the United States, but it was during and after completing her M.F.A. that she began writing seriously and completed a collection of short stories that was published as *Incantations and Other Stories* (Virago, 1991; Rutgers UP, 1992). Next, she completed her novel, *Listening Now,* which was published in 1998 by Random House and was also published in India. Over her career, she has contributed stories to anthologies, including *The Forbidden Stitch: An Asian American Women's Anthology, Mirrorwork: 50 Years of Indian Writing 1947–1997, Such Devoted Sisters,* and *Oxford Book of Modern Women's Stories.* In addition, she has published stories in a variety of periodicals, including *Passport: Magazine of New International Writing, Webster Review, Calyx: A Journal of Art and Literature by Women,* and others. For her fiction, Appachana has won the O. Henry Festival Award in 1989 for her short story "Her Mother" and was awarded a National Endowment for the Arts Creative Writing Fellowship in 1995–96.

Appachana's fiction, represented by her major works, *Incantations and Other Stories* and *Listening Now,* is generally regarded as deviating from much of modern Indian writing in that it is seen as apolitical, focusing primarily on the domestic rather than political scene. She explains that she is interested in writing about "the internal landscape" so that "politics—of the kind we know—would be intrusive" (Nayar). The world that she carefully examines is one in which women are forced by repressive families, cultural traditions, and indifferent men to maintain "silence"; however, in her fiction, her female characters, although often depicted as living desperate lives, are complex, interesting women who demonstrate the value of female bonding and exploring choices that break the silence. Some critics argue that it is in giving voice to such women that Appachana's writing achieves political purpose, "not from its sweep or its claim to represent entire world-in-the making, but from its insistence on enacting in a realist idiom the lives and experiences of middle-class families, particularly those of the women who live within and are defined by the expectations of these families" and from its ability to "delineate forms of change and work to suggest imaginative alternatives to the circumscribed or traumatized lives of women who transgress the silences and proscriptions of 'traditional' cultural expectations" (Kaul 121, 134). In this attempt to dispel female silence, Appachana experiments, in her short and long fiction, with the point of view as a narrative technique for giving voice to multiple perspectives.

Incantations is a collection of stories told by women of various ages, experiences, and backgrounds. The stories are often told from an observer's perspective rather than the character undergoing the focal conflict. One story, "The Prophecy," told from the perspective of the main character's friend, involves a college student who is prevented by college officials from seeing a doctor for an abortion, and when she miscarries, she is forced to enter into a loveless marriage. "Her Mother" is narrated as a letter from a mother in India to her daughter in the United States; the mother struggles to understand her daughter's changes, secrets, and distance, longing to be close to her again. "Bahu" (daughter-in-law) is a story told from the perspective of a young woman who marries for love and moves in with her husband's family; she is subjected to abusive treatment from her in-laws, and realizing that she is sacrificing herself and losing her identity, she walks away from the family. In "Incantation," the narrator is a young girl whose sister confesses to her the misery of her arranged marriage, and eventually, her sister kills herself after castrating her brother-in-law who has repeatedly raped her.

In *Listening Now,* each chapter of the novel is told through the perspective of different characters involved in the life of Padma, the main character, who has experienced tragic love, involving an illegitimate child and rejection by her lover, his family, and her family. Through this use of multiple perspectives, Appachana creates "an imaginative mapping of the lives of urban middle-class women, their uneasy negotiations with tradition and modernity," suggesting "a continuance of tradition through women, each contributing her bit to it, though this contribution is hardly ever acknowledged in a patriarchal society" (Panwar).

The critical response to *Incantations* has been largely positive, both in terms of individual stories and the collection as a whole. Many critics applaud this as a collection that expresses insights into the world of relationships, particularly between women, and is "marked by understatement and a laconic humour" (Mukherjee). Suvir Kaul, focusing on the craft and themes of *Incantations* concludes that, through the consciousness of Geeti, who moves from adolescence to adulthood and, in contemplating her sister's story and its implications, decides to leave her unfulfilling marriage, Appachana masterfully creates a character who finally comes to posses "a critical distance from the life of her parents, a distance that allows her to move, at least temporarily, out of a marriage that has lapsed into an unfeeling stasis" (133). Kaul describes the prose in the entire collection as "often bleak and angry," but "supple enough to register—ironically, warmly—the nuances and cadences of speech and thought in a functionally bi- and tri-lingual world" (134).

Although *Listening Now* has received a more mixed critical response, it, too, has been widely praised. Some critics object to the overuse of coincidence and overly dramatic ending, reminiscent of a Hindi film, but praise the novel as "a nuanced reflection on gender relations and the high price of non-conformity for women" (Mukherjee 2). Panwar praises the novel for the effective "oscillating back and forth in time, between past and present" and the strong links "maintained through women who feel for each other through thick and thin deriving a strength and a holistic power to hear, thereby forging a bond of sisterhood that is therapeutic." Milton praises the "lilting rhythms, vivid imagery" of the narrators' language which makes it "luxuriantly poetic" but also "remarkably down-to-earth" as they talk of everything from the Evil Eye and good omens to the grinding daily hardships of their existence" (E1). Kaul concludes that Appachana's work is "a critique of Indian middle-class morality and gender relations from within, a bringing together of feminist conviction, cultural skepticism, and an eye for surface detail that asks us to ex-

amine again, to be less sanguine about, the codes by which we live our lives" (134).

Ruth Forsythe

Further Reading

Kaul, Suvir. "Who's Afraid of Mala Mousi? Violence and the 'Family Romance' in Anjana Appachana's 'Incantations.' " *Tulsa Studies in Women's Literature* (Spring 2000): 121–36.

Milton, Edith. "Women with Men." Rev. of *Listening Now,* by Anjana Appachana. *The Boston Globe Online* 3 May 1998: E1. <http://www.boston.com/globe/Search/stories/books/anjana_appachana.htm>.

Mukherjee, Meenakshi. "Listening Now." Rev. of *Listening Now,* by Anjana Appachana. *India-Star Review of Books* (2003) Mar. <http://www.indiastar.com/Mukherjee2.htm>.

Nayar, Pramod K. "Sound of Silence." *The Hindu* 10 July 2002. <http://www.hinuonnet.com/thehindu/mp2002/07/10/stories/2002071000380200.htp>.

Panwar, Purabi. "Female Bonding." Rev. of *Listening Now,* by Anjana Appachana. *Biblio: A Review of Books* 4.3–4 (1999). Mar. 2003 <http://www.biblio-india.Com/articles/ma99_ar14.asp?mp=MA99>.

Appadurai, Arjun

Arjun Appadurai is currently William K. Lanman, Jr., professor of international studies and director of the Initiative on Cities and Globalization at Yale University, where he teaches in the departments of anthropology, political science, and sociology. He was previously the Samuel N. Harper Professor in the Department of Anthropology and professor in South Asian Languages and Civilizations at the University of Chicago. He was also the Director of the Globalization Project at the University of Chicago. One of the founding editors, with Carol A. Breckenridge, of the journal *Public Culture,* Appadurai obtained his first degree in Intermediate Arts at the University of Bombay in 1967. He then moved to the United States, where he received his B.A. in history from Brandeis University in 1970 and his M.A. in Social Thought from the University of Chicago in 1973. He completed his Ph.D. in Social

Thought in 1976, also at the University of Chicago.

Having written and published extensively in the fields of sociocultural anthropology, globalization, and public culture, Appadurai's major contribution perhaps lies in the formulation of concepts, which allow the taking of an anthropological approach to questions of modernity, globalization, consumption, and public culture. Appadurai has consistently offered paths to move beyond traditional oppositions between culture and power, tradition and modernity, the global and the local, pointing out the vital role that imagination plays in our construction of the contemporary.

In his book, *Modernity at Large*, Appadurai demonstrates how the imagination works as a social force in today's world, providing new resources for identity and energies for creating alternatives to the nation-state, whose era some see as coming to an end. He argues, "The imagination is now central to all forms of agency, is itself a social fact, and is the key component of the new global order" (31).

One of Appadurai's strengths seems to be interdisciplinary thinking, which is most visible in his work, *Modernity at Large,* where he draws on a range of theorists from disciplines as far-flung as anthropology, history, literary studies, economics, and philosophy with remarkable aptitude and ease. Regarding modernity, Appadurai suggests that modernity is a phenomenon that is irregularly self-conscious and unevenly experienced rather than one single moment of break between past and present. He proposes a "theory of rupture" that takes media and migration as its two majors, exploring their joint effect on the work of imagination as a constitutive feature of modern subjectivity (1996, 2–3). Global cultural flows are viewed as composed of complex, overlapping, and disjunctive orders that do not allow any homogenized perspective. While, for instance, the Marxist tradition has tried to consider such flows as ultimately determined by capital flows, Appadurai puts a decisive emphasis on the role of mass migration and, even more importantly, on the role of electronic media. For Appadurai, the global situation is not dominated by one side but involves instead a certain level of interaction. Appadurai believes that the current global processes of migration and communication will lead to the *deterritorialization* of identities in a world, which will be made increasingly culturally hybrid by a growth of diasporic public spheres and the global flow of images, finances, technologies, and ideologies. He urges us to look at the relationship between five dimensions of global cultural flows: *ethnoscapes, technoscapes, financescapes, mediascapes,* and *ideoscapes.* By identifying the five *-scapes,* Appadurai offers a framework for considering the "new global cultural economy a complex, overlapping, disjunctive order that cannot any longer be understood in terms of existing center-periphery models" (*Modernity* 32). And by using the suffix *-scapes,* he wants to emphasize the fluid and irregular shapes of these landscapes. These are the shapes that according to him characterize international capital as deeply as they do international clothing styles.

Besides looking at global cultural flows, Appadurai is also interested in area studies, particularly South Asian studies. Area studies in his view reflect particular maps, marking groups and their way of living by culture and creating topographies of national cultural differences (*Modernity* 16). Appadurai sees the significance of area studies in reminding us that globalization itself is a historical, uneven, and even localizing process. Appadurai also attempts to replace the term *culture* by the adjectival form of the word, that is, "cultural." He argues that the concept of culture as a coherent entity privileges forms of sharing, agreement, and bounding, and thus neglects the facts of inequality and differences in lifestyles.

Appadurai's interest now lies in investigating the global resurgence of violent forms of national and cultural identification, which frequently lead to cultural warfare, even to ethnocide. He argues that the renewal of ethno-nationalisms on a global scale are not a simple reaction to globalization, but they certainly reflect anxiety about immigrants, fears about economic interdependence and concerns about the status of minorities everywhere (2000). Providing an alternative to the primordialist or tribalist perspective on large-scale ethnic violence and terror, he argues that the extreme violence that accompanied many recent ethnic wars is a product of radical uncertainty about key social identities, which produces a surplus of anxiety and rage about categorical betrayal. This sort of radical uncertainty is seen as being directly tied to the larger processes of globalization. The collection of essays in the latest book edited by Appadurai contributes to the increasingly heated debates surrounding the cultural dimensions of globalization. While exploring the way in which the complex transformations of space and time involve changes in the situation of the nation, the state, and the city, the contributors seek to answer the question, "what do we really understand by globalization?"

Sumati Nagrath

Further Reading

Appadurai, Arjun. *Worship and Conflict Under Colonial Rule: A South Indian Case.* New York: Cambridge UP, 1981.

———. *The Social Life of Things: Commodities in Cultural Perspective.* Cambridge: Cambridge UP, 1986.

———. *Modernity at Large: Cultural Dimensions of Modernity.* London and Minneapolis: U of Minnesota P, 1996.

———. "Dead Certainty: Ethnic Violence in the Era of Globalization." *Public Culture* 10.2 (1998): 225–47.

———. ed. *Globalization.* Durham: Duke UP, 2001.

Arranged Marriage by Chitra Banerjee Divakaruni

Divakaruni was born in India, educated in India and the United States, and now lives and writes in the United States. The writer's own immigrant condition inspires her to write stories of immigrant lives. *Arranged Marriage* (1995) is a collection of 11 short stories focusing mainly on Indian women whose lives are linked both to the Indian tradition of arranged marriage and the dramatic changes brought by immigration.

Many of the stories use metaphors as an effective device to describe the conditions of their protagonists. In "The Bats," a little girl and her mother, who is physically abused by the husband, leave home but return repeatedly, compelled by his false promises and the society's disapproval of women who leave their husbands. They stay with the mother's aging uncle in his village home after she leaves her husband after a particularly unbearable episode of physical abuse. The uncle had worked at a fruit orchard that was constantly attacked by bats. To get rid of the bats, he used poisonous traps, yet the bats continued to fly back to the same orchard, eventually getting killed. The uncle and the little girl, who had become very close, both wonder why the bats keep returning to the same place where death awaited them. Analogically, the mother is just as helpless as those bats, as she keeps going back to the same abusive husband again and again. In another story, clothes become symbolic of entrapment or liberation. As Mita in "Clothes" chooses to shed her traditional Indian sari and puts on Western clothes in her post-immigration life, she liberates herself from a life of servile widowhood. In "Doors," the simple act of closing or keeping doors open becomes emblematic of the different cultural values of an Indian American wife married to an Indian husband. In "The Ultrasound," an ultrasound becomes a life-changing experience for the two cousins living in two different continents. While Anju in America sees her unborn baby boy through the ultrasound and feels the power of her love for him, Runu in India fights her husband and mother-in-law who want her to abort her unborn daughter because of its gender. The docile Runu who settled into her limited life after her arranged marriage becomes a rebel after the decisive ultrasound.

In other stories such as "The Disappearance," "Affair," and "Meeting Mrinal," women leave their unhappy arranged marriages to get fresh starts in their stagnated lives. In "The Word Love," "A Perfect Life," and "The Maid Servant's Story," Indian women in America are seen choosing a westernized custom of living together with boyfriends without marriage or its promise. Yet, they struggle between old loyalties and new yearnings and feel uncomfortable with both. In "A Perfect Life," Meera is a successful Indian American professional who thinks she is liberated without marriage and motherhood, yet when a lost little boy finds his way into her life, she longs to be his mother above all else. "The Maid Servant's Story" presents a story within a story, and it raises the issue of men's sexual exploitation of women, which can affect women of any social station and any generation. The story "Silver Pavements, Golden Roofs" tells of a college student's dreams about America and a romantic marriage, her eventual disillusionment with experiences of racism, and her immigrant aunt's mismatched arranged marriage.

This collection of stories presents the struggles of women caught between tradition and change with deep pathos and passion. But the Indian custom of arranged marriage is almost completely rejected as unfair and unworkable. In order to create a classic immigrant narrative of hope, India is generally shown as something to shed, to leave behind; and America is un-failingly seen as the source of new hope, albeit, with a few complexities. This stance constructs binaries of East versus West, inferior versus superior, and constricted versus liberated, thus encouraging a kind of neocolonial approval of Western culture and society. Though the book advances a feminist cause, its east-west binaries impede post-colonial causes.

Arranged Marriage has received many favorable reviews in the United States. Many reviewers have praised its believable characterizations and evocative language. Donna Seaman writes in *Booklist:* "These are ravishingly beautiful stories, some profoundly sad, others full of revelation, all unforgettable" (1860). Rose Kernochan writes in *The New York Times Book Review* "Ms. Divakaruni's stories are as irresistible as the impulse that leads her characters to surface into maturity, raising their heads above floods of silver ignorance" (20). But Keronochan also thinks that Indian femininity plunges Divakaruni's heroines into a dream world from which America "revives" them, and that America's freedom is like "extra oxygen" (20). Such criticism shows how voices in the West easily pick up the binaries created in these stories, declare India the realm of the half-dead dazed and glorify America as the lifesaver. *Arranged Marriage* can thus function as neoimperialistic literature in the guise of immigrant narrative.

Husne Jahan

Further Reading

Albert, Janice. "How Now, My Metal of India." *English Journal* 86.5 (Sept. 1997): 99–100.

Allen, Kimberly G. Rev. of *Arranged Marriage. Library Journal* 120. 11 (June 15 1995): 97.

Kernochan, Rose. Rev. of *Arranged Marriage. New York Times Book Review* (July 16 1995): 20.

Kim, Elaine H. Rev. of *Arranged Marriage. Amerasia Journal* 22. 1 (1996): 249–51.

Seaman, Donna. Rev. of *Arranged Marriage. Booklist* 91 (July 1995): 1860.

Sethi, Robbie Clipper. Rev. of *Arranged Marriage. Studies in Short Fiction* 33.2 (Spring 1996): 287–88.

Asiatic Society of Bengal

In founding the Asiatic Society of Bengal on January 15, 1784, Sir William Jones inspired and organized the private research of a dedicated group of crown and East India Company employees, many had been encouraged by Governor-General Warren Hastings in the promotion of his Orientalist regime. The first members were administrators, merchants, soldiers, lawyers and judges; professional men such as Charles Wilkins, a senior company merchant, first European of his generation to learn Sanskrit, and translator of *Bhăgvăt-Gēētā* (1785); and Francis Gladwin, a soldier, gifted entrepreneur, and translator of the *A'in-i Akbari* (1783–86). These amateur researchers were not ivory-towered intellectuals, and Jones, aware that "wealth is not the only pursuit fit for rational beings," offered them a vast sphere of intellectual and imaginative space as he initiated Indology. The society's researches, bounded "only by the geographical limits of *Asia,*" should encompass "MAN and NATURE; whatever is performed by the one, or produced by the other" ("Discourse" 5).

To the society's journal, *Asiatick Researches,* which was distributed and pirated throughout Europe, Jones himself contributed papers on a polymathic range of subjects: Indian anthropology, archaeology, astronomy, botany, ethnology, geography, music, literature, physiology, languages and inscriptions, mythology, and religion. Jones's "Third Anniversary Discourse" (1786) maintained that the classical languages of India, the Near East, and Europe descend from a common source, an imaginative leap that marks the beginning of Indo-European comparative grammar and modern comparative-historical linguistics. Jones further challenged Eurocentric thinking by concluding that it is not possible "to read the Vedanta without believing that Pythagoras and Plato derived their sublime theories from the same fountain with the sages of India" (37). His 1793 "Discourse On Asiatic History, Civil and Natural," building on earlier work upon ancient monuments, coins, and inscriptions by Thomas Law, W. Paterson, William Chambers, and Charles Wilkins culminated in Jones's accurate correlation of Eastern and Western history, effectively giving India her past.

Despite their rediscovery of classical Sanskrit literature, Jones and Wilkins were very much aware of modern Bengal as a crucial site in the evolution of Hinduism, reflecting a vigorous continuity between Jayadeva's *Gitagovinda* and contemporary Hindu belief in the doctrine of *bhakti* (loving devotion). Jones, faithful to Hastings's vision and his own deist leanings, attempted to guide the Society toward an acceptance of the syncretic inheritance of Emperor Akbar and Dara Shikuh, by demonstrating that the metaphysics and theology of the Sufis were compatible with both Vedantic and Platonic traditions.

Jones's suggestions that Indians be allowed to join the Society were ignored and, despite *Asiatick Researches* being the first European journal to publish papers written by Indian scholars, it was only in 1829, on the nomination of Horace Hayman Wilson, that Indians were admitted as members.

Henry Thomas Colebrooke further adjusted the metropolitan construction of India. The first paper he gave to the Society in April 1794, on *sati,* was the last to be heard by Jones, who died before the month was out; a quarter of a century later in London he founded the Royal Asiatic Society in 1823. He cemented ties between the newly-established College of Fort William, where he was professor of Sanskrit and Hindu Law, and the Asiatick Society, of which he was the fourth president, effecting a somewhat ironic collaboration between both these bodies and the Serampore Baptist Mission, whose principal, the excellent linguist William Carey, wished to translate and publish ancient Sanskrit texts to fund missionary activity.

Horace Hayman Wilson became secretary of the Society in 1811; the leading Orientalist of the generation, he united the imaginative vision of Jones and Colebrooke's systematical examination of Indian philosophy, turning his attention to the medieval India of the *Puranas* and to the cultivation of the vernacular languages.

James Prinsep succeeded Wilson as secretary, moving both the Asiatic Society and Indology toward the interpretation of archaeological sites and finds, enabling further research by successfully deciphering the Asokan inscriptions.

The labors of these Orientalists shaped Western conceptions of the other, and Indian perceptions of the self. The dissemination by the Society of key Indian texts effected an Oriental renaissance in the West and a cultural revolution in India. Such were the early colonial contributions to Indological studies, the center and focus of which remains to this day the prestigious and research-led Asiatic Society of 1, Park Street, Calcutta.

Michael J. Franklin

Further Reading

Cannon, Garland. ed. *The Letters of Sir William Jones.* 2 vols. Oxford: Clarendon, 1970.

"A Discourse on the Institution of a Society." *The Works of William Jones.* Ed. Anna Maria Jones, 13 vols. London: Stockdale and Walker, 1807, III: 24–46.

Franklin, Michael J. " 'The Hastings Circle': Writers and Writing in Calcutta in the Last Quarter of the Eighteenth Century." *Authorship, Commerce and the Public: Scenes of Writing, 1750–1850.* Eds. E. J. Clery, Caroline Franklin, and Peter Garside. Basingstoke: Palgrave, 2002. 186–202.

Kejariwal, O. P. *The Asiatic Society of Bengal and the Discovery of India's Past, 1784–1838.* Delhi: Oxford UP, 1988.

Kopf, David. *British Orientalism and the Bengal Renaissance; the Dynamics of Indian Modernization, 1773–1835.* Berkeley: U of California P, 1969.

Raychaudhuri, Tapan. *Europe Reconsidered: Perceptions of the West in Nineteenth-Century Bengal.* Oxford: Oxford UP, 1988.

Shaw, Graham. *Printing in Calcutta.* London: The Bibliographical Society, 1981.

"The Third Anniversary Discourse: On the Hindus" (1786). *The Works of Sir William Jones.* Ed. Anna Maria Jones, 13 vols. London: Stockdale and Walker, 1807, III: 24–46.

B

Badami, Anita Rau

Anita Rau Badami was born in 1964 in the town of Rourkela in Orissa, India. After completing her B.A. in English at the University of Madras, she went on to study journalism at Sophia College in Bombay. Before pursuing a career as a full-time writer, Badami worked as a copywriter for advertising agencies in Bombay, Banglore, and Madras. She also wrote stories for children's magazines in India. Following her marriage in 1984 and the birth of her son in 1987, Badami moved to Canada in 1991 where she completed a master's degree in creative writing under the supervision of Canadian novelist and scholar, Aritha Van Herk. Badami's master's thesis, entitled "Railways and Ginger" was completed in November 1995. "Railways and Ginger" was an early version of her first published novel, *Tamarind Mem* (1996). Similarly, her short stories—"Tracks," "In Kammini's Room," and "Ajii's Miracle"—can be viewed as early writing experiments that Badami expands upon in her later novels. Badami currently lives in Montreal, Canada, where she is at work on her third novel, *Can You Hear the Nightbird Call?*

Tamarind Mem, later published in the United States as *Tamarind Woman* (2002), is loosely based on the author's own life, whose father, like that of her protagonist Kamini, was a mechanical engineer for railroads. The autobiographical elements that many of its critics have noted do not undermine the novel's broader social im-plications. The novel is divided into two parts to indicate the division between the perspectives of mother, Saroja and her daughter, Kamini. The two women reflect upon their own lives and their relationship with one another. Part one is told from the perspective of Kamini who lives in Calgary while the second half of the novel re-tells Kamini's story from Saroja's side in India. The differences between their stories that relate similar events comprise the novel's central tension: cultural affiliation versus individual desire. Following the critical acclaim her first novel received, Badami's much-anticipated second novel, *The Hero's Walk,* did not disappoint her fans. *The Hero's Walk* quickly became a bestseller in both the United States and Canada and won a series of literary prizes, including the 2001 Regional Common-wealth prize for best book, and Canada's Marian Engel Award for literary fiction. Like her first novel, *The Hero's Walk* de-velops the disjunction that occurs between parents and their children as a result of conflicting desires and commitments. Set primarily in South India—with a brief foray into Western Canada—the novel fo-cuses on the life and times of Sripathi Rao, a middle-aged man who has devoted his life to the well being of his incongruent family members. Maya, his beloved daughter, shuns family tradition and honor when she marries a non-Indian in Canada. The two never reconcile their differences. Only after Maya's death is Sripathi forced to face the mistakes of his decisions in the form of his silent and brooding granddaughter, Nandana. Caught between the cultural forces and social demands represented by Canada and India, Badami's fiction best illustrates the emotional tensions that underlie current notions of the South Asian diaspora.

While fiction continues to be the primary mode of Badami's writing, she has also written a number of nonfictional essays. "My Canada," published in the *Imperial Oil Review,* develops the author's commitment to her new home nation without leaving her birth nation, India, too far behind. Badami compares her relationship with Canada to "a beautiful, enigmatic woman who looks down demurely most of the time, but then surprises the watcher with a sudden glance from a pair of mischievous eyes." In other words, Badami observes the contradictions and splendor of Canada without disturbing or upsetting the mask it wears to protect it from external intrusions. After spending more than a decade in Canada, the country has become her home and she has, in her own words, come "to love it on its own terms for what it was, rather than what it wasn't." Although Canada is a muted presence in her fiction, it does represent both freedom and possibility, such things that are much needed in the lives of her otherwise hopeless Indian characters.

While operating primarily in the sentimental mode, Badami's fiction manages to develop an incisive critique of Indian cultural politics and custom. Through her characters, the reader is able to witness the consequences of the clash between the individual's desire for recognition and personal fulfillment with the politics of heritage and nostalgia. Badami's early fiction introduces readers to a number of quirky characters, which, through her use of direct address and stream of consciousness, she uses to develop an unmediated relationship between characters and read-

ers. "In Kannigi's Room" and "Ajii's Miracle," readers gain a glimpse into the interior spaces of typical Indian households where the lives of individuals joined by marriage and blood "is one big war." In these stories Badami focuses on the circumscribed role of the daughter in the household. Being an "obedient daughter" limits the imagination of her female characters and it is the limit that Badami's plot does not take her characters beyond.

In *Tamarind Mem,* however, Saroja and Kamini do find a way out of their circumscribed roles in the household. Divided into two parts, the novel offers the perspective of both women, mother and daughter, as they set out to examine the circumstances of their own and each other's lives. The disease of nostalgia infects Kamini as she creates an illusion of her childhood in India to comfort her as she weathers the frigid airs of Calgary. Viewing her mother from a perspective of great critical distance, Kamini offers the reader few insights into Saroja's mind. Indeed, the story Kamini tells of the past reveals that although she has traveled a great distance to further her education, she has not moved beyond the limitations of her youth. Saroja's entry into the narrative offers readers a remedy to Kamini's highly selective memory. Filling in the gaps left by her daughter's narrative, Saroja details the facts of their mutual past: her marriage to Kamini's father—the admirable "Dadda" of Kamini's memories—was a loveless one. Saroja's husband not only had little time to spend with his wife but he also went out of his way to make sure that she spent her time properly, performing the duties of a wife and mother without spending any on herself. Saroja's story allows the reader to realize that her daughter's fond memories of the past are based on a lie, and that if she does not heed her mother's oft-repeated warning she will endanger her prospects for a more rewarding future.

The dynamics of the mother-daughter relationship set forth in *Tamarind Mem* shifts to the fraught relations between father and daughter in *The Hero's Walk.* Once again reflecting upon circumstance and future possibility, Badami introduces her readers to a rather unlikely hero: Sripathi Rao. After having disavowed his beloved daughter following her departure to Canada, he is confronted with her sudden death. As a result of her death, Sripathi must reevaluate his commitment to tradition and custom—the primary cause of the dissolution of his relationship with his daughter. Sripathi is given the opportunity to make amends for his past mistakes when his young granddaughter, Nandana, enters his decaying household. Nandana's entry into both Sripathi's household and the narrative has the potential to transform both. And she does affect this transformation. Having spent her early years in a suburb on the west coast of Canada, Nandana transfers the values and love she had learned in the West to the East. The consequences of this transference, in the form of a child, cause each member of the Rao household to finally let go of their commitment to Indian tradition and embark upon a future that is, ultimately, unknown. The popular response to *The Hero's Walk* resulted in the reissue of her previous novel. To date, the novel has been translated into six languages and continues to be a bestseller.

Tess E. Chakkalakal

Further Reading

Chopra, Sonia. Interview. "Anita Rau Badami." *Curled Up with a Good Book.* July 2002 <http://www.curledup.com/trwinter.htm>.

Kozminuk, Angela. "A Conversation with Anita Rau Badami." *The Peak.* 7 Oct. 1996 <http://www.peak.sfu.ca/the-peak/96–3/issue6/anita.html>.

"My Canada." Imperial Oil Review, Summer 2000, Vol. 84, No. 437. <http:www.imperialoil.ca/thisis/publications/reviewed/437mycanada.htm>.

Nurse, Donna. "A Sweet and Sour Life." *Maclean's* 109.37 (1996): 53.

Richards, Linda. "Interview with Anita Rau Badami." *January Magazine Online.* <http://www.janmag.com/profiles/raubadami.html>.

Baldwin, Shauna Singh

The diasporic, Indo-Canadian writer Shauna Singh Baldwin is the author of the novel *What the Body Remembers* (Knopf, Canada; Nan Talese/Doubleday, USA; and Transworld, UK, 1999), set in Pakistan and India, which won the 2000 Commonwealth Writer's Prize for Canada and the Caribbean Region; and a collection of short stories, *English Lessons and Other Stories* (Goose Lane Editions, 1996; Harper Collins India 1999), set in India, Canada, and the United States, which won the 1996 Friends of American Writers Award. She is the co-author of *A Foreign Visitor's Survival Guide to America* (John Muir, 1992), set exclusively in the United States. Her fiction, essays, and poems have been published in diverse magazines worldwide: *Saturday Night, Books in Canada, Prairie Fire, Canadian Forum, Fireweed,* and *McGill St. Magazine* in Canada; *Manushi* in India; and *The Writer, Calyx, Rosebud, hum, India Currents,* and *Cream City Review* in the United States. The Canadian Broadcasting Corporation Radio has hosted stories from *English Lessons* on its drive-time shows, *Between the Covers* and *Morningside.* Other awards Baldwin has earned include the 1997 Canadian Literary Award for her short story "Satya;" the 1995 Writer's Union of Canada Award for Short Prose for "Jassie," a story from *English Lessons;* the Nehru Award (India) for public speaking; and the Shastri Award (India) for English Prose. Currently she is at work on a second novel, based on the life of Noor Inayat Khan, a Muslim resistance heroine in World War II, who was awarded the George Cross medal for bravery, and another collection of short stories.

Born in 1962 in Montreal, Canada, Baldwin moved with her parents to India in 1972, where she attended school and college in Delhi. After earning an M.B.A. from Marquette University in Milwaukee, Wisconsin, in 1983, she returned to Canada but was back in Milwaukee three years later and has made her home there ever since. Married to an Irish American restaurant designer, David Baldwin, she produced an independent East Indian radio show, *Sunno!* (Listen!) from 1991 to 1994. She has worked full-time at her e-commerce consulting business, Shauna Baldwin Associates, Inc., since 1992, while continuing to write and travel extensively to conduct research for her historical fictional narratives.

While much of the discussion of Baldwin's work has centered on *What the Body Remembers,* which has been translated into Catalan, Dutch, French, German, Greek, Hebrew, Italian, Spanish, and Turkish, the stories in *English Lessons* are worthy precursors to the novel. Largely vignettes of the lives of Sikh women in three countries, India, Canada, and the United States, the 15 stories range in time from 1919 to the present day. They trace the lives of characters as young as 10 (in "Family Ties"), through young immigrants in Canada and the United States (in "English Lessons," "Devika," and "Montreal 1962"), to Indian mothers whose children are studying abroad (in "Rawalpindi 1919" and "Simran"), to elderly women in India and Canada (in "A Pair of Ears" and "Jassie"). At the same time, they describe more directly the contact between Eastern and Western cultures within the context of women's roles, as in "Nothing Must Spoil this Visit," in which the American Janet visits India with her Indian husband. In all these stories, Baldwin demonstrates her thematic engagement with questions of women's survival, cultural displacement, and historical exigency, as well as her considerable technical skill at incorporating disparate narrative perspectives, sensuous descriptive writing, and a wry wit to address what she describes as her "two audiences—one for whom they [her books] are written, the other at whom they are written" (<http://www.umiacs.umd.edu/users/sawweb/sawnet/books/shauna_bookclub.txt>; available 26 January 2003).

Beginning life as the short story "Satya," Baldwin's novel *What the Body Remembers* is set in undivided Punjab between 1937 and 1947, thus chronicling both the last decade of British colonial rule in India and its culmination in the brutal Partition of 1947. Contesting the relative global silencing of subcontinental Partition history, Baldwin points out that until 1998 there were only about 600 nonfiction books and five novels in English on the Indian Partition compared to more than 70,000 books about the American Civil War and thousands of novels in English and other languages about World War II and the Holocaust (Sinha, "SAWNET Bio"). Considering patriarchal colonial and Indian nationalist discourse as well as the overwhelmingly male perspective in the Indian fiction of the Partition era, Baldwin writes into history a female script revolving around two women narrators, Satya (whose name means "truth") and Roop (whose name means "body"), co-wives of Sardarji, a wealthy, Anglicized Punjabi landowner whose family is violently displaced by the Partition. To challenge the ideological bases of the male generic tradition of the *bildungsroman* and to subvert patriarchal control of women's sexuality, Baldwin "re-members" a discourse of women's pain, desire, sadness, and happiness in the interlinked, personal stories of Satya and Roop as primary narrative, and another story that serves only secondarily as an allegory of the political, bloody coming-of-age story of postcolonial India and Pakistan. Further, her novel denounces the oppressions of colonial English as well as Hindi linguistics in various ways: by incorporating indigenous, Punjabi words, translations of local proverbs, transliterated expression, and local colloquialisms and word patterns, and omitting a glossary, Baldwin forges an idiom that accurately reflects pre-Partition Punjabi culture and sensibility. Not only, then, does Baldwin foreground Sikh women's voices as resistant and thus write an alternative version of subcontinental, pre-Independence national history as it is told by British and upper-class Hindu politicians and historians, but she also challenges the elitist bias of most Indian nationalist historiography through her focus on a host of lower-class characters from the small village of Pari Darvaza—Kusum, Huma, Mani Mai, Bachan Singh, and Abu Ibrahim, among others—who, after Satya, Roop, and Sardarji, are the chief actresses and actors of her script.

Since the terrorist attacks of September 11, 2001, on the World Trade Center and the Pentagon, Baldwin has done considerable activist work on behalf of Sikh Americans and other minorities who bore the brunt of the racist backlash in the United States. To both terrorists and racists she says: "Each of us is given the ability to create or destroy—I opt to create;" and to her readers she admits, "Writing helps," thus underlining the therapeutic and functional role of writing in a world torn asunder by religious, national, ethnic, racial, linguistic, gender-, class-, and caste-based, and economic/corporate ideologies among others (Fitzgerald, *The Writer* 23). And it is Baldwin's interest in history—based on her conviction that "the repetitions of history are most striking. How much has not changed, but merely been renamed"—as well as her awareness of the exclusions of women from the historical arena that keeps her "read[ing] [and, one might add, writing] in search of her story" ("In Search of Herstory").

Harveen Sachdeva Mann

Further Reading

Baldwin, Shauna Singh. "Author Essay." 26 Jan. 2003 <http://www.randomhouse.com/boldtype/1199/ baldwin/essay.html>.
———. "In Search of Herstory." 2 Oct. 2000 <http://www.powells.com/portals/GlobalWriting.html>.
———. "What I've Learned from Writing." 26 Jan. 2003 <http://www.umiacs.umd.edu/users/sawweb/sawnet/books/shauna_writing.html>.
Fitzgerald, Mark. "Expressing the Inexpressible: The Power of Words in the Face of National Tragedy." *The Writer* 114.12 (2001): 22–26.
Rennicks, Rick. "Borders.com Interview: Talking with Shauna Singh Baldwin." 27 Apr. 2000 <http://www.go.borders.com/features/rrsinghbaldwin.xcx>.
"SAWNET Bio: Shauna Singh Baldwin." 26 Jan. 2003 <http://www.umiacs.umd.edu/users/sawweb/sawnet/books/shauna_singh_baldwin.html>.
Sinha, Nupur. "Nupur Sinha Interviews Shauna Singh Baldwin." 26 Jan. 2003 <http://www.umiacs.umd.edu/users/sawweb/sawnet/books/ssb_031802.html>.

Bangladeshi Literature in English

There has been a notable rise of English writing in Bangladesh during the last couple of decades. The situation was rather different immediately after liberation of the country in 1971. The use of English in public life was drastically restricted with Bangla being declared the only official language and medium of education at all levels. English was reduced to the status of a foreign language, and English-medium schools were discouraged. Linguistic nationalism had emulated inspiration from examples of Bengali poets such as Michael Madhusudan Dutt (1824–73) who eventually became a greater poet when writing in his native language instead of in English. Writers were not encouraged to publish in English, since there were only a handful of connoisseurs within the country. And internationally, the interest in new literatures in English was yet to receive the momentum it has now reached. These are some of the reasons for the lagging of English writing in Bangladesh as compared to other South Asian countries. However, the recent change in the public attitude toward English has immensely improved the readership and practice of English in the country. Colleges and universities now offer English as a course of study, and English-medium schools have become more prevalent.

The tradition of English writing in Bangladesh owes much homage to writers such as Dutt, Begum Rokeya Sakhawat Hossain (1880–1932) and Nirad Chandra Chaudhuri (1897–1999) who were born in what is now known as Bangladesh. Dutt wrote many poems in the Miltonic manner, Hossain is known for her feminist satire, *Sultana's Dream* (1908), which is written in a Swiftian strain. After independence in the 1970s, poetry writing increased dramatically, as the poets began espousing the sufferings of the liberation war. Writers of the 1980s conscientiously dealt with contemporary issues of Bangladesh, and the 1990s saw an increase of women writers in English.

Some eminent short story writers in English of the 1970s were Sayeed Ahmad, Abu Rushd, Abu Jafar Shamsuddin, Shaheed Akand and Syeed Samsul Haque. Akand's "Option for a Single Prayer"; Haque's "The Dream-Eater"; Rushd's "Pangs" and Shamsuddin's "The Dinner"—were all published in the *Bangla Academy Journal* (1970). Farhana Haque Rahman has published a book on satirical pieces, *Stalking Serendipity and Other Pasquinades* (1990). Niaz Zaman published a collection of short stories *The Dance and Other Stories* (1996). Some of these stories were previously published abroad and received international acknowledgement. Her stories are told in a translucent and eloquent manner with an insinuation of fantasy folktale. Razia Khan Amin has edited a collection titled, *Short Stories from Bangladesh* (1997). Sayeema T. Hasan Tori (an undergraduate in the United States) has compiled a collection of short stories, *The Stage is Yours* (2000).

Short stories published by some remarkable writers in the international journal, *Six Seasons Review* (2001–02, 2 vols.,

Numbers 1, 2, 3, 4) are Khademul Islam's "Cyclone," which is a retrospection of his childhood and focuses on how the country had prepared for freedom and independence during the 1960s. "An *Ilish* Story" reflects on the Bengali saga of eating Hilsa fish with the background of a new country that has just attained independence. Syed Monzoorul Islam's "Keeping Watch" and "Extramarital" (from his stillborn English novel) are stories of ordinary Bangladeshi people cleverly told from a postmodernist perspective. Syed Badrul Ahsan's short story "Faces, Images, Bits of Life" is a kaleidoscopic vision of his colorful past narrated in a fascinating manner. His language is rich with personal and intellectual allusions. Nuzhat Amin's "Transformation" focuses on how a girl in Bangladesh goes through immense transformation in the process of an arranged marriage to a stranger. In "A Touch of Midsummer in the Night," Shahid Alam tries to capture the picture of Dhaka during the time of the war for independence. Currently a manuscript version of his English novel has been accepted by an American press and is in the process of publication. Alam has effectively transformed the language of Shakespeare to narrate a tale of Bangladesh. Nupu Chaudhuri's "Secret Vices" (from his English novel, *A Grand Wedding,* in progress) is a comic story of a matrimonial matter very typical of the subcontinent. Aali A. Rahman's "Waiting" is a story about a man arduously waiting for his expectant wife at the labor room. Most of these stories are based on contemporary issues of Bangladesh, the independence war in retrospect, coping with natural disasters, and family matters. Syed Maqsud Jamil's "The Homecoming" (2002) was published in *The Daily Star* literary page. The story is based on the experiences of a city dweller returning to his rural roots in the past. *Zuleikha's Dream and Other Stories* (2002) by Shamim Hamid is a collection of short stories, imbued with feminist fervor, about struggling women in Bangladesh. Ahsan Senan's *The Tenth Victim* (2003) is a contribution of detective stories written ingeniously in the Western genre of detective fiction.

There were some plays written in English in the 1960s. Sayeed Ahmad's plays have placed him at the forefront of Bangladeshi theatre. His first two plays *The First Thing* (1961) and *The Milepost* (1964) are based on the contest and companionship between nature and humanity, and the strife to survive in cyclone- and famine-struck Bangladesh. His third play *Survival* (1967) is polemical in theme. The play depicts the exploitation of the common masses by the government in a powerful metaphorical expression combined with Bengali folk stories. His last play in English, *The Last King* (1989) is a historical play on the defeat of the last Nawab of Bangladesh, Sirajudduala, at the battle of Plassey by Robert Clive of the British East India Company. His plays are influenced by the style of Chinese opera and Indian street theatre, and his language is firmly bound with elements of realism and the folk theatre of Bangladesh.

During the 1970s and 1980s, Bangladeshi novels dealt with contemporary issues of an independent nation. Rushd's novel, *The Unadjusted Tune* (1977) is a translation of his own Bangla novel. Niaz Zaman, originally a Punjabi married to a Bangladeshi, wrote a novel entitled *The Crooked Neem Tree* (1982) during her exile in the liberation war. The novel recapitulates the urban lifestyle of the upper middle-class in Dhaka during the 1960s. Zaman deserves compliment for compiling several texts of translated short stories on war and miscellaneous themes by Bangladeshi writers and translating fairy tales and folktales of Bangladesh. Abu Rushd's novel *The Aborted Island* (1985) portrays the struggling life of a slum woman. Sanjib Dutta's novel *Juda Tree* (1986) written in the modern style of stream of con-

sciousness depicts some of the unfathomable dimensions of life. Abdul Matin's memoir *When the Grass was Green* (1989) written in the form of a bildungsroman is about a village boy growing up in a conservative family. S. M. Ali has published two books, *Rainbow over Padma* (1994) and *After the Dark Night* (1974). The first book is a novel that depicts the struggle of a group of people trying to create a new future against all odds, chiefly challenging the rotten sociopolitical order in the country. *Seasonal Adjustments* (1994), a prize-winning novel by Adib Khan, a Bangladeshi expatriate in Australia, delineates a story about a Bangladeshi immigrant who returns to his homeland and tries to adjust with everything; it is a novel of diaspora tradition that links him with writers such as Salman Rushdie and Amitav Ghosh. Farhana Haque Rahman, in her novel *The Eye of the Heart* (1998), reproduces a detailed experience of a newly appointed Bangladesh ambassador to Washington through an exceptional eye for detailed narrative skill. Razia Khan Amin published an English novel, *Draupadi,* which she had translated from her own novel in Bangla (1998). The novel is a jovial representation of a triangular relationship between three protagonists juxtaposed by the underlying anxieties of the liberation war looming in the foreground. Sayema T. Hasan's novella *Ava* (1998) recreates the world of the Zamindars of the bygone days of Bengal. *The Storyteller* (2000) by Abid Khan resembles Salman Rushdie's *The Moor's Last Sigh.*

Poetry writing has developed more in Bangladesh than any other form of literature. Some noteworthy poetry collections of the 1970s are Ajit Kumar Niyogi's *Flashing Wings* (1972); Sanjib Datta's *Eyeless in the Urn* (1974); Datta's poems portray the hurtful realization of his father's murder by Pakistani soldiers during the war. Feroz Ahmed-ud-din's poems in

This Handful of Dust (1974) and *Passage to America* (1979) are characterized by irony, revealing a mixture of bemused detachment and inescapable fascination.

Michael Madhusudan Dutt (1824–73), a major Bengali poet of the nineteenth century was born in what is now Bangladesh. Before he started writing in his native tongue, he wrote several verses, essays, and letters in English. He even translated some of his plays into English. His unfulfilled ambition to become an English bard is often held as an object lesson of the folly for those who desired to forge poetry in a foreign tongue. "The Captive Lady" and "Vision of the Past" are two of his best long poems. The theme of "The Captive Lady" is based on Indian mythology and "Vision of the Past" focuses on Christian elements. It was Dutt's English poetry and his invaluable knowledge of devising classical epic poetry, mythology, Miltonic couplets and sonnets that garnered him wide acclaim.

Poetry writing during the 1960s was scarce, but during the 1970s, after the experience of the liberation war in 1971 and the gaining of the long cherished independence, poetry writing became more prevalent. The gloriously earned victory and the agony of loss alongside became the principal theme of poetry in Bangla and English as well. Ajit Kumar Niyogi's book of verse, *Flashing Wings* (1972) is romantic and almost sentimental, but weak in craftsmanship. Sanjib Datta's *Eyeless in the Urn* (1972) is a hurtful cognizance of the war in which he lost his aged father who was brutally murdered by the Pakistani army. Poems by Feroz Ahmed-ud-din in *This Handful of Dust* (1974) and *Passage to America* (1979) are written in response to America, characterized by low-key irony underscored with values of love and friendship.

Razia Khan Amin is a major figure in English poetry in Bangladesh who started writing poetry in the 1960s. In her two collections, *Argus under Anesthesia* (1976) and *Cruel April* (1977), she focuses on the atrocities of war and recreates the wasteland of T. S. Eliot using her own diction of a war-struck Bangladesh. The verse woefully portrays the gruesome reality of war and the unforgivable murder of the teeming millions in *Argus under Anesthesia*. Poems such as "The Grave of Time" and "I Buried You" speak of time, change, the poignant loss of love, and the end of adolescence. In the serial poem "Carmel" her psychological conflict invokes Christian spiritualism, particularly the tradition of the English metaphysical poets. The style that she adopts in these poems may be inspiring but finds consolation only in the limited circle of an educated class in Bangladesh. Regretfully, Razia Khan has stopped writing poetry and changed her focus to writing fiction.

The theme of Halima Khatun's *Silhoutte and Starlight* (1981) ranges from romantic to domestic ideas, underlined by an amiable tone of feminism. S. K. M. Hassan's poems in *Inner Edge* (1987) and *Ashes and Sparks* (1989) are poems of political interest. Nadeem Rahman's *Poems of Expiation* (1992) is an interesting collection of various forms of guilt transformed from a Bangladeshi platform yet stunningly fresh and universal in appeal.

Kaiser Haq is one of the most prominent poets who write in English from Bangladesh. He has published five slim collections of poetry of which *A Happy Farewell* (1994), *The Black Orchid* (1996), and *The Logopathic Reviewer's Song* (2002) have earned him much prestige in South Asian literary circles. Haq's poetry bears the stamp of contemporary society and culture, imagery of both familiar urban and rural Bangladesh. His use of subcontinental English diction, as in "Civil Service Romance," is distinctively hilarious. This particularly affiliates him with Indian poets like Nissim Ezekiel who have playfully experimented with the English language to infuse pleasure and humor into poetry.

Shawkat Haider has published two volumes of poems, *Graffiti* (1994) and *A Day with Destiny* (2002). His poems are based on the typical trial and tribulations of life, the innerscape of mind and even the vocation of poetry writing itself. He is influenced by archaic diction and traditions of romantic and Victorian poetry in English. He is at his best when writing on personal themes. Assafuddowlah's poems in *Rain Clouds* (2000) are influenced and coupled in the diction of Sufi tradition, eluding to mysticism and spiritualism. Mizanur Rahman has published two notable volumes of poems: *A Heart That Bleeds* and *Under the Same Sky under the Same Sun* (2002). Rebecca Haque's poems in *Commencement Poems and Occasional Essays* (2003) reflect some deeply felt personal grief. Neeman A. Sobhan has published some poems and essays on her travel experiences to Rome in *An Abiding City* (2002).

Nuzhat Amin's poem "Valentine: For Husband and Valentine: For Wife"; Farida Majid's "New York Poem I: Garbage Truck Blues" and "New York Poem II: An Insomniac's Prayer" (expatriate); Niaz Zaman's "Big Boys Don't Cry"; Razia Sultana Khan's "The Elusive Muse" and "Go and Open the Door"; Shafi A. Khaled's "Tick Tock" (expatriate); Tazeen M. Murshid's "Promises" (expatriate); Batool Sarwar's "Fulfillment"; Rumana Siddique's "My Thirtieth Season"; and Shihab Sarker's "Days and Nights of a Botanist" are all published in different volumes of *Six Season's Review* (2001–02). Some poetry collections by budding young poets are worth mentioning, such as Seema Nusrat Amin's *Ramblings* (1999), which reflects on global issues of the time, from AIDS to nuclear tests, incorporating her personal hopes and fears. Reshad Rabbany's *Moments of Surreality: Ballads of the Soul* (2002) is a mature endeavor. Rabbany is confident in his poetic expression, also stunning, imaginative, and sensitive. His poetry reflects the agonized human condition that is threatened by evil yet holds on to dreams to come true—"he will live on holding on to a fist full of dreams," he writes, in "Street Child."

Creative writing in English in Bangladesh is more focused on poetry than on other forms of writing. While the older generation of poets have dwelt more on local issues, the younger generation of poets are shifting their view toward more global and universal matters. The poetic course of Bangladesh is changing rapidly toward a subgenre and is thus challenged with a wider audience that is perhaps still to come. Although the number of poets writing in English has increased, the trend, except for a few exceptions, is yet to take a definite form to receive international acclaim.

Bangladeshi literature in English is largely a corpus of translated works, and creative writing in English is still sparse in the country because unlike other South Asian countries, Bangladesh is largely a monolingual country. Although books by several writers have been translated from Bangla and have received international recognition, the trajectory of literature in English from Bangladesh is still developing. Those who write originally in English, however, are more prone to writing poetry than fiction, although in recent years the practice of fiction writing is increasing and has begun to receive considerable attention.

Masrufa Ayesha Nusrat

Further Reading

Benson, Eugene and L. W. Conolly, eds. *Encyclopedia of Post-colonial Literature in English.* London: Routledge, 1994. 26–27; 627–28; 768–69; 1113–14; 1235–36.

Haq, Kaiser, et al., eds. *Six Seasons Review.* 2 vols. Dhaka: UP Limited, 2001–02.

Bond, Ruskin

Ruskin Bond remains one of many Indian writers who are relatively unknown in the West but are the mainstay of the Indian literary circle and popular with India's considerable reading public. He was awarded the John Llewellyn Memorial Prize in 1957 for the very first book he wrote, in 1951, while in Britain. Entitled *Room on the Roof* (1956), this novel, along with *Vagrants in the Valley*, offers the adventures of an Anglo-Indian boy who escapes the surrounding European community to take to the road. On the road, he encounters the varied and teeming Indian culture that is typified in the Indian market. As one would expect, these novels have been compared often with Rudyard Kipling's *Kim*. In 1992, Bond received the Sahitya Akademi Award for *Our Trees Still Grow in Dehra* (1992), a semi-autobiographical work that offers the kind of stories for which he is well known: stories very local in their interest, offering a social and geographical space that is specifically Dehra Dun and the surrounding Garhwal hills. His most recent award, the Padma Shri (1999), recognized him for his contribution to the cultural life of India. Over the last 40 years, he has written articles, novels, essays, poetry, children's books, and numerous short stories. In an interview given in June 2001, Bond, characteristically self-effacing, said of himself and his work: "I've written from the heart. I'm not the clever, clever sort" (Kohzhisseri).

Bond was born on 19 May 1934 in Kasauli, Uttar Pradesh. He grew up in Dehra Dun and Shimla. He is often referred to as an Anglo-Indian writer and given the fact that much of his writing is of Anglo-Indians, British India, (or the 'Raj' as many of the Britishers who were part of colonial India, a figure that appears often in his works, prefer to remember it), and of Indian spaces that continue to be pervaded by the architecture of colonialism, a noting of his racial inheritance would not be amiss here.

Bond has provided much information himself in interviews he has given to Indian newspapers such as the *Times of India* and *Hindustan Times* over the years. One of his grandfathers came out to India with his regiment in the 1880s during the Second Afghan War, married an Indian and settled in India. Both of Bond's parents were born in India. Bond's parents separated when he was very young and his father died soon after. This very personal history, and its impact on Bond, as well as other scenes of his childhood are to be found in *Our Trees Still Grow in Dehra* and his memoir, *Scenes from a Writer's Life* (1997), which covers the first twenty-one years of his life.

Bond has lived all of his life in India, with the exception of a three-year period in the 1950s when he went to England. In an interview given to Reeta Dutta Gupta at the launch of his *A Bond with the Mountains* in 1998, Bond explained his "return" to India: "The pull was very strong. I realized home was here where I grew up among friends. I knew subconsciously I could write better about India and not a line about England. India is more than a land; it is an atmosphere" (Gupta, *Times of India*). Following his return, he settled in a flat in Astley Hall and began writing while freelancing for newspapers. Bond's journalism, as well as his reflections on the 'writerly' self are collected in *The Lamp is Lit: Leaves from a Journal* (1998), which is a nostalgic remembering of the Dehra Dun of the 1950s, and *Rain in the Mountains: Notes from the Himalayas* (1993), in which Bond records the centrality of the local Himalayas to his conception of himself as a writer. In the mid-60s he moved to the hills around Dehra Dun and has lived in Mussoorie ever since. His most recent work that offers insight into the writerly self is entitled *Landour Days: A Writer's Journal* (2002).

Bond's writing is anchored in a profound interest in the spatial economy of the present, particularly as it testifies to the historical. The majority of his work draws on the Garhwal region of the Himalayas, with its mid-size city of Dehra Dun, that still displays colonial architecture in its street-scenes, markets, buildings and private schools, and the hill-station Mussoorie, with its churches and graveyards dating to the colonial era, and much more. At the same time, the transformation of the space that speaks colonialism in its decaying buildings (most noticeably) is something that is as much a concern in Bond's writings. The contemporary Dehra Dun with its Hindi signage, Bollywood-dictated urban culture, and the surrounding hill-culture is offered as the palimpsest that makes colonial history the partially erased and rewritten past that it is in the present. Amongst the best of such 'local' writings are stories collected in *The Night Train at Deoli and Other Stories* (1988), including stories of adolescent trials and youthful, small-town administrative officials and local troublemakers (goondas). In *When Darkness Falls and Other Stories* (2001), Bond revisits the Dehra Dun of the 1940s and 1950s, somewhat nostalgically. *Time Stops at Shamli and Other Stories* (1990) is also a collection of stories about small-town and village India and its people. There is little in these collections of the political center and concerns of metropolitan India. As Shashi Kamra has noted in an unpublished piece on Bond, "the positive feature" in Bond's fiction of the local is "the recurring sense of cultural continuity and the hold of tradition, both of which act as stabilizing forces." She also points out the suitability of the genre of the short story, with its interest in the momentary, to Bond's purpose: his "fictive universe" is one that dramatizes the "seemingly insignificant," and "momentary joys and sorrows" of the "average Indian."

Bond's abiding interest in natural space, and his ongoing attempt to articulate the interconnectedness he clearly values as an experience, manifests in poems such as "Living with Mountains" (in *A Bond with the Mountains*) and statements such as the following from "Mother Hill" (also in *Bond*): "I like to think that I have become a part of these mountains and that, by living here for so long, I am able to claim a relationship with the trees and wild flowers." This vital relationship spills over into ecological concerns. Over the years he has written articles that comment on the cultural significance of the natural, as for instance in "Trees Make You Feel Younger" (*Hindustan Times,* 25 Sept 1992) where the generic tree becomes an image that brings into focus his personal past, collective past as it is expressed in village India—and the centrality of the banyan tree to its agora-like public space—and asceticism. In another, "Of Birds in My Bushes" (*Hindustan Times,* 4 July 1992), he describes his own participation "in the middle of this civilized wilderness" as he sits on a bench he has made and watches the activity of birds in the bushes. In 1999 he co-produced a book entitled *Himalayan Flowers* in which the authors offer a comprehensive account of the flora and fauna of the region. At its largest level, this sense of interconnection with nature is invoked as a belonging in India—an India Bond believes is more correctly described as 'atmosphere,' not 'land.'

Bond is remembered most for his children's stories. Looked at as a whole, here too we find an interest in layering the present with the past, particularly its cultural texts. In addition to writing original works, Bond 'retells' Hindu myths, contemporary local ghost stories, ghost stories of colonial India, animal stories that are sometimes naturalistic and sometimes fable and stories that celebrate social spaces for their colour and communal celebrations such as Diwali. These include *The Blue Umbrella* (1974), *Road to the Bazaar* (1980), *Tales and Legends from India* (1982), *Grandfather's Private Zoo* (1989), *The Adventures of Rama and Sita* (1990), *Panther's Moon and Other Stories* (1991), the *Penguin Book of Classical Indian Love Stories and Lyrics* (1996), the *Rupa Books of Animal Stories* (2003) and *the Rupa Book of True Tales of Mystery and Adventure* (2003). All the Rusty stories, written over many years, have been collected as *Rusty, the Boy from the Hills* (Delhi: Puffin 2002). There are stories here of Rusty himself: a lonely and sensitive boy who lives with his grandparents in Dehra Dun and witnesses the daily parade of eccentric relatives at the same time as he pursues an interest in the animal world that surrounds him. There are stories also of Rusty's adventures with his father and stories of animals (including one about a python that is narcissus reincarnated—fascinated by his own image). Although his ghost stories do not necessarily fall under the category of children's writings, they are often included in here and are an interesting mix of the historical (ghosts of colonial India) and the native supernaturalism of the area. In *A Season of Ghosts* (1999), for instance, Bond includes tales about demons and fairies, of the oral culture of colonial India—with its stories of murder, mayhem and ghostly hauntings—and even a detective story.

Bond writes as an Anglo-Indian about the Raj era that he knew so well. While the colonial past is to be found in his stories on the local Garhwal hills and its peoples, in his ghost stories, in his stories on the railway (including his Penguin collection of such stories, entitled *The Penguin Book of Indian Railway Stories* [1994]) and of course his Rusty stories, it is also to be found in stories specifically about the Raj. For instance, *Strange Men Strange Places* (1992) relates stories of soldiers and mercenaries employed by the Raj in the eighteenth and nineteenth centuries and the *Penguin Book of Indian Ghost Stories* (1993) and *Ghost Stories from the Raj* (2002) offer stories of supernatural experiences of colonial India by, amongst others, Rudyard Kipling, Satyajit Ray and Arthur Conan Doyle. Collections such as these and Bond's retelling of stories that are part of the oral history and literary culture of the Dehra Dun area in particular emphasize his role as a storyteller.

Bond has yet to receive serious critical consideration. There is only one scholarly book length work in English on Bond, titled, *The Life and Works of Ruskin Bond,* by Meena Khorana. Bond has been interviewed by Indian newspapers a number of times over the last few decades. Finally, there is a festschrift published by Roli Books (Delhi). Titled *Days of Innocence: Stories for Ruskin Bond* (2002), the book derives from a writer's retreat on childhood at the center of which is Ruskin Bond. Writers represented in the festschrift include Namita Gokhale, Binoo John, Kanika Gahlaut and Bulbul Sharma.

Sukeshi Kamra

Further Reading

Gupta, Reeta Dutta. "And Climb Once More the Windswept Mountain Pass." *Times of India* 21 Feb. 1998.

Kamra, Shashi. "Ruskin Bond, Chronicler of a Vanishing Ethos." Unpublished article.

Khorana, Meena. *The Life and Works of Ruskin Bond*. Westport, Connecticut: Greenwood, 2003.

Kozhisseri, Deepa. "I Am Not the Clever, Clever Sort: Ruskin Bond." 29 June 2001 <http://news.indiainfo.com/2001/06/29bond.html>.

Krishnamurthy, Sarala. "Growing Up With Nature." *Deccan Herald.* 10 Nov. 2002 <http://www.deccanherald.com/deccanherald/nov10/book4.asp>.

Wadehra, Amar Nath and Randeep Wadehra. "No Orchids for Mr. Bond." *The Tribune* 15 Apr. 2001 <http://www.tribuneindia.com/2001/20010415/spectrum/main2.htm>.

The Book of Secrets by M. G. Vassanji

The Book of Secrets (1994), like some of Vassanji's other works, including *The Gunny Sack* (1989) and *Uhuru Street* (1992), is set in east Africa and describes the experiences of a fictional East Indian community, the Shamsis, uprooted from its homeland and relocated in Dar es Salaam and surrounding areas. Vassanji's own immigrant experiences have informed and inspired his writing as he was born in Nairobi, Kenya, to Indian parents and raised in Dar es Salaam, Tanzania, before immigrating to the United States and finally settling in Toronto, Canada, in 1978. He describes himself as "an East African Canadian of Indian origin" or "an African Asian Canadian" (Vassanji *Passages* 24). His body of work is preoccupied with understanding the dynamics of exile from one's home and self, attempting to retrieve the history of a formerly colonized people that is both complicated and frequently unrecorded.

This award-winning novel (Vassanji was the inaugural recipient in 1994 of Canada's most prestigious literary award, the Giller Prize) is a multigenerational tale that spans seven decades. The story moves back and forth through time from 1913, just prior to the World War I, to the late 1980s in the bustling city of Dar es Salaam, where retired schoolteacher Pius Fernandes, a Goan, finds himself at the center of a literary mystery connecting the past to the present. The novel details the discovery of a diary, long hidden in Feroz the shopkeeper's storeroom, belonging to a British colonial officer, Alfred Corbin, who is assigned in 1913 to the post of assistant district commissioner in the fledgling town of Kikono, situated near the border of British and German east Africa. Pius resolves to relate the unknown or forgotten stories of the lives the diary has touched, stating with conviction:

> I would—I told myself—recreate the world of that book. I would breathe life into the many spirits captured in its pages so long ago and tell their stories; and I would revive the spirit of the book itself, tell *its* own story. And so I would construct a history, a living tapestry to join the past to the present. . . . (8)

By the novel's end, the reader realizes that *The Book of Secrets* is, in fact, the fulfillment of Pius's quest, as the diary and the novel ultimately become one.

The novel is divided into two main parts, the first of which relates the story of Corbin, and is comprised of a clever mixture of omniscient narration and occasional interjections of Corbin's thoughts embodied in his diary entries. As Corbin and other European colonialists, including two missionary ladies, Miss Elliott and Mrs. Bailey, interact with and attempt to govern and civilize the African and Asian communities of Kikono, the reader witnesses the intrusive exploits of the British colonial initiative that works to eradicate, or at least temper, native customs, traditions, and systems of authority. Significantly, Vassanji is careful to not overtly demonize Corbin as the colonial oppressor or, conversely, to portray the colonized subjects as helpless victims of the imperial mission. Rather, he seems to treat all of his characters, including the British, unapologetically with a sympathy that allows for human failing. Discussing his controversial portrayal of colonial interlopers, Vassanji states: "the fact is that the British administrators too were human and I don't know if it is politically incorrect to say that. There is always a danger of wallowing in the victim syndrome—" 'Look what they did to us' " (Kanaganayakam *Config-*

urations 134). Corbin's diary concludes with the approach of the war in 1914 in which African and Asian colonial subjects under British and German rule were absurdly compelled to fight a European war to defend the right of European hegemony, in effect ensuring the continuation of their own subjugation.

Pius's primary interest in the diary has to do with the enigmatic figure of the young Mariamu, a Swahili girl with whom, it is speculated, Corbin had an affair leading to the birth of a fair-skinned, grey-eyed boy, Aku, who grows up to be known as Ali. Mariamu is wed to Pipa (who was the previous owner of Feroz's shop and the one to conceal the diary in the storeroom) before the birth of Ali, and Pipa is led to believe the child is his. Pipa, however, is haunted for the rest of his life, and especially after Mariamu's mysterious murder, by the suspicion that Ali is not his biological son. Pius wants to solve, for the sake of the historical record, for his own curiosity, and for the satisfaction of his former pupil Rita, who becomes Ali's wife and the mother of his two children, the riddle of Ali's patrilineage.

The second part of *The Book of Secrets* follows Pipa, after Mariamu's death, from Kikono, to Moshi, and finally to Dar es Salaam where he settles in the 1940s and 1950s, remarries, raises a family, and opens a spice shop. His relationship to Ali is tenuous and begins to disintegrate as the approach of independence from colonial rule transforms the world around them. Pipa's fears are realized when Ali breaks away from the family fold and strikes out on his own. Years later, after the failure of his first marriage, the middle-aged Ali meets and falls in love with Rita who is still Pius's student and, indeed, indifferent love interest. Ali and Rita flee to London to marry, dashing Pius's hopes and convincing Pipa that "the son becomes the father" (263); that is, that Ali has gone away to the land of Corbin to become an En-

glishman. The final sections of the novel describe Pius's own journeys as an immigrant living and teaching in east Africa and tell of his particular attachment to and fondness for not only the beautiful Rita, but also for Gregory, an abrasive homosexual Englishman and fellow teacher. Vassanji hints at the possibility of an unexplored sexual relationship between Pius and Gregory but, as with much else in the novel, never offers a definitive answer to the question of Pius's true feelings.

The story concludes with Pius's reluctant relinquishing of the diary and research on Corbin and Mariamu to the safekeeping of Rita, who decides that it is for the best that the past and the truth of Ali's father and her children's grandfather be buried and left undisturbed. Ultimately, while Pius succeeds in recreating the lives of those connected to the diary, Vassanji renders him incapable of solving the riddle of *The Book of Secrets*. Vassanji seems to suggest that reclaiming a past so fraught with interruption, violence, and uncertainty, as is that of any formerly colonized people, is problematic and never wholly possible. Questions remain, and as Vassanji says, "that is the historian-narrator's dilemma—how much *can* we know, how much *dare* we know. . . ." (Kanaganayakam *Configurations* 135).

Dana Hansen

Further Reading

Kanaganayakam, Chelva. *Configurations of Exile: South Asian Writers and Their World.* Toronto: TSAR, 1995.

Vassanji, M. G. "Canada and Me: Finding Ourselves." *Passages: Welcome Home Canada.* Ed. Rudyard Griffiths. Toronto: Doubleday Canada, 2002. 15–34.

British Raj

British rule in India, also known as the British Raj, is often dated from 1757, when Robert Clive defeated the Nawab of Bengal at Plassey. Other European powers—the Dutch, the Portuguese, the French—were still vying for a share of trade in India, however, and in 1759, Clive went on to defeat the Dutch at Biderra; Britain's struggle with France in India was not formally terminated until the 1763 Treaty of Paris. For much of Britain's rule in India, the East India Company was the focal point of power, though Warren Hastings, who succeeded Clive as its governor-general, was the first such to be appointed by the British parliament, and from this point on the British venture in India was less exclusively the domain of commerce. A number of governor-generals of the East India Company went on to help consolidate British rule across the subcontinent, prominent among them Warren Hastings (1774–85), Lord Cornwallis (1786–93), and Lord Wellsley (1798–1805). By 1818, the British controlled nearly all of India south of the Sutlej River, although the Sind and the Punjab were not conquered until, respectively, 1843 and 1849. The East India Company administered the profitable parts of the country—the rich areas with cities—while Indian princes ruled the rest; but practically speaking, the British controlled India.

One of the first important pieces of legislation involving India is Pitt's Indian Act of 1784, which called for a halt to the conquests undertaken by the company. The act was, however, too idealistic a statement of principle for the commercial interests of the company, but it was a strong signal that parliament would take an even more active hand in Indian affairs. Company officials were in agreement in the late eighteenth century that a policy of noninterference in Indian culture was both morally correct and a practical means of maintaining British control of the region. Yet, a number of British endeavors on the subcontinent in the first half of the nineteenth century, some technological and aimed primarily at furthering commerce,

some ideological and designed to influence, or Westernize, Indian society, were to have a profound impact in shaping colonial India and paving the way for the modern states that comprise the subcontinental area.

The British Raj introduced a number of advances and changes in India, many of them self-interested but many also benefiting certain sectors of the Indian population. On the technological front, the steamship was brought to India in the 1820s and launched, in 1828, in Calcutta. As well, thousands of miles of telegraph lines had been installed across India by 1855. In addition, the Grand Trunk Road was built as a link between northern India and Calcutta. One of the most important changes, however, occurred in education. The 1835 resolution that required that English be the language of higher education had a profound impact, helping to create and foster a growing middle class in India that was for the most part willing to work within the British system for advancement. Changes were also introduced in both civil and criminal law, which served to circumvent many of the local legal procedures across India that were particularistic in their judgment. In 1829, for example, a law forbidding *sati* was enacted, and while this might well be the most dramatic example of British values being imposed on Indian culture, it does suggest the potential for the clash of different cultural beliefs and practices. Still, by the nineteenth century a number of Indian intellectuals, most prominently Ram Mohan Roy, were urging the British to bring innovations and change, hoping for India to benefit from the British presence on their soil. But some of the changes made on the subcontinent were driven by evangelical and Victorian elements in England, for in many ways, the English who had come to India—however separately they might live their lives from the natives—were shocked by what they saw, particularly the emphasis upon bodily imagery in some religious depictions.

The changes the Raj brought to India began to make themselves felt among the various social strata, and in 1857 came the Indian mutiny among trusted Indian troops in the parts of India that had come most recently under British control, most prominently along the Gangetic plain. Still, the rebellion affected only a few parts of the subcontinent and was quickly suppressed, but it did lead to overdue modifications in how the British administered India. For one thing, control passed wholly to the crown and away from the company. The British government reached the conclusion that change had been brought too quickly to India, and one ironic outcome of the revolts is that those Westernized Indians who had been most favorably disposed toward the British were to become marginalized, owing to their facility with the English language and British ways.

The system of British control in India had taken the shape of a layered administration. A governor-general, appointed by the British parliament for only a few short years, was at the pinnacle, but beneath him were the district officers, each in charge of his population of about a million Indians; in effect, the district officers would only follow those edicts beneficial to their own local rule. Nearly all of the district officers belonged to the Indian Civil Service, though in 1854, the Service stopped filling its ranks with appointees from Britain and switched to a system of examinations for entrance; in 1869, the Indian was able to earn a slot among the thousand or so district administrators who served to govern India. Beneath the district officers, nearly all administrators were Indian. The civil authorities were in control of the small British military force in India of less than quarter million men, about two-thirds of whom were Indian; all the officers were British. In 1877, in a largely symbolic show, Queen Victoria was crowned Empress of India.

By the 1870s the Indian middle class created by the British system, whose most prominent voice was Surendranath Banerjea, began to focus its energies toward greater Indian participation in the rule of India. In 1885, the Indian National Congress was formed in response to the new governor-general's backtracking on promised reforms. The congress included doctors, lawyers, college teachers and their students, and journalists, and it would remain a viable presence in colonial India for decades to come; it was a moderate force for change that sought greater participation in the Indian Civil Service and legislative councils. More extreme advocates for change were arising in India at the same time, however; these forces, led by such men as B. G. Tilak and Aurobindo Ghose, mistrusted the British and advocated violence and a return to Hindu traditions and values as a means of countering the Raj. In 1906 an Indian Muslim League, which sought cooperation with the British as a safeguard, was created in order to foreground Muslim concerns about the Hindu majority on the subcontinent.

The early twentieth century saw clamoring voices and sporadic violence in India, with the British implementing a series of reforms that would finally lead to Indian independence. There were isolated acts of violence by Indian radicals, mostly young men, and in 1909, the Morley-Minto reforms widened Indian participation in legislation but also created separate Muslim constituencies. The Indian National Congress, which continued to be a largely moderate voice for gradual change, saw the Morley-Minto acts as a British means of fostering Hindu-Muslim conflict. The World War I received Indian support only in its early stages, and in 1917, the British parliament made the Montagu Declaration, announcing that its goal on the subcontinent was "responsible government." By this time Muslims were joining the Indian National Congress, which was becoming increasingly multivocal, with moderate and radical elements. With the 1919 Montagu-Chelmsford Reforms, which created what amounts to a "dyarchy," the British were perceived as moving far too slowly to satisfy much of the congress. In 1919, at the site of a protestation of a government order in Amritsar, the army fired on the crowds, killing four hundred and wounding another thousand.

Among the rising voices that challenged British rule, Mohandas Gandhi was able to achieve the most prominent role by leading nonviolent protest against the British through noncooperation. By situating the concerns of the common Indian masses at the forefront of his movement, he helped to spread the idea of an Indian nation; his emphasis on Hindu culture in his pronouncements, however, caused the Muslim League to move once again in opposition to the Indian congress. Moreover, Jawaharlal Nehru's insistence that the movement toward independence was secular, not religious, troubled the Muslim idea of statehood. In counterpoint to Gandhi, M. A. Jinnah and others began to organize their call for the eventual creation of a separate Muslim state. In 1935 the Government of India Act allowed for Indian provincial government, and in 1937, in the first election held in India under British rule, the Indian National Congress, led by Gandhi and Nehru, was able to form governments in seven of the eleven provinces; Muslims were able to secure three of the provinces. In the years of World War II, during which the British parliament was still moving too slowly toward a responsible government in India, more noncooperation was urged and a number of leaders of the Indian National Congress, which started the Quit India Movement, were jailed; Jinnah, on the other hand, had urged Muslim support for the British war effort. Finally, in 1947, India was partitioned. Nehru became the prime minister of a secular India, and Jinnah became the governor-general of Pakistan.

Michael W. Cox

Further Reading

Broehl, Wayne G. *Crisis of the Raj: The Revolt of 1857 Through British Lieutenants' Eyes.* Hanover: UP of New England, 1986.

Garraty, John A., and Peter Gay, eds. *The Columbia History of the World.* New York: Harper and Row, 1972.

James, Lawrence. *Raj: The Making and Unmaking of British India.* New York: St. Martin's, 1997.

MacMillan, Margaret. *Women of the Raj.* London: Thames and Hudson, 1988.

Quraishi, Burke. *The British Raj in India: An Historical Review.* Karachi: Oxford UP, 1995.

The Buddha of Suburbia by Hanif Kureishi

Hanif Kureishi's first novel, *The Buddha of Suburbia* (1990), returns to his reflections on race, sexuality, and identity, explored previously in his screenplays *My Beautiful Laundrette* (1985), which won him an academy award nomination, and *Sammy and Rosie* (1987). Born in Bromley, Britain, in 1955, to a Pakistani father and a British mother, Kureishi was intimately familiar with racism in Britain from his father's failure to achieve literary fame and social acceptance. His complex relationship with his father, and the his biracial heritage are recurrent tropes in Kureishi's oeuvre, shaping not only *The Buddha of Suburbia,* but also his more recent works such as *The Black Album* (1995), *Love in a Blue Time* (1999), and *Gabriel's Gift* (2001). *The Buddha of Suburbia* evokes a slightly earlier period than the films, depicting the Thatcher years in Britain. This period of the late 1970s already marks a transition for the South Asian immigrant community in Britain, in the first intimations of de-industrialization, the disintegration of the notion of the welfare state, and a rise in violence against immigrants.

The Buddha of Suburbia is a multilayered, polyphonic novel, offering us glimpses of multiple social realms, combining elements of the picaresque and satire. Infusing the main plot of a *bildungsroman,* the novel depicts the growth of the hero, Karim Amir, into an artist, with the riotous spirit of comedy. The title of the novel refers to Karim's father, and his career is an important element of the plot. Karim's father, referred to as "Dad," or "God," in the novel, immigrated to Britain in the 1950s, found employment as a clerk, married a working-class white woman, and settled down in a London suburb to raise two boys. The humdrum predictability of Dad's life is forever disrupted, when under the tutelage of Eva, he discovers his new vocation as a Buddhist guru, offering the consumerist inmates of London suburbia the desirable salve of oriental spiritual therapy. Dad's adventures as the Buddha are rendered through the point of view of Karim, the autobiographical voice in the novel. The Buddha, far from being a spiritual mystic, is a man in the throes of a very worldly mid-life crisis of love and personal identity. His yogic lectures are punctuated by sexual escapades with Eva, leading ultimately to his decision to leave his wife and sons. However, his audience, who are steeped in the modern, industrial Western expectations of the East as the esoteric other, unquestioningly laps up his message. Kureishi is conscious of the inherent irony of the situation in which a man, whose personal choices are distinctly secular and modern, is apotheosized as a spiritual guru.

The changes in Dad's life also pave the way for Karim's move from the suburbs to London, beginning his odyssey into the counterculture of the late 1970s, highlighted by rock music, drugs, and sexual adventure. In Shadwell's production of Rudyard Kipling's *The Jungle Book,* Karim gets his first break in acting as Mowgli, an Indian boy, who has lived in the jungle and has been nurtured by the wolves. So although Indian, he is a half-human creature. Shadwell dismisses Karim's first attempt at Mowgli as being "inauthentic," since Karim's accent is not Indian enough. Although Kureishi satirizes Shadwell's artistic and political limitations, he also offers a counterpoint by depicting the dangers of politically motivated art in the avant garde theater of Pyke. Pyke encourages his troupe of actors to be involved in the writing of the play by creating characters drawn from their intimate autobiographical material. Although outwardly very liberating, this company does not allow Karim to portray a character he creates from his personal experience of his father's friend, Anwar. The reason stated by Tracey, Karim's co-actor, is that such a portrait of a high-strung patriarch forcing his daughter into an arranged marriage would reinforce existing stereotypes and would be politically reactionary. Although deeply committed to a left-wing multicultural politics, Kureishi is acutely aware of the stifling impact of a regime of political correctness on artistic expression.

The character Karim ends up developing is that of Changez, the husband of his friend and sporadic sexual partner, Jamila. Changez begins as a caricature of the fresh-off-the-boat immigrant, who enters into an arranged marriage with an extremely reluctant Jamila. He soon discovers the unlimited possibilities of sexual-fantasy fulfillment in England, and despite Jamila's indifference and refusal of marital intimacies, he develops an unswerving devotion for his wife, unshaken even when she has a child by another man. He is a terrible disappointment to his father-in-law, shirking the immigrant work ethic and notions of patriarchal honor, but he retains a firm hold of the reader's sympathy, especially when he becomes the target of a vicious racial attack. In portraying the character of his friend, Karim betrays his promise not to ridicule him in public, but Changez accepts the betrayal genially.

Kureishi is quite critical of the mores of the artistic community, especially in the manipulation of the mass media that is deliberately embarked on in the creation of stars like Charlie Hero. Even a politically committed artist like Pyke embodies the contradictions between his support of working-class politics and the reality of his class privilege revealed in the elite schools he chooses for his children.

This novel is successful in its witty exposure of myriad social contradictions, its debunking of many traditional institutions, and its affirmation of the restless spirit of change. It won the Whitbread Book of the Year Award for the First Novel category, and it is now regarded as a classic text of postcolonial literature.

Lopamudra Basu

Further Reading

Kaleta, Kenneth. *Hanif Kureishi: Postcolonial Storyteller.* Austin: U of Texas P, 1998.

Kureishi, Hanif. "The Rainbow Sign." *London Kills Me: Three Screenplays and Four Essays.* New York: Penguin, 1992.

Moore-Gilbert, Bart J. *Hanif Kureishi.* Manchester and New York: Manchester UP, 2001.

Ranansinha, Ruvani. *Hanif Kureishi.* Tavistock: Northcote House, 2002.

C

The Calcutta Chromosome
by Amitav Ghosh

Amitav Ghosh's *The Calcutta Chromosome* begins with Antar, a clerk for the International Water Council, gazing into his neo-Orwellian computer, AVA, as it tries to reconstruct an old ID card. Antar begins to investigate the history of the lost owner of the ID card, Murugan, who disappeared from records in 1995. The reader meets Murugan in Calcutta on his quest for the history of malaria, where he accidentally meets Urmila and Sonali. As we are introduced to these characters, they become "diseased" and are compelled to play their part in the malaria story.

The story speeds like a thriller: Urmila, chasing a fishmonger's boy to exchange her rotten fish, bumps into Murugan again, who unravels Cunningham's (an Englishman investigating malaria in the late nineteenth century) story with the help of the ancient train timetable in which Urmila's fish was wrapped. Murugan explains to the bewildered Urmila, "Someone's trying to get us to make some connections; they're trying to tell us something; something they don't want to put together themselves" (Ghosh, *The Calcutta* 216).

Suddenly the pieces of the story fall into place as Murugan and Urmila discover that Laakhan or Lutchman, is the same person (or phantom) who worked for Cunningham as an assistant to his apprentice Mangala; together they experimented

with pigeons by infusing malarial germs into them, then transferring their blood to cure syphilitic patients, thereby creating the "Calcutta Chromosome." This addition to the traditional Mendelian chromosomes had the ability to transfer character traits across species. As Urmila and Murugan reconstruct history, it becomes clear to the reader that Mangala and Lutchman have been reincarnated once again. The story ends with Antar re-viewing Murugan's story, but with different characters as his neighbor Tara and her friend Maria replace Urmila and Sonali. This suggests that the story can never be quite over, for as each character ends a story, a new one begins.

One of the major themes of this book is the dichotomy between science/rationality (the West) and magic/irrationality (the East). However, unlike most other texts that explore this dichotomy, magic/irrationality is privileged over science/rationality. Mangala comes upon the cause of malaria by accident through methods that would be classified as unscientific, and thus forces a space for magic and chance within the rational discourse of science. Not only do Mangala and Lutchman give Ross the solution to the malaria problem, (Lutchman accidentally stumbles into Ross's laboratory), but they do it so artfully that he never suspects that he is being manipulated. Murugan explains Mangala's motives to Urmila, "She's not in this because she wants to be a scientist. She's in this because she thinks she's a god"

(Ghosh, *The Calcutta* 251), and this sharply illustrates their disparate modes of functioning.

This book has often been referred to as science fiction, but while it may use some external devices of the science fiction novel such as a space-age computer, the narrative that slips frequently between present and future in a clipped fast-paced style is more textured than the usual science fiction novel. For the novel is ultimately about the postcolonial subject's (Mangala) ability to speak in its own voice—that of magic/irrationality. Murugan, a product of Western science must undergo many trials before he is able to understand Mangala's story. Murugan then becomes the anchor on which the reader relies for a translation of his language into a language of cause and consequences, which the reader is better able to understand.

Most critical attention to the book has labeled it as science fiction, as an article in the *Science Fiction Weekly* states, "*The Calcutta Chromosome* is fast, subtle, funny, haunting; and there is just enough SF in the mix to make the whole thing work in genre terms" (Clute). As Ingraham suggests it is also a "compelling tale of suspense at the intersection of science and the paranormal" (101). Sudeep Sen categorizes the text as "a literary thriller that contains within its folds advanced science, intellectual exploration, and fertile imagination" (221). Though it does fit into the genre of science fiction, it is more than that: "[*The Calcutta Chromosome* is a] dazzling and haunting mix of science fiction, the history of malaria research, thriller, ghost story and postcolonial allegory" (Chew 47). It is the situation of the science fiction thriller in a postcolonial context that makes this novel more than a tall tale about malaria: it becomes a space for the enactment of subaltern histories.

Another major theme of the book is the intersection of private and public history. Though Ronald Ross's discovery of the cause of malaria is famous, as the novel draws out, Ghosh suggests the presence of other unrecorded histories. These histories though situated in the realm of the paranormal are presented as equally valid alternatives to the public history. As Clute writes, "Ghosh (who has specialized in medical journalism) cannot be over praised for the ingenuity of his presentation of 'real' and 'fictional' history at this point." As characters in the novel become involved with these personal histories, ironically enough, the public history begins to seem more unreal.

Amitav Ghosh was born on July 11, 1956, in Bangladesh. He studied history at St. Stephen's College, Delhi University, and went on to pursue his doctorate in anthropology at Oxford. He did an ethnographic study in the fellaheen village of Lataifa while at the University of Alexandria. He has taught sociology at the Delhi School of Economics, and has been teaching comparative literature at Queen's College, City University of New York since 1999.

Krupa Shandilya

Further Reading

Chew, Shirley. "The Calcutta Chromosome." *New Statesman* 125 (1996): 47.

Clute, John. "A Tale Decent Folk Can Buy." *Science Fiction Weekly* (1997). 11 Nov. 2002 <http://www.scifi.com/sfw/issue56/excess.html>.

Ingraham, Janet. "The Calcutta Chromosome." *Library Journal* 15 Sept. 1997: 101.

Kich, Martin, "Mosquito Bites and Computer Bytes: Amitav Ghosh's *The Calcutta Chromosome*." *Notes on Contemporary Literature* 30.4 (Sept. 2000): 9–12.

Sen, Sudeep. Review of *The Calcutta Chromosome* by Amitav Ghosh. *World Literature Today* 71.1 (Winter 1997): 221–22.

Chandra, Vikram

A novelist, short-story writer, screenwriter, and essayist, Chandra was born in Delhi in 1961. His father, Navin, is a successful businessman, and Chandra has been surrounded by writers in his immediate family: his mother Kamna has written for film, radio, and television, his sister Tanuja is a screenwriter and film director, and his sister Anupama is a film critic and journalist for the popular magazine *India Today.* This family background presumably influenced Chandra's own course as a writer, as well as his forays into writing for cinema. Having received his secondary education at Mayo College in Rajasthan, Chandra earned his bachelor's degree in English and creative writing from Pomona College (California) in 1984. He then began studies at Columbia University Film School in New York, but left to pursue advanced degrees in writing. He attained an M.A. at Johns Hopkins University and an M.F.A. at the University of Houston, where he studied under John Barth and Donald Barthelme, respectively. Currently, Chandra is teaching creative writing at George Washington University in Washington, D.C., and divides his time equally between Washington and Mumbai.

Composed over the course of his enrollment in graduate writing programs, Chandra's first novel, *Red Earth and Pouring Rain,* appeared in 1995 and met with widespread acclaim, receiving both the David Higham Prize for Fiction and the Commonwealth Writers Prize for Best First Book. The structure of the novel involves the alternating narratives of two characters: Abhay Misra, an Indian student recently returned from college in the United States, and Sanjay (or Parasher), an eighteenth-century Brahmin poet reincarnated as a monkey. As Sanjay is obliged to Yama, the god of death, to entertain a listening audience with a story, Abhay stands in for Sanjay when the monkey becomes too exhausted to continue. With the frame story of these narratives providing a commentary on the questions of authority and audience in storytelling, the tales themselves allow Chandra to make use of

history, mythology, popular culture, and current events in his novel. Critics have pointed to the influence of a wide variety of sources on the novel, from Indian poetry—the novel's title is taken from the *nom de plume* of a fourth-century Tamil poet—to colonial history to current literary fiction, which Christopher Rollason traces to novels by South Asian contemporaries like Salman Rushdie and Michael Ondaatje as well as tales by Jorge Luis Borges, Herman Melville, and Edgar Allan Poe.

Chandra's second book, the short-story collection *Love and Longing in Bombay,* was published in 1997, again to general critical approbation; it appeared on several newspaper reviewers' "best of the year" lists, made the shortlist for the Guardian Fiction Prize, and won the Commonwealth Writers Prize for Best Book the following year. The five stories in the collection are each named for precepts of Hindu philosophy: "Dharma" (duty), "Shakti" (strength), "Kama" (desire), "Artha" (economy), and "Shanti" (peace). Chandra has remarked that he sought to "see how these [abstract] principles . . . worked their way through ordinary lives" ("The Cult" par. 3), and indeed all the stories combine to present a portrait of contemporary Bombay that is thoroughly shaped by these ideals. More than in *Red Earth and Pouring Rain,* Chandra's short stories explore popular genres of fiction, including the ghost story, "Dharma," the detective story, "Kama," and the romance novel "Shanti," although, as in Chandra's novel, the different stories are united by a common narrator, in this case the retired civil servant Subramaniam.

Chandra's two books so far have several themes in common. One especially noticeable correlation is the emphasis on oral narrative, inasmuch as each text presents the ways in which, and the circumstances under which, we tell stories. Both books use frame stories in which the narrator begins each new tale by urging his listeners, and by extension, Chandra's own readers, to literally *listen*. Such a dramatic device underscores the interrelationship of narrator and listener/reader, thereby allowing Chandra's works to explore the possibilities and problems inherent in fiction writing. How does one adapt a tale to meet the audience's expectations? How much, and what, should the author expect of the audience? What can storytelling accomplish beyond mere entertainment (if anything)? In addition to such generic questions, Chandra's emphasis on oral rather than written narrative places his writing within the larger South Asian tradition in which Hindu epics such as the *Mahabharata* and the *Ramayana* take the form of dictations and in which songs and poems routinely address their idealized listeners directly. Thus, Chandra's works form a kind of, in his own word, "conversation" between the ancient storytelling traditions of the subcontinent and modern "world" literature.

This kind of conversation underscores a second theme in Chandra's fiction: the intersection, collision, and hybridization of different cultures. In *Red Earth and Pouring Rain,* for example, Sanjay must alter his preferred storytelling style—that of the traditional epic—to hold his audience of modern Indian children, who wear American football T-shirts and play video arcade games. More centrally, in his tale Sanjay describes his nearly metaphysical attraction to the English language and its literature, and the lengths to which he goes to master both. Similarly, Abhay's story (which also re-tells stories from his American undergraduate companions and other travelers) returns again and again to the sense of dislocation engendered by migrancy, especially manifested in carefully detailed titles of pop songs and television shows. In *Love and Longing in Bombay,* the story "Dharma" offers a dialogue of sorts between the storyteller, Subrama-

nian, and the much younger, unnamed first-person narrator, who works at a software company in Bombay (Chandra himself has worked as a computer software consultant, and he has included his E-mail address on the covers of both his books). The younger man argues against the old ways and for India to be brought into what he considers the modern world: "I spoke at length then, about superstition and ignorance and the state of our benighted nation, in which educated men and women believed in banshees and ghouls. 'Even in the information age we will never be free' " (Chandra, "Dharma" 4). The collection as a whole seems to counter that the romance of storytelling must coexist with the details of contemporary life, as Chandra refers to the presence of such commercial entities as MTV and Benetton clothing stores. In particular, the detective story "Kama," which features as a backdrop the rise of the Hindu nationalist group Shiv Sena, suggests strongly that such radical efforts to recapture a lost cultural purity are misguided, if not outright immoral.

Indeed, Chandra's perspective on the possibility of *Indianness* emerges quite clearly in his essay "The Cult of Authenticity." In this piece, Chandra recounts a public disagreement between himself and the Indian literary critic Meenakshi Mukherjee, in which Mukherjee accused Chandra of using mundane details of Indian life to signal Indianness to Western readers, thereby exoticizing (and demeaning) the experiences of ordinary native Indians. In the course of his response to this charge, Chandra discusses several common assumptions about authors who write Indian fiction in English: that writers who do not live full time in India are insulated from Indian experience and subject to nostalgia; that it is impossible to write properly about India in English at all, since regional languages necessarily better reflect the realities of Indian life; that writers of Indian literature in English are targeting (and are limited to) a Western audience; and that these writers do so solely in order to capitalize on the financial opportunities that attend publication in English. After noting that "the most vociferously anti-Western crusaders are inevitably the ones who are the most hybrid" (par. 37), Chandra goes on to say that the possibilities of Indian fiction should not be limited by prescriptions such as those that favor regional writing: "To be self-consciously anti-exotic is also to be trapped, to be censored. Be free. Give up nothing, and swallow everything" (par. 43). Instead, he aligns himself overtly with Borges, who similarly argued, in 1951, against fellow Argentines' ideology that true Argentine writing must eschew European traditions. To Chandra, an artist's purpose is to find ways of making material, whether traditional or Western or "exotic," one's own.

In 1996, Chandra's teleplay of the popular series *City of Gold* was produced; Chandra also cowrote the script for the film *Mission Kashmir* (2000), directed by the Indian filmmaker (and Chandra's brother-in-law) Vidhu Vinod Chopra. At press time, Chandra is reportedly writing a detective novel based on his character Sartaj Singh, the protagonist in the story "Kama" in *Love and Longing in Bombay.*

Scott D. Walker

Further Reading
Chandra, Vikram. "The Cult of Authenticity." *Boston Review* (February/March 2000). 9 July 2002 <http://bostonreview.mit.edu/BR25.1/chandra.html>.

"Chandra, Vikram. "Contemporary Authors." *Galenet.com.* 9 July 2002. <http://web3.infotrac.galenet.com>.

Rollason, Christopher. "Vikram Chandra's *Red Earth and Pouring Rain:* Entwining Narratives and Intertextuality." *IndiaStar: A Literary-Art Magazine.* 9 July 2002 <http://www.indiastar.com/rollason.html>.

Salvador, Dora Sales. "Vikram Chandra's Constant Journey: Swallowing the World." *Journal of English Studies II* (2000): 93–111.

Chatterjee, Partha

Partha Chatterjee teaches political science at the Center for Studies in Social Sciences, Calcutta, and he is also professor of anthropology at Columbia University, New York. He is a founding member of the Subaltern Studies group of historians who, in the 1980s, sought to interrogate the story of Indian nationalism as a predominantly elite (read colonialist or indigenous bourgeois) enterprise by exploring the autonomous domain of subaltern (indicating society's laboring populations and other oppressed classes) resistance to both colonialism and bourgeois nationalism. Chatterjee is also often credited with signaling the culturalist or poststructuralist shift (via postcolonial theory and cultural studies) in what began primarily as a Gramscian project aimed at making visible the neglected aspect of popular struggle against domination and exploitation.

His first book, *Nationalist Thought and the Colonial World: A Derivative Discourse?* (1986), a pioneering attempt to theorize Indian nationalism, is predicated on a refutation of dominant Western understandings of anticolonial nationalisms as entirely derived from European models. Rather, Chatterjee argues that the relationship between nationalist thought and colonialist knowledge is a complex one characterized by both imitation and difference. Evoking the Gramscian idea of passive revolution, he traces the evolution of bourgeois nationalist discourse in India through the writings of Bankimchandra, Gandhi, and Nehru. His point is that the political project of nationalism involved succumbing to Enlightenment values of modernity and progress, in service to a larger goal—that of ending colonial domination and constituting a bourgeois national state as the sole agent of capitalist development. In its inner or spiritual domain, however, the nation was considered sovereign, even superior to the West. This so-called *private* realm, protected from the compromises and humiliations to which the public arena of economics, statecraft, science, and technology was subject, provided the colonized with a platform from which to articulate their autonomy and difference from the imperial power.

Elsewhere in his writings, Chatterjee argues that this ideology of separate spheres operated in accordance with a gendered logic that recast middle-class women as subjects of a new, transformed patriarchy. As custodians of the home and by extension of the nation's spiritual and moral essence, women were projected in the nationalist imagination as autonomous agents engaged in a struggle for the preservation of the inner core of Indian culture. Colonial authority could not be allowed to invade this sacred realm, and so social reform agendas to end caste, class, and gender discrimination were reconfigured in exclusively nationalist terms and in keeping with the movement's larger goals.

It is the contestations and transformations within this so-called private sphere excluded from participation by the hegemonic imperatives of a nation-state project conceived of as upper caste, male, and Hindu that Chatterjee takes up for detailed examination in his second book, *The Nation and Its Fragments: Colonial and Postcolonial Histories* (1993). His foregrounding of an autonomous domain of subaltern (primarily peasant and lower caste) struggle, founded on community solidarity, borders, as critics have pointed out, on a somewhat uncritical valorization of "community identity" as essentially antimodern, fragmentary, plural, and tolerant, as opposed to the coercive, political machinery of the modern state. However, Chatterjee maintains his critique of modernity even in his more recent writings as he continues to problematize the idea of a nation as a necessary contradiction between capital and community.

Anuradha Ramanujan

Further Reading

Chatterjee, Partha. "More on Modes of Power and the Peasantry." *Subaltern Studies II: Writings on South Asian History and Society.* Ed. Ranajit Guha. Delhi: Oxford UP, 1983.

———. *Nationalist Thought and the Colonial World: A Derivative Discourse?* Delhi: Oxford UP, 1986.

———. "The Nationalist Resolution of the Women's Question." *Recasting Women: Essays in Colonial History.* Eds. Kumkum Sangari and Sudesh Vaid. New Delhi: Kali For Women, 1989.

———. *The Nation and its Fragments: Colonial and Postcolonial Histories.* Delhi: Oxford UP, 1993.

———. "Secularism and Tolerance." *Secularism and its Critics.* Ed. Rajeev Bhargava. Delhi: Oxford UP, 1998.

Chaturvedi, Vinayak, ed. *Mapping Subaltern Studies and the Postcolonial.* London: Verso, 2000.

Chatterjee, Upamanyu

Upamanyu Chatterjee belongs to the generation of urban Indians that, in his own words, "doesn't oil its hair." Born in 1959, in Patna, Bihar, Chatterjee graduated with a master's in English literature from St. Stephen's College in New Delhi. He taught English for a year at St. Stephen's College and then joined the Indian Administrative Service (IAS) in 1983, at about the same age as his protagonist, Agastya, in *English, August: An Indian Story,* Chatterjee's debut novel.

Before embarking on his novel, Chatterjee published short stories in *Debonair* and *London Magazine.* His best-known short story, "The Assassination of Indira Gandhi," was published as part of the William Heinemann Collection of Best Stories in 1986. It was later included in the anthology *Mirrorwork: Fifty Years of Indian Writing in English, 1947–1997* edited by Salman Rushdie and Elizabeth West.

In 1990–91, as a writer-in-residence at Darwin College of the University of Kent in Britain, he worked on his second novel, *The Last Burden.* He continued to work in the IAS, and in 1998 was appointed Director (Languages) in the Ministry of Human Resource Development. Two years later, Chatterjee published his third novel, *The Mammaries of the Welfare State,* the much-awaited sequel to *English, August.*

The Mammaries of the Welfare State is currently being adapted for the screen by Dev Benegal, who also directed the film version of *English, August* (1994). Benegal and Chatterjee cowrote the screenplay as well as the story for Benegal's second feature, *Split Wide Open* (1999).

The response to Chatterjee's first novel, *English, August,* was overwhelmingly positive. Critics in India and abroad instantly placed him in the emerging canon of Indian writing in English. Satirical, witty, and astute in his observations of life in the Indian Administrative Service, the novel's protagonist, Agastya Sen, is a young IAS officer from Delhi, who is posted for a year in the sleepy, backwater town of Madna. Though his friend Dhrubo warns him that he is going to get "hazaar fucked" (thousand times fucked), Agastya is not prepared to face the relentless boredom and absurd bureaucracy that soon define his life in Madna. Marijuana, masturbation, and mosquitoes become his constant companions in his shabby accommodation at the government guesthouse. A complete outsider in Madna, and unsure of his ambition or destination, Agastya drifts between states of quiet restlessness and drug-induced torpor. Despite its seemingly apathetic protagonist, the novel is not self-indulgent or solipsistic. Agastya's alienation in the Madna ("the real India") reflects on the distance between metropolitan sensibilities and small town realities. His struggle to articulate his feelings about his job to his uncle, father, and Dhrubo render him sympathetic.

Chatterjee's second novel, *The Last Burden,* explores the theme of alienation through dynamics of a family reunion in the contemporary Indian middle class. Jamun, the unmarried son of Shyamanand and Urmila, visits his parents' home when he hears his mother has been taken ill. The parents live with Jamun's brother, sister-in-law, and two nephews. Nobody in particular gets along with each other. Suspicion, misgivings, and blame constantly brew in the cauldron of obligation and duty. Jamun must also contend with the ghosts of his past (his ex-lover, and his Aya from childhood). Jamun resents his parents for continuing in a dead marriage. After many arguments, altercations, and significant events Jamun comes to accept his parents' limitations. The tone is more somber than wry. Chatterjee brutally shows us how the ties that bind can often become the nooses of our own undoing. By the end of the novel, the mother passes away, the brother's family shifts to Bombay, and Jamun agrees to look after his father. The last sentence of the novel, "Well, not a bad beginning, reflects Jamun" is judiciously hopeful.

Mammaries of the Welfare State once again returns to the story of IAS officer Agastya Sen, now eight years older than when we last met him in *English, August. Mammaries* is a far more sprawling narrative, more episodic than linear, darkly satirical, and less personal. While most critics in India reviewed it positively, the novel has not yet found an international publisher.

Chatterjee has chosen to live and write in India. Even though most of his work revolves around themes of alienation, it is not the type of diaspora alienation that informs the writing of authors like Salman Rushdie or Rohinton Mistry. Chatterjee's commitment to stay in India and write from within is reminiscent of the oft-quoted claim made by dislocated, urban, Jewish Indian poet-playwright, Nissim Ezekiel: "as others choose to give themselves in some remote and backward place, my backward place is where I am" *(Selected Prose).* Does Chatterjee believe that his voice is closer to the ear of his Indian audience? Are the cartoonist Sathe's words in *English, August* echoes of Chatterjee's own position in the debate about Indian writing in English?

> I want to suggest an Indian writer writing about India, after having spent many years abroad, or living there . . . I find these people absurd, full with one mixed-up culture, writing about another, what kind of audience are they aiming at? That is why their India is just not real, a place of fantasy, or of confused metaphysics, a sub-continent of goons. All their Indians are caricatures. Why is that? Because there are no universal stories, because each language is an entire culture.

Poised between an anglicized urban middle-class consciousness and a resolutely local bureaucratic world, Chatterjee's writing poses interesting questions about the role location plays in the specific contours of Indian writers in English.

Shuchi Kothari

Further Reading

"August Returns." Rev. of *The Mammaries of the Welfare State,* by Upamanyu Chatterjee. *India Today* (4 Dec. 2000): 70–72.

Ezekiel, Nissim. *Selected Prose.* Delhi: Oxford UP, 1997.

Hema, M. S. "Upamanyu Chatterjee's *The Last Burden.*" *The Postmodern Indian Novel.* Ed. Viney Kirpal. Bombay: Allied, 1996. 49–58.

Kumar, Sanjay. "The Nowhere Man: The Exiled Self in Upamanyu Chatterjee's *English, August: An Indian Story.*" *Post-Colonial Indian English Writing.* Eds. R. A. Singh and Sanjay Kumar. New Delhi: Bahri, 1997. 101–07.

Sengupta, C. "Upamanyu Chatterjee's *English, August:* Metaphor of Contemporary Youth's Quest for Self-realization." *Indian Literature Today.* Ed. R. K. Dhawan. New Delhi: Prestige, 1994. 110–21.

———. "Upamanyu Chatterjee's *The Last Burden:* The Burden of Family and the Burden of Language." *Indian Fiction of the Nineties.* Ed. R. S. Pathak. New Delhi: Creative Books, 1997. 29–40.

Chaudhuri, Amit

Amit Chaudhuri was born in 1962 in Calcutta and was raised in Bombay. After

Amit Chaudhuri. Photo by Jerry Bauer.

graduating from University College, London, he went on to receive his doctorate in critical theory and the poetry of D. H. Lawrence from Balliol College, Oxford. He was then awarded a Creative Arts Fellowship at Wolfson College, Oxford, as well as the Harper Wood Studentship for English Literature and Poetry at St. John's College, Cambridge. He taught commonwealth literature at Cambridge and continued to shuttle between England and Calcutta for several years. In 1999, he relocated back to Calcutta permanently, where he lives with his wife and daughter. Among other things, he is an accomplished singer trained in the Hindusthani classical music tradition and has produced two albums under the aegis of the HMV music company.

Chaudhuri has published fiction, poetry, and book reviews in several well-known publications such as *The Guardian, London Review of Books, Times Literary Supplement, The New Yorker,* and *Granta* magazine. His first book, *A Strange and Sublime Address,* was published in 1991 to much critical acclaim and won the Betty Trask Award and the Commonwealth Writers' Prize for the Eurasia region. He was also short listed for the Guardian Fiction Prize. *Afternoon Raag,* Chaudhuri's second novel published in 1993, won the Southern Arts Literature Prize and the Encore Award for best second novel. After a hiatus of five years, in 1998 he wrote *Freedom Song,* a novel. The U.S. edition of *Freedom Song,* published as a collection of all three novels to date, won the LA Times Award in 2000. Chaudhuri then followed this with *A New World,* another novel. *Real Time,* published in 2002, is a collection of short stories and a verse memoir ("E-minor") set in Bombay and Calcutta. He has also edited the *Picador Book of Modern Indian Literature* (2001), a selection of works in English, and English translations from Indian languages by Indian authors.

Chaudhuri is one of a new wave of Indian authors with deep roots in post-Emergency, contemporary India, who came to prominence during the 1990s. His fiction, while sometimes partly set in foreign locales such as London or Oxford, demonstrates a preoccupation with the Indian urban middle class (and in particular the Bengali middle class) in a contemporary social-realist setting. Three issues characterize his fiction: a narrative that lacks a conventional plot; a sustained, almost loving focus on the quotidian activities in the lives of the characters; and a reposeful, meditative quality of prose. In his books, there are no direct accounts of catastrophic events either in the character's lives or in the world around them, and if such events are mentioned, they are only filtered through in a remote or passing manner via conversations or observations. Instead, he provides through the eyes or reveries of his characters, gentle, detailed vignettes of quotidian city life, interactions between family members and servants, Indian culture, food, and even

Indian classical music. At a muted and subliminal level, however, Chaudhuri also explores themes of displacement and belonging through characters that are transplanted to locales that are tantalizingly familiar yet not quite home.

A Strange and Sublime Address recounts the experiences of a young Bengali boy from Bombay who is visiting his relatives in Calcutta. Descriptions of ordinary, daily rituals such as bathing, eating, visits to relatives, and servants at their work, seen afresh through the boy's eyes, abound. The main character of *Afternoon Raag* is an Indian student at Oxford; the only book written entirely in the first person, it alternates between descriptions of the main character's daily life and encounters with other people in Oxford. The narrative is interspersed with reminiscences and descriptions of people and places in Calcutta and Bombay. *Freedom Song* is an account of the relationship between two families and their search for a bride for one of the characters. In this book, Chaudhuri departs a little from his relentless focus on the ordinary and quotidian by filtering through the observations of his characters the impact of the Babri-Masjid Hindu-Muslim riots. In these three books, the main characters either live in India or have recently been living there. Their instinct, thought, and memory are basically Indian, if not necessarily always quintessentially Bengalis raised in Calcutta.

In *A New World,* the point of departure is that the main character, Jayojit, is an expatriate who is now visiting Calcutta after several uninterrupted years of living in the United States. Thus, India is for him and his son (who cannot speak Bengali) a "new world," overlaid with memories of another new world and (in the case of Jayojit) the original "old world." In *Real Time,* Chaudhuri's collection of short stories contains an interesting excursion into verse by way of a memoir ("E-Minor").

As a relatively recent and low key postulant for entry into the South Asian literary canon, critical reviews of Chaudhuri's works have mainly been limited to book reviews and articles in literary magazines and newspapers. Critics in the United States and Britain have been appreciative of Chaudhuri, even making comparisons with Proust and Joyce, and calling his work prose poems. Michiko Kakutani of the *New York Times* described the U.S. edition of *Freedom Song* as "a Proustian tapestry of quotidian moments." Tim Adams of the *Observer* says of *A New World:* "At times, reading some of these passages, you can be reminded of reading Joyce's *Dubliners* for the first time, where every sentence can seem a small act of beauty. The wider world rarely impinges on these everyday epiphanies." However, some critics, particularly from the subcontinent, have dissented, objecting to the relentless focus on minutiae. For example, Gargi Bhattacharjee wrote of *A New World* in the *Telegraph:* "What makes Chaudhuri's narrative style so tedious is the fact that while he has a fine eye for detail, he is completely non-discriminatory in his choice of focus." The consensus opinion, however, is that Chaudhuri is extraordinarily adept at using snapshots of everyday life to build images of lasting meaning and value.

Padma Chandrasekaran

Further Reading

Adams, Tim. "A God of Small Things." *The Observer.* 28 June 2000, <http://books.guardian.co.uk/reviews/generalfiction/0,6121,333327,00.html>.

Bhattacharjee,Gargi. "A New World: Review." *The Telegraph, Calcutta.* 3 Mar. 2000: 17.

Deresiewicz, William. "Book Review Desk: Seeing India, Business Class." *New York Times* 21 Sept. 2002: 7.

Ratna, Kalpish. "An Unending Afternoon in Chaudhuriland." *Biblio India* VII (July-Aug. 2002): 14.

Cinnamon Gardens by Shyam Selvadurai

Shyam Selvadurai was born in Colombo, Sri Lanka, in 1965 and left the island for Canada with his parents at the age of 19 after the riots of 1983. He holds a B.F.A. from York University and has contributed to television and journals. His first book, *Funny Boy,* won the W.H. Smith/Books in Canada, the First Novel Award in the United States, and the Lambda Literary Award for Best Gay Men's Fiction. His second novel, *Cinnamon Gardens,* was published in 1998. He lives and works in Toronto.

Cinnamon Gardens is situated in the late 1920s when the colonial government instituted Donoughmore Commission to study all aspects of life in Ceylon in order to recommend reforms. Annaluckshmi, who is impatient with the constraints of her class and gender, successfully combats her father's dictates that she should marry her cousin. Though attracted to men, like Chandran Mackintosh and Seelan, she does not commit herself to a relationship, choosing instead to spend her time furthering the causes of women and labor unions. At the end of the novel, she is left pondering whether to go abroad and teach in Jaffna or become better acquainted with the artistic, Bohemian friends she had recently met in Colombo.

Balendran (Annaluckshmi's uncle) is the scion of a powerful mudaliyar and married to an attractive, intelligent cousin; however, these trappings mask deep psychological scars, which are the results of his father's breaking up his relationship with Richard Howland, in England, and forcing him to marry Sonia. Unlike his rebellious brother Arul, who was ostracized from the family for marrying a servant, Balendran is completely dominated by mudaliyar Navaratnam. Consequently, when his father requests him to approach Howland (now in Sri Lanka with the Commission) to help the Tamil cause, he cannot refuse. Although their meeting leads to a reawakening of their love for each other, Balendran's sense of familial responsibility prevents him from taking the relationship any further. Still, this reencounter gives him the strength to stand up to his father on occasion and (when necessary) to take independent action. Selvadurai has chosen to rewrite the sociopolitical and cultural scene of the late 1920s from perspectives not attempted by other novelists. In addition to examining issues like communal differences, class consciousness, and the position of women, he also explores the theme of homosexuality that is his major concern in *Funny Boy.*

Mudaliyars have become the butt of many contemporary Sri Lankan writers. Since they belonged to the native elite and enjoyed considerable privileges during the colonial period, they are prime candidates for satire. Navaratnam, who is jingoistic, pompous, self-seeking, hypocritical, and much more besides, is no exception. His forcing Balendran to terminate his affair with Howland, but having no compunction in asking the latter for a political favor and his ostracizing his eldest son for marrying a servant whose mother Navaratnam had abused sexually are just two examples of his two-faced nature. Such an authorial strategy is ultimately problematic, however, because the mudaliyar represents an entire class in this novel. The elite shared Navaratnam's weaknesses to varying degrees, but the island would not have been on the verge of becoming the first non-white British colony to be granted Universal Adult Franchise if not for the agitation carried out by the self-same class. Selvadurai also sentimentalizes the role of the labor leaders and ignores their self-seeking agendas, which A. Sivanandan has exposed in *When Memory Dies.*

The homosexual theme that is examined so convincingly in Selvadurai's previous novel is treated cursorily here. Since Balendran is gay, sex with his wife is anathema to him, and he can only obtain satisfaction by having surreptitious encounters with men. This issue, which apparently vitiates his marriage, inexplicably ceases to become a factor as Balendran eventually establishes a wholesome relationship with his wife. Howland is in Sri Lanka with a gay partner, but this partner graciously leaves soon after Balendran reappears on the scene. Finally, Howland and Balendran have an idyllic, passionate sexual engagement in an estate; yet, the affair does not last their return to Colombo with Balendran somewhat histrionically severing their relationship in a hotel.

Cinnamon Gardens is set up as a novel of growth and change. The lives of individuals are considerably transformed no doubt, but the *growth* is of a limited kind. Balendran can stand up to his father at the end of the novel and recognize the falsity behind the respectable façade. But this so-called socially conscious individual continues to enjoy the privileges of the elite. Since Annaluckshmi is rebellious by nature, one would have expected her to develop considerably by the time of the novel's conclusion. Though she resists all attempts at forcing her into marriage and realizes that the liberal philosophy espoused by her principal and mentor Miss Lawton does not extend to encouraging Ceylonese women to become principals themselves, Annalukshmi is at the end of the novel presented with several options but appears irresolute.

Cinnamon Gardens has not received the critical attention, or acclaim, accorded to *Funny Boy.* Perera, while acknowledging the importance of Selvadurai's situating the novel is a specific historical period when differences between the Sinhalese and Tamils first appeared, disputes Selvadurai's contention that the elite was totally self-seeking. Wickramagamage's review focuses on Annaluckshmi and wonders whether Selvadurai is "gesturing towards this documented history of women's activism in Sri Lanka by making a conscious narrative decision to 'retard' Annalukshmi's evolution into an unequivocally feminist individualist in terms of her practice as well as rhetoric" (139).

S. W. Perera

Further Reading

Perera, S. W. "In Pursuit of Political Correctness: Shyam Selvadurai's *Cinnamon Gardens*." *The Sri Lanka Journal of the Humanities* 24, 25 (1998–99): 1–2, 87–111.

Perera, Sonali. "(Where) Language Acts in *When Memory Dies*." *Nethra* 4.3, 4 (2000): 101–07.

Sivanandan, A. *When Memory Dies*. London: Arcadia, 1997.

Wickramagamage, Carmen. " 'A Fish without a Bicycle'?: Annalukshmi's Choice in Selvadurai's *Cinnamon Gardens*." *CRNLE JOURNAL: Sri Lankan and Indian Diasporic Writing* (2000): 130–40.

Clear Light of Day by Anita Desai

Anita Desai, one of India's best-known authors, was born in Mussorie, India, in 1937 to a Bengali father and a German mother. Educated in Delhi at Queen Mary's Higher Secondary School and Miranda House, Delhi University, she received a B.A. in English literature. Desai, who published her first story at the age of nine, has written several collections of short stories, children's books, 10 novels, and extensive journalism, and her books have been translated into most of the world's major languages. Three of her novels—*Clear Light of Day* (1980), *In Custody* (1984), and *Fasting, Feasting* (1999) have been shortlisted for the Booker Prize; and she has received the 1978 Sahitya Akademi Award, the (Indian) National Academy of Letters Award, for *Fire on the Mountain* (1977), the Guardian Award for Children's Fiction for *The Village by the Sea* (1982), and the Padma Sri (1990) among many other literary prizes. She has been a Visiting Fellow at Girton College, Cambridge, in England and has taught at Smith College and Mount Holyoke College in the United States; since 1993, she has been teaching creative writing at Massachusetts Institute of Technology.

Of all Desai's works, *Clear Light of Day* remains the most often discussed and taught. Set in Old Delhi in the 1970s, the novel tells the story of a middle-class Hindu Das family, paralleling their past estrangements to the partition of India and Pakistan in 1947. Tara, the younger sister, returns home on vacation from Washington, D.C., where she lives with her diplomat husband, Bakul, and two teenage daughters. This becomes the occasion for the predominantly retrospective plot in which she and her older sister, Bim, a college lecturer of history, relive and finally come to terms with their past, thereby finding their respective "clear light of day." The novel, which traces the narrative perspective not only of Bim and Tara but also of such minor characters as Aunt Mira, Baba, and Bakul, is structured in four parts, which Desai likens to the parts of a classical play.

Part I treats the present moment of Tara and Bakul's visit in the 1970s and sets the stage for the examination of the major themes: the complications of family relationships, the lingering effects on nations and families of the larger partition of countries in 1947, and the role of women in modern India.

Part II moves back in time to that portentous "summer of '47" to examine the political upheaval as Hindus and Muslims are pitted against each other and the personal tumult as Bim is cast aside by her older brother, Raja, in favor of their Muslim neighbors, the Hyder Alis, and their daughter, Benazir. Moreover, Mrs. and Mr. Das die in a diabetic coma and a traffic accident, respectively, both veritable strangers to the children in death as they had been in life; Mira Masi, the widowed aunt and caretaker of the Das household, turns to alcohol as she finds herself overwhelmed by familial responsibilities; Tara marries young to escape the moribund life around her; and Bim turns down an offer of marriage from Dr. Biswas because she does not want to be bound to domesticity and motherhood.

Part III burrows further back in time to narrate the birth of the younger, autistic brother, Baba. The narrative reveals the sordid history of Mira Masi, married as a child and widowed at 12, who is exploited and oppressed ever since. It traces the contrast in the temperaments of the female siblings, Tara desiring only to marry and settle down with a family of her own and Bim wanting to be financially independent and "to do things" (140).

Finally, Part IV moves the narrative back to the present in which Bim forgives Raja as well as Tara for forsaking her as she "see[s] . . . by the clear light of the day that she felt only love and yearning for them and, if there were hurts . . . it was only because her love was imperfect" (165).

Whereas earlier critics like Ramesh Srivastava and Madhusudan Prasad praised *Clear Light of Day* for it psychological probity and imagistic lyricism (3, 369), more recent critics schooled in contemporary theory are given to reading the novel as a feminist, postcolonial text, one that portrays middle-class "postcolonial women in the larger context of their subjectivity during complex phases of nation formation" (Parekh 282); that embraces a multitude of languages, literary and musical traditions, and genres which "figure the contradiction at the centre of emerging ideals of nation and femininity" (Mohan 50); and that examines "the structural function of gender in the political discourse and performance of colonialism and postcolonialism" (Ray 137). Whatever their particular interest, most readers and critics would agree that *Clear Light of Day* remains one of the best novels of its time.

Anthony Thwaite concludes that Desai, ever the "consummate artist," is able in *Clear Light of Day,* as in many of her other works, to suggest "beyond the confines of the plot and the machinations of her characters, the immensities that lie beyond them—the immensities of India" (38).

Harveen Sachdeva Mann

Further Reading

Mohan, Rajeswari. "The Forked Tongue of Lyric in Anita Desai's *Clear Light of Day.*" *Journal of Commonwealth Literature* 32.1 (1997): 47–66.

Parekh, Pushpa Naidu. "Redefining the Postcolonial Female Self: Women in Anita Desai's *Clear Light of Day.*" *Between the Lines: South Asians and Post-Coloniality.* Eds. Deepika Bahri and Mary Vasudeva. Philadelphia: Temple UP, 1996. 270–83.

Prasad, Madhusudan. "Imagery in the Novels of Anita Desai: A Critical Study." *World Literature Today* 58.3 (1984): 363–69.

Ray, Sangeeta. "Gender and Discourse of Nationalism in Anita Desai's *Clear Light of Day.*" *Genders* 20 (Fall 1994): 96–120.

Srivastava, Ramesh, ed. *Perspectives on Anita Desai.* Ghaziabad, India: Vimal Prakashan, 1984.

Thwaite, Anthony. "India Inside." *New Republic* (18 Mar. 1985): 37–38.

Colonialism

Colonialism is most often considered in relationship to the expansion of trading interests by a number of European powers beginning in the fifteenth century. The most prominent countries include Spain, Portugal, France, the Netherlands, and England; the latter three countries, especially, frequently chartered commercial ventures that were responsible for exploration and the negotiation of a nation's interests. These countries and entities set up trading posts and colonies throughout the world, often at the expense of the native inhabitants. This colonial phase of world history lasted approximately five hundred years, though some political theorists to this day ably demonstrate a colonialist tendency in certain hegemonic states throughout the world.

Several European powers have been involved with the Indian subcontinent since the early sixteenth century. The earliest of these European ventures would be the Portuguese capture of Goa in 1510, which became a prosperous port city later in the sixteenth century; sovereign India did not actually gain control of Goa until 1961. The British East India Company was chartered by Queen Elizabeth I in 1600, but was confined to the subcontinent fairly early on, in part because of stiff resistance from the Dutch in the East Indies. Other British traders, called interlopers, were also vying for control of the subcontinent during the seventeenth century, though by the early eighteenth century, the British East India Company was able to merge with some of these interests and became the sole British commercial entity on the subcontinent. Textiles were the chief export of the company, and the presidencies of Madras, Bombay, and Calcutta had been established. The British East India Company for a time had a serious rival in its French counterpart, the French East India Company, though Roger Clive, ultimately defeated the French during the mid–eighteenth century, and a treaty was signed in 1765. At the same time, the British were fighting the Indian Moguls in order to protect their own commercial interests.

The history of colonialism in India is directly tied to the history of the British East India Company well into the nineteenth century. Beginning with Warren Hastings, who succeeded Roger Clive as governor-general of the British East India Company, the British Parliament was responsible for making all the appointments. Hastings, Cornwallis, Wellsley, and other administrators were able to consolidate the Company's holdings south of the Sutlej River by 1818, with holdout territories being the Sind and the Punjab, which were conquered in 1843 and 1849. Still, the British Parliament assumed an increasingly active role in the affairs of the Company and so in the affairs of India. In 1784, for instance, the first important piece of legislation was passed, which called for a halt to the conquests of the company. This was impractical, however, though Company officials did agree in principle at this time that it should not influence Indian culture. Yet, the British Parliament could not itself refrain from trying to bring technological innovations and social change to the subcontinent. This was partly owing to the phenomenal level of success, commercially speaking, that the British were having in India and elsewhere in the world; as well, the Victorian society of England was becoming increasingly construed as the pinnacle of world civilization, and the British partly believed it was their duty to help other, lesser cultures become enlightened.

The British brought a number of changes to India. New technology in the nineteenth century included new methods of textile production, steam vessels, railroad lines, and the telegraph. A roadway was built that linked Calcutta to the north. But such changes, while important, were not necessarily widely felt across the subcontinent. More importantly, both criminal and civil law was changed, away from a particularistic approach and toward a more universalistic system. The British, in part in response to calls from Indian intellectuals, abolished *sati*. Perhaps the most significant change the British imposed, however, was the change in 1835 to higher education, which would henceforth be taught in the English language. The impact of this act was the creation of a new middle class in India that was eager to adapt itself to the British system of commerce and government. The system for administering the Indian subcontinent included a governor-general and approximately one thousand civil servants—district officers—beneath him, each in charge of a million Indians. Until 1854, all district officers were English, and they received their

British soldiers executing men tied to cannons, 1890. Courtesy of Library of Congress.

charge through patronage. It would be another 15 years, however, before the first Indian was able to receive a district appointment. Beneath the district officers, nearly all administrators were Indian. The British army in India, fairly small until World War I, was two-thirds Indian; all officers were British. The army was under the control of administrators. In 1857, an Indian Mutiny was fairly quickly squelched but brought about many needed changes in the British rule of India, most important among them that the Crown would henceforth assume the reins of power.

The British East India Company was dissolved in 1874, but the British colonial presence in India would continue for another 73 years. Many critics of the British regime believe that the English increasingly exploited differences between Hindus and Muslims in the twentieth century in order to cling to power, a practice that eventually led to the splitting of the subcontinent into separate nation-states. Yet, many also believe that the British presence was instrumental in helping to modernize Indian culture, though this modernization was not without cost. In some ways, the British presence was relatively benign and even beneficent, and in some ways, ignorable. Ranajit Guha uses the term "dominance without hegemony" in order to describe the paradox of British colonization on what he terms "elite" and "subaltern" Indian populations: "the originality of the South Asian colonial state lay precisely in this difference . . . an autocracy set up and sustained in the East by the foremost democracy of the Western world. And since it was nonhegemonic, it was not possible for that state to assimilate the civil society of the colonized to itself" (xii). Guha points to British imperialism in India as signifying "the historic failure of capital to realize its universalizing tendency under colonial conditions, and the corresponding failure of the metropolitan bourgeois culture to dissolve or assimilate fully the indigenous culture of South Asia in the power relations of the colonial period" (xii).

In an analysis of the social and political vision of Sri Aurobindo, K. D. Verma lists a number of questions that intellectuals like Aurobindo asked about the nature of colonialism in India, which "pertained to fundamental humanistic values and moral principles underlying the essential structure of British colonialism." Among the questions is this: "Why is the Christian ideal, according to which the denial of human rights is supposed to be an offense to God, generally considered to be compatible with the political reality of colonialism?" (49). According to Verma, for Aurobindo, Indian nationhood was an "immediate and irrevocable necessity" for eliminating the colonial presence of the British. Aurobindo's "staunch conviction" was that "imperialism and colonialism, whether mercantile or political, are manifestations of repressive egoism or hubris on the part of a nation or group who simply happened to possess an expedient superiority of means over its relatively less favored subjects" (47).

Michael W. Cox

Further Reading

Garraty, John A., and Peter Gay, eds. *The Columbia History of the World.* New York: Harper and Row, 1972.

Guha, Ranajit. *Dominance Without Hegemony: History and Power in Colonial India.* Cambridge: Harvard UP, 1997.

Verma, K. D. *The Indian Imagination: Critical Essays on Indian Writing in English.* New York: St. Martin's, 2000.

Commonwealth Literature

Commonwealth literature refers to the literature produced by writers belonging to the Commonwealth, an organization of 54 sovereign nations. The term *commonwealth* originally referred to the areas under the governance of British imperialism, but since the dissolution of the British Empire and the London declaration of 1949, the term is now applied to a voluntary association of sovereign states. Typically, the term commonwealth literature indicates literature written in English or translated into English by writers belonging to the decolonized nations of the British Empire. It includes writing from countries in the Caribbean, the Indian subcontinent, settler colonies such as Australia, Canada, New Zealand, African nations including South Africa, Kenya, Nigeria, and Uganda, and Pacific Ocean, and Southeast Asian states such as Malaysia, New Guinea, and Singapore, as well as the United Kingdom. (For a complete listing of all 54 states, please see <http://www.thecommonwealth.org/dynamic/Country.asp>). The current usage of this term replaces the previous practice of using the term to indicate literature from secondary regions of the United Kingdom, such as Ireland, Scotland, and Wales.

Commonwealth literature became visible chiefly during the 1960s within the academe, and usually within the English department, as more decolonized countries began to find and establish a national voice. Another reason for the rise of Commonwealth literature is the fact that American literature had begun to be offered as a course of study alongside British literature in countries across the world. This development in English studies displaced the assumed universal centrality of British and European literature, and it made it possible for other indigenous literatures to believe that they could, similarly, contribute significantly to world literature and sustain serious scholarly study.

The first commonwealth literature studies conference was held in the British city of Leeds in 1964, and The Association for Commonwealth Literature and Language Studies (ACLALS) was formed at this conference. Today, there are chapters of the ACLALS worldwide that promote and facilitate scholarship in the field (for more details, refer to <http://www.aclals.org/>). Journals devoted to commonwealth literature such as *The Journal of*

Commonwealth Literature (1965), *World Literature Written in English* (1966), *Ariel* (1970), and *Kunapipi* (1975) have been both longstanding as well as influential within the field.

The common themes of commonwealth literature across national boundaries are usually a shared historical heritage of British rule as well as an attempt to render topical and local experiences such as nation building and identity explorations through the medium of English. In seeming contradiction, anticolonial as well as anglophile tendencies coexist in most commonwealth literary texts. Studies of commonwealth literature have a propensity to range themselves around the literature of a specific commonwealth country or grouping of commonwealth countries, a comparative model between the commonwealth and more established literatures, or shared themes such as economic hardship, cultural conflict, and women's empowerment.

Two strange anomalies in the study of commonwealth literature in the period prior to the 1990s are worth noting: first, literature produced in indigenous languages by writers belonging to the commonwealth was rarely counted as commonwealth literature; second, although the United Kingdom was a central founding member of the Commonwealth, British literature was seldom included under the rubric of commonwealth literature. These and other similar misgivings have been heatedly debated within the field. And it would seem that the definition and use of the term has been refined by debate and argued consensus. For instance, the bizarre, early distinction between the *white* commonwealth—composed of settler colonies such as Canada and Australia and *black* commonwealth composed of states previously subject to colonial occupation such as India and African countries, is no longer in use.

Since the last two decades of the twentieth century, there have been increasing

demands that the term *commonwealth* be replaced by a term that is less evocative of the colonial heritage of governance by the British Empire. Substitute terms that have been proposed include World Literature Written in English, New Literatures in English, and Postcolonial Literature.

The term *postcolonial* has come to be increasingly substituted, since its sensibility lies in acknowledging colonialism while simultaneously interrogating it, and it is capable of incorporating both literary works as well as theory and criticism. However, scholars and critics who prefer the term *commonwealth* point out that since *postcolonial* primarily implies a way of reading rather than of producing a literary text, it is not quite cognate with the generality provided by commonwealth literature, and further that the term *postcolonial* privileges the moment of colonial contact much as the term *commonwealth* seems to prolong it.

Rather late in the history of commonwealth literature, the Commonwealth Writers Prize was instituted in 1987 by the Commonwealth Foundation (est. 1965) and has served to bring several worthy writers such as Rohinton Mistry, J. M. Coetzee, Vikram Seth, Olive Senior, Peter Carey, Festus Iyayi, Zadie Smith and others to international notice. However, it is worth noting that writers who are grouped under the rubric commonwealth have on occasion registered their concern at the over use of the term. In his 1983 essay titled "Commonwealth Literature Does Not Exist," the writer Salman Rushdie sees the presumed separation between commonwealth literature and English literature as an act of ghettoization and segregation. More dramatically, in 2001, the writer Amitav Ghosh withdrew his book *The Glass Palace* from the Commonwealth Writers Prize competition, where it had been entered on his behalf by the publishers, due to his distaste for historical and elitist implications of the term *commonwealth.*

Prathima Anandan

Further Reading

Jones, J. Terranglia. *The Case for English as World Literature.* New York: Twayne, 1965.

King, Bruce, ed. *Literatures of the World in English.* London: Routledge, 1974.

McLeod, A. L., ed. *The Commonwealth Pen: An Introduction to the Literature of the British Commonwealth.* Ithaca: Cornell UP, 1961.

Rushdie, Salman. "Commonwealth Literature Does Not Exist." *Imaginary Homelands.* London: Granta, 1991. 61–70.

Rutherford, A., Petersen K. Holst, and H. Maes Jelinek, eds. *From Commonwealth to Postcolonial.* Aarhus and Sydney: Dangaroo, 1992.

Thieme, John. Ed. *Commonwealth and Postcolonial Literatures: A Select Bibliography.* London: The British Council, 2000.

Communalism

The Oxford English Dictionary defines communalism as social or political organization pertaining to and revolving around local communes or communities of citizens (Pandey 7–8). By contrast, in the context of South Asia since the late colonial period, the term has come to denote identity and functioning around a notion of discrete religious, linguistic, and/or ethnic communities locked together in a relationship of mutual conflict and antagonism.

Theoretical approaches to communalism are many and seek to understand the emergence and development of the phenomenon in relation to concepts as varied as primitivism and religious fundamentalism, colonialism, nationalism, modernity, and secularism. Colonialist scholarship underscored religion as the primary driving force and marker of identity for communities in South Asia and conceptualized communalism in essentialist terms as inherent and endemic to *native* populations. In his book *The Construction of Communalism in Colonial North India* (1990), Gyanendra Pandey reverses this orientalist argument by reading communalism as "a form of colonialist knowledge" (6) produced by an imperial discourse as a means of dividing the subjugated and thereby legitimizing and extending the interventionist authority of a centralized colonial state. He demonstrates that all social unrest and clashes between individuals or groups in civil society were stripped of their contextual specificity and subsumed under an undifferentiated notion of Hindu-Muslim conflict, thus deflecting attention and responsibility from protests and uprisings that, in actuality, had nothing to do with communalism but rather represented the people's disenchantment with the colonial state and its repressive administrative and legal machinery. Furthermore, he points out that assertions of Hindu or Muslim identity in the late-nineteenth or early-twentieth centuries (which subsequently resulted in an irreparable split between the Muslim League and a Hindu-dominated Congress, a demand for a separate Muslim-majority state in 1940 and culminated, seven years later, in the partition of British India along religious lines) amounted to a reaction against both the state's homogenizing thrust, its attempts at unification by undermining the autonomy of communities, and missionary denigration of Indian history and culture as inferior, irrational, and barbaric.

Arguing from a somewhat different perspective, Marxist historians Bipan Chandra and Sumit Sarkar cite material causes for religious antagonisms, which, they hold, were exacerbated by manipulative colonial divide-and-rule policies. They emphasize that communalism, like nationalism, is a modern ideology based on a politics of popular mobilization that reconfigures structures from the past to construct a new discourse whose roots lie in social, economic, and political imperatives. In his groundbreaking work *Communalism in Modern India* (1984), Chandra defines the phenomenon as "the

The Golden Temple in Amritsar. Courtesy of Library of Congress.

The Jamamasjid Mosque, Delhi. © Helene Rogers/TRIP.

belief that because a group of people follow a particular religion, they have, as a result, common social, political and economic interests" (1). For him, as for Partha Chatterjee, communalism emerges as a potent force when nationalism fails to adequately address and unite the interests of all groups in society. Thus nationalism's inability to bridge disparities by transforming existing socioeconomic structures in postcolonial South Asia, and its tendency to play off communal prejudices against one another in the interest of electoral politics (Hindus against Muslims, Sikhs and Christians in India, Sinhalas versus Tamils in Sri Lanka) have led to a middle-class and petty bourgeois crisis of identity and economic competition between groups that perceive themselves and their interests as mutually antagonistic.

However, while Chandra attributes communalism's rise to a failed democracy once conceived of as socialist and secular, sociologists Ashis Nandy and T. N. Madan question the validity of a state-imposed secularism on the grounds that its relegation of religion to the realm of the private alienates believers, fosters intolerance and bigotry as reactions, and creates a gulf between the state and civil society. In its undermining of "religion as faith" (premodern, fluid, and tolerant), Nandy argues, secularism, a Western import, breeds "religion as ideology" (modern, monolithic, intolerant). His critique of statecraft terminates in an *in toto* rejection of modernity and the adoption of an uncritically indigenous stand that valorizes religious communities as, by definition, democratic, plural, and tolerant of dissent and difference. In treating such communities as homogeneous rather than as complex entities intersected by vectors of class, caste and, gender, Nandy's position runs the risk of legitimating communal formations that claim for themselves the sole right to speak on behalf of all members of a group (Hindutva male ideologues for all Hindus,

fundamentalist Islamic institutions for all Muslims). Such a unilateral critique of modernity, as Nandy's, could also lead to a conflation and simultaneous debunking of movements as diverse in intent, purpose, and organization as nationalism and feminism, as well as struggles aimed at ending class and caste oppression, solely on the grounds that they derive a portion of their energy and inspiration from the discourse of modernity.

Communalism, as feminist scholars like Tanika Sarkar and Urvashi Butalia have pointed out, is also a gendered ideology with specific implications for women who are deemed crucial to the formation and preservation of religious communities. Designated bearers of tradition and cultural value (which are continually reconfigured in accordance with larger socioeconomic and political imperatives but not necessarily for the empowerment of women themselves), on them falls the burden of upholding community honor and authenticity particularly in times of real or anticipated crisis. In such contexts, the female body becomes a contested site on which struggles for masculine control between communities are enacted. The equation of women with *property* that must be safeguarded at all costs necessitates social regulation of their sexuality and fertility. By the same logic, violation (through rape or abduction) of women of the *enemy,* becomes an act of collective aggression calculated to achieve dominance over an emasculated *other.*

Arguing against antisecular and antimodern positions such as the one outlined above, Sumit Sarkar calls for the urgent need to distinguish between nationalism and communalism on the grounds that to see the latter as no more than "another authoritarian version of the nation-state project" (Sarkar 361) is to ignore the violence, inequality, and hate that go into the careful and deliberate cultivation of the communal mindset. His genealogy of communalism consists of two important phases that serve to mark it as distinct from secular nationalism—the crystallization of a firmly bounded religious identity and the assumption of conflict (with an antagonistic *other*) as primordial and inevitable. For true democracy to be achieved, both the state and civil society must be secularized. Yet, in what terms this secularism must be conceptualized so as to ensure the right of every citizen and community to self-determination without fear of discrimination or coercion (on the part of the state or society), given the alarming upsurge of communalism in the region today, remains a contentious and much-debated issue in South Asia.

Anuradha Ramanujan

Further Reading

Chandra, Bipan. *Communalism in Modern India.* Delhi: Vikas, 1990.

Ludden, David, ed. *Contesting the Nation: Religion, Community, and the Politics of Democracy in India.* Philadelphia: U of Pennsylvania P, 1996.

Nandy, Ashis. "The Politics of Secularism and the Recovery of Religious Toleration." *Secularism and Its Critics.* Ed. Rajeev Bhargava. Delhi: Oxford UP, 1999.

Pandey, Gyanendra. *The Construction of Communalism in Colonial North India.* Delhi: Oxford UP, 1990.

Sarkar, Sumit. *Writing Social History.* Delhi: Oxford UP, 1997.

Sarkar, Tanika and Urvashi Butalia. *Women in the Hindu Right: A Collection of Essays.* New Delhi: Kali For Women, 1995.

Cosmopolitanism

To understand the function of cosmopolitanism in a South Asian context, it is important to first trace its etymology as well as its critical genealogy. Literally meaning "citizen of the world," (from *cosmo* which means world and *politan* which means citizen), cosmopolitanism usually implies an identity free from the restrictive ties of nationality. Its original association with the Stoics and Kant secures the term to the normative values of the Enlightenment and a belief in a problematic universality. Critics of cosmopolitanism argue that the term imposes the beliefs of the Enlightenment on a universal scale thereby erasing the diversity within the cultures it seeks to encompass.

Cosmopolitanism, however, has also developed as a contemporary mode of understanding global cultures. In a multicultural world, where nationality is often fluid and subject to change, cosmopolitanism becomes a useful way of thinking about citizenship, national affiliations, and cultural allegiances. Two names come to mind here: Martha Nussbaum and James Clifford. The former's essay on cosmopolitanism, entitled "Patriotism and Cosmopolitanism," was republished in an anthology edited by Joshua Cohen entitled *For Love of Country: Debating the Limits of Patriotism* after it appeared in the *Boston Review* in 1994. Nussbaum's essay engendered a flurry of debate with Judith Butler and Sissela Bok among others (see Cohen for more information on this debate), criticizing her assertion that cosmopolitanism is freedom from the quotidian concerns of localism (Cohen 15). James Clifford in his well-known essay entitled "Traveling Cultures" characterizes cosmopolitanism as the "portrayal of local/global historical encounters, co-productions, dominations, and resistances" (*Routes* 24). Cosmopolitanism, according to this definition, then emerges as a multinational and multicultural rather than a transnational and universal sensibility.

How is cosmopolitanism relevant to a study of South Asian culture? Through the consequences of Empire in the form of migration and diaspora, the Indian subcontinent has had a long tradition of intercultural contact. South Asian literary and cultural theorists are increasingly evoking cosmopolitanism as a paradigm with which to examine cultural exchange. Although the idea of cosmopolitanism as a multinational and multicultural sensibility has particular currency in the South Asian diaspora, it is not exclusively associated with culture traveling out from South Asia, but also with culture traveling into South Asia.

Two anthologies are particularly important in their effort to develop cosmopolitanism as a coherent theoretical entity in South Asia. In the fall of 2000, an entire issue of the journal *Public Culture* devoted its contents to the theme of cosmopolitanism. Edited by South Asian critics Arjun Appadurai, Carol Breckenridge, Sheldon Pollock, Homi Bhabha, and Dipesh Chakrabarty, this issue sought as a collective project to excavate nuanced definitions of the term cosmopolitanism. At least four full-length essays in this collection are either by scholars of South Asian origin or it addresses the development of cosmopolitanism in South Asia. The introductory essay in this volume by Pollock, Bhabha, Breckenridge, and Chakrabarty—all scholars of South Asia—defines the parameters of the term and emphasize the influence of "nationalism, globalization, and multiculturalism" (*Public Culture* 578) on the character of cosmopolitanism. Arjun Appadurai's essay in this collection is entitled "Spectral Housing and Urban Cleansing: Notes on Millenial Mumbai." Focusing on how Bombay's cosmopolitanism "has been violently compromised in its recent history" by a spate of ethnic riots, Appadurai claims that citizenship in this Indian city is unstable because "global wealth and local poverty articulate a growing contradiction" (*Public Culture* 630). Historian Sheldon Pollock's essay, entitled "Cosmopolitan and Vernacular in History," attempts to locate cosmopolitanism as a daily practice in ancient India while South Asian critic Dipesh Chakrabarty's essay, entitled "Universalism and Belonging in the Logic of Capital," engages with the contentious relationship between universalism and cultural relativism in the discourse of cosmopolitanism.

Cosmopolitan Geographies: New Locations in Literature and Culture is the second important anthology on cosmopolitanism. Edited by South Asian literary critic Vinay Dharwadker, the anthology seeks to effect a "multi-layered treatment of cosmopolitanism" (*Cosmopolitan Geographies* 3). Dharwadker's introductory essay, while summing up the project of the collection, also advances a critical definition of the term: "a validation of inclusive, egalitarian heterogeneity, of the tolerance of difference and otherness . . . or very simply the unqualified practice of fairness, kindness, and generosity" (*Cosmopolitan Geographies* 7). Like Pollock before him, Dharwadker searches for cosmopolitan possibilities in ancient India particularly locating these in the inclusive order of monks initiated by the Buddha (*Cosmopolitan Geographies* 6). Dharwadker also traces the difference between various types of South Asian cosmopolitanisms, arguing that Gandhi "ruralized cosmopolitanism" by retreating to the villages even while he was shaped by such multinational entities such as "London, and South Africa, the New Testament, and the Bhagavad Gita, Tolstoy and Mill, and Ruskin and Thoreau" (*Cosmopolitan Geographies* 9). Nehru, on the other hand, depicted the more urban as well as urbane traits of cosmopolitanism by his investment in modernity and development. In the same collection, South Asian theater scholar Una Chaudhuri's essay entitled "Theater and Cosmopolitanism: New Stories, Old Stages" argues that the stage is always rich with cosmopolitan possibility, especially when it engages with the cosmopolitan thematics of diasporic and multicultural drama such as Peter Brook's adaptation of the *Mahabharata*.

The multicultural composition of South Asia as well as the "traveling cultures" of its diaspora facilitates vast networks of cosmopolitan interaction. While writers such as Salman Rushdie, Anita Desai, and Amitav Ghosh have most frequently been described as cosmopolitan, critical theorists of cosmopolitanism have also attempted to situate the term in the unexpected, such as in the cultures of ancient India, and in the neglected, such as trade in Bombay. Cosmopolitanism, even in its contemporary manifestation, has, however, not been accepted without disapproval. Most notably Timothy Brennan has criticized the rootless aspect of cosmopolitanism and the problematic manner by which the postcolonial migrant, Rushdie being Brennan's emblematic example, becomes the universal voice of the Third World.

Pallavi Rastogi

Further Reading

Breckenridge, Carol A., Sheldon Pollock, Homi K. Bhabha, and Dipesh Chakrabarty, eds. "Cosmopolitanism." *Public Culture* 12.3 (Fall 2000): 577–803.

Brennan, Timothy. *Salman Rushdie and the Third World: Myths of the Nation.* New York: St. Martin's, 1989.

Clifford, James. *Routes: Travel and Translation in the Late Twentieth Century.* Cambridge: Harvard UP, 1997.

Cohen, Joshua, ed. *For Love of Country: Debating the Limits of Patriotism.* Boston: Beacon, 1996.

Dharwadker, Vinay, ed. *Cosmopolitan Geographies: New Locations in Literature and Culture.* New York: Routledge, 2001.

Robbins, Bruce and Peng Cheah, eds. *Cosmopolitics: Thinking and Feeling beyond the Nation.* Minneapolis: U of Minnesota P, 1998.

Cracking India by Bapsi Sidhwa, film *Earth* by Deepa Mehta

Deepa Mehta's *Earth* (1998–99), a film based on Bapsi Sidhwa's novel *Cracking India* (published in the United States in 1991 and in Britain as *Ice-Candy Man* in 1988), chronicles the life of a Parsi family on the Indian subcontinent at the time of independence from British rule and the subsequent partition of the subcontinent into India and Pakistan. It is the second film in a planned trilogy of which *Fire* was

A film still from Deepa Mehta's film *Earth.* Courtesy of Photofest.

the first. *Fire* takes on the Indian tradition of the arranged marriage showing how two sisters-in-law, unhappy in their marriages, fall into a lesbian relationship with each other. *Earth* is the much more colorful and political second film of the trilogy.

The story of *Earth* centers on Lenny-baby, a polio-stricken child whose Parsi parents try to shelter her from the violence that is breaking out around her in the city of Lahore. Lenny is protected and taken care of by an *ayah,* or maidservant, who is considered to be part of the family. The story is an autobiographical treatment of Bapsi Sidhwa's life. Sidhwa grew up with polio at the time of Indian independence and partition. Ayah is Hindu and in the film portrayed by the stunning Nandita Das. Both the local masseur and the "ice-candy man," a man who sells ice cream, Dil-Nawaz, portrayed by Amir Khan, are attracted to her. There are poignant scenes of Lenny playing in the park unsupervised while ayah receives the attentions of the men coming in and out of the park. Lenny's mother, Kitu Gidwani, tries to encourage ayah to leave, even giving her jewels that she could sell to survive. As all of Lahore seems to be burning because of religious rioting, it is almost too late to save ayah who had planned to run away with Dil-Nawaz. The men, jealous of her attraction to him, form a mob and march to the Parsi house demanding to know why they, the Parsis, are sheltering a Hindu.

Their Muslim cook emerges trying to protect her. But the mob manages to trick little Lenny into blurting out that ayah is hidden in the bathroom. They drag her out, presumably to be raped and/or butchered as the masseur was. The film ends on the note of the author, Bapsi Sidhwa, walking out on to the park, Queens Park, Lahore, which she remembered playing in as a child.

The Parsis (sometimes spelled Parsee) are a small minority community that immigrated to India from Persia 1,200 years ago because of Muslim persecution. When the Parsis arrived on the coast of Gujarat, they told the Hindu rajah that they would mix with the Indian people like milk mixes with sugar. This story is recounted in the dinner scene at the beginning of both the novel and the film. It is a traditional story that is told in Parsi culture repeatedly. The Parsis are followers of an ancient Persian religion called Zoroastrianism. Zoroastrianism believes in the purity of the fire and in three tenets, "good thoughts, good words, and good deeds." Being neither Hindu nor Muslim, the Parsis were usually on the outside of the religious factionalism that tore India apart at the time of Indian independence. They usually watched from the sidelines and considered themselves neutral, "like Switzerland," Sidhwa writes in the novel, and Deepa Mehta who wrote the film script keeps this line. However, in this novel and film they get caught between the two religious factions. This was indeed the case historically, where many Muslim or Hindu friends sought refuge in the homes of Parsi friends in order to not be persecuted by either religion.

The opening dinner scene in both the novel and the film depicts a conversation among the dinner guests at the Parsi home, a British couple, a Sikh, and a Muslim. Lenny-baby (Maia Sethna) is the child narrator through whose eyes both the novel and the film are told, though of course because of the difference in the medium,

Lenny is not as much the narrator of the film as she is of the novel. Little Lenny, who hobbles along quite touchingly with her polio boot in the film, clambers under the table to listen to this conversation, which she instinctively knows is important. She hears the adults arguing and the Sikh thumping on the table as the British gentleman, stiff as his bow tie, expresses the fear that the "native" peoples will be unable to rule themselves. Lenny's father is apt to agree. Although there is no overt nostalgia for the British Raj rendered in the film, there was a sense among the Parsis that India would have been better off continuing to be ruled by the "outsiders," and this theme definitely pervades both the novel and the film. We see the Muslim characters—especially the sullen masseur Hasan who himself is butchered and left in a body bag that the child discovers—as being treacherous individuals. The Sikhs and Hindus also seem particularly violent. But such was the nature of Partition. Deepa Mehta has repeatedly referred to it as "our holocaust" in interviews. Since Muslim men are circumcised, Hindus and Muslims are said to have stripped men of their pants to determine their religion. Dominique La Pierre and Larry Collins's book *Freedom at Midnight* documents this. Muslims wanted a homeland of their own since they felt marginalized by India's Hindu majority. But Hindus, Muslims, and Parsis had lived side by side for at least a century. It was hoped that when the British left they would continue to live together peacefully. But as depicted in Paul Scott's *The Raj Quartet* the novel and the film, as well as this novel and film, the violence and killings were gruesome.

Deepa Mehta says that it was the sectarianism of the moment that drew her to Bapsi Sidhwa's novel: "The reason I wanted to do a film about the partition is that fifty-two years after we are still struggling with the same issue in Rwanda and Kosovo" (Churi, "Interview with"). Metha made this comment again in her interview with Richard Phillips in which she compared Kosovo and Ireland with what had happened in India, saying *"Earth* is a direct statement against nationalism and separatism, not just in India, but everywhere" (Philips, "Interview with"). Interestingly, even the actors in this film seem to have taken on acting as a way to make a point about religious sectarianism. In an interview entitled, "Of Earth and a Star," on June 3, 1998, published on www.rediff.com, Amir Khan says his favorite piece of dialogue that Deepa had written was, "It was not a question of Hindu, Muslim or Sikh. All of us are like caged beasts waiting for the cage to open. And when that happens only God is *maalik* (Lord)" ("Of Earth"). The opening cage of course refers to when the British leave and let the beasts out. This is why I say that there is indeed a sense of nostalgia for the order that the British kept. Communal rioting continues to plague India today, and communal feeling especially as connected with religious identity continues even to permeate discussion of this film. C. J. S. Walia claims that Mehta manages to distort the complex history of partition: "It follows her controversial *Fire,* which was severely criticized for presenting a distorted view of Hindu culture" (Indiastar.com). Mehta responds by saying she set out to portray the partition because she feels there has been a silence about this tragedy among Western filmmakers. Her theory about this silence is described in an interview with Richard Phillips:

I think it is bound up with a number of attitudes that prevail in Western countries about India. Obviously I'm not including everybody in this generalization, there are many exceptions, but there are several conceptions that prevail in the West about India. There is firstly the spiritual India—a place where you go to find Nirvana. Secondly there is the conception that India is entirely poverty stricken, with a permanent kind of begging bowl attitude. There is the India of the Maharajahs, princes and queens and the India that comes from the nostalgia for the Raj. And there is always the prevailing pressure that people should feel superior to some other place: "look how bad India is with all the beggars, aren't we lucky to be better off."

Because she felt that it was "uncomfortable and difficult for some film makers to produce works that destroy these perceptions," ("Interview with," Phillips) Mehta set about to make this film.

Deepa Mehta has herself been a victim of sectarian religious feeling. The Indian government stopped the third film of the trilogy because they felt that it was insulting to Hindus. Yasmine Yuen-Carrucan's "The Politics of Deepa Mehta's *Water"* published in the *Bright Lights Film Journal* details all the atrocities committed against the film crew. Moreover, the film set was destroyed and dumped in the Ganges by protesters who did not like her treatment of Hindu widows in Varanasi.

Deepa Mehta was born in India. She went to a prestigious boarding school in Dehra Dun. Later she undertook a degree in philosophy at the University of Delhi. Her father was a small film distributor and she seemed to go into filmmaking quite naturally. In 1991, she directed her first feature film *Sam and Me* in Canada about the friendship of an Indian immigrant and an elderly Jewish man. She won the very first honorable mention in the Camera D'Or category at the 1991 Cannes Film Festival. In 1992 she directed a one-hour episode of the *Young Indiana Jones Chronicles,* "Benares," produced by George Lucas who then gave her other episodes to direct. George Lucas also came to her rescue decrying her treatment at the hands of the Indian government when she was filming *Water.*

The Ganges River at dawn, Varanasi. © Helene Rogers/TRIP.

Bapsi Sidhwa was born in 1938 in Lahore, now in Pakistan. She belongs to the illustrious Parsi family called the Bhandaras and is of the priestly class. The family was involved in sheltering and assisting both their Hindu and Muslim friends during partition. Sidhwa now lives in Houston with her husband, Noshir, and their two daughters. She is also the author of *The Bride* (1983) and the *Crow Eaters* (1980).

Feroza Jussawalla

Further Reading

Bahri, Deepika. "Telling Tales: Women and the Trauma of Partition in Sidhwa's *Cracking India.*" *Interventions: International Journal of Postcolonial Studies* 1:2 (1999): 217–33.

Churi, Maya. "Interview with Deepa Mehta." 21 January 2004 <http://www.indiewire.com>.

Collins, Larry, and Dominique Lapierre. *Freedom at Midnight.* New York: Simon and Schuster, 1975.

Dhawan, R. K., and Novy Kapadia, eds. *The Novels of Bapsi Sidhwa.* New Delhi: Prestige, 1996.

"Of Earth and a Star." Interview. 3 June 1998 <http://www.rediff.com>.

Phillips, Richard. "Interview with Deepa Mehta." *World Socialist Web Site.* 6 August 1999 <http://www.wsws.org>.

Sidhwa, Bapsi. *Cracking India.* Minneapolis: Milkweed, 1991; *(Ice-Candy Man)* London: Heinemann, 1991.

Yuen-Carrucan, Jasmine. "The Politics of Deepa Mehta's *Water.*" *Bright Lights Film Journal* 28 (April 2000). <http://www.brightlightsfilm.com>.

D

Dalit Literature

The word *dalit* literally means the ground down, broken, depressed, and down trodden. Dalit literature has become the forum and medium for expression of the experiences of the communities that have been excommunicated, exploited, and humiliated for ages in Indian society. Dalit literature reflects dalit experience and sensibility attempting to define and assert dalit identity from a dalit point of view. Dalit literature faithfully mirrors the stark realities of the dalit situation and becomes an important weapon to strengthen the dalit movement.

The first dalit writer about whom information is available is Chokhamela of the thirteenth century, the only prominent *untouchable* in the Bhakti Movement in Maharashtra. His *abhangas* do suggest some protest against the concept of untouchability, even though the great numbers of them reveal only the traditional devotion and piety of the bhakta. The origins of dalit literature in the contemporary usage of the term, which is largely written and published in Indian regional languages except for a few translations into English, are in the late nineteenth century. The writings and activities of people such as Mahatma Jotirao Phule and Babasaheb Ambedkar (or Dr. Bhimrao Ramji Ambedkar) introduced a tremendous change in the lives of dalits, and Ambedkarist thought is still the life and blood of dalit literature. Although in the early twentieth century dalit was greatly influenced by Gandhian thought and reformist ideology, dalit literature gradually turned into a movement literature, demanding alteration of the caste-based and discrimination-ridden society.

Dalit literature attempts to rewrite history by saying that dalits were the original inhabitants of India and the builders of the Indus Valley Civilization. Some minority Christian and Islamic writers, apart from exposing the alienation that they are subjected to in a Hindu dominated society, put forth the argument that they were also originally dalits who were compelled to convert to other religions because of the discrimination and inhuman treatment meted out to them in their own religion. They express solidarity with the suffering and fighting dalits.

Dalit literature subverts the popular notions, literatures, and images that have been thrust on Indian society for ages now by the dominant castes and classes. Colors such as black and images like the bat, which have been given negative connotations, become positive in dalit interpretation. They adopt some of the images from classical literature to show how dalits have always been isolated and exploited. One image that is used to focus on the upper-caste atrocities is that of Sambhuka from *Ramayana,* a lower-caste man who was doing *tapas,* a practice that was prohibited for him on the grounds of his caste and who was brutally killed by Rama at the insistence of the Hindu sages while he was meditating. Another image is that of the character of Ekalavya from *Mahabharata,* a tribal, who learnt archery, which again he was not permitted to learn from a brahmin guru, Drona, but which he learnt in the presence of his guru's statue. But, in order to see that his kshatriya disciple Arjuna should be the best archer in the world, Drona asked for Ekalavya's right thumb as *gurudakshina,* which Ekalavya happily surrendered, thus ending his brilliant career as an archer. These two instances, which epitomize the exploitation and mercilessness of the upper caste and class, become the reiterated subjects of dalit literature.

Influenced by its long tradition of storytelling, song, and street theatre, dalit literature echoes the spirit of dalit experience and dalit sensibility. Dalit literature, which revolts against the conventions and rigidities of society, also resists literary conventions and language rigidities and tries to create its own poetics against the set politics of the classical literature of the upper strata of the society. Dalit literature uses spoken language, the dialect that is specific to dalits of that region, wherever possible and emphasizes the faithful reflection of the complex and heartrending dalit experience in terms as simple as possible. Dalit writing prioritizes subjective narratives in contrast to the norms of the existing standard literature that concentrates on the objectivity and universality of literature.

Dalit literature mainly stands on the foundation of its tradition of storytelling and song, and many Indian languages have witnessed the publishing of dalit autobiographies and dalit theatre. It is in poetry and fiction that dalit literature vociferously argues for justice, condemning the age-old atrocities and contextualizing the same in the contemporary situations of massacre and elimination.

Another prominent feature in dalit literature is that very few women writers have spoken, but these few have made a strong impact on the literary scenes of various regional languages. The typical experiences of dalit women from different walks of life—where gender is added to the double bind of caste and class—sharply touch the readers of this writing. Especially the autobiographies of Kumud Pawde in Marathi and Bama in Tamil have been revealing and path breaking.

Bama's *Karukku,* an autobiographical novel, explores the experience of leaving the religious order. The novel is structured as a series of memories and recollections whereby the author examines her own experiences first as a Roman Catholic and then as a woman and a dalit. The novel does not follow a linear path and often adopts the *confessional* mode as its narrative strategy. In many ways, it is a re-reading of the Christian scriptures in the light of specific dalit problems. The narrative is a polemic between the self and the community and deals with the issue of caste oppression specifically within the Catholic Church and its institutions. Like all dalit literature, this novel draws from the oral traditions of folk songs and work-chants. Her style opposes the formalities of written language to include colloquialisms. Bama often breaks the rule of written grammar and spelling to demand an alternate and oppositional way of reading and understanding her text.

While dalit literature attacks the past and criticizes the present, it also expresses hope in the future. Voices that have been silenced for ages now refuse to identify themselves with the Hindu religion that they have been part of, accusing it to be the source of discrimination and segregation. They point out that the nation they are singing of offers them only alienation and humiliation, but they proudly declare that the glorious history of this country was built by the dalits.

K. Suneetha Rani

Further Reading

Ambedkar, B. R. *Annihilation of Caste.* Bombay: Bhushan, 1936.

Anand, Mulk Raj and Eleanor Zelliot, eds. *An Anthology of Dalit Literature.* New Delhi: Gyan, 1992.

Bama. *Karukku.* Trans. Lakshmi Holmstrom. Ed. Mini Krishnan. Chennai: Macmillan India, 2000.

Dangle, Arjun, ed. *Poisoned Bread: Translations from Modern Marathi Dalit Literature.* Hyderabad: Orient Longman, 1994.

Ilaiah, Kancha. *Why I Am Not a Hindu.* Calcutta: Samya, 1996.

David Davidar. Photo by Dinesh Khanna.

Davidar, David

David Davidar has been a major figure in the world of publishing for many years, well before his first novel, *The House of Blue Mangoes,* was published in 2002. This novel grew out of an earlier piece written about Davidar's grandfather, which was published in the newspaper *The Hindu.*

The novel itself weaves a piece of the Indian tapestry from a new angle: it narrates history from the point of view of *history,* that is, from the perspective of individuals: sometimes committed, like Aaron Dorai, to the freedom struggle; or totally impervious to its implications, like his brother David, as they live through these crucial years. It can almost be said that the freedom struggle is the façade, and Davidar takes the long route to unravel the complex network that allows the official history to exist. Thus, we have the horrendous scene in which the would-be hero of the independence struggle is broken in captivity and subjected to the most excruciatingly humiliating treatment. Meanwhile, in an attempt to recover their common legacy, David Dorai becomes so involved in building a colony that he remains oblivious of the national ferment. In a similar manner, there is the personal involvement of Kannan, David's son, in a British-owned tea plantation, which allows

the author to explore at length the social and political reality of the British presence in India. Davidar has said in one of his interviews that sometimes he had to read a whole book in order to write just one paragraph. Indeed, this fact perhaps accounts for the encyclopedic quality of the novel.

Despite this, or because of the immense terrain it covers, the novel is structurally kept together by three main sections, each of which covers the fate and fortunes of one of the three generations of the Dorais, from Solomon Dorai to David Dorai and finally to Kannan. From these narrational positions, the novel also charts the social landscape—from the caste wars that confront the landowner, Solomon Dorai, to the professional success achieved but abandoned by his doctor-son David in pursuit of a dream (the Dorai colony) to the further professional ventures of the third generation Dorai (Kannan) who becomes manager of a tea plantation.

While some critics have faulted the novel for the scant attention paid to its female characters and others for its total disconnectedness from the usual modes of treating the independence struggles, Debashish Mukherjee, writing for *The Week,* seems to claim for the book a unique significance:

In its bubbly tale-weaving, it reinvents English as a language of India. *The House* tells us unequivocally [that] it's time we accepted and owned up to English, garnished with tumeric, as our very own language. Tainted and tinted, it comes to life in this novel, more than anywhere else, as the language we are wont to speak, wont to hear. Both the imaginary characters and the author himself make brilliant use of the primarily Indian idiom—spoken English . . . . Fundamentally, this novel could not have been conceived in any language other than English, India's English that is.

The fact that David Davidar had a working network of links within the publishing community in no way means that his novel has been given the easy route to literary recognition. He avoided such unnecessary controversy by sending his manuscript to different publishers under the name of S. H. Jeyakar, an anagram of his own middle name, so that the book would be judged on its literary merit and not on its author's contacts in the world of publishing. Indeed, David Davidar is well known in the world of publishing as the CEO and publisher of Penguin Books, one of the country's leading trade and general publishers, and a subsidiary of the Penguin Group. He was a founding member of the company, and at age 26, not only was he the youngest major publisher in India, but one of the youngest anywhere in the world. In May 2000, he was also appointed managing director of Dorling Kindersley India, the Indian subsidiary of a leading illustrated reference publisher.

During his time at Penguin Group in India, he has published some of the best-known Indian authors in the world, including Vikram Seth, Arundhati Roy, R. K. Narayan, Khushwant Singh, Shashi Tharoor, Rohinton Mistry, Shoba De, Upamanyu Chatterjee, Ramachandra Guha, Sunil Khilnani, Vikram Chandra, Shashi Deshpande, Kiran Desai, Romila Thapar

and Mark Tully. Before he went to Penguin, he was executive editor of *Gentleman* magazine in Bombay.

David Davidar obtained his bachelor's degree in science from Madras University and has a diploma in publishing from Radcliffe College/Harvard University. He has attended senior management and finance programs at top management schools such as the Indian Institute of Management, Ahmedabad, and INSEAD, Fountainbleau, France.

Nandini Bhautoo-Dewnarain

Further Reading

"Beguiled by Chevathar Magic." Rev. of *The House of Blue Mangoes*, by David Davidar. *The Book Review* Mar. 2002: 26.

Lal, Nandini. "Over-Ripe Fruit." Rev. of *The House of Blue Mangoes*, by David Davidar. *Biblio: A Review of Books* Jan.-Feb. 2002: 14.

Mukherjee, Dabashish. Rev. of *The House of Blue Mangoes,* by David Davidar. <http://www.pugmarks.com/week/24 Aug 17/html>.

Desai, Anita

Anita Desai was born in Mussorie, India, in 1937 to a Bengali father and a German mother. Educated in Delhi at Queen Mary's Higher Secondary School and Miranda House, Delhi University, she received a B.A. in English literature. The following year, she married Ashvin Desai, a businessman, with whom she has lived in Delhi, Bombay, Calcutta, and other Indian cities. The couple has four children, one of who, Kiran Desai, is now a writer in her own right, author of *Hullabaloo in the Guava Orchard* (1997).

Anita Desai has written several collections of short stories, children's books, and 10 novels. Her books have been translated into most of the world's major languages. Three of her novels—*Clear Light of Day* (1980), *In Custody* (1984), and *Fasting, Feasting* (1999) were short-listed for the Booker Prize. She received the 1978 Sahitya Akademi Award—the (Indian) National Academy of Letters Award, and the

Guardian Award (United Kingdom) for Children's Fiction in 1982. Her other awards include the Winifred Holtby Prize (Royal Society of Literature, 1978), the Hadassah Magazine Prize (United States, 1989), the Padma Sri (India, 1990), the Literary Lion Award (New York Public Library, 1993), the Neil Gunn Fellowship (Scottish Arts Council, 1994), and the Moravia Award (Rome, 1999). Desai has been a member of the advisory board for English of the Sahitya Akademi in Delhi, a member of the American Academy of Arts and Letters, and a Fellow of the Royal Society of Literature in London. She has been a Fellow at University of Cambridge, England, and has taught at Smith College and Mount Holyoke College in the United States; since 1993, she has been teaching creative writing at Massachusetts Institute of Technology and splitting her time between the United States, England, and India.

In a 1983 talk titled, "Indian Women Writers," given to the London Commonwealth Institute, Anita Desai outlined the complex characteristics of a "feminine standpoint in literature" like hers. Pointing out that women writers "tend to place their emphasis differently from men, that their values are likely to differ, . . . whereas a man is concerned with action, experience, and achievement, a woman writer is more concerned with thought, emotion and sensation," yet she admitted that "this is by no means always so," especially in the West. Citing Henry James and D. H. Lawrence as examples of "exquisitely feminine" writers and Doris Lessing, Muriel Spark, and Iris Murdoch as examples of writers who "display much the same concerns and style as contemporary male writers do," Desai, following Coleridge—as well as Virginia Woolf, advocated an androgynous literature as the ideal. However, she was quick to point out that in India, social, cultural, and political conditions were still not conducive to the production of such literature, so Indian women novelists were "still exploring their feminine identity and trying to establish it as something worth possessing," and writing about "feminine" subject matter, which "makes the reader, whether man or woman, understand and feel what it is to be a woman, know how a woman thinks and feels and behaves . . . prob[ing] into layers of consciousness and explor[ing] what is at the core, at the root of being" ("Indian Women," 54, 57–58).

It comes as no surprise to the contemporary reader, then, that the common critical consensus in the 1970s and 1980s regarding Desai's early work, an opinion strengthened by the writer's own claims such as the ones above, was that she wrote purely subjective, psychological novels, which employed introspective language. One of the post-independence urbanized and "westernized" elite women writers in English, who display no immediately identifiable predominant nationalist sentiment or populist revolt in their works, Desai was generally seen as an exponent of private rather than public themes and as a proponent of a feminine sensibility rather than masculine ideas. For example, Salman Rushdie, in 1984, noted that "the subject of Anita Desai's fiction has, thus far, been solitude. Her most memorable creations—the old woman, Nanda Kaul, in *Fire on the Mountain,* or Bim in *Clear Light of Day*—have been isolated singular figures. And the books themselves have been private universes, illuminated by the author's perceptiveness, delicacy of language and sharp wit, but remaining, in a sense, as solitary, as separate, as their characters" (*Imaginary Homelands,* 71).

Such an exclusive emphasis upon Desai as a woman writer is further reinforced and perhaps even occasioned by Desai's own disclaimers regarding the label of *feminist.* Beginning to write as she did in the early 1960s, she readily admits that early in her career she "wasn't even aware of such a concept as feminism" for "the feminist movement in India is very new" (Bliss 524, Jussawalla 166), an observation borne out by the formalization of the modern Indian Women's Movement as recently as the early- to mid-1970s. Further, interpreting feminism as a constricted movement unified by an evangelical, even militant ideology, Desai declares, "I find it impossible to whip up any interest in a mass of women marching forward under the banner of feminism. Only the individual, the solitary being is of true interest" (Dalmia 13). Finally, subscribing to the notion of a circumscribed feminism that fails to integrate women's issues within the larger national movement for universal civil liberties and democratic rights, she asserts, "I don't have much patience with the theory that it's women who suffer. As far as I can see, men suffer equally" (Bliss 524).

Those critics who take Desai at her word above, however, fail to consider her distinction between the (gendered) kinds and spheres of suffering of Indian men and women. Whereas women "have a life presented to them," men, she notes, are "expected to be active, to forge a life for themselves and their families;" whereas the former are limited to "exercis[ing] whatever control they can within those parameters," the latter are "expected to move further beyond them—and there lies danger" (Bliss 524). Furthermore, in her more recent remarks in interviews and journalistic pieces, Desai displays a keener understanding and appreciation of the feminist movement in India, even as she notes the difference between Western and Indian feminism: "Few Indian feminists really contemplate total change," she points out; "working towards an adjustment through the traditional role is much less drastic, much more Indian. I think Indian feminism is more practical than theoretical . . . expedient rather than ideological," she concludes ("A Sense of Detail," 168).

More recent critics schooled in contemporary theory, therefore, are increasingly given to reading Desai not as a quintessentially feminine novelist of sensibility, but as a feminist, postcolonial writer, who is critical of patriarchy. Such interpretations reflect Desai's own strong criticisms of gendered reality in India, especially as these issues are discussed in her recent political journalism and interviews as well as her belief that critical theory "when it follows a work of art . . . makes a great deal of sense," because "theorists can make all kinds of discoveries and arrive at an understanding of a text which you would not have otherwise" ("A Sense of Detail," 171).

Taking my cue from Desai's statement above regarding the translative-interpretive task of the critic—the latter rooted in her particular historical-ideological moment of the early twenty-first century—I review Desai's key novels as significant discourses on modern Indian feminism. As Desai portrays the discord between chiefly ratiocinative, stolid male characters and predominantly sensitive, introspective female protagonists, she documents the pernicious gender-based polarities of intellect and instinct, rationalism and passion, culture and nature prevalent in modern India. But amid the traditional structures of patriarchy, she also charts the evolving sensibility of the *new* middle-class Indian woman, delineating progressive degrees of female resistance in her fiction. *Cry, the Peacock* (1963), her first novel, recounts the story of Maya, a high-strung childless woman who murders her husband, an unsentimental, aloof lawyer twice her age, and then regresses into an infantilism and subversive madness before she commits suicide. In *Voices in the City* (1965), Monisha is an intelligent, self-aware woman who, alienated from her philistine husband and stifled by her mean existence in an orthodox Bengali extended family, also chooses suicide over a lingering death of the soul. Her sister, Amla, a commercial artist, belongs, by contrast, to the younger generation of professional, urban Indian women. Economically independent, she is nonetheless sexually circumscribed and soon learns that the pursuit of selfhood, of "something more rare, more responsible" than the "security" of marriage exacts in return disillusionment, bitter compromise with life, and abiding isolation.

In *Where Shall We Go This Summer?* (1975), Desai progresses beyond the self-destructive actions of Maya and Monisha to the depiction of a more radical female revolt by the middle-aged Sita, a modern version of her mythic namesake in The Ramayana. During her fifth pregnancy, Desai's character flees from the imprisoning domestic and societal round to her childhood home in order to effect what she terms "the miracle of not giving birth," of protecting her unborn child against the falseness and vicissitudes of the world (31). But at the narrative's end, seeking neither heroism nor martyrdom, she returns to home and husband to prepare for the birth of her child; having recognized that she is part of nature, she opts for life over death. *Fire on the Mountain* (1977) examines the protest of two generations of women: Nanda Kaul, a retiree who, casting off her domestic and familial responsibilities after long servitude, leads a hermetic, pared-down existence; her contemporary, Ila Das, a single genteel but impoverished social worker who is raped and murdered when she opposes child marriage in a north Indian village; and Nanda's great-granddaughter, Raka, a temperamental recluse and rebel who has been abandoned by an abusive father and a deranged mother. Whereas the older generation has arrived at nonconformity "by a long route of rejection and sacrifice," the narrative informs us, the younger generation, represented by Raka, is oppositional "by nature, by instinct," having been "born to [rebellion] simply" (48).

The anarchic energy of Raka gives way in *Clear Light of Day* (1980) to a courageous self-realization and self-acceptance in Bim, the novel's protagonist. In contrast to her sister Tara, who marries to escape an unhappy home life, Bim rejects the circumscription of marriage—its economic dependence and sexual and biological subjugation—choosing instead the life of a single, professional woman. Contradictorily judged by conventional patriarchal standards as an admirable self-abnegating woman who has devoted herself to the lifelong care of her aged aunt and retarded brother or as a self-willed woman who has forsaken salvation by forgoing marriage and motherhood, she disregards both societal approval and disapproval to resist, challenge, even subvert patriarchal norms and institutions. Combining both intellect and sensitivity, she transcends the stereotypical binary opposition of the sexes to approximate in human terms Desai's literary ideal of the Ardhanarishwara, the androgynous Hindu mythological figure who embodies the union of Shiva and Shakti, of male substance and female energy.

In a 1990 interview, Desai responded to a question regarding her "very deliberate" choice of male protagonists in two of her recent novels, *In Custody* and *Baumgartner's Bombay* by confessing that "I felt that as long as I wrote about women, and just had my chief characters as women leading traditional women's lives in India, I was restricting myself to home and family. And if I wanted to walk out into the wider world and bring in history and experience and events and action I simply had to write about male characters" (Libert 54). *In Custody*—for which Desai also wrote the screenplay for the 1993 film version, directed by Ismail Merchant—focuses on the male-male, guru-disciple relationship of Nur, an Urdu poet, who has fallen on hard times, and Deven, a lecturer of Hindi, who realizes that his one-time idol is neither the literary genius nor the man he had imagined him to be, while the depiction of the decline of Urdu and of Muslim culture more generally also enables Desai to "follow the tangled roots of Indian history" (Kenyon 39). And *Baumgartner's Bombay* (1988), which not only has a male protagonist but also draws on Desai's mother's memories of pre-war Germany and is her attempt to write about India from a foreign perspective, tells the story of Hugo Baumgartner, a displaced Jewish businessman. Escaping the Nazis of his youth, Baumgartner, however, ends up living in poverty in India and is brutally murdered by a German hippie whom he befriends.

Journey to Ithaca (1995) continues Desai's interest in non-Indian characters and in male figures through whom she questions gender stereotypes as she spans several continents and decades to chart the pilgrimages to India of three Europeans: Mateo, the romantic Italian dreamer, always dependent on women, Sophie, his German wife, and the Egyptian-French Laila, known as Mother, now the spiritual head of an ashram. As in the relationship between Nanda and Raka in *Fire on the Mountain,* the link between Mother and Sophie is one of protofeminist and feminist, the older woman paradoxically renouncing domesticity and maternity to become the "Mother" to her followers, the younger woman eventually finding freedom in her acceptance of her role as mother, both to her husband and her children. And Desai's latest novel, *Fasting, Feasting* (1999), in a move that underscores her own current position between East and West, is set in both India and the United States, as it tells the story of Uma, who lives with her parents, MamaPapa, in a small provincial Indian town, and her brother, Arun, who is studying and living as a paying guest in Massachusetts. Although the U.S. segments of the story are somewhat stereotypically cast, the sections

on India remain utterly convincing as they trace Uma's story of thwarted desires for a career, for leaving home, and for living on her own.

As they portray the continuing sexual and economic dependence of women in a rapidly industrializing world; the pernicious division of Indian society between the public and private sphere and the concomitant propagation of the myth of the ideal daughter, wife, and mother; the clash between marriage, career, and self-fulfillment, and the efficacy or otherwise of women's rebellion against domestic and social oppression, Desai's novels sunder variously the "old orthodoxies" of religion, caste, and family that she alludes to in her essay "Indian Fiction Today" through their political and politicized narratives. Thus, her works prove to be those very exceptions to novels that maintain the gender status quo in Indian nationalist culture, "exceptions" that Desai regards as highly desirable ("Indian Fiction," 207, 208).

Harveen Sachdeva Mann

Further Reading

Bliss, Corinne Demas. "Against the Current: A Conversation with Anita Desai." *The Massachusetts Review* 29.3 (1988): 521–37.

Dalmia, Yashodara. "Interview with Anita Desai." *The Times of India* 29 April 1979: 13.

Desai, Anita. "Indian Fiction Today." *Daedalus* 118 (Fall 1989): 207–31.

Desai, Anita. "Indian Women Writers." *The Eye of the Beholder: Indian Writing in English.* Ed. Maggie Butcher. London: Commonwealth Institute, 1983. 54–58.

Jussawalla, Feroza and Reed Way Dasenbrock, eds. "Anita Desai." *Interviews with Writers of the Post-Colonial World.* Jackson: UP of Mississippi, 1992. 156–79.

Kenyon, Olga. "Anita Desai." *The Writer's Imagination: Interviews with Major International Women Novelists.* Bradford, UK: U of Bradford P, 1992. 35–43.

Libert, Florence. "An Interview with Anita Desai." *World Literature Written in English* 30.1 (1990): 47–55.

Rushdie, Salman. "Anita Desai." *Imaginary Homelands.* London: Granta, 1991. 71–73.

Desai, Kiran

Beyond a few basic facts, very little is known about the life of author Kiran Desai. Born in 1971, Desai is one of four children of world-renowned author, Anita Desai. After immigrating to the United States at the age of 14, Desai went on to complete a degree in creative writing at Columbia University as a Woolrich Fellow. Although Desai has a home in Manhattan, she also spends her time in India and the United Kingdom, feeling at home in all three locations.

The meager focus on Desai's private life has been offset by the enormous attention given to her one published work, *Hullabaloo in the Guava Orchard* (1999, Faber and Faber, U.K.; Grover Press, U.S.). Inspired by the real story of a hermit who lived in a tree, in this 209-page novel, Desai focuses on a similar story of Sampath, a young boy, who escapes the complications of his home life by climbing and residing in a tree. Interestingly, when she first began writing the novel, Desai had been moving in an entirely different direction.

Desai often felt stifled by the constant rerouting of writing workshops and the irregular pattern of student life, which constantly interrupted her writing rhythm. To jumpstart her writing, Desai took a year off from school. In the end, the four years Desai devoted to her novel have been well repaid by a remarkable debut, on a level craved by any new author. Writer Salman Rushdie lauds Desai's novel as "welcome proof that India's encounter with the English language continues to give birth to new children, endowed with lavish gifts." Robbie Clipper Sethi of *Little India* writes: "She is a novelist with great potential and promise, one of a rising generation of writers whose parents have achieved renown in the literary world—David Updike, Susan Cheever, Andre Dubus III. Among these Desai holds the most promise of

joining her mother, Anita Desai, as a world-class author." Excerpts of Desai's text were also included in Rushdie's post-colonial anthology of Indian literature in English, *Mirrorwork,* as well as in *The New Yorker's Special Issue on Indian Writing.* The high caliber of her writing is further evidenced by its nomination for the *Dublin IMPAC Literary Award* in 2000 and its translation into nine other European languages.

One of many young female Indian writers dominating the current global literary market, Desai distinguishes herself by identifying herself specifically as an Indian writer living in the United States. Furthermore, while writing *Hullabaloo in the Guava Orchard,* Desai made a concerted effort to locate her own voice, apart from those of contemporary and previous Indian writers. Despite her split residential situations, she notes that her relationship to India has always been central to her identity. "My own relation to India is a very natural one," she observes in an interview for *The New York Times.* "I find it very easy to reach into my past and write about India, because it is my heritage. It's in my blood." That same blended vision is reflected in her perceptions of writing, in which the borders between writer and art are rendered almost indistinguishable, yet, remain integrally complementary. "I really felt that in writing one really has to know both how to lose your self-consciousness and absorb yourself in your work and then also to regain it and take a step back and look at your work critically," she notes (Dixon).

Despite the hullabaloo over Desai's novel, many have criticized *Hullabaloo in the Guava Orchard* for the lack of depth in its characters and for its rather odd ending. Needless to say, the lack of any such literary skills only conceals Desai's nascent, developing abilities, and, with the current pace she has set for herself, certainly, time will prove her to be a serious writer to be reckoned with.

V. G. Julie Rajan

Further Reading

Dixon, Martin. *Pure Fiction.* 1998 <http://www.pcug.co.uk/~fiction/newrev/intervie/desai.htm>.

McRandle, Paul. *The Second Circle.* <http://www.thesecondcircle.com/pwm/briefs.html>.

Rothstein, Mervyn. "India's Post-Rushdie Generation: Young Writers Leave Magic Realism and Look at Reality." *New York Times,* 3 July 2000 <http://www.indianembassy.org/ind_us/news_media/post_rushdie_jul_03_00.htm>.

Sethi, Robbie Clipper. "Review of Kiran Desai's *Hullabaloo in the Guava Orchard.*" *Little India* <http://www.asanet.com/achal/archive/Nov98/Literary.htm>.

Deshpande, Shashi

Shashi Deshpande, an eminent Indian novelist in English, was born on August 19, 1938, in Dharwad, Karnataka. After her schooling in Dharwad, Shashi Deshpande graduated in Economics from Elphinstone College, Bombay. Thereafter at Government Law College in Bangalore she won two gold medals; and after serving briefly as a junior lawyer, she took a master's degree in English literature from the Mysore University. She took a diploma course in mass communication in Bombay leading to three more medals and then had a short career in journalism.

Shashi Deshpande's father, Adya Rangachar, better known as Sriranga, was a highly reputed Kannada dramatist and Sanskrit scholar. His liberal attitudes (he never let the family members identify themselves in terms of caste or religion) had an enormous impact on his daughter. But her fiction cannot claim any influence of the father's works. It is said that Sriranga's plays deal with ideas, whereas Shashi Deshpande could never separate ideas from people, even for artistic purposes.

Shashi married D. H. Deshpande, a professor of pathology, whose progressive outlook and unconventional ways equal those of her father. At the end of a year with him in England, when he was a Commonwealth scholar, she described their term abroad in three articles sent to her father, who in turn sent them to *The Deccan Herald* where they were immediately published. A series of short stories followed, which were eventually published as an anthology entitled *The Legacy.* This collection has been well received by both the academic world and the reading public. Since then, Shashi Deshpande has published four other collections of short stories—*It Was Dark, It was the Nightingale, The Miracle and Other Stories,* and *The Intrusion and Other Stories.* An avid reader and admirer of Enid Blyton, Deshpande has also written short-story volumes for children—*A Summer Adventure, The Only Witness, The Hidden Treasure,* and *The Narayanpur Incident.* They were initially inspired by her need as a mother to provide suitable Indian stories for her own children to read. In addition, she has published several essays in books, scholarly journals, popular magazines, and newspapers. An edited volume of her significant essays is soon to be published by Penguin India.

Shashi Deshpande's remarkable success with the literary form of the short story gave her the confidence to deal with the larger canvas of the novel. In her short stories, Deshpande had tried some unconventional subjects such as rape within marriage, reversal of gender roles, forbidden love, burden of motherhood, and female sexuality.

Roots and Shadows (completed 1978, published 1983), Deshpande's first novel, won the Thirumati Rangammal prize for the best novel of 1982–83. Indu, its protagonist, is an independent writer in quest of her selfhood. She marries (outside her caste and language background) Jayant, a man of her choice, but soon realizes that this relation allows him to have power over her. She feels a sense of disintegration within herself because of her unhealthy dependence in marriage. She even turns to an extramarital relationship with Naren to arrive at a better understanding of herself and of the power of love for another human being. But she finally realizes that though love involves an element of surrender, it need not promote vulnerability. Her introspection leads to an awareness of the masks put on by the so-called liberated people including herself, and also, ultimately, to her recognition that love can strengthen as much as weaken a person.

Indu becomes aware of her autonomy as a writer and as a woman having stable relationships within the institution of family. She restores her connection with Jayant, with the understanding that a relationship can be a trap or a healthy bond depending on the ability to tap into one's own courage and make one's own choices. Her inheriting of the ancestral home from Akka, an elder member of the family, allows Indu to assume a matriarchal role, reawakening her vital connection with the roots that she had earlier rejected in her pursuit of shadows. Indu can now distinguish between bonds and bondage and reach out to Jayant. Her rootedness gives her a better understanding of the self and society.

The Dark Holds No Terrors (1980) is Deshpande's second novel, although it was published before *Roots and Shadows*. The novel is in a way an expanded version of her short story "A Liberated Woman" included in the volume *The Legacy*. The novel grows out of the marriage of Manu, who had degenerated from a promising poet and actor into a mediocre English teacher in a third-rate college; and Saru, a successful physician who falls victim to Manu's frustration and sexual sadism. Manu's wounded pride and feelings of inferiority to Saru lead to his use of sex as an instrument of revenge and result eventually in marital estrangement. Saru re-

turns to her father's house that she had rejected 15 years earlier, and the time away from her husband and two children leads to a review of her own unhappy childhood.

Saru's mother had always considered her a burden, a responsibility, and a problem, with no right to any choice in life. To break free of her mother's authoritarianism, Saru becomes a doctor and marries Manu in defiance and in self-assertion. Saru hesitates to deal with increasing marital problems because to admit defeat is to prove her mother right, and there is no reconciliation with her mother even at the time of the latter's death. Saru thus remembers her mother obsessively with a sense of guilt and defeat.

Moving still further back in time, the novel shows that Saru had been a victim of gender discrimination at home. Her brother, Dhruva, was the mother's precious child. Accompanying Dhruva at play one day, Saru carelessly and passively allows her brother to drown, thus perhaps revealing her subconscious desire, and justifying her mother's claim that Saru is, by intent, a murderess.

The Dark Holds No Terrors moves around the uncertainty of events like Saru's responsibility for the death of her brother, Manu being the predator and Saru the prey. Saru attempts a blackout of experiences that lie between reality and unreality. The novel ends with a call to Saru's sense of profession that steadies her and gives her the courage to confront reality. Attending to illness is significantly placed at the end of the novel. The doctor in her is more important than her role as the wife or mother. Assertion of her career is likely to help Saru confront the terrors within, light up the situation and declare that the dark holds no terrors.

Deshpande has written two detective novels that were originally serialized in magazines. The author herself considers them total failures. *If I Die Today* (1982) deals with the campus life fraught with dangers in the residential quarters of a hospital. The slim novel is crowded with characters, including Dr. Ashok (husband of Manju, the narrator); Guruji, a terminally ill cancer patient; Prabhakar Tambe, a selfless leader of mill workers who dies mysteriously; and Dr. Vidya, whose responsibility for several disturbing deaths is finally revealed. But the narrative is too flimsy to take on all its twists and turns, and the whodunit element in the novel does not produce the desired effect.

Come Up and Be Dead (1983) has a girls' school as its setting. The novel exposes the evil of sexual exploitation in an educational institution that exists to empower girls to seek and offer justice. But the characterization is far below Deshpande's standards. These characters fall into mere categories of preys, predators, and accomplices. The good people lurk in the dark and are ineffectual.

With *That Long Silence* (published by Virago, London in 1988, and winner of the Sahitya Akademi award the following year), Deshpande became better known as a novelist outside of India. The novel begins with a crisis in a middle-class family. The husband, Mohan, is accused of business malpractice and his wife, Jaya, is forced to go into hiding with him to her family apartment in Bombay. The present routine is upset and the future is bleak and uncertain. Jaya enters into self-analysis and regrets frittering away her potential as a writer. Haunted by the fear of failure, she takes lessons of conformity from her father's many unsold books. At Mohan's suggestion, she writes successful, humorous, acceptable "Seeta columns" for local magazines.

But education has not helped Jaya extricate herself from the stranglehold of tradition. As a wife, her unreserved support to her husband is taken for granted. Corrupt or not, her husband is a "sheltering tree." This deep-rooted notion is challenged when she realizes how she has also participated in its perpetuation with lies and deceit. Her marital loyalty is under threat when she is drawn to the well-read, sensitive critic, Kamat. Kamat is all that Mohan is not. He is clumsy in looks but is a keen intellectual and a sensitive listener. It is he who helps her identify the lack of anger and punch in her story of a child widow who had been rejected by many publishers. She is surprised at her own free self-revelation to Kamat. Her long silence and submission have served as her mode of communication with Mohan. Kamat helps her to acknowledge her fear of failure as a writer. Such a forbidden relationship that can be emotional, intellectual, and physical is destined to be clandestine and face eventual extinction. The disturbing presence of Kamat is conveniently removed from Jaya's life and from the novel. Mohan's telegram regarding reinstatement in his job brings relief to Jaya and reopens the possibility of return to her former routine. But the experiences in the family flat have given her self-assurance and resurgence of strength.

In *The Binding Vine* (1993), the protagonist Urmila is a college teacher whose husband, Kishore, is away on service in the navy. Urmila realizes that a love marriage does not guarantee permanent emotional oneness: her husband can reach out to her only through her body. One day she discovers the poems and diary notes of her long dead mother-in-law, Mira, which had been hidden away years earlier. Urmi realizes that Mira had been trapped in a marriage where she had been the object of obsessive lust and controlling love. Creativity was Mira's only escape and refuge. At about the same time, she comes into contact accidentally with Shakutai, the mother of a rape victim, Kalpana, who has been reduced to a near-dead existence. In Urmi's consciousness, Mira and Kalpana come together as powerless victims of rape who desperately seek a voice. Past and present coalesce and Urmila interprets love as an obsessive need to control and exert power over the object of love. In a patriarchal society, the beauty of the victim becomes the cause of her plight. Urmi reconstructs the life of Mira that is submerged in her poems and makes a public campaign out of Kalpana's condition to create awareness in the people. Because of her genuine concern, she is able to achieve more than her sister-in-law who is a social worker. Despite the depiction of agony, the novel ends in the hope of integration. Urmila recognizes that being left to grow up with her grandmother was not an act of rejection by her mother, but a punishment meted out to her mother for leaving the child with a male servant while going out. Urmi learns to feel a shared togetherness with her family. Her ability to reach out to people makes life meaningful.

In *A Matter of Time* (1996), Deshpande focuses for the first time on the psyche of a male character. The main character, Gopal, without rational explanation leaves his home, his wife Sumi, and his three teenage daughters, Aru, Charu, and Seema, forcing them to relocate in Sumi's parental home. But the parents, Kalyani and Shripati, have fallen into non-communication. Their mentally retarded son had wandered away from Kalyani in a crowded railway station 35 years earlier and Shripati holds her responsible. Thus Sumi's distress at the departure of her husband is intensified by the need to adapt to an unpleasant domestic situation.

Sumi is aware that the reason for Gopal's angst and his subsequent detachment lie deep within him. She had sensed his gradual move toward this stage, which is the result of his feelings of human aloneness. She can understand his impelling urge and can easily deal with his absence. In fact, Gopal's absence brings about the realization of her own creative ability, self-reliance, and empowerment. Her play, "The Gardener's Son," written for a school function, is just the beginning of her cre-

ative ventures. She can create and also subvert existing creative material to celebrate feminine causes. Sumi's position as a teacher and her riding a scooter with her father is another suggestion of hope and integration. Unfortunately her life and creativity come to an abrupt halt when she and her father are killed in an accident.

After the death of Sumi and her father, Sumi's eldest daughter, Aru—previously rebellious in attitude because of the absence of her father Gopal—modifies and changes from her earlier antagonism in an attempt to reach out to the remaining family members. She decides to take care of her grandmother, Kalyani. At the same time she begins to acquire an understanding of her father and his actions. Gopal's feelings of alienation had resulted from tangled relationships in his own family, producing anguish in him that he was unable to deal with. As Aru develops a fuller awareness of the problems in her family background, she moves toward a better understanding of people and of the necessity to bond.

Small Remedies (2000) is an ambitious novel that deals with many issues relating to the human condition of aloneness. On one hand, the novel is about personal loss and memory and the possibility of its retrieval. On the other hand, it is about the creative process and different versions of truth. The protagonists in this novel are women, and they face challenges because they refuse to conform to society. Madhu Saptarishi is separated from her husband, Som. She has also lost her only son, Aditya in a post-Ayodhya bomb blast. She is laden with guilt and grief as her son had left the house in anger on hearing of the rift between his parents. Eventually Madhu sets out on a commissioned assignment of writing the biography of Savitribai Indorekar, an older Hindustani vocalist. Madhu realizes that a biography can reveal as much as conceal information. In narrating her life to Madhu, Savitribai chooses to maintain a deliberate rift between her public and her private image, and to negate the existence of her daughter, Munni. Her unmoved rejection and loss of her only daughter is parallel to the irreparable loss of Madhu's son, Aditya. Both he and Munni fall victims to the same communal violence. But the maternal reactions are totally different. It is not Bai's achievements but her negation of motherhood that becomes the enigma central to Madhu's project.

Another significant nonconformist is Madhu's aunt, Leela, a woman who has the courage to live her principles. Her activism counters caste bigotry, male chauvinism, and selfish materialism within and outside her communist party. While Savitribai manipulates her ways to break into the male bastion of power and position, Leela walks out of her party to prove her principles. Savitribai's life is self-centered; Leela strives to give voice to the weak. This comparison offers Madhu a better perspective on the meaning of life.

Madhu learns that truth is not simple or singular, and that subjective narration alone is possible. In the process of writing Savitribai's life story, Madhu increasingly reveals more of herself, and the work becomes a biography within a biography. Writing of the biography itself is thus therapeutic for Madhu, a small remedy for the pain that she has experienced. Remedies come in small doses, in the little acts of concern that one gets from unexpected sources.

Thus, the novel ends with the realization that while memories may torment, they can also be a source of strength. Experiences cannot be repeated or undone. Life itself is reconstructed memory. But memories can quicken the healing process and make survival possible. The exposure to the lives and experiences of others gives Madhu a renewed perspective on life, suggestive of a renewed relationship with her husband.

The female centrality in the novels of Shashi Deshpande has led to the labeling of her works as feminist fiction. Deshpande sees in this labeling a divisive tendency to categorize creative writing by gender and render works by women irrelevant for male readers. Her primary interest in the novels is human relationships in and out of the family structure. When she writes about a society caught between tradition and modernity, it is natural for women to occupy center stage as the victims of inequality. While dealing with the complexities of male-female relationships, she maintains commendable objectivity and refrains from generalizations. Deshpande does repudiate women's faithful acceptance of the secondary position given to them. Societal prescriptions are often received from the mothers, and Deshpande, perhaps more than any other Indian writer, pays special attention to this mother-daughter relationship in her fiction.

Most of Deshpande's protagonists are educated middle-class women who have careers of their own. With the altered demands on women and men in society, power relations within the family need to be renegotiated. The institution of family is sacred but not without its basic requirement of love and understanding. When transformation becomes impossible, rejection becomes necessary. The best form of freedom comes with choices and responsibilities.

The protagonists in Deshpande's novels are also on the road to self-discovery. Usually some domestic crisis propels them in this quest. They may or may not reach the desired destination by the end of the novel, but there is often hope and determination. Their struggle is to realize their identity as persons, not as daughters, wives, or mothers. Shashi Deshpande's novels also frequently ruminate over the condition of human alienation and the vicissitudes of time. Past resides with the present, and the novels often digress into Indian myths, fables, and folktales that show the power of tradition and the society's reluctance to change. But her novels are infused with a rich inclusiveness, which in itself enhances the possibilities of the hope with which many of them end.

Premila Paul

Further Reading

Atrey, Mukta and Viney Kirpal. *Shashi Deshpande: A Feminist Study of Her Fiction.* Delhi: B. R. Publishing, 1998.

Dinesh, Kamini. "Moving out of the Cloistered Self: Shashi Deshpande's Protagonists." *Margins of Erasure: Purdah in the Subcontinental Novel in English.* Eds. Jasbir Jain and Amina Amin. New Delhi: Sterling, 1995. 196–205.

King, Adele. "Shashi Deshpande: Portraits of an Indian Woman." *The New Indian Novel in English: A Study of the 1980s.* Ed. Viney Kirpal. New Delhi: Allied, 1990. 159–68.

Pathak, R. S., ed. *The Fiction of Shashi Deshpande.* New Delhi: Creative Books, 1998.

Sebastian, Mrinalini. *The Enterprise of Reading Differently: The Novels of Shashi Deshpande in Postcolonial Arguments.* New Delhi: Prestige Books, 2000.

Desirable Daughters by Bharati Mukherjee

Bharati Mukherjee was born in Calcutta, India, in 1940. She has an M.A. from the University of Baroda, an M.F.A. and a Ph.D. from the University of Iowa. She has written six novels, two nonfiction works, and two collections of short stories, one of which won the National Book Critics Circle Award. She is a professor of English at the University of California, Berkeley. She is married to writer Clark Blaise, and they have two sons.

Mukherjee's novel *Desirable Daughters,* narrated by the 36-year-old Indian American protagonist Tara, explores, in her words, "the making of a consciousness" (5). The youngest of three beautiful and well-cultivated daughters of a wealthy engineer, Tara was raised in a close-knit, upper-class Bengali family of orthodox

Brahmins living in Calcutta. At the age of 19, she marries Bishwapriya (Bish) Chatterjee, the perfect husband selected by her father.

In the Unites States, Tara rejects her traditional Indian life. She divorces her multimillionaire husband of 10 years when she concludes that her marriage does not fulfill "the promise of life as an American wife" (82). Sacrificing the comfort and privileges of her life in a prestigious neighborhood, Tara moves to San Francisco with her 12-year-old son, Rabi. Everything in Tara's life changes. She starts working, and after a number of short-term relationships with men, finally welcomes Andy, a Hungarian Buddhist contractor, as her live-in lover.

As Tara begins to feel comfortable in her newly transformed American self, a young man, Chris Dey, unexpectedly enters her life. Claiming to be the illegitimate son of her eldest sister, he threatens the safe assumptions on which her new life is partly founded. His mysterious appearance forces her into a period of intense self-examination. Suddenly she finds that her happy and glorious past "seemed now the darkest cave" and members of her family "blind stumbling creatures" (*Desirable* 133). She realizes for the first time the tremendous differences in worldview and lifestyle that separate the sisters in spite of their earlier common training. After Andy moves out of her life, Tara also realizes she has misunderstood her ex-husband and moves closer to him.

One night, Tara and Bish are attacked in her house by explosives planted by the person who had falsely identified himself as Christopher Dey. To recover from this traumatic incident, Tara returns with Rabi to her parents in India, leaving America with an enhanced understanding of her connection to her Indian roots.

In *Desirable Daughters,* Mukherjee makes a departure from her earlier novels in several significant ways. Unlike her other Indian protagonists, Tara tries to find her identity in the United States without wanting to obliterate her former identity. She desires to combine her past Indian and her present American selves to invent her own new self, and succeeds in doing so. Like Mukherjee herself, Tara welcomes this painful and difficult process and meets it with poise and strength.

To know herself, Tara traces with pride and affection the story of her ancestors, especially female ancestors. She does not ignore the subjugated position of these Indian women, yet they do not appear as victims, but as intelligent and sensitive people struggling to empower themselves within their limited world and opportunities. This theme arises in the story of Tara's ancestor, Tara Lata Gangooly, a saint and a freedom fighter. Like "each generation of women in [her] family" Tara discovers "in her something new," and uses her story as a source of inspiration and to continue the chain of family unity (*Desirable* 289).

Tara desires to get rid of everything in her past that is false and superficial, whether of culture, class, or caste. This challenging process requires her to reassess her society, which is not easy for her given her privileged background. She stumbles and occasionally falls, but she is determined to look squarely at her own weaknesses and those of her family members. Nor does she allow these insights to dampen or destroy her ongoing search for identity.

Although Tara learns to reconnect with her sisters in new ways, they do not reciprocate, and they continue to criticize her brashly and unjustly, while she remains silent. This unwholesome aspect of their relationship produces a sense of incompleteness in Tara's mission. On the other hand, Tara's ability to communicate openly with Rabi, Bish, and Andy, which is a result of her self-expansion in America, helps to provide some beautiful moments in the novel. Her renewed understanding

of the Hindu concept of dharma helps her to see Bish in a new light, and her love for her son helps her to accept his homosexuality. Her relationships with these three men reflect her peaceful and understanding nature, which help them to reveal the best in themselves.

Once again, for Mukherjee, America serves as a transformational stage for her characters. Free from the authoritarian grip of her father, living in multicultural America, Tara is able to remake herself in a remarkably successful way, unlike her previous protagonists who survive by a costly amputation of the past. She acts out her part with a grace and wisdom that some of the earlier characters lacked.

This absorbing, eloquent, and compassionate narrative, enriched by Mukherjee's sense of history and humor, will be important to readers of many backgrounds.

Desirable Daughters has received favorable reviews by most major newspapers. These reviews have noted Mukherjee's sound expansion of her earlier themes, such as the self-transformation of the immigrant and the collision of cultures. She has also been highly praised for her skillful narrative and her artful handling of history and geography.

Sartaz Aziz

Further Reading
"Expat Exuberance." Rev. of *Desirable Daughters*, by Bharati Mukherjee. *Biblio: A Review of Books* July-Aug. 2002: 15.

Dhondy, Farrukh

Farrukh Dhondy is a filmmaker, columnist, novelist, children's writer, and commissioning editor. Having discovered him as a children's writer when I was teaching children's literature, I interviewed Dhondy in his office at Channel 4 TV in London in 1988. There was general celebration and jubilation that day as a film he had commissioned, Mira Nair's *Salaam Bombay,* had just won the Palm d'Or at Cannes. Dhondy was brimming with genuine pride. He has been the first Parsi writer to get serious recognition abroad, especially for his children's and adolescents' books, and the first to be written up in reference works such as Gale's *Something about the Author.*

Dhondy was born and raised in Pune, India, in 1944. He moved to England at the age of 20 to study science at Cambridge, but later switched to studying literature. He later became a dedicated English teacher writing about the students he taught in the East End of London. His first book, *Come to Mecca* (Fontana, 1978), is a children's book in which Dhondy focuses on "Black British," children—not just those racially black, but the Asians and Middle Easterners, all of whom the British lump together as "Black." These were the children on "Free Dinners," (there is a story by that title in *Come to Mecca*), Bangladeshi, Caribbean, living in Brick Lane, eating at "Iqbal's Café," trying to understand Shakespeare, but also trying to adopt him: "I like Urdu poet. Most sweetest language in the world, just next to Bengali and English. Iqbal, Tagore, Nazrul, Shakespeare, all artists, all brothers" (49). One of the little boys he created in the story, "Salt on a Snake's Tail," a Bangladeshi called Jolil, lives in the British elementary school curriculum through a little story taught over and over called "Kiss Miss Carol," an obvious play on "Christmas Carol," where Jolil is asked to play Tiny Tim and does not know how to tell his poor Bangladeshi father who is a tailor and who needs Jolil's help sewing pockets. Besides, his conservative Muslim parents would not want him to act, let alone in a Christmas play. Through a series of misadventures, he ends up acting anyway. While this story may seem foreign to an American elementary school audience, in many ways it portrays the cross-cultural encounter based on language and religion. In this sense it is similar to Rudolfo Anaya's *Bless Me, Ultima,* which focuses on marginalized Chicano gang kids performing in a Christmas play, probably the arch assimilation device in all minority literature, taking its cue from the Christmas recital in James Joyce's *The Dead.*

East End at Your Feet (1976) and *Trip Trap* (1982) gave birth to the generation of literature about the characters Hanif Kureishi has called "cockney-Asians"—*Asians* meaning mostly Indians and Bangladeshis (not Chinese and Japanese). Dhondy created and legitimated characters that would then appear in the fiction of Hanif Kureishi or Zadie Smith. Assimilation and fitting in are the themes of these stories. " I don't know much Hindi, but I have to speak to my granddad in Hindi 'cause he don't know nothing else," the character tells us in "East End at your Feet," the title story. "I used to pretend I couldn't speak Hindi when I was with the lads" (*East End* 52). "The Lads," on the other hand, are deciding whether to "roll" a "Paki geezer." In *Trip Trap,* one of "the lads" justifies himself:

> I knew you used to think I was right prejudiced, but that's because you only joined our school in the fourth year and I was a skin at the time. We had to do it. I'll tell you, I don't think you teachers knew what was going on down there. We was in the minority, right, and it was our country, but you wouldn't allow us to say it. And the Asian kids, they came flash. "Sikhs rule," and all this, and there was so many of them you only opened your mouth if you wanted a taste of knuckle sandwich. (15)

This quotation reinforces what Kamala Markandaya had once said to me about her book *Nowhere Man:* "Hybridity: they won't allow it." These themes of culture clash and of culture conflict in the schools now outdated in Britain are surprisingly contemporary in the United States today and are ideal for teaching tolerance and showing how the world changes with the influx of immigration. *Poona Company* (1982) on the other hand is juxtaposed with these works, because almost in an R. K. Narayan–like fashion, it portrays the more peaceful, lighthearted conglomeration of young men in the bazaars and boys going to Catholic schools, a world wide apart from that in "East End." Salman Rushdie, quoted on the book blurb, says, "It's a beautiful collection, full of affection, malicious exact detail, dialogue perfectly caught; and it is an extremely funny book."

But Farrukh Dhondy is a Parsi writer, raised in a Westernized, British school, who, though he writes about Parsis in *Bombay Duck* (1990), turns to his Western education, specifically the Parsi love of English literature to write about Shakespeare and Marlowe in *Black Swan* (1993). While addressing a group of students Dhondy said, "*Black Swan* is an attempt to get truly away from the Asian subject." When one student asked about nationalism, Dhondy joked, "I think it was a literary mistake. I say characters can have it, but writers can't. There is a writer who wrote *Mein Kampf,* very nationalistic." But he added, " I think it is a non-sequitur to think of *hybridity.*"

Dhondy's career can be divided into three stages: college lecturer, school teacher, and novelist (at Leicester College and teacher and Head of the English department at Archbishop Michael Ramsay's school, 1968–84), who was writing about his students; commissioning editor at Channel 4 TV, U.K. (1984–97) who made possible award-winning films such as *Salaam Bombay* (Dir. Mira Nair), *Immaculate Conception* (Dir. Jamil Dehlavi), *Mississippi Masala* (Dir. Mira Nair), *Bandit Queen* (Dir. Shekhar Kapur), and playwright; and now, 1997 onward as a columnist, independent filmmaker, literary critic, and theorist writing about the Carib-

bean socialist, C. L. R. James. His debut as a screenwriter was in *Split Wide Open,* which was produced and directed by Dev Benegal. His plays include *The Bride and other Plays for T.V.* (Faber and Faber), *Vigilantes* (Hobo Press), *Mama Dragon* (stage play, Arts Theatre and ICA, London), *Shapesters* (Cottesloe at the National Theatre), *Film, Film Film* (Shaw Theatre, London). His TV series include *Come to Mecca, No Problem, Tandoori Nights, Empress and the Munshi, King of the Ghetto,* and *Annie's Bar.*

In an E-mail to me, this is how Dhondy characterized his current work:

> I quit Channel 4 at the end of 1997 and have been writing since. My latest books are a biography of C. L. R. James (Weidenfeld) and *RUN* a novel for young adults, about a boy called Rashid Rashid, whose grandfather dies and leaves a boy with a dual identity (Bloomsbury 2002). I have since gone on to writing films: the *Alexandria Quartet* based on Lawrence Durrell's books—three films are yet to be produced, the first is out—and *The Rising,* a story of the Indian Mutiny (1857) [on which the critical theoretical term *subaltern* is based], with Ketan Mehta directing and Aamir Khan acting. Have finished another children's book called *BAD.* Tara Press in India has published a collection of short stories *Adultery and Other Stories.*

Dhondy's life of his Caribbean friend C. L. R. James entitled, *C. L. R. James: Cricket, the Caribbean and World Revolution* (Weidenfeld and Nicolson, 2001) and *C. L. R. James: A Life* (Random House, 2002), have been published to great acclaim especially since there is so much interest in James's notion of "crossing boundaries"—those metaphoric and literal, as on a cricket field. Dhondy first met James at a Black Panthers' movement meeting in the late 1960s. In the 1970s, James lived with Dhondy and the two became good friends. In two recent columns, one before 9-11 and one after, Dhondy seems to have run afoul of the Black British Muslims he struggled to help and support in the 1970s and 1980s. In July 2001, he wrote in *The Guardian* that an Islamic academy was needed in Britain to address the needs of Muslims in Bradford and Brick Lane. He then criticized the British for their policy of anglicizing Muslim natives of Britain. In "Our Islamic Fifth Column" (Autumn 2001, Vol. 4), he wrote of radical Islamic clerics recruiting British teenagers, causing much consternation in the Islamic community who thought that because his name sounds Muslim that he was betraying them. He was not in fact betraying them and has undertaken a commission from YTV to write a script portraying the racism involved in the brutal attack on Sarfraz Najeib in Leeds by two soccer players, Woodgate and Boyer. But Farrukh Dhondy is a Parsi Zoroastrian from India, a "pukka sahib," a true gentleman, who in fact has assimilated in Britain as "the good Parsi," as the British said in the nineteenth century, a term used flatteringly to describe the accomplishment and success of such Parsis as the industrialist, J. R. D. Tata.

Feroza Jussawalla

Further Reading

Albertazzi, Sylvia. "Spaghetti alla Bolognese e antara di Bombay." (A conversation with Sylvia Albertazzi) *Linea d'ombra* XIV, 114 (1996): 31–35.

Chanda, Tirthankar. "Code Switching in Farrukh Dhondy's *Bombay Duck*." *Commonwealth* 20.1 (Autumn 1997): 45–54.

James, C. L. R. *Beyond a Boundary.* Durham: Duke UP, 1993.

Jussawalla, Feroza. "Hybridity, Our Ancestral Heritage: Minority Indian Writers Speak of Their Diversity." Ed. Monika Fludernik. *Hybridity and Postcolonialism.* Tübingen: Stauffenburg Verlag, 1998.

Kumar, Narendra. *The Parsee Novel.* New Delhi: Prestige, 2002.

Diaspora

During the last decade, exilic and diasporic discourses have emerged in relation to contemporary examinations of the nation and postcolonial migration within cultural criticism, resulting in shifting definitions and usages of the terms. With an increasing critique of the racialized formation of national identity, scholars in such diverse fields as feminist, postcolonial, and cultural studies have questioned the rooted, static, and sedentary logic of modernity. Challenging narratives of purity and rootedness, diasporic discourses are positioned to dismantle nationalist constructions of belonging, linking body and space in seamless tales of blood and family with land and territory. While diaspora also emerges in discussions of globalization and transnationalism, it has not always been fully linked to economic and material analyses.

From its Greek roots, *diaspora* means literally to scatter or sow across. *The Oxford English Dictionary* traces its usage to a reference in the Old Testament (Deut. 28:25) to the dispersal of the people of Israel across the world. The classic definition of diaspora, based on the Jewish model, presumes that dispersal is due to forced exile from a homeland to which people desire to return eventually. Recent usages of diaspora refer simply to the migration of an ethnic community. Attempts to define diaspora more stridently by outlining its characteristic traits have led to contentions regarding the central features of diasporas. William Safran suggests that diasporas are characterized primarily by the relationship between the dispersed people and the "original homeland" to which they hope to return (84–85). One notable absence in Safran's defining features is the lack of specification about the cause of migration; in other words, his definition does not make a distinction between forced or voluntary dispersal. For many, the historical conditions of migration such as colonialism cannot be separated from the diasporas that they engender. Furthermore, scholars, such as Robin Cohen, have proposed typologies of diaspora that distinguish not only between voluntary and forced dispersal, but also between the conditions of acceptance and acclimation. For example, though the condition of postcoloniality provides some parallel to the African diaspora and its history of slavery, South Asian diasporas, resulting from various modes of displacement including indentured servitude, colonialism, and uneven capital development, produce heterogeneous formations of diaspora and diasporic politics. The predominant feature of Safran's definition is the extensive emphasis on the connection with and return to the homeland. Recent interpretations of diaspora articulate less stringent requirements regarding the relationships between dispersed communities and homelands. Khachig Tölölyan posits that "it makes more sense to think of diasporan or diasporic existence as not necessarily involving a physical return but rather a *re-turn,* a repeated turning to the concept and/or relation of the homeland and other diasporan kin" (14). Tölölyan, rather than eliminating or evading diaspora's relationship with the homeland, unfetters it from a permanent physical return in favor of diverse connections to the homeland.

In the case of the African diaspora, the Negritude movement, represented by writers such as Aimé Césaire and Leopold Senghor, attempted to link the diaspora in its essential and oppositional blackness to Africa. Negritude advanced a return to Africa via cultural roots and aesthetic forms, more than it promoted a physical and political return. However, many African diasporic intellectuals critique the Negritude movement as narrowly based on essentialist notions of authenticity and purity. Stuart Hall argues that diaspora does not have

to evoke "those scattered tribes whose identity can only be secured in relation to some sacred homeland to which they must at all costs return, even if it means pushing other people into the sea. This is the old, the imperializing, the hegemonizing form of 'ethnicity' " (401). Therefore, Hall removes homeland from the center of diaspora in order to avoid the essentialism associated with the Negritude movement, posing diaspora as a rupture to the racist British formulation of the nation. Similarly, Paul Gilroy's concept of the "Black Atlantic" does not focus on the return of Africans to the homeland, but instead recognizes the exchanges and connections between diasporic communities. Thus, these more recent articulations of the African diaspora construct alternative architectures of diaspora based on cultural difference and hybridity, rather than homeland. Echoing the sentiment, "it ain't where you're from, it's where you're at," their works focus primarily on the developing situation of diasporic location as home. In doing so, they have produced narratives that decouple diaspora from homeland in hope of avoiding essentialist narratives of belonging and origins. James Clifford comments that the "centering of diasporas around an axis of return overrides the specific local interactions (identifications and 'disidentifications,' both constructive and defensive) necessary for the maintenance of diasporic social forms. The empowering paradox of diaspora is that dwelling *here* assumes a solidarity and connection *there.* But *there* is not necessarily a single place or an exclusive nation" (322). These differences indicate the expanded contemporary use and classification of diasporic discourses. Like Clifford, some scholars see diasporas as fecund sites of creative cultural, social, and intellectual production.

Citing the cosmopolitan transnational politics of the African and Jewish diasporas as exemplary, Gilroy emphasizes forced dispersal as a foundational component, while simultaneously divorcing diaspora from its conservative and essentializing modes (such as Zionism and Indian diasporic Hindu nationalism or Hindutva) in order to construct an idealized political formation that positions itself between nationalisms of the homeland and of the places of residence. In *Against Race,* Gilroy argues that diaspora produces a diasporic identity which is "focused, less on the equalizing, pre-democratic force of sovereign territory and more on the social dynamics of remembrance and commemoration defined by a strong sense of the dangers involved in forgetting the location of origin and the tearful process of dispersal" (123–24). Critiquing the nation-state, Gilroy writes diasporic consciousness "stands opposed to the distinctively modern structures and modes of power orchestrated by the institutional complexity of nation-states. Diaspora identification exists outside of and sometimes in opposition to the political forms and codes of modern citizenship" (124).

Building on terms such as multiculturalism, globalization, postcoloniality, and ethnicity, cultural studies theorists have posited diaspora as an oppositional theoretical concept in relation to the nation. In these formulations, diaspora is utilized to challenge the "natural" connection between a place and a people that is articulated in exclusionary national narratives. Narrations of the nation often employ temporal and spatial tropes that link people together and to a land through claims of shared ancestry and culture. These narratives therefore assert connections between purity and belonging, between blood and soil. Referring to the joined tropes of genealogy and place, Jewish scholars Jonathan and Daniel Boyarin remark, "Race and space together form a deadly discourse" (714). To speak of the nation and its territory is to speak in racialized terms. In response to these tropes,

the Boyarins position diasporic hybridity and difference as strategies of resistance against the claims of authenticity and purity in national narratives. For the Boyarins, diaspora can function as the renunciation of territorial sovereignty in conjunction with the maintenance of a minority or ethnic identity and culture. Additionally, Gilroy in *The Black Atlantic* relates the African diaspora, based on the shared inheritance of slavery, as relating a counterhistory of modernity and the nation-state. Thus, Gilroy and the Boyarins disenfranchise diaspora from a homeland, emphasizing instead its contestation of authenticity and purity by hybridity, its insistence on heterogeneous communities, its foregrounding of incommensurability and cultural difference, and the productivity of diasporic displacement.

Diaspora is positioned by scholars as a check to the dominant discourses of *rootedness* that support the exclusionary narratives of nation formation in modernity. Opposing essence, purity, and sedentarism, these discourses of diaspora privilege hybridity and mobility as strategic forms of resistance. Based on Derrida's concept of *differance* and Gramsci's concept of a war of positions, Hall proposes diasporic cultural identity as a politics of positioning and identity characterized by hybridity and heterogeneity (395). "Diasporic identities are those which are constantly producing and reproducing themselves anew, through transformation and difference. . . . Far from being eternally fixed in some essentialized past, they are subject to the continuous 'play' of history, culture, and power" (Hall 401). Diaspora poses a range of analytic possibilities that challenge many categories of modernity such as the nation and national identity, but differ from postmodernist critiques in foregrounding complex histories of slavery, exile, colonialism, and postcoloniality.

Jigna Desai

Further Reading

Boyarin, Daniel and Jonathan. "Diaspora: Generational Ground for Jewish Identity." *Critical Inquiry* 19.4 (Winter 1993): 693–725.

Clifford, James. "Diasporas." *Cultural Anthropology* 9.3 (1994): 302–38.

Cohen, Robin. *Global Diasporas: An Introduction.* Seattle: U of Washington P, 1997.

Gilroy, Paul. *Against Race: Imagining Political Culture Beyond the Color Line.* Cambridge: Harvard UP, 2000.

Hall, Stuart. "Cultural Identity and Diaspora." *Colonial Discourse and Post-Colonial Theory.* Eds. Patrick Williams and Laura Chrisman. New York: Columbia UP, 1994. 392–403.

Safran, William. "Diasporas in Modern Societies: Myths of Homeland and Return." *Diaspora* 1.1 (Spring 1991): 83–99.

Tölölyan, Khachig. "Rethinking *Diaspora*(s): Stateless Power in the Transnational Moment." *Diaspora* 5.1 (Spring 1996): 3–36.

Divakaruni, Chitra Banerjee

Chitra Banerjee Divakaruni is an Indian American writer who emerged on the world literary scene in 1990 and has prolifically published since then, writing poetry, short stories, and novels. Divakaruni was born on July 29, 1956, in Calcutta (Kolkata), India. She received a B.A. in English in 1976 from Calcutta University, an M.A. in English in 1978 from Wright State University, and a Ph.D. in Renaissance English literature in 1985 from University of California, Berkeley. She has taught creative writing and English literature at Diablo Valley College, Foothill College, and University of Houston. She also cofounded Maitri, an organization that works with South Asian women dealing with situations of domestic violence. She volunteers her time to Maitri and to Chinmaya Mission, a spiritual and cultural organization.

Moved by the dual forces of the preimmigration and postimmigration conditions, touched by the pains of women in male-dominated societies, and inspired by the desire to preserve memory, Divakaruni first began writing poetry, then moved on to short fiction, and eventually to novels.

Her major publications include three volumes of poetry: *The Reason for Nasturtiums* (1990), *Black Candle* (1991), and *Leaving Yuba City* (1997); two collections of short stories: *Arranged Marriage* (1995) and *The Unknown Errors of Our Lives* (2001); three novels: *The Mistress of Spices* (1997), *Sister of My Heart* (1999), and *The Vine of Desire* (2002); and a children's book *Neela: Victory Song* (2002). She is also the editor of two multicultural readers: *Multitude* (1993) and *We, Too, Sing America* (1998). *The Mistress of Spices* has been adapted as an audiobook and has been optioned for an English-language film. *Sister of My Heart* has been optioned for a Tamil-language television serial. Critics have lauded Divakaruni's storytelling powers, evocative language, and poignant characterizations. They have also appreciated her for retelling the dilemmas of immigration and portraying the diverse lives often marginalized by mainstream American society. Her popularity with readers has been proven repeatedly through her best-selling books.

Black Candle, true to its name, poetically chronicles scorched lives of women. It is declared to be a collection of poems about women from India, Pakistan, and Bangladesh. The book is traversed by women in purdah, women whose marriages are arranged to their detriment, childless women enslaved by their husband's families, outcast widows, women whose female fetuses are aborted, women burnt for dowries, women beaten by husbands, Muslim women whose husbands marry second wives, Hindu women burnt at their husbands' funeral pyres, living goddesses whose lives are sacrificed to the service of the temple: suffering women of the above named countries whose lives Divakaruni attempts to hold up to the light— to chronicle and expose the oppression to which patriarchal hegemony has subjected them. However, as Divakaruni's book speaks for women of these south Asian countries, it also limits women's lives in these places only to experiences of pain. For all the pain and oppression in the traditions, myths, and histories that she invokes, the poet fails to find anything redeeming, inspiring, or liberating. As far as this book is concerned, the literary, cultural, and political traditions of the Indian subcontinent have never produced any resistance to women's oppression in its entire history.

Arranged Marriage is a collection of eleven short stories focusing on Indian women whose lives are linked both to the Indian tradition of arranged marriage and the powerful changes brought by immigration to America. These stories portray, with deep pathos and passion, the struggles of women caught between tradition and change. But the Indian custom of arranged marriage is rejected as invalid. To create an immigrant narrative of hope, India is generally shown as something to shed, to leave behind; and America is unfailingly seen as the source of new hope, albeit, with a few complexities. This stance constructs binaries of East versus West as inferior versus superior and primitive versus advanced, a procedure which helps develop neoimperialism on behalf of Western culture and society. Though the book advances a feminist cause, its East-West binaries impede postcolonial causes.

The Mistress of Spices, Divakaruni's first novel, juxtaposes magic and realism, fuses an enchanted past into a contemporary ethnic spice shop in Oakland, and brings together the lives of the magical Tilo and many other immigrants whom she is destined to help through powers of spices. But when Tilo falls in love with Raven, a Native American, she is confronted with her own desires and a need to help herself. Thus, she has to choose between a life governed by a distant mystical power and the reality of her current life. Tilo's dilemma is an allegory for the dilemma of the immigrant who is pulled between the charm of the past and the call of the present.

In *Sister of My Heart,* two cousins are brought together by destiny to be born in the same house on the same night, and they grow up together as inseparable sisters in their hearts. Closer to each other than anyone else, they share their joys and pains and are willing to make the biggest sacrifices for one another. The story is told in the alternate voices of Sudha and Anju, each one being the narrator of each alternate chapter. The beautiful Sudha is gentle and quiet. She reveres old myths and weaves them into her narration to interpret life's realities, while Anju is rebellious, always questioning the old tales that Sudha reveres. Yet, when Sudha is put to the test, she makes the biggest sacrifices and walks the boldest path. This novel portrays two beautiful and passionate protagonists, taking readers into the core of their hearts' desires as well as bringing through their voices fiery criticisms of society's injustices against women. Its language is metaphoric and sensuous. Although some aspects of the plot are melodramatic and some characters appear formulaic, the sisters speak poignantly to most readers' hearts. But again, to make immigration the destiny of the heroines, India is seen as the land they must forsake and America as the land at the end of the rainbow.

The Vine of Desire is a continuation of the saga of Sudha and Anju, the two cousins from *Sister of My Heart.* Far from the comforts and troubles of Calcutta, the women are now caught up in the anticipations and disenchantments of immigrant life in California. In the first book, many forces test their devotion to each other. Now they face new challenges: a baby born and a baby lost, Anju's husband's treacherous attraction to Sudha's beauty, and Sudha's difficulty in finding a true home for herself. Language rich in imagery and lyricism and characters created with convincing emotional reality enrich this book.

In *The Unknown Errors of Our Lives,* a collection of nine short stories, Divakaruni goes past the East-West binaries found in *Arranged Marriage* and shows various lives in a range of complexities. An elderly woman writes a letter to her friend in India, disguising her disillusionment with life in America with a son who has grown distant and his family to whom she has little value. A sister is unable to talk about her mother's terminal illness with her uncommunicative brother. An unmarried Indian woman tries to carve a life of her own in California, away from the watchful eyes of her family. A young Indian American woman tries to find an answer to an emotional crisis through the religious myths her Indian grandmother passed on to her. An Indian woman with an American husband visits her village in India to reconnect herself and her new family with her old roots. These are some of the complex life stories rendered in this volume.

Divakaruni's first children's book, *Neela: Victory Song,* looks at the Indian anticolonial movement from the perspective of a 12-year-old girl.

Divakaruni has been critically well received, especially in the United States. She has won many awards for her poetry and fiction. Most of her writings have elicited appreciative reviews for her dexterous fusion of lyricism, realism, myth, and powerful emotion. However, the unmistakable glorification of the adopted society at the cost of denigrating the Indian society she left behind is evident in some of her writings, such as *Black Candle, Arranged Marriage,* and even *Sister of My Heart.* But she has moved away from that predisposition in her newer writings *The Vine of Desire* and *The Unknown Errors of Our Lives.* In a conversation with Rajini Srikanth for the *Asian Pacific American Journal* (99), Divakaruni has defended all her portrayals as being guided by truth and

honesty, and compassion for her characters.

Husne Jahan

Further Reading

Chitra Banerjee Divakaruni. 29 Nov. 2002 <http://www.chitradivakaruni.com/>.

"Chitra Banerjee Divakaruni." *Literature Resource Center.* 10 Apr. 2002 <http://www.galenet.galegroup.com/>.

Farmanfarmaian, Roxane. "Writing from a Different Place: Chitra Banerjee Divakaruni." *Publisher's Weekly* 248. 20 (14 May 2001): 46–47.

Moka-Dias, Brunda. "Chitra Banerjee Divakaruni." *Asian American Novelists.* Ed. Emmanuel S. Nelson. Westport, Conn.: Greenwood, 2000. 87–92.

Srikanth, Rajini. "Chitra Banerjee Divakaruni: Exploring Human Nature Under Fire." *Asian Pacific American Journal* 5.2 (1996): 94–101.

Dramatists of India

This study offers a critical assessment of six contemporary Indian dramatists: Asif Currimbhoy, Mahesh Dattani, Girish Karnad, Pratap Sharma, Vijay Tendulkar, and P. S. Vasudev.

Asif Currimbhoy, born on August 15, 1928, is one of the leading Indian English playwrights with almost 30 plays in his repertoire. Currimbhoy descends from a baronet family of khoja Muslim industrialists in Goa. His liberal educational/familial background, his study and work abroad, and his extensive travel through India in his executive job for Burma-Shell have made his dramatic art diverse and unique. His first play *The Tourist Mecca* (1959) deals with the East-West relations seen in terms of an ideal love relationship. With *Doldrummers* (1960), he gained notoriety for his free representation of love and sex. In his next play *The Dumb Dancer* (1961), Currimbhoy projected the tragedy of a Kathakali dancer who identifies himself with the role he performs. *Thorns on a Canvas* (1962) airs strong views on censorship that makes a mockery of true art. In *Goa* (1964), Currimbhoy juxtaposes a passionate but tragic love story with the topical events of the Indian annexation of the Portuguese colony.

Asif Currimbhoy's Bengal plays begin with *Inquilab* ("Revolution" 1970), which probes the tensions of the Indian youth triggered by the Naxalite's zeal to establish a new-world order. The satirical *Darjeeling Tea?* (1971) is a two-act comedy about tea planters and the many East-West contradictions that their colonial living manifests. *Sonar Bangla* ("Golden Bengal," 1972) is a potent play about the Bangladeshi Liberation War. *Om Mane Padme Hum!* ("Hail to the Jewel in the Lotus!" 1972) retells, in flashbacks and dream sequences, the story of the end of Lamaism in Tibet. *This Alien . . . Native Land* (1976) is a kind of memory play that probes into family conflicts.

Currimbhoy's other dramas include televised and one-act plays. The one-act *The Hungry Ones* (1966), an off-Broadway success, gives a moving portrait of an environment of poverty and violence. His other short plays—*The Refugee* (1971), *The Clock* (1959), and *The Miracle Seed* (1973)—are appreciated for their thematic variety, technical virtuosity, and experimental form and technique. He is considered an original voice in Indian drama.

Mahesh Dattani, born on August 7, 1958, is a Bangalore-based playwright writing in English. Dattani worked as copywriter in an advertising agency and also assisted his father in the family business. Theatre was always close to his heart from his childhood. His aptitude for crafts and dance was encouraged in his family. Dattani's active involvement in the Bangalore Little Theatre in his college days and his fond learning of Bharatnatyam and ballet helped him when he finally decided to turn to theatre. In 1984, he started his own theatre group called Playpen, which became the site for his acting, playwriting, and directorial ventures. Dattani won the

Sahitya Akademi award for his first collection of plays *The Final Solutions and Other Plays* (1994). He has nine dramas to his credit: six full length plays, two radio plays, and a one-act play.

Where There's a Will (first produced, 1988) is a provoking exhibition of patriarchal control, as seen in a Gujarati family. The story of family conflicts, especially between the father and the son, ends with the family's final rejection of paternal authority. *Dance Like a Man* (1989) retells in two acts—time present and time past—the inner struggles of a dancing couple. *Bravely Fought the Queen* (1991) explores family turmoil and questions the social roles of the man and the woman. *Tara* (1995) is a poignant story of a family's collective sin of maiming a female child in order to make her twin brother healthy. Dattani analyses the problems of social injustice and female infanticide with a feminist's zeal.

The Final Solutions (1993) is an exposition of communal hatred and violence inherent in common people. It is a commentary on the religious hypocrisy found in even liberal-minded people. *On a Muggy Night in Mumbai* (1998) is a frank portrayal of gay relationships. Dattani's two radio plays, *Do the Needful* (1997) and *Seven Steps around the Fire* (1999), are powerful in their appeal. The former reveals the futility in man-woman relations in the empty life of a gay husband and his flirtatious wife. The second radio play exposes social prejudices and pretensions in the Indian milieu.

Dattani's plays have evinced interest both in India and abroad. His use of innovative staging techniques assimilated in a well-constructed story reflecting modern Indian concerns has brought a new vitality to Indian drama in English.

Girish Karnad, born on May 19, 1938, is the prime playwright of contemporary Indian stage. Karnad is a native of Matheran near Bombay, and was brought up in Dharwad, Karnataka. As a child, he grew up seeing the indigenous folk plays in his small town. He received a Rhodes scholarship (1960–63) and also won a Fulbright Scholar-in-Residence award for 1987. He chaired the Film and Television Institute of India, Pune, in 1974, and also chaired the Sangeet Natak Akademi, New Delhi, from 1988 to 1993. Karnad writes his plays in Kannada and then translates them into English. He also acts and directs in films and television.

Girish Karnad's first play *Yayati* (1961) in Kannada still remains untranslatable. The play reflects his attempt to relate contemporary issues to old myths. Here, the Mahabharata story is of a son's exchange of youth with old age in order to fulfill his father's desire for eternal youth. Karnad's second play *Tughlaq* (1964) is a theatrical success and considered a classic. Karnad turns to history and dramatizes the ebbing fortunes of the fourteenth-century sultan of New Delhi, Mohammed Tughlaq. The theme of a king's enthusiastic idealism gradually fading into tyrant misrule is often linked to the post-Independence loss of faith in Nehruvian idealism.

Karnad's third play *Hayavadhana* (1971, English 1975), which won the Natya Sangh and Sangeet Natak awards, is based on a Sanskrit story that he discovered in Thomas Mann's story of transposed heads. Karnad's ingenuity lies in capsuling an ancient story in an experimental form and in the Indian folk theatre tradition. With his heroine, Padmini, Karnad centers a woman into his play for the first time. The existentialist theme of search for identity and perfection is reflected in a double plot—in the consequences of the transposed head as seen in the two friends and in Hayavadhana's struggle to get rid of his horse head. The futility of the search is also reflected in both the plots, with Padmini performing sati in the funeral pyre of the two friends, and with Hayavadhana turned into a complete horse rather than man.

Anjumallige (1971), a play based on incest, was not a theatrical success. *Nagamandala,* his second play with a female protagonist, is a retelling of two Kannada folktales by a woman in the oral tradition. Like Padmini (*Hayavadhana*), Rani too is caught in a dichotomous situation, between the reality of a tyrannical husband and the illusion of a snake lover. The multiple viewing of the story and its metatheatrical form leave a rich commentary on the conflation of the epic and the dramatic narratives.

The Sahitya Akademi award winning *Tale-Danda* (1990), meaning "death by beheading" is about a twelfth-century Kannada poet's attempt to set up a caste-free society. *The Fire and the Rain* (1998), commissioned by the American Guthrie Theater, won him the Jnanpith award. The play belies the issue of fratricide viewed in a socioreligious backdrop. The tales of fraternal jealousy and violence in the Yavakri-Paravasu and Indra-Vishwarupa myths from Mahabharata are retold in a play-within-a-play framework.

Karnad's dramatic works are noted for their stageworthiness and contemporaneity. They have been widely translated and directed in several Indian languages including Hindi, Marathi, Telugu, and Tamil. His ingenuity lies in capsuling ancient myths in an experimental form and Indian folk theater tradition, thereby creating "a bridge between the elite and the folk" (Ramaswamy, "Indian Drama" 278).

Vijay Tendulkar, born on January 7, 1928, is a versatile and prolific Marathi playwright. He began his career as journalist and gradually changed over to playwriting. Tendulkar's powerful plays in Marathi are widely translated and performed. They have won him the prestigious Sangeet Natak Akademi award and the Padma Bhushan title. Tendulkar has written 28 full-length dramas, 24 one-act plays, and 11 children's plays, many of which have been translated into English.

Vijay Tendulkar's first major work that gave him recognition was *Manus Navache Bet* ("An Island called Man," 1955). It projects the inherent violence in the modern self-alienated man. *Gidhade* ("The Vultures," 1971) is a bold portrayal of the controversial subject of extramarital relations. *Shantata ! Court Chalu Ahe!* ("Silence! The Court is in Session," 1968) dramatizes a shocking mock trial of a woman accused of illicit relations. Tendulakar explores, within the play-within-a-play mode, the vulnerability of his heroine (Leela Benare) silenced by the vulgar hypocrisies of the people surrounding her. The collective destruction of the woman's integrity, the hypocrisy of the Indian middle class and its innate sadism, the social alienation, failure and ennui in modern human life are some issues that unfold as the play progresses.

Sakharam Binder (1972) faced strong censorship for its shocking depiction of naturalism. *Ghasiram Kotwal* (1973) employs the ballet form to project the violence, the sensuality, and the corrupting power games played by men. *Kamala* (1981) is a satire on the success-oriented modern world and its pursuit of goals at the expense of human values. The play reevaluates the institution of marriage in the light of women as victims of men's success.

Vijay Tendulkar treats human complexities and dangerous transitions in the Indian middle-class life, especially in an industrialist society. Like Currimbhoy's works, his plays are depictions of his keen observation of the people around him. He is considered one of the most productive and consistent Indian playwrights. His contribution to Indian drama is unique. He has brought revolutionary changes in the Marathi stage. Through his plays, he has created vital commentaries on the Indian political, social, economic, and moral degeneration and on the tragic plight of the suffering individual, especially the female.

Pratap Sharma, a novelist and dramatist, is known for his successful but controversial plays: *A Touch of Brightness* (1968) and *The Professor Has a Warcry* (1970). *A Touch of Brightness* focuses on Bombay's brothels and its debased inhabitants. *The Professor* once again dramatizes a controversial issue, that of child rape. The horrific scenes have made his plays unpalatable to Indian theatre enthusiasts. This fact is probably responsible for their unpopularity on the Indian stage.

P. S. Vasudev is a minor playwright, whose short play *The Forbidden Fruit* (1967) is noteworthy. This miniplay is a farcical satire on corruption in the government offices. Vasudev makes use of the myth of Adam and Eve in order to present the evils of sexual passion. The play is critically acclaimed for its compactness, clarity of presentation, and its sensational building up of suspense and climax.

Mala Renganathan

Further Reading

Benson, Eugene, and L. W. Conolly, eds. *Encyclopedia of Post-Colonial Literature in English.* 2 vols. New York: Routledge, 1994.

Bhatta, S. Krishna. *Indian English Drama: A Critical Study.* New Delhi: Sterling, 1987.

Dodiya, Jaydipsinh, ed. *The Plays of Girish Karnad: Critical Perspectives.* New Delhi: Prestige, 1999.

Iyengar, K. R. Srinivasa. *Indian Writing in English.* New Delhi: Sterling, 1985.

Naik, M. K. et al., eds. *Perspectives in Indian Drama in English.* Madras: Oxford UP, 1977.

Narasimhiah, C. D., ed. *The Makers of Indian English Literature.* Delhi: Pencraft International, 2000.

Pandey, Sudhakar, and Freya Barua, eds. *New Directions in Indian Drama.* New Delhi: Prestige, 1994.

Ramaswamy, S. "Indian Drama in English: A Tentative Reflection." *The Makers of Indian English Language Literature.* Ed. C.D. Narasimhiah. Delhi: Pencraft International, 2000. 275–301.

E

East India Company

On December 31, 1600, a group of English merchants who had incorporated themselves into an institution formally titled the "Governor And Company Of Merchants Of London Trading Into The East Indies" (from 1600 to 1708; later the "United Company Of Merchants Of England Trading To The East Indies") were given monopoly privileges by Queen Elizabeth to trade in goods from India and the East Indies. The company was specifically formed to share in the Southeast Asian spice trade, which had been a monopoly of Spain and Portugal until the defeat of the Spanish Armada (1588) by England brought a chance of breaking the monopoly. The ships of "The Honourable East India Company" first arrived in India at the port of Surat in 1608. Sir Thomas Roe reached the court of the Mughal emperor, Nooruddin Muhammad Jahangir (son of Akbar, the original great mogul), as the emissary of King James I in 1615 and gained for the British the right to establish a factory at Surat.

The company met with opposition from the Dutch in the Dutch East Indies (now Indonesia) and the Portuguese. The Dutch virtually excluded company members from the East Indies after the Amboina Massacre in 1623 (an incident in which English, Japanese, and Portuguese traders were executed by Dutch authorities), but the company's defeat of the Portuguese in India (1612) won them the prime trading position with the Mughal Empire. Over the years, they saw a massive expansion of their trading operations in India. "John" Company had a monopoly of this trade until 1694 when the House of Commons passed an act that enabled all British firms to trade with India. The East India Company retained its dominant position and continued to make large profits from India, and by 1720, 15 percent of Britain's imports came from India, mainly cotton, silk, indigo, saltpeter, and, later on, tea from China. Numerous trading posts were established along the east and west coasts of India, and several English communities developed around the three presidency towns of Calcutta, Bombay, and Madras surrounded by the barracks of troops mostly recruited from the surrounding country. In 1717, the Company achieved its most notable success when it received a firman (royal charter) from the Mughal emperor exempting the Company from the payment of custom duties in Bengal.

The Company saw the rise of its fortunes and its transformation from a trading venture to a ruling enterprise when one of its military officials, Robert Clive, defeated the forces of the Nawab of Bengal (present day Bangladesh and the Indian state of West Bengal), Siraj-ud-daulah, at the Battle of Plassey in 1757, thus gaining suzerainty of an area the size of France, one of the richest in India. A few years later, the Company *Bahadur* ("Brave": as it was known to its native troops before they grew disillusioned with their chances for advancement in its ranks) acquired the right to collect revenues on behalf of the Mughal emperor; but the initial years of its administration were calamitous for the people of Bengal. The Company's servants were largely a rapacious and self-aggrandizing lot, and the plunder of Bengal left the formerly rich province in a state of utter destitution. The famine of 1769–70, which the Company's policies did nothing to alleviate, may have taken the lives of as many as a third of the population. The Company, despite the increase in trade and the revenues coming in from other sources, found itself burdened with massive military expenditures, and its destruction seemed imminent. State intervention put the ailing Company back on its feet, and Lord North's India Bill, also known as the Regulating Act of 1773, provided for greater parliamentary control over the affairs of the Company, besides placing India under the rule of a governor-general; the first was Warren Hastings. Under his watch, the expansion of British rule in India was pursued vigorously. Hastings remained in India until 1784 and was succeeded by Cornwallis, who initiated the "permanent settlement," whereby an agreement in perpetuity was reached with *zamindars,* or landlords, for the collection of land-based revenue in addition to the continued profits from trade. In its time such luminaries as John Stuart Mill, Arthur Wellesley (Duke of Wellington), and Elihu Yale, whose money founded Yale University, all worked for the Company.

After the mid–eighteenth century, the cotton-goods trade declined, while tea became an important import from China. Beginning in the early-nineteenth century, the company financed the tea trade with illegal opium (grown in India) exports to China. Chinese opposition to this trade precipitated the first Opium War (1839–42), resulting in the Chinese defeat and the expansion of British trading privileges. In India the Company had ceased trading (in 1834) and instead acted as a managing agency actively engaged in attempts to eliminate Indian rivals. Rivals abroad, such as the French, would be defeated in fields far from India, and missionary groups at home who tried to gain converts under the safety net of the Company soon found themselves under censure for disrupting British rule by stirring up religious anger. Consideration of underlying social and political conditions in Britain and India reveals that the debate was concerned less with missions and political security per se than with power. It became a focal point for the struggles between the Church of England and the Dissent, and between the Company and the Crown over who was ultimately to control India, religiously and politically. As for the Indians themselves, major victories were achieved against Tipu Sultan of Mysore and the Marathas, and finally the subjugation and conquest of the Sikhs in a series of Anglo-Sikh wars in the 1840s led to de facto British occupation over the entirety of India. In some places, the British practiced indirect rule, placing a resident at the court of the native ruler who was allowed sovereignty in domestic matters. Lord Dalhousie's notorious doctrine of lapse, whereby a native state became part of British India if there was no male heir at the death of the ruler, was one of the principal means by which native states were annexed; but often the annexation, such as that of Awadh (Oudh) in 1856, was justified on the grounds that the native prince was of evil disposition. The annexation of native states, harsh revenue policies, and the plight of the Indian peasantry all contributed to the Rebellion of 1856–57, referred to by British commentators at the time as the Sepoy Mutiny. In 1858, the administration of India became the responsibility of the Crown; the Company lingered on until 1873 when it was dissolved and its offices at East India

House in Leadenhall Street were taken over by Lloyd's.

Abid Vali

Further Reading

Joseph, Betty. *Reading the East India Company, 1720–1840: Colonial Currencies of Gender.* Chicago: U Chicago P, 2003.

Lawson, Philip. *The East India Company: A History.* Studies in Modern History. London: Longman, 1993.

Misra, Maria. *Business, Race, and Politics in British India 1850–1960.* Oxford: Oxford UP, 1999.

Wild, Anthony. *The East India Company: Trade and Conquest from 1600.* Guilford: Lyons, 2000.

English, August by Upamanyu Chatterjee

When Agastya Sen (the protagonist), called August in the novel, leaves his middle-class urban Delhi environment to join the Indian Administrative Service (the most powerful bureaucratic branch of the civil service in the government of India), he enters the near-foreign terrain of rural life in Madna (the hottest place in India)—situated in the heartland of India—where he has to undergo his year-long training. Central to *English, August* is a harsh critique of the malfunctioning of the bureaucracy, and Agastya's unwillingness to engage with it; his alienation is a result of his upper-middle class, urban, Westernized upbringing. His mentors are presented as ridiculous figures, all much older than the 24-year-old protagonist. Agastya trains under Srivastava, who is the collector of the district (the most important government official in an area) and meets an assortment of people in the administration; the aim of the senior officers, as the narrator says, was to "explain, to impress, to tutor, to justify" (Chatterjee 21). The bureaucratic system is still what the British have left behind, made evident in that the *Madna District Gazetteer* has not been updated since 1935. As readers, we are presented with an assortment of characters: Kumar, the superintendent of police;

Shankar, a deputy engineer in minor irrigation whom Agastya meets at the Rest House (accommodation provided by the government for its officials); Sathe, a cartoonist of Madna; John and Sita Avery, an Englishman with an Indian wife visiting Madna for personal reasons—amongst others. The absence of any linear narrative does not detract us as the novel is made of numerous episodes and encounters. Agastya does what he has to, but most of what his job entails—meeting with officials and visitors—seems to be incomprehensible to him, and he refuses to negotiate with the sociocultural environment of Madna. Instead, he escapes to his hotel room, into his secret world of erotic fantasy and contemplation, preferring to smoke marijuana, masturbate, daydream, and read Marcus Aurelius's *Meditations.*

But gradually, even as he makes sense, Agastya desires to escape Madna and flee to Delhi and contemplates joining a publishing house. Eventually, he decides to remain in Madna and learns how to live his official life with petitions, "application, requests" (250). But even as he settles down, he tells Sathe that his past always haunts him with "alternative, happy images" that seem to mock him (284). At the end, however, he decides to leave. His angst is a result of not knowing his own positionality within the larger social life of India; Sathe tells him quite appropriately, "You see, no one, but no one, is remotely interested in your generation, August" (286).

It would not be erroneous to describe this work as a psychological novel, delving into the mind of Agasyta as he makes his way through his training in Madna. The story, thus, is about a particular generation of young, cosmopolitan Indians—alienated from mainstream India and unsure as to where it would be going. Undoubtedly, the young protagonist's class position determines the novel, and the angst that is evident is a result of being in between cultural spaces. Agastya is too Westernized, too urbanized to fit in anywhere within India, or with any individual not sharing his same elite background. Agastya tells Dhrubo, his friend from college,

> Amazing mix, the English we speak. Hazaar fucked. Urdu and American," Agastya laughed, "a thousand fucked, really fucked. I'm sure nowhere else could languages be mixed *and* spoken with such ease. (Chatterjee 1)

What Chatterjee draws our attention to is the creation of hybrid cultural spaces, evident in how the characters use language, mixing English with local linguistic usage. But this in-between space refers to a very static concept of cultural hybridity, as Agastya is unable to extend outside this space.

Satire is a dominant tonal quality in the novel, and Chatterjee's critique is not only against the bureaucracy that runs India, but extends to the peasantry and every meaningful institution. The characters are fleshed out—not completely, but enough to be lampooned in a stringent fashion. And though there is an absence of linear progression of a storyline, there are vivid descriptions of different towns and villages in India that form a constant background.

Like Agastya Sen in the novel, Uapamanyu Chatterjee himself joined the Indian Administrative Service in 1983, and is presently Director (Languages) in the Ministry of Human Resource Development, Government of India. He was born in Patna, India, in 1959 and studied English Literature in St. Stephens College, Delhi, India. In 1990, he was Writer in Residence at the University of Kent, Britain. His story "The Assassination of Indira Gandhi" was published in the William Heinemann collection of Best Stories 1986.

English, August often features in courses on Indo-Anglian and postcolonial literatures that examine postcolonial states and subject formations. But the novel can be difficult as the text is rather local, preventing the Western reader from fully comprehending the subtleties of the narrative. Considering that the sequel to *English, August, The Mammaries of the Welfare State,* was not well received in the West—to the extent that it has not been released by the Western press—one can conclude that undoubtedly, publishing houses do determine literary tastes. What is also revealed is the hegemony of a certain kind of postcolonial literature within the Euro-American academia, which often excludes those texts that do not conform to certain paradigms.

Tapati Bharadwaj

Further Reading

English, August. Screenplay by Upamanyu Chatterjee. Dir. Dev Benegal. Twentieth Century Fox, 1994.

Kirpal, Viney, ed. *The New Indian Novel in English: A Study of the 1980s.* New Delhi: Allied, 1990.

"My Writing Is Not Scatology; It's Comic." 30 Nov. 2002 <http://www.india-today.com/chat/200012/upamanyu.html>.

The English Patient by Michael Ondaatje, film by Anthony Minghella

We are unusually fortunate to have detailed analyses of *The English Patient* by both its renowned editor, Walter Murch, and the novelist on whose work it was rather freely based. More remarkable still is that many of their revelations occurred in the course of conversations spanning a number of years. In the second edition of Murch's *In the Blink of an Eye* (2001), he devotes a great deal of space to the crisis and subsequent period of adjustment that led to his abandoning the KEM manual technology with which he had started editing Minghella's film and adjusted to the new Avid digital-editing technology. It is not with a little pride that he announces:

A film still from *The English Patient,* based on Michael Ondaatje's book. Courtesy of Photofest.

"after all the turbulence and uncertainty that we went through during this period, *The English Patient* went on to win nine Oscars, one for editing" (Murch 104–05).

Even before Michael Ondaatje had completed the series of conversations with Murch that turned into a very well-received book, I had the opportunity to ask Ondaatje whether his highly visual style of narration owed anything to his love of cinema and his own experience as a filmmaker. To this he replied that his visual style might just as well have come from encounters with Conrad, but that he found film editing far more sophisticated than that of most novels. Thus, although unsurprising, it is a matter of considerable interest that the film's engagement with the novel occurs most significantly at the level of editing. So radical are the shifts in characterization that the novel's secondary plot, with its intricate flashback structure, comes to dominate the two hours and forty minutes left of nearly sixty given to Murch as raw footage by Minghella. In Murch's condensation the two love stories no longer alternate as suggestively as in the novel, and the romance between the Ca-

nadian nurse, Hana, and the Sikh bomb-diffuser, Kip, seems to have gradually paled to relative insignificance beside the David Lean–like epic sweep of the story of the English patient and his forbidden love. In fact, it is not the simplified revelation of treachery in the film, or its greater linearity in plot structure, that Ondaatje mentions as his one great disappointment, but the dramatic reduction of Kip's role. From the conversations between writer and editor one gets the powerful sense that Ondaatje not only rejoiced in a deep appreciation of the nature of the medium into which his novel was being translated, but that he also encouraged, even urged, Minghella's changes.

In his preface to *The Conversations: Walter Murch and the Art of Editing Film* (2002), Ondaatje emphasizes the role of chance in a collaborative medium (something less intrinsically available to a writer). In the same scene in which Caravaggio loses his thumbs, Willem Dafoe, who plays the tortured spy, at one instant implores: "don't cut me." In the course of his wide reading, Murch had come upon an assertion in Curzio Malaparte that above all the Nazis hated signs of weakness in their enemies. Thus, from Minghella's 15 takes of the scene, Murch selected one in which Dafoe's voice quavers. Extracting the sound, he added a second exclamation after his first plea. Thus is the Nazi's casual threat transformed into "what he now has to *do*." It is at this point that Murch withdraws all sound from the scene except the room tone.

Controlled chance, then, is one of the principal sources of the film's distinction, for its flavor depends a great deal on the expressions and gestures improvised by the outstanding actors, even those movements lost but still vaguely present as shadow (such as Juliette Binoche's Hana turning around, her whole body expressing grief at Kip's eventual departure, a scene Murch abbreviated reluctantly). Equally felicitous is the seamless, rhythmic alternation between past and present, for as Murch points out the 40 transitions, "a huge number," are many more than even the second part of *The Godfather,* which Murch also edited. Here again, the latitude granted to him by directors such as Coppola and Minghella is as surprising as it is productive. Only seven of the forty transitions occur as they were written in Minghella's screenplay. Yet, these later changes, too, reveal themselves as part of a collaborative exercise, as is one instance when the editor felt that some element was missing from a scene. Minghella had scripted a private conversation between the English patient and Caravaggio, in which the latter more or less reveals his true identity, a scene barely suggested in the novel. That in the film as it now exists Hana overhears it is yet a further departure, and a tribute to the flexibility of both director and editor in being a very late addition in the editing process. Yet it clarifies a later scene, as Murch observes, for when Hana now administers a final dose of morphine to her patient, she does so with the "weight of that knowledge."

Yet another dimension of the film in which it expands on the novel is its use of sound. Murch began his career as an expert in sound montage, and the particularly dense and yet logical use of sound is characteristic of his approach. To simulate the weathered piano on which Hana plays one of Bach's *Goldberg Variations,* thus summoning Kip, who rushes forth in a comical manner, warning her of the dangers of thumping on pianos abandoned by Germans, Murch had the piece rerecorded on a detuned piano. Subtler still are the uses of sounds such as the chirping of birds and distant bells, all of which reappear with symbolic resonance, as do Murch's famed silences. It is fitting that Ondaatje seems just as entranced by the film editor's craft as he was with mapmaking and desert exploration when he wrote the novel.

To speak of the critical reception of the film is tantamount to redundancy, but it is certainly the best known and most honored film based on the writing of a South Asian author of the present generation (Rabindranath Tagore's works were the basis of two of Satyajit Ray's most important films). While the acclaim that it has received is certainly disproportionate in relation to a number of other notable adaptations, its indisputable merits and its courageously dialogical relationship with Ondaatje's celebrated novel transcend its occasional concessions to the less edifying aspects of popular taste.

Anthony R. Guneratne

Further Reading

Murch, Walter. *In the Blink of an Eye: A Perspective on Film Editing,* 2nd ed. Los Angeles: Silman James, 2001.

Ondaatje, Michael. *The Conversations: Walter Murch and the Art of Film Editing.* New York: Alfred A. Knopf, 2002.

Roberts, Gillian. " 'Sins of Omission': *The English Patient* and the Critics." *Essays on Canadian Writing,* 76 (2000), 195–215.

"The Patience of Making *The English Patient*." Comments by Anthony Mingella and interviews of Kristin Scott Thomas and Juliette Binoche. Spliced Online. <http://www.spliced online.com/features/englishtalk.html>.

Thomas, Bronwen. " 'Piecing Together a Mirage': Adapting *The English Patient* for the Screen." Eds. Giddings, Robert and Erica Sheen. *The Classic Novel: From Page to Screen.* Manchester: Manchester UP and St. Martin's, 2000.

Tötösy de Zepetnek, Steven. "Social Discourse and the Problematics of Theory, Culture, and Audience." Eds. Joret, Paul and Aline Remael. *Language and Beyond: Actuality and Virtuality in the Relations between Word, Image and Sound / Le Langage et ses au-delà: Actualité et virtualité dans les rapports entre le verbe, l'image et le son.* Amsterdam: Rodopi, 1998.

Eurocentrism

The term *Eurocentrism* is a recent coinage that considers a European-based perspective on the world. That such a term was needed demonstrates how varied and multiple the world has become. The term has arisen in part because of the growing influence of colonial and postcolonial approaches to history and literature, and Eurocentrism is often counterposed to other such bases or perspectives as Afrocentrism and Islamism. In short, a Eurocentric point of view is one that considers Europe at the center or, more so, as the pinnacle, of achievement or progress in the world. Belton defines Eurocentrism as "the tendency to see European culture and history as the norm and all others as marginal" (Belton).

Many historians and critics have recently commented on Eurocentrism. Bobby Sayyid discusses Eurocentrism in the context of a number of ethnocentrisms. Sayyid writes, "Eurocentrism is a project to recentre the West, a project that is only possible when the West and the centre are no longer considered to be synonymous" (128). In essence, Eurocentrism as a cultural phenomenon exists because the West is no longer at the center, and yet it has the need, apparently, to restore its privileged but vacated position. "The logic of eurocentrism," Sayyid argues, "is committed to closing the gap between the West and the centre; it is opposed by and opposes projects which widen this gap and operate in this space created by the gap" (129). Sayyid goes on to write that the logic of Islamism, on the other hand, "necessitates the provincialization of the West and its relocation as one center among many. . . . Europe is just one culture among others."

Arif Dirlik argues that no critique of Eurocentrism is complete without a critique of capitalism, which has helped to ensure the continued dominance of Eurocentrism in the world. As well, the emphasis on culture rather than on political economics in postcolonial and postmodern studies—however inclined toward cultural critique—helps to maintain eurocentric dominance by ignoring the real site of power. As well, Eurocentrism is hardly confined to Euro-America, for the machinations of capitalism have spread throughout the globe. For that matter, many scholars and businesspeople from Third World countries have located themselves inside Euro-America and are working within its systems, sometimes as "critics" of Eurocentrism, but only in an institutionally sanctioned way. From this perspective, globalism itself is not an attempt to understand other cultures so much as it is a means by which to sell goods.

Dirlik points out that, were it not for capitalism, Eurocentrism might well have been considered just another of many possible forms of ethnocentrism. He argues that "spheres of cultural hegemony that more or less coincided with economic and political domination have been present all along, defining a 'Chinese' world, an 'Islamic' world, 'Arabic' and 'Indic' worlds, and so on. In spite of real or imagined hegemonies over vast territories, however, none of these worlds were in the end able to match Eurocentrism in reach or transformative power" (34). At the same time, Dirlik shows that, from a Eurocentric perspective, the reason offered for a Euro-American dominance of the world would not be owing to capital, but would be owing to "the superiority of Euro-American values." He cites such an answer in order to show the futility of cultural explanations for power. One could think of Eurocentrism as an ethnocentrism that has been rendered into a "universal paradigm," and thus any critique of it requires taking into account "values and structures that are already part of a global legacy" (36).

Michael W. Cox

Further Reading

Belton, Robert J. *Words of Art.* 2002. 26 Nov. 2002 <http://www.ouc.bc.ca/fina/glossary/e-list.html>.

Dirlik, Arif. "Is There History after Eurocentrism? Globalism, Postcolonialism, and the Disavowal of History." *History of the Three Worlds.* Eds. Arif Dirlik, Vinay Bahl, and Peter Gran. Lanham: Rowman and Littlefield, 2000.

Goonatilake, Susantha. *Anthropologizing Sri Lanka: A Eurocentric Misadventure.* Bloomington: Indiana UP, 2001.

Sayyid, Bobby S. *A Fundamental Fear: Eurocentrism and the Emergence of Islamism.* London: Zed Books, 1997.

Shohat, Ella, and Robert Stam. *Unthinking Eurocentrism: Multiculturalism and the Media.* New York: Routledge, 1994.

F

A Fine Balance by Rohinton Mistry

Dina Dalal has had an unfortunate childhood as she lost her father when she was only 12. Nusswan (Shroff), Dina's brother who is 11 years older than she is, takes to running the household, and he gradually brings Dina around to attend to all the domestic chores and to facilitate her in doing them, he stops her schooling and dismisses the maid servant.

The righteousness and bossiness of Nusswan add to the oppressive atmosphere at home for Dina. And she tries to find solace in the public library and the concert halls. In one of her evenings in the music hall, Dina meets Rustom Dalal, a pharmaceutical chemist. Their friendship develops into love. And, as a result, frustrating Nusswan's hope of getting her married to one of his own friends, Dina marries Rustom and moves into his flat. She lives with him for three years very happily.

On their third wedding anniversary, Nusswan with his wife Ruby and his two sons come to dinner. And Rustom, after dinner, cycling to buy the children some ice cream, is killed in an accident. After a period of mourning, Dina returns to her flat from her brother's house. She seeks the help of Rustom's Darab uncle and Shirin aunty to find means for her livelihood. Shirin aunty happily gives away her sewing machine and introduces Dina to her own customers. Thus, for a while, Dina manages to live on her own with the income from tailoring.

However, as time passes, Dina's eyesight grows poor and she finds sewing difficult. Unwilling to ask her brother to support her, Dina seeks ways in which she can retain her independence. Through her schoolmate Zenobia, Dina gets the idea of hiring two tailors to do piecework for Mrs. Gupta's *Au Revoir,* a garment export company. In addition, Zenobia suggests that Dina should get a paying guest, and that it will solve her problem. And she herself recommends Maneck, son of Farokh and Aban Kohlah. Aban, another schoolmate friend of the two women, is now married and settled in a hill station in the north.

The Kohlahs have lost some of their property with the Partition and at present have been doing moderately well with the running of a store. Mr. Kohlah produces soft drinks in his store, and it has been very popular until other big companies and new brands of colas flood the market and edge out Kohlah's cola. As business becomes dull, Mr. Kohlah thinks of sending his son to the city for a higher education in hopes of reviving the failing family business. Maneck wants to stay at home and modernize the store, but his father insists on his going away for an engineering course.

Maneck Kohlah, thus, comes to the city to study refrigeration and air conditioning. Of his hostel mates, except for Avinash who teaches him how to play chess, Maneck finds hostel life quite unfriendly. He vacates his hostel room and moves in with Dina Dalal as a paying guest. And Maneck finds a second home in Dina's apartment. On the same day that Maneck visits Dina's flat, the two tailors, Ishvar Darji and Omprakash, also arrive at work.

Ishvar and Omprakash belong to the Chamaar caste, a low-caste community that tans and seasons dead animals' skin as cobblers, and has been treated as untouchables by the upper castes. Ishvar's father, Dukhi Mochi, and his mother, Roopa, have suffered the most unfair and cruelest oppression by the upper-caste pandits and thakurs. And angry with such treatment, Dukhi seeks to work elsewhere far away from his village. Then one day he meets Ashraf, a muslim tailor, who offers to apprentice his sons, Ishvar and Narayan. Dukhi gratefully sends his two sons to Ashraf.

Ishvar and Narayan return as tailors to their village. Narayan gets married to Radha and settles down in the village, while Ishvar continues as an assistant at Ashraf's Muzaffar Tailoring Company. Narayan becomes famous as a tailor andhe, especially, is the pride of the chamaars. Narayan and Radha become the proud parents of a son, and when he grows up to be a boy, Ishvar takes him along to apprentice him in tailoring.

During the elections, because Narayan insisted on his ballot paper to exercise his vote, he is murdered by Thakur Dharamsi's men, and his whole family is burnt alive. Since Ishvar and Omprakash, uncle and nephew, were in the city with Ashraf, they escape. As business at Ashraf's tailoring shop becomes dull (owing to the sudden craze for ready-made garments among people), Ishvar and Omprakash look for a job in the city because they cannot go back to their village. They finally find Dina's offer worthwhile and start working for her.

Thus the foursome—Dina Dalal, Maneck Kohlah, Ishvar and Omprakash—come to share their lives in Dina's flat. The prime minister's declaration of Emergency coincides with their coming together, and the trauma that they experience during those two dark years form the central part of the novel.

The government's efforts at clearing the slum and beautifying the city render Ishvar and Omprakash homeless and at the mercy of the Beggermaster. The Beggermaster, who employs a hoard of beggars in the city and sponges on their alms, acts like a corporate executive and is quite powerful with the police. When the shacks get demolished and the inhabitants are taken to a forced labor camp, Beggarmaster comes to rescue his people. On an agreement to pay a weekly installment from their tailoring income, Ishvar and Omprakash are rescued by Beggermaster. Thus, the hope of putting up in a shack in the slum and earning and saving enough to go back home and start their own tailoring shop in their village becomes impossible for them.

After much persuasion from Maneck, Dina relents and allows the two tailors to stay in her verandah. And, afraid of the landlord and his rent collector catching her illegally housing two tailors, Dina permits the tailors to eat with her and Maneck, instead of their going out to eat their meals. Meanwhile, the two tailors keep searching for accommodation.

The four of them together under one roof assuages Dina's sense of loneliness, and she feels she is living in a family. And, as Maneck and Omprakash are of the same age group, they get along very well with their own private jokes and escapades. Seeing his nephew forget the gruesome murder of his parents, Ishvar feels relieved and thankful for that fact, however brief the respite.

Though intervened once by Beggermaster, Dina is able to retain her flat against her landlord's notice to vacate. She gets caught alone and helpless when Maneck has gone home after completing his exams and the two tailors have gone to their village to find a suitable bride for Omprakash. Dina finally vacates her flat and goes to live with her brother.

In the village, Thakur Dharamsi, the family enemy, sees Ishvar and Omprakash, and the old family rancor is revived. Thakur Dharamsi with his increased power now gets uncle and nephew forcibly taken to the family planning camp where the former is operated upon for birth control and the latter is castrated.

Maneck goes to Dubai and earns money. He returns for his father's funeral and promises his mother that he will come back and run the store and be with her. On his way back to the city, he visits Dina aunty in her reduced status. And he also sees Ishvar maimed for life and Omprakash unnaturally bloated, as a consequence of the surgeries they underwent. They are both professional beggars. Haunted by the words that "Everything ends badly," Maneck kills himself by jumping on the tracks in front of a speeding train.

The unfinished quilt that Dina has been stitching, with the waste-cloth from the tailoring she does for *Au Revoir,* can be seen as a suggestive structural parallel that the author has intended for his narrative. And there are so many varied characters in the novel that such a reading of the novel will not be quite unwarranted. Much like the unfinished quilt, the novel leaves the reader depressingly disturbed.

Mistry's use of Balzac for his novel's epigraph has drawn much critical attention, as it has made reviewers and readers regard Mistry's writing to be realistic. Much as in his *Such a Long Journey,* here also, Mistry is seen to draw abundantly from Indian history, but more purposefully to rewrite the history of the marginalized and the oppressed. While questioning subtly the authenticity of history like a new historicist, Mistry's novel, especially with its epigraph, is intended to be history veiled as fiction.

N. Poovalingam

Further Reading

Ball, John. "Taking the Measure of India's Emergency." *The Toronto Review of Contemporary Writing Abroad* 14.2 (Winter 1996): 83–87.

Dodiya, Jaydipsinh, ed. *The Fiction of Rohinton Mistry: Critical Studies.* New Delhi: Prestige, 1998.

Kesavan, Mukul. Rev. of *A Fine Balance* by Rohinton Mistry. *The India Magazine* 16.6 (May 1996): 80–81.

Mantel, Hilary. "States of Emergency." *The New York Review of Books* 43.8 (20 June 1996): 4, 6.

Nair, Rukmini Bhaya. "Bombay's Balzac." *Biblio* (March 1996): 14–15.

Thorpe, Michael. Rev. of *A Fine Balance* by Rohinton Mistry. *World Literature Today* 71.1 (Winter 1997): 224–25.

Freedom Song by Amit Chaudhuri

Freedom Song, set in Calcutta in 1993 during the turbulent times of the Hindu-Muslim riots after the Babri-Masjid episode, is an account of two families and their search for a bride for one of the characters.

Khuku, her husband Shib, and their son belong to one family. Shib is a retired businessman who works as a part-time consultant. The couple's son lives in America. Mini is Khuku's friend from her childhood days and is staying with them while recuperating from arthritis. The other family consists of Khuku's brother Bhola, his wife, and their children. One of their sons, Manik, lives and works in Germany while Bhaskar, their second son and Piyu, their daughter, live with their parents.

Mini and Khuku read old Bengali novels and reminisce about their childhood, families, and friends. From time to time, they talk about major national events such as the Babri-Masjid and Hindu-Muslim riots. Shib is languidly exercised by his efforts to reform business practices at a public sector biscuit factory, and the muted but powerful inertia among the staff that resists his efforts.

Bhaskar has recently joined the Indian Communist Party and has also become active in street theatre. These developments worry his parents and relatives, who feel this will jeopardize his prospects for a respectable arranged marriage. Bhaskar's mother receives photographs of nubile young women, over which she pores with her husband.

Compared to Chaudhuri's earlier books, there is more than a suggestion of a plot—a beginning (the families), events, and a conclusion (a marriage). However, even this is not much of a plot or narrative in the conventional sense, as the book meanders through impressionistic descriptions of streets, houses, people, and daily activities. Desultory conversations hint tantalizingly at past or current events of personal or national importance. Once again, the attention of the writer is on creating images and atmosphere using background details, rather than on the foreground of a story.

Freedom Song was first published in 1998. In the United States, it was published as part of a collection together with *Afternoon Raag* and *A Strange and Sub-lime Address* in 2000, and won the LA Times Award. The collection received acclaim from critics on both sides of the Atlantic, inviting comparisons with Proust, R. K. Narayan, and Satyajit Ray.

Born in 1962 in Calcutta, Amit Chaudhuri was raised in Bombay and graduated from University College, London. He did his doctorate from Balliol College, Oxford. Chaudhuri lives in Calcutta with his wife and daughter. Chaudhuri has published four novels and a short-story collection and has written for several well-known publications such as *The Guardian* and the *London Review of Books*. He has been the recipient of several awards for his writing, including the Betty Trask Prize, the Commonwealth Writer's Prize for Eurasia and the LA Times Award. Chaudhuri is also the editor of *The Picador Book of Modern Indian Literature* (published 2001).

Padma Chandrasekaran

Further Reading

Cole, Dorothy, and Lee Jeffrey. "Speed Reader" *Alibi Arts* (10–16 June, 1999). Weekly Wire <http://www.alibi.com/alibi/1999-06-10/speeder.html>.

Cronin, Richard. "Handfuls of Dust." *London Review of Books* 20.22 (12 Nov. 1998): 37–38.

Kakutani, Michiko. "Books of the Times." *New York Times* 26 Feb. 1999: 48–49.

G

Gabriel's Gift by Hanif Kureishi

Hanif Kureishi was born in 1954 in Bromley, Kent, and at the age of 14 decided to become a writer. He attended Ravensbourne College of Art for A levels, and studied philosophy at Lancaster University, but was expelled at the end of his first year. Though he is of South Asian ethnicity and the son of an immigrant, he considers himself thoroughly English and his writing "part of English literature. . . . Whatever I've written about, it's all been about England in some way, even if the characters are Asian or they're from Pakistan or whatever" (Kaleta 3). Kureishi has written screenplays, novels, short stories, and plays; he was awarded the Whitbread Prize for his first novel, *The Buddha of Suburbia,* and received an Oscar nomination for his first screenplay, *My Beautiful Laundrette.*

Gabriel's Gift focuses on a white family in London, in particular on the title character, Gabriel, who is 15 years of age. Gabriel is a dreamer who likes to draw and who has the ability to make the objects he depicts come to life and then, at the turn of a sheet of his artist's paper, disappear. He often communes with his dead twin brother, Archie, who passed away at the age of two and who left an emotional hole in the family's life; part of the poignancy of the novel comes in Gabriel's not being sure, in fact, if he wasn't switched with Archie, and if it wasn't Gabriel himself

who died. Gabriel lives at home with his mother, Christine, who has given his father the boot. Christine drinks too much and occasionally brings home men whose names she cannot remember in the morning, and so Gabriel notices that she substitutes vague endearments when she has to call them something. Gabriel's father, Rex, was a glam rock musician in the seventies, for the most part, though he is fond of talking about the sixties with a kind of reverence, Gabriel notes, that older men use for referring to war. He played guitar in a band that sounds very much like David Bowie's Ziggy Stardust and the Spiders from Mars, though he fell off his elevated shoes one night while playing onstage, and had to quit touring. Things were never quite the same for Rex, though for years he wrote to Lester Jones, the leader of that band, in the hopes of rekindling his relationship and being taken back into the fold. Like David Bowie, Lester has had a long and chameleon-like career, taking on any number of personas and building a larger and larger fan base over the decades. Lester, who takes a liking to Gabriel in part because he thinks the boy has artistic talent, is perhaps off-puttingly self-absorbed—he fairly casually, for instance, tells Rex that once he kissed Christine, then allows that it was a long time before Rex entered the picture. The most vividly depicted character in the novel, though, might well be Hannah, Gabriel's governess (acquired in the wake of Rex's being kicked out), who speaks a kind of Eastern European Pidgin English and who likes to eat (that's pretty much all that Christine can promise her when Hannah takes the job, a roof over her head and all the food that she can eat, which turns out to be, at least from Gabriel's point of view, something of the rub); she keeps a keen and unnerving eye on Gabriel. The plot itself is fairly straightforward: Rex has been kicked out, and it is Gabriel's mission to reunite his parents, who are, in the scheme of things, perfect for one another—provided, that is, that Rex gets a job (there are other small problems Christine has with the man, but a job that brings a little self-respect would solve them all). But Gabriel is able to take care of this little problem as well, finding Rex employment (teaching music to a rich man's son). Gabriel even manages to get his parents to the altar.

The strength of the novel is in the sympathetic nature of the characters and the tender moments between them. Readers see the characters through Gabriel's 15-year-old perspective, and in part, of course, his naiveté informs our own perception of these people, who seem complicated but for the most part pleasantly and dreamily so. One of the more understated but emotionally powerful moments in the novel unfolds beautifully as Gabriel and Rex make their way to see Lester at the hotel where he is staying. A crowd of journalists and fans waits outside the hotel, eager for a glimpse of the middle-aged but still-potent rock star. Rex tells his son that this is what it was like in the old days, when crowds of people would wave and shout and want to touch him and the other members of the band. Rex speaks, hoping for the crowd to let him and Gabriel pass, and the photographers turn and aim their cameras, hesitating:

No one moved. There was a puzzled pause.
"Is he anyone?" a voice asked.
"Is he? Is he?" said other people.

"No, no one," was the authoritative reply, at last.
"No one," someone echoed.
"No, no one."
A sigh of disappointment fluttered through the gathering.
"We are someone." Dad put his hand on Gabriel's arm. He whispered, "If anyone asks us anything . . . say 'No comment.' Right?"
"No comment," repeated Gabriel.
"That's it." (64)

Deftly Kureishi prepares us to experience what Rex and Gabriel feel in this moment: for Rex, first the possibility that someone, anyone might recognize him as having played in Lester's band decades before; and then the deflation of spirit that accompanies the repetition of "no one" from the photographers; and finally his need to assert his and his son's right to self-esteem. For Gabriel, the pain of knowing how the journalists' words must affect his father, and then the realization that saying "no comment" is more effective in this situation, surrounded by reporters, than actually bothering to say who it is they really are. The novel is filled with many such moments, and Kureishi vividly depicts these present-day Londoners as well as the dimming memory of their glam past.

Critical reviews for the novel have been largely positive. There was nearly universal praise for the writing itself—particularly the dialogue and characterization—and the warmth of the relationship between the characters. In *Review of Contemporary Fiction,* Brian Budzynski notes that "the intimacy of familial relationships is at the front," and that the novel includes a "genuine and perfectly tender rendering of an ordinary family breaking to bits and calling on its youngest member . . . to fix it" (235) In *Book,* Kevin Greenberg notes that Kureishi's "ability to cultivate richly nuanced relationships is a thing of wonder" (68–69). Some critics, however, while praising the book, felt that it was somewhat thinly imagined or too sparing in its details, though Budzynski rationalized this by noting how much Kureishi is able to accomplish without the use of "exhaustively specific detail" (235). While generally praising this novel, Ray Olson, in *Booklist,* notes that "Kureishi's other career as a screenwriter-director shows all over this endearing, dialogue-and-blocking-heavy book that would make— surprise!—a heartwarming movie" (192).

Michael W. Cox

Further Reading

Budzynski, Brian. Rev. of *Gabriel's Gift. Review of Contemporary Fiction* 22.2 (2002): 235.

Greenberg, Kevin. Rev. of *Gabriel's Gift. Book* Nov.-Dec. 2001: 68–69.

Kaleta, Kenneth C. *Hanif Kureishi: Postcolonial Storyteller.* Austin: U of Texas P, 1998.

Moore-Gilbert, Bart. *Hanif Kureishi.* Manchester: Manchester UP, 2001.

Olson, Ray. Rev. of *Gabriel's Gift. Booklist* 15 Sept. 2001: 192–93.

Ganesan, Indira

Indira Ganesan was born November 5, 1960, in Srirangam, India. When she was five years old, her family moved to the United States, first to St. Louis, Missouri, and then to New York. Ganesan graduated from Vassar College with a B.A. in English. She completed an M.F.A. from the Iowa Writers' Workshop in 1984, and is currently assistant professor of English at Southampton College, Long Island University. There, in addition to teaching creative writing at both undergraduate and graduate levels, Ganesan taught a course entitled "Wicked Women and Wayward Girls" and organized a lecture series by the same name. Ganesan's first novel, *The Journey,* for which she was a finalist in the Granta Best Young American Novelist Award, was published by Knopf in 1990. Her second novel, *Inheritance,* was published by Knopf in 1998.

The Journey and *Inheritance* are both set on the mythologized Prospero's Island,

or Pi for short, "a chunk of India that is not quite India torn free to float in the Bay of Bengal" (*Journey* 17). *The Journey* commences with the death of Rajesh, cousin of Renu Krishnan, a 19-year-old college student who lives in New York with her mother and 15-year-old sister Meenakshi. The death reunites the Krishnan's extended family in the home of grandfather Das on Pi. Renu lives in the past and in her dreams, an introverted caretaker of both her widowed mother and her lively younger sister. Meenakshi, who has renamed and reinvented herself as Manx, lives in the present. Following their arrival, Renu falls ill with grief over the loss of her cousin. She spends her days recuperating in the garden, "lost in a net of nostalgia" (*Journey* 31). She suffers fitful nights, alternating between sleeplessness and uninterpretable dreams of three women who swallow stones and beckon to her to join them. In contrast, Manx is restless and "eager for scars" (*Journey* 131). She spends her days wandering through the bazaar with her transistor radio tuned to the BBC hit parade. There, she meets Freddie Flat, an "itinerant American" in his thirties. Manx and Freddie strike up a friendship that eventually blossoms into a love affair. Eventually, Renu releases her reluctance to embrace the present. The lessons that she learns throughout the novel about the fruitlessness of living in the past culminate in a dream-hallucination in which she rejects the act of sati—self-immolation on the altar of the past—out of loyalty to Rajesh. The novel ends with Renu about to embark on a new journey, back to New York and into the future. The theme of travel, variably depicted throughout the novel as pilgrimage, wandering, running away, tourism and migration, is here reenvisioned as life in flight: "Weightless travel, metaphorical soul soaring, a shedding of swallowed stones, a mobility that can hold the keys of the universe" (*Journey* 174).

Inheritance continues several themes found in *The Journey,* in particular, migration, hybridity, and the embrace of life. A bildungsroman, *Inheritance* tells the story of Sonil, a "half brown, half white," fragile 15 year old who lives with her guardian aunts in Madras and visits Pi for a summer at her grandmother's house. Whereas her grandmother is her "mothering muse," Sonil is estranged from her enigmatic mother, Lakshmi, who has a reputation for madness and wantonness, having given birth to three daughters by different men. Sonil imagines her absent American father as a cowboy. Sonil harbors several goals: to attend Radcliffe and become a zoologist, to travel and find adventure, to someday meet her father, and to solve the riddle of her neglectful mother. In fact, she is so fascinated with and frustrated by her mother, Lakshmi, that she spies on her and sifts through her belongings. When the vacation grows dull, Sonil entertains herself with forays to the market or a café. She meets an American man named Richard who is studying ayurvedic medicine. Soon thereafter, Sonil and Richard become lovers. When Richard abruptly leaves to travel to Ethiopia, Sonil is distraught. Ultimately, her experience of loving and losing Richard expands her capacity to understand her mother's life. Her empathy for her mother evolves more fully when her grandmother dies, and she witnesses her mother weeping. Sonil ruminates: "[m]y sorrow [is] reincarnated as compassion for my mother" (*Inheritance* 168). Her mother responds by revealing herself through her life stories. Sonil's maturation involves the lessons of learning to cope with the loss of love, and of the importance of holding her family close to her while pursuing her goals.

Favorable reviews of both novels are plentiful, but critical analyses of either *The Journey* or *Inheritance* have yet to be published. While the *San Francisco Chronicle, Los Angeles Times, New York Times Book Review,* and *Booklist* praise both of the novels, *Publishers Weekly* offers a more balanced and critical review of each. When

The Journey was reissued in paperback in April 2001, a *Publishers Weekly* reviewer wrote: "Despite her turmoil, Renu remains obscure, difficult to picture and understand, as do many of the other characters. Readers who need to know a character thoroughly to love a book will find this novel frustrating, but those interested in a subtle—sometimes touching, sometimes comedic—tale of our nomadic, crossbred lives will be happy it is now available in paperback" (*Publishers Weekly* 78) The reviewer of *Inheritance* wrote in 1997 that while many of the novel's characters are "robust, if exotic," Lakshmi, Renu's mother, "is an infuriating character: her purposeful silence seems excessive when she finally reveals the secrets of her past, which are less dramatic than one anticipates" (*Publishers Weekly* 55).

Kellie Holzer

Further Reading

Chander, Harish. "Indira Ganesan." *Asian American Novelists: A Bio-Bibliographical Critical Sourcebook.* Ed. Emmanuel Nelson. Westport: Greenwood, 2000. 99–104.

Ganesan, Indira. "Food and the Immigrant." *Half and Half: Writers on Growing Up Biracial and Bicultural.* Ed. Claudine Chiawei O'Hearn. New York: Pantheon, 1998. 170–80.

"Indira Ganesan: A Conversation." 14 November 2002 <http://www.southampton.liu.edu/person/faculty/iganesan/iview.htm>.

Review of *Inheritance,* by Indira Ganesan. *Publisher's Weekly* 10 November 1997: 55.

Review of *The Journey,* by Indira Ganesan. *Publisher's Weekly* 19 March 2001: 78.

Gay and Lesbian Literature

The term *gay and lesbian literature* is used to define literary production from the perspective of sexual minorities. Traditionally, the conception of romantic love depicted in mainstream literary conventions and canons has been predicated on heterosexual normativity and its consummation in matrimony. Gay and lesbian literature seeks to challenge such representations by depicting alternative forms of sexuality, love, and commitment in same-sex relationships. While forms of same-sex relationships are an intrinsic part of many South Asian cultures, the concept of literary production from this perspective is a relatively new one. In the 1980s and 1990s first-generation diasporic writers from India, Pakistan, and Sri Lanka—Suniti Namjoshi, Hanif Kureishi, Shyam Selvaduari, and Vikram Seth, to name only a few—wrote fiction, poetry, and drama foregrounding same-sex relationships. Most of this work was published abroad; the literary acclaim won by these authors rested not so much on it being the first work of its kind to highlight proscripted same-sex desire but because this was the post–*Midnight's Children* boom era of South Asian writing in English. Thus it is useful to remember that these works were categorized as South Asian literature in English and not "South Asian gay and lesbian literature in English." If the latter label can now be applied to them, it is only because in the past decade there has been a bourgeoning of literature deliberately embracing a form of this category as a political gesture.

For instance, three works using *gay* and *lesbian* as a political rather than a literary label, titled *A Lotus of Another Color: An Unfolding of the South Asian Gay and Lesbian Experience* (1993), *Facing the Mirror: Lesbian Writing from India* (1999), and *Yaarana: Gay Writing from India* (1999), include stories, poems, extracts from plays that fall within the purview of the literary as well as opinion pieces, interviews, reports of organizations working in this area, accounts of meetings and conferences, and reinterpretations of history, mythology, and folklore. The editor of the earliest published anthology states that the book has the dual purpose of "increas[ing] our visibility in both the South Asian and the gay and lesbian communities" and that of "empowerment,"

since "Until now, the mainstream world has defined us, as it does with any subgroup, within its parameters. . . . This book offer[s] us an opportunity to define ourselves. The power of self-definition is awesome [sic] because words are tremendously effective tools for reconstruction" (Ratti 26). When speaking of gay and lesbian writing in South Asia it is imperative to expand the connotations of traditional definitions of *literature*. Thus gay and lesbian literature is not only limited to the clearly identifiable genres of poetry, fiction, drama, and the essay but also includes other genres not strictly included under the category of the literary. Ashwini Sukthankar, editor of the first anthology of lesbian writing in India, mentions both the activist agenda underlying this compilation as well as its expansion of generic conventions: "The pieces that were produced for this book are the abiding public affirmation of lives far too often lost on the sidelines . . . for the purposes of this compilation, 'writing' signifies the gritty imperfect media through which the body, with its yearning and its suffering, spoke out. . . . Somewhere in the convergence of all these nebulous realms—of 'Indian', 'lesbian' and 'writing'—in the free confluence of fiction, essay, poetry, and memoir, this project resides" ("Introduction" xxi).

Following this redefinition, it is valid to consider activist material as another form of gay and lesbian literature. In the Indian context this has taken the form of publications such as *Less than Gay: A Citizen's Report on the Status of Homosexuality in India* (1991) published by the AIDS Bhedbhav Virodhi Andolan (ABVA), involving a campaign for anti-discrimination against AIDS victims; *Humjinsi: A Resource Book on Lesbian, Gay and Bisexual Rights in India* (1999) by the India Center for Human Rights and Law; and the CALERI (Campaign For Lesbian Rights in India) report entitled *Khaamosh! Emergency Zaari Hai, Les-*

bian Emergence: Campaign For Lesbian Rights, A Citizen's Report (1999). An instance of activism leading to literary production is Rajesh Talwar's play *Inside Gayland.* Talwar states that the idea for the play occurred to him when he filed a public interest litigation on behalf of the ABVA in the Delhi High Court seeking relief measures concerning spread of AIDS among male inmates of a Delhi prison in 1992. The blurring of the lines between literary and activist discourse is evident in a recent re-publication of this work containing an extended version of the play, appendices reprinting the ABVA petition, the full text of a judgment on gay rights by the European Court of Human Rights, and previously cited judgments on gay rights delivered by that court.

Within traditional definitions of literature, there is a proliferation of works of fiction and some poetry and drama depicting alternative sexualities. However, the literary acclaim of most of these writers rests only marginally on their representation of gay and lesbian lives, and predominantly on their stylistic innovations, exploration of social and political conditions in South Asia, and/or a delineation of the South Asian diasporic experience. Namjoshi, who lives in and publishes from England is famed as a poet, fabulist, and satirist primarily for her reworking of folk material from a feminist perspective in *Feminist Fables* (1981), *The Blue Donkey Fables* (1988), and invention of feminist utopias in *The Conversations of Cow* (1985) and *The Mothers of Maya Diip* (1989). Her explicitly lesbian feminist poetry in *Flesh and Paper* (1985), coauthored with her partner Gillian Hanscombe, is less well known. Seth also lives and publishes from outside India. Though his literary output is multigeneric (including three collections of poetry, a travel account, a translation of Chinese poetry, a libretto, a reworking of folktales, a novel in verse, and two prose novels) it is

his fictional oeuvre: *The Golden Gate* (1986), a novel in verse, and his more recent publications, *A Suitable Boy* (1993) and *An Equal Music* (1999), which are better known. Seth's most explicit presentation of alternative sexuality is in the failed relationship between Phil and Ed in *The Golden Gate.* Some of the poems from his early collection *Mappings* (1981) and *All You Who Sleep Tonight* (1991) also refer to same-sex love. Kureishi's fictional, filmic, and dramatic work explores the intersection of race and sexuality in the lives of sexual minorities of color, especially first- and second-generation Pakistani immigrants in Britain, where he lives and writes. The depiction of a gay South Asian man in his film *My Beautiful Laundrette* has been hailed as an exemplum of a radical cultural politics. His first novel, *The Buddha of Suburbia* (1990), won similar critical commendation for the delineation of second-generation South Asian gay, lesbian, and bisexual experience in Britain. Selvadurai, whose family emigrated from Sri Lanka to Canada in 1983, presents the experience of growing up gay amidst ethnic conflict in postcolonial Sri Lanka in his critically acclaimed first novel *Funny Boy* (1994). His second work of fiction, *Cinnamon Gardens* (1999), refers back to colonial times to present a skillful weave of concerns of sexuality and race, the personal and the political, in the life of its closeted gay protagonist. Some of the writers of South Asian gay and lesbian literature in English are the Parsi Indian author Firdaus Kanga whose works speak of a multiple marginalization since he is gay and handicapped. The Indian playwright Mahesh Dattani has received national and international acclaim for exploring many controversial issues, among them those concerning the lives of sexual minorities such as gays, lesbians, bisexuals, and the *hijra* community in India. In poetry, some of prominent gay and lesbian poets writing in English are the academics Ruth Vanita, Hoshang Merchant, and R. Raj Rao.

The canon of South Asian gay and lesbian literature in English is as yet in its formative stage. In the last two decades there has been a proliferation of works foregrounding socially and culturally tabooed same-sex desire in many regions in South Asia. An interrogation of this proscription takes the form of a reexamination of mythology and scripture, as in Giti Thadani's *Sakhiyani: Lesbian Desire in Ancient and Modern India* (1996), and of indigenous historical and literary traditions in Ruth Vanita and Salim Kidwai's edited collection, *Same-Sex Love in India: Readings from Literature and History* (1999). Perhaps critical work is the best indication of the arrival and acceptance of a literary category. There is some evidence of this in the form of an analysis of a few of the works mentioned. However, the construction of a subcategory gay and lesbian literature in the field of South Asian literature in English still awaits creative, critical, and institutional validation.

Kanika Batra

Further Reading

Murray, Stephen, and Will Roscoe, eds. *Islamic Homosexualities: Culture, History, and Literature.* New York: New York UP, 1997.
Ratti, Rakesh, ed. *A Lotus of Another Color: An Unfolding of South Asian Gay and Lesbian Experience.* Boston: Alyson, 1993.
Sukthankar, Ashwini, ed. *Facing the Mirror: Lesbian Writing from India.* New Delhi: Penguin, 1999.
Vanita, Ruth, ed. *Queering India: Same-Sex Love and Eroticism in Indian Culture and Society.* London: Routledge, 2002.

Ghosh, Amitav

Amitav Ghosh was born on July 11, 1956, in Bangladesh. He grew up in Bangladesh, Sri Lanka, Iran, and India. He studied history at St. Stephen's College, Delhi University. After graduation, Ghosh wanted to pursue a literary career, but the situation in India did not permit him to do so. He therefore worked as a journalist at *The In-dian Express,* the closest approximation to being a writer. In 1980, he pursued a doctorate in social anthropology at Oxford, in the course of which he traveled and studied at the University of Alexandria. While in Egypt, he did an ethnographic study in the fellaheen village of Lataifa, which was later transformed into the novel, *In an Antique Land.* Ghosh's interest in medical history and anthropology has provided the foundation for many of his novels. He has taught sociology at the Delhi School of Economics and has also taught at the University of Virginia and Columbia University. He has been teaching comparative literature at Queen's College, City University of New York since 1999.

Sen writes about the recurrence of landscapes as a motif in Ghosh's work: "Those familiar with Ghosh's earlier work will at once recognize the macrocosmic links his latest work has with the earlier ones, not in terms of similarity (in fact, stylistically the novels are entirely dissimilar) but in terms of linking various landscapes and vocation" (*The Calcutta* 221). In *The Circle of Reason,* Alu connects rural Bengal to al-Ghazira in the Middle East, through his own travels. The notion of drawing together disparate places becomes very important in *In an Antique Land,* as Ghosh the anthropologist is able to recognize cultural similarities between Nashawy and India. The close commercial and cultural exchanges shared by these communities have been erased from the collective consciousness of their people today. In *The Shadow Lines,* places are drawn together in the imagination of the narrator through the many stories—real and imaginary—told by the characters. As Aldama writes, "Ghosh's novels blur boundaries between genres—fiction and archival fieldwork—to complicate postcolonial identity." Meenakshi Mukherjee in an analysis of *The Glass Palace* notes a similar phenomenon: "Casually mentioned details get linked across space and time to form haunting patterns, their cumulative effect staying with the reader long after the novel is over."

Another important theme that is played out in Ghosh's work is the dialectic between public and private history. In an interview with Aldama, Ghosh describes the symbiotic relationship of *fiction* (a personal invented history) with *nonfiction* (public history), "the institutional structure of our world presses us to think of fiction and nonfiction as being absolutely separate . . . the techniques that I've brought to bear on nonfiction, essentially come from my fiction. . . . In the end it's about people's lives; it's about people's history; it's about people's destinies." This relationship is played out in *In An Antique Land,* which is part nonfiction and part fiction, as the narrator retrieves the history of Ben Yiju and his slave from public history and reconstructs it as a personal story between two people, from which emanates the history of two cultures. In *The Shadow Lines,* Tridib is suspicious of public history and teaches the narrator the necessity of inventing private histories. Ironically, it is Tridib's death that requires the narrator to disregard the public history of the riots of 1964 and create his own personal history. In *The Calcutta Chromosome,* Murugan is impelled by personal reasons to reinvestigate the public history of the malaria problem. The history he reconstructs with Urmila veers on the fantastic, but stands as a very concrete alternative to the standard history of the "malaria problem."

Characters in Ghosh's novels are wanderers; migration therefore becomes an important theme of these novels. Alu is introduced to the reader as a migrant at the beginning of *The Circle of Reason,* and this sets the tone for his subsequent journeys. He is one of several illegal immigrants in al-Ghazira, the mythic city of plenty in the Middle East. Toward the end of the novel, he is compelled to immigrate to the city of El-Oued in Algeria, and each of his journeys serves to impact his identity. In *The Shadow Lines,* Ila and Tha'amma are migrants who have crossed national boundaries in search of home. However the narrator and Tridib are the real migrants of the story, for they travel through the imagination: "It seemed to me still that Tridib had shown me something truer about Solent Road a long time ago in Calcutta, something I could not have seen had I waited at the corner for years—just as one may watch a tree for moths and yet know nothing at all about it if one happens to miss that one week when it bursts into bloom" (56–57). Ghosh writes that the act of intellectual migration becomes essential for the writer: "to even perceive one's immediate environment one must somehow distance oneself from it . . . to locate oneself through prose, one must begin with an act of dislocation" *(Kunapipi).*

Migrations, also lead to an implicit discussion of politics in *In an Antique Land,* where the Gulf War is discussed in terms of the emigrants from Nashawy. In *The Shadow Lines,* politics—the Partition and the riots of 1964—are filtered through the consciousness of individual characters. In *The Glass Palace,* Ghosh once again deals with politics through people. The political histories of three nations—Burma, India, and Malaya—are bound together through the narrative of the characters. Ghosh's nonfiction deals with politics in a more explicit manner. *Countdown* explores different responses to the Pokhran nuclear tests—these are not only the responses of political figures (George Fernandes), but also of the ordinary people of Rajasthan who were directly affected by the aftermath of the nuclear tests.

Newspapers and journals across the globe have critically acclaimed Ghosh's work. Sudeep Sen writes, "Amitav Ghosh not only corroborates his reputation as being among the best writers of his generation in India, but also confirms his position as one of the finest literary writers on the contemporary international scene" (*The Calcutta* 222). Ghosh's work has not only been evaluated for its literary value, but also for its contribution to anthropology. Vishwanathan commends Ghosh's *In an Antique Land* for its originality of methodology and perspective: "he challenges the convention of the questioning, omniscient and value-neutral ethnographer who can pry information from his subjects at will . . . Ghosh finds a model of syncretism no longer available in the modern age, where religious and cultural differences so overwhelm the possibilities of all dialogue." Ghosh's curious tales of alternative histories of medicine have been acclaimed by science fiction journals as well, "*The Calcutta Chromosome* is fast, subtle, funny, haunting; and there is just enough SF in the mix to make the whole thing work in genre terms" (Clute). Ghosh's work, in all its experimentation with difference genres, paves new directions for postcolonial writing today.

Krupa Shandilya

Further Reading

Aldama, Frederick Luis. "An Interview with Amitav Ghosh." *World Literature Today* 76.2 (Spring 2002): 84–90.

Clute, John. "A Tale Decent Folk Can Buy." *Science Fiction Weekly* 1997 <http://www.scifi.com/sfw/issue56/excess.html (29/11/02)>.

Kunapipi, *A Journal of Post-Colonial Writing* (U.K.), Vol. XIX, No. 3.

Mukherjee, Meenakshi. "Of Love, War and Empire," *The Hindu* 1 October 2000.

Sen, Sudeep. Rev. of *The Calcutta Chromosome* by Amitav Ghosh. *World Literature Today* 71.1 (Winter 1997): 221–22.

Viswanathan, Gauri. "Beyond Orientalism." *Stanford Humanities Review* 5.1 (1995): 19–32.

Gidwani, Bhagwan S.

As a novelist, Bhagwan S. Gidwani thrives on controversy. His first novel, *The Sword of Tipu Sultan,* created a commotion in India among fundamentalists because of his praise of Tipu, a Muslim ruler of Mysore, India, in the eighteenth century. The novel has had 44 reprints and sold more than 200 thousand copies—a record for novels published in India. Gidwani's second novel—*Return of the Aryans*—is more ambitious, with a 1,000-page story of the beginnings of Hinduism in 8000 B.C.E. and the origin of Aryans in India in 5000 B.C.E.

Gidwani, born on November 11, 1923, is a bureaucrat turned novelist. He was India's Additional Director General of Tourism and Director General, Civil Aviation till 1978; India's Counsel at International Court of Justice, The Hague; and Representative of India on ICAO (United Nations) and Director of ICAO (UN) from 1978 to 1985. Since retirement, he lives in Montreal, Canada.

Tipu Sultan, maligned by historians as a cruel and bigoted despot, emerged in Gidwani's *The Sword of Tipu Sultan* (1976) as a humane, enlightened ruler who believed that all religions deserve equal respect. Gidwani established Tipu as the first among Indian nationalists who died on a battlefield while fighting the British. He could have saved himself, but he wanted his sacrifice to serve as an example for future generations of India.

Protests against *The Sword of Tipu Sultan* turned into a virtual storm with the announcement of an upcoming TV series based on Gidwani's screenplay. Fundamentalists went to great lengths to stop the TV series. The Vishwa Hindu Parishad organized demonstrations, and the government appointed a historians committee. Gidwani presented massive evidence and records from England, France, and elsewhere showing that there is more historical truth about Tipu in his novel than in all other published books. He claimed that charges against Tipu of forced conversion of Hindus were fraudulent; Tipu had a Hindu temple in his palace compound and gave large land grants to Hindu institutions; his prime minister and many of his other ministers and generals were Hindus.

A Hindu festival. UN/DPI Photo.

Eventually, the high court and the historians committee dismissed the fundamentalists' petitions to block the TV series; and *The Sword of Tipu Sultan* was telecast in 1990 in 52 episodes, running for four years continuously in India and repeatedly thereafter. It was also telecast in principal cities in western Asia, the United Kingdom, Europe, and the United States.

Gidwani's novel—*Return of the Aryans*—published in 1994 by Penguin Books, continues to be popular and has had several reprints. Within a highly entertaining story, it presents the drama of the birth and the beginnings of Hinduism *(Sanatana-Dharma)* prior to 8000 B.C.E. with a thrilling account of how, in 5000 B.C.E., the Aryans originated from the Indian subcontinent (and from nowhere else) and why they moved out to travel abroad: their adventures, trials and triumphs in Iran, Sumeria, Egypt, Russia, Lithuania, Turkey, Finland, Sweden, Italy, Greece, and Germany, and finally, their return to their homeland and heritage of India. Gidwani effectively demolishes the theory of an Aryan invasion of India from the west or north. He traces the ancestry of Aryans from 8000 B.C.E. and shows that Aryans originated from the Bharat Varsha (Indian subcontinent) and were effectively anchored in the timeless foundation of the Hindu faith.

Besides, the novel unfolds the drama of prehistoric Indian civilization and presents glimpses of its art, culture, music, abstract thought, philosophical leanings, and spiritual values, along with fascinating stories behind the origins of *Om, namaste, the swastika, Gayatri Mantra,* and *Soma wines.* It tells how Tamil and Sanskrit developed and influenced world languages; it also has tales of the discovery and disappearance of the Saraswati River; the founding of the Sindhu, the Ganga, and Dravidian civilizations; and it describes the battles that led to the fall and rise of Benaras, Hardwar, and many other cities.

The novel speaks of the prehistoric establishment of constitutional systems, as well as the material advancements of pre-ancient India. For instance, the development of ships, harbors, gold mines, chariots, yoga, mathematics, astronomy, medicine, surgery, drama, art, and architecture are just some of the subjects addressed in the novel.

Gidwani's *Return of the Aryans* approaches Hinduism with deeply felt respect. It speaks of ideals that took shape in early times to become the foundation of *Sanatana Dharma,* including the recognition of the spiritual nature of man *wherever* he is from; the acceptance of *every* culture as an expression of eternal values; and man's obligation to respect and protect the environment and all creatures, tame and wild.

All literature on India begins with the Vedic Age. Gidwani's *Return of the Aryans* is the very first to trace India's drama far back to pre-Vedic roots. Many reviewers have furiously criticized Gidwani for questioning the Aryan invasion theory and his view that Aryans originated from India. Others have eulogized him for those assertions.

A bizarre aspect about Gidwani's novels is that though they are clearly and unmistakably labeled as fiction, almost all reviewers have fallen into the trap of discussing and analyzing whether assertions and statements made in the novel are true or false. To some extent, Gidwani himself has led reviewers astray by referring, in an introduction or a preface, to his extensive and intensive research with the aim to separate "the lie from truth." Also, he invests his stories with many surrounding details and incidents, with quotations or references to historical testimony, archeological records, or *memory songs* and oral history traditions, so that much of what he says carries an air of plausibility. Even so, reviewers should treat such assertions simply as a novelist's ploy, and Gidwani's novels should be read as fiction and be reviewed as such.

Mamta Bherwan

Further Reading

"Awkward Pastiche." Rev. of *The Sword of Tippu Sultan,* by Bhagwan S. Gidwani. *Indian Review of Books* 15 Apr.-16 May 1995: 28–29.

Chhibber, V. N. Rev. of *The Sword of Tippu Sultan,* by Bhagwan S. Gidwani. *Indian Literature* Jan.-Feb. 1978: 126–31.

Raju, Anand Kumar. "Fiction and the Use of History: A Thematic Study of Bhagwan S. Gidwani's *The Sword of Tippu Sultan.*" *Journal of Asian Studies* Mar. 1987: 131–40.

Tilak, Shrinivas. "Mother India's Returning Children." *New Quest* Jul.-Aug. 1995: 225–30.

Globalization

Globalization has become a commonplace term to describe a vast and complex contemporary phenomenon: one whose history and consequences is now debated across the humanities and social sciences, as well as in the media. At its most general, *globalization* refers to the growing interconnection of economic, social, cultural, and political relations around the world, such that local events have global contexts and vice versa. Political scientist Benjamin Barber, author of *Jihad vs. McWorld,* argues that globalization is fueled by four main imperatives: capitalism's quest for new markets (the spread of multinational corporations and transnational finance); the ever-growing need for shared resources; the bridging of time and space produced by information technology; and the pressing world ecological crisis (whereby one's country's environmental problems inevitably affect not only its nearest neighbors but potentially countries and peoples halfway across the world). Critics of globalization often focus on the homogenization of culture that attends the spread of capital and information technology, pointing to the worldwide omnipresence of American products and services such as Coke and McDonald's, and the resultant conformity, excess consumerism, and demise of local cultures and traditions.

So-called developing regions like South Asia are thought to be particularly ill-served by the economic forces of globalization, not only because of their Westernizing and Americanizing cultural effects but, more specifically, because of the frequently disastrous impact of global finance mechanisms, such as the International Monetary Fund (IMF) and the World Trade Organization (WTO), on these regions. Critics of these institutions point out that instead of creating opportunities for development, restrictions imposed on countries such as India in exchange for loans and investments end up enhancing the trading power of developed countries, often at the expense of the poorest inhabitants of the developing one.

Though globalization has been studied most closely as an economic concept, literary studies increasingly view globalization as a crucial concept in understanding the function of culture and the circulation of literature. Those interested in the cultural implications of globalization differ widely, however, on globalization's genealogy and on whether its effects are potentially positive or solely destructive. While the concept of globalization is relatively new (the word appeared in the 1960s, according to the *Oxford English Dictionary*), some critics trace the origins of globalization to premodern times, with the development of exploration and maritime travel. Others, such as Anthony Giddens, see it as continuous with the logic of modernity and the rise of the nation-state. Still others, Michael Hardt, Antonio Negri, and Arjun Appadurai for instance, understand it as a distinctly postmodern phenomenon: a decisive break with the past in which power dislodges from the static structures of the nation-state to circulate in *flows* of capital and information. While many believe that the increased disembodiment of power makes it harder to

harness, contributing to the continued disenfranchisement of indigent people worldwide and heralding the end of hopes for a fully realized democratic governance, others argue for the progressive potential of "globalization from below." Appadurai, for example, proposes that the fluidity of knowledge and information under globalization makes those forces more widely available to marginalized peoples who can then turn them to their own advantage. Rather than seeing non-Western cultures as passive consumers of Western (particularly American) culture, he suggests that we should attend to the way different cultures actively reshape dominant forms and adapt them to local ends. Paul Jay points out, however, that the ability to appropriate and refashion hegemonic cultures is often the prerogative of urban audiences and does little to change the lives of the rural poor: those whose lives are most drastically and adversely impacted by the dynamics of the world market. To avoid replicating the Western dominance of other cultures that characterizes globalization, critics in literary studies stress the dialectical relationship between British and American and non-Western literary cultures and call for a more active and reciprocal dialogue between critics and writers across national and cultural boundaries.

The cultural impact of globalization on South Asia has included the spread of global Hinduism and Islamic fundamentalism, and the frequent intensification of religious conflict on the subcontinent as a result; the *fatwa* launched against Salman Rushdie after the publication of his *Satanic Verses* in 1989, for example, illustrated the growing rift between modernizing and traditionalizing forces in the wake of globalization. However, the prevalence of South Asian literature in international literary markets, and the impact of both that literature and of South Asian literary theorists on current Western conceptions of the literary canon and of literary study, is evidence that globalization is not merely a Western-dominated phenomenon, but one that can be productive of truly hybrid and novel cultural forms and ideas. Alongside literature, other South Asian cultural productions—such as Bollywood cinema and bhangra pop music—that creatively synthesize South Asian and Western influences find a growing audience in markets worldwide.

The field of literary studies itself has been, and continues to be, reshaped by globalization. Because of the prevalence of postcolonial and ethnic literatures in English departments, "English," as many departments now acknowledge, no longer refers to a body of English national literature, as it originally did, but increasingly to literatures merely written in English. In order to supplement and replace older ideas of national and cultural coherence as contexts for literary study, then, critics increasingly emphasize transnational, diasporic, and postcolonial contexts and argue that both the longer history of globalization and its contemporary incarnations should be used to understand literary texts. The question of how to mediate effectively and equitably between local and global contexts is central to these new methodologies and one that unites those interested in globalization studies across disciplines.

Tanya Agathocleous

Further Reading

Appadurai, Arjun. *Modernity at Large: The Cultural Dimensions of Globalization.* Minneapolis: U of Minnesota P, 1996.

Barber, Benjamin. *Jihad vs. McWorld.* New York: Times Books, 1995.

Giddens, Anthony. *The Consequences of Modernity.* London: Polity, 1990.

Hardt, Michael, and Antonio Negri. *Empire.* Cambridge: Harvard UP, 2000.

Jameson, Fredric, and Masao Miyoshi, eds. *The Cultures of Globalization.* Durham: Duke UP, 1998.

Jay, Paul. "Beyond Discipline? Globalization and the Future of English." *PMLA* 116 (2001): 32–47.

The God of Small Things by Arundhati Roy

Born on November 24, 1961, and brought up in Kerala, Arundhati Roy left home at 16 and lived in a squatters' camp in a small hut within the walls of Delhi's Ferozshah Kotla selling empty beer bottles. She joined the Delhi School of Architecture where she met her first husband Gerard Da Cunha. They eked out a living, selling cakes on the beaches of Goa for around seven months. Back in Delhi, she was cast in the role of a tribal bimbo in a film, *Massey Saab,* by Pradeep Krishen, her second husband. Following the publication of her novel, *The God of Small Things* (1997), Roy has come out strongly on several contemporary sociopolitical issues in her subsequent writings: "The End of Imagination" (1998), "The Greater Common Good" (1999), "The Algebra of Infinite Justice" (2001), and *Power Politics* (2002).

The God of Small Things won the Booker Prize in 1997. The novel opens with 31-year-old Rahel returning to Ayemenem, a village in Kerala, to meet her fraternal twin Esthappen, begotten of an unhappy short-lived marriage between an alcoholic father and an attractive mother, Ammu. Denied college education, marriage for Ammu meant an escape from her "monstrous suspicious bully" (180) of a father, Benaan John Ipe and embittered mother Soshamma, referred to as Pappachi and Mammachi in familiar terms. Ammu and her children's arrival at the old Ayemenem house is regarded contemptuously by her parents, Ammu's sexually frustrated spinster aunt, Navomi Ipe, known as Baby Kochamma, the vitriolic cook, Kochu Maria and her hugely selfish brother and Rhodes scholar, Chacko. The single mother and her twins fade into further insignificance in course of the eagerly awaited arrival of Chacko's former British wife, Margaret, and their daughter Sophie Mol. However, this visit turns into a nightmare as Sophie Mol is drowned while ferrying across a river with Estha and Rahel. Meanwhile Ammu has been having a clandestine physical relationship with Velutha, an untouchable working in Mammachi's factory. The discovery of their affair coincides with the death of Sophie Mol, and the unwanted guests are readily evicted. The rigidly defined caste hierarchy, the establishment of the Anglican Church to reorder this division, and the rise of the Communist Party serve as an intrusive backdrop to the sequence of events in and around the old Ayemenem house.

Transgression or the fear to transgress dictates the fate of the members of the Ipe family, making them social outcasts or sociopaths. Filial, religious, educational, legal, political, and patriarchal institutions are caricatured as tools of self-preservation and oppression used to castigate or contain the transgressor. There results a fractured family history wherein lives are colonized in a circuslike spectacle with indelible "Edges, Borders, Boundaries, Brinks and Limits" (3). The History House, witness to the brutal assault on Veutha's rebellion against the Order, becomes a frightful symbol of "human history, masquerading as God's Purpose" (309).

The narrative structure and elements of this "anti-Bildungsroman" (Thruax) serve as a commentary on the nature of memory strongly interlaced with the cancerous nature of guilt imported by childhood trauma. The nonlinear plotline is dotted with symbols associated with terror like the decaying river, the History House on the other side of the river, and the ghost of Pappachi's moth that was never named after him. The jagged movement in time is also forever haunted by incidents like Estha being forced to aid the masturbating Orangedrink Lemondrink Man, Sophie Mol's death, and Ammu's adulterous relationship with Velutha. The varying degrees of madness seen as a family ailment become an extension of the all-pervasive physical and moral decay. With the passage of time, Rahel develops a frightening apathy and Estha withdraws into a deathly silence. The suggestion of an incestuous encounter between brother and sister, at 31, underscores the one's tacit and complete physical and emotional understanding of the other that everyone else is a stranger to. Life has come a full circle as they can once more imagine themselves as "We or Us" and not "Them" (2–3).

The chaos of incident is furthered by upheaval in language as the writer invents her own linguistic idiom couched in playful irony. Roy tells her readers precisely what she wants to and not what words allow her to (Choubey 125). The author's ingenious use of similes conjures up images that stimulate more than one, sometimes all the reader's senses simultaneously: "Strange insects appeared like ideas in the evenings and burned themselves on Baby Kochamma's dim 40-watt bulbs" (9–10).

These surprises, however, appear overdone and tend to lose their flavor beyond a point. Roy's syntactical somersaults in the form of deliberate typographical irregularities, breaking down of words—"Prer NUN sea ayshun" (36)—repetition, neologisms—"Locusts Stand I" (57), sentences spelled backward, palindromes, verse, listing of recipes, and even the curious ways in which the author refers to her young characters, "E(lvis) Pelvis, and Ambassador S(tick). Insect" (139), are devised to appropriate and parody the received tongue.

The apparition of The God of Small Things in Ammu's dream being a one-armed cheerful man holding "her close by the light of an oil lamp," capable of singular action, is a complete inversion of an Almighty God. Roy lets diminutive figures in society, the untouchable, the fallen woman, and children brazenly articulate and act out their aspirations and fears. The spirit of the text is remarkably captured as "Small God," likened to a "rich boy in shorts," whose laughter is a "hollow laugh" tinged with sorrow at its own insignificance, and the source of whose "brittle elation" is the "relative smallness of his misfortune" (19).

The book received rave reviews worldwide and was heralded for its "extraordinary, morally strenuous, and imaginatively supple" narration (Thruax). Though certain Indian academics have taken issue with Roy for pandering to a Western audience (Dwivedi 1) there is unequivocal admiration at her uninhibited linguistic foreplay.

Suhaan Mehta

Further Reading

Choubey, Asha. "The Magic Wand of Arundhati Roy." *Arundhati Roy's Fictional World: A Collection of Critical Essays.* Ed. Amar Nath Dwivedi. Delhi: B. R. Publishing, 2001.

Dhawan, R. K. *Arundhati Roy.* Delhi: Prestige, 1999.

Dwivedi, Amar Nath, ed. *Arundhati Roy's Fictional World: A Collection of Critical Essays.* Delhi: B. R. Publishing, 2001.

Simmons, Jon. *Arundhati Roy Unofficial Web Site.* 20 Nov. 2002 <http://www.arundhatiroy.org.uk/>.

Thruax, Alice. "A Silver Thimble in Her Fist." Rev. of *The God of Small Things,* by Arundhati Roy. *New York Times Online.* 25 May 1997. 20 Nov. 2002 <http://www.nytimes.com/books/97/05/25/reviews/970525.25truaxt.html>.

Gooneratne, Yasmine

Poet, novelist, essayist, academic, biographer, literary critic, editor, and bibliographer, Yasmine Gooneratne was born in 1935, in Sri Lanka, of a Sri Lankan father and a Trinidadian mother of Indian origin. She studied at Bishop's College, graduated from the University of Ceylon in 1959, and received a Ph.D. from Cambridge University in 1962, where her thesis traced the development of the English-language literature of Ceylon between 1815 and the end of the 1870s. After teaching for 10 years at the University of Peradeniya, she moved to Australia in 1972 with her hus-

Yasmine Gooneratne. Photo by Effy Alexakis.

band, the physician and historian Dr. Brendon Gooneratne, to join Macquarie University in New South Wales. In 1981, the university conferred on her its first ever degree of Doctor of Letters. In 1988, she became the founder-director of Macquarie's Centre forPostcolonial Studies, and in the early 1990s she was appointed to a personal chair in English. After her early retirement in 1999, she was made professor emeritus. In 1990, Gooneratne was made an officer of the Order of Australia (AO) in recognition of her distinguished service to literature and education and, in that same year, she was invited to become the patron of the Jane Austen Society of Australia. She has been a visiting professor or specialist at the Edith Cowan University, the universities of Yale, Princeton, and Michigan, Jawaharlal Nehru University, and the University of the South Pacific. Through all of this, her links with Sri Lanka remain: after her move to Australia, she continued to edit the journal she had started in 1970, *New Ceylon Writing;* in 1999 she became a founder-trustee of the Pemberley International Study Center in Sri Lanka, an institution that offers residency to selected writers, scholars, and creative artists; and she is currently working on the preparation of the first scholarly edition of Leonard Woolf's novel set in Sri Lanka, *The Village in the Jungle*. In 2001, Gooneratne was awarded the prestigious Raja Rao Award.

Her works include four volumes of poems: *Word, Bird, Motif* (1970), *The Lizard's Cry and other Poems* (1972), *6,000 Ft. Death Dive* (1981), and *Celebrations and Departures;* two novels, *A Change of Skies* (1991), which won the Marjorie Barnard Literary Award for Fiction in 1992 and was short-listed for the Commonwealth Writers Prize, and *The Pleasures of Conquest* (1995), which was short-listed for the Commonwealth Writers Prize in 1996; her family history, *Relative Merits: A Personal Memoir of the Bandaranaike Family of Sri Lanka* (1986); several edited anthologies, including, *New Ceylon Writing* (1973), *Stories from Sri Lanka* (1979), and *Poems from India, Sri Lanka, Malaysia and Singapore* (1979); as well as critical studies of Jane Austen, Alexander Pope, and Ruth Prawer Jhabvala.

A Change of Skies, the final draft of which was edited while Gooneratne was a Writer's Fellow at the Varuna Writer's Center, traces the influence of displacement and cultural dislocation on the lives of a young Sri Lankan academic, Bharat, and his wife, Baba, who move to Australia. In Baba's attempts to learn Australian, we witness a marked involvement with orality that brings into the text a sense of the Sri Lankan reality, the latter heightened by an ample Tamil-Sinhalese vocabulary, with the sociocultural context of the narrative movement facilitating the successful reception of this lexical fidelity. As Bramston says, this is a work in which "the writer draws on her own largely positive, cross-cultural experience in order to represent the traps and difficult processes of cross-cultural adaptation to the main-

stream of Australian readership" (*A Change* 19). A self-reflective piece of work, the narrative engages with the very act of writing and all that it entails—as do many of her poems.

Gooneratne's second novel, *The Pleasures of Conquest,* focuses on Euro-Asian relations against the background of Ceylon's transition from a British colony to an independent democracy. Focusing on both the historical and the contemporary, it engages with aspects of global academia, and the politics of neocolonialism. Undergirding this larger theme is a quieter narrative marking a passionate relationship between an old colonial, an English civil servant and a local woman, a poet who writes in Sinhala.

In 1999, Gooneratne coauthored, with her husband, the biography of Sir John D'Oyly (1774–1824), the man upon whom the fictional civil servant of *The Pleasures of Conquest* had been modeled. This work also reveals the identity of the Sinhala poet, an artist from an earlier age whose work survives to this day.

Relative Merits sees Gooneratne revisiting her family—the distinguished Bandaranaike family of Sri Lanka—opening with a family tree encompassing six pages, the various branches of which she then proceeds to elaborate upon in the most objective manner through the rest of the book. This desire for balance is evident in her co-opting five other family members, whom she refers to as her five "co-authors" in her postscript. As Gooneratne says, "*Relative Merits* has been shaped by our joint recollections, while it records incidents of which we retain different impressions, and personalities of whom we maintain contradictory opinions" (245). Here, Gooneratne reveals the impulse behind the choice of her field of research at Cambridge: her father's suggestion that she work on the writings of *his* grandfather, the nineteenth-century scholar and man of law, James D'Alwis (128).

As with her prose, Gooneratne's poetry, too, is self-reflective to a great extent, one of its themes being poetry itself. Fernando and Raheem draw our attention to her "technique and style [which] reveal a superb command of English literature. She moves with ease and poise from the sonnet form . . . to the song . . . to the looser, episodic structure of the longer [poems] based on the traditional Sri Lanka [sic] verse form of the "sandesa" (a message borne by a courtly messenger)" (269).

The body of her work, considered as a whole, reveals, among other things, the influence of, and a sustained engagement with, the splicing of an English literary tradition with her Sri Lankan heritage, the dynamics of the past in the present, the energy of the immigrant experience, and the intimacy of the very act of writing—all of which denote an engagement with the personal, the known, the lived. This, one might say, is the sic passim evident in her work.

Dipli Saikia

Further Reading

Bramston, Dorothy. "A Sri Lankan Writer in Australia: Gooneratne's *A Change of Skies*." *New Literature Review* 31 (1996): 19–32.

Gooneratne, Yasmine. *Relative Merits: A Personal Memoir of the Bandaranaike Family of Sri Lanka*. London: C. Hurst, 1986.

Raheem, R. and S. Fernando. "Women Writers of Sri Lanka." *World Literature Written in English* 17 (1978): 268–78.

Rama, R. P. "A Conversation with Yasmine Gooneratne." *SPAN: Journal of the South Pacific Association for Commonwealth Literature and Language Studies* 38 (1994): 1–18.

The Great Indian Novel by Shashi Tharoor

The Great Indian Novel (1989) by Shashi Tharoor recasts the 2,000-year-old Indian epic, the Mahabharata, with fictional but highly recognizable events and characters from twentieth-century Indian politics. Written as a hilarious satire, the novel is as much against Indian foibles as the bumbling of the British rulers. From the book jacket we learn that the narrative depicts "a dazzling marriage of Hindu myth and modern history" bringing together the events of political India through the greatest political saga, the Mahabharata, which is probably the earliest account of the struggle for power and control. It is the story of the great war of Kurukshetra fought between the Pandavas and the Kauravas to establish a claim over the Indian throne. The underlying theme of the epic is the eternal conflict of Dharma versus Adharma (good versus evil; right versus wrong conduct).

The Great Indian Novel is primarily a political saga. The author, through the voice of Ved Vyas, takes the reader through the major events that shaped India's destiny in the period that eventually culminated in freedom from the British. The second half of the book focuses on the trajectories of independent India and the woman who ruled the nation (Indira Gandhi ruled India for almost two decades from the 1960s to the 1980s). It takes the characters out of the Mahabharata, paints them with unmistakable traits of modern Indian politicians and in the process provides a new perspective with which the Mahabharata and Indian nationalist politics can be read. This is significant, as accounts of the Mahabharata and the nationalist struggle have permeated the national consciousness of India.

As was the case with the Mahabharata, *The Great Indian Novel* is narrated by a Mr. Ved Vyas, or V. Vji, as he is more commonly known, to a big-nosed South Indian by the name of Ganapati. The Mahabharata's indomitable Bhishma earlier known as Gangaputra (having been born of Ganga to King Shantanu) is the central character in this book. Loin clad, bald-headed, bespectacled, Gangaji as he is known in the book, is a most humorous cross between the patriarch of the Maha-

The Meenakshi Temple in Madurai. © Fiona Good/TRIP.

bharata, the man who began it all and Mahatma Gandhi, the father of modern India. Dhritarashtra is Gangaji's protégé within the Kaurava Party (the Congress party), his heir apparent, the nation's golden boy. Oxford educated and suave, the author leaves no doubts as to his modern day equivalent: he is none other than Jawaharlal Nehru with Gandhari the Grim as the ailing, all suffering Kamala Nehru. Amidst scenes of lightning and torrential rain, jackals baying in the jungle and vultures circling the skies, Gandhari, who had been expecting a hundred sons, gives birth to a daughter. They name her Priya Duryodhani. It is proclaimed that Gandhari's daughter shall one day grow up to rule the nation. Priya Duryodhani is none other than Indira Gandhi.

Tharoor coalesces myth, dreams, folklore, religion, and legend in this first person, near-death life narration of Ved Vyas. The reader suspends disbelief as the garrulous old man omnisciently relates secret conversations, lustful couplings, the assassination of Ganga Datta/Gandhi, and the intimacies of Lord and Lady Drewpad (read Mountbatten). Intermittently humorous, satiric, and fantastic, with wordplay and recurrent verse, this work is most effective when discussing Datta/Gandhi: his enemies, celibacy, hunger strikes, and political tactics. Mohammad Ali Karna's epical narrative is collapsed with the trajectory of Jinnah while Pandu's defiance to Ganga Datta and his death is linked up with Subhash Chandra Bose and his animosity to Gandhi. Hence, ManiMir is Kashmir, Snup-ing, the capital of Chakra is Peek-ing, the Chinese capital. Interwoven within the subtext of the novel is an inherent critique of all the leaders such as Mahatma Gandhi, Nehru, and Indira Gandhi who have been deified within the Indian national pantheon. In this vein, Tharoor reveals that Mahatma Gandhi believed in the power of truth, his truth, for he assumed his truth was the universal truth. Nehru was well meaning but allowed himself, perhaps not entirely unwillingly

Mahatma Gandhi and Jawaharlal Nehru in 1946. Courtesy of Library of Congress.

to be pulled into the petty struggle for power and dominance. Indira Nehru Gandhi made the grievous mistake of believing she was indispensable and she alone held the key to Indian problems.

The Great Indian Novel skillfully weaves together in its narrative the genres of the epic, the sonnet, the novel and the folktale, just as history and myth, dream and reality intertwine in every chapter, calling into question the validity of categories. Tharoor has similarly used different narrative strategies in his other novels *(Show Business, Riot)*. Throughout, Tharoor appropriates titles, phrases, and figures from the work of a pantheon of first-world writers, ranging from E. M. Forster and Rudyard Kipling to Ernest Hemingway and Arthur Koestler, a subtle but potent reversal of the traditional tide of cultural colonialism. Tharoor has also

undertaken a parody of British writing about India, with chapters titled the "Bungle Book" or "The Duel With the Crown." Ronald Heaslop from E. M. Forster's *A Passage to India* appears again and again as a particularly hapless civil servant. Indian literature is also not spared—other chapters carry titles like "The Rigged Veda" or "Midnight's Parents." Since there exists a sufficient amount of hagiography about the Indian nationalist heroes and there is a great deal of reverence for the ancient epics, the genre of satire allows the novel to reinvent both the epics and the history cynically—the great ideas, the great stories, and the great men or women are recast in a light that is so unfamiliar that it immediately provokes a fresh way of looking at them, which is serious, hilarious, and entertaining.

"One must be wary of history by anecdote," warns the narrator; one must be wary of "history" itself, suggests Tharoor. History to Tharoor as portrayed in *The Great Indian Novel* is, however, the history of nationalist leaders and colonial officials, and politics to Tharoor is merely the sum of all transactions between the masters themselves. Hence, Tharoor reproduces ideas in history textbooks that primarily emphasize the role of the nationalist leaders in securing Indian independence. This is precisely the historiography that subaltern historians have critiqued, as it is conspicuous with the absence of the *subaltern* role in the freedom movement. Also, Tharoor's stereotypical treatment of British and Indian characters, reiterates elite interpretations that the domain of colonial and Indian politics was unified and homogenous.

The Great Indian Novel's account of complex Hindu-Muslim relations, the legacy of which continues in present India, is sketchy and inadequate. In spite of fusing the narratives of Mahabharata and the nationalist movement, the characterizations are predictable. Hence, Tharoor replays the process of *othering* by sketching Karna as Jinnah and Pandu as Subhash Bose. Though Tharoor manages to make the Mahabharata current while making modern Indian politics somewhat understandable, the novel keeps in mind the urban, middle-class English-speaking reader. Without prior knowledge of the narratives of the Mahabharata and the nationalist movement, the reader would miss the humor, satire, and various characterizations of the novel. The novel, however, does provide a cursory insight into ancient and modern Indian history. The facts as presented in this novel are a work of fiction frequently *transcreated* to suit the author's fancy, but this particular device is of limited literary merit and can veer toward being dull and predictable.

The author's biographical subjectivity as one who is educated in India and the United States and works for the United Nations in New York also influences the construction of what is *great* in this novel. Hence, the metanarratives of the Mahabharata and the freedom movement become the ideal playing field of writing a novel on India. Above all, the novel highlights the author's constant process of self-interrogation about India and the anxiety of *Indianness* within him, a point reflected in the title of the novel. Nonetheless, the novel attempts to reveal the parallels between the past and present India.

Nayanika Mookherjee

Further Reading
Chowdhury, Kanishka. "Revisioning History: Shashi Tharoor's Great Indian Novel." *World Literature Today* 69.1 (Winter 1995): 41–48.

Gorra, Michael. "*The Great Indian Novel.*" *The New York Times Book Review* (24 March 1991): 16.

Pousse, Michel. "Shashi Tharoor in *The Great Indian Novel:* A Selective Iconoclast." *Commonwealth Essays and Studies* 18.2 (Spring 1996): 46–55.

Guha, Ranajit

Ranajit Guha is the founding editor of the Subaltern Studies Series and author of a number of celebrated books. He has held various research and teaching positions in India, England, the United States, and Australia. At the end of the 1970s, Ranajit Guha and a group of young historians based in Britain embarked on a series of discussions about the contemporary state of South Asian historiography (Chaturvedi 364). Founded in 1982, the Subaltern Studies Collective has become one of the leading voices in postcolonial studies, critiquing both colonial and postcolonial history.

From the onset, the underlying principle that united the group was a general dissatisfaction with the official historical interpretations of the freedom movement of India, which celebrated elite (both Indian and British) contributions in the making of the Indian nation while denying the politics of the people—the laboring population or the subaltern classes. Subaltern Studies was conceived as a historiographical negation of both a rigidly formulaic orthodox Nationalist Marxism, which glossed over real conflicts of ideas and interests between the elite nationalists and their socially subordinate followers and the Namierism of the Cambridge School in Britain, which propounded a skeptical view of Indian nationalism. Both of them failed to account for "the subaltern as the maker of his own destiny" (Guha: Subaltern Studies III, 1984: vii), and "the contributions made by people on their own that is independent of the elite to the making and development of this nationalism" (Guha: Subaltern Studies I, 1982: 3).

Unlike the Cambridge and nationalist schools, which conflated the political domain with the formal side of governmental and institutional processes, Guha claimed that there was in colonial India an "autonomous" domain of the "politics of people" that was organized differently than the domain of the politics of the elite. By explicitly rejecting the characterization of peasant "consciousness" as prepolitical, and by avoiding evolutionary models of consciousness, Guha was prepared to suggest that the nature of collective action against exploitation in colonial India was such that it effectively led to a new constellation of the political (Chakravarty). Examining for instance over a hundred cases of peasant rebellions in British India between 1783–1900, Guha showed in his *Elementary Aspects of Peasant Insurgency in Colonial India* (1983) that these always involved the deployment by the peasants of codes of dress, speech, and behavior that tended to invert the codes through which their social superiors dominated them in everyday life.

In his *Dominance without Hegemony: History and Power in Colonial India* (1998), Guha points out that the colonial state in South Asia was fundamentally dif-

ferent from the metropolitan bourgeois state that sired it. He argues that while Britain ruled India by force as a colony, it never achieved hegemony over most of the population. So, although the British had the power of coercion, they were never able to persuade the urban poor and the rural masses that they ought to be ruled by a foreign presence. Thus the colonial state, as Guha defines it in this closely argued work, was a paradox—dominance without hegemony. On the nationalist side, a structural split between the elite and subaltern domains of politics led to the consequent failure of the Indian bourgeoisie to integrate vast areas of the life and consciousness of the people into an alternative hegemony. In both endeavors, the elite claimed to speak for the people constituted as a nation and sought to challenge the pretensions of an alien regime to represent the colonized. In his *History at the Limit of World-History* (2002), Guha attempts to find alternatives to statism by emphasizing the need to address the historicality of everyday life.

Guha's work and the Subaltern series, while emerging with various interdisciplinary followers, have been scathingly criticized. In Guha's formulation, colonialism and nationalism appears to be a single, unified, discursive structure of power (Ludden 14). The hard dichotomy between elite and subalterns alienated subaltern studies from social histories and popular movements. Instances from movements for women's rights or of lower-caste protest show that these movements were not constituted by such binaries and in fact are influenced and even utilize aspects of colonial administration and ideas as resources in their struggle against colonialism itself. Furthermore, subaltern politics retains the status quo by being unable to threaten a political structure. The dichotomy between domination and resistance according to O'Hanlon carries the marks of a dominant discourse in its insistence that resistance itself should take necessarily the virile form of a deliberate and violent onslaught. Also peasant consciousness is rendered supra historical by Guha as it is not determined by any objective historical forces (Ludden). This has enabled the subaltern to be a creation, a reification of historians (Ludden). Sarkar has pointed out a tendency toward *essentialising* the categories of "subaltern" and "autonomy" and non-Western "community consciousness" as the valorized alternative of critiques of Western colonial power knowledge. The separation of domination and autonomy disallows immanent critiques of structures that have been the strength of Marxist dialectical approaches. In *Chandra's Death* the community that was unraveled through Guha's moving study of the death (through enforced abortion after an illicit affair) of a low-caste woman was one of conflict and brutal exploitation of power relations "sited at a depth within the indigenous society, well beyond the reach of the disciplinary arm of the colonial state" (Subaltern Studies V 1987). Indian Marxists also charge that the postmodernist valorization of the fragment in subaltern historiography hurts the cause of the unity of the oppressed and helps Hindu extremists.

Guha's work and Subaltern Studies is the first Indian historiographical school whose reputation has come to be evaluated primarily in terms of audience response in the West. Nonetheless, disparate readings exist among readers in other South Asian countries who might tend to read Subaltern Studies as an Indian national project. Also South Asian readers outside the matrix of big city universities and research centers might tend to value the project's global success inversely to its local credibility. Nonetheless, Guha's work has provided (or rather, made more visible) productive ways of looking at larger issues: for example, subaltern/peasant violence as an agential rather than an irrational act.

Nayanika Mookherjee

Further Reading

Chakravarty, Dipesh. *Habitations of Modernity: Essays in the Wake of Subaltern Studies.* New Delhi: Permanent Black, 2002.

Chaturvedi, Vinayak, ed. *Mapping Subaltern Studies and the Postcolonial.* London: Verso, 2000.

Ludden, David, ed. *Reading Subaltern Studies: Critical History, Contested Meaning and the Globalization of South Asia.* New Delhi: Permanent Black, 2001.

O'Hanlon, Rosalind. "Recovering the Subject: Subaltern Studies and Histories of Resistance in Colonial South Asia" *Modern Asian Studies* (22:1) 1988. 189–224.

Sarkar, Sumit. "The Decline of the Subaltern in Subaltern Studies." *Writing Social History.* Ed. Sumit Sarkar. New Delhi: Oxford UP, 1997. 82–108.

Gunesekera, Romesh

Romesh Gunesekera was born in Sri Lanka in 1954 and was educated briefly in Colombo before moving to the Philippines with his parents. He settled down in London in 1972. Gunesekera's collection of stories, *Monkfish Moon,* was a New York

Romesh Gunesekera. Photo by Barbara Piemonte.

Times Notable Book of the Year while his first novel, *Reef,* was short-listed for the Booker Prize. His other novels include *The Sandglass* and *Heavens Edge.*

Monkfish Moon provides a variegated collection of stories based in Sri Lanka and England. Among those that stand out are "A House in the Country," which focuses on the complicated interactions between Ray, who returns to Sri Lanka from England, and Siri, his carpenter cum servant, and the way in which they are threatened by the political turmoil in the country; "Batik," which characterizes the problems faced by a Sinhalese and Tamil couple living in England when the ethnic conflict in Sri Lanka careens out of control; and the title story, where Peter, a successful Sri Lankan businessman, begins to show the extent to which his life has been transformed by wealth when he interacts with friends and family at a dinner party. Other stories include "Captives," "Ullswater," "Storm Petrel," "Ranvali," "Carapace," and "Straw Hurts."

In *Reef,* Gunesekera's first novel, Triton, a successful restaurant owner in England, looks back at his beginnings as a servant in Salgado's home in Sri Lanka. Despite his poverty-stricken background, Triton won the favor of his master on account of his efficiency as a servant and skills as a chef. Interspersed with Triton's bildungsroman, however, is an account of life in the island from the 1960s to the 1980s. What is described is by no means positive: the lower classes are generally uncouth, the middle class only interested in hedonistic pursuits, and the guerrillas who carried out the armed insurrection against the state, mostly inarticulate, irrational, and destructive. Opposed to these negative attributes one finds the alluring seascape in Sri Lanka and the comparatively calm atmosphere in England that Triton and his well-meaning but ineffective master retreat to when life becomes intolerable in Sri Lanka.

The Sandglass, too, deals with the troubled state of Sri Lanka, although here the author, in tracing the activities of the Ducals and Vatunas over several generation, indicates that corruption and exploitation have been endemic in the island long before independence was achieved. The other differences in this novel are the mode of narration, which is reminiscent of a detective novel, and the substantial space given to accommodate expatriate themes. In the lives of Pearl, Ravi, Jason, and Chip, the narrator, Gunasekera shows different versions of expatriate experience—none of which is totally sustaining or wholesome. The message of the novel is that only expatriates of the second or third generation can obtain fulfillment. *The Sandglass* is similar to *Reef* in that it, too, depicts Sri Lanka as a country that is plagued by ethnic riots, war mongering, and various kinds of greed, a land in which honest individuals are easily swept aside.

Heaven's Edge is Gunesekera's latest novel. Although the author has claimed at readings and on other occasions that the setting is a collage of various locales, it is evident that this futuristic novel is for the most part situated in a Sri Lanka (once again depicted as a fallen Eden) that has been devastated by war, bad government, and anarchy. Although born and bred in Britain, Marc is adrift, haunted by the island that his grandfather left and to which his pilot father returned only to be shot down while on a mission against rebels. Marc arrives on the island to "find" himself, and also to secure a haven from the odious, "pointless" life he leads in England. But he discovers all too soon that he would need to fight like his father to discover the serenity his grandfather spoke about. Although he enjoys a brief Edenic existence with Uva, an eco-activist he meets soon after arrival, their world is shattered by militants who destroy all that they had created. Marc and Uva are separated and he becomes increasingly involved in a campaign that he cannot really understand, an engagement that takes him through the better part of this alluring but devastated island. Such a strategy enables the author to explore a myriad number of themes: peace that has been forced by war, the uneasy relationships among different people who are brought together under trying circumstances, and violence in its many manifestations. Although the lovers are reunited at the end, their reunion is far from the idyllic affair that they had enjoyed previously—they have suffered too much individually and collectively to relish such luxury.

When *Reef* was short-listed for the Booker Prize and received plaudits in England, some Sri Lankans pointed out that the author took a jaundiced view of the country and was equally guilty of exoticising it. What is significant is that European critics like Paula Burnett sprang to his defense, suggesting that Gunesekara's was an honest portrayal of what had happened to Sri Lanka in the recent past. The controversy continued after the publication of *The Sandglass.* Paul Binding's comment in reviewing the novel that "Sri Lanka compels the leaving of it" because "it is unable to provide a home for its inhabitants" (29) would appear to vindicate the negative critiques leveled at Gunesekara's work by Sri Lankans. *Heaven's Edge,* though favorably received in England, has not generated the same critical attention in Sri Lanka.

S. W. Perera

Further Reading

Binding, Paul. "A Tear-Shaped Homeland." *The Independent on Sunday: Review Books* (22 Feb. 1998): 29.

Burnett, Paula. " 'The Captives and the Lion's Claw': Reading Gunesekara's *Monkfish Moon.*" *The Journal of Commonwealth Literature* 32.2 (1997): 3–15.

Perera, Senath Walter. "Images of Sri Lanka through Expatriate Eyes: Romesh Gunesekera's *Reef.*" *Journal of Commonwealth Literature* 30.1 (1995): 63–78.

———. "The Perils of Expatriation and a 'Heartless Paradise': Romesh Gunesekera's *The Sandglass.*" *Commonwealth: Essays and Studies* 22.2 (2000): 93–106.

Gupta, Sunetra

Born on March 15, 1965, Sunetra Gupta, referred to by fellow novelist Amit Chaudhuri as "one of the very few genuinely talented writers to have emerged from that aggressively marketed group of practitioners called Indian writers in English," returned to Calcutta, the city of her birth, as a teenager after spending a childhood in Ethiopia, Zambia, and Liberia (28). Through her father, a professor of history, Gupta became interested in the works of Rabindranath Tagore, the famous Bengali poet and thinker whose lyrics appear as emotional touchstones throughout Gupta's works. Propelled into a world of art, literature, and film, Gupta herself began to write science fiction stories in Bengali.

In 1984, Gupta left Calcutta to attend Princeton University where she majored in biology while taking creative-writing courses with Joyce Carol Oates. After receiving her undergraduate degree in 1987, Gupta went on to obtain a Ph.D. from the University of London. Married and mother of two daughters, Gupta currently writes in London while working as a reader in Epidemiology of infectious diseases in the zoology department at Oxford University. Gupta's oeuvre of English works includes four novels, a bevy of articles on immunology, as well as scientific reviews. Her first novel, *Memories of Rain* (1992), published when Gupta was 27, garnered the 1996 Sahitya Akademi award. Her most recent text, *A Sin of Color* (1999), earned the 2000 British Southern Arts Literature Prize.

Characterized by its stream-of-consciousness style, Gupta's prose focuses on the interior lives of her characters. Affiliated more often with modernist writers than with her postcolonial compatriots,

Gupta's works engage with fundamental questions regarding the nature of truth, love, memory, loss, and writing's ability to represent these shifting realities. The focus of Gupta's tales is not just what happens but also how and why things happen. This is not to argue, however, that Gupta's writings do not comprise a literature of displacement: all four of her texts span different locales and multiple continents, containing writing that travels through time, space, and point of view to reflect the characters' dislocations from their homes, hearts, and desires.

In what Shashi Tharoor calls "Gupta's remarkable first novel," *Memories of Rain,* Gupta presents a rewriting of *Medea* (3). Through a series of memories and present-time ruminations, readers follow the main character, Moni, as she decides to take her daughter back to India and abandon her English husband, who is having an affair. The story describes Moni and Anthony's whirlwind romance in Calcutta, the transition to England, and the slow decay of their passion into abiding affection. In Tharoor's estimation, the text is "an elegiac rendering of the cultural loss that emigration entails" and describes not only love's loss but also the inability to reside—emotionally as well as physically—in two lands (3).

In her second novel, *The Glassblower's Breath* (1993), Gupta spans one day's goings-on in an epic-length elegy that brings readers into "the cultural milieu of . . . expatriation, multiculturalism and globalization" (Fludernik 279). This text's central unnamed woman protagonist is rendered both through the sustained use of the second person—a rare narrative technique—and via interactions with the four men who love her. The narrator's shifting desires and affections—her first love and Indian cousin, Avishek; her American poet muse, Jonathan Sparrow; her part-Persian husband, Alexander; and her new English lover, Daniel—are configured through the

central loss of the text, the death of the narrator's sister from cancer. For this reason, Monika Fludernik views the book as elaborating "the equation of passionate love with annihilation" (282). The text's central motif, a broken wineglass that leads back to the glassblower, is taken from a Jelaluddin Rumi poem and signals the shards of love and the urge to follow desire to its source. Yet, as all the characters discover, desire itself is seen to be a cancer: in this text, breath and death intertwine.

Moonlight into Marzipan (1995), Gupta's third novel, builds on the vocabulary of alchemy and myth. Readers follow the attempts of the central character, Promethesh, to replicate his Calcutta laboratory transformation of gold into grass. But Promethesh cannot repeat the experiment in England. To add to despair, his wife, Esha, throws herself under the tube in London, committing suicide. A text that ironically refers to itself as a biography in the making, this novel traces many failures—including that of authorship itself: "you had hoped to weave the threadbare events of my past into a system of helices to encoil those prurient readers who would buy my experiences for little more than the price of a song" (132). Through its world of clashing myths—evocations of Prometheus and Eurydice amongst others—readers understand that lives cannot be captured in one telling nor delineated into scientific models. In the end, *Moonlight into Marzipan* describes not only Promethesh's failure but the inability of writing and storytelling to represent life, to determine a beyond-market value, and to enable transformation.

Gupta continues to explore the theme of life's limitations in her most recent novel, *A Sin of Color.* In an intergenerational saga, Gupta renders the parallel stories of Debendranath Roy and his niece, Niharika. In the house of Mandalay, Debendranath falls for his sister-in-law, Reba.

To escape overwhelming desire, he perfunctorily marries an Englishwoman and chooses to live in London. One day he decides to disappear: his niece Niharika later writes her vision of his story of disappearance. In an ironic conversion of stories, Niharika herself is in love with the married man who was the last to see her uncle alive. A tale of love's boundaries and crossings, *A Sin of Color* paints the spectrum of emotions where "decay had become nectar" (6). Gupta's novels depict pain, love, and life through the intersection of bitter and sweet, a space where even hope and possibility are threaded with decay.

Social and political events—such as the partition of Bengal and the need to sell Mandalay to developers—are etched through the impact they bear on the characters' choices and options. As Sarah Curtis explains, Gupta's "interest lies in the inner worlds her characters inhabit, although she indicates that their dilemmas stem in part from the social pressures to which they conform" (26). Thus, Debendranath's mother's inability to take her school exams—her mother-in-law had forbidden it—despite her desire to be educated is traced through an erosion of self and an eventual madness that consumes. The political and social is registered in Gupta's novels through the particular impacts made on individual lives.

Across Gupta's texts, blindness, real and figurative, functions as a central conceit. Debendranath reappears in his former life because he is becoming blind; and Anthony cannot see Moni's imminent departure. For readers, these blind spots are apparent: we view what the characters lose sight of. Yet, Gupta's style of writing—added to the overt references to writing's limitations in reflecting whole lives—indicates that both writers and readers participate in acts that represent only partial truths. Gupta uses the language and images of science and disease as well as the range of storytelling forms (fairy tales, myths, songs, and lyrics) to inscribe the limits of human possibility and of writing. Stories are always vulnerable to breach by other points of view and precedent. Gupta's works thread together memories and lives across cultures in a syntax complicated by desire and multiple dislocations.

Lauded for her unique voice in the contemporary canvas of South Asian writers in English, Gupta is best known for her lush, sensuous language. In praise of her painstaking style, Gupta has been affiliated by publishers and critics with many a renowned writer: Virginia Woolf, Henry James, T. S. Eliot, James Joyce, as well as Jean Rhys and Anita Desai. The constant links made between Gupta's writing and her literary predecessors prove one point—that Gupta's novels are immersed in a conversation with the expanses of literature produced in English. Gupta's works, with their emphasis on form and allusions to other literary productions, assert this topography themselves, beckoning critics to comment on her contributions to language and form.

Writer Amit Chaudhuri observes that Gupta's audience is divided "into either admirers or detractors" (28). Gupta has been praised, often lavishly, for the sheer luminosity of her prose. But she has been taken to task for short shifting her narrative plots and characters. Tharoor praises Gupta's innovative writing while offering a small critique regarding character development in her first novel, asserting that Gupta is "better at evoking a mood than at submitting its elements to rational scrutiny, more skilled at depicting human frailty than at explaining her character's tolerance of it" (3). Part of this incompleteness of character is intrinsic to Gupta's writing style—the depiction of changing memories and identities is a liquid, not a fixed state. This is partly a philosophical point—feelings and emotions are not always definable or captured through outside referents.

The lack of defined characters aside, most complaints lodged against Gupta's writing bemoan its overlyricism, its indulgence in language and syntax, which allows paragraphs to span pages and the point of view to be muddied. Claire Messud admits that Gupta possesses clear literary talent but that her style often obfuscates, stating, "Gupta never uses one word where she can find ten for the purpose, and this seems all too often a matter of naïve principle rather than of considered necessity" (29). Like Messud, some critics have found Gupta's longwinded paragraphs, use of repetition and unfamiliar syntax to be stultifyingly dense—a real plot-stopper where the result is "the use of language in such a heightened and evocative way that nothing is left *except* language" (Taylor 38).

Yet these alleged faults are central to the power of Gupta's complex writing, indicates Chaudhuri. In a nod of appreciation to the fellow novelist, Chaudhuri observes that Gupta's language presents a "tension between two seemingly incompatible registers—the firm grip, through exact observation and evocation, on reality, and then the almost helpless loosening of that grip" (29). Chaudhuri values these texts because they do not allow reading to be easy: complex writing should challenge readers to engage and participate in the representation and enactment of complexity. Writing, such as Gupta's, which interpolates cultures, histories, as well as human understandings and experiences of reality, need not be transparent but rather fulfilling and substantial. Gupta's fiction successfully shifts the central preoccupation of South Asian writing from the representation of identity to the mapping of a process of experience and feeling.

Purvi Shah

Further Reading

Chaudhuri, Amit. "The Road from Mandalay." *The Spectator* (3 July 1999): 28–29.

Curtis, Sarah. "From Calcutta to Oxford." *TLS, The Times Literary Supplement* (18 June 1999): 26.

Fludernik, Monika. "Colonial vs. Cosmopolitan Hybridity: A Comparison of Mulk RajAnand and R. K. Narayan with Recent British and North American Expatriate Writing (Singh-Baldwin, Divakaruni, Sunetra Gupta)." *Hybridity and Postcolonialism: Twentieth Century Indian Literature.* Ed. Monika Fludernik. Tubingen: Stauffenburg-Verlag, 1998. 261–290.

Messud, Claire. "No Skull beneath the Skin." *The Guardian* (29 June 1993): 29.

Taylor, D. J. "Fool's Gold." *New Statesman and Society* (19 May 1995): 38.

Tharoor, Shashi. "Out of India: A Thirst for the Past." *Book World* (29 March 1992): 3.

Gustad, Kaizad

Born in Bombay in 1968, Kaizad Gustad was raised by his wealthy Parsee-Iranian family in Bombay and Karnataka. During this time, Gustad's schooling occurred as much in the family's cinema halls as it did at boarding school. At 16, he and his family moved to Sydney, and at the age of 18, he began to travel. *Of No Fixed Address* (1998), the travelogue based on his journal from this time, was published 10 years later. Gustad entered NYU film school where he made his short films *Corner Store Blues* (1994) and *Lost and Found* (1995). He took four years to finance and complete his first full-length feature film, *Bombay Boys* (1998). This box-office hit was seen to mark the emergence of a new English language cinema in India for a cosmopolitan upper-middle-class audience. Gustad also coauthored the Filmi Fundas Manifesto that outlines the ideologies and guidelines of Indian independent cinematic production. Gustad's latest project, the film *Boom* (2003) focuses on high fashion models and the underworld in Mumbai.

Gustad's major texts, *Bombay Boys* and *Of No Fixed Address,* develop overlapping themes such as the search for self-identity through travel, the relationship between diaspora and the homeland, and the meaning of home. *Of No Fixed Address,* a collection of stories, begins in Mumbai with an obsession for a silent underage sex worker with eyes "big as land" (1) and ends with a New York subway ride. What seems significant about the moments in between is not the object of the search, but the search itself, framed as a "set[ting] out to get lost" (231), an attempt to escape from the world "at breakneck speed" (242). In *Of No Fixed Address,* place is less significant than displacement. The subject is made and remade through the journey, while identity is in flux. Interweaving metaphorical and material homelessness, in the last story "The A Train," the homeless narrator stands above the clamor of the subway tracks and creates a giant web of migratory routes for postcolonial travelers, connecting Mumbai to New York, Moscow to London, so that "every road met here. Every river coalesced here. Every memory began and ended here" (242). Capitalizing on his cosmopolitan identity, he is mobilized, like capital, from one global city to another in a world where he needs no fixed address.

Though it distinguishes diasporic Indians from other India-bound Western travelers, *Bombay Boys* fondly parodies the return of diasporic men to the homeland in search of roots, family, romance, and fortune. It centers on three second-generation boys (from New York, London, and Sydney) all arriving in Mumbai in search—one for fame in Bollywood, another for his brother, and the third for himself through music and a coming to terms with his same-sex desires. The film satirizes the "return" to the homeland by "these Indians who are Indians but have never been to India" ("Interview" Smith). Gustad quips, "There is a large hippie culture that says it [India] has all the answers, so go and find it there. And I just thought, wait a minute, India should start charging for these rights. It was literally a cheap shrink to all of the world's lunatics . . . no wonder it's the filthiest country in the world today because everybody comes and dumps their emotional baggage here" ("Interview" Smith). The film simultaneously mocks this desire for roots and is empathetic to the predicament of the diasporic displacement and desire for belonging.

Gustad's critique extends also to diasporic writers who return to India only in their literary productions. In "Apprenticeship of an Author," Rustomji, a character from a Booker Prize winning Parsee Canadian's pen, comes alive in Mumbai and travels to Toronto to respond to these literary representations. He goes to ask how Cawas Byramji, the writer, can receive Western accolades and write about a home that he has not visited in more than 20 years. Not a simple argument about essentialism, authenticity, or accuracy, the book problematizes the question of national belonging, especially for Parsees. Byramji justifies: "What proved most difficult was this notion of 'home' that he toyed with in the first collection. There, it was clear that home was somewhere between two continents, one foot in each, buried over the Atlantic. . . . But the Parsees are the only ones left on this good earth who haven't a land to call their own" (194). But neither home accepts his allegiance, and both challenge his belonging in separate moments of violence, the first in which Byramji suffers serious injury in a hate crime, and the second when 60-year-old Rustomji docks him a blow, sending him reeling and crashing. In this case, the embodied homeland literally challenges the authority of the diasporic author.

Gustad's texts are interrogations of the trope of home, reflecting the ironic postmodern understanding that home is not a geographic place: "thinking as always of home, . . . whatever that might mean and wherever that might be" (154). The title of the book emerges as a response to the ubiquitous question asked of racialized diasporic South Asians: "Where are you from?" The narrator recoils from the inquiry: "I am unable to respond to that question, even if its rhetoric is innocuous, its answer obvious. I realize suddenly it is the *necessity* of asking the question itself that rankles me the most." Recognizing the desires behind the question, the narrator sells his story for a loaf of bread, thus foregrounding the commodification of racialized and transnational cultural narratives. Thus, Kaizad Gustad's literary and cinematic texts self-reflexively comment on their insertion into and location within larger global processes that produce postcolonial diasporas.

Jigna Desai

Further Reading

Desai, Jigna. "Bombay Boys and Girls: The Gender and Sexual Politics of Transnationality in the New Indian Cinema in English." *South Asian Popular Culture* 1.1 (April 2003): 45–61.

Grossman, Andrew. "The Boyz of Bollywood: Kaizad Gustad's *Bombay Boys*." 1 Dec. 2002 <http://www.brightlightsfilm.com/32/bombay boys1.html>.

Smith, Caroline. "Interview with Kaizad Gustad, Writer and Director." 16 Jan. 2001 <http://www.e.bell.ca/filmfest/98/exclusive/content/inter/gustad.htm>.

H

Half a Life by V. S. Naipaul

V. S. Naipaul, the acclaimed homeless cosmopolitan writer of high magnitude, is concerned with certain resonant themes as abandoning one's homeland in search of the lost self, locating oneself in a foreign land, longing for a sense of belonging, and nurturing an ineradicable feeling of dislocation. Naipaul's aspiration for an elusive world that would give him wholeness and purpose seems congenital. Naipaul was born in Trinidad but he is not happy about the spiritual and cultural poverty of the country. He is of Indian parentage yet he does not feel at home in India. He had his education in the Port of Spain and Oxford University; however, England with its colonial stigma fails to relate him to its values and give him a sense of identity.

"I will say I am the sum of my books," affirms Naipaul in his Nobel lecture. And it is not easy to rule out autobiographical elements in his works. In *Half a Life,* Naipaul reiterates the predicament of dislocation and reinvention of the self. The protagonist, Willie Chandran, is in a quest—right from seeking to know the connection behind his middle name "Somerset," to the physical abstinences of his father in comparison with his own sexual inadequacy. The novel comprises two stories; the first, where the deluded father tells his story to his son in the Indian background, and the second, where the son narrates his story in the backdrop of London and Portuguese Africa. Culturally, the protagonist lives a partial life among people of three countries, and accordingly, the novel is neatly divided into three parts, namely, "A Visit from Somerset Maugham," "The First Chapter," and "The Second Translation."

The life of the father, lived just by chances, and by lies perpetuated to resemble truths, is fraught with comic ironies. The father explains his life principle: "It sometimes happens that when you make a slip of the tongue you don't want to correct it. You try to pretend that what you said was what you meant. And then it often happens that you begin to see that there is some truth in your error" (4–5). Coming from a line of high-class Brahmin priests, he idles away in the university but uses Mahatma Gandhi's call to boycott universities as a cover to give up education. Later, in the name of abolishing caste hierarchy, he marries a "coarse-featured, almost tribal in appearance, noticeably black" (11) girl of low caste, though he despises her backwardness. Having triggered the ire of people of both castes, he finds a hideout in the temple and uses penance as his weapon. It is during one of those pretentious days that Somerset Maugham meets him and makes him the spiritual source of *The Razor's Edge.* Since Willie was conceived during this period, despite his father's vow of sexual abstinence, the novelist's name sticks to him.

Right from birth, Willie has the sense of half a life, due to the duality of his mixed inheritance. It spoils everything, whether going to school in India or attempting sexual encounters with females in England. Knowing fully that his hybrid existence cannot give him breathing space, especially in a country where caste is everything, and disenchanted with his earlier ambition of becoming a missionary by his education in a Mission School, Willie secures a scholarship and leaves for London.

In the late imperial Britain he hopes to live a full life, as the country liberates him from the old rules and holds of the Indian caste traditions: "he was free to present himself as he wished. He could, as it were, write his own revolution" (60). Willie busies himself in his remaking process. He joins the immigrant bohemian society of Nothing Hill, gets an opportunity to write radio pieces for the BBC; he boldly attempts sexual affairs with his friends' girlfriends, June and Perdita, though both find his performance culturally inhibited. Finally, he starts writing stories, partly imagined and faintly disguised plagiarisms from popular film and fictional scenarios. Scorned by a friendly critic, published still, Willie himself wishes that his book should fade away, as it is "artificial and false" (123). In order to escape humiliation and a rudderless life in London, he marries one of his fans, Ana, a guileless woman of mixed African descent, who finds in his stories moments of her past life, and he moves to her family estate in a large Portuguese colony on the east coast of Africa (Mozambique). He spends 18 years of his life in a "half-and-half world," during the last days of colonialism, with half-and-half friends, "people of the second rank" (160).

In Africa, Willie yields to his wild sexual impulses, with a hope to convert them into sexual prowess, by frequenting prostitutes, even without the knowledge of Ana, until he sees the little maid, Julio, lined up with the prostitutes. At that moment, he realizes he has "betrayed Ana, sullied her, as it were, in her own house" (191). Willie's sexual exploration does not end there; he strikes another passionate liaison with Graca, the new manager's wife. However, the change of the political scenario when the guerillas take over and an accidental slip from the front steps of Ana's decrepit plantation-home make Willie come to his senses. His sister, Sarojini, who is content with her international marriage with an elderly German photographer, Wolf, invites him to stay with them in West Berlin. Willie decides to lean on the strength of his sister and hopes to live another life this time.

Willie runs from one country to another to define and reinvent himself, yet wherever he goes, he is painfully reminded of the country that he came from. His outcast status remains unaltered, and he cannot fully participate in any of his lives—in India, in England, in Africa. The novel ends at the moment of his decision, in his forties, to leave Africa. Willie painfully admits that he had lived yet another life that was not his own. He regrets: "But now the best part of my life has gone, and I've done nothing" (228). Thus the novel literally covers only "half a life." Perhaps, as pointed out by Willie's friend Roger, "Life doesn't have a neat beginning and a tidy end. Life is always going on. You should begin in the middle and end in the middle, and it should all be there" (83).

While there are critics who find *Half a Life* one of the "truly outstanding works of literature, in the classical sense" (Moore 1) and praise the novelist's "sharp eye and limpid prose" (Kumar 3) and consider that the novel "confirms Naipaul's stature as the greatest living analyst of the colonial and post-colonial dilemma" (Wood 1), there are others who feel that *Half a Life* is just a distillation of Naipaul's familiar themes of exile and alienation, and hence is disappointing for "those expecting an epic tale full of social insight" (Golden 2). Yet as it has been rightly pointed out, "For the reader coming to Naipaul for the first time, *Half a Life* can be fresh and exciting, and it is representative of his ideas" (Sheridan 3).

Though *Half a Life* bears many resemblances to most of Naipaul's earlier works, particularly, *A House for Mr. Biswas* and *The Mimic Men,* what sets the novel apart from the rest is the vigor in which sex is used as a tool for reinvention of self. Where before, Naipaul assumes remarkable restraint in references to sex and thereby keeps it at the periphery, here, Willie's sexual exploits bring it to the center. Mindless sex, used as an escape from any emotional involvement, ironically, ends in an acceptance of it. And for those readers who grieved that Naipaul's earlier masterpieces are devoid of sexual intimacies, *Half a Life* is full of life!

T. Ravichandran

Further Reading

Golden, Renata. "Always the Outsider: 'Half a Life' is a distillation of V. S. Naipaul's dichotomies." <http://www.chron.com/cs/CDA/printstory. hts/ae/books/reviews/1140293>.

Kumar, Amitava. "The Critical Eye." Frontline 18:24, 24 Nov.–7 Dec. 2001. <http://www. flonnet.com/fl1824/18240740.htm>.

Moore, Auggie. Rev. *Half a Life,* by V. S. Naipaul. <http://largeprintreviews.com/halflife.html>.

Sheridan, Anne. "*Half a Life*: V. S. Naipaul." <http://www.culturevulture.net/Books2/Halfa Life.htm>.

Wood, James. "Saving Vidia: *Half a Life*—Review." *New Statesman* 1 Oct. 2001. <http://www. findarticles.com/cf_0/m0FQP/4557_130/790 29930/print.jhtml>.

Hamid, Mohsin

Mohsin Hamid was born in Lahore, Pakistan, in 1971 and went abroad for his university education. While attending Princeton, he participated in a fiction workshop with novelist Toni Morrison, and it was there that he began working on his first novel, *Moth Smoke*. After graduating, Hamid went to Harvard Law School, where he came in contact with Professor Richard Parker who taught a law and literature seminar. Every year, Parker supervises about a dozen students who submit works of fiction for their third-year papers. Hamid reworked the long fiction piece he began in Morrison's workshop under Parker's tutelage, emphasizing the courtroom aspects of the story. After receiving his Juris Doctorate in 1996, Hamid accepted a position with McKinsey and Company in New York City, where he worked as a management consultant.

While working at McKinsey and Company, Hamid revised his third year paper during lunch hours and on weekends. In 1998, a friend brought the manuscript to a literary agent, and the novel was published by Farrar, Strauss, and Giroux as *Moth Smoke* in 2000. Overseas rights have been sold, and publication in Hamid's native Pakistan is forthcoming. He has also published numerous articles in *The New York Times, Outlook India, Nerve.com, Dawn,* and *Time.* Many of his articles deal with the political situation in Pakistan, where "the state isn't delivering on its most basic responsibilities: infrastructure, security, education" ("Where Chaos Foils Ambition"). In writings such as "Mistrust in the West" and "The Usual Ally," Hamid cites the fluctuating relationship between the West (the United States in particular) and Pakistan as a major source of the latter's troubles. Hamid recalls one such policy shift after the Soviet withdrawal from Afghanistan:

> I went to college in America soon after the Soviets were defeated. Surprisingly, few Americans I met seemed to think of Pakistan as an ally. Fewer still knew where Pakistan was. After the war, America turned its back. Aid and military supplies were cut off. My friends back home were shocked by this. I, living in America, was less surprised. In America, the murky, unknown places of the world are blank screens: stories of evil

can be projected on them with as little difficulty as stories of good. ("The Usual Ally" 3)

This excerpt also illustrates another theme in Hamid's work: the anxieties of the emerging transnational professional class. Although a Pakistani citizen, Hamid works in the United States on an H-1B work visa. Many middle- and upper-class Pakistanis go abroad for their college education, and most return to work in banks or large international corporations. Hamid, however, is representative of a newly emerging international elite. In a *New York Times* article entitled "International Relations," Hamid recounts his experience in trying to obtain a travel visa to visit his girlfriend in Italy. In order to get the visa, Hamid would have to submit a copy of his Italian girlfriend's passport and a notarized letter. The article posits discrimination based not on race, as one would expect, but one based on nationality:

> Race has become too clumsy a shorthand for the legal boundaries that divide liberal democracies like the United States. Nationality, unless overcome by wealth, is a far more acceptable proxy. Nations deemed prone to poverty and violence are walled off to consume themselves, to fester. And national discrimination has taken its place alongside racial discrimination, denying both our common humanity and our unbelievably varied individuality as it frisks at the border. ("International Relations")

His debut novel *Moth Smoke* fictionalizes this transnational upper crust in the context of contemporary Pakistan. The novel is set amidst the back-and-forth nuclear testing between India and Pakistan in the summer of 1998. It follows, through various narrative voices, the decline and fall of Daru, a young Lahori banker who is fond of hashish and his best friend Ozi's wife, Mumtaz. After losing his job because he was disrespectful to an important client, Daru quickly descends into a world of adultery, drug dealing, and robbery. He is eventually framed by Ozi for vehicular homicide and convicted. The novel ends with Mumtaz, under her pen name of Zulfakir Manto, writing the *real* story of the accident.

Moth Smoke is a fast-paced debut novel that has received critical acclaim both in the United States and abroad. Because the novel is a recent publication, there is very little scholarly material published on it. Western reviewers are generally positive and tend to focus on Hamid's narrative technique and darkly evocative voice. South Asian critics have a more mixed reaction. They question Hamid's motives in publishing the narrative in a Western market. Samina Choonara claims that *Moth Smoke* "is an index to the ills besetting Pakistan, carved out for the overseas English speaking markets where Indian literature has carved out a niche for itself" (6). Despite Choonara's elision of India and Pakistan, the critique of Hamid is not hers alone. Singh Gill has leveled the same charges at Hamid, and wonders if "most Indo-Anglian [sic] writers write for themselves, or western readership?" (14). On the other hand, Umbereen Beg Mirza cites it as "without a doubt the best book I have read this year" (4).

Donovan S. Braud

Further Reading

Choonara, Samina. "Reviewing Mohsin Hamid." Matteela.com. <http://matteela.com/review.html>.

Gill, Himmat Singh. "The Classic Love Tragedy." *Tribune India.* 18 June 2000. 24 June 2002 <http://www.tribuneindia.com/2000/20000618/spectrum/books.htm#1>.

Hamid, Mohsin. Mystery Park Arts. Pakistani and South Asian Discussion Forum. 158.15 1 Oct. 2001. 24 June 2002 <http://mysteryparkarts.org/forums/Virsa_Forum/posts/44.html>.

———. "Where Chaos Foils Ambition." *New York Times.* 18 March 2000: A-15.

———. "International Relations." *New York Times.* 6 Aug. 2000: sec. 6 p. 66.

Mirza, Umbereen Beg. "Moth Smoke—Mohsin Hamid." *Visage* 9.33. 24 June 2002 <http://visagepk.com/archive/iss33_vol9/article4_bk review.html>.

Heat and Dust by Ruth Prawer Jhabvala, film by James Ivory

By the time the Merchant-Ivory-Jhabvala filmmaking team came to make *Heat and Dust,* it had already accumulated successes spanning almost 20 years (the first being the 1965 *Shakespeare Wallah*). Although in the interim the trio had in a sense relocated to upper-class Euro-American settings, until *The Bostonians* of 1984 the move seemed impermanent. Ironically, for a career that started in India, Ivory's films subsequently became synonymous with Europeanate historical grandeur: opulent in setting and populated with a richly costumed *haute bourgeoisie.*

One of the most striking features of Ivory's *Heat and Dust,* other than a *mise-en-scène* that at times picturesquely conveys the aridity of the title, is its fidelity to the complex narrational structure of Ruth Prawer's (she was later to drop her married last name) Booker Prize–winning novel. For while sequential juxtapositions of parallel storylines are not uncommon to the classical plot-subplot structures of Hollywood's films, alternations of events in separate time frames are indeed rather rare (D. W. Griffith's *Intolerance* of 1916 and the second of Coppola's *Godfather* films, made nearly 60 years later, in 1974, being famous examples). Less concerned with the moral underpinnings of history repeating itself as in those films, Prawer's novel treats the quasi-Zolaesque situation of a woman and her husband's granddaughter by his second wife suffering a remarkably similar fate, the difference of the outcomes in their stories being as much a matter of a changing of era as of individual personality.

For Ivory, plump advisors to Nawabs become thin, government officials become landlords, the seasons pass briskly, and opulence is concentrated in boudoirs and around dinner tables. Yet the film's essential textures remain faithful to their source, with even the first-person journal entries mirrored in the direct address of its protagonist-narrators. Indian-born Julie Christie, playing the descendent Anne, starts the viewers off on the journey of historical rediscovery, and the object of her curiosity, Olivia, thus summoned, faces the camera to initiate her own story. As in the novel, it is Olivia's tale that is much more interesting, for she succumbs to passion while Anne, one feels, succumbs to boredom and indirection. Or so at least Ivory would have it for his handsome Nawab (for whom the svelte Harry has fallen and not Olivia alone) is far more glamorous than poor Anne's simpering Inder Lal.

There is, however, a rather interesting insight that Ivory has drawn from the novel and amplified in his film: this is that while the European men scurrying about trying to be administrative spend a lot of time swathed in dust, it is their womenfolk who are constantly and fatefully in heat. Save for the Nawab who seems to change costumes with vivid effect in scene after scene, the men are as drab and colorless as their attire (even Harry, trying to escape him by taking refuge in the home of Olivia Rivers and her husband George, behaves strikingly like the abject Renfield character does with his master Dracula when the Nawab arrives to reclaim him). Even the simian Chad, a religious convert from the Midlands (Ivory converts him further to an American Midwesterner), is denied his priapic pleasures with the obliging Anne, who in the film brushes him aside and heads for browner pastures.

Moreover, Shashi Kapoor's Nawab, boyish and graceful, embodies more than a hint of sexual ambivalence, his amorous attentions to Olivia becoming something

A film still from the adaptation of Ruth Prawer Jhabvala's novel *Heat and Dust*. Courtesy of Photofest.

of a political gesture. This is never clearer than in the scene in which Olivia confesses her pregnancy and is horrified to discover that his transports of joy derive entirely from his certainty of the shock it would deliver to her husband. Nor is Greta Scacchi's Olivia quite the same independent, willful woman of the novel, who is used to being looked at and treated in a certain way, for here she appears to derive an almost masochistic delight in the Nawab's vigorous courtship (he, one imagines, may have been a connoisseur of the methods of his contemporary, Valentino). The moment of seduction occurs under a tree where she muses on the story told to his British guests at a dinner party, his voice serving as narration as he recounts with mordant relish an ancestor who nursed so powerful a grudge as to massacre the entire entourage of a rival despot. When the montage of ferocious stabbings ceases, she finds the Nawab standing over her and yields to his kiss. When they return to his royal apartments he seems somewhat uncertain about the intricacies of female undergarments, and she has quite literally to assist in her undoing.

Perhaps because of its brisk storytelling, the film was (and continues to be) well received by critics. Besides its provocative themes, which might well have set in motion the miscegeny-in-the-Raj cycle that presently overtook British film and television, its visual values were the finest of the Mechant-Ivory-Jhabvala partnership up to that time. If critics, overcome by the sights and sounds of India, missed something, it is Ivory's suggestive translation of his screenwriter's gender conflicts into gender ambiguities, finding contrasts between the female protagonists, for instance, where the novelist suggested convergence. Perhaps the subtlest, most purely cinematic evidence of this comes near the end of the film. After the denouement of Olivia's story, the pace of the intercutting between tales quickens until Anne finally finds herself in the mountains, at the very house provided for Olivia by the Nawab where she lived out her days. Peering through a glass windowpane, Anne hears the youthful Nawab's laughter as he raises a glass of tea to his lips, and when Olivia starts to play the piano behind him he continues to smile contentedly and to gaze outward, his eyes at one moment seeming to meet those of Anne whose reflection passes across both of them.

While Olivia radiates the elegant

beauty of a Renaissance portrait, her descendent has a countenance that though beautiful has much stronger lines, as if it is she who has lived through and suffered more. With the help of a passing man Anne then walks toward her intended destination, going, as her narration informs us, to the same mountain clinic where Olivia went to die, albeit in her case to give life.

Anthony R. Guneratne

Further Reading

Gooneratne, Yasmine. "Film into Fiction: The Influence of Ruth Prawer Jhabvala's Early Cinema Work upon Her Fiction." *Still the Frame Holds: Essays on Women Poets and Writers.* Eds. Sheila Roberts, and Yvonne Pacheco Tevis. San Bernardino: Borgo, 1993. 173–89.

Lenta, Margaret. "Narrators and Readers: 1902 and 1975." *ARIEL: A Review of International English Literature* 20:3 (July 1989): 19–36.

Muraleedharan, T. "Women/Migrants/Victims in the Male Empire: The Redeployment of Racist and Patriarchal Notions in Raj Cinema." *Critical Arts: A Journal of Cultural Studies* 10:2 (1996) 91–104.

Rodríguez, María Cristina. "Narrators in Narration in Fiction and Film: Ruth Prawer Jhabvala's *Heat and Dust.*" *Canadian Review of Comparative Literature/Revue Canadienne de Littérature Comparée* 23:3 (Sept. 1996): 803–08.

Roy, Parama. "Reading Communities and Culinary Communities: The Gastropoetics of the South Asian Diaspora." *Positions: East Asia Cultures Critique* 10:2 (Fall 2002): 471–502.

Hegemony

While the term *hegemony,* which originates from the Greek verb *hēgeisthai* (to lead), has been in use since the nineteenth century to denote political domination, especially the leadership or domination of one state over others, it was not until the rediscovery and rehabilitation in the 1970s and 1980s of Italian Marxist Antonio Gramsci's *Prison Notebooks* that hegemony became a widespread, popular, and influential concept much debated in contemporary critical and literary theory.

Moving beyond the strict economism of a Marxist approach to understanding the exercise of power in Western society, Gramsci sought, in the 1930s, to examine the ways in which the domination, or hegemony, of one class over others was achieved not only through economic might but also through a combination of political and ideological means. In his analysis of power relations, Gramsci, as critic Robert Bocock points out, rejects the deterministic Marxist notion that "assumes that once a change in the ownership of the main economic means of production, distribution and exchange has been accomplished there will be no major obstacles to a truly democratic, and free, society" (35). Such a shortsighted assumption, in Gramsci's estimation, fails to address the equally if not more significant ideological factors contributing to the establishment of class hegemony. The domination of the bourgeois middle classes, he asserts, owes less to the possession of state coercive power and more to the capability to convince others of the value and rectitude of the ideas and institutions of a capitalist vision. Writing during an era of extreme political unrest among the working class proletariat in Italy and across Europe, Gramsci concludes that the successful deposal of the capitalist regime depended upon the proletariat's enactment of a project of counterhegemony that would establish for the working classes an ideological authority to counteract that of the bourgeoisie. In other words, before attempting to challenge official state power the revolutionaries would have to secure, through the diligent work of Marxist intellectuals, popular moral approval, effectively winning over the masses to the merits of an anticapitalist worldview.

According to Gramsci's understanding then, the preponderant influence of one social class or group manifests itself in two ways: as " 'direct domination' or command exercised through the State and 'juridical' government" (12), and as " 'intellectual and moral leadership' " (57) exercised through the instruments of civil society, which include a broad range of educational, religious, political and associational institutions. It is through the various institutions of civil society, Gramsci claims, that the dominant social group initially wins the necessary " 'spontaneous' consent" (12) of the dominated masses by convincing them that the interests of the ruling class—the prevailing so-called norms—represent the interests of all. In this way, hegemony or leadership is subtly achieved by *consent* rather than force as the ideas and values that derive from religious doctrine, educational institutions, the law, the media, from political movements and so on, are employed by the dominant group to shape and direct the psychological, philosophical, intellectual and emotional thoughts and responses of those it wishes to govern (Bocock 35).

The idea of hegemony as rule by consent, as opposed to force, has become in the past three decades an essential analytic concept in the study of literature defined as *postcolonial,* and in the development of a body of theory pertaining to the experiences of colonization, decolonization, nationalization, and neocolonialism. This important component of Gramsci's theory of power relations has proved constructive in examining the dynamics of imperial conquest and the seemingly inexplicable "success of imperial power over a colonized people who may far outnumber any occupying military force" (Ashcroft, Griffiths, and Tiffin 116). The British colonization of the Indian subcontinent from the mid-1700s to the independence of India in 1947, during which time millions of Indian subjects were governed by a relatively small group of British colonial officials and administrators, serves as one example of the subjugation of a people through the hegemonic instruments of "intellectual and moral leadership." The success of the British imperial mission in India, as elsewhere, relied in large part upon the interpellation or "hailing" (Althusser 245) of

Indian individuals as subjects of the British Raj. As such, they were recruited, through the various institutions of a transplanted British civil society, as active members (though marginalized) of a hegemonic project designed to bring civility to a supposedly savage land. Illustrating the dynamic of hegemonic rule by consent, colonial official J. Farish hubristically concluded in 1938 that "The Natives must either be kept down by a sense of our power, or they must willingly submit from a conviction that we are more wise, more just, more humane, and more anxious to improve their condition than any other rulers they could have" (qtd. in Viswanathan 436).

In a landmark study of the conquest of India through words and ideas—a study that owes much to Gramsci's understanding of hegemonic activity—Gauri Viswanathan argues that one of the primary methods employed by colonial rulers in the garnering of consent from subaltern groups was the implementation, under the Charter Act of 1813, of a system of education based on the values and convictions of Western civilization and conveyed through the medium of English literature. As an instrument of sociopolitical control, English literature provided a nonthreatening, noncoercive means by which to disseminate among colonial subjects, as guiding principles, the treasured knowledge and beliefs of European civilization while concealing the less-than-benevolent aspects of the colonial initiative. As Viswanathan notes, "The introduction of English literature marks the effacement of a sordid history of colonialist expropriation, material exploitation, and class and race oppression behind European world dominance" (20).

The introduction of English studies in India and other former European colonies in the nineteenth century has had a profound and lasting impact that continues to fuel debate among contemporary scholars and writers as to the role of language and literature in the formation of nations and national identity. Critics continue to question whether English should be regarded, in the wake of the colonial experience, as a legitimately Indian language, or whether it remains a damaging vestige of European imperial hegemonic oppression. Are writers of South Asian origin including, among others, Salman Rushdie, Anita Desai, and Rohinton Mistry, who choose to write in English rather than their native tongues, pandering to Western literary tastes thereby undermining vernacular traditions and the vital work of the formation of national culture in formerly colonized countries?

Hegemony, or the consolidation of leadership through the transformation of the dominant group's ideology into common practices and beliefs, remains an important analytic concept in postcolonial and, more recently, globalization studies as scholars such as Edward Said, Homi Bhabha, Stuart Hall, and Ernesto Laclau strive to understand and articulate the manner in which nations, cultures, and peoples interact, exchange knowledge, and for better or for worse, negotiate power.

Dana Hansen

Further Reading

Althusser, Louis. "Ideology and Ideological State Apparatuses." *Critical Theory Since 1965.* Eds. H. Adams and L. Searle. Gainesville: Florida State UP, 1986. 238–50.

Ashcroft, Bill, Gareth Griffiths, and Helen Tiffin. *Key Concepts in Post-Colonial Studies.* New York: Routledge, 1998.

Bocock, Robert. *Hegemony.* Chichester: Ellis Horwood Limited, 1986.

Hoare, Quintin, and Geoffrey Nowell Smith, eds. *Selections from the Prison Notebooks of Antonio Gramsci.* New York: International Publishers, 1971.

Viswanathan, Gauri. "The Beginnings of English Literary Study in British India." *The Post-Colonial Studies Reader.* Eds. Bill Ashcroft, Gareth Griffiths, and Helen Tiffin. New York: Routledge, 1995. 431–37.

———. *Masks of Conquest: Literary Study and British Rule in India.* New York: Columbia UP, 1989.

Hosain, Attia

Attia Hosain was born on October 20, 1913, in Lucknow, India, into one of the oldest *taluqdar* (landowing) aristocratic Muslim families of Oudh. After her father died, when she was 11, her mother took charge of running the family estate. Raising the children under strict Muslim tradition, her mother ensured close ties to their roots with regular family visits to the ancestral village. The family observed the traditions at home of *purdah* (literally, curtain), the practice of women not appearing in public, and of living in the *zenana* (women's quarters). However, her family, like other privileged Indians exposed to British colonial culture, lived with both Eastern and Western cultures. Both her father and brother studied at Cambridge; Hosain had an English governess and attended the exclusive La Martiniere School for Girls and Isabella Thoburn College, in Lucknow. She also had lessons at home in Urdu, Persian, and Arabic, and had the distinction as the first taluqdar Muslim woman to graduate from college, in 1933.

In the 1930s, Hosain was inspired by India's national movement for independence and influenced by her friends and cousins who were returning from their studies in England as left-wing activists. She was attuned also to the Progressive Writers' Group in India, Marxist poets and writers, who spoke out against social injustice, advocating social change. In fact, she was at the first Progressive Writers' Conference in India, but did not, as she says, "actively enter politics as [she] was . . . tied and restricted in many ways by traditional bonds of duty to the family" (Desai xii).

Despite the fact that Hosain felt bound by duty to her family, seeing women come out of the privacy of their homes into public space to participate in India's national movement encouraged Hosain in her own quest for independence. She defied the traditional norm of an arranged marriage by choosing her own husband, Ali Bahadur Habibullah, a Cambridge graduate. After marriage, Hosain wrote stories and published articles in the Indian newspapers, the *Statesman* and the *Pioneer,* and worked as a broadcaster and journalist in India until 1947, the year she moved with her family to London where her husband was posted to the Indian High Commission. A broadcaster for the BBC, Hosain presented her own woman's program on its Eastern service, read news in Hindi, translated Shakespeare into Urdu and Hindi, appeared on television and the West End stage, in addition to giving lectures on the commingling of Indian and Western cultures. Both her son, Waris Hussein, and daughter, Shama Habibullah, were influenced by their mother's artistic abilities; both work in film, as film director and as film producer, respectively.

Growing up in a feudal home governed by patriarchal ideology, Hosain had become increasingly aware of gender and class oppression, which she voices in her collection of short stories *Phoenix Fled: and Other Stories* (1953) and her novel *Sunlight on a Broken Column* (1961). Set against India's political turmoil of independence and partition, both books deal with the fading aristocracy and the plight of servants, *purdah, izzat* (honor), and *sharam* (dishonor) and children. Revealing an underlying feminist and class-conscious ideology, Hosain explores the exploitation and oppression suffered by women, children, and servants in both the novel and the short stories.

Categorized as one of the first generation of diasporic writers who wrote in English after India's political independence, Hosain's uniqueness lies in the fact that she wrote the first novel in English about the taluqdar North Indian Muslim culture and society caught between tradition and modernity. In some ways, both India and England were part of her life even before she went to England: witness the fact that, on the one hand, she had read all the classics of English literature, especially the women writers, and was impressed by Virginia Woolf (Anand vi), and, on the other, she had read Urdu literature and was surrounded by a culture in which Urdu poetry was read and recited. She imported the cadences of Urdu poetry into her crisp, sensitive prose and translated into English the rhythms of Urdu metaphors. Her English schooling and Muslim cultural upbringing had exposed Hosain to both Indian and Western cultures, making her life a curious blend of both.

Her novel has been a source of inspiration for writers, among others, Vikram Seth, whose novel, *A Suitable Boy,* was set in Lucknow and who "visited many of the families that my mother chronicled in her books," remarks Hussein (Advani 1). *Sunlight on a Broken Column* centers on Laila, the orphaned daughter of a feudal family, brought up in her grandfather's home by two aunts. Depicting the ways in which the lives of women in a feudal Muslim family were circumscribed, confined to the *zenana,* the novel highlights Laila's personal and political concerns. Laila is caught between the desire to break free of traditional norms and her sense of duty, as a daughter, to uphold her family's honor and respect. *Sunlight on a Broken Column* echoes a diasporic writer's nostalgia for a lost world, with fond memories of Hosain's childhood and a feudal way of life with its old world charm; at the same time it confronts the suffering of servants, the stoic acceptance by women of their fate, and questions the cultural norms and myths that define women's roles and underlie constructs of women.

Attia Hosain died on January 25, 1998.

Hena Ahmad

Further Reading

Advani, Mira. "A Passage to India." 1–3. <http://www.the-week.com/98aug16/enter.htm>.

Anand, Mulk Raj. "Introduction." *Sunlight on a Broken Column.* Attia Hosain. New Delhi: Arnold-Heinemann, 1961. Introduction, 1979 edition.

Burton, Antoinette. *Dwelling in the Archive: Women Writing House, Home, and History in Late Colonial India.* New York: Oxford UP, 2003.

Desai, Anita. "Introduction." *Phoenix Fled: And Other Stories.* Attia Hosain. London: Virago, 1953. Introduction, 1988 edition.

Jain, Jasbir, and Raj Kumar Kaul. *Attia Hosain: A Diptych Volume.* Jaipur: Rawat, 2001.

Needham, Anuradha. "Multiple Forms of (National) Belonging: Attia Hosain's *Sunlight on a Broken Column.*" *Modern Fiction Studies* 39.1 (Winter 1993): 93–111.

Palkar, Sarla. "Beyond Purdah: *Sunlight on a Broken Column.*" *Margins of Erasure: Purdah in the Subcontinental Novel in English.* Eds. Jasbir Jain and Amina Amin. New Delhi: Sterling, 1995. 106–18.

A House for Mr. Biswas by V. S. Naipaul

The 2001 Nobel Prize citation lauds V. S. Naipaul for the "giant stride" that he took with *A House for Mr. Biswas,* hailing it as "one of those singular novels that seem to constitute their own complete universes, in this case a miniature India on the periphery of the British Empire, the scene of his father's circumscribed existence." Published in 1961, and critically applauded as one of the best novels written in the twentieth century, *A House for Mr. Biswas* opens a window to the vibrant complexity of the multicultural society of colonial Trinidad. Karl Miller describes it as "one of the few virtually perfect novels in our language" and the Modern Library places it among the top hundred novels of the century.

The novelist delves deep into the reservoir of his own personal childhood experiences for subject matter and theme, the protagonist Mr. Biswas being closely modeled on his journalist father, Seepersad Naipaul, who had similar writing aspirations. Naipaul himself avows: "Of all my books *A House for Mr. Biswas* is the one closest to me. It is the most personal, created out of what I saw and felt as a child." It is in the creative transformation of this intensely personal experience that he calls up the balancing quality of detached involvement that he treasures so much, to produce a work that is a commendable blend of autobiography, documentary and fictional narrative.

The story is about Mohun Biswas born, unfortunately, as the inauspicious six-fingered fourth child of a poor Brahmin laborer on a Trinidadian plantation. Losing his father early, an unnatural death by drowning for which he is unwittingly responsible, Biswas is forced to grow up as a poor dependent relation, living on the whimsical charity of a wealthy but extremely stingy uncle and aunt. Thus, with nothing going for him, he blunders through a largely irrelevant colonial education of learning the spelling of *oasis* (osis according to Biswas) and warbling alienating songs of the white masters ("in the snowy and the blowy" and "Bingen on the Rhein"). Thereon, he moves to becoming a lesser satellite in the totalitarian Tulsi universe, bullied into a loveless marriage with a giggly, spineless Tulsi daughter.

The tyrannical colonizing efforts of the Tulsis, one of the most powerful Hindu families of Trinidad, comes as a menacing clampdown on any aspirations to individuality, their efforts being to push him to the brink of emotional and psychological breakdown and annihilation. The Tulsis as a "microcosm of a slave society" (Satendra Nandan) represent the heavy odds that the hapless, utterly ordinary and buffoonish hero has to confront. The struggle to make something of his life, to build up an independent identity is epitomized in his "vision of the house" (494). The early enunciation of his aspirations, "I am going to get a job on my own. And I am going to get my own house too. I am finished with this" (64), and his dogged pursuance of this desire, transforms the house into a potent, directing romantic symbol.

In a land where success is measured by the money one makes and by the way corrupt practices and base *comprador* subservience to the colonial master are exploited to make this upward mobility a reality, Biswas seems to be a failure. His early efforts at constructing his own house are catastrophic because they are either built on Tulsi land or with Tulsi material. Most importantly, he has not yet forged a sound bond of kinship with the other five members of his immediate family: his wife, Shama, and his four children. It is only when this is achieved, that he can truly break away from the Tulsi stranglehold and buy his own house on Sikkim Street. Conned into buying this "jerry-built" ramshackle house by a swindling solicitor's clerk, this house may seem to be a limited achievement yet, for whatever it is worth, it is an accomplishment. It is, at once, a harsh comment on a dead-end island society that offers no opportunities, and a positive assertion of Biswas's success. It is left to the next generation, his son Anand, to truly break away and escape to a country with better openings, as Naipaul himself did in real life.

The tone of the narrative is primarily humorous, irony becoming the main literary tool, ably used by the novelist who himself believes this novel contains some of his funniest writing. Naipaul vigorously proclaims, "I have no higher literary ambition than to write a piece of comedy that might complement or match this early book." He emerges as a Dickensian caricaturist, deftly outlining and building up idiosyncratic and unforgettable characters in the service of satire aimed at a highly inimical social set-up. Yet, his sensitive, compassionate handling of an "Everyman's" tragic-comic struggle, raises this bildungsroman, which follows Biswas through the 46 hard years of his life, to the level of high humanistic literature. Moving from one thankless job to another (rum-shop worker, apprentice pundit, sign painter, shop owner, plantation overseer, finally a reporter for the *Sentinel)* and from one house to the other (the obliterated laborer shanty of his father, the back traces of his Aunt Tara, the single-room accommodations in the various Tulsi properties: Hanuman House, the Chase shop, the barracks in Green Vale, and the houses at Port of Spain and Shorthills, and finally to his own house), Biswas manages to garner the sympathetic attention of both his creator and the reader.

Displaying an exquisite command over the English language, Naipaul emerges as one of the best stylists in the language. His ability to write clearly and precisely about the futility and absurdity of human aspirations in the context of a derelict society makes *A House for Mr. Biswas* a creative offering that is universally acclaimed as the Nobel Laureate Naipaul's masterpiece.

Meenakshi Bharat

Further Reading

Hamner, Robert D., ed., *Critical Perspectives on V.S. Naipaul*. London: Heinemann, 1977.

Miller, Karl. Introduction to *A House for Mr. Biswas*. London: Everyman's Library, J. M. Dent, 1995.

Nandan, Satendra. "The Diasporic Consciousness." *Interrogating Postcolonialism: Theory, Text and Context*. Shimla: Indian Institute of Advanced Studies, 1996.

Panwar, Purabi, ed. *V. S. Naipaul: An Anthology of Recent Criticism*. Delhi: Pencraft International, 2003.

Swedish Academy, The Nobel Prize Citation 2001. 11 Oct. 2001.

I

Imperial Myth

The term *imperial myth* is most commonly employed in colonial discourse analysis to designate narratives that served the interests of modern European imperialism. These narratives justified economic exploitation, territorial ambitions, exercise of political and cultural hegemony, and the erasure of indigenous modes of social, political, and cultural production.

The term *myth* itself merits some consideration here. Roland Barthes has offered us a politically directed reading of myth, noting its power to determine social and political reality in his comment that myth is "depoliticized speech" (142). That is, as it is employed in the modern world, myth reconstitutes the historical into the conceptual, a process that involves the distortion of meaning. For Barthes, this process serves a political function, namely that of arresting historical process itself, in order that the concept at stake may dominate. Thus, for instance, the common image of imperial France he offers as example, of a black soldier giving the French salute, serves to naturalize French imperialism. The moment of naturalizing is the moment that marks the moment of myth itself: it is when the "myth exists" (130).

The European imperialist project is one in which British colonialism participates, both politically and philosophically. British imperialism in India is generally dated back to Robert Clive's victory at the Battle of Plassey in 1757. However, what is probably *the* imperial myth by which British colonialism in India is remembered is not as easily ascribed to a particular date. It is a myth made famous by Rudyard Kipling in a poem where he employs the term "the white man's burden" (136) to describe the civilizing mission of the West in its colonies. The paternalistic relationship imagined in the term and poem only marks the conclusion of a lengthy process that takes in sixteenth century travelogues, the historiography of G.W. F. Hegel, and the philological writings of the preeminent orientalist, William Jones. Equally, it informs Macaulay's 1835 Minute on India ("Indian Education"), James Mill's *History of British India* as well as the very popular oriental tales in circulation in eighteenth- and nineteenth-century Britain. In all of these works, we witness variations of a pattern of representation described at length in Edward Said's *Orientalism,* the Indian, as the "Orient" in general, is a savage, uncivilized other of the European cultured and civilized self. Problematic in itself, this representation is invariably accompanied by a statement of the moral burden this assumption of superiority placed on the latter: the uncivilized, it was argued, required the civilizing effort of the West.

The terms of engagement laid out in the phrase "white man's burden" serves to recast economic ambitions, arguably the prime motivation behind the drive to colonize, as ethical imperative. In the first instance, then, the phrase is employed to justify first the ambition to colonize and later colonialism itself, primarily for the "home" audience. The fact that these very terms are repeated—concretized as duty, self-sacrifice, benevolence and, above all, destiny—in colonial texts of different generations testifies to the less than secure sense of the legitimacy of the script itself.

While the civilizational imperative as inscribed in the phrase "the white man's burden" was meant to reassure the critical home audience, it was seemingly differently housed for the colonized, in a phrase: "we are your ma-bap" (literally "mother-father"). This phrase is, however, readable as a domestication of the trope of the white man's burden for the purposes of an audience presumed to be more familiar with the rhetoric of the familial. These related, and paternalistic myths—the white man's burden and mother-father—justify in the same terms and posit the same and benevolent end to colonial history: a *willing* relinquishing of the colony at some future date, when it arrives at maturity/civilization. Further, an application of Barthes' conclusion about the political intention of myth, a mode identifiable by its function of arresting historical process, leads to the conclusion that this myth naturalizes colonial occupation and erases the history of violence and conflict that informs colonial Indian history.

Of the social and political consequences of this imperial myth in both forms, probably the most critical has been in the area of education and hence culture. The civilizing mission, in India, took the form of a radical intervention in existing educational systems by the establishment of English curriculum and language as a medium of instruction. The year 1813 marks the beginning of the *education question* if you will. In this year, the Charter Act allotted 10,000 British pounds annually for the promotion of education for Indians. In the decades following, education was the subject of much debate with the Orientalists arguing in favor of education based in indigenous languages and subjects and the Anglicists arguing in favor of Western education. Macaulay's 1835 Minute settled the debate in favor of the latter. The argument that Macaulay invoked, not surprisingly, was the by then familiar one of the superiority of Western forms of knowledge, a superiority that made it an act of morality and responsibility to establish a Western curriculum in the colony. Given that the legitimacy of Western culture and its traditions and texts was beyond question (and we remember his famous pronouncement: "a single shelf of a good European library was worth the whole native literature of India and Arabia"), the only question that remained to be settled, according to him was: "Simply whether, when it is in our power to teach this language [English], we shall teach languages in which, by universal confession, there are no books on any subject which deserve to be compared to our own."

The other arguably equally critical area in which the civilizing mission had a critical impact was that of social practice and custom. One that has proved to be very popular in the colonial imagination is *thugee*. The term refers to a cult and its practice of ritual slaying as part of its worship of the goddess Kali. Although the cult and practice were eradicated during the governor-generalship of William Bentinck (1927–35), the image was recirculated and recycled in nineteenth- and twentieth-century imperialist literature as proof of the barbaric practices of oriental India (Chowdhry 133). Another area that merits consideration is where one best witnesses the paternalism so critical to the myth: the white man's task was that of "saving brown women from brown men" (Spivak 296). The place where this form of moral justification was most mobilized, as Lata Mani points out, is in the debate over sati sati (widow burning). References to this practice in numerous eighteenth- and nineteenth-century European imperial texts routinely act to legitimize arguments for colonization and introduction of Western social laws. Not surprisingly, this motif too appears in much Raj fiction well into the twentieth century (M. M. Kaye's *The Far Pavilions,* for instance).

There are, of course, other powerful imperial myths that form part of colonial South Asian history. These are recognizable also for their overall function of justification, but they indicate subtle shifts in emphasis, particularly in the narrative of justification itself. Two that merit mention are the myth of the "savage Hindoo and Muslim," that dominated in the post-Mutiny era for a while, and the myth of the "Great Game," that pervades late nineteenth- and early twentieth-century imperial literature respectively. The rebellion, now referred to as the First War of Independence, resulted in a radical shift in the reading of the colonized: from being mild and requiring education, the Indian (male) was now imagined as the violent and threatening other against whom the domestic economy had to be secured, using violence if necessary (Sharpe). Thus, the myth quickly turns into a justification of the violence of colonial rule. The myth of the great game belongs specifically to the era that also witnessed the British fear over a loss of the North-West Frontier Province to Russia. It not only offered the seductive rhetoric of adventure that led many to a career in the colony but reflected another shift in the narrative of justification: British India was essential as a bulwark against Russian ambitions in the area (Chowdhry).

Imperial myths as they manifest in all types of cultural texts identify culture itself as an important locale of imperialism. It is here that the rhetoric and narrative that enabled colonialism is given body, an issue that was necessary to gain the public support for colonial rule in the Indian subcontinent. It was critical, that is, to the manufacturing of consent.

Sukeshi Kamra

Further Reading

Barthes, Roland. "Myth Today." *Mythologies.* Trans. A. Lavers. New York: Noonday, 1972.

Chowdhry, Prem. *The Making of Empire Cinema.* New Delhi: Vistar, 2000.

Kipling, Rudyard. "The White Man's Burden." *A Choice of Kipling's Verse.* London: Faber and Faber, 1941. 136–37.

Mani, Lata. "Contentious Traditions: The Debate on Sati in Colonial India." *Recasting Women.* Eds. K. Sangari and S. Vaid. New Delhi: Kali for Women, 1989. 88–126.

Said, Edward. *Orientalism.* New York: Vintage, 1979.

Sharpe, Jenny. *Allegories of Empire: The Figure of Woman in the Colonial Text.* Minneapolis: U of Minnesota P, 1993.

Spivak, Gayatri. "Can the Subaltern Speak?" *Marxism and the Interpretation of Culture.* Eds. C. Nelson and L. Grossberg. Basingstoke: Macmillan, 1988. 271–313.

In Custody by Anita Desai, film by Ismail Merchant

During the glittering years Paris enjoyed in the 1920s, when it served at once as font of creativity and watering hole to the inspiration-parched *literati* of Europe and the Americas, one of its brightest denizens, F. Scott Fitzgerald, *bon vivant* and friend to all, had but one enemy: his wife Zelda. It is widely rumored that it was her passionate jealously and her own quasi-literary aspirations that led to the stifling of the writer's talent (in the years following *The Great Gatsby*) under tirades of withering criticism. In Anita Desai's masterpiece of subtle irony, Nur Shahjehanabadi, greatest of the living Urdu poets of chaotic, post-Independence India, faces at least twice as many problems as Fitzgerald, for he has two domineering, contentious wives. And unlike Fitzgerald's Gatsby, a creature of the light who flutters in a shimmering mansion, Nur spends his days in a world, which like the language of his poems, has contracted into shadow.

A film still from the adaptation of Anita Desai's novel *In Custody.* Courtesy of Photofest.

The sense of helpless claustrophobia that pervades the novel is captured elegantly in Ismail Merchant's film, the first fictional feature in which he stepped out of the role of producer for his long-time collaborator, James Ivory. There is no small *frisson,* in fact, in the recognition that the corpulent, Oblomovian figure of Nur, is that same lithe princeling, Shashi Kapoor, who scarcely more than a decade earlier had ravished the Botticellian Greta Scacchi in Ivory's adaptation of Ruth Prawer Jhabvala's *Heat and Dust.* Yet it is this later performance, full of world-weary self-loathing, that is by far the greater achievement—perhaps the finest of a great career, for nature seems to have intended him for it as Indian cinema's most public portrait of corrupted flesh. Nor are the baleful Om Puri, another of the great actors who played many a fine role in the New Indian Cinema of the 1970s and 1980s and its greatest female star, the predatory, golden-eyed Shabana Azmi, overmatched by Kapoor (although it is he who walked off with the major awards of India's film industry).

To some degree the roles, too, have shifted to accord with the personalities of the actors. In the novel, when Deven first encounters Nur, age has granted the latter a certain solidity, but he is not yet in helpless decline (whereas from the beginning Merchant's film transforms him into a beached whale). The political allegory of a condemned culture is more evident in the novel, where Nur's atelier has turned into a crumbling den of intrigue in the midst of a celebrated Delhi slum, while in the film he is marooned in a mazelike edifice in picturesque, tragic Bhopal. Merchant, the maker of masterly documentaries and in a sense Ivory's cinematic protégé, accomplishes these translations with the same consummate attention even to squalid detail that has made the richly textured *mise-en-scène* of *A Room with a View* and *Howard's End* justly famous. He has contrived also to grant the poet and the schoolteacher some moments of intimacy, whereas the novel has Nur perpetually surrounded by remora-like disciples, sponging off him while making no effort to conceal their detestation of the "Hindi-wallahs" ruling Delhi. The timid, hero-worshipping Deven, who in the novel scarcely notices that in his self-mockery Nur's face assumes a "mask of decay," no longer needs to conceal his sense of failure through harshness to a dowdy, nagging wife. Even the pigeons that in one of Merchant's more eloquent flights of fancy are torn from their roosts by the frustrated younger begum, are of a more lyrical sort than the rapacious, Hitchcockian creatures of Desai's novel.

In a talk given shortly after the release of the film (the text of which she has kindly sent me), Desai does more than merely approve of the changes. In translating her work into a screenplay she confesses that compression first took the form of "picking up an axe and . . . chopping off great chunks, reducing it to a stump." In "reassembling" it in another form, she discovered a "miraculous new way of writing . . . in sound and images." Further unanticipated changes were suggested by veteran actors long-versed in the arts of improvisation. Parikshit Sanhi insisted that his incarnation of Desai's "seedy Mr. Siddiqui" would never gamble with cards and instead ended a scene by dismissing his musicians and companions and playing a "wonderfully atmospheric riff on the *tabla.*" Unhappy with the "monochrome of her role as a neglected wife," Nina Gupta added to her part greatly, making Om Puri's transformation of Deven into a caring father all the more credible. Most transformed of all is the shrill harpie, Imtiaz Begum. According to Desai Azmi's feminist beliefs lent conviction to her final confrontation with Deven, thus turning a letter cast aside in the novel into the climax of the film. Even earlier, noting Nur's clandestine departures for his interviews by Deven, Imtiaz casts a look of such magnificently feline vindictiveness that the sudden interruption by the poets-in-waiting of the next interview seems quite explicable.

While Desai is satisfied that much of the charm of the film derives from moments of improvisation, not all are as felicitous. As she admits, the choice of the poetry of the great Faiz Ahmed Faiz for

the "dissolute Nur," though approved by surviving relatives, proved controversial. And rather slyly (although not unexpectedly for a novelist famed for the psychological depth of her female characters) she hints that the ambiguity as to whether Imtiaz is justified in her self-assessments, lost when Merchant has her steal her better poetry from Nur and invent verses only suited to a Bombay musical, was indeed important to balances of characterization.

Despite minor limitations, the film is an eloquent recreation of a justly celebrated novel, filled with memorable performances. That the influential film critic Leonard Maltin calls the film "nonsensical" is something of a compliment, as all non-Western films that for him attempt anything but simple storytelling are similarly nonsensical. In contrast, most European and American critics were quick to note its merits, but forgot it just as quickly. That a film that also won India's National Film Award is not numbered among Ismail Merchant's credits in Ephraim Katz's otherwise authoritative *Film Encyclopedia* is astonishing. It most assuredly deserves greater recognition.

Anthony R. Guneratne

Further Reading

Desai, Anita. "Ismail Merchant's Adaptation of *In Custody.*" Prepared talk, unpublished, 1995.

Kirpal, Viney. "An Image of India: A Study of Anita Desai's *In Custody.*" *ARIEL: A Review of International English Literature* 17:4 (Oct. 1986): 127–38.

Merchant, Ismail. "Britain's Foremost Maker of Indian Films, Reflects on a Subcontinent's Change as Seen through His Lens." Article by Merchant retitled and published in *New Statesman* (London, England: 1996) v. 126 (15 Aug. 1997) 29.

Panigrahi, Bipin B., and Viney Kirpal. "The Dangling Man: Deven in Anita Desai's *In Custody.*" *The New Indian Novel in English: A Study of the 1980s.* Ed. Viney Kirpal. New Delhi: Allied, 1990. 271–78.

Sen, Sharmila. "Urdu in Custody." *South Asian Review* 22 (2001): 57–70.

Indian Men Poets

Indian male poets who write in English are interesting as a category only in that they construct an India quite different from that of the Indian women poets. From Henry Louis Vivian Derozio's early nineteenth century call to Indian nationalism (decades before Indian nationalism would enter Indian languages), Indian-English poets have written the nation into their verse. Derozio (1809–31) whose sonnets "The Harp of India" and "To India—My Native Land" are still anthologized since they signal the birth of a nationalist consciousness in India, though paradoxically in the language of the colonizer and in the hands of a poet who is only a quarter Indian, his father being of mixed Portuguese and Indian descent and his mother English. It would not be an exaggeration to say that modern India came into being in the English poetry of Indian male poets of the nineteenth century and after. It would also be true to say that this poetry is rooted in and symptomatic of the phenomenon of cultural dislocation. The pioneering poets had to seek a language that would express their complex positioning within India, even as they followed the example of Anglo-Indian (i.e., British poets in India) poets who were catering to a market that hungered for the exotic East. Among the poets whose complex transactions with colonialism and Orientalism make for fascinating study of the construction of modern Indian consciousness, one must name the Bengal poets—Kashiprasad Ghose (1809–73); Michael Madhusudan Dutt (1824–73), who famously relinquished English for Bengali and achieved the lasting fame that he was seeking, fathering modern Bengali poetry with revolutions in form (introducing the sonnet and blank verse) and diction even as he continued with his search for the masculine technological Hindu; the Anglicized Dutt family, consisting of the brothers, Govin Chunder (1828–84, father of the famous Toru Dutt),

Hur Chunder (1831–1901), and Greece Chunder Dutt (1833–92), who along with their nephew, Omesh Chunder (1836–1912), brought out a collection of poems, *The Dutt Family Album* (1870); their cousin Shoshee Chunder (1825–86), a prolific writer of both poetry and prose; and the brothers, Manmohan (1869–1924) and Aurobindo Ghose (1872–1950), the latter being the famous seer Sri Aurobindo. Colonial Indian poetry moved to other centers as well—especially Madras and Bombay producing among others, A. M. Kunte, who published in Poona, B. M. Malabari (1853–1912) from Bombay, G. K. Chettur (1898–1936), who published in Mangalore, and the Goan poet Joseph Furtado, whose comic use of Indian words in English foreshadows the ways in which the language has been used in recent fiction.

While many of these poets have been dismissed as mere apprentice poets, their works and their lives are of great interest because of the new cultural mix from which they wrote. Bengal saw the earliest impact of colonization, and Bengalis took to the English language even before the English saw fit to impose it on the subcontinent. Calcutta was a multilingual multicultural metropolis already, and the English and the Indians (many of them new converts to Christianity) studied in the same schools and were thus trained in the same Orientalist framework. Thus, their transactions with the colonial language and culture is of great interest—their nationalist consciousness makes them part of the process of redefinition of Indianness and Hindu masculinity and valor, and they use their education and training, the colonizer's language and methods to delineate and claim their India(s). Their hunt for Hindu heroes from the past, heroes who fought the Muslim outsiders valiantly, collaborates with Orientalist historiography and archival research—for instance, borrowing from James Tod's *Annals and Antiquities of Rajast'han or the Central and*

Western Rajpoot States of India (1829). The Bengal poets thus collaborated in the construction of an authentic Hindu India, even if this was because of the displaced hostility engendered by colonialism (the Muslim raiders substituting for the British rulers). Manmohan Ghose is unique among the male poets because he did not publish from the margins but the center itself. Hailed as a leading talent of his generation by Oscar Wilde, Manmohan Ghose was a contemporary of Laurence Binyon and his poetry is truly English in that he was actively involved in the literary scene of London and Oxford at the beginning of his career, and his poetry written in India after his forced return in 1894 reads like poetry written in exile. However, his brother, Aurobindo, participated in the same nationalist program of the other Indian male poets, and reclaimed his Sanskrit heritage so well that after a short career as a revolutionary, he became famous around the world as a seer and a guru. Aurobindo's mystical poetry, of which the epic *Savitri* is a prime example, has become a convenient dividing point between what is seen often as two periods in Indian-English poetry—the colonial and post-Independence. Curiously, there is a great deal of mystical and religious poetry written in English during colonial times by Indian male poets, including Swami Vivekananda (1863–1902), which calls for investigation. Was this a logical extension of the Orientalist project, with the Indian men actively seeking and playing the role of the Eastern mystics, or was this the logical extension to the construction of identity necessitated by the disjunctions and displacements caused by colonialism as has been argued? In any case, colonial poetry by Indians is dismissed by many as insipid, imitative, Orientalist, and inauthentic. Thus, they see the true birth of Indian-English poetry taking place only after Indian Independence in 1947. Curiously, the first generation of post-Independence poets, too, seem to be involved in the same practices of definition of the nation, a nation that would accommodate their English-educated and writing selves in it, even if they are no longer seeking acceptance from the British or asserting equality with them.

Nissim Ezekiel (b. 1924), who is the Yudhishtra of the Mahabharata of post-Independence Indian-English poetry, setting its standards, devotes a major part of his poetry to playing the harp of the nation, constructing a modern urban India as a space for the Westernized Indian male who can from its anonymity assert his right to belong and to contest and critique other spaces and positions both inside and outside the nation. Ezekiel uses his Jewish descent to write himself a natural outsider-insider position in India, but asserts his sense of belonging. He is the poet of modern Bombay and modern India and to underline his right to this space, even tried his hand at translating Marathi poetry. This contestation of the nation plays a major role in the poetry of the first generation of post-Independence male poets. This is the generation that was under attack both by Hindi nationalists and regional language writers. Their cultural practices, their writings, and their very lives were seen as alien and unpatriotic. The India that had been born in English now wanted to manifest itself in other avatars, other languages. Many of the male poets thus saw themselves as having to defend their positions, even if they sympathized with some of the theoretical positions ranged against them. What was at stake was their very right to exist as poets. Hence while women poets had used the distance offered by English to explore their sexuality and explode their gendered worlds, the male poets were making desperate attempts to defend their nationalist turf. (Is this why women poets seem more at ease with the language, not only in control but also molding it into their own personal languages the way male poets do not seem to be able without a sense of defensiveness or the nudge of theory?) Nissim Ezekiel who played the role of a gentle patriarch and encouraged many poets, reading their works and commenting on them, identifying and nurturing talent, leads this defensive nationalistic pack, but R. Parthasarathy (b. 1934) has a whole corpus of poetry in English that is about the futility of writing in English and the frustration of his desire to write in his mother tongue Tamil, which has become unworthy of serious poetry! He is one of the major figures who participated in the frenetic anthologizing work that took place during the 1970s when Indian-English poets anthologized each other in collections titled *Indian* rather than *Indian English* poetry and the nation belonged to them. Parthasarathy was hugely influential because of his position as editor at Oxford University Press.

By now, it should be clear that even as this generation of poets asserted their rights to the English language and to India, they felt defensive about both, their tongue was in English chains and they could not articulate specific Indian cultural locations with ease. The male poets did not *chutnify* the language; when they did attempt Indian English it was only to achieve comic effects, not to evolve their own language. The sense of disjunction allows them to adopt ironic postures with ease, one of the hallmarks of modern poetry. The attempt of this generation of male poets is thus to evolve a personal theoretical position and poetic subject matter that would allow them to connect with their specific Indian language traditions, their literary pasts. A. K. Ramanujan (1929–95) is the most successful example of this trend, his poetry traversing the terrain between Tamil Sangam poetry and Anglo-American modernism, his Indian past and his American life. Even he does not attempt anything very much with the English language, using the language itself as a distancing device,

which would aid his ironic positioning. This allows him to put the lid on violent emotions and schism within, but his poetry on childhood has often been misread as poetry of nostalgia or of Hindu belonging. Jayanta Mahapatra (b. 1928) is the only one of the male poets of this generation, even though he began to write later, who seems to write in an Indian English, but he has been accused often enough of simply not having enough control over the language. Mahapatra is the poet of Cuttack, in Orissa, and his poetry charts the familiar course of belonging and not belonging but within a specific cultural and geographical location. He also differs from other modern Indian-English poets in that his poetry is highly emotive and full of personal symbolism. Mahapatra is Christian and this is what adds the poignancy to his poetry of loss. Keki N. Daruwalla (b. 1937) is the leading figure in Indian-English poetry today, and his poetry has always been an unapologetic part of the Indian environment. His other profession as a police officer seems to have kept his feet firmly on the ground, so he has always known where he stands—in the modern, complex and conflictual, wonderful and wonderfully corrupt India, where else? His may be existentialist poetry of skepticism, but he seems to assert his right to all his heritages more and more, from the Parsi to the Western literary. With great skill and control, he writes poetry that encompasses the world he knows. There are other notable poets—Adil Jussawalla (b. 1940), Saleem Peeradina (b. 1944), and Arvind Krishna Mehrotra (b. 1947) who follow soon after. Each of them has left a mark as anthologist while the first and the third are better-known poets in India. Mehrotra has an impressive corpus of poetry, and he for one demonstrates certain impatience with both the English literary tradition and Indian English modernism, having moved to French surrealism for inspiration because he could not get his English to bend

Agha Shahid Ali. © Fine Arts Work Center.

enough to convey his reality. On the other hand, Jussawalla uses his postcolonial predicament as subject matter for his poetry as most famously in *Missing Person*. Peeradina has always tried to be Ezekiel-like in his poetic concerns and techniques. His is a poetry that tries for equipoise that is imbued with an ethical consciousness.

There is an interesting group of poets who demonstrate their belonging in this cradle of multiculturalism by writing poetry in two languages—two of those prominent among them are Dilip Chitre (b. 1938) and Arun Kolatkar (b. 1932), who write in English as well as Marathi. Their creative bilingualism is worthy of study because the pressures exercised by the cultural environment and the language of their choice of the moment force their poetic landscapes into interesting shapes. It should be noted that Jayanta Mahapatra flirted with Oriya poetry late in his career but seems to have shifted back to English. Arun Kolatkar's *Jejuri,* which won the Commonwealth Award, is a book of poems that has defined the generation of urban, Westernized secular Indians with their religious skepticism, mainly because it is a Hindu's look at Hindu pilgrimage consumerism.

Plowing a different field in this generation is Dom Moraes (b. 1938), who like Manmohan Ghose, saw himself for a long time as an English poet. His poetry again belonged to the center and shows a similar difference from that of his contemporary Indian poets like Ghose too took part in the currents of literary change in England. As King says, "Moraes was the darling of England" is the 1950s and the mid-1960s. He too, like Ghose, shows "unusual mastery over the harmonies and rhythms of traditional English verse" (296). In India now for many years, he is still an outsider poet, at home only in his poetry.

It is with Agha Shahid Ali (1949–2001) that one gets a really fresh whiff of air, the sign of a new generation of poets. Here is poetry from a different axis altogether, poetry that does not argue for or establish belonging but that which arises confidently from the cultural mix that produces it. But this is also the poetry that is born in fragmentation and reaction—a world where cultures are dying and need to be celebrated to be kept alive, where the poet has to evolve his identity not in terms of national politics but in terms of subnational belonging or a transnational sense of literary and cultural heritage. Agha Shahid Ali's movement as a poet is from that of an urban Indian poet celebrating the traditions of Urdu poetry and singing to that of a diasporic Kashmiri poet addressing the loss of belonging. He can and does play with language and form, encouraging many poets to write the (Urdu) Ghazal in English. While his American sojourn saw him change his identity as a poet, it is interesting to see what role his homosexuality plays in his poetry. Another interesting writer is Vikram Seth (b. 1952), who has established himself as a novelist, but it is as a poet that I think his reputation will survive. One can see the ease with which the Indian-English writer moves in the transnational world of his writings. His poetry has come out of varied experiences in different parts of the world, and it is said often that it is only his name that identifies his poetry as Indian. Quite like Manmohan Ghose and Dom Moraes, Seth displays a mastery unsurpassed by native Anglo-American poets of his generation, evolving or reinventing forms and even genres (*The Golden Gate,* for example, a novel in verse with 14-line stanzas). Seth has written children's verse as well and is also open about his homosexuality in his poetry. There are two other poets who now write openly about the gay preferences— Hoshang Merchant (b. 1947) and R. Raj Rao (b. 1955). While Hoshang Merchant seems to revel in playing to the gallery, Raj Rao writes a highly emotive poetry, what has been termed by King as a mixture of "Swiftian satire and gay activism" (343).

A truly impressive poet is Manohar Shetty (b. 1953) who has evolved a personal style—his poetry is quiet and explores the world of the observed. Among the newer poets writing in Indian English, Bruce King identifies the following male poets—Ranjit Hoskote (b. 1969), Jeet Thayil (b. 1959), C. P. Surendran, Vijay Nambisan, R. Raj Rao, Bibhu Padhi (b. 1951), Tabish Khair, and G. J. V. Prasad. This is a varied crop of different ages. While the age of the Indian-English novel seems to have brought no greater visibility to Indian-English poetry, these poets do demonstrate that poetry still has a space and that it is reaching out in different directions. If the nation space is still a contested space, it is so not because the poets write in English but because the Indian nation was contested quite hotly in the last two decades of the twentieth century. Thus, the poets play their personal quests out in their poetry and the ease with which the younger poets show the language to be their own shows us a generation has come of age and dropped any defensiveness about using English. If Hoskote's poetry has an explosive quality and is perhaps demonstrative of his interests as an art critic

and of his readings in other Indian poetry, Bibhu Padhi writes a Mahapatra-like regional, small-town poetry, quiet and contemplative; Thayil and Surendran and Raj Rao write from an urban, cosmopolitan space. Thayil is positioning himself as more of an international poet, heir to the many traditions of cosmopolitanism, while Surendran is an exciting new voice who articulates the angst of living in contemporary times holding nothing sacred or immune to his attack. Tabish Khair, a diasporic poet now living in Denmark, writes the poetry of an intellectual, one who analyses and has a vision, but the poetry of one with not only the eye for the light and the ironic, but also a deft touch with the language. Along with Agha Shahid Ali, he is a major Muslim Indian poet in English, but like Ali, his poetry is that of the secular intellectual. Nambisan's poetry shows great skill and a distrust of emotional or linguistic excess. This is a poet who has published little but whose poetry is worth exploring. G. J. V. Prasad's poetry is seen by King to bring over "into poetry many of the ways of mapping and representing India found by such novelists as Rushdie and Seth." (352). His attempt is to write a more accessible poetry, an oral poetry that uses the conventions of light verse for serious themes. The poets of the last decades of the twentieth century have thrown into the dustbin of history the questions of authenticity of Indian-English poetry, and of the suitability of the language to represent Indian (even if individual) realities. If the pioneering male poets defined the nation and established their rights to the language, the first generation of post-Independence male poets defended the national turf even as they continued to refine the language without taking too many risks, while the next generation has more personal and political axes to grind, contests the making of the turf, and is more interested in cultivating individual flowerbeds, be they in different diasporic gardens altogether.

G. J. V. Prasad

Further Reading

Choudhuri, Rosinka. *Gentlemen Poets in Colonial Bengal: Emergent Nationalism and the Orientalist Project,* Calcutta: Seagull Books, 2002.

King, Bruce. *Modern Indian Poetry in English: Revised Edition,* New Delhi: Oxford UP, 2001.

Naik, M. K. *A History of Indian English Literature,* New Delhi: Sahitya Akademi, 1982.

Naik, M. K., and Shyamala A. Narayan. *Indian English Literature: 1980–2000 A Critical Survey.* New Delhi: Pencraft International, 2001.

Prasad, G. J. V. *Continuities in Indian English Poetry: Nation, Language, Form.* New Delhi: Pencraft International, 1999.

Indian Women Poets

While the number of Indians writing novels in the postcolonial period burgeoned beyond anyone's imagination, the ranks of poets have remained conspicuously tiny, probably on account of the age-old reason that poetry does not sell and cannot guarantee a ready market, either in India or abroad. Some of India's male poets writing in English made their mark globally under the tutelage of their mentor, Nissim Ezekiel, the best known and most widely acclaimed of that small minority. Women poets, on the other hand, are confined to a miniscule coterie and their works are little known outside their own country.

The fact that they are women becomes a necessary theme in the writings of most of these women—some to a greater degree than others. Kamala Das, Mamta Kalia, Imitiaz Dharker, and Eunice de Souza, for instance, are frankly feminist. Others, like Melanie Silgardo, Sujata Bhatt, and Smita Agarwal, eschew their own femininity, eluding only slightly to the fact of their gender in a curiously sexist society. Almost all of them have identity issues to confront and autobiographical references are found uniformly in their oeuvre.

Kamala Das is one of the most recognized and decorated of Indian poets writing in English. Born in 1934, she has published extensively in English and in her mother tongue, Malayalam, under the pseudonym Madhavikutty. The most senior of these poets whose works have been successfully published in India, she has a poem entitled "An Introduction," in which the "I" of the speaker is clearly the poet herself. She writes:

> I am Indian, very brown, born in
> Malabar, I speak three languages,
>   write in
> Two, dream in one. (de Souza, *Nine Indian Women Poets* 10)

Later in the same poem, she refers candidly to the English versus Malayalam tug-of-war that has frequently confronted her and justifies her reasons for choosing to write in English. Das's poetry is a vehicle for the exploration and exposure of her frustrated dreams and desires. As a mature woman, she looks back on her innocent youth, regretting the willingness with which she gave herself up to a callous lover who cared not that she "shrank pitifully" from his embraces and the roles that society forced her to assume. Fighting against the stereotypical duties of wife, mother, beast of burden, she "wore a shirt and my / Brother's trousers, cut my hair short and ignored / My womanliness" (de Souza, *Nine Indian Women Poets* 10). Still Das did not fit in. As she grew older, the anguish in her poetry became more menacingly self-destructive. Her images grew far more graphic. Consider, for instance, her poem entitled, "The Maggots," which depicts Krishna and Radha making love on the riverbank:

> Radha felt
> So dead that he asked, What is wrong,
> Do you mind my kisses, love? And she
>   said,

No, not at all, but thought, What is
It to the corpse if the maggots nip?
(de Souza, *Nine Indian Women
Poets* 13)

In the poem, Das uses familiar figures
from Hindu mythology to reflect upon her
own unsatisfactory sexual unions and the
endless frustration of attempting to find
compatibility with those through whom
she sought emotional and sexual intimacy.
In having humanized Radha's sexual dis-
satisfactions, Das makes human inability
to achieve conjugal fulfillment much more
easily understandable. Frequent references
to the lust of her own partner color Das's
perspective of him, such as in her poem
entitled, "Three P.M." Das has a keen eye
for the tiniest detail. Sensual imagery
abounds in references to the female body.
There are frequent allusions, for instance,
to "the musk of sweat between the
breasts," wombs, and "the warm shock of
menstrual blood" (de Souza, *Nine Indian
Women Poets* 15). She continually seeks a
way to satisfy her "endless female hungers" (de Souza, *Nine Indian Women Poets*
15). Poetry becomes the agency through
which she gives voice to her anxiety: for
instance, in "The Looking-Glass," she renders reflections of images from her own
unhappy past.

Since the publication of her autobiography in 1976 entitled *My Story,* critics
and readers have attempted to find parallels between the characters in her poems
and the real-life individuals who made up
the bulk of her emotional experience.
While this is always a dangerous exercise,
it is clear that Das, like most Indian
women poets, only thinly disguises her
own personae in her writings, so that it is
fair to say that the poetic experience is
very likely her own.

What Das did succeed in doing
through her poetry was opening the path-
ways for other Indian women poets to become openly confessional, in the tradition

of such female stalwarts as Anne Sexton
and Sylvia Plath. Eunice de Souza states,
"she mapped out the terrain for postcolonial women in social and linguistic
terms. Whatever her vernacular oddities,
she has spared us the colonial cringe"
(*Nine Indian Women Poets* 8). The "vernacular oddities" that de Souza refers to
here concern the notorious tendency that
Das had to leave off the definite article,
perhaps a result of her mother-tongue in-
terference. In her book, *The Endless Female Hungers,* critic Vrinda Nabar took
objection to this cavalier attitude toward
grammar, and Das was taken to task for
ignoring the purists. However, it is this defiance of grammatical correctness, this
tendency to allow Malayalam to color the
idiomatic quality of her lines that gives the
poems their peculiarly distinctive essence
and allows her to claim them uniquely as
her own.

Always known for courting controversy, Das has turned to politics in recent
years, seeking a seat in parliament, which
has, so far, eluded her. Her conversion to
Islam in 1999 resulted in a change of
name. She is now known as Kamala Su-
rayya. She received the P.E.N. Prize in
1964, the Kerala Sahitya Akademi Award
for fiction in 1969, the Chaman Lal award
for journalism in 1971, the Asian World
Prize for literature in 1985, and the Indira
Priyadarshini Vrikshamitra Award in
1988.

Eunice de Souza, born in 1940, herself
a critic as well as a poet and an anthologist
(she edited a collection called *Nine Indian
Women Poets* in 1997), has made her ethnicity a major theme in her writings. Her
first book, *Fix,* published in 1979, underscored her struggle to find a way by which
she could perceptibly belong to the mainstream—whatever that means—in cosmopolitan Bombay, where she has lived for
most of her adult life. In her poem "De
Souza Prabhu" *(Fix),* the speaker of the
poem states that regardless of the fact that

her name is Greek, surname Portuguese, and language alien, "There are ways / Of belonging" (de Souza, *Selected and New Poems* 17).

It is clear that de Souza, like most other contemporary poets of Goan origin, still finds it difficult to deal with the multicultural aspects of her being. At least until the late 1970s, these poets, who were Roman Catholic by religious upbringing and Bombay-based by geographical location (among others Santan Rodrigues, Melanie Silgardo, Raul de Gama Rose), were still struggling to come to terms with what they looked upon as the incongruous elements of their heritage (Portuguese Goan Roman Catholics based in Bombay). De Souza's poems frequently bear reference to her Goan roots. She is aware that de Souza Prabhu, the subject of her poem, is making valiant attempts to choose a last name that will placate both segments of the Goan population—those nostalgic people who harbor fond memories of Portuguese colonial rule and still express loyalty toward their erstwhile masters, and the contemporary nationalists who wish to erase all remnants of Goa's imperial past.

Departing from the poetic conventions of their Goan Catholic predecessors who spoke nostalgically of Goa's swaying palms, idyllic sunsets on unspoiled beaches, and the fragrant red earth of post-monsoon evenings, de Souza and her former student Melanie Silgardo confront issues that reportedly offended the sensibilities of their own ethnic group. One does not find picturesque descriptions or quaint vignettes of Goan village life in their poetry as one did in the poetry of their Goan predecessors. Instead, they deal with their own personal dilemmas and the paradoxes that remain unresolved. Because both of them are of Goan Roman Catholic heritage, their background becomes an intrinsic part of their work and tints their perceptions. Indeed, in poem after poem, they refer to their "Goanness"—

the customs and traditions (particularly mortuary ones), social mores, upbringing, and inherited lifestyle—and they repeatedly express their discomfort with and anger at it. Yet, much as they would like to merge with the mainstream and indeed alienate themselves from what they perceive as the hypocrisy, dogma, fetters of convention and tradition that accompany their Catholic upbringing, and the ludicrous habits, lack of intellectualism, and banal behavior of the Goan community, these continue to intrude upon their world. Much as they may resent this phenomenon and wish to deny it, this Goanness ironically also presents them with some of the most original and interesting motifs of their poetry.

Take, for instance, 1956-born Melanie Silgardo's poem "Goan Death" *(Three Poets)* in which she grimly recalls her father's funeral. As he lay "encoffined. / Cotton stuffed in nostrils / ice below" (Silgardo, 19), her glance falls on her relatives. She writes:

. . . vultures clustered round
in lace and satin blacks,
weeping salt,
. . . .
mumbling incoherent prayers . . . (19)

They misjudge her mother who "wept no salt-corrosive." Silgardo's brilliant image of relatives hovering around the casket, like vultures, "picking entrails neatly" stands out for its originality and the predatory connotations it conveys. Were it not for the fact that she is a Goan Catholic, Bombay-born, and U.K.-settled since 1985, accustomed to images of black-clad women mourners reciting rosaries around coffins, she would have been deprived of one of the finest images in her poetry. The same Goan Catholic symbols and metaphors provide her poem "Sequel to Goan Death" *(Three Poets)* with equally meaningful religious allusions. Silgardo bends over to kiss her father's face that is "cold as the marble church / across the road." She concludes that "This death is a Christian duty, / slipping into eternity with the final prayer" (20).

In her introduction to Silgardo's poems in her anthology *Nine Indian Women Poets,* de Souza states that "Though Melanie Silgardo started writing . . . poems . . . when she was an undergraduate, there is nothing of the apprentice in any of them" (27). It is difficult to disagree with her. Silgardo has such a firm grip on the craftsmanship of poetry, such a confidence with which she inserts image and symbol into her lines, such an unfailing ear for the subtlety of nuance that her poems, while being deeply thought provoking, are entirely a pleasure to read or indeed to listen to. This ability only grew as she honed her skills. In later poems, such as "Cat" and "Bird Broken" *(Skies of Design)* in which she focuses more on impersonal themes, she continued to display her enormous creative talents.

Images of graves, epitaphs, crucifixes, coffins, gravel, and so on, echo through these poems, easily providing the reader with thematic unity. In de Souza's poem "My Grandfather's Death" *(Selected and New Poems),* for instance, she recalls the burial of her grandfather and provides abundant pen-pictures of the Catholic solemnity of such an occasion. Mercifully, de Souza does not perceive her relatives as carrion birds of prey and is thankful that the gravediggers allowed her to grieve alone.

De Souza's poems are clever, intellectual exercises in which her tone is always intolerant, caustic and unflinchingly critical of the shortcomings of her community. One rarely finds in them, however, the succinct metaphor, the memorable image that would raise her observations and reflections to the level of great poetry. She is not the only Indian writer to have exposed the idiosyncrasies of her own ethnic minority. Nissim Ezekiel, for instance, has done so

memorably of Bombay's Jews in his poems (as has Rohinton Mistry of Bombay's Zoroastrians in his novels). But while Ezekiel and Mistry use the lightest of touches and an abundance of humor to soften the eccentric portrayals, de Souza is merciless in her critique, clearly not given to suffering fools gladly.

Though she might be a lapsed Catholic, one finds frequent images of Catholicism in this poetry. She is never reluctant about expressing her distance from and the distaste she feels at such a pervasive presence in her life. Thus, her discomfort with the icons of her religion is made a frequent subject of her poetry. Furthermore, she expresses deep hurt at the humiliations she suffered at the hands of diverse Catholic nuns and priests while still a child. In one of her more recent poems entitled "Eunice" *(Selected and New Poems),* she remembers "Embroidery Sister" who ridiculed her during her needlework class for "seams that are worthy of an elephant" (29). De Souza dismisses her venomously as a "Silly bra-less bitch" (29). In an earlier poem, "Sweet Sixteen" *(Selected and New Poems),* she wrote about a nun who screamed, "You vulgar girl / don't say brassieres / say bracelets" (5), and who "pinned paper sleeves / onto our sleeveless dresses" (5). In the same poems, she recalls with much bitterness the preacher who thundered: "Never go with a man alone / Never alone / And even if you're engaged / only passionless kisses" (5). In "The Road," she recalls that she "clutched Sister Flora's skirt / and cried for my mother / who taught across the road" (36). The Catholic clergy are not well regarded by de Souza who apparently was at the receiving end of a great deal of moral stricture from them, but who ironically enough, spent the bulk of her professional life as a lecturer in English in a Jesuit Catholic college, an environment which, by all reports, nurtured such creative talents in its students and faculty and encouraged such candid self-expression. Her growing years seem to have been punctuated by a heavy sense of loss, frequent separation from loved ones, and a form of education that regarded female sexuality as dirty. Her surrogate caregivers, the Catholic clergy, failed to satisfy her childhood and adolescent needs for affection. In her adult years, de Souza attacked their callousness with a vengeance. Breaking the fetters of propriety that rendered them sacrosanct and suppressed the expression of any resentment against them, she hits out fearlessly, sparing no insult.

De Souza also expresses the same anger, this time indulging in sarcasm as well, when she describes the procedure that some Goan Catholics adopt when trying to find a suitable husband for their kith and kin. The speaker who tells the reader about her cousin, Elena, in de Souza's poem, "Marriages Are Made" *(Selected Poems),* cringes from the customary practice of examining family histories for "T.B. and madness" (4), after Elena has had "her eyes examined for squints / her teeth for cavities / her stools for the possible / non-Brahmin worm" (4). Though these cultural caricatures might be exaggerated, the poet does not spare any thrusts. Her attack is vicious and the effect is powerful as she holds up a mirror to the practice of traditional arranged marriage.

It is not just death or Catholicism that provides de Souza with uniquely ethnic and cultural images. The pervasive culture, the joy of life expressed by other Goan Catholics, for some odd reason, also seems to evoke in her the same sense of outrage and nonbelonging, of standing on the periphery as an outsider, looking upon the scene with disdain, unable to identify with it. Nor does she want to. Indeed, there is profound cynicism with which she beholds this scenario. Clearly, her intellect has alienated her from fellow members of her own ethnic minority, and one cannot mistake the superciliousness with which she

comments on the antics of this group. The best example of this poem occurs in her "Bandra Christian Party" *(Selected Poems):*

> The gathered goans giggle.
> Dirty jokes:
> Hot stuff and sex.
> .   .   .   .
> now the party'll go men go
> says Fred (7)

De Souza approximates the typical linguistic idiom of this group—Goan Catholics from Bombay, or more particularly, Bandra, as her title indicates—and while she attempts to present verisimilitude in their speech, she yet manages to convey, by their use of language, that she considers them somewhat inferior to herself and to the mainstream because they belong to a subculture of which she can never be a part. The poem continues:

> Fred is the life of the party.
> Come on men Fred Give us
> A song calls Mabel. (7)

What de Souza seems to rebel against, through this poem, is the distilled Goanness of Dominic, Fred, Mabel, and Hetty—the result of the dilution of their native Goan culture with Bombay's cosmopolitan spirit. These poems have been described by Keith Fernandes as "funny, yes, but blackly so" (Fernandes, x). In fact, they are examples of scathing satire against Bombay's Goans whose love of partying, drinking, singing, and laughing is being criticized. Clearly, the reporter is uncomfortable within this *milieu.* Irish writers have chosen to depict a similar fondness for the bottle, devotion to music and song, dance and high jinks that characterize the vital social life of European Roman Catholics. But while they look upon this *joie de vivre* with a sense of national and communal indulgence and celebrate it in their literature, de Souza finds it offensive and satirizes it in her work.

The same superciliousness character-izes her poem "Conversation Piece" *(Se-lected Poems)* in which the speaker writes of her "Portuguese-bred aunt," who picked up a clay *shivalingam* and asked the sales-man if it was an ashtray. She was obviously nonplussed when the man responded: "No . . . this is our god" (9). De Souza leaves a great deal unsaid in this poem, but the implications are enormous. The aunt's ignorance of Hinduism, a result of her immersion in Western, for example, Por-tuguese culture, and her stubborn alle-giance to it, alienates her from the culture of the Indian, for example, Hindu, main-stream. Through the character of the aunt, de Souza implies that it is time Goan Cath-olics shed the vestiges of their colonial roots and immerse themselves in the cul-tural mainstream.

Autobiographical innuendo, while tempting the reader to arrive at obvious conclusions about the poet's own life, must be ignored because such conclusions might not always be sound. The exception to this rule is the odd poem that is clearly entitled "Autobiography" or, as in the case of Kamala Das, "An Introduction." How-ever, one might generalize and state that family affiliations play a major role in this body of poetry, as indeed they do in most Goan Catholic homes. These poets deal with family feuds, the inability to com-municate with one another and the emo-tional chasms that result, with brutal honesty—in total disregard of the social taboo that prevails in most such homes against the notion of airing dirty family laundry in public.

Both Silgardo and de Souza write *con-fessional* poems that deal with the enor-mous burden on their psyche of the unfinished business of trying to bury their past with their dead. Silgardo is successful in doing so, but de Souza still seeks rec-onciliation. Indeed, Silgardo is more sym-pathetic toward her father in her poem, "For Father on the Shelf" *(Three Poets)*, but then, her perceptions are tinged with nostalgia because he is no longer alive and it is difficult to think poorly of the dead. She refers to his love of fishing, smoking and drinking—stereotypical facets of Goan Catholic males, portrayals that re-mind one very much of the protagonists in most of the short stories of Raymond Carver—but there is little rancor in her portrait. She seeks his forgiveness, though a little too late, for calling him "cad" and "bastard," "fifty times inside," maturity and loss softening her impressions of him. But Silgardo has suffered through her re-jection of her father for she expresses her anguished pain: "You never knew I wet my pillow / oftener than I had ever wet my bed" (de Souza, *Nine Indian Women Poets* 32). She tries, in her later years, to rec-oncile his failings with the things that she is happy to have inherited from him:

> Father, you will be proud to know
> You left something behind.
> The year you died
> I inherited a mind. (31)

Finally, she acknowledges that though he was unable to meet her emotional needs for intimacy and affection, he was "both villain and hero of the piece" (32) because her deprived childhood made her an intel-lectual soul doomed to question and probe the void left by his abandonment of her through his death.

De Souza feels no such sympathy to-ward her mother. While she begs forgive-ness in "Forgive Me, Mother" *(Selected and New Poems)* for having left her "a life-long widow / old, alone" (16), she admits candidly, "In dreams / I hack you" (16). Yet, in a later poem "She and I" *(Selected and New Poems)*, she muses "Perhaps he never died / We've mourned him sepa-rately / in silence / she and I" (28). Clearly estranged because they have been unable to articulate the loss they have separately felt—of husband and father respectively—not even a common grief enables de Souza to bond with her aged mother, nor, through her poetic imagination with her long-dead father. De Souza lost her father when she was three, and in the manner of Sylvia Plath writes a number of poems in which she seeks to *find* this man that she cannot remember. Regardless of the social scandal that will inevitably ensue as a result of their "airing their crotches" in this manner, as de Souza puts it in her poem "My Students" *(Selected and New Poems),* these poets expose the ones closest to them with candor and truthfulness. Keith Fernandes refers to Philip Larkin's line "They fuck you up, your mum and dad," when he points to the ambivalent emotions these poets feel in relation to their parents—"on the one hand the more acceptable emotions of caring and regret, and on the other, anger because of the maiming harm that they inflict" (Fernandes).

In her later poems, de Souza turns away both from her endless communal and deeply personal psychological scrutiny so that her sweep is broader. In "Outside Jaisalmer" *(Selected and New Poems),* she presents images of a medieval desert city that are never simply picturesque or touristy. In "Landscape" *(Selected and New Poems),* she comments on the flotsam and jetsam that make up "the stretch marks of the city" (53). In these poems, she reveals the artist's eye for the memorable image and manages to convey these with a delightful elegance.

Imtiaz Dharker's ethnicity is also a frequent subject of her poems but she is far less strident about it than are de Souza and Silgardo. Born into a Muslim family in Lahore, Pakistan, in 1954, she was raised and educated in Britain, and upon marriage to an Indian Maharashtrian Hindu, has lived in Bombay for the past three decades. Her first book of poetry, *Purdah,* was published in 1989, while her second, *Postcards*

from God, came out in 1994. An artist, an illustrator, and a documentary filmmaker, her creative talents have been revealed through a variety of media, in all of which she has proclaimed her distinctive multicultural and multiethnic voice. In fact, the publication of *Purdah* was accompanied in India by an exhibition of drawings and paintings that confronted the same theme—that of the suppression of women by societal forces. As de Souza puts it in her introduction to Dharker's poems, Purdah is seen "not just as concealing garment but as state of mind" (*Nine Indian Women Poets* 48).

Dharker herself defines *Purdah,* one of the most Islamic of female images, in these terms: as "a kind of safety." The poet's compassion for the women who are concealed within this shroud and unable to bare their thoughts, knows no bounds. Realizing that but for her own fortunate circumstances she might have been one of this suppressed lot, she feels for them and understands that this same symbol of oppression is also embraced by these women as a safety device, through which their own outrage against societal strictures is concealed. There is no attempt to tear apart the social hypocrisy that renders these women mute; rather there is an attempt to reach out and empathize with their suffering.

In "Battle-line" *(Purdah)*, a brilliant poem in which images of lovers on a sheet-strewn bed coalesce with soldiers' remains strewn carelessly on a battlefield, Dharker's compassion resurfaces once again. For her "the body becomes a territory / shifting across uneasy sheets" (de Souza, *Nine Indian Women Poets* 51). She goes on to say, "It's the same with lovers / after the battle-lines are drawn: / combatants thrown / into something they have not / had time to understand" (51).

Her Islamic heritage is reflected similarly in the poem entitled "8 January 1993" *(Postcards from God)* when Bombay burned following the riots that plagued the country in the aftermath of the assault upon the Babri Masjid when Muslims were hunted out like rats by Hindu fanatics. Vividly, the lens of her poetic eye captures what Wilfrid Owen would have described as "the pity of war"—albeit a communal one.

> The bolt bangs in.
> A match is struck and thrown.
> The burning has begun.
> Afterwards
> The bodies are removed
> One by one. (de Souza, *Nine Indian Women Poets* 56)

In this poem, Dharker has underlined the precariousness of the lives of Indian Muslims in a country that has turned savagely communal. In the light of the more virulently anti-Muslim climate that has characterized India following the massacre at Godhra, this poem acquires even more sinister overtones. Nowhere does Dharker's tone become sarcastic nor does she strike a pose of superiority in which she disassociates herself from such narrow mindedness. On the contrary, by implication, she includes herself among this haunted, hunted minority. "The List" *(Postcards from God)* is equally ruthless in emphasizing the manner in which Muslims were singled out for cruel treatment by their own Hindu neighbors. She comments: "This must be how war feels: / When ordinary things lose / their sense of gravity" (57). The purdah image continues to be exploited in her lines: "Your name is there/ It settles on you like a shroud" (57). This is religious poetry of a very striking and deeply poignant kind.

In like manner, her poem "Minority" *(Postcards from God)* is autobiographical in the same vein as Das's "An Introduction" and Silgardo's "1956–1976 A Poem" *(Three Poets)* She writes:

> I was born a foreigner.
> I carried on from there

> To become a foreigner everywhere
> .   .   .   .
> I don't fit,
> Like a clumsily-translated poem; (58)

Dharker makes it clear in such poems that she will continually confront identity issues and remain marginalized by them. Her religion and ethnicity provide her with a variety of metaphors that she continually exploits to startling effect in her poems. Your typical *nowhere* man, she is, ultimately, a citizen of the world though never completely at home anywhere in it.

Mamta Kalia, born in 1940, has also made significant contributions to the body of Indian women's poetry in English. Her poem "Tribute to Papa" (from a collection of the same name that came out in 1970) underlines, but does not attack the father in the poem for his stereotypical ambitions for his daughter. Kalia is cross at her father for toeing the bureaucratic line and, therefore, always remaining "an unsuccessful man." She does not disdain him who "always lived a life of limited dreams" because it is clear that he had ambitions that he would attain vicariously through his daughter's success. The speaker's love for her father is acute enough to recognize this, and though as an adult she informs him that "These days I am seriously thinking of / disowning you, Papa, / You and your sacredness" (de Souza, *Nine Indian Women Poets,* 20), the reader is aware that she is too fond of this man, too devoted to him to do anything that will crush him. Hence, she will live her life in accordance with his notions of bourgeois respectability and middle-class morality. Kalia evokes the reader's sympathy for this upright conception of human decency. In fact, the reader's sympathy is drawn both by the image of this ordinary Indian father who wants nothing but the best for his daughter, and her own helplessness at being unable to conform to the image of the daughter that he wished to have created.

Both characters in this poem are losers and, therefore, the reader's sympathy is evoked.

In "Sheer Good Luck" *(Tribute to Papa),* she writes an autobiographical poem in which she talks about all the misfortunes that could have been her fate like that of many uneducated women in India's male-dominated society. Instead, she celebrates the fact of her ordinariness, saying that:

> . . . nothing ever happened to me
> Except two children
> And two miscarriages. (21)

Ideas of rape, abandonment, illiteracy, and violence of all kinds against women frequently appear in Kalia's poems. While she feels fortunate to have escaped the kind of fate that she knows has been the lot of scores of Indian women, she is aware also of the compromises many Indian women have made in their positions as daughter, wife and mother. Like Das, she writes of unhappy marriages and the frustration of putting up a facade instead of facing up to her own endless female hungers. In "After Eight Years of Marriage," she talks about the complacency with which parents expect a daughter to be happy for they focus only on her "two sons / Hopping around like young goats" (25). The fact that the woman has given birth to two healthy sons automatically proclaims the fact of her conjugal bliss. Because they find pride and happiness in the fact of her motherhood, they assume that she has done so too. The fact that she has sublimated her own desires, hopes, dreams, and ambitions for the greater good of her family would seem to them to be the most normal, most laudable thing to do—the ultimate sacrifice of a loving wife and mother in a traditional joint family. Hence, the speaker cannot confide in anyone or attempt to alleviate her own unhappiness. She instead "swallowed everything / And

smiled a smile of great content" (26). Kalia's female subjects have learned the power of "Positive Thinking" *(Tribute to Papa and Other Poems),* the title of one of her more sarcastic poems in which an unhappy wife suppresses her thwarted desires in a mundane marriage by keeping her sights firmly fixed on her material acquisitions—"A comfortable home / Your air-conditioned office / Our quarter-dozen children / Your bank balance / The Race Course nearby" (25). Thus, the speaker concludes by stating, "Who cares for primal disappointments?" (25). But suppression has its price and finally the speaker, who all along might have been the poet Kalia herself states, in "Anonymous" *(Hers):* "I no longer feel I'm Mamta Kalia" (26). Having negated her own sense of self and become a cipher in the crowd, Kalia has relinquished the privilege of questioning who she really is, who she would truly want to be. Poems like these are frankly confessional as well as autobiographical and take us unmistakably into the landscape of these women's minds, allowing us to penetrate the barriers of politeness and refinement that they have erected around themselves and allowing us to lay bare their broken dreams. Also bilingually creative (in Hindi and English), Kalia's colloquial idiom is owed in large measure to her fluency in the vernacular and her ability to transit effortlessly between these two modes of expression. Like Kamala Das, there is a distinctively piquant tone to her poetry, which makes a critic like Bruce King state in *Modern Indian Poetry in English:* "the present contemporary manner appears to have been initiated by Mamta Kalia" (155).

Unlike most of the women poets discussed above, the work of Smita Agarwal, who was born in 1958, is refreshingly impersonal. Neither hung up on identity issues nor tussling with ethnic discomfort or psychological and emotional inadequacies, her poetry is a comment on the littlest stimuli that touch her life daily. Her only collection of poems to date entitled *Wish Granting Words* was published in 2002 in New Delhi. In it, she indulges in fantastical scenes in which characters from history indulge in hypothetical conversations, such as in "Kasturba Talks of Life with Gandhi" and "Samyukta at Khajuraho." Occasionally, a serious comment on conjugal incompatibility does enter into the sphere of her consciousness, as in her poem "Discord," in which she describes two individuals who skirt around their conflicts, going nowhere, achieving no resolution. The poem concludes: "They've been at it again / like two crossed knives, husband and wife" (de Souza, *Nine Indian Women Poets,* 68).

In the poems of Agarwal, one truly hears the deep resonance, the lyricism of intriguing poetry. There is sophistication in her phraseology that is unusual in contemporary Indian poetry in English. Take, for instance, her poem "The Word-worker" in which she states: "Fixed for ever in the / Slim gap between alphabets / I am the saboteur, the hit-man" (65), or in "The Lie of the Land: A Letter to Chatwin" where several lines enchant and delight the reader. In her complex imagery and the use of elaborate but enormously succinct diction, Agarwal's poetry challenges the reader to unravel the various threads that make up her poetic compositions. One has very little insight into her personal life at the end of the day, but her ear for the music of words is finely tuned and sharp, and she ultimately achieves a level of success that few other poets reach. De Souza's students, who supposedly wondered where they could find the *poetry* in the work of Indian women poets, might do well to look for them in Agarwal's lines.

The same might be said for the poetry of Sujata Bhatt, who was born in 1956, and who has lived in different parts of the world before making Germany her home.

There is a great tendency on her part to intertwine the rhythm of vernacular Indian languages (such as Gujarati) with the scansion and meter of European languages such as German. Bhatt's multilingual abilities are at her service and she exploits this facility to interesting effect rather ingeniously. Her collection of poetry, *Brunizem* (1988), shows remarkable evidence of this ability. To ascertain the success with which superior poetic effects are achieved by employing such a technique, critics and readers would also need to be multilingual. Her other collections include *Monkey Shadows* (1991) and *The Stinking Rose* (1994). A truly diasporic poet, Bhatt's subjects, like Agarwal's, are impersonal. In "Kankaria Lake" *(Monkey Shadows),* for instance, she presents a wonderfully visual perception of still waters.

> It is more like skin;
> A reptile's skin—
> Wrinkled and rough as a crocodile's
>   And green.
> Bacterial green, decomposed
> Green—opaque and dull. (de Souza,
>   *Nine Indian Women Poets,* 79)

These delightful images of the lake remain with readers long after they stop thinking about the boy in the poem who occasions such musing. Again, in "Something for Plato" *(Brunizem),* she contemplates the antics of a rhinoceros in a Delhi zoo, presenting this unstately animal in noble guise—"He's so pleased / with the virile cut of his new sports jacket" (76). Again, in "White Asparagus" *(Monkey Shadows),* she enters into the consciousness of a pregnant woman who erotically relives her state of sexual fulfillment.

> Who speaks of the strong currents
> Streaming through the legs, the breasts
> Of a pregnant woman
> In her fourth month? (78)

Bhatt's images are unforgettable. She speaks of "the green coconut uterus" and "the green coconut milk that seals / her well, yet flows so she is wet / from his softest touch" (79).

This entry is hardly all-inclusive. It merely attempts to give readers an account of the wide spectrum of subjects that have preoccupied the minds of Indian women poets during the last three decades. It also assesses the overall technical merits and achievements of this body of writing. As the country continues to grow more fiercely divided on religious and communal grounds, as more atrocities are perpetrated against women, as Indian poetry finds an audience beyond national shores, the themes we will encounter will undoubtedly reflect shifting paradigms. The recurring problematics that concerned women poets during the last quarter of the twentieth century will certainly give way to newer, less narrowly feminine ones. Indian women's poetry of the future is likely to encompass all manner of human existence and will articulate it with sophistication and confidence.

Rochelle Almeida

Further Reading

Bajaj, Rashmi. *Women Indo-Anglian Poets: A Critique.* New Delhi: Asian Publishing, 1995.

Chavan, Sunanda P. *The Fair Voice: A Study of Indian Women Poets in English.* New Delhi: Sterling, 1984.

De Souza, Eunice, ed. *Nine Indian Women Poets: An Anthology.* New Delhi: Oxford UP, 1997.

De Souza, Eunice. *Selected and New Poems.* Bombay: St. Xavier's College, 1994.

Dharwadker, Vinay, and A. K. Ramanujan, eds. *The Oxford Anthology of Modern Indian Poetry.* New Delhi: Oxford UP, 1994.

Fernandes, Keith. "Introduction." *Selected and New Poems* by Eunice de Souza. Bombay: St. Xavier's College, 1994.

King, Bruce. *Modern Indian Poetry in English.* Rev. ed. New Delhi: Oxford UP, 2001.

Silgardo, Melanie. *Three Poets.* Bombay: Newground, 1978.

Zide, Arlene R. K., ed. *In Their Own Voice: The Penguin Anthology of Contemporary Indian Women Poets.* New Delhi: Penguin, 1993.

Indigenous Languages

The seven countries that officially constitute South Asia (as members of the intergovernmental organization SAARC, the South Asian Association for Regional Cooperation)—Bangladesh, Bhutan, India, the Maldives, Nepal, Pakistan, and Sri Lanka—are remarkable for the rich diversity of their indigenous languages. To begin with the classical languages of South Asia, Sanskrit, Pali, Prakrit, and Tamil each had a considerable body of literature by the sixth century A.D., and two more classical languages came to South Asia with the advent of Muslim rule in north India in the twelfth century A.D.: Arabic and Persian. Just as Sanskrit had fulfilled an elite, pan-Indian role in the ancient Hindu era, Persian served as the language of higher administration through the medieval period, from around the founding of the Mughal Empire in 1526 until English superseded it in 1837.

Of the older South Asian languages, Sanskrit is preeminent both for the sophistication of its grammar and the richness of its vocabulary and literature; it was described by the first orientalist Sir William Jones as "of wonderful structure, more perfect than the Greek, more copious than the Latin, and more exquisitely refined than either." Among the major literary works in Sanskrit are the foundational epics, the *Ramayana* and the *Mahabharata* (which includes the *Bhagavadgita*), the plays of Bhasa, Kalidasa (including the *Abhijnana-shakuntalam*), and Bhavabhuti, the prose narratives of Bana Bhatta, and a lively tradition of works on poetics beginning with Bharata's *Natya-shastra*. Sanskrit was also the language of Hindu scriptures including the *vedas,* the *upanishads,* and the *puranas,* and of treatises on subjects such as social organization, statecraft, medicine and erotics: the *Manusmriti,* the *Arthashastra,* the *Charaka-samhita,* and the *Kamasutra.*

Pali remains important for having been the language of early Buddhist teachings including the *Dhammapada*. Prakrit, a more natural and popular form of Sanskrit with which it had from the beginning coexisted (as in Sanskrit plays in which some characters spoke in Sanskrit and others in Prakrit), later mutated and lived on while Sanskrit died, allegedly under the weight of its own refinement. The various forms of Prakrit spoken over north and Central India formed a bridge between Sanskrit and the dozen or more modern Indo-Aryan languages that evolved into their distinct forms broadly between 1000 A.D. and 1400 A.D. These include Assamese, Bengali, Gujarati, Hindi, Marathi, Oriya, Panjabi, and Sindhi, as well as the relatively less widely spoken Kashmiri, Konkani, Manipuri, and Nepali. Besides Tamil, three other Dravidian languages also came into being at about the same time if not a little earlier: Kannada, Malayalam, and Telugu. A notably hybrid language, Urdu, with a grammar identical to that of Hindi but a vocabulary derived largely from Arabic and Persian, came into existence as a form of bazaar or camp parlance but developed into an attractive medium of literary expression in the eighteenth century.

The 17 modern languages named in the last paragraph together with an 18th, Sanskrit, are each recognized as a national language in the Constitution of India (besides English, which continues as an alternative official language to Hindi.) It is a measure of the preponderance of India in the South Asian region that these 18 Indian *national* languages happen to include the national/official languages of most of the other South Asian countries as well: Bengali (Bangladesh), Nepali (Nepal), Urdu, Panjabi and Sindhi (Pakistan), and Tamil (Sri Lanka). The only other notable South Asian languages are Sinhala, the major language of Sri Lanka, and Divehi, the language of the minuscule Maldive islands,

of which Sinhala too derives from Sanskrit and Prakrit while Divehi derives in turn from Sinhala. Such comprehensive commonality of linguistic matrix right across South Asia is an index of the high degree of literary and cultural cohesiveness of the whole region.

While it is not possible here to offer even the briefest outline of the literatures of the 18 or 20 modern South Asian languages, it may be no exaggeration to say that at least 10 of them possess a history of literary development quite as extensive as English does, and a body of literature comparable in substance and variety with English literature. Each of these major languages, typically, possess several epics written between, say, the eleventh and the sixteenth centuries, a period of *bhakti* or devotional literature spanning some three or four centuries that also saw the production of a variety of secular verse, and thereafter, following the colonial impact, a modern period marked by the rise of the novel and of discursive prose, and of indigenized forms of Marxist, modernist and postcolonial writing, among others. The only Nobel prize in literature so far awarded to a South Asian was to the Bengali poet Rabindranath Tagore in 1913, but the growing body of translations into English of the works of many other writers has not yet won South Asian literature any notable attention in the West.

On the scale of the 3,000-year-old history of Sanskrit or even the half-millennium-old histories of the modern Indian languages, South Asian writing in English seems to have been born but yesterday, is yet able to fill only a couple of shelves, comparatively speaking, and is accessible to less than 5 percent of the population of South Asia who know English. While a vast proportion of the literature produced and read in South Asia is even now in the indigenous languages, it is this tiny, elitist (and often diasporic) anglophone fraction by which South Asian literature is increasingly known abroad. This may be thought even more iniquitous in view of the fact that, in contrast with the overlapping term *postcolonial* (which is by definition oriented to highlighting writing in the language of colonization, English), the term *South Asian* is associated (as in the names of university departments in the United States and now increasingly also in England and Europe) with the older literature and culture of the region and with knowledge acquired at the ground level through learning the indigenous languages.

Harish Trivedi

Further Reading

Das, Sisir Kumar. *A History of Indian Literature.* Vol. 8 (1800–1910) and Vol. 9 (1911–1956). New Delhi: Sahitya Akademi, 1991, 1995 (other volumes in progress).

Pollock, Sheldon, ed. *Literary Cultures in History: Reconstructions from South Asia.* Berkeley: U of California P, 2003.

Tharu, Susie, and K. Lalita, eds. *Women Writing in India: 600 B.C. to the Present.* 2 vols. New York: Feminist P, 1991, 1993.

Interpreter of Maladies by Jhumpa Lahiri

Jhumpa Lahiri was born in 1967 in London to Indian parents. Her parents moved to the United States after she was born, and Lahiri grew up in Rhode Island. Her father was a librarian and her mother was a teacher. Lahiri's collection of short fiction, *Interpreter of Maladies,* won her the prestigious Pulitzer Prize in the year 2000. Three of the stories in this collection had been previously published in the *New Yorker,* which also adjudged her as one of the 20 best writers under the age of 40. Apart from the Pulitzer Prize, she has also won a few other awards such as the Transatlantic Review Award from Henfield Foundation, and the Fiction Prize from *Louisville Review.* She has a Ph.D. in Renaissance studies and had initially toyed with the idea of becoming an academic. A

Jhumpa Lahiri. Photo by Sanjay Kothari.

stint as a fellow in the Fine Arts Center in Provincetown, Massachusetts, helped her to decide that her passion lay in storytelling and not in research. She is currently working on a novel.

Interpreter of Maladies is a collection of nine short stories of which three are set in India and six in the United States. The author has assumed upon herself the role of an interpreter of stifled emotions. In her own words, "the title best expresses the predicament at the heart of the book—the dilemma, the difficulty, and often the impossibility of communicating emotional pain and affliction to others, as well as expressing it to ourselves" *(To Heaven without Dying).* Emotional pain and nostalgia form the basic ingredient of *Interpreter of Maladies.*

The role of an interpreter for dialogue between nations is an extremely vital one. The impassive neutrality on the features of an interpreter speaks of the tremendous effort involved in the job. Inefficient interpretation can result in international disquiet. Lahiri places herself in a similar position though her interpretation camouflages the undercurrents of personal emotional strain. As a child of immigrant parents, she has borne the brunt of living two lives, one in India and the other in the United States. The title story is about a young couple caught too early in the tangles of matrimony and parenting. Lahiri allows us to interpret them through the eyes of Mr. Kapasi, who is their driver cum guide on their visit to Orissa in India. They are children of immigrant parents, who were clandestinely led into a commitment by their parents who probably feared an onslaught of American culture if the children were left unharnessed. The result was a mechanical marriage, a furtive romance, a boy born out of an illegitimate alliance, and a self-acclaimed mental trauma. Lahiri's neutrality sometimes cracks because she allows an almost palpable note of censure in her depiction of immigrant children. In "Temporary Matter," there is again the portrayal of a soured marriage apparently brought about by the loss of a baby. Shoba and Sukumar are again children of immigrant parents who have lost their skill to communicate with each other except when in darkness. The title is perhaps a comment on the nature of marriages in the Western world where there is always an escape route from an unpleasant situation. Marriages fail everywhere, and while both the stories are an illustration of failed marriages, the perspective offered in each is different. While the former carries a note of despair due to unstable rooting, the latter carries a subtle note of connivance in which the super efficient Shoba uses the pretext of her miscarriage to distance herself from the easy going husband who continues to be a student at 35. "Mr. Pirzada Came to Dine" is a story about a Pakistani scholar on a study grant who visits an Indian family regularly in New England. The

little girl of the family finds the bonhomie between her parents and the visitor strange, especially since they belong to different countries. Lahiri allows her personal sense of being marginal, both in India as well as in America, to encroach upon her work in the following line when she describes the girl's parents and Mr. Pirzada sharing the anguish of the Indo-Pak war in 1971 as they watched it on television: "Most of all I remember the three of them operating during that time as if they were a single person, sharing a single meal, a single body, a single silence, and a single fear." Peter van der Veer's opinion, that people who do not think of themselves as Indians before migration become Indians in the diaspora is rather cynical when we consider the above sketch of the three displaced individuals who are bound together by their concern for their motherland. "Sexy" is a blatant statement on the amoral tendencies of Indian men in the permissive American society, while "The Blessed House" includes an element of secularism in a marriage. "Mrs. Sen's" is about a desperately homesick Indian woman who comes to terms with her own nostalgia, and a 10-year-old boy, Eliot, who is inadvertently drawn into the unfamiliar warmth of her environment while she baby-sits him. In "The Third and the Final Continent," Lahiri sums up the diasporic experience in a rather vehemently conclusive manner by suggesting that the exiled must assimilate in order to survive in a strange land.

"The Real Durwan" and "The Treatment of Bibi Haldar" are based in India, but the marginality of the protagonists in both cases (Boorie Ma and Bibi Haldar) hints at the common skein that runs through all the stories. That inability to cohere can result in rejection, not only on foreign soil but also in one's own land, is Lahiri's message in the two stories. She has interpreted the maladies of various characters and has also offered a remedy through the process of assimilation.

Suneeta Patnayak

Further Reading

Lahiri, Jhumpa. *To Heaven without Dying.* FEED Books Issue. Essay 7.24.2000 (Internet source)

McCurdy, Amy. Rev. of *Interpreter of Maladies* by Jhumpa Lahiri. *IndiaStar Review of Books.* 25 Jan. 2004 <http://www. indiastar.com>.

Taylor, Charles. Rev. of *Interpreter of Maladies* by Jhump Lahiri. 25 Jan. 2004 <http://www. salon.com/books/review/1999/07/27/lahiri>.

van der Veer, Peter, ed. "Introduction." *Nation and Migration: The Politics of Space in the South Asian Diaspora.* Philadelphia: U of Pennsylvania P, 1995.

Wallia, C. J. S. Rev. of *Interpreter of Maladies* by Jhumpa Lahiri. *IndiaStar Review of Books.* 25 Jan. 2004 <http://www.indiastar.com>.

J

Jhabvala, Ruth Prawer

Ruth Prawer Jhabvala was born of Polish/ Jewish parents, Marcus Prawer and Leonora Cohn Prawer in Cologne, Germany, on May 7, 1927. Even during her school days in Germany, she tried her skill at short-story writing. In 1939, when Ruth was 12, the family migrated to England as refugees. She soon learned to communicate with ease in English. In 1951, she took a master's degree in English from the University of London.

The condition of displacement continued into her adult life. The initial displacement was one of survival but the later moves were a conscious choice. In 1951 Ruth married Cyrus S. H. Jhabvala, a Parsi architect from India, and moved to New Delhi. Her three daughters, Renana, Ava, and Firoza were born in India. After a 24-year-long tussle with India, she has made yet another home for herself in New York.

When Jhabvala was still in India, she was asked to write the screenplay for films and television programs directed by James Ivory and Ismail Merchant. This invitation for collaboration was too exciting a prospect to turn down. The film version of her novel, *The Householder,* was the first such venture. Her other successful films include adaptations of her novel, *Heat and Dust,* Henry James's *The Europeans,* Jean Rhys's *Quartet,* E. M. Forster's *A Room with a View,* and *Howards End.* Some of the other significant films for which she has written scripts are *Shakespeare Wal-* *lah, The Guru, Bombay Talkie, Autobiography of a Princess, Roseland, Hullabaloo over Georgie and Bonnie's Pictures, The Bostonians,* and *Madame Sousastzka.* She also wrote the script for television films such as *The Place of Peace, An Experience of India,* and *Jane Austen in Manhattan.* This successful teamwork with Ivory and Merchant has now lasted for more than three decades, and it keeps her in New York. However, she still maintains her connection with both England and India.

Jhabvala started narrating her reactions to home, the loss of it, and the lack of it in her short stories during her student days in England. The context of displacement and the clash of cultures have remained her obsessive concern throughout her literary career of over half a century. Her 24-year life in India and her love-hate relationship with it have made her what she is as a creative writer. In the essay "Myself in India," which prefaces two volumes of her short stories, *An Experience of India* and *Out of India,* Jhabvala talks about the inescapable cycle that any European in India gets into and the different stages in a European's relationship with India. One slips from the tremendous enthusiasm for India to a stage when everything Indian is abominable. Renewal of the cycle is possible or one can get stuck in the last stage of detesting India. The essay provides useful insights into some of the Western characters in her fiction. It also helps us trace the evolution of her changing attitude toward India as revealed in that fiction. Whether in or out of India, she cannot get India out of her consciousness. She feels a compulsive need to interpret India and all that is Indian in her fiction—to the Western readers in particular. Jhabvala's distant perception and detached depiction of India have led critics to label her as an inside-outsider or an outside-insider. In spite of her identifying herself as a European writing on India, the India-related themes recurrent in her fiction and her daughter-in-law status have encouraged literary scholars to include her in anthologies of Indian fiction in English.

Jhabvala is acclaimed as a novelist of high literary repute. International recognition has come to her in the form of the Booker Prize for her novel *Heat and Dust* in 1976. She was a recipient of the John Simon Guggenheim Memorial Fellowship in 1976, the Neil Gunn International Fellowship in 1979, and the MacArthur Foundation Fellowship in 1986. She has also received many awards for her scriptwriting. She was awarded a doctorate of literature by the University of London.

Jhabvala's first four novels were published in quick succession. In them, she has translated her early Indian experiences and observations into social comedies. They reveal an ironic humor and a compassionate understanding of the urban temperament of India. In *To Whom She Will* (1955, published in the United States as *Amrita,* 1956), Jhabvala presents the life of an upper-class Hindu Pandit Ram Bahadur Saxena's family with elaborate accounts of their rituals, their food habits, and their family relationships. In a tradition-bound society, reactions against parental decisions are normal. But in this novel, the love relationships do not go beyond exaggerated declarations of love. Amrita and Hari Sahni profess to be in love and wallow in sentimentality. But it is not difficult for them to settle for the partners decided for them by their elders. This

Ruth Prawer Jhabvala with James Ivory and Ismail Merchant. Courtesy of Photofest.

sense of accommodation springs from their innate trust in the established institutions, such as the arranged marriage, and the lack of will to go against community norms and parental authority.

The Nature of Passion (1956) presents India as a bundle of contradictions, modern and conservative, spiritual and materialistic. Lala Narayan Dass Verma (Lalaji), a successful contractor, has lost his Punjabi village to Pakistan and has settled down in Delhi. He has all that money can buy. Western fads and fashions have no use for him and his sense of security stems from his Indian values. But his children have different goals. His daughter Nimmi wants to be independent of her indulgent father and make her own choices in life. His son Viddi wants to be a writer to avoid the family business. Being success orientated rakes up issues of principles and responses to corruption. But Lalaji's obsession with acquisition of

A film still from the adaptation of Ruth Prawer Jhabvala's novel *The Householder.* Courtesy of Photofest.

wealth is redeemed by his genuine love for his daughter.

Esmond in India (1957) contrasts the lives of Har Dayal and Ram Nath who had been classmates in Cambridge. Har Dayal is thoroughly anglicized and develops into a crass materialist, whereas Ram Nath sacrifices his life for Indian freedom. Har Dayal's daughter Shakuntala revels in pseudosophistication, whereas Ram Nath's brilliant doctor son, Narayan, dedicates his service for the villagers. The novel also presents the pompous Esmond flaunting his imperial arrogance in India. His married life with his Indian wife, Gulab, is marked more by their differences than by their affinities. They are divided by their habits, attitudes, and food. Esmond represents the colonial, male arrogance whereas Gulab, Indian and female, represents passivity. Esmond's frequent assaults on Gulab's self-respect and individuality fail to jolt her out of her smugness. He treats both his English mistress Betty and the adolescent Shakuntala as mere conquests. Finally, it is his failure to play the role of a husband and protect Gulab from the lecherous servant that prompts her to leave him for good. The man-woman relationships in the novel are based mainly on sensuality and lead to no commitment. Jhabvala mocks the pseudosophistication of the upper-class Indians who either glorify or downgrade their own culture in order to appeal to the Westerners. Esmond tutors the European women of social importance on Indian art, culture, and Hindi. He is both shallow and snobbish, and Jhabvala does not hesitate to make him an object of ridicule in the eyes of both the Indians and the Westerners.

The Householder (1960) deals with a diffident Hindi teacher Prem, in a private college in Delhi, who comes to terms with his lower-middle-class life. His life is marked by his awareness of his deficiencies, money concerns, and the inability to assert himself anywhere except at home. His diffidence is seen in the way he plays his role as a teacher, social being, and as a householder. He is unable to seek a raise in his salary or get his house rent reduced. The novel also introduces European seekers and Indian Swamis and the uneasy relationship between the two, a subject that Jhabvala returns to time and again in her later novels.

Jhabvala visited England in 1960 after nine years. Her absence from India altered her perception of the country on her return. This change is also reflected in her fiction. She can no longer present a merely amused observation of Indian life. In the novels published after 1961, there is an acute awareness of India's social problems and the oppression of the self by Indian society. She describes her characters' struggle to retain their individuality and protect the sanctity of the self.

Get Ready for Battle (1962) focuses on the ruthlessness of the moneyed class and the exploitation of the poor. Sarla Devi responds to her call to fight against social injustice. Her husband Gulzari Lal's materialistic goals and calculated moves to realize them bring about a rift between the two. His subsequent relationship with an attractive widow, Kusum Mehra, evokes no bitterness in Sarla. She concentrates on the need to protect the hapless hutment dwellers in Bundit Busti from the real estate dealers and industrialists who threaten to drive them out of their homes. Fighting their cause is to fight against her husband, a prospective buyer of the land. Her son Vishnu fails to support the cause of the downtrodden, but Gulzari Lal's mistress is eager to do her part and thwart her lover's plans of evicting the poor from their land. Sarla's brother Brij Mohan uses Tara, a prostitute, for his needs, and sheds her with no compunction. It is Sarla again who seeks Tara out to offer help. The novel presents the complex relationships of its characters and the many acute social problems of India. But there is hope in the relentless battle fought by noble characters like Sarla Devi, and Gautam, an environmentalist.

A Backward Place (1965) presents poverty as the overwhelming Indian reality. Jhabvala is critical of the Westernized Indian intellectuals who feel no moral responsibility toward the predicament of the poor. She contrasts the Indian and the Western attitudes but refrains from generalization of any kind. Judy falls in love with Bal when he attends a conference in London and settles for a middle-class Indian life with him in a joint family. Judy's adaptability is a contrast to the pampered Bal's immature ways. Bal is obsessed with his film world contacts even when his son Prithvi is fighting high fever. Judy is a caring and dutiful wife and mother and demands responsibility out of Bal. She finds Bal's resilient spirit and enthusiasm for life endearing. Etta, a Hungarian who changes lovers frequently, is a contrast to Judy. Etta sees India as a backward nation, a view endorsed by the visiting professor of economics, Hochstadt, and his wife. The pair has gone through an enthusiastic stage of admiring Indian art and Indian spirit, but is ready now to quit. In spite of Judy's ability to relate to Bal's relatives and live in a joint family situation, the novel shows how impossible it is to integrate the Western and the Indian attitude to life.

A New Dominion (1972, published in the United States as *Travelers,* 1973) is Jhabvala's seventh novel. The earlier edition of the novel provides a list of characters labeled Indian or Western. Disillusioned with the mechanized, materialistic life in the West, three girls, Lee, Evie, and Margaret, shuffle aside the security of home, and set out on a spiritual quest. They are fascinated by the rich heritage of India. Unfortunately, they run into a Swami whom they take to be the very source of spiritual sustenance. He destroys them systematically by tempting them to see the spiritual in the sensual. They are convinced that oneness with the Swami could be achieved only when the body is surrendered. They vie with one another to achieve this end. In the process, Margaret dies of callous neglect. Lee loses herself totally in an attempt to realize the meaning of life. The narrative is episodic and moves from Delhi to the holy city of Benares to the Rajasthani town of Maupur. There are many Indian and Western characters in the novel. Miss Charlotte, a Christian missionary, is happy to return to her home in England after her 30 years of service in India. She feels that education and economic amelioration alone can save the country. Raymond, the rationalistic English tourist, makes futile attempts to free the three Western girls from the spell of the Swami. He experiments with life in India, maintaining his European detachment. Asha, an aged beauty, craves for sensual attention to renew her youth. Gopi, a college student, is full of sexual desires. The novel abounds in carnality and spirituality serves as a snare for sexual appeasement.

Heat and Dust (1975) is the last novel that Jhabvala has written from India. It is still considered her best and won the prestigious Booker Prize. The novel deals with the experiences of two socially very different Western generations in India. The young unnamed British narrator comes to India to solve the enigma of a scandal associated with her step-grandmother, Olivia Rivers. Olivia comes to India as the wife of the subcollector of Satiapur, Douglas Rivers. Her boredom with her social class drives her to an illicit relationship with the Nawab. She is compelled to elope with him when her pregnancy is exposed. The narrator makes judicious use of Olivia's personal letters to her sister, Marcia. At the end of the novel, the enigma remains unsolved. But the narrator emerges as an expectant mother. She takes this to be part of her rich store of Indian experiences. She is content to alternate her journal entries with Olivia's letters. She does not interpret Olivia's India or evaluate Olivia's actions in moral or cultural terms. She merely tries to relive Olivia's experiences in the same places in an attempt at a better understanding of Olivia and India. As a result, two neat characters are sketched out. The carefully worked out parallelism seems labored and contrived and it brings out the contrast more than the similarity between the two women.

Heat and Dust discusses India and its effect on the Westerners at length, particularly the question of "staying on." The novel abounds in Indian aspects that could appeal to the Raj nostalgia. In spite of genuine attempts made by both the Indians and the English, the characters find it impossible to cross cultural barriers. Beneath all social cordiality lie the preconceived notions about India and the West. Jhabvala betrays a certain amount of anxiety to caution a Western seeker from getting seduced by India. The characters never appeal to us as persons but remain merely as either British or Indian throughout the novel. Jhabvala has made use of the heat of the sun and the heat of human blood and has raised dust about them to clarify her own responses to India.

Jhabvala's disillusionment with India is evident in the short stories she published in the 1960s and 1970s as well. They appear in the collections *Like Birds, Like Fishes* (1962), *An Experience of India* (1966), *A Stronger Climate* (1968), and *How I Became a Holy Mother* (1976). These stories contain in a nutshell the themes that she has elaborated in her novels. A collection of her selected short stories has been published under the title, *Out of India* (1987).

After moving out of India and after a gap of eight years, Jhabvala has published four novels. These are set in the United States, England, and India. *In Search of Love and Beauty* (1983) deals with the life of German Austrian Jewish immigrants in New York and their sense of displacement, which had been a significant part of Jhabvala's own past. The immigrants try to recapture and relive the grandeur of their lost European heritage by getting together to remember anniversaries and by decorating their apartments with German furniture. The pragmatic ones realize that prewar Germany is lost forever, and therefore, a return home would not be possible or useful. Jhabvala juxtaposes characters of different time periods and they are in search of love and beauty. Her continued interest in, and fear of, spiritual leaders is also revealed in this novel. Leo Kellermann, the founder of the Academy of Potential Development, a self-styled spiritual counselor, is the American version of a Swami who has the ability to lure people to damnation. He tries to establish a link between the physical and the spiritual and uses the impressionable, gullible disciples for his sexual gratification.

Louise and Bruno Sonnenblick, their daughter Marietta, and their grandchildren, Mark and Natasha, are all on a quest. While the older people bemoan the loss of a home, the younger ones take dislocation as a condition of modern life. Louise attempts to fill her void by relating to the sensual Leo Kellermann. Mariatta has no qualms about a similar search for love. It leads her to a series of lovers, to Leo, and then to India. Natasha, a Jewish orphan, the adopted sister of Mark, is the only one who emerges as a contented person. Jhabvala's inability to cast off her Indian connection is seen in the way she transports her characters to India.

Three Continents (1987) has been dedicated to James Ivory and Ismail Merchant who are primarily responsible for Jhabvala's entry into the United States and the film world. The 19-year-old idealistic twins, Harriet Wishwell and Michael Wishwell, inherit a large fortune. But they seek more than what money or their divorced parents can offer. They meet the Indian leaders of Transcendental Internationalism—Rawul, Rani, and the charismatic Crishi—in the United States. The twins feel irresistibly drawn to them. Michael sees in the spiritual movement the possibility of world unity. The twins surrender all their wealth to the Indian group and follow them to England and then to India. It is in India that they become aware of the fraudulence of these "transcendentalists." Michael is willing to retrace his steps, but Harriet, hopelessly in love with Crishi, is ready to give up her values, her brother, and herself to be with him. Her irrationality destroys her sense of judgment. The seeming support system offered by the fake gurus snaps the familial bonds. The sexual gratification that Crishi rations out to Harriet reduces her to needing and longing. Michael longs for a better ideology and a new social order. His knowledge of the criminal activities of the holy trio results in his murder. Harriet collaborates with them in disguising it as a case of suicide.

The novel reverses the role of the colonizer and the colonized. The American twins are enslaved and they find it impossible to free themselves from the devious, power hungry Indian trio. Crishi colonizes Harriet's body and mind. On the Fourth of July, Rawul hoists his Sixth World Flag alongside the Stars and Stripes. He sings his own anthem and not the national anthem of the United States.

Poet and Dancer (1993) explores the complex power relationship between the first cousins, Angel and Lara. Angel is plain looking, submissive, and caring, whereas Lara is beautiful but utterly irresponsible. The vibrant Lara can evoke both desire and devotion. Lara has an unhealthy love affair with Angel's father, Peter Koenig. Angel does all that is possible to protect Lara but does so in vain. The novel also depicts the life of the many immigrant communities in Manhattan.

In *Shards of Memory* (1995) Jhabvala again tries to integrate her three backgrounds represented by New York, Hampstead, and Bombay. She returns to the recurrent figure of a charismatic spiritual leader and his influence on four generations of Americans. Elsa Kopf deserts her husband, Kavi, an Indian poet in New York, and goes to Hampstead with her friend, Cynthia, to spread her spiritual guru's message. The death of her guru coincides with the birth of a son to Renata, Elsa's granddaughter in New York. The child, Henry, has the same looks and charisma of the guru. This leads to the search for family heritage, the discussion of shared memories, and the human need to trust.

In all the four novels written in the United States, Jhabvala points out the weak will, the vulnerability, and the lack of direction of Western youth. She is critical of those who romanticize India and turn to the East for spiritual answers. When one is disillusioned with one's culture, it is easy to get attracted to anything that is exotic. She is equally critical of the Indians who hanker after Western ideas of sophistication and materialism. One needs to have strong roots in one's own culture to be able to absorb the good in another. Jhabvala has experienced cultural tensions sharply and continually, and that experience has proved to be a rich store for her creativity.

Premila Paul

Further Reading

Chakravarti, Aruna. *Ruth Prawer Jhabvala: A Study in Empathy and Exile.* New Delhi: B. R. Publishing, 1998.

Crane, Ralph J. *Ruth Prawer Jhabvala.* New York: Twayne, 1992.

———. ed. *Passages to Ruth Prawer Jhabvala.* New Delhi: Sterling, 1991.

Gooneratne, Yasmine. *Silence, Exile and Cunning: The Fiction of Ruth Prawer Jhabvala.* New Delhi: Orient Longman, 1983.

Jha, Rekha. *The Novels of Kamala Markandaya and Ruth Jhabvala.* New Delhi: Prestige, 1990.

Shepherd, Ronald. *Ruth Prawer Jhabvala in India: The Jewish Connection.* New Delhi: Chanakya, 1993.

Sucher, Laurie. *The Fiction of Ruth Prawer Jhabvala: The Politics of Passion.* London: Macmillan, 1989.

Jones, William

William Jones (1746–94) was born at Beaufort Buildings, Westminster, on September 28, 1746, the youngest child of William "Longitude" Jones FRS (1675–1749). His father, the distinguished Welsh mathematician and friend of Newton and Halley, died before he was three, leaving him only modest financial resources. But a significant intellectual patrimony connected the young Jones with the polymathic Lewis Morris who, together with his Anglesey circle, pioneered a Welsh renaissance. The progressive educational ideas of his mother Mary (née Nix) were also instrumental in nurturing this prodigy and, having won a scholarship to Harrow in 1753, Jones rapidly displayed remarkable linguistic skills in the classics, Hebrew, and modern European languages, which earned him the sobriquet of "the Great Scholar."

Entering University College, Oxford, in 1764, Jones initiated what was to be a lifelong practice of collaborating with native informants by using the proceeds of a prestigious Bennet scholarship to employ Mirza, a Syrian, to help him translate *Mille et une nuits* back into Arabic. Delighting in the manuscript treasures of the Pococke collection and in his discovery of Sa'di, he explored the linguistic connections between Arabic and Persian. He made the acquaintance of Bishop Robert Lowth whose *De Sacra Poesi Hebræorum* (1753) encouraged Jones to see in the Old Testament a masterpiece of Oriental literature. He was, in his own words, "with the fortune of a peasant, giving himself the education of a prince" (Teignmouth Memoirs, *Works,* I. 59). Education was in his blood, and he augmented his fortune by accepting in 1765 the post of tutor to Viscount Althorp, the son of Earl Spencer, gaining a lifelong friend and correspondent, access to an impressive library, and an entrée into the society of influential Whig magnates.

He rapidly established his reputation as an Orientalist: to his first book, *Histoire de Nader Chah* (1770), a prestigious commission from Christian VII of Denmark, he appended an important "Traité sur la poësie orientale." This was closely followed by *Dissertation sur la littérature Orientale* (1771) and the best-selling *Grammar of the Persian Language* (1771), influential works of cultural proselytism, recommending that Europe look beyond Graeco-Roman classicism to invigorating Arab and Persian traditions. "Persian" Jones's *Grammar* blended the poetical—inaugurating Romantic Orientalism—and the practical—being adopted by the East India Company for the training of its writers in the language of the Mughal courts. 1772 saw both his election to the Royal Society and the publication of *Poems, Consisting Chiefly of Translations from the Asiatick Languages;* a fascinating mixture of original poems developing the genre of the Oriental verse tale; accurate translations from writers such as Sa'di, Háfiz, and Mesihi; and two essays that established the primacy of lyric in the new poetics of Romanticism. The following year Jones failed to secure the post of ambassador to Turkey, but was elected to Dr. Johnson's Turk's Head Club by Burke, Gibbon, Goldsmith, Reynolds, and other illuminati.

Irritated by his dependence on aristocratic connections, Jones chose law as a career in which merit might rival privilege and was called to the Bar at the Middle Temple in 1774. Jones practiced on the Welsh circuits, and the lessons learned there prepared him for his role as an imperial administrator. Detesting the arbitrary power of the Anglicized squirearchy, his egalitarian principles and Celtic sympathies were apparent in his legal representation of the colonized Welsh. Simultaneously, a series of works including his *Speeches of Isaeus Concerning the Law of Succession to Property in Athens* (1779), *Essay on the Law of Bailments* (1781), and *The Mahomedan Law of Succession to the Property of Intestates* (1782) established Jones as one of the first comparative lawyers specializing in the protection of the individual, his person, and property.

In his recreational hours, Jones transformed conceptions of the pastoral with his acclaimed translation of the pre-Islamic *The Moallakát, or Seven Arabian Poems* (1782), and he enhanced his reputation as a writer of occasional verse with a pronounced radical bias. His opposition to the American war and the slave trade; his standing as a Whig candidate to represent Oxford University in 1780; his energetic support for Wilkes; and the powerful polemic of *Speech on the Nomination of Candidates to Represent the County of Middlesex* (1780), and *Speech on the Reformation of Parliament* (1782) secured the friendship of men such as Franklin, Adams, Priestley, Price, and Cartwright. But these writings seriously blighted his prospects of appointment to the Bengal judicature where he might combine his linguistic and legal expertise. The representations of Lords Ashburton and Shelburne finally prevailed, and in the spring of 1783 Jones was appointed, knighted, and married to Anna Maria, eldest daughter of Jonathan Shipley, the radical bishop of St Asaph. Even as they sailed to India, Jones's radical pamphlet *The Principles of Government* (1782) was the subject of a notorious seditious libel trial written at Wrexham.

Arriving in Calcutta on September 25, 1783, Jones immediately rose to the intellectual challenge of "the vast regions of Asia." By January 1784, his enthusiasm and reputation galvanized the small but dedicated group of East India Company employees encouraged by Warren Hastings into the pioneering Asiatick Society of Bengal. This effectively marked the beginnings of Indology, and its research program encompassed Indian languages, literature, philosophy, civil and natural history. The organ of the society, *Asiatic Researches,* transformed Western conceptions of a marginalized subcontinent, placing India at the center of European Romanticism. Inheriting Hastings's project to codify Muslim and Hindu law, Jones's close collaboration with native informants and his friendship with Charles Wilkins, translator of *Bhagvat-Gita* (1785), inevitably led to his learning the "language of the gods."

Within six months of beginning Sanskrit, Jones's "Third Anniversary Discourse" (1786) introduced the startling thesis that the classical languages of India and Europe descend from a common source language no longer extant. Such disconcerting notions of linguistic kinship between the rulers and their black subjects were underlined by Jones's claim that there existed a familial relationship between Vedantic thought and Platonism. Jones's original "Hymns to Hindu Deities" (1784–88) and his path-breaking 1789 translations of Kalidasa's entrancing play *Sakuntala* and Jayadeva's erotic allegory *Gitagovinda* constructed a Romantic mythical image of India for a rapidly orientalizing Europe. In collecting, translating, and printing Sanskrit materials, Jones and his fellow Orientalists were making accessible in the secular public domain texts formerly subject to exclusive Brahmanical control. Thus Orientalism, through its retrieval of Sanskrit texts and its reconstruction of India's past, shaped the way Indians perceived themselves, ushering in the Bengal Renaissance. Underwriting this contribution to Hindu cultural rebirth, and justifying British commercial and imperial intervention in Indian affairs, was an enlightened historicist critique of feudalism and decadent court government in Europe, and an accompanying desire to cleanse corrupt administration abroad.

Jones's principal task of preparing an exhaustive digest of Hindu and Muslim law was only partially completed with the publication of *Al Sirájiyyah: or, Mohammedan Law of Inheritance* (1792) and the *Institutes of Hindu Law: Or, the Ordinances of Menu* (1794). But his commitment to the idea that Indians should be governed by their own laws was nothing less than total. The fruit of six years of Jones's tireless editorial and collaborative labors, Jagannâtha Tarkapañcânana's *Vi-*

vãdabhangãrn.ava, or "Oceans of resolutions of disputes," was completed shortly after Jones's death. Brahman pandits wept openly with Muslim maulavis at the news of this tragically premature death on April 27, 1794.

Michael J. Franklin

Further Reading

Cannon, Garland, ed. *The Letters of Sir William Jones,* 2 vols. Oxford: Clarendon P, 1970.

———. *The Life and Mind of Oriental Jones* Cambridge: Cambridge UP, 1990.

Franklin, Michael J. *Sir William Jones.* Cardiff: U of Wales P, 1995.

———. ed. *Representing India: Indian Culture and Imperial Control in Eighteenth-Century British Orientalist Discourse,* 9 vols. London: Routledge, 2000.

———. ed. *The European Discovery of India: Key Indological Sources of Romanticism,* 6 vols. London: Ganesha, 2001.

———. "Cultural Possession, Imperial Control, and Comparative Religion: The Calcutta Perspectives of Sir William Jones and Nathaniel Brassey Halhed." *The Yearbook of English Studies* 32 (2002): 1–18.

Leask, Nigel. *British Romantic Writers and the East: Anxieties of Empire.* Cambridge: Cambridge UP, 1993.

K

Kamani, Ginu

Bombay-born essayist and fiction writer Ginu Kamani's first book-length publication, *Junglee Girl,* is a collection of stories exploring sexuality, sensuality, and power. Kamani has published fiction and essays in various anthologies, literary journals, newspapers, and magazines and has taken part in readings and lectures. Her essays and talks focus on gender and sexual self-knowledge in the context of the dual identities of hyphenated American subcultures. A self-described thinker and writer, Kamani credits the popularity of her book as responsible for her involvement in a spectrum of cultural excavation, investigation, and activism. In her role as an activist, she aims to expose areas of shame that imprison culture and society. Her book has been used as a text in different courses of literature, writing, and the social sciences.

Kamani was born in Bombay in 1962. She came to the United States when she was 14 and earned a master's degree in creative writing in 1987 from the University of Colorado in Boulder. After living in Bombay from 1987 to 1991 to work on film projects, Kamani returned to the United States to write full time. She has been teaching at Mills College, Oakland, since 1997 and is now a visiting assistant professor. She conducts fiction workshops in creative writing, courses at both graduate and undergraduate levels, and also teaches a literature course titled The Craft of Fiction. Frequently invited to lecture and teach, Kamani finds such academic activities expanding her cross-cultural, cross-disciplinary, and historical analyses. From May 1995 to March 1996, for example, Kamani gave 50 readings in 18 cities on three continents. In these readings, Kamani assumes the role of the performer where she simulates the tone and mannerisms of her characters' voices by putting on Indian accents and the highly emphatic manner of communication that marks Indian English. Underscoring the power of such playacting, Kamani regrets the lack of performing skills among many contemporary authors: "With all the emphasis on the quality of the written word and the push to get published, very few authors actually work on any aspect of performance as part of their creative process. We've managed to forget in this time and age how crucial the storytelling process is, with all the emphasis on writing" (qtd. in Tenzer).

Junglee Girl is a collection of 12 short stories that center on female protagonists in India. Although these women differ in class, sexual orientation, and age, all the protagonists have one thing in common—society labels them "junglee" girls and condemns them for being wild and uncontrollable women. Each story is presented in almost vignettelike form, showing us a glimpse of a woman's life and revealing the moment of sexual awakening. Many of them are told in the first person. The women in these stories are, in their own way, seeking to break the mold of the asexual, passive Indian woman. Within these situations lurk the unspoken erotic and sexual undercurrents that Kamani uncovers in her writing. Adolescent fantasies raise a mundane servant into an object of desire in "Maria." In "The Tears of Kamala," the one hundred tears she counts and sheds mark a bank teller's day. By night, she is stubbornly tearless and bears the curses of her abusive husband with dry eyes. "Lucky Dip," a story that effortlessly recreates the atmosphere of a suburban, English school in Bombay, is tinged with sexuality that one finds hard to pin down or give a name. "Waxing the Thing" is a humorous tale of a beauty salon assistant who earns her living waxing pubic hair off rich Bombay socialites. The salon assistant is introduced to this lucrative business by Mrs. Yusuf, "who said very sweetly, that only young girls like me [the main character] are pure enough in the heart to wax down there" (120). Some of the tales border on the bizarre and fantastic such as "Shakuntala" where a servant of that name does her household chores with a cat hidden under her peasant skirt and is accidentally discovered when the precocious child of the house tries insinuating her toes between Shakuntala's thighs. In "The Cure," a female doctor tells a mother that her taller-than-average daughter is "fundamentally over-sexed. Danger to society. Sex hormones out of control. Look how she tempts" (46). The girl is subsequently referred to a sexologist, Dr. Doctor, who diagnoses her tallness to be a case of "a one-in-a-million imbalance of the feminine fluids" (48). He recommends a weekly visit alone with the daughter "only to make it less painful to you, madam, being the girl's mother and all" (48). The young girl and her brother in "The Smell" rebel against the rigid orthodoxy of a vegetarian Gujarati household by eating eggs on toast in their servant's quarters. Their inquisitive grandmother tries every morning to catch them at it. It becomes a game

that never ends. The grandmother cautions the girl, "Eating meat is not good for women. Unnecessarily you will pollute your unborn son" (194). But it is already too late. Rani not only enjoys meat but vows to herself "When I grow up, I will never marry. I will smell the meat on men and the smell will keep me hungry" (196).

Kamani's prose is bold and incisive. It grabs and holds the reader till the very end, providing a window into Indian society and depicting gender relations within Indian culture. At the heart of Kamani's book is a picture of a woman caught at a crossroads, choosing in a single moment whether to flaunt convention and become a junglee woman or to close the door and quietly return home. However, the theme tends to get a bit repetitive and tiring toward the end. Some of the characters, like the Gujarati woman in "Ciphers," seem more like a caricature and less like someone one might actually meet on a train in India. The same is true of the characters in "Just Among Indians" and "This Anju." Like villains in a Hindi movie, they seem stereotyped and one-dimensional.

Kamani's agent in Los Angeles submitted the manuscript of *Junglee Girl* to several corporate publishing houses that would not take it on the excuse that it would be difficult to market. Then Aunt Lute, the independent multicultural women's press in San Francisco, approached her about publishing the book. Based on such experience, Kamani finds the dichotomy between mass-marketed and independent fiction to be increasingly disturbing: "Publishing houses such as HarperCollins, owned by multinational media conglomerate Rupert Murdoch, have changed the nature of the work they'll publish in the past 20 years to make the maximum amount of money at the expense of diverse styles and the content of the writing" (qtd. in Morgan). She did not feel that the corporate publishers rejected her because she was a woman or because she was writing about India. She believes that the reason she was rejected had more to do with the complexity of her work. "I'm trying to take a look at everything without being judgmental. You must have noticed that my stories don't provide resolutions. That's one of the reasons that my publisher was attracted to the work in the first place," she explains. In a 2001 interview, Kamani confided that she had put off her work on her novel and was writing a collection of interrelated stories while continuing to write for the *San Francisco Examiner.* She has also been involved in scripting some film projects.

Rebecca Sultana

Further Reading

Kamani, Ginu. Interview with Gina Bacon. "Crossing Culture." Nervygirlzine.com July-Aug. 2001. 21 Nov. 2002 <http://www.nervygirl zine.com/nervy/july_2001/features.html>.

Kamani, Ginu. "In the Junglee: Public Outings of a Private Writer." *Night Light Articles.* 23 Dec. 1998 <http://www.cleansheets.com/archive/archarticles/junglee_12.23.98>.

Kamani, Ginu. Interview with Livia Tenzer. Aunt Lute Web site. 23 Jan. 2003 <http://www.auntlute.com/k-interview.htm>.

Morgan, Fiona. "Interview." *University of Washington Online Daily,* 20 Feb. 97. 27 Nov. 2002 <http://www.wsu.edu:8080/~brians/anglophone/wlresearch.html>.

Khan, Adib

Living and writing in Australia, Adib Khan is gradually transforming from a best-selling novelist within Australia to a critically acclaimed one within anglophone literature. He also writes on multiculturalism, race relations, and other issues faced by the growing body of Third World immigrants. Among other subcontinental writers attaining fame in English literature, Khan especially attributes Salman Rushdie for the sudden interest in writing from this region for, "He made us realize we could reinvent the language which shook the West" (Condon 2).

Khan was born in Dhaka, now in Bangladesh, on January 29, 1949. He arrived in Australia in 1973 as a postgraduate student at Monash University where he completed his master's degree on the poetry of Robert Browning. He became a permanent resident in 1977 and an Australian citizen in 1978. He has taught English and history at Damascus College in Ballarat. Currently he teaches creative writing at the University of Ballarat. He also appears frequently on talk shows on Australian radio and television. He is married and has two daughters.

Khan's first short story, which he wrote at 19, was broadcast on the BBC World Service. Khan's novel writing, however, started much later when he was in his late forties. While confronting his sense of displacement and pondering the future of his creative and academic life, writing became a creative outlet that also served as a therapeutic process. He usually handwrites his first draft as it allows him to "crumple up papers" and also because there is "something very primitive and fundamental about it" (Karim 8). At the suggestion of a bookseller friend, Khan sent his first completed draft to a publisher. Taking an alphabetical list of Australian publishers, Khan sent it first to Allen and Unwin who soon called to confirm publication. Commenting on this initial success, Khan said to Sullivan, "Had I known then what I know about the publishing world now I wouldn't have had the courage. I went into it in a state of total naivety" (7). Khan's literary career started through the publication of his first novel and by winning several awards for it.

Khan's first novel reveals the profound sense of emotional and physical dislocation that permeates his later works as well. In *Seasonal Adjustment,* Iqbal Chaudhary, a Zaminder descendent, abandons a privileged life of wealth and social standing to migrate to Australia. Dismayed and disillusioned by what he considers the vengeful barbarity committed by the people of war torn Bangladesh, Chaudhary leaves his home and family to escape to Australia. The novel recounts Chaudhary's return to Dhaka after a period of 18 years and his subsequent failure to rekindle the ties that he had severed. *Seasonal Adjustment* sets the tone for the lonely course of Khan's troubled heroes. Both philosophical and bitter at the same time, Chaudhary sums up his position among other men: "Do you know what it means to be a migrant? A lost soul forever adrift in search of a tarnished dream?" (143). He discovers an unrecoverable gulf between himself and the rest of his family as they struggle to accept him at his own terms. Cultural and social norms that he had not encountered for 18 years now seem antiquated. Chaudhary's agnosticism is greeted with shocked indignation when he reveals his daughter's lack of religious conformity, his own inability to pray, and his blatant skepticism of his mother's blind devotion for a "holy man." He finally understands that, "You get sick of wearing masks to hide your confused aloneness. You can never call anything your own" (143). The novel is vaguely autobiographical as Khan relies much on his own childhood memories. These memories become fragile and pristine for Khan when he detects discrepancies between his former memories of home and the actual reality that he confronts once he finds himself physically present there. Besides critical acclaim, the novel has also won several awards. In 1994, the novel won the Christina Stead Award for fiction and the Australian book of the year prize. The novel was also short-listed for the Age Book of the Year Award. In 1995, the novel won the Commonwealth prize for the best first book.

Khan's second novel *Solitude of Illusions* focuses on memories as well as on family, home, love, and death. This novel, too, is set in the Indian subcontinent. Khalid Sharif is a successful businessman from Calcutta who is visiting his son in Melbourne. Stricken with terminal illness, Sharif takes the time to reassess his life. He recalls his youth in the turbulent 1940s when he had met a beautiful courtesan, Nazli, and had fallen in love with her. His separation from her, enforced by an indignant family, leaves him overwhelmed with guilt and self-reproach, which still haunts him the rest of his life. *Solitude of Illusions* has also won a number of awards, including the Tilly Ashton Award for the best Braille Book of the Year Award. The novel was short-listed for both the 1997 Christina Stead Award and the New South Wales Ethnic Commission Award.

Khan's third novel, *The Storyteller,* reverts from diasporic themes to describe Vamana, a very ugly dwarf, who tells stories in the streets of New Delhi; and through his fictional characters, he reinvents himself into a heroic figure. As he gradually fails to distinguish between reality and the illusion that he creates for himself, he gets himself into trouble. Khan draws a hideous picture of a deformed human being with a humpback, scarred face, scaly lips, huge head, jagged teeth, and floppy ears replete with animal metaphors. Yet, Vamana is perceptive enough to realize the impact his appearance has on others, which is at once repulsive and fascinating. By showing other characters such as eunuchs, transvestites, prostitutes, and corrupt police, the story also illuminates issues such as intolerance and prejudice, the price of progress and the inequity of wealth and power (Haas 36). In her review Annie Greet has commented, "Vamana is a metaphor, a reminder of our creative natures and an indictment on how we have crippled and distorted ourselves, failing our potential as human beings" (11).

The troubled voices in all three novels, always in search of a tangible homeland in both geographical as well emotional terms, can be found in Khan's personal writings as well. In his essay, "Writing Homeland" Khan emphasizes the need for a place called home as "It fills those gigantic gaps in the past and makes the present more bearable because it diminishes that sense of loss" (24). The place need not be one's birthplace for "that creation is essentially an illusion, and deep inside one knows that the purpose will not be fulfilled because illusions are transient" (24). Iqbal Chaudhary, thus, returns to Australia having realized that the illusion of home that he had carried within him back to Bangladesh has been lost forever. When Sharif reminiscences about his past, Khan's own words better fit his fictional character: "It is an amalgamation of remembrances, half-truths, fragmented images, gaunt shadows, snatches of conversations and yearnings structured into a shimmering mirage by an imagination that feeds itself uneasily on an awareness of the discrepancy between the way it was and the way it possibly is" (Khan "Writing Homeland" 25). Although a frequently discussed issue among many Third World writers, racism as a topic, however, does not interest Khan. In a review of *The Storyteller* in *The Age Extra,* Jane Sullivan writes about Khan's lack of racial experience. Sullivan quotes Khan: "It's a peculiar thing here. If you can speak the idiomatic language, you're pretty right. If you know the language of abuse and sweating, unfortunately it works." Although his immigrant characters rarely face bigotry, experience as such when depicted, are more a consequence of general human ignorance rather than incidents of racial or cultural hatred.

Character for Khan is of fundamental importance, far more important than the story or the plot. Describing his creative style, Khan says that he weaves words like "candy floss" where he lets the character take over rather than himself dictating the turn of the story. Characters that appear in Khan's fiction, subcontinental or otherwise, are mostly off beat and eccentric creations rather than average middle-class characters.

Since Khan is a relatively new writer, mostly reviews and comments have been written on his works. On the blurb of *Seasonal Adjustment* Tim Winton describes Khan's first book as: "A startling heady novel about the sticky web of attachment and belonging." Annie Greet, who calls Khan "Brilliant," finds *The Storyteller* "confident of winning gold in an impressive number of areas" (11). One of the greatest achievements that she finds in the book is that, "in his focus on extreme ugliness and perversion, the antitheses of our fancied 'norm' for the human condition, Khan pinpoints the sad, twisted nature of the species as a whole" (11).

Because all three of his published novels are set in the Indian subcontinent Khan has, at times, been criticized as being too exotic. Jane Sullivan has compared Khan with two other Indian writers, Rohinton Mistry and Vikram Chandra, especially for his "unashamedly 'exotic' writing" of *The Storyteller* (7). Elsewhere, in his otherwise favorable review of *Solitude of Illusions,* Andrew Riemer, too, had expressed his hope "that there will be nothing about the Indian subcontinent in his next novel: he is far too good a writer to remain predictably 'exotic' " (Sullivan 8). Aware that such comparison only attempts to compartmentalize him even more, Khan has repeated subcontinental characters in *The Storyteller.*

Critically acclaimed for all his three novels, Khan's reviews too have been largely favorable, as publishers have actively sought after his books. Four publishers had bid for *The Storyteller* when it was auctioned, with HarperCollins winning the contract. But even with such remarkable success as a writer, Khan is apprehensive about the novelty of his future writing. Although he is already thinking about plots of future novels, his biggest concern remains whether "he might try out a 'bone dry' style, like J. M. Coetzee" (Sullivan 7).

Khan is currently working on a novel about a Vietnam veteran's battle to cope with posttraumatic stress disorder. His agent auctioned the manuscript and HarperCollins won the rights for Australia, New Zealand, and Britain. The working title of the novel *Journey of Shadows* may be changed at the time of publication in October 2003. Khan has received $50,000, to be awarded over two years, from the Australian Council for the Arts to complete this book. Khan's agent is already contemplating on taking the edited version to the United States. Khan is very optimistic about the outcome of his latest project in terms of content and style and claims it to be quite different from his previous novels. He is collaborating on the book with one of Australia's foremost fiction editors, Judith Lukin-Amundsen.

Amitava Kumar.

Rebecca Sultana

Further Reading

Greet, Annie. "Angels and Demons." Rev. of *The Storyteller. The Age* 9 Sept. 2000: 11.

Haas, Lynette. "Life Write Large." Rev. of *The Storyteller. Sunday Mail* 24 Sept. 2000: 36.

Khan, Adib. Interview with Matt Condon. "An Encounter with A Charismatic Street Performer inspired Adib Khan's *The Storyteller.*" *Sun-Herald* 15 Oct. 2000: 1–2.

———. "Writing Homeland." *Australian Book Review* May 1995: 24–25.

O'Connor, Shaunagh. "Dwarf Tells Tall Story." *Herald Sun* 12 Aug. 2000: 18–19.

Perry, Susan. "Adib Cooks himself a Winner." *Sydney Morning Herald* 1 Oct. 1994: 13.

Sullivan, Jane. "Outside Edge." Rev. of *The Storyteller. The Age Extra* 2 Sept. 2000: 7–8.

Kumar, Amitava

Born in Bihar, India, Amitava Kumar grew up in Patna, and received master's degrees from Delhi and Syracuse Universities and a Ph.D. from the University of Minnesota. An itinerant academic, he now teaches English at Penn State University. Kumar has published a volume of poetry *No Tears for the NRI* (1996), the multigenre work *Passport Photos* (2000), and more recently *Bombay–London–New York* (2002). He has also written journalistic pieces; edited collections of scholarly essays, *Poetics/Politics: Radical Aesthetics for the Classroom* and *Class Issues: Pedagogy, Cultural Studies, and the Public Sphere;* and scripted and narrated "Pure Chutney," a video about the hybrid lives of Indo-Trinidadians, which was directed by the filmmaker Sanjeev Chatterjee.

In all his work, Kumar is concerned with the intermarriage of politics and aesthetics, and as he writes in his preface to *Poetics/Politics,* he is interested in productively mining the tensions between art and politics, bringing them to a constructive dialogue with each other. As a teacher in an American classroom, he, along with the volume's other contributors, wonders about the goals of academics and searches intensely for pedagogical strategies that will enable struggles to be waged inside and outside the classroom. *Passport Photos* contains Kumar's musings on the poetics and politics of the immigrant condition. Kumar variously calls his book a "report on postcolonialism" (x), his "own brand of anthropology and autobiography" (56), and most importantly a "forged" document, one that speaks against the official languages of the state, and subverts the categories in a passport that attempt to fix identities narrowly in boxes. This work, while mimicking the organizational structure of a passport, is a collage of poetry, newspaper articles, photographs, photo captions, postcolonial Marxist and feminist theory, literary and cultural criticism, letters to the editor, and personal reflections, that is extremely attentive to the way in which the local and the global always intersect in an increasingly transnational and globalized world order. Kumar includes within his narrative many poems that were published earlier in *No Tears for the NRI* in which he tries to make visible precisely those histories that get left out in dominant narratives of the state, whether they be of the poor migrant worker who sends money home from one of the Gulf states, or the South Asian taxi driver in the United States whose narrative gets erased in all the talk of "model minority."

Moving between various locations, Kumar explores, in a self-conscious, even flamboyant manner, the following issues among others: borders and transnationalism; migrant women workers in the United States exploited in global circuits of capital; South Asian women in the United States as they negotiate new identities between an oppressive home and the racialized world of the "host" country. *Passport Photos* ends with a list of immigrant support groups and organizations, a testimony to the new assemblages and solid communities that immigrants create to counter the racial politics of their adopted country. *Bombay–London–New York* also picks up some of these same themes. The book opens with the sentence, "This book is about recent Indian fiction in English" (1). But it is also, as Kumar says a few pages later, about his "struggle to become a writer" (15). In this "literary journey," Kumar constructs a portrait of the memoirist as a literary and cultural critic, as literary artist and social historian. Focusing on the three cosmopolitan cities that figure prominently in the reality and imagination of writers of the South Asian diaspora, Kumar also chronicles stories from other lost smaller towns and villages; other histories of migration and displacement as inflected by class and gender; and also acts of resistance in the diaspora. In this book about diasporic realities, Kumar meditates on the constructive as well as oppressive force of nostalgia, the importance of the past in shaping one's present identity, the prominent appearance of the "diaspora aesthetic" in the Bollywood films of the 1990s, and the works of many writers including Mahatma Gandhi, R. K. Narayan, V. S. Naipaul, Hanif Kureishi, Salman Rushdie, and Manil Suri. Demonstrating his familiarity with writing in vernacular Indian languages, as well as with Indian writing in English, Kumar tries to create a space for himself as a writer in these traditions.

Kumar's deep commitment to the issues he writes about has been recognized by various scholars. M. V. Ramana calls *Passport Photos* a "charming, exhilarating, thought-provoking attempt at understanding and speaking about the immigrant experience" (35). Similarly, a reviewer of *Poetics/Politics* comments that "Ultimately the value of Kumar's collection is that it traces two predominant understandings of the relation between the aesthetic and the political in smart and sophisticated ways, and it forces us out of a complacent sense that there's not a lot we can do about their mutual implication" (Bernard-Donals 177).

Anupama Arora

Further Reading

Bernard-Donals, Michael. Rev. of *Poetics/Politics: Radical Aesthetics for the Classroom,* ed. Amitava Kumar. *College Literature* 28:3 (Fall 2001): 177.

Ramana, M. V. "Two Nations and One World." Rev. of *Passport Photos* by Amitava Kumar. *Kala* 5:2 (Winter 2001): 35–36.

Kunzru, Hari

Hari Kunzru was born in 1969 in Woodford Green, England, to an Indian father and English mother. He has been a regular contributor to many British and international publications, writing about technology, cultural change, electronic music, and art. During 1999 and 2000, he presented a magazine program about electronic arts on Sky TV. He was an associate editor at *Wired* and was named the Observer Young Travel Writer of the Year in 1999. He is a contributing editor to *Mute* magazine and music editor at *Wallpaper.* However, Hari Kunzru is best known for his debut novel *The Impressionist,* published in 2002 to great critical acclaim, after a transatlantic tug-of-war for publication.

The novel focuses on the significance of multiculturalism as an individual experience. It is a simultaneous attempt to explore a part of his ancestry—the Indianness of his being, the reality of empire domination, and the fragmented center that creates doubts. But beyond the Indianness, it is the formation of the mindset that accompanied the deeds of empire, which he explores through the story of Pran/Jonathan.

However, this novel is in the tradition of both Walter Scott's *Waverley* and Saratchandra Chattopadyay's *Srikanta.* It has at its narrative center an absent hero who functions as an excuse for chronicling the world around him as he travels on his picaresque journey throughout the land. In *Srikanta* this journey was through India; in *Waverley,* it is the world of Scotland that is explored. In Kunzru's *The Impressionist,*

the setting is the vast scope of the British Empire. But the journey is not only a physical journey: it involves countless mental somersaults as the hero moves from one extreme of cultural absolutism to another and to another, and so on, until he reaches the point of total annihilation of center and meaning and allows himself to be abandoned to the flux of time.

The novel recounts the story of Pran/Jonathan: born of mixed parentage but brought up within a strictly orthodox Hindu family. His world of privileges and petty domination crashes when the truth of his conception is revealed and he is thrown out on the streets. To escape the streets, he is directed by a beggar to a brothel, but from there is sold to the Fatehpur Royal family. This section of the narrative allows the reader to enter the world of decadence of the Indian aristocrats and their frolicking with the British in all the glorious incompetence of both groups, as the one tries to maintain control and the other to wrest power over a land that neither of them really cares about. It takes time for Pran Nath to escape, and when the escape comes, the color of his skin leads to strange encounters and allows him the most daring of impersonations. This fact permits him to travel to England, appropriate the identity of Jonathan Bridgeman, and enter the seat of empire through an educational institution that resembles the world of Cambridge Dons and Cambridge rituals.

There are obviously many subtexts to Kunzru's narrative: the reader cannot miss references to E. M. Forster, Charles Dickens, Evelyn Waugh, Rudyard Kipling, and others. The author says that these references were both a way of dealing with the sociopolitical reality of the Raj—the novel is set mostly in nineteenth-century India—and a natural outcome of the literary reality that "our imagination, especially in India, has been largely constructed by those authors, who are by and large British authors" (Kunzru).

It has to be noted that Kunzru himself was a student at Oxford University, Wadham College, where he read for a degree in English literature. Subsequently he went to Warwick for a master's in philosophy and literature. Before Oxford, though, Kunzru was at Bancroft school. This experience with both the public school tradition and at Oxford is put to direct use in his novel. As Pran/Bridgeman learns to find his way through the successive closed circles of elite British educational establishments, his obsession with impersonation brings him closer and closer to theories of racist supremacy, which he appropriates as a joke in order to obliterate his mixed ancestry. But this racist supremacy translates as anthropological superiority when he joins an expedition to Africa to study the Fotse. Lined, drawn and quartered, both the anthropologists and the natives exist in confrontation. But at the moment of final obliteration, Bridgeman discovers that the center he had been traveling toward is but make believe and vacuous. In this realization comes annihilation and a new beginning: in his near-death state he is taken into the mystical world of the Fotses who save his life and give him entrance into a new world of reality.

Kunzru's novel is an interesting exploration about the constructed nature of the self. He says of the novel: "It's a retrospective way of understanding how I came to exist and to be born the way I was to parents I was. So the whole idea of tradition and influence and whose history and whose tradition were very important to me." Kunzru has his own Web site (<http://www.harikunzru.com>) where he publishes both journalistic and fictional short prose. Kunzru is working on his second novel, *Transmission,* to be published by Penguin in 2003.

Nandini Bhautoo-Dewnarain

Further Reading
"Don't Laugh." Rev. of *The Impressionist* by Hari Kunzru. *London Review of Books* 8 Aug. 2002: 22–23.
Kunzru, Hari. <http://www.harikunzru.com>.
"The Mimic Man." Rev. of *The Impressionist* by Hari Kunzru. *Biblio: A Review of Books* May-June 2002: 4–5.
"Myriad Avatars." Rev. of *The Impressionist,* by Hari Kunzru. *The Book Review* July 2002: 5–6.

Kureishi, Hanif

Hanif Kureishi was born in Bromley, England, in 1954. The son of a Pakistani immigrant father and English mother, Kureishi grew up experiencing firsthand the racial and cultural clashes that constitute the main theme of his work. Much of his work is derived from his own experiences as a hybrid of two different races and cultures. Kureishi wanted to be a writer ever since he was a teenager. He studied philosophy at the University of London at which time he supported himself by writing pornography under the pseudonym Antonia French. Kureishi began his career in theater as an usher for the Royal Theater. Eventually he became the theater's writer in residence.

His first play *Soaking up the Heat* was produced in 1976 at London's Theater Upstairs, and his second play, *The Mother Country* won him the Thames Television Playwright Award in 1980. His first major breakthrough, however, came with his play *Borderline* (1981), performed at the Royal Court Theater, and his next play *Outskirts* (1981), performed by the Royal Shakespeare Company, which won him acclaim as a playwright.

Kureishi's success as a playwright illuminates the fact that his own hybridity and concern with the lives of immigrants living in London defines his writing. He claims that in England there is a new national identity:

I'm British. . . . But being British is a new thing now. It involves people with names like Kureishi or Ishiguro or Rushdie. . . . And we're all British too. . . . But most critics in England don't understand that. So there isn't any understanding of Britain being a multicultural place. They think that I'm, let's say, a regional writer or writing in a sort of sub genre. They think writers like (me) are on the edges. We are still marginalized culturally. . . . They don't see that the world is now hybrid. (Kaleta 7)

However, even though Kureishi's plays deal with the problems of race relations in England, they are products of the rich heritage of English theater. Like Ben Jonson, Kureishi criticizes social hypocrisy. Like the plays of Oscar Wilde, his plays deal with class barriers and sexual tensions.

In an early essay *The Rainbow Sign* (1986) Kureishi recalls his own experiences as a misfit growing up in a racially torn England. The essay is divided into three sections set in England and Pakistan, and it reflects the ambiguities of Kureishi's own identity, which is neither at home in England nor at home in Pakistan. The essay is an autobiographical examination of the author's exile and the ambiguities of identity as defined by color.

The prejudices of race and class distinctions form the subject matter of his two screenplays and films, *My Beautiful Laundrette* (1985) and *Sammy and Rosie Get laid* (1988). In *My Beautiful Laundrette* (directed by Stephen Frears), Kureishi explores and articulates the predicament of migrancy and race relations through the problematic concept of *home,* where white British youth subcultures clash with black immigrants and jostle for space. In this film, multiple notions of home emerge against the backdrop of Margaret Thatcher's England. *My Beautiful Laundrette* is a story of a young Pakistani boy, Omar, and his white working class lover, Johnny. Omar is torn between two worlds—Pakistan and England; and two philosophies—the idealistic socialism of his father Hussein and the get-rich-quick philosophy of his uncle Nasser.

A film still from the adaptation of Hanif Kureishi's novel *My Beautiful Laundrette.* Courtesy of Photofest.

The film is also about the conflict between immigrants and the youth cultures in London. In fact, the film redefines questions of national identity and belonging. Thus, gangsters like Ghengis and Moose signify the breakdown of consensus, and their aggression successful Pakistanis like Nasser and Salim is a reflection of their sense of displacement and their hopeless attempts to reclaim a sense of community. However, for Hussein, there is another dilemma:

> The lack of possibility in Pakistan leads him to pursue his intellectual and political ideals in England where he encounters a society eroded by racial tension and a new enterprise culture of money-making. This lack of possibility in his adopted "home" leaves him in a perpetual state of limbo . . . it is clear Hussein is in a permanent state of exile. (Sampat-Patel 13)

The sense of contingency or provisional belonging that characterizes the dilemma of Hussein and his brother Nasser is completely contrasted with Kureishi's main characters: Hussein's son Omar and his white working-class boyfriend Johnny. Both Johnny and Omar share a relationship that subverts conventional notions of heterosexual love and rearticulates them in new forms of political identities and alliances. Omar is willing to forgive Johnny's right-wing past, and unable to identify with his father's and uncle's ties with Pakistan, he is driven by a deep desire to succeed financially.

In *My Beautiful Laundrette,* love triumphs and ambitions are achieved. In Kureishi's next film, *Sammy and Rosie Get Laid* (also directed by Stephen Frears), questions of social/political class and racial identity are more complex. The film contains a wide variety of characters (punks, socialists, lesbians, anarchists, patriarchal father figures, ruthless property

A film still from the adaptation of Hanif Kureishi's novel *Sammy and Rosie Get Laid.* Courtesy of Photofest.

owners, suburban women) that interact with the protagonists, Sammy and Rosie. They come from different class, racial and social backgrounds with different histories, political commitments, and sexual preferences so that "the codes of heterosexual love are mocked and political inconsistency is privileged as the characters release themselves from boundaries of imposed sexual, social and political roles" (Sampat-Patel 26). Critic Leonard Quart writes:

> It's Kureishi's belief that a life of spontaneity—free of guilt and crass self-interest—which the films set in opposition to all that is respectable, repressive and calculating in society. Friars' directorial style reinforces this vision by making use of split screen, rapid, rhythmic crosscutting, shock cuts—a barrage of visual and aural fireworks to

help disrupt our sense of order and affirm a life lived without conventional constraints. (Kaleta 53)

Thus, the film's bold juxtapositions of visual and political messages (riot scenes set against the background of Thatcher's speeches calling for harmony) are vivid representations of urban squalor, violence, repression, and racial tensions that characterized Thatcher's London.

In 1991, Kureishi made his debut as a film director with the release of his film *London Kills Me,* which is, once again, a story of contemporary London. This time Kureishi's main character is Clint, a white grifter and drug dealer who lives in squats, has sex with a liberal feminist, uses friends and robs his employer to get a pair of shoes that would enable him to get a respectable job away from his working-class Notting Hill neighborhood. The film received many negative reviews and unsuccessfully recalled the 1970s nostalgia of youth revolutions.

In his next film *My Son the Fanatic* (1993), directed by Udayan Prasad and based on a short story of the same title, Kureishi depicts the story of a reticent taxi driver and immigrant, Parvez, who is having an illicit love affair with an English prostitute. Parvez has a son, Farid, who is engaged to the white daughter of a local policeman. Farid breaks off his engagement and immerses himself in a fundamentalist and devout Muslim subculture that provides him with a sense of identity and solidarity. This film indicates Kureishi's growing interest in the area of fundamentalism, particularly as a reaction to the liberalism of immigrants who had moved to England in the 1950s and 1960s.

Kureishi continues to explore the familial and racial conflicts in his novel *The Buddha of Suburbia,* published in 1990. This book tells the story of Karim, a teenager of an Indian father, Haroon, and English mother growing up in London.

Hanif Kureishi directing *London Kills Me.* Courtesy of Photofest.

Karim is besotted by his father's girlfriend Eva's son, Charlie, who becomes famous in a punk band. Haroon is the "Buddha" of the story and sees himself as some sort of New Age guru. Both Karim and Haroon package themselves as false Indians appropriating popular notions of "Indianness." Both are trapped in their confused and mistaken notions of identity and strive to move from the peripheries to the center. Karim is constantly reminded of his hybridity and soon learns that a pure English identity is something he will never achieve. Haroon, on the other hand, is greatly disappointed with England since it does not conform to any of his images. Ultimately both father and son are trapped in a pathetic yet hilarious search for authentic identities. *The Black Album,* published in 1995, once again deals with issues of a young Asian growing up in London. However, it is not as lighthearted as *The Buddha of Suburbia* and is set in the sordid backdrop of student digs in Kilburn. The book is also about the clash between Islam and liberal Western culture, and Shahid, the central character in the novel is informed by the conflicting forces of Islamic fundamentalism represented by his guru, Riaz, who can put him in touch with his roots and the liberal intellectual forces at the college. There is a third force at work in Shahid's life as well—the drug culture of 1968, often known as the "summer of love," which is incompatible with his Muslim identity. The novel is clearly a critique of fundamentalism and censorship (there are references to the Rushdie affair) and a sharp and convincing portrait of the rootlessness experienced by British Asians.

In *Intimacy,* published in 1998, Kureishi explores the problems of midlife crisis. Jay, the narrator of the novel, decides to leave his complacent middle-class life and family to pursue his dreams. This novel is different from his other novels because it is a purely subjective narrative of self-analysis where Jay's dreams, desire for freedom, and erotic fantasies reveal an almost childlike protagonist who is completely self-absorbed and deluded. Critics have commented on the strong autobiographical content of this novel and have compared the antihero to Salinger's adolescent hero in *The Catcher in the Rye.*

Hanif Kureishi's most recent novel, *Gabriel's Gift,* published in 2002, is very different. Like his earlier novels, *The Buddha of Suburbia* and *The Black Album,* this novel reflects Kureishi's interest in pop, rave, ecstasy, and rock music and the culture of drugs, parties, clothes, politics, and sexuality that went with it. It is the story of Gabriel who is recovering from the breakup of his parents' marriage. His father, Rex, is a talented guitarist, and neither he nor Gabriel's mother, Christine, are able to come away from a bohemian lifestyle and face the real world where people pay rents and go to work. Gabriel, of course, is more realistic and hopes, some day, to become a filmmaker. He communicates with his dead twin brother while he is left to look after his parents. Unlike Rex and Christine, Gabriel does not live in the world of the 1970s and is not marked by their nostalgia and disappointment.

Hanif Kureishi has also written many essays and two collections of short stories, *Love in a Blue Time* (1997) and *Midnight All Day* (1999), and a play, *Sleep With Me,* that premiered in 1999. In 1995, he co-edited *A Faber Book of Pop* with Jon Savage.

Niti Sampat-Patel

Further Reading

Kaleta, Kenneth. *Hanif Kureishi: Postcolonial Storyteller.* Austin: U of Texas P, 1998.

Sampat-Patel, Niti. *Postcolonial Masquerades: Culture and Politics in Literature, Film, Video, and Photography.* New York: Garland, 2001.

Spivak, Gayatri Chakravorty. "In Praise of *Sammy and Rosie Get Laid." Critical Quarterly* 31.2 (1989): 80–88.

Yates, Robert. "London Necropolis of Fretful Ghosts." *Sight and Sound* 6 (June 1994): 12–16.

L

Love and Longing in Bombay
by Vikram Chandra

Born in Delhi in 1961, Chandra was raised by his father Navin, a company president, and his mother Kamna, a screenwriter and playwright. Chandra attended school at St. Xavier's College in Mumbai (formerly Bombay), then obtained a B.A. from Pomona College, an M.A. from Johns Hopkins University, and an M.F.A. from the University of Houston; he also attended film school at Columbia University before pursuing a career as a writer. In addition to *Love and Longing in Bombay,* Chandra has published the novel *Red Earth and Pouring Rain* (1995); authored the popular Indian television series *City of Gold* (1996); and coscripted a film, *Mission Kashmir* (2000), directed by his brother-in-law, Vidhu Vinod Chopra. He is at present teaching creative writing at George Washington University, and divides his time between Washington and Mumbai.

Love and Longing in Bombay is composed of five short stories, two of which are lengthy enough perhaps to be considered novellas. Each story is named for a precept of Hindu philosophy: "Dharma" (duty, or right action), "Shakti" (strength), "Kama" (love or desire), "Artha" (economy), and "Shanti" (peace). Chandra has written that his intention in thus titling his stories was to emphasize the ways in which such abstract concepts play out in the contemporary world: "That's precisely what I like about the titles [. . .] the bur-nished glow of the Sanskrit, their seeming distance from the gritty landscapes of the stories themselves" ("The Cult of Authenticity," par. 3). Although it is misleading to suggest that the stories are parables of these concepts, since each tale is too complex for so limiting a label, it is nonetheless accurate to note that each of these principles infuses the story with a degree of philosophical significance. On the other hand, the tales also occupy recognizable genres of fiction, from the ghost story to detective fiction to romance.

The narrator of all the stories is a retired civil servant named Subramaniam, who relates each story to the younger Nanjit Sharma. In the first story, "Dharma," Major General Jehangir "Jago" Antia is a war hero, a born soldier (apparently) who lost his leg in the 1971 Indian-Pakistan war, but who still leads his men through his iron control and force of will. Jago resigns and returns to his desolate family home to recuperate, only to discover that the house is haunted. Through flashbacks we learn both that Jago amputated his own leg in order to continue to lead his troops during battle, and that he was involved in the accidental death of his elder brother Soli. Upon confronting the spirit, Jago discovers that it is his seven-year-old self with whom the adult Jago seems in the end to affect a kind of reconciliation.

"Shakti" relates the tale of an epic struggle between two Bombay socialites, Sheila Bijlani and Dolly Boatwalla.

Snubbed by the established Dolly, the *nouveau riche* Sheila decides to retaliate. Each subsequent maneuver by the rivals has escalating ambitions and consequences, from prevented marriages to business takeovers. Ultimately, Sheila's victory (brought about by her servant Ganga) culminates in a marriage as well as a business partnership between the two families. This story, with its emphasis on the connection between public affairs and domestic politics, has evoked for some readers the work of Edith Wharton and Marcel Proust.

"Kama" is essentially a detective story that centers on the efforts of detective-inspector Sartaj Singh, a Sikh policeman, to solve a deceptively simple murder case. As Sartaj delves deeper into the facts surrounding the murder, he becomes embroiled in a labyrinth of political machinations (specifically, the fascist group Shiv Sena) and discovers his own uncomfortable relationship to the case, as the details of the underlying sex scandal remind him all too much of his tangled involvement with his ex-wife, Megha. This story's evocation of the Bombay underworld is reportedly so strong for Chandra that he is currently at work on a crime novel featuring Sartaj Singh as a protagonist.

"Artha" concerns the relationship between its protagonist, Iqbal, a computer programmer, and his lover, Rajesh, who has mysterious ties to a construction magnate named Ratnani. The plot revolves around two mysteries: a computer bug that threatens to derail Iqbal's consulting project and Rajesh's sudden disappearance. Iqbal discovers the sabotage that has wrecked his efforts to construct his computer program, but his efforts to locate Rajesh, though they lead him unexpectedly into the Bombay underworld, are never rewarded. Underlying "Artha" is the theme of the drive for money, and the more metaphorical exchange of allegiances and betrayals.

"Shanti" concludes the collection with a romance set against the backdrop of war-time loss and violence. The main character, Shiv, yearns for his twin brother, killed in the Hindu-Muslim sectarian riots prior to India's independence; at a train station, he spies Mrs. Shanti Chauhan, a beautiful woman who is crisscrossing the country in search of her missing husband, a fighter pilot who has gone missing in Burma. As Shiv and Shanti fall in love through trading stories, it becomes evident that Shiv is Subramaniam himself, telling the story of how he met his wife. At the end of the collection, the stories Ranjit has heard seem to have transformed him from a somewhat callow young man, disdainful of tradition and superstition, into someone whose appreciation of stories allows him to embrace life.

Although relatively little academic criticism has been directed toward *Love and Longing in Bombay,* book reviewers have consistently noted its contrast to Chandra's novel *Red Earth and Pouring Rain,* which appeared two years earlier. Where the latter was labeled a magical-realist epic that yoked together Indian narrative tradition and more contemporary literary styles, *Love and Longing in Bombay* received its praise primarily for its depiction of the lived experience of urban India and its skillful interweaving of apparently dissimilar tales. Ultimately, the book collectively speaks to the various types of love and loss we can experience in our modern, chaotic lives, and the role of stories in restoring us to ourselves.

Scott D. Walker

Further Reading

Chandra, Vikram. "The Cult of Authenticity." *Boston Review* Feb.-Mar. 2000. 9 July 2002 <http://bostonreview.mit.edu/BR25.1/chandra.html>.

"Chandra, Vikram 1961– ." *Contemporary Authors.* Galenet. 9 July 2002 <http://web3.infotrac.galenet.com>.

Sethi, Robbie Clipper. Rev. of *Love and Longing in Bombay* by Vikram Chandra. *IndiaStar: A Literary-Art Magazine.* 9 July 2002 <http://www.indiastar.com/sethi3.htm>.

M

Macaulay's Minute on Education

In 1835, the governor-general of India, Lord William Bentinck, invited a respected British man of letters, Thomas Babington Macaulay, to recommend a suitable educational system for the colonized people of the Indian subcontinent. Macaulay, who had arrived in India as a law member of the governor-general's council in June 1834, had by December of that year also been appointed president of the General Committee of Public Instruction. In response, he turned out a lengthy rhetorical document declaring that India could be reshaped in England's image through education.

In what has become an often-studied statement of colonial arrogance, Macaulay's Minute recommended that English become the official language of India as well as the medium of educational instruction in all educational institutions. Imbued with a strong belief in liberalism and radical universalism, Macaulay asserted that British culture alone represented civilization. As Sara Suleri notes, Macaulay's statement is "infamous for the ease with which it obliterates cultural nuance and consequently fails to see any continued vitality in indigenous Indian languages and modes of learning" (33).

Four main themes emerge in Macaulay's Minute. To begin with, Macaulay argues that English should replace Persian, the language of the Mughal emperors, as the official language in India. Although he did not claim to have any firsthand knowledge of Arabic or Sanskrit, Macaulay is quite confident that neither of these languages or their literatures have anything to recommend them. Further, he claims to have the word of Orientalists that "the entire native literature of India and Arabia" is not equal to "a single shelf of books in the English language."

Second, he advises that English should be introduced as the medium of instruction in all the institutions of learning, for that language alone "has ready access to all the vast intellectual wealth which all the wisest nations of the earth have created and hoarded in the course of ninety generations." Macaulay advises that a language of the sciences be used to promote "knowledge of the sciences" according to the India Act of 1833.

Third, he insists that translating Western knowledge into vernacular languages that are not properly developed would not be useful. He finds neither Arabic nor Sanskrit suitable for the transmission of scientific and technological knowledge. Rather, Indians acquainted with Western knowledge and science would surely have "the inclination and the ability to exhibit European knowledge in the vernacular dialects" and would eventually help to develop a vernacular literature in the country within 20 years.

Macaulay's fourth point follows logically from the third: Indians taught through the medium of English would take care of the education of their countrymen and would themselves become "a class of persons, Indian in blood and colour, but English in taste, in opinions, in morals and intellect." Thus was born the trickle-down system of education, which sadly, had not reached the level of elementary school by the time independence was granted in 1947; thereby too, evolved the huge number of clerks and writers who kept the records of the vast bureaucracy needed to govern the British Raj.

Macaulay, like other liberal idealists of his day, including James Mill and his son, John Stuart Mill, looked forward to the day when India might be politically independent, its society and culture having been completely transformed by exposure to English education and law. Yet, as Thomas Metcalf suggests, this project was flawed: "the more fully non-European peoples were accorded the prospect of future equality, the more necessary it became to devalue and depreciate their contemporary cultures" (34). Despite the fact that an ancient civilization clearly existed, Macaulay felt compelled to insist that India was currently "sunk in the lowest depths of slavery and superstition." A century and a half later, the West rediscovered the richness of South Asian culture.

Janet M. Powers

Further Reading

Cohn, Bernard S. *Colonialism and Its Forms of Knowledge: The British in India.* Princeton: Princeton UP, 1996.

Ghosh, Suresh Chandra. "Bentinck, Macaulay, and the Introduction of English Education in India." *History of Education* 24:1 (Mar. 1995): 17–24.

Metcalf, Thomas R. *Ideologies of the Raj.* Cambridge: Cambridge UP, 1995.

Suleri, Sara. *The Rhetoric of English India.* Chicago: U of Chicago P, 1992.

Teltscher, Kate. *India Inscribed: European and British Writing on India: 1600–1800.* Delhi: Oxford UP, 1995.

Viswanathan, Gauri. *Masks of Conquest: Literary Study and British Rule in India.* New York: Columbia UP, 1989.

Magical Realism

The oxymoron magical realism (or magic realism) is a balance of two opposing discursive practices: realism and fantasy. The term was first used by German art critic Franz Roh in 1925 to describe an art movement that responded to the enigmas of reality. It was later adopted by the literary community but interpreted in different ways. The Cuban novelist Alejo Carpentier's "real maravilloso" (or marvelous real) defined a particular form in Latin American fiction that conveyed the marvelous aspects of American reality. Tommasa Scarano says of Carpentier: "he proclaims the authentically marvellous character of the real, as opposed to the false marvels of what is unreal" (Linguanti, Casotti, and Concilio 14). In 1954, the term *realismo mágico* (magical realism) was used by Ángel Flores in an academic context to focus on the amalgamation of realism and fantasy in Spanish American literature. Tommasa Scarano describes this amalgamation as "the naturalization of the unreal, and the supernaturalization of the real," involving the use of "techniques such as alienation, deformation or exaggeration to narrate the real as marvellous, prodigious, and magical" (Linguanti, Casotti, and Concilio 17, 18).

Magical realism has been described in various ways in order to differentiate a certain body of fiction from fantastic narratives. John Erickson explains: "In narratives marked by magical realism . . . two diametrically opposed ontologies coexist on equal terms: the empirical world of reason and logic and the supernatural world of unreason" (Zamora and Faris, 428). Where fantastic narrative "through its characters and narrator, conveys doubt, anxiety and crisis, the magical-realist narrative insinuates the absence of doubt" and "narrates the supernatural event without any ambiguity . . . [and is] not in conflict with reality" (Tommaso Scarano in Linguanti, Casotti, and Concilio 24).

Günter Grass and Franz Kafka are well-known magical-realist writers; the latter influenced Gabriel García Márquez, whose *One Hundred Years of Solitude,* published in 1967, is perhaps the most commonly known work described as magical realist. In this parody of European travel narratives, Marquez's magical realism subverts the mythological image of New World discovery, and in so doing critiques political reality. Since *One Hundred Years of Solitude,* writers not confined to Latin America have used magical realism as a literary device in diverse ways, such as Salman Rushdie's *Midnight's Children,* Ben Okri's *The Famished Road,* Peter Carey's *Illywhacker,* and Isabel Allende's *The House of the Spirits,* to name a few. The fusion of individual forms of myth, legend, or folklore (unique to each writer) with *realism* acts to contest the cultural assumptions of traditional Western narratives.

This methodology is the framework to Salman Rushdie's *Midnight's Children,* published in 1981, a text that significantly changed the representation of India in Western literature. The juxtaposition of history and fiction, the construction of oral narrative as a means of storytelling within the written narrative, and Rushdie's use of hybridized English and Indian allusions, can be regarded as a means of liberation within a postcolonial literary context. This work has been significant in representing the complexities of colonization, decolonization, migrancy, and hybridity, and has been instrumental in influencing recent Indian novelists and also in instigating theoretical debates and critical works of Asian literature in English. The combination of reality and magic in Rushdie's novels is a metafictional device drawing from both Western and non-Western sources, and it

questions the validity of fixed myths through a manipulation of their meanings. The influences of both Márquez and Günter Grass are apparent in Rushdie's fiction. Magical realism is used as a satirical means to playfully subvert both the realist novel and the myth, while social reality is critiqued within the structure of a deliberate literary artificiality.

Stephen Slemon explains this device, used as a strategy within a postcolonial context, with reference to the novels *The Invention of the World* by Jack Hodgins, and *What the Crow Said* by Robert Kroetsch. Slemon explains that these texts "comprise a positive and liberating engagement with the codes of imperial history" (Zamora and Faris 422). The disruption of Western narratives places magical realism in a subversive context, however, as Michael Valdez Moses suggests, it can also be regarded as a mediator between cultures in a global sense. Various novelists articulate the mix of the realistic and the fabulous in differing ways, but the common link is perhaps the combination of traditional realism with varying aspects of cultural traditions. In other words, the two traditions of narrative writing—the European realist novel, and the indigenous, heterogeneous aspects of folk narratives—fuse together in magical realism. In this sense, the author can be considered as a mediator between the dominant literary forms and the various cultural traditions from diverse societies. The worldwide popularity of magical realism as a discourse lies in the adaptability and possibility of articulating the representation of individual cultural practices from specific locales, alongside the Western literary conventions. The oxymoron *magical realism* further reveals the paradox of maintaining cultural distinctions through a global literary practice (Moses). In this way magical realism as a mediating strategy can be interpreted as breaking down boundaries between literary formations and cultural discourses.

Melanie A. Murray

Further Reading

Durix, Jean-Pierre. *Mimesis, Genres and Post-Colonial Discourse: Deconstructing Magic Realism.* Basingstoke: Macmillan, 1998.

Linguanti, Elsa, Francesco Casotti, and Carmen Concilio, eds. *Coterminous Worlds: Magical Realism and Contemporary Post-Colonial Literature in English.* Amsterdam: Rodopi, 1999.

Moses, Michael Valdez. *Magical Realism at World's End.* 2001 <http://www.angelfire.com/wa2/margin/nonficMoses.html>.

Zamora, Lois Parkinson, and Wendy B. Faris, eds. *Magical Realism: Theory, History, Community.* Durham: Duke UP, [1995], 1997.

Markandaya, Kamala

Kamala Markandaya is the pseudonym of the Indo-British novelist, born Kamala Purnaiya in the princely kingdom of Mysore in South India in 1924. Markandaya had a privileged upbringing in India—a Purnaiya having been a *dewan* (prime minister) in the court of Tipu Sultan. Ruth Montgomery's few biographical notes in the *Wilson Library Bulletin* inform us that she hails from a fairly orthodox Hindu Brahmin family. Her father's family, "whose records go back to the seventeenth century, were landowners, financiers and administrators; her maternal grandfather was a member of the old Indian Civil Service" (Montgomery 296).

Casting aside his illustrious ancestry, Markandaya's own father chose to rebel and went into government service as an employee of the Indian Railways (at that time, of course, under the control of the British)—as did another brother before him. His unlimited travel facilities were indirectly responsible for Markandaya's flowering into a creative writer as they allowed her the luxury of vacationing in various Indian locales throughout her growing years—locales that provided the inspiration for the settings of her novels.

Her father's frequent transfers to locations around India meant that Markandaya's own education was "intermittent and casual" (Montgomery 296) including a number of schools in India as well as the services of private tutors. Much of her early schooling was obtained in Coimbatore in South India (in the modern-day state of Karnataka) where the family lived for at least eight years at a stretch between 1931 and 1939 until Markandaya was 15. They took summer vacations in the hills of Ootacamund. In 1940, she entered the University of Madras with the intention of taking a degree in history, which was her enduring interest; but she was sidetracked in her scholastic pursuits by an increasingly strong inclination to write.

This desire was, undoubtedly, fueled by the political upheaval around her at the time. In another two years, the struggle for Indian independence from the British would intensify into the sometimes violent protests of the Quit India Movement—a process that would inevitably draw into its vortex all thinking, concerned Indians. Markandaya was no exception. These early experiences provided material for her creative writing so that critics are quite justified in drawing parallels between the life of her female protagonist, Mira, in *Some Inner Fury* (1955), and her own. Her firsthand insight into Indo-British race relations during this very critical period is perhaps the reason why the confrontation of Eastern and Western forces is a frequently recurring theme in her novels.

Abandoning her academic studies before earning her undergraduate degree, Markandaya joined a small weekly paper in South India as a journalist. This paper, unfortunately, closed down for financial reasons, after which "largely out of curiosity" (Montgomery 296) she lived for an extended period of time in a South Indian village. This phase of her life, often referred to on the jackets and blurbs of her novels as "the period of her experiment in rural living" was responsible for the creation of *Nectar in a Sieve* (1954), which most critics consider to be her literary *tour de force* and upon which her reputation in the West rests. Her village experience possibly explains the authenticity of Markandaya's characters in the same novel, Rukmani and Nathan, who, like Job, their Biblical counterpart, reveal boundless patience and resignation in the face of adversity. Dr. Kennington's sense of indignation, in this novel, against Rukmani's unresisting tolerance of injustice, possibly reflects Markandaya's own bewilderment with the long-suffering nature of Indian peasantry that she witnessed firsthand while living in their midst.

In 1948, Markandaya sailed for England hoping to support herself as a journalist, confident that her few months with a minor Indian periodical would launch her directly into the prestigious inner circles of Fleet Street! Of course, such miracles did not happen, and, in an article entitled "Childhood Memories" in *The Illustrated Weekly of India,* she recalled this bleak period in her life: "For a long time while I wrote prodigiously and earned next to nothing and lived in a gaunt bed-sitter in Bloomsbury cooking myself dreary meals on a gas-ring, I dreamed of dining on *pilaus* and *crepes suzettes.* Especially *crepes suzette*" (26–27).

Her early years in England resulted in a series of "dull but amiable jobs" ("Childhood Memories" 26) as she continued to write with the fervent hope of, someday, finding a publisher. The novel she wrote third, *Nectar in a Sieve,* was the first one to be published by Putnam in London in 1954, and, with its publication, she achieved immediate international success. This book still continues to be the most widely prescribed of her novels in courses on modern South Asian literature and civilization in the West.

Little is known about her life in England after 1948. She met and married an Englishman, one Taylor, and has chosen to live in England as an expatriate, though she has since then taken British citizenship—which is why Uma Parmeswaran refers to her as a "native-alien" (*A Study of Representative Indo-English Novelists* 86). She has raised her daughter, Kim, an only child, in England and lives a very private life in Dulwich, in Central London. Despite many attempts by scholars to probe deeper into her personal life, she has remained adamantly silent about it, even reclusive. In a summer 1987 interview, through the services of the British Council, she talked about her novels but refused to discuss her personal life. Now rather frail and keeping very indifferent health, plagued with migraine attacks (as she recently confided to me during a telephone conversation), she keeps a very low profile and avoids the press or scholars' queries completely. She has completely given up writing—a pursuit, she said, which belongs to a very long ago time in her distant past.

As a preamble to her account of a rare interview that Markandaya granted Naseem Khan in London, she reports that she is "a keen theater-goer and an avid reader of history, particularly Greek, Persian and Mughal history" (Naseem Khan 3). This accounts for her vivid recreation of Indo-British history during the Raj in *The Golden Honeycomb* (1977). Markandaya, Khan says, describes herself as "Hindu-Brahmin in religion" and "anti-colonist, anti-imperialist in politics."

Kamala Markandaya is certainly a prolific writer, having published 10 novels to date. In addition, she has published a few short stories in Indian and foreign periodicals and has written several journalistic articles.

Set in a nameless South Indian village, *Nectar in a Sieve* takes us into the lives of a rural family headed by Nathan who has an arranged marriage with a child of 13 years, Rukmani. The novel has been hailed as a fine testament to the enduring quality of family values such as loyalty, fealty, and mutual concern among India's peasant poor. Apart from being a profound love story on the endurance of family ties, it is a fine sociological document that draws attention to the impact of the monsoon on India's agrarian economy, the trials and tribulations of arranged marriage and dowry in India, and the urgent need for rural development and social reform.

Considered a highly autobiographical novel by many, *Some Inner Fury* focuses on the cultural difficulties involved in an interracial relationship that develops between Mira, a young girl raised in the city of Madras, and Richard Marlowe, an Englishman. This novel emphasizes the havoc played by cultural differences in the lives of young Indians at a time when the country was going through a massive transition. Set in the early 1940s, it depicts the questioning of values that many Indians needed to undertake in attempting to identify the side with which their loyalties ought to lie. Her ability to identify with the thoughts and feelings of Mira so effectively makes it seem as if Mira is an autobiographical reincarnation of the author herself.

In *A Silence of Desire* (1960), Markandaya takes us into the home of a young urban Indian couple. Dandekar makes his living as a petty clerk. Sarojini, a housewife, tries her hardest to manage the household on his frugal income until she is diagnosed with a serious medical condition, an abdominal tumor. Dandedar would prefer to see his wife treated by a physician. He is disappointed, instead, to discover that she has placed herself in the hands of a faith healer, a local swami, to whom she begins to pay frequent visits. The crux of the problem in *A Silence of Desire* lies in the clash between tradition and modernity. Dandekar, who considers himself a modern man, has faith in Western medicine while his wife, a tradition-

alist, puts her faith in miracles and spirituality. Their inability to reach a compromise destroys their conjugal harmony. Markandaya's focus in this novel is clearly the dilemma posed by a new India that finds itself quite suddenly on the verge of a revolutionary way of thinking, as it becomes more modernized and moves further into the twentieth century.

Set in the city of Madras in South India and in London, England, *Possession* (1963) is the story of a highly talented Indian artist named Valmiki who is born into a modest Hindu family. His talent is recognized by the local swami who befriends him, becomes his mentor, and fosters his skills. Through the efforts of the swami, Valmiki comes into contact with Lady Caroline Bell, a ruthlessly materialistic Englishwoman who decides to promote the struggling artist. Though his elderly mother begs Valmiki not to leave her alone in India, Caroline whisks him off to her grand home in London's fashionable Belgravia district, where the sudden acquisition of money, power, and attention produces terribly negative effects upon his personality. *Possession* presents another example of the clash between traditional values and monetary ones. It also represents the confrontation between Eastern philosophy and Western materialism. In Valmiki's decision to leave the comforts of England and return to his own culture, Markandaya proves that monetary seductions can have only a temporarily lulling effect upon the psyche of an artist who needs complete freedom of expression to be most creative.

In many ways, *A Handful of Rice* (1966) might be looked upon as the urban counterpart of *Nectar in a Sieve*. Set in the city of Madras, the novel takes an intimate look at the lives of India's urban poor in the decades immediately following the independence of the country. In this novel, the male protagonist, Ravi, born into a poor rural family, leaves his village to seek his fortune in the city. *A Handful of Rice* deals with the harmful sociological effects of India's rapid urbanization. Through this novel Markandaya attempts to show that mass migration from the rural to the urban areas in India (a phenomenon that continues unabated to this day) only resulted in the evils of overcrowding, lack of sanitation, homelessness, and so on. She proves that the lack of basic infrastructure in the cities made rural migrants often feel as if they had jumped from the frying pan into the fire. The novel also focuses on the criminal nexus of India's underground mafia dons and the hold that they exerted on innocent young people, who willingly fell into their clutches by hanging their aspirations for instant riches upon the promises made by these criminals.

Also set in South India, *The Coffer Dams* (1969) brings the reader into the world of rapid rural development in the two decades immediately following independence. *The Coffer Dams,* one of the least known of Markandaya's novels, is a powerful indictment of the imperialist attitudes and policies that continued to reign supreme in India long after the departure of the British. It presents an unlikely love triangle and the politics of an unhealthy marriage against the backdrop of the heady desire for agrarian development that characterized the spirit of early independent India. Through this work, Markandaya questions the price at which rural development was achieved in India and raises ethical issues that were so often ignored in the country's determination to become a strong economic power in the postcolonial years.

In *The Nowhere Man* (1972), Markandaya focuses poignantly and sensitively on a situation with which she was well acquainted. Through her Indian protagonist, Srinivas, Markandaya presents the peculiar dilemma faced by first-generation immigrants who find themselves misfits in every society. Having left their native land

early in life to assimilate into the foreign culture of their adopted homes, they eventually find themselves belonging nowhere. In *The Nowhere Man,* Markandaya experiments with narrative technique. The action moves back and forth between India and Britain, and through the use of flashbacks, she reconstructs Srinivas' past life in India while juxtaposing it against his present anguish in England. The novel deals squarely with the issues of diasporic *angst,* psychological and physical displacement, and hyphenated identity that became popular themes for literary and critical inquiry among later postcolonial critics.

Two Virgins (1973) is Kamala Markandaya's most controversial writing, because in it she deals for the first time with subjects never previously covered by the Indo-English novel. Set in the village of Chingleput in South India, it takes us into the sheltered world of two sisters, Saroja and Lalitha. In scenes that hint of autoeroticism, the young sisters experiment with their gracefully awakening sexuality—with which they are delighted. *Two Virgins* is Markandaya's comment on the need for greater sex education among India's rural communities.

The Golden Honeycomb (1977) is Markandaya's most ambitious novel, by virtue of the wide time span that the plot covers and the broad scope of its subject matter. Dealing with a world with which she was somewhat personally acquainted—the royal households of South India—it traces three generations in the family of an Indian Maharaja. Bawajiraj II of the fictional princedom of Devapur rules over a prosperous and adoring kingdom, despite being under the scrutiny of the British regent, Sir Arthur Copeland, who is posted in his court. Markandaya has filled this novel with a great deal of local color. The exotic backdrop and the gallery of characters from the world of India's erstwhile monarchy do not detract from the intriguing nature of the novel's plot. Markandaya shows the manner in which the conscience of Indian rulers was changed as the nineteenth century gave way to the twentieth. While former members of royal families meekly cooperated with British interests, the later ones joined the national effort to rid the country of British power. They became sensitive to the roles that destiny required them to play once the country was free of foreign shackles. This novel is also important for the vast amount of historic research that Markandaya poured into it, often juxtaposing important real-life events against the fictional background of her created *milieu.*

With *Pleasure City* (1982; known as *Shalimar* in the American edition), Markandaya returns to some of her favorite themes, such as the encounter between East and West, the clash of cultural ideologies, and the ethics involved in the exploitation of Indian peasantry and labor for commercial profit. Based in South India, the novel's setting is the construction of a luxury hotel, "Shalimar," on an Indian beachfront by AIDCORP, a British firm hired to design and manage the venture. As a postcolonial comment on the affinity toward the East that was experienced by many Westerners, *Pleasure City* is unique. It presents a sympathetic Englishman, Tully, whose genuine affection for India and its people transcend considerations of racial and cultural affiliation.

Rochelle Almeida

Further Reading

Almeida, Rochelle. *Originality and Imitation: Indianness in the Novels of Kamala Markandaya.* Jaipur: Rawat, 2000.

Joseph, Margaret. *Kamala Markandaya.* New Delhi: Arnold Heinemann, 1980.

Khan, Naseem. "The Maharajas: Pomp without Power." *National Herald III* (8 May 1977).

Markandaya, Kamala. "Childhood Memories." *The Illustrated Weekly of India* (23 July 1967): 26–27.

Misra, Pravati. *Class Consciousness in the Novels of Kamala Markandaya.* New Delhi: Oscar, 2001.

Montgomery, Ruth. "Kamala Markandaya." *Wilson Library Bulletin* 38.3 (Nov. 1963): 296.

Parmeswaran, Uma. *Kamala Markandaya.* Jaipur: Rawat, 2001.

Prasad, Madhusudhan, ed. *Perspectives on Kamala Markandaya.* Ghaziabad: Vimal Prakashan, 1984.

Mehta, Ved

A prolific writer who has written in various genres including autobiography, biography, travel narrative, and nonfiction prose, Ved Mehta was born in 1934 in Lahore in undivided India. At the age of three, he became blind following a severe bout of meningitis, then at the age of five, Mehta entered a school for the blind away from home. This dislocation was but the beginning of many others in Mehta's life. When the British partitioned India in 1947, his family was forced to abandon their home in Lahore in the newly formed Pakistan and flee as refugees to Delhi. From living in Delhi, Mehta was transplanted once again and sent off to another school after which he gained admission to the Arkansas School for the Blind in the United States. While most schools in the United States turned Mehta down because they believed that migration would only add to the social and cultural maladjustment of a young blind Indian child, Arkansas accepted him. After spending three years in Arkansas, Mehta moved on to Pomona College where he received his bachelor's degree only to migrate to England to study modern history at Balliol College. Returning to the United States, he joined *The New Yorker* as a staff writer in 1961, where he stayed until the early 1990s. Mehta's impressive oeuvre includes a series of autobiographies and familial biographies titled "Continents of Exile"; several books that focus on the culture and contemporary politics of India; and also reflections on contemporary British and other Western theologians, philosophers, and historians, among other subjects. *All for Love* (2001), the ninth volume in his autobiographical series, recounts the anguish, complications, and contradictions of his romantic relationships with four women in the 1960s. The tenth and most recent book in this series, *Dark Harbor* (2003), is set in Isleboro, a small island off the coast of Maine. This is a personal narrative in which Mehta describes, among other things, the follies of building a house, his struggles as a writer, and his love affair with the woman he marries and the children they raise. The eleventh volume in this series, *The Red Letters,* is to be published in 2004.

While Mehta has experimented in various genres, it is the autobiographical form that he has returned to again and again in his search for identity and his attempts to make some sense of his self. His first autobiography, published in 1956, titled *Face to Face,* is divided into three sections—India, Pakistan, and United States—and addresses Mehta's multiple migrations. *Face to Face* was followed by *Sound Shadows of the New World* (1986), *The Stolen Light* (1989), and *Up at Oxford* (1993), autobiographies that expand on themes and memories that Mehta only touches upon in *Face to Face.* In *Sound Shadows* and *The Stolen Light,* Ved Mehta recalls his time in Arkansas and Pomona respectively. In these narratives, Mehta is aware of being a "lonely foreigner" in the United States, even as he constantly attempts to make sense of the traumas of Partition and its very real material effects on his family. Mehta is initiated into the U.S. racial hierarchical politics when, in addition to being called "primitive" and "heathen," his partially sighted classmate racializes him specifically as " nonwhite": "Here you are first white or not white and I see that you ain't white" (*Sound Shadows* 43). His growing consciousness of racial difference in Arkansas in the 1950s leads

Mehta to contemplate his place in the race hierarchy: "I wondered . . . where I fitted into the social puzzle . . . where I stood in the shading from white to black, to connect myself to the rest of the world" (74). Mehta's compulsive impulse to revise and write his story that results from a loss of identity or assignation of a new racialized identity in the adopted home also has a therapeutic value. Continuing his project of self-invention, in *Up At Oxford,* Mehta recalls his undergraduate days at Oxford, his meetings with famous personages, and his Anglophilia: "At Oxford, I had come to deny my Indianness, even my Americanness, and tended to adopt unwittingly the mannerisms and attitudes of the people I admired" (428).

In *Vedi* (1982), Mehta reconstructs through memory the painful recollections of his time at the Dadar School for the Blind, while in *The Ledge Between the Streams* (1984), he offers a vivid and harrowing account of the Partition of India. In *Daddyji* (1972) and *Mamaji* (1979), Mehta details the lives of his parents and traces their genealogies. He reveals his awe of his upwardly mobile and hardworking Anglophile father, who is a senior medical officer in the colonial government. On the other hand, he portrays his mother as traditional, less educated, and conservative in outlook. In addition to these autobiographies, Mehta has also written a series of books on India, trying to see how the homeland he has left behind has fared since Independence. *Walking the Indian Streets* (1960), *Portrait of India* (1970), *Mahatma Gandhi and His Apostles* (1977), *A Family Affair: India Under Three Prime Ministers* (1982), and *Rajiv Gandhi and Rama's Kingdom* (1994) deal variously with the (ir)relevance of Gandhian idealism to contemporary India: the unfinished tasks since Independence: the failures of the postcolonial Indian nation-state in the domain of politics, governance, and gender; the state's apathy toward the socially or religiously disenfranchised; and a critical look at some political decisions and government policies.

While all of Mehta's work has been praised by scholars across various disciplines, it is his autobiographical project that has received the highest critical regard. David Scott Philip writes, "This series of rambling recollections is a type of therapy through meticulous and painstaking remembrance in which the same events may be covered again and again" (142). John Slatin also comments on Mehta's project of endless autobiography: "No other writer that I know of . . . has felt it necessary to revise his own autobiography so extensively" (175). Janet Malcolm calls *Vedi* an "extraordinary memoir," and adds, "Not the least of *Vedi*'s originality is . . . stylistic denial, which amounts to an approximation of the experience of blindness" (3).

Anupama Arora

Further Reading

Dong, Stella. "Ved Mehta." *Publishers Weekly* (3 Jan. 1986): 57–58.

Malcolm, Janet. "School for the Blind." Rev. of *Vedi,* by Ved Mehta. *New York Times Book Review* (7 Oct. 1982): 3–5.

Mehta, Ved. *Sound Shadows.* New York: Norton, 1985.

Philip, David Scott. *Perceiving India: Through the Works of Nirad C. Chaudhuri, R. K. Narayan and Ved Mehta.* New Delhi: Sterling, 1986.

Slatin, John M. "Blindness and Self-Perception: The Autobiographies of Ved Mehta." *Mosaic: A Journal for the Interdisciplinary Study of Literature* 19.4 (1986): 173–93.

Midnight's Children by Salman Rushdie

After his first novel *Grimus* (1975) proved to be unsuccessful both critically and commercially, Salman Rushdie sought to refashion himself as a writer by using his fiction to revisit the place of his birth. Born in Bombay on June 19, 1947, to Anis Ahmed and Negin Rushdie, Rushdie's nostalgia for the city he identified as his home was to form the kernel of *Midnight's Children* (1981), the novel that would turn him into a literary celebrity. Like the novel's narrator Saleem Sinai, Rushdie grew up in a wealthy Muslim family on a colonial estate. Throughout his schooling at Rugby, his family's immigration to England and then Pakistan and his degree at Cambridge, Bombay was the home with which Rushdie most identified. As such, *Midnight's Children* stands as a homecoming of sorts, a literary and emotional return to familiar territory depicted with such flair that it won him the Booker Prize in 1981. While *The Satanic Verses* (1988) established Rushdie's international notoriety, *Midnight's Children* secured his status as a preeminent author and a compelling voice of postcolonial literature.

Midnight's Children is the story of Saleem Sinai, who by accident of his birth at the stroke of midnight of August 15, 1947—the moment on which India gained independence—is blessed with the power to read minds and cursed with the constant linkage between his life and the history of the subcontinent. In the novel's frame, Saleem is 30 years old, working in a pickle factory, and using the evenings to write his autobiography. The drama of the novel progresses as he attempts to discuss his place in history as the mirror image of India, which is under intense pressure from familial strife, border wars, and state repression. Through the veil of his own predetermined and privileged sense of connection with India, Saleem's narrative explores the extent to which the lives of individuals and nations intertwine and in turn are constrained by the state. Rushdie makes a figurative connection literal through a self-conscious intermingling of history and fiction, using Saleem's family story to touch upon some of India's most defining twentieth-century moments. For instance, in 1919, Saleem's grandfather is a witness to the Amritsar Massacre, and in

1942, he joins an anti-Partition alternative to the Muslim League, whose leader is assassinated during the Quit India movement. The correspondences between Saleem and India continue throughout the novel.

1947: Saleem's family (along with a number of other well-to-do Indians) agree to purchase houses on the estate of William Methwold, who offers a very cheap price on the condition that everything in them is left intact until the transfer of power; Amina Sinai (Saleem's mother) decides that she will win a contest for giving birth to a baby at midnight on August 15, when India gains independence, which she does; India gains independence and suffers its territorial sundering and the mass murder of its citizens in the Partition; Baby Saleem Sinai receives a letter from Prime Minister Nehru that greets him as "the newest bearer of that ancient face of India which is also eternally young."

1948: Mahatma Gandhi is assassinated, the news of which ruins the premier of Saleem's uncle Hanif Aziz's suggestive new film and sends the Sinais fleeing for safety.

1957: During this election year, Saleem begins to tune into the thoughts of the midnight's children (see below); Saleem triggers a riot between Gujarati and Marathi speakers in the preamble to the partition of Bombay; finally, India flirts with the Communist Party in the elections, while Amina flirts with her first husband, who has become a Communist Party candidate.

1958: Saleem begins to hold nocturnal meetings in his mind for the midnight's children; Staying with his aunt Emerald and his uncle General Zulfikar, who has grown rich on abandoned Hindu property in Pakistan, Saleem helps map out and then witnesses the coup that ushered martial law into Pakistan under General Ayub Khan.

1962: As tensions with China increase, Ahmed Sinai suffers a heart attack; back in India, Saleem attempts to reconvene the M.C.C., but the midnight's children—sensing that he has something to hide—abandon Saleem, as the Indian army is being beaten soundly by the Chinese army; Saleem's sinuses fill up with each new wave of Indian jingoism; the Chinese stop their advancement and Saleem's parents have his sinuses drained, causing him to lose forever his telepathic powers; Saleem gains a preternatural sense of smell.

1965: Back in Pakistan, Saleem's entire family—except for his sister and his Uncle Mustapha (who had remained in India)—is wiped out by Indian bombs during the Indo-Pakistan war of that year; Saleem is knocked unconscious and loses his memory and his ability to feel.

1971: Saleem, now a member of a Pakistani antisubversive military unit, is transported to the East Wing of Pakistan, assists in the arrest of Sheikh Mujibur Rahman (who would go on to lead in the creation of Bangladesh), and witnesses/participates in the atrocities in Dacca; returns to India and settles in Delhi with a troupe of magicians.

1975: Indira Gandhi declares Emergency, Saleem's son-who-is-not-his-son Aadam Sinai via his marriage to Parvati is born; Parvati's labor has lasted 13 days, from the guilty verdict of the Allahabad court to the arrests on the night of the June 25, 1975; Baby Aadam is stricken with tuberculosis, which lasts until the Emergency is lifted in 1977.

1976: The magician's ghetto in which Saleem is living is razed by bulldozers; Saleem is arrested by Shiva and imprisoned in Benares with the rest of the midnight's children.

1977: Saleem and the midnight's children are surgically sterilized, which robs the children of their magical powers; Indira Gandhi calls for elections, and Saleem is released; Morarji Desai becomes prime minister; Saleem returns to Bombay and writes his life story.

Rushdie's method of folding historical moments into his fictional narrative extends to the outright appropriation of a mainstream historical text, Stanley Wolpert's *A New History of India,* which David Lipscomb characterizes as a method of critique: "By inscribing fragments of Wolpert's textbook in his 'imaginary homeland,' Rushdie picks an epistemological fight not just with this expert but, above all, with the [Western] discourse the expert's work faithfully embodies" (170). This act of incorporating and defamiliarizing history extends in a number of directions: Gandhi is largely excluded from the narrative, and the largest single scene devoted to him is his assassination (Saleem later admits that he got the date wrong). Instead of the heroic resistance and self-sacrifice represented by Gandhi, Rushdie's rescripting of Indian history has a much more critical focus; he replaces a nationalist-redemptive narrative with an elitist-satirical one. Filling the gap created by the lack of a Gandhi-centered narrative, the process by which Saleem's family takes possession of (and in turn are taken possession by) William Methwold's estate comprises the satirical high point of the novel. Methwold, a toupéed eccentric and admitted relic of the Raj, offers a group of upper-class Indian prospective buyers a deal: he will sell to them his villas, each named after a European grand palace, for an astonishingly low price if they preserve everything in them exactly as is until the transfer of power on midnight, August 15. This image of a wealthy cast of characters occupying abandoned British property and adopting British accents and habits presents a compromised and transitional independence, a key moment in the disillusionment Rushdie will articulate later on in the novel.

By far, the most striking invention of the novel is the midnight's children themselves, a group of 1,001 youths from all corners, castes, classes, and religious communities who were each born at the midnight hour of India's independence and who depict a cross-section of a new nation in all of its diversity. The midnight's children represent on one hand a unified national promise, "a vision of the country [Rushdie] wants India to be" (Gorra 113), a view also supported by Josna Rege: "An interviewer once reported that Salman Rushdie kept on his writing desk a little sculpture of an unpartitioned India. Even as he wrote of the realities of a divided subcontinent, he couldn't help but persist in holding on to India's geopolitical wholeness as both an idea and an ideal" (361). However, the midnight's children as an idealized vision of India is explicitly a limited one: they argue about class, caste, region, language, and their purpose, and they represent national promise only through a dangerous form of exceptionalism and assumed centrality that Rushdie identifies with Indira Gandhi. In these ways, the midnight's children might just as easily comprise a deadend for Rushdie, a promise of new nationhood that is left unredeemed. For Rushdie, the blame for this failure is placed squarely on the state. The novel thus reads as a mourning of sorts, as we see India distanced from the democratic ideals of its founding to a bleaker, more authoritarian entity.

In his invention of the midnight's children, Rushdie produces both a celebration of Indian national possibilities and a critique of the ways in which they were realized by the state; in short, the midnight's children bear such symbolic weight as to make their narrative presence larger than even the sprawling historical landscape depicted in the novel. As such, they also are the most prominent example of Rushdie's incorporation of magical realism. Kumkum Sangari distinguishes Rushdie's technique from that of García Márquez, claiming that the latter author offers an alternative reality that exists outside of and in resistance to prevailing political conditions, whereas Rushdie's vision remains subsumed within them. Nevertheless, the midnight's children, Saleem's telepathy, and Shri Ramram Seth's prophecy all contribute to the magical real narrative of *Midnight's Children,* a novel that in its description of—appropriately enough—the inhabitants of New Delhi's Magician's Ghetto sums up its own craft: "[T]he magicians were people whose hold on reality was absolute; they gripped it so powerfully that they could bend it every which way in the service of their arts, but they never forgot what it was." Rushdie's magical realism contains possibilities not only for the liberation of imagination from political and cultural constraints, but also for the dramatic and destructive reassertions of those constraints. In its dual focus on both national potential and its destruction, the magical realism of *Midnight's Children* is a double-edged sword of hope and pessimism.

A deeper sense of mourning also pervades the novel, stemming from the founding trauma of modern Indian history—Partition: if the Emergency represents a disaster for the liberal-democratic state, Partition represents a broader disaster for the nation and its people. Saleem's initial narrative of Partition is quite circumspect, as he deliberately states his refusal to focus on its events in favor of describing his birth. However, we find that images of truncation, fragmentation, in short, partition, are to be found throughout *Midnight's Children.* Saleem vividly imagines his slow cracking and eventual disintegration into dust; Aadam Aziz falls in love with his patient and future wife, Naseem, one piece at a time via a sheet with a hole in the middle (through which he must examine her to preserve her decency); Amina Sinai learns to love her husband by concentrating with all her will on one piece of

him at a time; Pakistani soldier Shaheed is literally partitioned by a flying hand grenade in the last minutes of the Indo-Pakistan war of 1971; finally, Saleem and the other midnight's children are castrated, sterilized, and drained of hope. Thus, Rushdie disperses references to Partition and its effects through a variety of images of fragmentation rather than through the single-minded description of a geopolitical nightmare.

Midnight's Children was a tremendous critical success. After winning the Booker Prize in 1981, it went on to win the Booker of Bookers (for the prize's first 25 years) in 1993. The praise Rushdie received, however, was not without its problematic elements. In the heat of Rushdie's accomplishment, critics celebrated Rushdie as the best and only voice in Indian literature. In addition, even though *Midnight's Children* questioned mainstream representations of India, it became tempting for readers—especially those not familiar with Indian history—to use the novel as a substitute for what it had dislodged and thus domesticate its resistant potential. There is also some evidence that Rushdie was disappointed with some aspects of the novel's reception in India, as he describes in *Imaginary Homelands* how he received letters reprimanding him for leaving out further considerations of language and Dalit issues or for the pessimism of his novel.

Despite such criticisms, Rushdie was overwhelmingly hailed as a path breaker—a writer who articulated with a great deal of stylistic flair the imperatives of renarrating history in a postcolonial context—and his influence can be seen in authors who followed him. For example, Mukul Kesavan's *Looking through Glass* is a direct descendant of *Midnight's Children's* skewed and individualized reexplorations of Indian history, as its narrator magically falls backward through time to the Quit

India movement and lives through India's Partition. Arundhati Roy's *The God of Small Things,* while not (as the author herself has protested, despite her admiration of Rushdie's work) patterned after *Midnight's Children,* is linked to it in its spirited wordplay. However, beyond the authors for whom Rushdie may have opened creative vistas in linguistic experimentation or historical revision, the achievement of *Midnight's Children* is twofold: it boldly fashioned a language that conveyed politically incisive historical narrative with the structure of an epic saga and the voice of bemused and rambling confession, and it created a greater space for Indian authors and subjects in Western literary markets. In this way, the revolution of *Midnight's Children* extends much further past its literary merits. It is also worth noting that *Midnight's Children* continues to develop as a text. Years after some unsuccessful attempts to film it for television, in 2002 Rushdie joined with Simon Reade and Tim Supple to adapt his novel to a play performed by the Royal Shakespeare Company, thereby comprising a new phase in the reception of the work, which is still considered to be Rushdie's finest.

Jason Howard Mezey

Further Reading

Gorra, Michael. *After Empire: Scott, Naipaul, Rushdie.* Chicago: U of Chicago P, 1997.

Islam, Syed Manzurul. "Writing the Postcolonial Event: Salman Rushdie's August 15, 1947." *Textual Practice* 13.1 (1999): 119–35.

Kortenaar, Neil. "Postcolonial Ekphrasis: Salman Rushdie Gives the Finger Back to the Empire." *Contemporary Literature* 38.2 (1997): 232–59.

Lipscomb, David. "Caught in a Strange Middle Ground: Contesting History in Salman Rushdie's *Midnight's Children.*" *Diaspora* 1.2 (1991): 163–89.

Rege, Josna. "Victim into Protagonist? *Midnight's Children* and the Post-Rushdie National Narratives of the Eighties." *Studies in the Novel* 29.3 (1997): 342–75.

Sangari, Kumkum. "The Politics of the Possible." *Cultural Critique* 7 (1987): 157–86.

The Mimic Men by V. S. Naipaul

V. S. Naipaul is overtly concerned with the depiction of the harrowing effects of colonialism upon the people of the Third World, but "His is not that sooths but sears" (Wattas, 4). Naipaul finds the postcolonial men in a state of limbo, lingering between a defunct world abandoned by the colonizers and a powerless world possessed by the colonized. In their attempt to transform themselves from the slavery of colonialism to the owners of independent states, they first imitate their colonial masters. In *The Mimic Men,* Naipaul reacts sharply to this tendency to mimicry that produces only hypocrites and self-contradictory individuals, who deprive themselves of their own inherent identities. These "mimic men" belong to a newly independent country, the island of Isabella, in the West Indies. Naipaul uses "island" as a metaphor to indicate the insulated existence of the people there, unlike those of their past rulers in the mainland; and hence, the need for imitation out of personal insecurity and cultural instability.

Ralph Singh, a representative of these dislocated, dangling men, narrates the story of the novel in autobiographical mode. He is a disillusioned cabinet minister from the newly independent multiracial Isabella, who has fled to London to seek refuge and live as an exile in a hotel. He writes his story as he begins to reevaluate and invent order in an apparently haphazard life. The novel spreads into three parts: the first two, comprising seven chapters and the last, containing nine. Part one commences with Ralph's first arrival as a student in London during World War II. He stays in the boarding house of Mr. Shylock and starts living a false Bohemian dandy life. Despite his meager income, he boasts of his family's liaison with Coca Cola and pretends to be "the extravagant colonial, indifferent to scholarship" (19). He has an affair with Lieni, the Maltese housekeeper, who puts on the pose of a "smart London girl." She helps him in his playacting of "the rich colonial," which includes having indiscreet sex with prostitutes and other women whose language he does not understand. Later, in an exhausted, oppressed mood of waste and helplessness, he marries Sandra, a strong-willed woman and trusts her ability to relieve him of disintegration and fluidity. He returns to Isabella with Sandra at war's end. Sandra is an unwelcome guest here since Ralph has not informed his mother about his marriage. His mother refuses to accept Sandra, and the initial dismay continues throughout the rest of the narrative. Nevertheless, Ralph has an innate cleverness for real estate business, and soon he becomes one of the richest young men on the island. Money gives ample space for detachment and introspection. Ralph realizes that Sandra too has a forlorn feeling, and that they had actually come together for self-defense. He revives his habit of seeking physical gratification with women of various races. Yet, he does so with a painful awareness that Sandra too might be in search of similar solace. By the time his cherished Roman house is built, he loses his home, and Sandra leaves for other relationships and other countries.

The second part of the novel focuses on his boyhood and schooldays in Isabella. It shows how such boys deal with their mixed parentage. Ralph's reading influences his attitudes, in which he adopts a European view. At unease with his Indian name, Ranjit Kirpal Singh, he chooses a Western one, Ralph Singh. He secures the friendship of Browne, a Negro, who shares his shame of a racial past. Similarly, there is an attractive boy, Hok, who feels humiliated when his pose of Chinese ancestry is broken with his Negro mother's appearance. Ralph's mother comes from a family that belonged to the group of "Isabella millionaires," whereas his father is a poor schoolteacher. Cut off from his real

country, Ralph feels that his father "had in some storybook way been shipwrecked on the island and that over the years the hope of rescue had altogether faded" (94). He cherishes his mother's family, though in secret he is the son of his father, a Rajput, who reads about Aryans and stories of knights. His father fails to return home one day and soon Ralph's family comes to know that he has become "Gurudeva," the leader of a revolutionary group. Conversely, Ralph's yearning for an ideal Aryan past receives a sharp jolt when he realizes that his father has performed the greatest of the ancient Hindu sacrifices, *Asvamedha,* the horse-sacrifice, in his killing of Tamango, the race horse owned by the Deschampsneufs. He confesses, "Chieftaincy among mountains and snow had been my innermost fantasy. Now, deeply, I felt betrayed and ridiculed" (153).

The third part of the novel essentially deals with the height of Ralph's political career and his ill-fated fall. Politics is combined with personal identity in the novel. As William L. Sachs points out, "Politics provides a clue to understanding mimicry" (3). During their college days in London, Browne had been a political pamphleteer with unconventional ideas. On Isabella, Browne convinces Ralph to invest money in a newspaper, *The Socialist,* that he has founded. They start with a feature commemorating the dockworkers' strike and Ralph's father's exodus to the hills. To their astonishment, they realize that they have kindled a mass political awakening. Soon Browne is elevated to the status of a "folk-leader" and even prime minister. Ralph becomes a cabinet minister and gains immense popularity by handling certain critical projects, such as the renegotiation of the bauxite contract with the Americans. Yet, Ralph is forced to do the impossible and face his humiliation when he has to work out the nationalization of sugar industries. Subsequently, he is ousted by other power-mongers who categorically reveal his public imposture. He accepts the offer from the new leaders of a free and safe passage to London again by air, with 66 pounds of luggage and 50 thousand dollars—a fraction of his fortune.

In this way, the novel progresses with the protagonist's attempt to assimilate his identity but ends when he is only half way to is goal, just at the age of 40, estranged from both cultures and left with a splintered self from which he can never fully recover. Ralph repeatedly alludes to the image of "shipwreck," which implies that his life on the island is unreal: he has been washed up there, but his true "magic" home is elsewhere. In order to put an end to his "shameless fantasies" he leaves on a scholarship to London, thinking he will never return. But, ironically, he continues to feel like a shipwrecked passenger even in the "great city." Ralph's anglicizing of his name, his marriage to an English woman, and his later refuge in England are attempts to find order from the English tradition. Yet, Ralph remains an exile in England as he was in Isabella. London does not welcome him; he fails to integrate into the ideal culture presented to him through books. Even the sexual promiscuity and role-playing in which he indulges in order to fight the sense of loss, do not give him any permanent gain. His isolation becomes acute and his marooned status ultimate. This is the common plight of the colonized, the mimic men, who emulate the colonizer.

Chandra B. Joshi argues that Ralph's personality traits are representative of his author and that "through this work and through this character Naipaul comes finally to terms with his own placelessness" (176). According to Clark Blaise, "Ralph Singh does not fully convince, either as an ex-politician or an exile" (124). Nonetheless, as a novel, *The Mimic Men* is acclaimed for its realistic portrayal of postcolonial nationalism. For Robert M. Greenberg the novel "appears to accurately reflect the multiethnic societies and political fragmentation that typifies Trinidad, British Guyana, and Suriname" (16). Minor flaws apart, as V. S. Pritchett puts it, "Mr. Naipaul's book gets down to the entrails of a colonial agony and is as exciting as it is penetrating" (5).

T. Ravichandran

Further Reading

Blaise, Clark. "The Commonwealth Writer and His Material." *Awakened Conscience: Studies in Commonwealth Literature.* Ed. C. D. Narasimhaiah. New Delhi: Sterling, 1978. 118–26.

Greenberg, Robert M. "Anger and the Alchemy of Literary Method in V. S. Naipaul's Political Fiction: The Case of The Mimic Men." *Twentieth Century Literature* (Summer 2000). <http://www.findarticles.com/cf_0/m0403/2_46/67315273/print.jhtml>.

Joshi, Chandra B. *V. S. Naipaul: The Voice of Exile.* New Delhi: Sterling, 1994.

Pritchett, V. S. "Crack-Up." Rev. of *The Mimic Men,* by V. S. Naipaul. *The New York Review of Books* (11 Apr. 1968). <http://www.nybooks.com/articles/11733>.

Sachs, William L. "V. S. Naipaul and the Plight of the Dispossessed." *Christian Century* (17 Nov. 1982): 1167. <http://www.religion-online.org/cgi-bin/relsearchd.dll/showarticle?item_id=1354>.

Wattas, Rajnish. "Enigma of a Nobel's Arrival: Finding the Centre Despite a Million Mutinies." *The Sunday Tribune* (21 Oct. 2001). <http://www.tribuneindia.com/20011021/spectrum/main1.htm>.

Mimicry

One of the world's foremost contemporary intellectuals, Homi K. Bhabha devised the theory of colonial mimicry. The main body of his work involves theorizations of colonial subjectivity, colonial discourse, and postcolonial identity, a group of ideas in which mimicry plays a central role. Another writer of South Asian origin, Nobel laureate V. S. Naipaul's 1967 novel, *The Mimic Men,* centered around colonial mime; this novel demonstrates the key attributes of Bhabha's conception of colonial mimicry through the central character, Ralph Singh, who, on the opening page, reflects: "I thought Mr. Shylock looked distinguished, like a lawyer or businessman or politician. He had the habit of stroking the lobe of his ear and inclining his head to listen. *I thought the gesture was attractive; I copied it. . . .* I offered Mr. Shylock my fullest, silent compassion" (7; emphasis added). Bhabha claims that colonized subjects are often expected to take on the behaviors and dress, the values, knowledge, and attitudes of the colonizer. In colonial South Asia, this meant Indians were to attempt be like or imitate English gentlemen and gentlewomen. Bhabha calls this mode of colonial discourse *mimicry.*

An oft-cited work of imperial discourse in which we see this imitative pretext for colonial subjects confirmed is the 1835 Minute on Indian Education in which Thomas Macaulay states: "We must . . . form a class who may be interpreters between us and the millions whom we govern, a class of persons Indian in blood and colour, but English in tastes, in opinions, in morals and in intellect." This excerpt shows how colonial mimicry not only involves desire on the part of the colonized—"*I thought the gesture was attractive; I copied it.*"—it also reflects the express aims of the colonial power. According to Macaulay, the British ought to create mimic men and women who will function as middlepersons between themselves and the "millions [they] govern." Furthermore, this shall be achieved through a carefully organized colonial pedagogy with English literature occupying a central place. Bhabha's theoretical formulations involving "mimic men" are underpinned by the Lacanian notion of mimicry as a kind of mottling (85). For Lacan, the mime is not veiled or masked but camouflaged, an intermixture of what it *is* and what it *imitates.* In Bhabha's terms, "colonial mimicry is the desire for

a reformed, recognizable Other, *as a subject of a difference that is almost the same, but not quite*" (86). The colonized impersonator *cannot* become the colonial subject since "to be Anglicized is emphatically not to be English" (Bhabha 87). Thus the "copied subject" produced through mimicry is *inexact,* and this inexactness amounts to a fundamental flaw, a palpable rupture in the machinery of colonial authority.

This underlines a crucial insight in Bhabha's work—the subversive potential of colonial mimicry and other aspects of colonized subjectivity. As a postcolonial theorist, Bhabha is less concerned with the subjugation and violence of colonial authority and far more interested in exploring the radical promise inherent in colonized identity and its potential to undermine colonial subjectivity and discourse. One of the best examples of this is in his conception of mimicry. The one who copies the powerful, like Naipaul's character, threatens and undermines that power. An unintended authority is conferred upon colonial mimes, they possess a type of influence or potential that cannot be contained within the rubric of colonial dominance. Thus, the copier threatens to displace that which he or she copies. Because of this dynamic, Bhabha argues that Macaulay's institutional plan to produce mimic men contained the germ of its own destruction because it was a hybridized plan reliant upon the threatening character of the mimic man/woman. When colonized subjects mimic imperial representatives, they also mock them. Bhabha insists that mimicry is not representation but *repetition*—as with a mime repeating the precise bodily movements and facial expressions of an individual standing before them. This kind of imitation produces laughter in onlookers because it is a form of humorous teasing, or mockery. As such, when colonized subjects mimic they also mock, such as Naipaul's mimic man who imitates the action of "stroking the lobe of his ear and inclining his head to listen." In Bhabha's words, this type of mimicry contains "resemblance *and* menace" (86). This means the effects of mimicry—its excess—are outside the oppressor's control. Its outcomes are irrepressible, disobedient, and disorderly. "[T]o be effective, mimicry must continually produce its slippage, its excess, its difference" (Bhabha 86). Being beyond colonial control, mimicry in the forms of English language and literature *learning*—the very plan prescribed by Macaulay—in time become English language and literature *production,* such as the creation of counter discourses, like postcolonial literature in English.

Maureen E. Ruprecht Fadem

Further Reading

Ashcroft, Bill, Gareth Griffiths, and Helen Tiffin, eds. *Post-Colonial Studies: The Key Concepts.* New York: Routledge, 2000.

Bhabha, Homi. *The Location of Culture.* New York: Routledge, 1994.

———, ed. *Nation and Narration.* New York: Routledge, 1990.

Childs, Peter, and Patrick Williams, eds. "Chapter 4: Bhabha's Hybridity." *An Introduction to Post-Colonial Theory.* Essex, England: Prentice Hall, 1997. 122–56.

Macaulay, T. B. "Minute by the Hon'ble T. B. Macaulay, Dated the 2nd February 1835." *Project South Asia.* <http://www.mssc.edu/projectsouthasia/history/primarydocs/education/Macaulay001.htm>.

Naipaul, V. S. *The Mimic Men.* New York: Macmillan, 1967.

Mishra, Pankaj

Pankaj Mishra was born in 1969 and grew up in the historic town of Jhansi, Bundhelkand. He received his B.A. at Allahabad University and his M.A. and Ph.D. at Jawaharlal Nehru University. He currently divides his time between New Delhi and Simla. As the former chief editor of Harper Collins, India Division, Mishra made good use of his editorial choice by discovering the manuscript of *The God of Small Things* and signing up its author, Arundhati Roy. Later, Mishra became well known as a political journalist through a series of probing and lucid articles on Kashmir that were published in *The New York Review of Books.* His reputation as a literary critic grew further with his essays in the *Times Literary Supplement* and *The New York Review of Books,* especially his essay on Naipaul entitled "A House for Mr. Naipaul," which is now collected in *The Humor and Pity,* a collection of essays edited by Amitava Kumar. Also noteworthy in this regard is Mishra's essay on Edmund Wilson, which appeared in the *Picador Book of Modern Indian Literature* (2001). Mishra has published two books: *Butter Chicken in Ludhiana* (1985) and *The Romantics: A Novel* (2000). Currently, he is working on a book on Buddha.

Mishra's first book *Butter Chicken in Ludhiana* recounts his travels through 19 small towns of India—Muzafarnagar, Mandi, Pushkar, Jhansi, Ajmer, Shimoga, and Kottayam. In this compelling book, Mishra charts the social, economic, and political climate of small-town India and correlates its "new aggressiveness" to the new wealth and the new poverty, as well as to the new cultural identities in the making that he witnesses there. The young politician that Mishra encounters in Mandi in his "Arrow shirt, Woodland shoes, Park-Avenue shoes, and VIP briefcase" may or may not resemble his big city counterparts, but he is typical, Mishra claims, of the "new kind of businessman created by the recent liberalization of the economy, the wholesale marketing of India . . . unabashed in their self-love, their frantic hankering after wealth, fame and status" (41). In this book, Mishra does not just point to the ascendant forces of this new capitalism, or to the small-town orientation toward fast-food restaurants and MTV, or to loss of local culture in small-town India. Rather, he renders these visible contrary currents and this new ambivalence through concrete evocations of people and their social voice. There is the police officer who, on seeing the author read Iris Murdoch's *Word Child,* wants to know "whether she is Rupert Murdoch's wife"; and then, there are Mahesh and Rajkumar in Pushkar who want the guesthouse "to be mentioned in *The Lonely Planet.*" This aspect of small-town India that Mishra offers is in every way different from earlier symptomatic imaginings of it.

While *Butter Chicken in Ludhiana* retains its form as a travel narrative—a road trip narrative—it has also the quality of a memoir. Instead of fixing India in images, as knowable through encounters with what he sees, Mishra presents small-town India as knowable only by a kind of continuous investigation where the shape and meaning of the journey are revised with each new experience. Mishra finds his certainties of analysis repudiated when he meets the peasant activists, Rajesh and Ragubhir, who are "mobilizing people for a anti-GATT rally to be held in Patna" or when he meets on the train "a seven year old Sitaram "whose narrow thinly-covered shoulders shiver in the breeze and whose hair has turned the colour of rust from malnutrition" but "who still . . . goes to school" and "proves his newly acquired abilities by writing in a large wavering hand the first five letters of the Hindi alphabet." When Sitaram points out that Mishra's writing of the alphabet is "not in the right order," Mishra feels that he has been "taught what he thought he knew by heart and had long forgotten" (276).

Mishra's writing has a sharp surge to it, a social conscience that is different in style from the urban sophisticated, modernist aesthetic ideals of what has come to be called the "St. Stephen school of fiction": the work of writers like Amitav Ghosh, Mukul Kesavan, Rukun Advani, Shashi Tharoor, and Khuswant Singh. Yet, Mishra's mode of social realism cannot really be contrasted with the urban modern-

ism (typified by St. Stephen school) in so much as his first novel *Romantics* (2000), that won him the L.A. Times Art Sidenbaum Award for Best First Fiction, shows Mishra forging a set of strategies drawn from both these conflicting discourses, strategies suitable to both his aesthetic and his political concerns.

Padmaja Challakere

Further Reading

Bhattacharjea, Aditya, and Lola Chatterjee, eds. *The Fiction of St. Stephen's.* New Delhi: Ravi Dayal, 2000.

Mishra, Pankaj. "Kashmir: The Birth of a Tragedy." *The New York Times Book Review* XLVII, 15 (5 Oct. 2000).

———. "Edmund Wilson in Benares." *The Picador Book of Modern Indian Literature.* Ed. Amit Chaudhuri. New Delhi: Picador India, 2001. 355–72.

Mistry, Rohinton

The ever-dwindling Parsi community of Mumbai, India, is central in the fiction of Rohinton Mistry, a Canada-based writer of Parsi descent. His works, while being firmly contextualized within the framework of India's turbulent post-Independence history, raise and address important questions about Parsi identity in a turmoil-ridden world. This fact, coupled with his astonishingly vivid, sensitive, and compassionate portrayal of middle-class life in India, makes Mistry one of the leading postcolonial writers of the Indian diaspora.

Born in 1952, Mistry spent his early years in Mumbai. He graduated with a degree in mathematics and economics from the University of Mumbai and in 1975, at the age of 23, just one month after a state of emergency had been declared in India, Mistry emigrated to Toronto, Canada. Not entirely content with his job in a Toronto bank, he enrolled in part-time courses in English and philosophy at the University of Toronto.

In 1983, Mistry took to writing short stories in his spare time and his first draft of *One Sunday* brought him instant recognition at the University of Toronto's Hart House Literary Contest. Mistry was awarded the first prize in two successive years, and his work was also anthologized in *The New Press Anthology: Best Canadian Short Fiction,* winning the Canadian Fiction Magazine's Annual Contributor's Prize for 1985.

Mistry's first collection of interconnected short stories, *Tales from Firozsha Baag* (1987), revolves around a Parsi apartment complex, transporting its readers to the Zoroastrian world of "dustoorjis" (priests), "agyaaris" (Fire-temples), "navjotes" (Zoroastrian initiation ceremonies), "dhandar-paatyos" and "sali-botis" (both Parsi specialties). The linguistic hybridity and the use of colloquialisms—*"Arre, please yaar, why harass an old man? Jaane de, yaar"*—lend the stories greater authenticity. Mistry showcases a startling variety of characters, each with a distinct personality and idiosyncrasies characteristic of Parsis. Adding considerably to the humor in the stories is the eccentric, even comical, figure of the "Bawaji" of which "Rustomji the Curmudgeon" is the perfect embodiment. There is also the touching, almost poignant, relationship between young Jehangir, "the Bulsara boy . . . who sat silent and brooding, every evening, watching the others at play." ("The Collectors" 79) with the elderly Dr. Burjor Mody. It is through the character of Kersi that Mistry directly addresses issues concerning Western migration and the feeling of guilt associated with it. For instance, in "Lend Me Your Light," Kersi states: "I am guilty of the sin of hubris for seeking emigration out of the land of my birth, paying the price in burnt-out eyes: I Tiresias, blind and throbbing between two lives, the one in Bombay and the one to come in Toronto" (180). This quote is a brilliant illustration of the feeling of displacement that is so pronounced, not only in this particular short story, but in Mistry's novels as well. Mistry has written three novels, all of which have been short listed for the prestigious Booker Prize. Though each novel is distinctly different in its plot, treatment of characters and other details, there are striking similarities between them. All three novels foreground the metropolitan and focus on family problems amidst economic hardships. There emerges a certain thematic unity as they all deal with the recurrent themes of loss, displacement, home and the eternal struggle between the traditional and the modern. Most important, however, is the questioning of religious beliefs in an attempt to define the identity of the minority Parsi community in the wider Indian context.

Published four years after his collection of short stories, Mistry's first novel, *Such a Long Journey* (1991), launched him into the international literary scene. It won the Commonwealth Writers Prize for Best Book, amongst other awards. It has been translated into German, Swedish, Norwegian, Danish, and Japanese and has been adapted for a film by Sooni Taraporevala, which was released in 1999. Set in Mumbai, the novel has as its political backdrop the Indo-Pakistan war, over what was later to become Bangladesh. The plot has been constructed as a close parallel to the real-life Sohrab Nagarwala scandal that rocked the Indira Gandhi government in 1971. As the novel traces the protagonist, Gustad Noble's involvement with his friend Major Billimoria's supposed embezzlement of a large sum of money, the public turmoil of the period is effectively mirrored in the private world of the Noble family.

Mistry's technique of weaving the private dimension of his characters into the macrocosmic political canvas is at its best in his second novel, *A Fine Balance* (1996). While chronicling the state of emergency declared in 1975 by the then prime minister, Indira Gandhi, until her assassination in 1984, Mistry does not spare his characters any of the atrocities that were inflicted upon the common Indian citizen in that period. His depiction of the dismal quality of life is rendered with exceptional realism. Jennifer Takhar remarks, "Mistry emphasizes pure veracity, as he sees it, underlining the most unsightly and hideous aspects of life: its poverty, despair and violence." Mistry's choice of protagonists reveals a deliberate attempt to privilege the marginalized sections of Indian society. Dina Dalal is an admirably resilient Parsi widow, who struggles to make ends meet in a hostile city, ostensibly Mumbai. In a desperate attempt to preserve her "fragile independence" (*A Fine Balance* 13), she takes in a paying guest, Maneck Kohlah, a Parsi student, and hires two tailors, Ishwar and Omprakash Darji. The lives of the tailors bear testimony to the irrevocable damage for which the MISA (Maintenance of Internal Security Act) with its forced sterilizations was responsible. Loss and the inevitability of death loom at large in the lives of the protagonists. The solace and warmth that they find, as their lives intersect, is only fleeting.

Shashi Tharoor asserts that though "*A Fine Balance* was deservedly praised . . . it was also weighed down by tragedy." Comparatively, in Mistry's latest novel, *Family Matters* (2002), "the most moving parts of the book have less to do with death than with the ennobling power of life." Set in the mid-1990s, this novel center-stages the domestic life of Nariman Vakeel's extended family. The cast of characters spreads across three generations. While the opening chapter presents a meticulously detailed portrait of Nariman Vakeel, an aged Parsi widower suffering from Parkinson's disease and a fractured foot, the book closes with the narrative of his youngest grandson, Jehangir Chenoy. Mistry's portrayal of different relationships, especially that between Nariman and Je-

hangir, has been rendered with great sensitivity and tenderness. As the novel traces the profound changes that each character undergoes, attention is drawn to the Parsi community's struggle to preserve its identity, in the face of the threat posed by intermarriage and Westward migration. Mistry's representation of the city of Mumbai is remarkably authentic, with frequent references to Iranian restaurants, overcrowded trains, and the 1992–93 riots that rocked the metropolis. The novel, in the words of Shashi Tharoor, is "a superb work that confirms Rohinton Mistry's reputation as a novelist of the highest quality" (10).

Rachana Aggarwal

Further Reading

Bharucha, Nilufer E., and Vrinda Nabar, eds. *Mapping Cultural Spaces: Postcolonial Indian Literature in English: Essays in Honor of Nissim Ezekiel.* New Delhi: Vision, 1998.

Dodiya, Jaydipsingh, ed. *The Fiction of Rohinton Mistry: Critical Studies.* London: Sangam, 1998.

Jain, Jasbir, ed. *Writers of the Indian Diaspora: Theory and Practice.* New Delhi: Rawat, 1998.

Tharoor, Shashi. "The Pain and Joy of Being Homebound." *The Asian Age* (Nov. 2002): 10.

The Moor's Last Sigh by Salman Rushdie

The Moor's Last Sigh (1995) is a sprawling family saga. The novel was short listed for the Booker Prize and won the Whitbread Novel of the Year Award. All of Rushdie's novels to date display the influences of such diverse writers and works as Lawrence Sterne, James Joyce, G. V. Desani's *All About H. Hatterr,* Gunter Grass's *The Tin Drum,* and Gabriel Garcia Marquez's *One Hundred Years of Solitude.* This is the case with *The Moor's Last Sigh,* which employs the narrative techniques of postmodernism to reflect on family, art, fundamentalism, and mortality. Divided into four sections, the novel is narrated by Moraes Zogoiby, youngest son of Abraham and Aurora Zogoiby. Moraes, the Moor of the novel's title, suffers a curious affliction: he ages at twice the rate of a normal person, a condition that is a striking trope for the burden of mortality. The novel begins with Moraes in the mountains of Andalusia, near death, and works backward to relate his story and that of his family, particularly his parents, Aurora and Abraham Zogoiby.

In the first section, "A House Divided," Moraes backtracks to the early histories of his parents and grandparents. Both Aurora da Gama and Abraham Zogoiby are from old Indian families, but, significantly, their families are old immigrant families. Aurora is descended from the original Portuguese colonists of India, while Abraham's ancestors were Jews expelled from Spain; additionally, there is the suggestion that Abraham may be a descendent of Boabdil, the last sultan of Granada, who was expelled by Ferdinand and Isabella of Spain. Moraes's heritage is thus not only one of conquest and domination, but of banishment and exile. His parents' marriage brings together the three major Western religions: Christianity, Judaism, and Islam. In addition to telling the stories of Aurora and Abraham's courtship and Aurora's development as a painter, the novel's first section reflects upon India's multicultural history by relating the stories of their respective families. Finally, the first section introduces Vasco Miranda, an artist friend of Aurora's who will be important to the novel's climax.

The first third of "Malabar Masala," the novel's second section, details Moraes's birth and early life. Moraes enters the world with a club for a right hand, an affliction that echoes Oedipus's famous clubfoot and indicates the importance Aurora will have in his life. The middle third of the section relates the origin of Aurora's most famous painting, her "Moor" series, in which the Moor is Moraes and the paint-

ings become reflections by his mother on his life, his relation with her, and the life and history of his family. Aurora's paintings reflect Moraes's life, even as they influence it. Magical, and irreverent, the paintings reflect the techniques of Rushdie's own fiction. The last third of the second section tells the story of Moraes's doomed love affair with Uma Sarasvati, a parodic postmodern artist who turns out to be mentally unbalanced.

"Bombay Central," the novel's third section, occurs against the rising tide of Hindu nationalism and violence in India. Moraes discovers that Abraham, whom he had thought was employed importing and exporting spices, is in fact a crime lord. The novel thus links the spice trade, the origin of the West's interest in and conquest of India, with the criminal. Moraes goes to work for Raman Fielding, Rushdie's caricature of the Hindu nationalist leader Bal Thackeray, as hired muscle. Aurora dies in a fall from the roof of the family house, apparently assassinated, Moraes learns, by Fielding. Moraes avenges Aurora by beating Fielding to death. This already violent section ends with the violent assassination of Abraham Zogoiby in one of a series of explosions that destroy the houses and buildings associated with him, as well as the gallery holding most of his dead wife's paintings. Moraes flees India for Spain, where Vasco Miranda is supposed to have stolen copies of her paintings.

The novel's last section, "The Moor's Last Sigh," occurs entirely in Spain, the place from which Moraes's father's ancestors were once exiled. Moraes thus seeks out his mother's missing paintings in the land of his fathers. Moraes finds Vasco living in an enormous castle whose rooms have been modeled on Aurora's paintings; in entering the castle, he literally steps into her art. Moraes is held captive by Vasco, who reveals the true identity of Aurora's assassin: Abraham. On the verge of killing Moraes, the hypertrophied Vasco explodes, and the novel ends with Moraes, near death, completing its final lines.

The novel explores, among other things, the nature of life, death, history, art, fame, and the many complicated guises of love that are manifested in the contemporary world. The central point, however, that the novel seems to focus on is the issue of hybridity. In terms of cultural representations of reality, hybridity implies a mixture or fusion, where the notion of fixity, purity, or original essence is continually contested. Rushdie, in all his works, has been a vociferous advocate of hybridity: for instance in *Midnight's Children,* the themes of intermixing are epitomized in the idea of "chutnification"; and the entire narrative of *The Satanic Verses* revolves around a central axiom, pronounced early on, "a little of this and a little of that; that is how newness enters the world." In *The Moor's Last Sigh,* the issues of heterogeneity and syncretism are brought to the forefront. On one level the novel renders the pluralism and hybridity in contemporary India, but it also goes through great pains to show the corruption and violence that fundamentalism and communalism have engendered. In this sense, Rushdie offers a critique of fundamentalist practices and shows how those who have refused to espouse hybridity have actually thwarted the vision of a secular Indian nation. Rushdie, to a large extent, laments the current state of the nation, and the narrative becomes an important satirical statement about what happens when hybridity is undermined by dangerous fundamentalist rhetoric.

Though not quite as well studied as Salman Rushdie's earlier novels, there is a good introductory discussion of *The Moor's Last Sigh* in Cundy. Kuortti and Sanga's works offer more complex, though rewarding, analyses of the novel.

John Langan

Further Reading

Cundy, Catherine. *Salman Rushdie.* New York: St. Martin's, 1997.

Kuortti, Joel. *Fictions to Live By: Narration as an Argument for Fiction in Salman Rushdie's Novels.* New York: Peter Lang, 1998.

Rushdie, Salman. *Imaginary Homelands: Essays and Criticism 1981–1991.* London: Viking, 1991.

Sanga, Jaina. *Salman Rushdie's Postcolonial Metaphors: Migration, Translation, Hybridity, Blasphemy, and Globalization.* Westport: Greenwood, 2001.

Moth Smoke by Mohsin Hamid

Mohsin Hamid's *Moth Smoke* is a brisk first novel set in Lahore, Pakistan, amid the nuclear saber rattling between India and Pakistan in 1998. Hamid is a native of Lahore who graduated from Princeton, where the seeds of the novel were sown in a fiction workshop led by Toni Morrison. Hamid then went on to Harvard Law School where he submitted a revised draft of *Moth Smoke* as his third-year paper. After graduating, Hamid went to work in New York as a media consultant. From 2000 onward, he wrote for various magazines and newspapers and had the final version of *Moth Smoke* published as a novel. The novel centers on a young banker, Daru, who is consumed by his desires (like the moth in a flame) for drugs, alcohol, his friend's wife, and an upper-class, Westernized lifestyle. His first person narrative forms the bulk of the book, while the "testimony" of other principal and minor characters a is spliced into that narrative. Hamid states, "The book explores the idea of how you arrive at truth with conflicting narratives, which is what you do in law" (qtd. in Rice 2).

The multiple points of view, as well as the drug-induced unreliability of Daru's narration make *truth* hard to establish in the novel. The story begins with the reunion of Daru and his childhood friend, Ozi, a privileged son of Lahore's upper class, and Ozi's new wife Mumtaz (who secretly writes investigative articles under the pen name Zulfakir Manto). While Daru stays in a Pakistani university, Ozi and Mumtaz study abroad in the United States and return to live the jet-set lifestyle that Daru aspires to, complete with SUVs, mobile phones, imported sushi, and contraband liquor. Daru, however, seems to be more interested in his hashish habit than in office work, and is fired from his bank job within the first 25 pages of the novel. He then begins a downward spiral—dealing drugs to get by financially, becoming sexually involved with Mumtaz, and eventually developing a heroin addiction. During this slide, Daru witnesses Ozi drive through a red light, striking and killing a young cyclist. He also becomes involved with a pseudocommunist rickshaw driver/robber baron named Murad. Together they hold up a boutique and the reader is left unsure as to whether or not Daru shoots a small boy trying to escape.

> No one gets out, that's the rule. No one gets out.
>   My hand. Hand's rising. Hand with the gun in it. [. . .]
>   The sound of an explosion and the glass of the door becomes opaque with cracks but doesn't shatter.
>   Was that me? (223)

The police come for Daru the next day; however, he is accused of Ozi's crime. The chapters from other characters' points of view that punctuate Daru's narrative tell the reader the "truth" of the matter: Ozi discovered Daru and Mumtaz were having an affair and framed him with running the red light and killing the cyclist.

It is in these interstitial chapters that Hamid makes his most striking social commentaries. Ozi serves as an example of the corruption that plagues Pakistani business and government. During his testimonial chapter, he says, "People are rob-bing the country blind, and if the choice is between being held up at gunpoint or holding the gun, only a madman would choose to hand over his wallet rather than fill it with someone else's cash" (184). A more populist sentiment comes from Murad: "[T]he right to property is at best a contingent one. When disparities become too great, a superior right, that to life, outweighs the right to property. Ergo, the very poor have the right to steal from the very rich" (64). Murad's position becomes less tenable when we see it in action—he uses this philosophy to justify robbing cabs and boutiques.

Hamid uses another narrative device to give the book a political dimension. The entire novel is framed by the story of the Mogul emperor Shah Jahan and his four sons, who fought a war of succession after his death. The principal combatants in this war were Dara Shikoh (Daru's full name) and Aurangzeb (Ozi's full name). Hamid explained the symbolism of the story thus: "My story posits that Pakistan faces a similar choice today. But my Aurangzeb represents the entrenched elite—an impediment to the country's development. Darashikoh in my story is his opposite, the violent backlash to that system. He's secular, but his angry reaction stands for Pakistan's religious movements, its violent crime" (qtd. in *Newsweek International* 62). What then, is an option for the people of Pakistan? Hamid seems to posit no viable alternative, except perhaps for Mumtaz. She leaves Ozi and writes a story about the trial as Zulfakir Manto, exercising agency enough to shun the "entrenched elite," while simultaneously lifting the onus of violence from the "backlash to that system."

Hamid has been criticized in the South Asian press for his portrayal of Pakistan in this fashion. Samina Choonara claims that *Moth Smoke* "is an index to the ills besetting Pakistan, carved out for the overseas English speaking markets where Indian literature has carved out a niche for itself" (6). Despite Choonara's elision of India and Pakistan, the critique of Hamid is not hers alone. Singh Gill has leveled the same charges at Hamid and wonders if "most Indo-Anglian writers write for themselves, or western readership?" (14). Reaction to Hamid is not uniformly negative in South Asia, however. In the West, critical reception has been positive, but to date there has been little scholarly work done on Hamid's novel.

Donovan S. Braud

Further Reading

Choonara, Samina. "Reviewing Mohsin Hamid." Matteela.com. 24 June 2002 <http://matteela.com/review.html>.

Gill, Himmat Singh. "The Classic Love Tragedy." *Tribune India.* 18 June 2000. 24 June 2002 <http://www.tribuneindia.com/2000/20000618/spectrum/books.htm#1>.

Hamid, Mohsin. "A Call to Arms for Pakistan." Interview with Anon. *Newsweek International* 24 July 2000: 62.

Hamid, Mohsin. *Moth Smoke.* New York: Picador, 2000.

Mirza, Umbereen Beg. "Moth Smoke—Mohsin Hamid." *Visage* 9.33. 24 June 2002 <http://visagepk.com/archive/iss33_vol9/article4_bk review.html>.

Rice, Lewis. "A Novel Idea." *Harvard Law Bulletin.* Summer 2000. 24 June 2002 <http://www.law.harvard.edu/alumni/bulletin/backissues/sum 2000/article5.html>.

Mukherjee, Bharati

Born in 1947, the author of more than a dozen acclaimed books and numerous articles in international journals, Bharati Mukherjee has the distinction of being one of the leading and, perhaps, most influential of Indian women writers in America. Her first novel, *The Tiger's Daughter,* was published in 1971 but it was only in 1988, with her prize-winning *The Middleman and Other Stories,* that she came into the limelight. Since then, her reputation has steadily grown.

Mukherjee belongs to an affluent upper class Bengali family from Calcutta. Barring a few years spent with her family in the United Kingdom, she spent the first two decades of her life in India. At the age of 21, she left home for the University of Iowa, where she registered for the Creative Writing Program and later received her Ph.D. from the Department of English and Comparative Literature. It was here that she met and married the Canadian writer, Clark Blaise, in 1963.

Clark Blaise and Bharati Mukherjee moved to Canada where Mukherjee took up a teaching assignment in McGill University in Montreal. However, she was not happy in Canada, which to her was claustrophobic, narrow minded, and racist. She felt that she was treated with suspicion on account of her color. Finally, the couple moved to the United States and took up teaching at the University of Iowa in Iowa City. Since then, the two writers have lectured in several universities across the American continent. Each has played a supportive role in the other's career. While pursuing their independent writings, they have also produced two nonfiction books in collaboration: *Days and Nights in Calcutta* (1977), and *The Sorrow and the Terror: The Haunting Legacy of the Air India Tragedy* (1987). Mukherjee has successfully combined a career in creative writing with her teaching profession; she is currently a professor at the University of California in Berkeley.

For Bharati Mukherjee the choice to move from Canada to the United States was a liberating one. With enthusiasm, she embraced the openness of the American culture and its respect for individuality, expressing her views without inhibitions in her writings. Simultaneously, she has gone on record, stating emphatically that she would like to be treated as an "American" writer rather than a "hyphenated" or an "ethnic" one. In other words, she would like her novels to be appreciated regardless of her ethnic background and by the same yardsticks as those applied to mainstream novelists.

Nonetheless, Mukherjee has made an important contribution to the multiethnic literature of the United States. As a writer who has moved from one geographical and cultural space to another, from India to the American continent (first to Canada, then to the United States), her writings speak of the inevitable changes involved in such transitions. She is concerned with migrations, dislocations and relocations, the consequences of these displacements, and cross-cultural encounters and the changes they effect in the identities of those who are part of such movements. Inevitably, her works are preoccupied with the notion of belonging, the idea of rootlessness, the feeling of alienation, and the search for a home. There is also a questioning of biases and prejudices, a deconstruction of social, cultural, and national stereotypes, and a re-visioning of ideas and concepts that belong to two antipodal worlds. Her novels constantly juxtapose symbols and ideas from the two worlds in a bid to explore their validity in the lives of the individuals that people her stories.

In her early writing, Mukherjee begins with cultural encounters between India and the United States. Her later works shift the focus to other multicultural encounters that take place in America: the protagonists are not necessarily South Asian, but nearly all of them are new arrivals in America. The first novel, *The Tiger's Daughter,* narrates the story of Tara who spends many years in the United States, gets married to an American, and returns to India briefly, only to find that she can no longer belong to her mother country. The story has strong autobiographical overtones with the life of the female protagonist paralleling Mukherjee's own life in more ways than one.

Whereas the stories of *Darkness* (1985) present the experiences of Indian immigrants in the United States, *The Middleman and Other Stories* (1988), her best-known book, focuses on immigrants from different ethnic groups who are part of the American salad bowl, whether they come from Philippines, Italy, Israel, India, or Trinidad. They may be minority voices, but together they form a sizable body in the nation of immigrants, representing the various tributaries that flow into the great American mainstream. These stories explore the multitextured quilting of the American society, the changing face of America as these ethnic groups move from the margins to the center. As they assimilate into the milieu, they also bring about changes in their environment.

The 1993 novel *The Holder of the World* moves silently through space and time: geographically between India and the United States, and historically between contemporary times and the seventeenth century, even as it speaks of romantic relationships across different sociocultural barriers. In contrast, her next novel, *Leave It To Me* (1997), is the story of a female child abandoned by her mother, who was a hippie from California on a love-and-peace flower trip to India. The father is probably from the Indian subcontinent, a "guru" with a questionable background. Obsessed with a desire for revenge on the parents who abandoned her, the protagonist determines to seek them out. The revenge story is interwoven with the question of identity, presented through the twin motifs of Kali and Electra, taken from the East and the West, as Mukherjee explores the hyphenated individual's dilemma in the multiethnic potpourri of America.

In her latest novel, *Desirable Daughters* (2002), the dual concerns are, again, female identity and the rerooting of the self, as the author follows the story of three Bengali sisters in the United States, weaving into the narrative memories from their childhood along with scenes from India's history. Thus the major concerns remain the same through Mukherjee's career: she continues to be fascinated by the plight of the Indian expatriate in America, by the female experience, the question of identity, and other related issues.

Bharati Mukherjee has received grants and awards from different institutions, including the Guggenheim Foundation. In 1981, she was awarded the National Magazine Award for her essay "An Invisible Woman." The most prestigious, however, was the 1998 National Book Critics Circle Award for best fiction, awarded to *The Middleman and Other Stories,* which firmly established her as a distinguished voice of the Indian diaspora in America.

While there is no doubt that Mukherjee is a talented writer, at ease with the subjects she chooses to focus on, scholars and critics are not always comfortable with her insistence on being treated as a mainstream American writer. Mukherjee's argument is that most of her adult life she has lived in the United States, so she should be considered American. The counter argument of her critics is that her formative years, growing up, education, and early influences, were all molded in India—a factor that also contributes to the predominant themes exploited endlessly in her stories; and the concern with being "housed," "unhoused," and "rehoused,"

which recurs in her works is the result of her personal experiences, dependent on the fact that she has geographically relocated from India to the American continent. So the hyphenated factor or the ethnic origins simply cannot be ignored. For this reason she is placed in the Asian American category, the slot that deals with diasporic writings from India, despite her vehement protests. Much of the critical reception accorded to her undeniably rests on this factor.

Manju Jaidka

Further Reading

Chua, C. L. "Passages from India: Migrating to America in the Fiction of V. S. Naipaul and Bharati Mukherjee." *Reworlding: The Literature of the Indian Diaspora.* Ed. Emmanuel S. Nelson. Westport: Greenwood, 1992.

Dhawan, R. K., ed. *The Fiction of Bharati Mukherjee: A Critical Symposium.* New Delhi: Prestige, 1996.

Fakrul, Alam. *Bharati Mukherjee.* New York: Twayne, 1995.

Nelson, Emmanuel S. *Bharati Mukherjee: Critical Perspectives.* Garland Reference Library of the Humanities, Vol. 1663. New York: Garland, 1993.

Wickramagamage, Carmen. "Relocation as Positive Act: The Immigrant Experience in Bharati Mukherjee's Novels." *Diaspora* 2.2 (Fall 1992): 171–200.

N

Naipaul, V. S.

Nobel laureate Vidiadhar Surajprasad Naipaul is one of the most controversial and prolific writers of the twentieth century. He was born in rural Chaguanas, Trinidad, on August 17, 1932, a third generation West Indian of East Indian descent. His grandfather, a Brahmin Hindu, was one of the North Indian immigrants who arrived in Port of Spain as an indentured laborer in the latter half of the nineteenth century. As Naipaul's link with India weakened with the passage of time, he sought a sense of belonging in the Western literary tradition. His father, Seepersad Naipaul, shaped Naipaul's literary ambitions significantly. A reporter for the *Trinidad Guardian,* and a short-story writer as well, Seepersad provided the first models for his son's literary and journalistic interests.

Naipaul's Eurocentric intellectual training dramatically influenced his perception of his identity as both a West Indian, and as much an East Indian. Consequently, as observed by Robert Hamner, what followed was the emphatic rejection of both, "Hinduism and the colonial society into which he was born" (xvi). Naipaul vowed to escape from Trinidad and at the age of 18, a hard-earned scholarship to Oxford University led him to England.

Naipaul has operated from his adopted residence ever since he took his degree of Bachelor of Arts in 1953. His daunting literary output, comprising novels, short stories, essays, travelogues, and documentary works has been received with the highest critical acclaim as well as bitter condemnation. Among the many literary prizes that he has been awarded are the Booker Prize in 1971 and the T. S. Eliot Award for Creative Writing in 1986. He is an honorary Doctor of St. Andrew's College and Columbia University and of the Universities of Cambridge, London, and Oxford. In 1990, he was knighted by Queen Elizabeth, and he was awarded the Nobel Prize for Literature in 2001.

Chandra B. Joshi remarks that Naipaul, "is an Indian by ancestry, a Trinidadian by nativity and British by residence as well as intellectual training and inclination" (14). Despite these established ties with three different continents, themes of homelessness, spiritual isolation, and "perpetual exile" reign supreme in Naipaul's works. In fact, Joshi proceeds to state, "Naipaul's creative talent has been shaped by the acute and anguished perception of his own deracination, rootlessness and displacement." After having rejected both Trinidad and India, "it dawned on him that the literary tradition he had grown up accepting as his own belonged to an alien society. The alien vision made him see his own society as petty and ridiculous" (16).

Yet, Trinidad provides the setting for his earliest books. His first three books, *The Mystic Masseur* (1957), *The Suffrage of Elvira* (1958), and *Miguel Street* (1959)

V. S. Naipaul. © The Nobel Foundation.

are light, satirical comedies. The books are also social history, showing the start of protest politics during the late 1930s and how Trinidad began to change during and after World War II. Such social change is treated amusingly, without the more analytical perspective found in his later novels. There are extensive references to local events, characters, and such politicians as Uriah Butler, Albert Gomes, Arthur Cipriani, and Naipaul's two uncles, Rudranath and Simbhoonath Capildeo in his novel, *The Mystic Masseur.* The masseur Ganesh Ramsumair follows an erratic trajectory. Following a succession of failures, his ironic rise to international eminence ultimately results in "jaded disillusionment" (Hamner xvi).

Robert Hamner writes, "Accidents, eccentricities, chicanery, and bribery pave the road to an equally unsavory victory in *The Suffrage of Elvira*" (xvi). Set in an isolated region with a predominantly Indian population, this novel presents the picture "of a rootless society, imitative and aim-

less in values" (xvi). Chittaranjan, the one character to achieve dignity, is one of the losers in a society obsessed with material gains, even if they are achieved at the cost of self-respect.

Miguel Street, a volume of linked short stories, has for its subject an impoverished area of Port of Spain. Miguel Street is a racially mixed community, predominantly black, brown, and Indians, but with some Spanish, Portuguese, and "Whites." While play-acting in public and eccentric self-display is tolerated, even appreciated, "style," as Bruce King puts it, "is the underdog's way of being unique, a way to assert identity, a mask for failure" (18). It seems that the only hope amidst stifling urban poverty is escape.

Naipaul's fourth book, one of his most outstanding novels and considered by many to be among the best novels in English literature, is *A House for Mr. Biswas* (1961). This novel, one of epic proportions, is constructed very recognizably around the facts of his father's life. Brilliantly capturing authentic West Indian life, the novel focuses on one man's desperate fight to have a house of his own, an act "symbolic of man's need to develop an authentic identity" (Hamner xvii). Mohun Biswas, the protagonist is an Everyman, a universal figure transcending regional boundaries and evoking themes of universal significance. In fact, Bruce King comments, "Biswas brings to mind Lear, unhoused, rejected by his family, alone with the Fool, unprotected from the violence of nature. . . . Both the novel and the play are about individuals who thought they could stand on their own and find that once they are unhoused, powerless, outside society, madness follows" (38). However, while *King Lear* is unequivocally a tragedy, *A House for Mr. Biswas* has an ambivalent conclusion. The manner in which the novel has been written is comic, despite Naipaul's bleak worldview.

Naipaul's first nonfictional assignment led to the publication of *The Middle Pas-*

sage (1962). Naipaul received the proposal in 1960 when he was on a three-month government scholarship in Trinidad. The book was completed in 1961 and even before it could be published, Naipaul had embarked on another journey—to India. This journey too resulted in the publication of another book, and thus, the pattern was set. Joshi states, "Travel became his means and nonfiction his mode of examining the societies of the Third World" (40).

The first of his travel books, *The Middle Passage,* reflects Naipaul's extremely critical and unflattering view of West Indian life. He is of the firm opinion that the British settlers have failed to bring about any constructive changes in Trinidad. On the contrary, the importation of slaves and indentured laborers in large numbers without provision of adequate means to improve their living conditions has resulted in mimicry of the colonizer, racial resentment, and violence. Naipaul asserts: "Colonialism distorts the identity of the subject people, and the Negro in particular is bewildered and irritable. Racial equality and assimilation are attractive but only underline the loss, since to accept assimilation is in a way to accept permanent inferiority" (*The Middle Passage* 181, qtd. in Bruce King, 53).

A clear departure from the West Indies, Naipaul's fifth novel, *Mr. Stone and the Knights Companion* (1963), once again returns to themes of human isolation and man's search for an authentic identity. It won the prestigious Hawthornden Prize. The novel was written in Kashmir in 1962 during a year when Naipaul was examining his relationship to India. While Naipaul's journey to India had been made in the hope of discovering his roots, his experiences there only confirmed his rootlessness. He states: "I was not English or Indian; I was denied the victories of both" (98). In "*An Area of Darkness*" (1964), Naipaul attacks India severely. He

launches a strong critique of the poverty and squalor that he witnessed, vividly describing beggars defecating in public. Commenting on the "collective blindness" (70) of the onlookers, Naipaul conveys the urgency of the need for better sanitation. He also condemns the practice of the caste system in India, blaming it for causing segregation, insulation, and ruthlessness. Naipaul is extremely critical of both Mahatma Gandhi and Jawaharlal Nehru in his comparative analysis of them. He has been strongly criticized, especially by Indian writers, for the negative light in which he portrays India. Dilip Chitre, for instance, complains bitterly that Naipaul employs "the vocabulary of savage but cold condemnation" (Sharma 200) when he writes on India.

Three years later Naipaul published *The Mimic Men* (1967), which was followed by a collection of short stories called *A Flag on the Island (*1967). *The Mimic Men,* as the title suggests, focuses on the theme of colonial mimicry. Gail Minault explains: "Despite the end of political dependency on the colonizer country, the newly emerging independent nation continues to be culturally and economically dependent. This continued dependence leads, according to Naipaul, to the responses of mimicry" (193).

Cultural mimicry, in the setting Naipaul chooses to portray, occurs at a horrifyingly early stage in people's lives. At school, the children are prepared to be Mimic Men of the New World. Consequently, individuals' sense of identity is strongly influenced by the colonizer's perception of them. This is well illustrated in the comment: "We became what we see of ourselves in the eyes of others" (20). The novel has a complex narrative structure, with the protagonist, "Ralph" Kripal Singh piecing together fragments of his life to give his autobiography some semblance of chronological order. Singh's "feeling of abandonment at the end of the empty world" (106) highlights the familiar theme of alienation predominant in Naipaul's fiction.

His extended work, *The Loss of El Dorado* (1969), merges together journalism, reportage, history, and fiction. It examines the early history of Trinidad after its discovery by Europeans. In his book, *In a Free State* (1971), Naipaul, referring to the capital of an African state, comments, "Everyone in it was far from home" (Joshi 1). The book is a collection of two journal entries, a novella, and two long short stories, all of which are instrumental in developing the significance of the title. Ultimately the free state does not represent a political entity, but a state of being.

The Overcrowded Barracoon (1972) is a collection of previously published essays and reviews spanning the years from 1958 through 1972. Both *Guerillas* (1975) and *A Bend in the River* (1979) dwell on the detrimental impact of colonialism and emerging nationalism in the Third World. *Guerillas* is a novel based on the report on the murder of a white woman, Gale Ann Benson, that Naipaul had written for the *Sunday Times* of London. The portrayal of Africa in *A Bend in the River* has been compared to Conrad's *Heart of Darkness*. T. R. S. Sharma states: "He [Naipaul] shares with Conrad a literary form and his many concerns—his feeling for 'lost' souls, 'lost' countries" (201).

Naipaul returns to India repeatedly in both *India: A Wounded Civilization* (1977) and *India: A Million Mutinies Now* (1990). In *Finding the Center* (1984), "the center is now the creation and discovery of the self rather than external in an ideal society" (King, 136). *A Turn in the South* (1989) presents Naipaul's reexamination of his former prejudice toward the southern United States. While his novels *The Enigma of Arrival* (1987) and *A Way in the World* (1994) are to a great extent autobiographical, *Among the Believers* (1981) and *Beyond Belief* (1998) are critical assess-

ments of Muslim fundamentalism in non-Arab countries such as Indonesia, Iran, Malaysia, and Pakistan. Naipaul's latest novel, *Half a Life* (2001), portrays the ironical existence of diaspora through the story of William Somerset Chandran.

Commenting on his literary output in an interview with Ronald Bryden in 1973, Naipaul stated: "All my work is really one. I'm really writing one big book" (qtd. in Joshi, 41).

Rachana Aggarwal

Further Reading

Hamner, Robert, ed. *Critical Perspectives on V. S. Naipaul.* Washington, D.C.: Three Continents P, 1977.

Joshi, Chandra B. *V. S. Naipaul: The Voice of Exile.* India: Sterling, 1994.

King, Bruce. *V. S. Naipaul.* London: Macmillan, 1993.

Minault, Gail. "Through a Glass Darkly: Naipaul's Post-Colonial Travel Accounts." *Critical Responses: Commonwealth Literature.* Dept. of English, Osmania Univ. Hyderabad. New Delhi: Sterling, 1993. 192–99.

Sharma, T. R. S. "Naipaul's Version of Post-Colonial Societies." *Critical Responses: Commonwealth Literature.* Dept. of English, Osmania Univ. Hyderabad. New Delhi: Sterling, 1993. 200–208.

Theroux, Paul. *V. S. Naipaul: An Introduction to His Work.* London: Andre Deutsch, 1972.

White, Landeg. *V. S. Naipaul.* London: Macmillan, 1975.

Nandy, Ashis

It is difficult to situate the prolific Ashis Nandy within segregated disciplinary boundaries. Variously described as a "social theorist" or a "political psychologist," Nandy's work supercedes these prescriptive designations: his scholarly oeuvre explores the complexity of Indian political and cultural life, especially in its efforts to search for an identity that goes beyond the hegemonic influence of Western imperialism. Nandy is currently director of the Centre for the Study of Developing Societies (Delhi). The many books he has authored include *Alternative Sciences* (1980), *The Intimate Enemy* (1983), *Traditions, Tyranny and Utopias* (1987), *The Tao of Cricket* (1989), *The Illegitimacy of Nationalism: Rabindranath Tagore and the Politics of Self* (1994), *The Savage Freud and Other Essays in Possible and Retrievable Selves* (1995), and *An Ambiguous Journey to the City: The Village and Other Odd Ruins of the Self in Indian Imagination* (2001). Books edited by Nandy include *Science, Hegemony and Violence: A Requiem for Modernity* (1988) and *The Secret Politics of our Desires* (1998).

Instead of attempting the impossible task of addressing the immensity and complexity of Ashis Nandy's entire opus, it is more practical to focus on excavating key themes in two important books by Nandy that have special relevance to South Asian political culture: *The Intimate Enemy* and *The Savage Freud.*

The Intimate Enemy (1983) is often considered to be Nandy's most important contribution to both postcolonial studies as well as to studies of South Asian cultural life. Subtitled "The Loss and Recovery of Self Under Colonialism," this book examines the diverse possibilities of anti-imperial resistance advocated by colonial Indians such as Mohandas Gandhi and Shri Aurobindo. Like many other postcolonial critics, Nandy argues that the experience of colonialism is that of a negotiated dialectic rather than a simple binary of power and powerlessness. To that end, the main agenda of *The Intimate Enemy* is to focus on the "psychological resistance to colonialism" (xii). However, Nandy does not claim to be interested solely in the colonial encounter. He is also interested in exploring the deferred implications of colonial contact: "Indian traditions which have emerged less innocent from the colonial experience" (*Intimate* xvi). Although Nandy considers colonialism a "battle for the minds of men" (*Inti-*

mate 6–7), he suggests that colonial violence also developed the psyche, and not just the mind, into a war zone. Gandhi, then, becomes an exemplary figure of anticolonial resistance, not only in terms of his striving for political independence, but also in his efforts to create for himself an identity that surpassed Western modalities of subjectivity (*Intimate* 54–55).

The Savage Freud was first published as a separate book in 1995 and then republished in 1998, along with *Alternative Sciences* and *The Illegitimacy of Nationalism,* under the title *Return From Exile.* Subtitled "And Other Essays on Possible Retrievable Selves," *The Savage Freud* recalls *The Intimate Enemy* in its effort to locate an identity that surpasses those identities created by the violence of the imperial encounter. *The Savage Freud,* therefore, defines itself as a text engaged in an act of "social criticism" (Preface, v). This collection also includes Nandy's polemical essay on *Sati* or widow burning. Nandy analyzes the discourse of "self-righteousness" and "anger" (*Savage* 32) engendered amongst the urban elite after the teen-age widow Roop Kanwar immolated herself in 1987. Nandy claims that the civic discourse regarding Roop Kanwar's sati revolves around the modernity versus tradition debate, in which the supporters of modernity endorse themselves as "bastions of rationality," thereby maintaining the "legitimacy of their social and political dominance" (*Savage* 33). The title essay of this book refers to Girindrasekhar Bose who "pioneered the discipline [of Psychoanalysis] in India" (*Savage* 83). According to Nandy, Bose's "unique response" to Freudian methodology was determined by the conflicts within the genre of psychoanalysis as well as by the "psychological contradictions that had arisen in Indian culture due to the colonial impact" (*Savage* 83). Here, then, we observe another example of how colonial Indians sought to express the fractured identities engendered by colonialism as well as to recover a sense of indigenous self.

Even though *The Intimate Enemy* and *The Savage Freud* span almost a decade in Nandy's scholarly career, they collectively demonstrate important thematic concerns that are repeatedly configured in Nandy's other books: an examination of the complex link between Indian public life and Indian culture; the impact of Western culture on the Indian imagination; and a corresponding effort to create a new holistic identity that can transcend, though never negate, the violence engendered on the colonized psyche by the forces of colonialism.

Nandy is perhaps not so well known in the larger field of postcolonial studies, but he is widely recognized for his contribution to South Asian studies both in India and abroad. Correspondingly, there has been an increased critical response to Nandy's work. In addition to Ziauddin Sardar's extensive essay on Nandy entitled "The A, B, C, D (and E) of Ashis Nandy," Vinay Lal has edited an entire collection of essays, entitled *Dissenting Knowledges, Open Futures: The Multiple Selves and Strange Destinations of Ashis Nandy,* that analyzes Nandy's work in comprehensive detail.

Pallavi Rastogi

Further Reading

Lal, Vinay, ed. *Dissenting Knowledges, Open Futures: The Multiple Selves and Strange Destinations of Ashis Nandy.* New Delhi: Oxford UP, 2001.

Sardar, Ziauddin. "The A, B, C, D (and E) of Ashis Nandy." Introduction. *Return from Exile.* New Delhi: Oxford UP, 1998.

Naqvi, Tahira

Tahira Naqvi was born in Iran to Pakistani parents. She was raised and educated in Lahore, Pakistan, and has lived in the United States for over three decades. She has taught English at Western Connecticut State University and is currently teaching English at Westchester Community College, New York. She has also taught Urdu at Columbia University and is presently teaching Urdu at New York University. She received an M.A. in psychology from Government College, Lahore, and an M.S. in education from Western Connecticut State University. She lives in New York with her husband and three sons.

Naqvi is one of the few Pakistani American fiction writers in the United States. Naqvi's short stories appeared in Asian American anthologies such as *The Forbidden Stitch* (1989) and *Imagining America: Stories from the Promised Land* (1991), and in early collections of South Asian American fiction including *Her Mother's Ashes* (1994) and *Living in America* (1995). Naqvi has also received attention in the United States as a translator of Urdu writings into English, especially the literary works of Ismat Chughtai and Sa'adat Hasan Manto.

Naqvi's first collection *Attar of Roses and Other Stories of Pakistan* includes 14 stories that evoke the author's memories of the sights, smells, and sounds of Lahore, recast as those of her protagonists. She depicts middle-class family life and social relations in Pakistan: the attempts to gain love or arranged marriages and concerns of sexual repression and gender segregation. In an interview, Naqvi admits that her fiction is autobiographical and depends on memory, and that unlike Chitra Divakaruni's representations of South Asian women's "misery and despair" in *Arranged Marriage,* Naqvi attempts to depict the "joy and fulfillment in our lives," since "Romance among cousins is an integral part of Muslim societies, especially in India and Pakistan, and as I have often told my students here, we are not all hijab-wearing, persecuted, inexperienced, naïve women as the world would have us be. We do get to have some fun!" (Devi)

In her second collection, *Dying in a Strange Country,* Naqvi's fiction shifts in both locale and subject matter to the United States, while depicting characters who are largely suspended between the two worlds of Pakistan and the United States or, more specifically, Lahore and Westchester, Connecticut. This collection had been originally planned and advertised under various titles including *Amreeka, Amreeka* and *Beyond the Walls, Amreeka.* Naqvi's stories describe the everyday lives, loves, sorrows, and amusing, but pathos-filled, family encounters in the lives of Pakistanis living in America, as well as their aging relatives—such as Sakina Bano who is afraid of dying in a strange country while visiting her Americanized son. Naqvi's tragicomic vision and her gentle, humorous, irony, is evident in her best stories: "Thank God for the Jews" and "Dying in a Strange Country." The stories, interconnected through similar settings and characters belonging to the same extended family, have the feel of a loosely structured novel. Most stories are from the point of view of the middle-aged Pakistani American wife and mother, Zenab, and portray her preoccupation with domestic chores such as cooking and child-rearing, and her reflections on issues of public concerns such as the interpretation of the Koran, or the fear of being buried in foreign soil. She has recently finished writing her first novel.

Although her voice is described as "gentle and poetic" (Reale), Naqvi's fiction is not as well known as works by contemporary Indian American women writers who have gained widespread readership among Asian American readers and critics—including Jhumpa Lahiri, Bharati Mukherjee, and Chitra Divakaruni—and whose writings have appeared or been reviewed in popular media such as the *New York Times* or *The New Yorker.*

Naqvi's fiction, perhaps, resonates more specifically for those familiar with life experiences in Pakistani and Pakistani American households that she describes so vividly. For instance, Pakistani American scholar Fawzia Afzal-Khan gives a positive review and praises Naqvi's "lyrical, suggestive prose" in *Attar of Roses* and suggests that reading her "moving collection of stories should be an act of atonement all readers of South Asian literature willingly undergo." Bapsi Sidhwa praises Naqvi's debut collection's "nuanced expression" and "imaginative sense of humor and playfulness," and some stories as "compulsively readable." But Marilyn Booth harshly criticizes the protagonists of *Attar* as "merely the vehicles that convey a political agenda" and some of the endings as "a bit too cute."

Nalini Iyer rightly praises Naqvi's "ability to create finely nuanced characters such as Zenab and her retinue of aunts," in *Dying in a Strange Country,* and her skill as she "balances the absurd with the profound, the comic with the potentially tragic moments." But Schurer's review states that stories in *Dying* are "repetitive," providing "individual snapshots with not enough significance" and "not enough tension to hold the reader."

Lavina D. Shankar

Further Reading

Afzal-Khan, Fawzia. Rev. of *Attar of Roses and Other Stories of Pakistan. World Literature Today* 73.1 (Winter 1999): 219–20.

Booth, Marilyn. Rev. of *Attar of Roses and Other Stories of Pakistan. Middle East Women's Studies Review* 13. 3 (Fall 1998): 20.

Devi, Gayatri. "Tahira Naqvi: Sprinkling the Attar of Pakistan over Amreeka and the World." 17 June 2002 <http://www.monsoonmag.com/interviews/i3inter_naqvi.html>.

Iyer, Nalini. "Young Pakistani Mother Holds Immigrant Stories Together." Rev. of *Dying in a Strange Country* by Tahira Naqvi. *International Examiner* 30 Apr. 2002: 5.

Reale, Michelle. Rev. of *Dying in a Strange Country* by Tahira Naqvi. *Little India* 11.9 (30 Sept. 2001): 43.

Schurer, Norbert. Rev. of *Dying in a Strange Country* by Tahira Naqvi. *World Literature Today* 76.1 (Winter 2002): 142.

Sidhwa, Bapsi. Rev. of *Attar of Roses and Other Stories of Pakistan* by Tahira Naqvi. *The Journal of Asian Studies* 58.1 (Feb. 1999): 242–43.

Narayan, R. K.

R. K. Narayan is considered one of the foremost modern Indian writers writing in English. His lifespan of 94 years (1906–2001) encompasses a rich creative output that has won him an undisputed place among international writers. He has written extensively, traversing a range of genres that includes 14 novels, 12 volumes of short stories, 3 books of travel writings, several essays, as well as memoirs and reflections, written from 1935 to 1993. His prolific career has won him numerous honors and awards: the A. C. Benson Award by The Royal Society of Literature in 1980; honorary membership in the American Academy and Institute of Arts and Letters; an honorary doctorate by the Mysore University; the Sahitya Academy Award in 1958 for his novel *The Guide*. He has also received several nominations for the Nobel Prize.

R. K. Narayan's major novels deal with a range of material, exploring the intricacies and often the comical complications of living in a traditional society. Thus, topics such as the following recur: kinship structure of the extended family and the rebellious cogitations of youth's struggle *(Swami and His Friends, The Bachelor of Arts);* the husband-wife frictions *(The Dark Room);* the tragic consequence of losing a loved one *(The English Teacher* and *Grateful to Life and Death);* the life of the common man engaged in local trades and the impact of modernization *(Mr. Sampath: The Printer of Malgudi, The Financial Expert,* and *The Painter of Signs);* the moral order of the universe *(The Man-Eater of Malgudi, The Guide,* and *The World of Nagaraj).*

Narayan's short-story collections offer a vibrant and humorous look at the human follies and foibles enacted at the cusp of a transforming yet continuously reiterating the world of the past. Some examples are *Malgudi Days* (1982); *Under the Banyan Tree and Other Stories* (1985); *A Story-Teller's World: Stories, Essays, Sketches* (1989); *The Grandmother's Tale: Three Novels* (1993); *Salt and Sawdust: Stories and Table Talk* (1993).

Notable essay collections and travel memoirs reveal an honest perspective on various topics. A recurring preoccupation is with the need to escape the fast acceleration of an institutionalized, mechanized way of life, both in India and the West. Some of these collections are *Next Sunday: Sketches and Essays* (1960); *My Dateless Diary: An American Journey* (1964); *My Days* (1974). As a writer, Narayan has left a record of his own fondness for the personal essay in *A Writer's Nightmare: Selected Essays 1958–1988* (1988). He has translated two major Hindu epics into simplified prose, *The Ramayana: A Shortened Modern Prose Version of the Indian Epic* (1972) and *The Mahabharata: A Shortened Modern Prose Version of the Indian Epic* (1978).

A man of such repertoire started off with a first novel that almost reached a watery grave but for the good will of a friend in London who passed on the manuscript to a young British writer, Graham Greene. The stories of Greene's recognition and glowing support of R. K. Narayan are legendary. The fact that Narayan conceded to Greene's suggestion that he shorten his name from Rasipuram Krishnaswami Narayan to R. K. Narayan testifies to Narayan's enduring regard for Greene. This literary mentorship led to the publications of several of Narayan's early novels. A major event that spelt disaster for Narayan was the death of his young wife, Rajam, whom he had married by choice rather than the traditional system of arranged marriage. The recovery and spiritual strength gained subsequently is the subject of his fourth novel, *The English Teacher*.

From then on, Narayan has consistently been a productive writer.

The literary merit of Narayan's work rests on his envisioning of a small mythical town, Malgudi, in Southern India, which he invested with such detail and specificity that critics and readers have speculated on actual towns in Mysore to be the origin. Malgudi is a functional device, a material location, as well as a philosophical conceptualization. Centering his narratives in this small town allows Narayan's writings to include precolonial, colonial, and post-colonial time frames of India's history, as well as a spatial configuration that traverses from mythical Mempi forests and caves, legendary Rama's journeys along Sarayu River, and the site of Buddha's preachings to the colonial Railway lines and institutions of industrial capitalism.

A recurring preoccupation in Narayan's narratives is the persistence of an indigenous way of life as well as a pervasive sense of changes that have remapped Malgudi, and by extension India, through specific historical junctures. One such phase is the British colonial presence. In the pre-Independence narratives, this issue is pursued as a way to understand a protagonist's personal growth, often depicted as caught between the magical allure of colonial fantasy and the robustness of indigenous ways of life. In *Swami and Friends*, Narayan's first novel, the young schoolboy, Swami tries to forge his growing awareness of politics and social ills within a colonial system while resisting the real attractions of material progress and sense of superiority imposed by the colonial institutions. Layered with the double consciousness of the colonized, Swami and his friends are products as well as potential critics of their colonized reality. They are influenced by the Albert Mission School, but they also resist it, becoming victims of its punishing faith in "educating" the native to hate himself. The comic-ironic vein of the narrative reveals

Swami's struggles as he embarks upon resisting all kinds of authority, both within his home, at school, as well as within the social and political level.

Narayan projects the wisdom of village communal life and ultimately its simplicity as the strength of the Indian way of life, although he often perceives India from mainly a Hindu-dominant perspective. His early novels reiterate this belief. His male protagonists, from whose perspective we enter the life of Malgudi, are often critical of the idiosyncrasies and contradictions of a small village life, yet ironically, in performing their individual acts they confirm the processes of communal affirmation.

Framed within the context of Hindu philosophy, Narayan's world is reformulated in terms of the stories of Hindu gods such as Ganesha and Shiva. In *Mr. Sampath: The Printer of Malgudi* (1949), Lord Ganesha is evoked both as an icon of Srinivas's ancestral and maternal past (the icon is given to him by his mother), which can transform even the arid environs of a small, rented room in a city into a sacred space of private, family and communal power through faith. Shiva too can transform evil with the gaze of his third eye— the eye that disables the value of mere physical and intellectual life untouched by spirituality, and thus can collapse the entire universe into nothingness. These stories and myths so central to Hindu cosmology emerge from the spaces and interspaces of Malgudi, and ultimately validate its convergence of all disparities into one unrecorded, undocumented, unappropriated mass of spacelessness.

Narayan's narratives project certain themes and symbols. One such persistent topic is focused on the home as a concretization of the family structure in a traditional Hindu household, an extended family where several members of the family reside under the same roof. In his autobiography *My Days* (1974), Narayan recounts how he himself grew up first in his uncle's house, along with his grandmother, and later moved to his parents' in Mysore. Narayan, in his narratives, identifies with his protagonist's sense of values and liabilities involved in all such kinship bonds.

The Financial Expert (1953) exposes the encroachment of colonial bureaucracy into rural Malgudi. Margayya's native business skills and sharp insight into the impracticality of the colonial system become means for personal gain. However, when his projects become large-scale ventures, the impersonal and unconscionable nature of capitalism takes away the pleasures of conducting one to one business with villagers of interestingly varying mental capacities, with whom he can haggle and score a point. His final rejection of unscrupulous and unethical practices, in order to ensure the safety of his son and his family, bring him back full circle to his starting point. Margayya's utopian dreams are concretized in that impulse that ultimately posits an alternative, indigenous-based ethos of success against importation of Western capitalism. In *The Financial Expert*, Margayya's home is the place where human bonds are tested and ultimately accepted above and beyond material possessions.

For Narayan a novel is not a "sociological study or a social document," as he himself points out in "Reluctant Guru," an essay collected in *A Writer's Nightmare* (101). He touches the very pulse of life in an Indian milieu with a keen and decided finger, and what he reveals is its significance in the very chaos of living it. Competing identities are explored in *The Guide* (1958): from "Railway Raju" to tourist guide, to Rosie's lover to agent, to forgerer of legal documents, to prisoner, and finally to saint, Raju's journey traces the direction of self definition within the confines of Malgudi's record of colonial and postcolonial history. Raju, in many ways, oper-

ates as the trickster figure, like the Narada of Hindu mythology and cosmogonyî (Parekh 184–85). Raju may not have achieved sainthood but his journey, however accidental to begin with, results in confirming the close proximity of our material and spiritual natures. In Narayan's perspective, these mythmaking tendencies are the evidence of our faith in the possibilities of human enactment of spiritual values.

In Narayan's last novel, *The World of Nagaraj* (1990), the spiritual, philosophical, and historical dimensions of a Hindu world find a harmonious blend in the main protagonist's struggles. Nagaraj's main goal is to write a book on the Sage Narada, "The celestial sage who had a curse on his back that unless he spread a gossip a day his head would burst" (3) Nagaraj's thesis is to ultimately find the "cosmic perspective" in such clashes and destruction. However, ironically, Nagaraj's own progress in writing the book is impeded by several peripheral preoccupations and interruptions, besides his own habitual lack of discipline. A series of family crises, devastating to his artistic goals, provide obstacles to his project. After a number of complications and family feuds, Nagaraj accepts the primacy of the family instead of the individual self. As Nagaraj knows, even the most insignificant or the most destructive forces of life prove "beneficial in a cosmic perspective" (3).

Critical reception of Narayan's works has been varied. Several critical assessments range from book length studies and collections of essays to journal articles. Most early critics tended to focus on Narayan's apolitical preoccupations and "universal" humanistic themes, recognizing his inimitable comic-ironic style. In the West, critics responded to elements within Narayan's work that could be identified as representations of Hindu philosophy, spirituality as well as its extended family structure, and so focused on works like *The English Teacher* (which deals with

Krishnan's psychic reconciliation with his dead wife, Susila), *The Bachelor of Arts* (dealing with a young man's journey growing up in an extended family system), and *The Financial Expert* (which highlights the family quarrels within this system). *The Guide* allowed the West to understand the East in Indian terms rather than orientalist portrayals. William Walsh's two books, *R. K. Narayan* (1971) and *R. K. Narayan: A Critical Appreciation* (1982) provide such Western perspectives. V. S. Naipaul who has been constantly evoked as a critic of Narayan, saw Narayan's Malgudi as a limiting world. Naipaul claimed that Narayan's Malgudi "did not prepare me for the distress of India," charging Narayan for depicting poverty as "seen but not abhorred" in *Malgudi Days* (12). Among Indian critics, there is an attempt to place Narayan in the context of Puranic texts or examine him in relation to other major writers of his era, Mulk Raj Anand and Raja Rao. Reza Ahmed Nasimi's *The Language of Mulk Raj Anand, Raja Rao and R. K. Narayan* (1989) examines these authors through a focus on their use of language. Additionally, critics like Feroza Jussawala and Viney Kirpal provide a grounded analyses of Narayan's stylistic and structural, as well as symbolic, use of language, such as Indian English, as well as the archetypal landscape. Atma Ram's *Perspectives on R. K. Narayan* (1981) provides inroads into defining the emerging field of Indian writing in English by including a range of Narayan criticism. Lakshmi Holmstrom's *The Novels of R. K. Narayan* (1973) notes the realism of Narayan's works as based on recognizing "every man with ideals, plans, and illusions is Quixotic and funny, because these plans will come into collision with the fixed and determined" (125). Among recent critical works, there is a greater intersection of scholars from the West and India, allowing for a rich dialogue of perspectives. Geoffrey Kain's *R. K. Narayan:*

Contemporary Critical Essays (1993) is a major collection that includes new critical approaches. American and Indian scholars examine Narayan's works from cultural, postcolonial, feminist, and socialist-materialist perspectives. Since Narayan's death in 2001, several journal articles have appeared, commemorating his contributions. Narayan has been the topic of various academic research studies, such as dissertations (Manorama Pandit, Feroza Jussawala, for example) and continues to invite further critical attention.

Pushpa N. Parekh

Further Reading
Holmstrom, Lakshmi. *The Novels of R. K. Narayan.* Calcutta: Writers Workshop, 1973.
Kain, Geoffrey, ed. *R. K. Narayan: Contemporary Critical Essays.* East Lansing: Michigan State UP, 1993.
Narayan, R. K. "Reluctant Guru." *A Writer's Nightmare: Selected Essays 1958–1988.* India: Penguin, 1988. 99–105.
Ram, Atma. *Perspectives on R. K. Narayan.* India: Vimal Prakashan, 1981.
The South Asian Review. 23: 1(2002). (Commemorative issue devoted to R. K. Narayan).
Walsh, William. *R. K. Narayan.* England: Longman, 1971.
———. *R. K. Narayan: A Critical Appreciation.* Chicago: U of Chicago P, 1982.

Nationalism

Nationalism first emerged as an influential historical force in the eighteenth century, with the contestation of the divine right of monarchs in Europe and the spread of European settlements in the Americas. The rise of print culture aided the dissemination of secularist ideals—such as the sovereignty of the people and "no taxation without representation"—and momentous events such as the American and French revolutions, permeated by nationalist rhetoric, influenced other national movements in turn. Marxist critics emphasize nationalism's instrumental value in this period to bourgeois elites in particular, who sought to protect their mercantile interests by forming cross-class alliances within newly bounded territories. In the nineteenth century, nationalism proved to be a defining political force in Europe, with the unification of Italy and Germany and the rise of imperial competition between the major powers. By the meeting of the League of Nations in 1920, Benedict Anderson notes in his widely influential work, *Imagined Communities,* that the nation had become the only acceptable state form. The postcolonial movements of the twentieth century, wielding the nineteenth-century legacy of nationalist struggle against the European powers that had dominated the previous century, resulted in a host of liberated nations worldwide, while the two world wars radically redrew the boundaries and territories of existing countries, producing new ones (such as Israel) in the process. At the beginning of the twenty-first century, ethnic nationalisms continue to proliferate as the unified nations of the recent past increasingly splinter apart. Many argue, however, that the future of the nation—in its most positive guise as a political entity that safeguards the rights of its people—is now under serious threat from the forces of globalization.

Nationalism is often defined as a political outlook, as that "principle which holds that the political and national unit should be congruent" (Gellner 1). Because the term also describes a deeply felt sense of commitment and belonging to the aggregate of people that shares, or seeks to share, a territory and government, however, it is best understood in cultural as well as political terms. Historian E. J. Hobsbawm argues that nationalism always precedes the formation of the national-political entity: "Nations do not make states and nationalisms but the other way around" (10). Like many theorists of nationalism, Hobsbawm emphasizes its constructed and unstable nature and the importance of nationalism's cultural myth-

making to the perpetuation of the nation: as Anderson's book reminds us, the nation is first and foremost an "imagined community."

Despite the fact that nationalism is an essentially modern phenomenon, contemporaneous with the rise of vernacular languages and the spread of print, it often perpetuates the idea of a country's ancient past and of a purported collective memory of that past. A common language, religion, culture, ethnicity and race might also be evoked to underpin the feelings of belonging essential to nationalism, and these qualities are frequently used to naturalize community membership in nationalist discourses (though not all or any of them are essential to the existence of nationalism). Anderson's analysis of nationalism stresses the importance of technological changes, such as the advent of print culture, to its emergence and resonance. The novel and the newspaper, for example, produce a concept of the nation by allowing for the perception of simultaneity across time, thus enabling people to envision themselves as members of the same civic space. In evoking the sensation of what Anderson calls a "deep, horizontal kinship," these forms pave the way for the kind of solidarity that inspires citizens to go to war and to die for their country.

Because of its appeal to essentialist categories of belonging and its necessarily exclusionary character, theorists and historians of nationalism are wary of its potentially negative repercussions. Hobsbawm, for instance, argues that "no serious historian of nations and nationalism can be a committed political nationalist . . . (n)ationalism requires too much belief in what is patently not so" (12). Even as nationalism functions as the site of collective action and of great emotion, these tend to be most frequently and effectively mobilized at times of war and imperialist expansion; Nazi Germany is thus an oft-cited example of the potential depravities and excesses of nationalism. In her powerful essay on "The Decline of the Nation-State and the End of the Rights of Man," Hannah Arendt argues that the violent exclusions of nations and nationalisms, such as those of World War II, produce stateless people who are deprived of basic human rights: rights guaranteed only to citizens within the boundaries of states.

Despite the efforts of the United Nations to uphold a universal human rights bill, no international body currently wields the power to enforce these rights within individual nations so that nationalisms, particularly ethnic ones, continue to produce the kinds of exclusion Arendt noted over half a century ago. Feminist and queer theorists have also launched powerful critiques of nationalism. While nationalist movements can be modernizing projects that further women's rights, nationalism also tends to rely on an ideology of separate spheres in which women are regarded as the biological and cultural reproducers of the nation, while men are called upon to protect them from external aggression. Because heteronormativity and traditional gender roles most effectively guarantee the reproduction of further citizen-subjects, nationalism tends to reinforce itself upon the language and ideology of both. Organizations such as "Queer Nation" thus respond to the problematic category of the nation by inviting the formation of local and transnational versions of community rather than strictly national ones.

Despite the range and virulence of critiques of nationalism, some theorists argue that it remains as an important check on the rapacious forces of capitalism—a bond of cohesion that allows for the continuance of civic participation and engagement at a time when individual political agency appears to be increasingly eroded by the vast power and influence of multinational conglomerates. Nationalism also has potentially positive connotations for those invested in postcolonial movements.

While the boundaries imposed on colonies by European imperialists created problems for the nations that would arise within them, contributing to the ethnic rivalries and economic crises that continue to trouble postcolonial regions today, the language of national solidarity originating in postcolonial liberation movements, and the theories of influential Third World nationalists such as Frantz Fanon and Amilcar Cabral, continue to provide valuable inspiration. Many contemporary critics strive to face the problems of postcolonial nationalism directly, however, by focusing on its fissures; by studying voices silenced by traditional nationalist historiography (the *Subaltern Studies* project is a noteworthy example of such work); and by emphasizing the transnational movements (such as pan-Africanism and the nonviolent resistance movement) that accompanied the rise of nationalism. Partha Chatterjee's *The Nation and its Fragments,* for instance, teases out some of the contradictions inherent in anticolonialist Indian nationalism, showing that while nationalists fought to erase cultural difference in the domain of state power, they strove to retain it in the spiritual domain in order to assert their agency, and difference from the colonial power. Chatterjee's argument overlaps with feminist critiques of both European and postcolonial nationalisms in its focus on the ways in which the opposition between material and spiritual spheres within the nation works to reify the cultural and social roles of women.

The relationship between nationalism and literary production has been much debated in literary studies since Anderson's linkage of the novel and nationalism, particularly in the context of South Asian and other postcolonial literatures. Marxist theorist Aijaz Ahmad, in his book *In Theory: Nations, Classes, Literatures,* influentially argued against Fredric Jameson's claim that Third World literature should be read as national allegory, pointing to the ways in which Western literary studies suppresses difference within Third World literature and constructs it falsely as a unitary object of knowledge. While he argues against the mapping of literary onto national form in Third World literatures, Ahmad also contends that the cultural nationalism that arose in response to imperialism in colonized countries must not be lightly dismissed before it has been fully inhabited. Ahmad calls, therefore, for a fully differentiated theory of postcolonial literature that also acknowledges the importance of nationalism to postcolonial identities.

The prevalence of the term *South Asian* in discussions about literature of the region itself points to a departure in literary and postcolonial studies from the nationalist model that has prevailed until recently. While the idea of a South Asian literature might be said to reproduce the Western tendency to homogenize non-Western cultures for the convenience of study that Ahmad points to, the term also performs the salutary function of emphasizing cultural and historical commonalities: commonalities whose existence testifies to the violence inherent in the national boundaries that now divide the subcontinent. As many critics point out, however, South Asian studies must strike a delicate balance between identity and difference in its understanding of cultures that fall under its scope, while also avoiding the pitfall of becoming merely a synonym for Indian literature at the expense of the study of other national and regional traditions in South Asia.

Tanya Agathocleous

Further Reading

Ahmad, Aijaz. *In Theory: Classes, Nations, Literatures.* New York: Verso, 1994.

Anderson, Benedict. *Imagined Communities.* New York: Verso, 1983.

Arendt, Hannah. *The Origins of Totalitarianism.* New York: Harvest, 1973.

Chatterjee, Partha. *The Nation and Its Fragments: Colonial and Postcolonial Histories.* Princeton: Princeton UP, 1993.

Gellner, Ernest. *Nations and Nationalism.* Ithaca: Cornell UP, 1983.

Hobsbawm, E. J. *Nations and Nationalism since 1780.* Cambridge: Cambridge UP, 1990.

Neocolonialism

Postcolonialism has caused a great deal of debate among its protagonists and antagonists since it seems to imply that the issues of the colonial era can safely be relegated to the verdict of history. The use of the term *neocolonialism* is one of the ways theorists wish to emphasize the importance of keeping discussions about colonialism and its effects current. Critics such as Ella Shohat and Arif Dirlik fault the term *postcolonial* for glossing over contemporary global power relations. In Dirlik's estimate, postcolonialism is to be counted among the progeny of postmodernism, and many postcolonial critics' most original contributions consist in their rephrasing of older problems of Third World–ism in the language of poststructuralism; but they have deliberately avoided examining the relationship between postcolonialism and global capitalism. While giving postcolonial critics full credit for engaging "in valid criticism of past forms of ideological hegemony," Dirlik takes them to task for their complicity in covering up "contemporary problems of social, political, and cultural domination" (296). Shohat takes issue with the term *postcolonial* for its implication that "colonialism is now a matter of the past" (326), which inadvertently conceals the fact that global hegemony persists in forms other than overt colonial rule. In her rigorous interrogation of postcolonialism, both as a term and as an emergent discourse, Shohat addresses the problems of its origin, contradictions, and political failures. From her point of view, the term *postcolonial* fails to address the issue of contemporary power relations; it lacks a political content that can account for imperialism in the eighties and nineties. Despite differences and contradictions among and within Third World countries, Shohat prefers the term *Third World,* for it contains a common project of allied resistances to neocolonialisms, usefully evoking "structural commonalities of struggles" (332) among diverse peoples. She further objects to the term *postcolonial* for its premature celebration of the pastness of colonialism, and to her, part of the reason for the curious ubiquity of the term is its academic marketability, for it sounds more palatable to the authorities of universities than *Third World studies,* or studies in *neocolonialism.* In her assessment, the term *postcolonial* would be more precise if it were "articulated as a 'post–First/Third Worlds theory' or 'post-anti-colonial critique,' as a movement beyond a relatively binaristic fixed and stable mapping of power relations between 'colonized/colonizer' and 'center/periphery' " (329).

Yet the term *neocolonialism* is in itself extremely contentious because it is multifaceted and loosely used, often as a synonym for contemporary forms of imperialism, and, in a polemical way, in reaction to any unjust and oppressive expression of Western political power. Lying underneath all these various meanings of neocolonialism is a tacit understanding that colonialism should be seen as something more than the formal or physical occupation and control of territories by a Western metropole. Hence, while formal methods of control like the implementation of structures of governance, the stationing of military forces, and most importantly the incorporation of the natives as subjects of the metropolitan government, suggest an obvious, more or less easily quantifiable form of control, neocolonialism suggests an indirect form of control through economic and cultural de-

pendence and exploitation. In this case, neocolonialism describes the continued control of former colonies through ruling native elites compliant with neocolonial powers, populations that are exploited for their labor and resources in order to feed an insatiable appetite for finished physical or cultural commodities made by the metropole.

Scholars in postcolonial studies generally agree that the term *neocolonialism* originated with Kwame Nkrumah, Ghana's first post-independence president. As part of a burgeoning movement of consciousness developing among postcolonial elites in Africa, Nkrumah became aware that the gaining of political independence and national sovereignty by African states was purely token and in no substantial way altered the relationship between the colonial powers and the colonized state. Nkrumah argues in the introduction of *Neo-Colonialism: The Last Stage of Imperialism:*

> The Neo-Colonialism of today represents Imperialism in its final and perhaps its most dangerous stage. The essence of Neo-Colonialism is that the state which is subject to it is, in theory, independent and has all the outward trappings of international sovereignty. In reality its economic system and thus its political policy is directed from outside. (ix)

In effect, the formal granting of independence created a more manichean system of dependency and exploitation since the old imperialism was retaining economic control after being forced to cede direct state power. As Nkrumah noted, neocolonial methods are "subtle and varied" and neocolonialists "operate not only in the economic field, but also in the political, religious, ideological, and cultural spheres" (239).

While Nkrumah does not provide a solution to neocolonialism in his book, he makes a number of tacit suggestions, including the need for pan-African (and, by implication, pan–Third World) unity in making the task of hegemony more difficult for neocolonialism. By doing so it may become possible to counter the extent to which late capitalism has invented more sophisticated strategies of containment to repress oppositional culture; *neocolonialism* in the form of economic and technological revolution possesses unprecedented capacity to conquer. Never before has Western imperialism been so successful in infiltrating and consolidating European American master narratives of history; never before has the majority of Western society been so unanimously bound together (for all the postmodern angst and disintegration that it displays) by the structure of feeling that, to borrow a phrase from Edward Said, "we are number one, we are bound to lead, we stand for freedom and order, and so on" (xvii); and never before have non-Western countries been so awe stricken by the sense of the Western world's superiority in technology and economy and therefore resentful when they consider their own colonial and modern subjugations to that superiority.

Abid Vali

Further Reading

Amin, Samir. *Eurocentrism.* Trans. Russell Moore. New York: Monthly Review, 1989.

Dirlik, Arif. "The Postcolonial Aura: Third World Criticism in the Age of Global Capitalism." *Contemporary Postcolonial Theory: A Reader.* Ed. Padmini Mongia. New York: St. Martin's, 1996.

Hardt, Michael and Antonio Negri. *Empire.* Cambridge: Harvard UP, 1989.

Nkrumah, Kwame. *Neo-Colonialism: The Last Stage of Imperialism.* Atlantic Highlands: Humanities Intl., 1965.

Said, Edward. *Culture and Imperialism.* New York: Knopf, 1993.

Shohat, Ella. "Notes on the 'Postcolonial.' " *Contemporary Postcolonial Theory: A Reader.* Ed. Padmini Mongia. New York: St. Martin's, 1996.

O

Ondaatje, Michael

While traversing Sri Lanka, gathering information to assemble his family chronicle, *Running in the Family* (1982), Michael Ondaatje visits many relatives and friends. They are all engaging characters but Ondaatje writes with particular poignancy about one woman: Aunt Dolly is 80 years old, and she, together with her brother Arthur, were close friends of Ondaatje's father, Mervyn. Ondaatje writes about his delight at meeting her—"suddenly all these journeys are worth it" (111). The old house Aunt Dolly stays in is under repair, and the garden seems to have crawled into the house; she is a delicate woman staying in a fragile home. Ondaatje has to force himself "to be gentle with this frailty in the midst of [his] embrace" (112). This is a touching moment in the text. It also offers a paradigm for the way in which Ondaatje, the traveler, embraces his homeland Sri Lanka—a circumspect, tentative grip of a place and its people.

Philip Michael Ondaatje was born in 1943 on a tea estate in Kegalle, Ceylon, now Sri Lanka. When he was 11, he left to study in England soon after his parents' divorce. In 1962, he immigrated to Canada. Though his ancestry is a mixture of Dutch, Sinhalese, and Tamil, the family "was solidly British colonial in outlook" (Jewinski 23). Ondaatje's Ceylonese and English educational background formed the British streak in him. In Canada, however, he awoke to a new, robust literary tra-

dition. Ed Jewinski, a biographer of Ondaatje, writes: "For the young poet there was now a sense of a new tradition being formed, a new, vigorous, and vital outlook on the world" (31), one that was linked but different from the British tradition he knew. He attended Bishop's University and then the University of Toronto where he received his B.A. in English in 1965. Having received his M.A. in 1967 from Queen's University, he began teaching in the English department at the University of Western Ontario, and later joined the faculty of Glendon College, York University. He currently resides in Toronto. Though Ondaatje has won some of Canada's most prestigious literary awards with texts such as *The Collected Works of Billy the Kid (1970)* and *Coming Through Slaughter* (1976), he acquired international renown when his novel *The English Patient* (1992) won the Booker Prize. Besides being a documentary filmmaker and critic, the novelist is also a prolific poet, and his poetry collections include *The Dainty Monsters* (1967), *Rat Jelly* (1973), *Secular Love* (1984), *The Cinnamon Peeler: Selected Poems* (1991), and *Handwriting* (1998).

It is Ondaatje's diasporic background that determines the themes in his works. Notions of home, identity, travel, history, and migration find a prominent place in his writings. True of the diasporic sensibility with its narrative of dislocation, Ondaatje's need to articulate home and identity is textualized into the very fabric of his writings, which in turn makes his works highly textured and complex. Not surprisingly, Ondaatje's representations of his first home, Sri Lanka, and the Sri Lankans in his narratives, generate heated debate. Critics like Arun Mukherjee comment on what they see as Ondaatje's ahistorical and atemporal treatment of the island. Ondaatje, says Mukherjee, "does not get drawn into the acts of living, which involve the need to deal with the burning issues of his time" ("The Sri Lankan Poets" 34). His success "has been won largely through a sacrifice of his regionality, his past and most importantly, his experience of otherness in Canada" (Mukherjee, "The Poetry" 50). Kanaganayakam writes that a weakness in *Running in the Family* is the text's refusal "to participate actively in the referential" (40). At the same time, however, there are critics who challenge these views and Suwanda Sugunasiri takes Ondaatje's dissenters to task, saying that the writer's works must be located within his particular sociopolitical context of the elite bourgeoisie, which he depicts so vividly in his texts. Despite some reservations, Kanaganayakam is also compelled to say that *Running in the Family* manifests "the complexity of a colonial inheritance" (41), acknowledging the text's engagement with history and location.

The divergent responses to Ondaatje's works are understandable given the author's background and ambivalent relationship to his island home. He tells us in *Running in the Family:* "I am the foreigner. I am the prodigal who hates the foreigner" (79). This statement captures the insider-outsider dilemma that plagues the diasporic individual in his relation to his original home—he belongs and yet does not belong. This is evident in *Running in the Family* in which the Ondaatje clan, colorful but rootless, are contrasted with the Sri Lankan natives who seem privileged by a special kinship with the land. This bit-

tersweet memoir also traces the writer's own search for selfhood. Though not all conflicts are resolved at the end of the book, there is certainly a deeper consciousness of the self. The protagonists in Ondaatje's novels are also caught in worlds that overlap and mingle but still display a fervent desire to find self- and place-identity. *Anil's Ghost* (2000) discusses the need to reconcile origins and the immigrant experience so as to discover a sense of self. In this novel, Anil Tissera, after years spent abroad studying in England and the United States, returns to her homeland Sri Lanka to solve a series of unexplained deaths in the island. Alongside this narrative of political intrigue, is a riveting story about a woman who courts foreignness, but finds herself having to explore her own uncertain relationship to her home space and to understand her current identities. Like Ondaatje, she must return to her homeland to recover a sense of self. In the overlap of cultures and spaces that distinguish the diasporic individual, identity then, is, as theorist Stuart Hall describes it, always a matter of "becoming" and not just "being" (394).

The Ondaatje protagonists are always in a state of flux and the places they reside in are equally mobile and transient. For instance, there is no detailed description of Sri Lanka in *Running in the Family*. A sense of place is created by atmospheric nuances evoked by the abundant sights, sounds and smells that surround the writer—the monsoon rains, old newspaper cuttings, buildings, even a gesture, "The outline of a large fish caught and thrown in the curl of a wave" (69). Spatial representation is an interesting feature in *The English Patient*. The novel, like its predecessors, is about identity. A Canadian nurse, Hana, tends to an English soldier who is burnt beyond recognition in a World War II battle. A Sikh bomb-disposal expert, Kip, and Caravaggio, a friend of her father, soon join her. These three different people form a bond of love around the dying man, trying to discover his true identity. Though set in Italy at the end of the World War II, all the characters in the narrative are transported to different places and times as the past merges with the present in a seamless flow. The incongruous mingling of locations and times in *The English Patient* is fascinating as it implodes conventional constructs of time and space. The novel, just like Ondaatje's other texts, asserts that it is in the weaving of fact and fiction, the merging of different modes of discourse, and the overlap of the personal and the public that spaces for self-definition are created.

Indeed slippages, ruptures, discontinuities, retelling, and retracing are characteristic features in Ondaatje's narratives, as the writer composes in a postmodern style and pays close attention to language and narrative structure. Themes of flux and change are textualized into his narrative so that form and meaning are integrated in Ondaatje's text. His books defy generic distinctions so as to portray alternative realities, truths, and spaces. *The Collected Works of Billy the Kid,* for instance, is a collage of prose, poetry, and illustrations that deconstruct the popular portrait of the American outlaw. *Coming Through Slaughter,* about the legendary American jazz musician Buddy Bolden, is a poetic narrative in prose that the author says wrestles against what would be a documentary portrayal of Bolden. Ondaatje often presents his reader with a meta-narrative that critiques processes of representation and narration. His works dispute the kinds of representation that revolve around principles of sameness and linearity, and also problematize the idea that there is a fixed authorial voice providing unity.

Yet, for all the features in Ondaatje's narratives that gesture toward a postmodern sensibility with its portrayal of multiplicity and a borderless world, his writings also possess a postcolonial dimension. He does not disavow the formative experiences of the local and the past in his writings. In all his novels, the writer does not, indeed cannot, overlook historical realities that shape narratives of identity. In *Running in the Family,* we see the lingering effects of colonialism on the Sri Lankans. *Anil's Ghost,* set in 1990s Sri Lanka, captures the turbulence in the war-torn island as it faces ethnic strife. Indeed the disruptions and omissions that appear in Ondaatje's texts reflect the fractures that necessarily characterize diasporic history. These works prove, contrary to common opinion, that Ondaatje's books do not elide the physical and historical realities of the island state. Though postmodern writers question and often negate the possibility of such a place as a home, Ondaatje's narratives show that the diasporic writer, by imposing imaginary homelands on an actual geographical location, may seek out firmer ground than abstractions to build ways of belonging to places.

Carol E. Leon

Further Reading

Hall, Stuart. "Cultural Identity and Diaspora." *Colonial Discourse and Post-Colonial Theory: A Reader.* Eds. Patrick Williams and Laura Chrisman. London: Harvester Wheatsheaf, 1993. 392–403.

Jewinski, Ed. *Michael Ondaatje: Express Yourself Beautifully.* Toronto: ECW P, 1994.

Kanaganayakam, Chelva. "A Trick with a Glass: Michael Ondaatje's South Asian Connection." *Canadian Literature* 132 (1992): 33–42.

Mukherjee, Arun P. "The Sri Lankan Poets in Canada: An Alternative View." *The Toronto South Asian Review* 3.2 (1984): 32–45.

———. "The Poetry of Michael Ondaatje and Cyril Dabydeen: Two Responses to Otherness." *The Journal of Commonwealth Literature* 20.1 (1985): 49–67.

Ondaatje, Michael. *Running in the Family.* 1982. New York: Vintage, 1993.

Sugunasiri, Suwanda H. J. " 'Sri Lankan' Canadian Poets: The Bourgeoisie That Fled the Revolution." *Canadian Literature* 32 (1992): 60–79.

Orientalism

Edward Said identified the concept Orientalism in his 1978 book *Orientalism: Western Conceptions of the Orient* as a mode of discourse that authenticated domination over the Orient by the West. He defines Orientalism in three ways: as an academic discipline, as a style of thought, and as a corporate institution. Said discusses the emergence of Orientalism as an academic discipline in the late eighteenth century and defines the Orientalist as "Anyone who teaches, writes about, or researches the Orient. . . . whether the person is an anthropologist, sociologist, historian, or philologist" (Said 2). Orientalism as a style of thought is based on a distinction between the East (the Orient) and West (the Occident) as a starting point for theories and cultural evaluations. The academic and the imaginative meanings are interrelated. The third meaning, as a corporate institution, deals with the Orient "by making statements about it, authorizing views of it, describing it, by teaching it, settling it, ruling over it: in short, Orientalism as a Western style for dominating, restructuring, and having authority over the Orient" (Said 3).

By using Michel Foucault's theory of the relationship between knowledge and power, Said suggests that the Orient as a textual construct creates knowledge and appears to describe reality. This emphasis on textuality relates to a reality formed within a framework of knowledge that has been established from previously written texts (Ashcroft and Ahluwalia 67) and through this representation establishes ideological concepts.

Said cites two Orientalist projects in the eighteenth century: Anquetil-Duperron's translation of Avestan texts revealing Oriental civilizations to the Europeans; and that of the magistrate and first president of the Asiatic Society of Bengal, William Jones, who in 1784 compared and codified the arts and sciences of Asia, both to enable developments in India and also advance knowledge at home (76–79). However, specific emphasis is placed on Napoleon's invasion of Egypt in 1798, which was "a truly scientific appropriation of one culture by another, apparently stronger one," as Napoleon's use of Orientalist scholars and their so called knowledge of the Orient was crucial in gaining the trust of the natives in order to deceive them. This, for Said, marks the beginning of modern Orientalism where knowledge is linked to political ambition (Said 42).

Orientalism is a system of knowledge created from a body of theory that has filtered through Western consciousness (Said 6). Orientalist theory is not objective knowledge but has been shaped by disciplines such as philology, based on formations and assumptions established in the past (Said 122). The Orient, then, is a textual creation, where the text creates knowledge based on existing writings, acquiring a *reality* determined by political means. The notion of European identity as superior over "Oriental backwardness" is linked by Said to Gramsci's theory of cultural hegemony, where political domination is gained not only by physical means but also by ideological consent (Said 7). Gauri Viswanathan suggests "English literary study had its beginnings as a strategy of containment," stating that British colonial administrators in India used English literature to control the natives through an educational system that instigated Christian values whilst avoiding the politically sensitive areas of secularism and Indian religion. In 1813 a selection of texts for the Indian curriculum, chosen for their piety and morality, enabled "voluntary reading of the Bible and at the same time disclaim[ed] any intentions of proselytizing" (Viswanathan in Ashcroft, Griffiths, Tiffin 435). Viswanathan quotes from Gramsci who wrote: "The supremacy of a social group manifests itself in two ways . . . as 'domination' and as 'intellectual and

The great Mosque of Vazir Khan in Lahore, 1895. Courtesy of Library of Congress.

moral leadership' " and is used to illustrate the assumption of English superiority through a literature that the natives "would freely learn" (Ashcroft, Griffiths, Tiffin 436).

Said speaks of a European discourse based on illusions and a system of truth situated in myth, which developed into a doctrine in the nineteenth century, saying "every European, in what he could say about the Orient was consequently a racist, an imperialist, and almost totally ethno-centric" (Said 203–4). This academic tra-dition proved to be useful in gaining authority over the Orient, he suggests. While claiming his work is not anti-Western, Said opposes an essentialist per-spective implied by a Western system of thought, which places the Orient under ob-servation as if from above that ignores the complexities and diversities of a hetero-geneous reality (333).

For Said the resistance is twofold: to know the Orient outside the discourse of Orientalism and to represent this knowl-edge to the Orientalists—in other words, to write back to them. Said's strategy of resistance is to challenge "the hegemonic nature of dominant culture," employing a critical consciousness that "detaches itself from the dominant culture . . . to discover and know, the force of statements in texts" (Ashcroft and Ahluwalia 73). This poses questions of Said's own position—can he stand outside the hegemonic system, and is he an imperialist? Rather than writing a "testimonial" for "subaltern status," Said insists he is critiquing "power using knowledge to advance itself" (336). If Said cannot objectively stand outside the aca-demic system, can he use knowledge to deconstruct this ideology, by disclosing paradoxes, without seeking an alternative voice? It is suggested that appropriation is

Snake charmers in India, ca. 1890. Courtesy of Library of Congress.

Nautch girl dancing with musical accompaniment, Calcutta, ca. 1900. Courtesy of Library of Congress.

a common form of postcolonial oppositional strategy (Ashcroft and Ahluwalia
81).

Many critics focus on the paradox of
attempting to challenge the dominant culture when one is not outside the system, as
Bill Ashcroft and Pal Ahluwalia reveal.
Said's privileged position in the West,
which enables him to theorize the marginality of diaspora, has been discussed considerably. Issues such as the implication
that there may be a real Orient that is
knowable and his use of the differing theories of Gramsci and Foucault are questioned, particularly the latter, as Said puts
different historical periods within the same
discourse. It has been suggested that Said's
own position is close to that of the Orientalist, an essentialist position, and that
his appropriation of a Western theoretical
tradition presents the problem of seeking
a counternarrative that avoids "Occiden-
talism" (Ashcroft and Ahluwalia 76–82).

By "writing back" Said seeks to challenge colonization, stating that the imaginative geographical separation of East and
West is central to his project. Historical experiences once based on this geographical
separation of people are now reformulated
in contemporary literary works (Said 353).
Although colonial administration made
use of Orientalist knowledge in South
Asia, it is argued that the "colonized subjects are not passively produced by hegemonic projects but are active agents whose
choices and discourses are of fundamental
importance in the formation of their societies" (Breckenridge and Van der Veer 4).
Ania Loomba also states: "The native intelligentsia certainly cannot be dismissed
easily as *either* revivalist or 'native informants' " (Williams and Chrisman 314). In
this context Orientalism has been instrumental in instigating further debates in academic postcolonial study, signifying its
continual importance to the contemporary
world.

Melanie A. Murray

Further Reading

Ashcroft, Bill, Gareth Williams, and Helen Tiffin,
eds. *The Post-Colonial Studies Reader.* London
and New York: Routledge, [1995], 1999.

Ashcroft, Bill, and Pal Ahluwalia. *Edward Said: The
Paradox of Identity.* London: Routledge, 1999.

Breckenridge, Carol A., and Peter Van der Veer. *Ori-
entalism and the Postcolonial Predicament:
Perspectives on South Asia.* Philadelphia: U of
Pennsylvania P, 1993.

Gramsci, Antonio. *The Prison Notebooks: Selections.* Trans. and eds. Quintin Hoare and Geoffrey Nowell Smith. New York: International
Publishers, 1971.

Said, Edward W. *Orientalism: Western Conceptions
of the Orient.* London: Penguin, [1978], 1995.

Williams, Patrick, and Laura Chrisman, eds. *Colo-
nial Discourse and Post-Colonial Theory: A
Reader.* Hemel Hempstead, UK: Harvester
Wheatsheaf, 1993.

P

Partition Literature

The historical events of India's Partition are complicated by the fact that so many different religious communities, as well as their British colonial masters, were players in the action. In August 1947 some 11 million persons immigrated to one side or the other of the hastily drawn border, with six million Hindus and Sikhs moving into what was to become India and five million Muslims into West Pakistan and East Bengal. Some were victims, some were aggressors, some were healers, and others observed from a distance. In his introduction to the revised 1988 translation of Bisham Sahni's novel of the Indian Partition, *Tamas,* Govind Nikhalani writes:

> A traumatic historical event usually finds the artistic/literary response twice. Once, during the event or immediately following it, and again after a lapse of time, when the event has found its corner in the collective memory of the generation that witnessed it. The initial response tends to be emotionally intense and personal in character, even melodramatic. On the other hand, when the event is reflected upon with emotional detachment and objectivity, a clearer pattern of the various forces that shaped it is likely to emerge. (5)

Nikhalani is, of course, writing about Sahni's novel, first published in Hindi in 1974, one of the first of the second-generation reflective responses to the wrenching Partition of India. But since then, Salman Rushdie's *Midnight's Children* (1980) has appeared, and also Bapsi Sidhwa's *Cracking India* (1991, first published under the title *Ice-Candy Man* [1988]), both in English.

The first generation of Partition writers, including Khushwant Singh, Manohar Malgonkar, and Saadat Hasan Manto, produced exactly the sort of literature that Sahni describes. Khushwant Singh's *Train to Pakistan* (1956), originally published as *Mano Majra,* was the first novel about the Partition to be published in English. Lurid and realist, it presents an undeniable historical fact: that trains arrived in Pakistan loaded with the dead bodies of thousands of refugees. Although Singh deserves recognition for calling attention to such despicable acts, he also reminds us that intercommunal relationships were not out of the question in pre-Partition India. Readers cheer the melodramatic sacrifice of the dacoit hero Jugga Singh, whose love for a Muslim girl named Nooran leads him to foil an attack on another refugee train. The helplessness of the police and the inattention of the British are both startling and historically accurate.

Manohar Malgonkar's novel, *A Bend in the Ganges* (1964), is noteworthy for its vividly represented background of militant resistance to British colonialism. Malgonkar pictures British repression stimulating acts of mob violence: "hundreds of instances of railway stations, post offices and police stations being burnt down, telephone and telegraph wires being cut and, in one place, of a policeman being burnt alive. Meanwhile those who had the power to restrain the people, to persuade them to refrain from violence, were kept securely locked up in prison" (277). Thus, implies Malgonkar, "the British were striving to convert the non-violence of the leaders of India into the violence of the terrorists; to discredit the movement in the eyes of the world by forcing it to become violent"(278). *A Bend in the Ganges,* offering little sense of hope, ends with the death of the hero, Debi-dayal, on a refugee train at the hands of an angry Muslim mob, followed by the slaughter of Hindu family members by Muslim militants.

In this novel, Malgonkar insists repeatedly, "in the midst of non-violence, violence persists" (277). This message was not one that Nehru's India, bent on building a secular state grounded in Gandhian ideals, really wanted to hear. Nor was it welcomed by the rest of the world, still starry-eyed with the idea of *satyagraha* and its possibilities for the American Civil Rights Movement. Yet the epigraph to *A Bend in the Ganges* is striking. Malgonkar quotes Gandhi himself, evoking a huge degree of irony and leaving readers with the sense that the Mahatma knew what would happen and let it happen anyway:

This non-violence, therefore, seems to be due mainly to our helplessness. It almost appears as if we are nursing in our bosoms the desire to take revenge the very first time we get the opportunity. Can true, voluntary non-violence come out of this seeming forced non-violence of the weak? Is it not a futile experiment I am conducting? What if, when the fury bursts, not a man, woman, or child is safe and every man's hand is raised against his neighbour?

Malgonkar raises important questions, and yet the novel, with the earmarks of a B-grade thriller, is not memorable. One continues, however, to ponder the possibility that Gandhi was irresponsible, an idea that recurs in the second-generation literature of the Partition.

The translated Partition stories of Saadat Hasan Manto first appeared in English under the title *Mottled Dawn: Fifty Sketches and Stories of Partition* in 1997. Yet most of them, originally published in Urdu, were written much earlier in Lahore, just after Independence, at a time when Manto, having left the Bombay film industry, could find no work. The sketches comprised a slim volume called *Siyah Hashye* (Black Fringe), published in 1950, which pictures the "single-minded dedication with which men killed men" (Manto xix) and also the way in which their "humanity occasionally and at the most unexpected times caught up with them" (Manto xxi). Individual stories are better known. Salman Rushdie and Elizabeth West selected one of them, "Toba Tek Singh," about the government-inspired exchange of Hindu and Muslim lunatics just after Partition, for *Mirrorwork: 50 Years of Indian Writing, 1947–1997.* The metaphor of a man/village lying between India and Pakistan, belonging to neither and yet to both, and its setting of lunacy, is the sort of irony at which Manto excels.

"The Woman in the Red Raincoat" tells the story of a former art student who, in his desire to take possession of a girl during a time of riots, inadvertently tried to rape a cooperative old woman, the principal of the art college, whose face he could not at first see clearly. "Bitter Harvest" works with a similar sort of irony as a Muslim, enraged by the murder of his young daughter, rushes into a Hindu house and ravages a young girl, only to discover that her father is his close friend. In Manto's "The Return," an exceedingly haunting story, a man who wakes from unconsciousness after an attack on a refugee train begins to search for his daughter. He

People visit a Mosque in Karachi. © Robin Graham/TRIP.

is helped by a group of eight young men, who drive to Amritsar, recover abducted women, and bring them back to Pakistan. When they find Sakina, however, they do not return her but keep her for their own enjoyment. When she is finally discovered, horribly ravaged and barely alive, her hands respond automatically to an innocent request, "Open the window," by loosening her shalwar strings. From Manto's stories, we come away troubled by violence and savagery, and full of unanswered questions about the unpredictability of human nature.

The second generation of writers, further removed in age from the events of Partition but clearly haunted by them, have had time to reflect on the meaning of events. Some, such as Bapsi Sidhwa, who has turned her childish misunderstanding of Partition events into a superb novel, were children in 1947. Others, like Salman Rushdie, were removed from the violence of the Punjab, both geographically and by economic class; yet his life was trans-

formed by his parents' decision to immigrate to Pakistan. Although Bhisham Sahni witnessed the turbulence of Partition as an adult, he did not write about it until 23 years later, preferring to think about and assess the complexities and nuances of the Partition experience. Because a writer who deals with Partition cannot essentialize or stereotype it without misrepresenting reality, the novels that have emerged from reflection on such historical complexity are of rare quality.

Tamas and *Cracking India* are set in Lahore, and its environs but were published, respectively, in India and Pakistan. The third, *Midnight's Children,* is set in both Bombay and Karachi. Sahni and Sidhwa, following in the steps of Manohar Malgonkar, continue to work at deconstructing the myth of Gandhi in order to reconstruct in its place a more accurate version of Partition events and a greater understanding of the attitudes and behavior, which generated communal violence. Salman Rushdie, however, sidesteps the is-

sue of Gandhi, dealing only with his assassination in any depth. Saleem Sinai, his
first-person narrator, notes, that he is avert-
ing his eyes "from the violence in Bengal
and the long, pacifying walk of Mahatma
Gandhi," and chides himself for being
"selfish" and "narrow-minded" in focusing
instead on his own birth, but "excusably
so"(130). Although some might question
whether *Midnight's Children* is a novel
about Partition, others submit that it is
about little else; for Rushdie goes beyond
the events of Partition to trace the effects
of dividing the subcontinent, and his judgment is harsh.

All of the second-generation novels,
however, and the earlier ones as well, emphasize the way in which the various religious communities lived harmoniously
prior to Partition. Some, in fact, are constructed around central characters that
share deep friendships and ongoing business relationships, reflecting a carefully
knit societal fabric, all the more surprising
for its sudden unraveling. Nor can readers
ignore the violent events of Partition, at the
heart of each of the novels, although represented in new ways. Sahni shows very
clearly how events were orchestrated and
emotions manipulated to generate violence, despite the voices of those who
tried to keep the peace and speak against
prejudice. Sidhwa's embedded, and ago-
nizingly true, story of a young Muslim survivor, in "Ranna's Tale," is complete in
itself. A quintessential Partition narrative,
it has also been lifted from Sidhwa's novel
and anthologized in *Mirrorwork*. A more
subdued sort of description of frozen family assets, the disruption of migration, and
the difficulty of maintaining relations with
family members on the other side of the
border.

Of the three philosophical strands that
emerge from Partition literature, the need
to deconstruct the heroic myth of Gandhi
appears in both generations of writers, but
it is particularly strong among the second

generation. The second theme, the notion
of a harmonious pre-Partition India, also
assumes mythic proportions. Although
things were never perfect, virtually all Partition writers insist on that harmony and
weave their stories around it. In extolling
a societal tapestry intricately woven over
time at great cost, they recognize that
something precious has been irretrievably
lost in its division.

The third theme, violence, never
seems to disappear from South Asian literature. Sidhwa and Sahni go beyond the
generalized violence of first-generation
writers in presenting the ravaged face of
Ayah and the Sikh women who calmly
jump into a well rather than submit to rape.
Rushdie does not deal with events of Partition violence per se, but does it with de-
layed violence of the psychological sort,
as his young hero copes with culture
shock. Each of these writers explores a different dimension of violence. Sahni offers
insight into how communal violence is orchestrated, while Sidhwa poses hard questions about the nature of good and evil.
Rushdie, jolted by sudden immersion into
a world of lies and unreality, explores the
severing of a finely textured culture. In all
Partition writing, however, one finds an ultimate irony: that humans inevitably turn
on each other to prove their loyalty to a
group.

Janet M. Powers

Further Reading

Hasan, Mushirul. "Partition: The Human Cost."
     History Today 47.9 (1997): 47–53.
Ibrahim, Huma. "The Troubled Past: Literature of
     Severing and the Viewer/Viewed Dialectic."
     *Between the Lines: South Asians and Post-
     Coloniality.* Eds. Deepika Bahri and Mary Va-
     sudeva. Philadelphia: Temple UP, 1996.
Mann, Harveen. "South Asian Partition Literature
     and the Gendered Rape and Silence of the Na-
     tional Body." *South Asia Review* 22 (2001):
     3–22.
Singh, Sujala. "Nationalism's Brandings: Women's
     Bodies and Narratives of the Partition." *Com-
     paring Post-Colonial Literatures: Disloca-*

tions. Eds. Ashok Bery, Patricia Murray, and Wilson Harris. New York: Macmillan, 2000.

Tharu, Susie. "Rendering Accounts of the Nation: Partition Narrative and Other Genres of the Passive Revolution." *Oxford Literary Review* 16.2 (1994): 69–91.

Tickell, Alex. "How Many Pakistans? Questions of Space and Identity in the Writing of Partition." *Ariel* 33.3 (2001): 155–80.

A Passage to India by E. M. Forster

Forster began writing *A Passage to India* after his first visit to India in 1912–13, but completed the novel after a gap of more than 10 years following his second visit in 1921–22 during the time he worked as private secretary to the Maharajah of the Hindu State of Dewas. The novel was published in 1924.

Forster studied at Cambridge University and became a member of intellectual groups such as the Cambridge Apostles and Bloomsbury Group. He traveled and lived in Greece, Italy, Egypt, and India. Inspired by liberal humanist thinking, he was critical of the repressive limitations of English culture and explored alternate worldviews in his novels. His other writings include *Where Angels Fear to Tread* (1905), *A Room with a View* (1908), *Howards End* (1910), and *Aspects of the Novel* (1927).

A Passage to India has three parts, titled "Mosque," "Caves," and "Temple." Within the first section of "Mosque," all the important characters—the Indian Muslims, Hindus, and the Anglo-Indians—are introduced along with the setting at Chandrapore city and the mysterious Marabar caves that lie temptingly within eye's reach. The period is believed to be between 1912 to 1922, coinciding with the times Forster was in India, a few decades before British colonial rule ended. In this milieu, we see the complexity of relations between different cultural groups through the part realistic, part abstract, and some-times seriocomic depiction of the novel's characters.

Miss Adela Quested and Mrs. Moore are two English ladies who are visiting Magistrate Ronny Heaslop. He is Mrs. Moore's son by her first marriage, and Miss Quested is considering marriage with him. Mrs. Moore chaperones Miss Quested to India so the lady can judge if life with Heaslop in India is agreeable. Both women have romantic notions about seeing the real India. But they are confronted with the shock of seeing the local British in their arrogant claims to power and prejudiced attitudes toward Indians. Collector Turton, Dr. Callendar, police superintendent McBryde, the officers' wives, and Heaslop have all become stereotypical, prejudiced imperialists believing the colonized Indians to be an inferior people. The social lives of the imperial administrators and the colonized Indians are as segmented as their living quarters. But Mrs. Moore with her goodness and Miss Quested with her curiosity and liberalism want to connect with the Indians. The "Mosque" section depicts several attempts at connection, ranging from the successful meeting between Mrs. Moore and Dr. Aziz, a Muslim Indian and a principal character of the novel, to the unsuccessful "Bridge" (bridging gap) party arranged for the mingling of British and Indians. Also introduced are college professors, Fielding and Godbole, the former British and the latter Hindu Indian. Apart from the visitors, Fielding is the only British character with a desire to have social relations with Indians. In Fielding's house, Aziz, wishing to be a host to the English visitors, suggests an expedition to the Marabar Caves.

The visit to the Marabar Caves and its consequences make up the "Caves" section of the novel. In the heat and the inscrutable monotony of the caves, when all sound is reduced to the echo "ou-boum," all spiritual values are reduced to sameness in Mrs. Moore's mind. Unable to experience this through a Hindu vision of cosmic unity, she suffers from spiritual despair. Meanwhile, Miss Quested goes inside a cave and imagines that Aziz has physically assaulted her. A contentious trial follows, during which she becomes confused about her own sense of reality at the caves, and she recants her charge. Throughout Aziz's trial, Fielding supports his innocence, breaking ranks with other Anglo-Indians, whereas Mrs. Moore's support is mystically felt by the Indians, although she herself had left Chandrapore.

In the "Temple" section, Aziz and Godbole are working at a Hindu princely state called Mau, rejecting the indignities of British India. Aziz has had reason to misunderstand Fielding in spite of the latter's loyal friendship. The two meet during the festivities celebrating the birth of Krishna, the god of love; and their misunderstanding is cleared. Their friendship is renewed, but only temporarily, as Aziz says they cannot be friends until every Englishman is driven out. A hundred voices issuing from everywhere say that friendship is not yet possible, and the sky also concurs.

Dealing with issues like the fundamental unfairness of British colonialism, the collisions and collusions of cultures and peoples, and the spiritual desire of humans to connect to something larger than life, *A Passage to India* has always been read as a complex novel. Among Forster's contemporary critics, Hartley sees it as "disturbing," Wright remarks that it deals with a "subject of enormous difficulty," and Priestly describes it as an "honest thing in three dimensions" (Bradbury 47–58). Over the years, criticism has generally focused on its depiction of sociopolitical realities or on its symbolic representation of humanity's spiritual angst, or sometimes on both. While earlier readings have seen the novel as a liberal-humanist's scathing critique of colonialism, some readings in the 1970s and 1980s have seen it as func-

tioning from within the discourse of imperialism even while attempting to question it (Parry 27–43). However, the approach exemplified by John Beer, seeing it as a versatile novel with many interpretive possibilities, best opens up this complex and wonderful text.

Husne Jahan

Further Reading

Beer, John, ed. *"A Passage to India." Essays in Interpretation.* Totowa: Barnes and Noble, 1986.

———. "Conclusion: *A Passage to India* and the Versatility of the Novel." *Essays in Interpretation.* Ed. John Beer. Totowa: Barnes and Noble, 1986. 132–52.

Bradbury, Malcolm, ed. *E. M. Forster—A Passage to India: A Casebook.* London: Macmillan, 1970.

Herz, Judith Scherer. *A Passage to India: Nation and Narration.* New York: Twayne, 1993.

Parry, Benita. "The Politics of Representation in *A Passage to India." Essays in Interpretation.* Ed. John Beer. Totowa: Barnes and Noble, 1986. 27–43.

A Passage to India. Dir. David Lean. Columbia, 1984.

Rutherford, Andrew, ed. *Twentieth Century Interpretations of A Passage to India.* Englewood Cliffs: Prentice-Hall, 1970.

Postcolonial Theory

Colonialism and its aftermath prompt a form of cultural studies that seeks to address questions of identity politics and justice that are the ongoing legacy of empires. Postcolonial theory has its origins in resistance movements, principally at the local, and frequently at nonmetropolitan, levels. Among its early thinkers, three seem of special importance: Antonio Gramsci, Paulo Freire, and Frantz Fanon. Antonio Gramsci (1891–1937) was a founder of the Communist Party in Italy. In his *Prison Notebooks* (1971), he wrote insightfully about the proletariat, designated by him as subalterns; his thoughts regarding the responsibilities of public intellectuals inspired many, and his notion of hegemony and resistance proved influential. Paulo

Freire (1921–97) was a Brazilian with a special interest in education. His *Pedagogy of the Oppressed* (1970) seeks to restore subjectivity to objectified, oppressed classes in society. Frantz Fanon (1925–61) was a psychiatrist of Caribbean descent who participated in the Algerian independence movement. His two books, *The Wretched of the Earth* (1963) and *Black Skin, White Masks* (1967) inspired many anticolonial struggles and investigations of racism's many manifestations.

Other important early influences would include Amilcar Cabral, Aimé Césaire, Léopold Senghor, José Carlos Mariátegui, Alejo Carpentier, Edward Kamau Brathwaite, C. L. R. James, Edouard Glissant, and Wilson Harris. The Kenyan novelist Ngugi wa Thiong'o, whose essays on the need for decolonizing the minds of those living in former colonies have been very influential, echoes Fanon's work and tempers it with experience from the anglophone world. Social theorists, economists, and anthropologists such as Stuart Hall, Samir Amin, Clifford Geertz, Benedict Anderson, and James Clifford have anchored important areas of investigation, developed in fascinating ways by writers such as Mary Louise Pratt and Tejaswini Niranjana. The names suggest the inescapable fact that postcolonial theory is a worldwide intellectual event, and not the product of any one cultural system.

The disparate investigations of these authors began to coalesce with the creation of the Subaltern Studies Project, under the direction of Ranajit Guha. Drawing its inspiration from these writers and others, including Michel Foucault and E. P. Thompson, the Subaltern Studies Project is a group of revisionist historians who attempt to write history from the point of view of those who had been forgotten: all oppressed groups without a voice or sense of agency. Most active from 1986 to 1995, much of their work, a "history from below," can be seen as one of recovery, a re-

discovery of voices that were always there but seldom attended to—in colonial documents, in oral discourse, in popular memory. One of the group's members, Dipesh Chakrabarty, notes that the peasant was already part of the political equation but was written out of its decisions. Insights such as these lead the group to consider cultural production as a potential neocolonialism. Among its other members are Gyanendra Pandey, Gautam Bhadra, David Hardiman, Shahid Amin, Partha Chatterjee, Arvind Das, Sumit Sarkar, Asok Sen, and Veena Das. Part of the project of the group is a critique of the elitism of nationalisms that perpetuate the silence of subalterns and their communities. The group has had imitators elsewhere, as in the Latin American Subaltern Studies Group, which was active from 1992 to 2000.

Though not a member of this group, the political psychologist Ashis Nandy, through his association with the Centre for the Study of Developing Societies in New Delhi, explores similar territory. This group was founded in 1963 by Rajini Kothari and seeks to oppose the hegemony of Western discourse. Nandy is equally critical of India itself, portraying its middle class as a neocolonial elite. In *The Intimate Enemy: Loss and Recovery of Self under Colonialism* (1983) and *The Savage Freud* (1995), he details his criticism of the ongoing Western imposition of a global consciousness that levels other modes of cultural expression.

Postcolonial theory came into its own as a revisionist project of the early 1990s, dominated until recently by Indian intellectuals and informed by a second trinity: Edward Said, Gayatri C. Spivak, and Homi K. Bhabha. Edward Said (1935–) was born in Jerusalem of Lebanese and Palestinian heritage. His family was wealthy, and he was raised a Christian and educated at Princeton and Harvard with degrees in history and literature; his dissertation was on Joseph Conrad. Gayatri Chakravorty

Spivak (1942–) was born in Calcutta and educated at Cornell and Cambridge. Her dissertation at Cornell was on William Butler Yeats, under the direction of Paul de Man. Homi K. Bhabha (1949–), a Parsee born in Bombay and educated at Oxford, is the nephew of the first director of India's nuclear program. He currently teaches American literature at Harvard. Even this brief listing suggests their privileged backgrounds and their training in European humanism, but also demonstrates the hybridized nature of their careers and cultural knowledge. Not too surprisingly, their life experiences also point the direction of their research interests.

In their writings these theorists emphasize issues arising from hybridity, exile, cosmopolitanism, and diasporic perspectives. Said, whose *Orientalism* (1978) set the terms for all further discussion of postcolonial theory, focuses attention on objectification by the West, identity politics (using the plight of the Palestinians as a case in point), and on the autonomous intellectual who finds him/herself in between nation states. Spivak, who translated Jacques Derrida into English and is consequently influenced by poststructuralism, explores issues of alterity and agency, asking who is served when differences are defined. She publicized in North America the work of the Subaltern Studies Group, thereby helping determine the vocabulary of postcolonial theory and solidifying its signature issues. Bhabha draws some ideas from psychoanalytic theory and rejects the notions of binary identities, discussing instead migrant sensibilities and the consequent necessity for performances of one's identity as a cultural mix. Given the subject matter of their graduate educations, it is not surprising that these three and others like them especially privileged literary studies in their initial forays into what is now termed *postcolonial theory,* including, for example, the politics of transla-tion, the choice of a language in which to compose, and the politics of travel literature.

One of the earliest expressions of postcolonial theory was the analysis of colonial discourse, the various conduits used by London, Paris, and the other imperial capitals to define a binary system of civilized world and savage jungle. In this cosmology, the world of the colonizer is seen as central, and that of India, Africa, and so on, as peripheral. The former is the location of high culture, the source of modernity, science, rationality; the latter is a seething darkness, ever threatening to pull all humanity back into superstition and chaos. Given this philosophy, the mandate to treat the rest of the world as something less than fully human seems inevitable, and colonization is presented as a God-given duty purportedly serving the colonized at least as fully as it enriches the colonizer.

Writers such as Said point out the broad generalizations that are employed by supposedly objective colonial proponents in their analysis of subject peoples, resulting in the infantilizing of entire peoples and the stripping away of individuality. More recently, analysts of colonial discourse have themselves been criticized as unwittingly generalizing the colonizer and the colonized alike, ignoring countertrends in some nineteenth-century documentation, and underplaying subaltern agency and resistance to the colonial juggernaut. A persistent issue that dogs prominent theorists is the authenticity of their voices, variously remote from indigenous agents.

Bhabha's contribution to colonial discourse analysis includes his discussion of mimicry, whereby England and other colonial powers trained a class of colonized peoples to serve the colonizer's interests while apparently remaining fully within the local culture. They accomplished this through the implied and sometimes explicit message, spread by the educational systems they established throughout the empire as well as by some Christian missionaries, that to adopt British manners and culture was an advance over one's own culture. In any event, such personal transformation was generally a step toward greater economic security. This resulted in a comprador class, left behind after decolonization as a neocolonial elite that kept the colonial institutions running, much as if nothing had changed.

At the heart of the various forms of postcolonial theory, therefore, is a determination that political modernity must be rethought through non-European eyes, using more than European philosophy to do so. This goal sets up an implied contest between the exoticizing that lines up under Said's concept of orientalism, and the search for a common humanity across cultures that is condemned or praised as universalism. The idea of an *essential* identity of any one culture or people remains contentious, used by various subaltern groups as a rallying cry for political representation, but condemned by others as a romanticized tribalism that flies in the face of the increasing hybridity of individual identities. This tension leads postcolonial theorists to consider questions such as these: if nations are lowering their borders, can their citizens be far behind in erasing their identifying characteristics? In other words, is a postcolonial identity becoming, through the forces of globalization, the hegemonic imposition of an inevitable Western, and increasingly American, cultural overlay? Can any ethnic or national grouping meaningfully resist what many postcolonial theorists condemn as neocolonialization? Those who answer in the negative frequently are among those who argue that there is no meaningful *post* in postcolonial theory—that is, that the legal maneuver of independence from imperial powers is only technical, a form without substance. Overlaying it are economic and other cultural forces that are as determinative as ever.

Much early postcolonial theorizing had to do with questions of nation-building, but Paul Gilroy's work on various issues having to do with the Caribbean has helped shift the focus from national identity to the importance of diasporas across the globe; these concerns have been further sparked by the many novelists currently writing about homelands they left many years ago. Increasingly, in the United States, expected postcolonial theorizing combines with border theory and issues arising from multiculturalism to produce a hybridized field that seeks to include that nation's many ethnic literatures into a broadened notion of what determines a condition of postcoloniality. The field is now less biased toward literary analysis and theory than it once was, and increasingly comparative and interdisciplinary; the social sciences contend for the lion's share of relevant topics for investigation. Consequently, areas such as film studies, gender and sexuality studies, historiography, epistemology, and the politics and sociology of representation, architecture, and even science and technology as they enable globalization, are also increasingly coming to the fore. As the field develops, it is moving from colonial discourse studies to transnational cultural studies, accommodating itself to an often contentious dialogue with advocates of globalization.

Elements of postcolonial theory have become so variously applied, in fact, that its prevalence can dilute its earlier claims to radical revisionism in the service of justice. Critics of the postcolonial movement, if it may be so designated, point to the problematic nature of its colonization by Western intellectuals (or those now living in the West). As Aijaz Ahmad, Arif Dirlik, and others point out, what began as a set of radical writings intended to change society has become a vehicle for academic promotion and high salaries for some, the latest chic chatter for the intellectual elite.

Recent theorists, such as Arjun Appadurai, Inderpal Grewal, Asha Varadharajan, Gauri Viswanathan, Chandra Mohanty, and Keya Ganguly, take these criticisms to heart and seek to reassert central postcolonial issues in new ways, introducing feminism and queer theory, theorizing globalization, and studying diasporic groups in the United States and elsewhere. Sisir Kumar Das and others are bringing increasing attention to writers like Mahasweta Devi who, by choosing to write in languages other than those of the colonizer, arguably stake a claim for a decentering of postcolonial theorizing.

John C. Hawley

Further Reading

Chaturvedi, Vinayak, ed. *Mapping Subaltern Studies and the Postcolonial.* London: Verso, 2000.

Loomba, Ania. *Colonialism/Postcolonialism.* London: Routledge, 1998.

Singh, Jyotsna G. *Colonial Narratives, Cultural Dialogues: "Discoveries" of India in the Language of Colonialism.* London: Routledge, 1996.

Srivastava, Sanjay. *Constructing Post-Colonial India: National Character and the Doon School.* London: Routledge, 1998.

Trivedi, Harish and Meenakshi Mukherjee, eds. *Interrogating Post-Colonialism: Theory, Text and Context.* Shimla, India: Indian Institute of Advanced Study, 1996.

Young, Robert J. C. *Postcolonialism: An Historical Introduction.* Oxford: Blackwell, 2001.

R

Rao, Raja

Raja Rao was born on November 8, 1908, to a family of Brahmins who had been advisers to the kings for generations. He learned Sanskrit and Indian philosophy from his grandfather when he was a young boy.

He attended Nizam College in Hyderabad from 1926 to 1929 and graduated with a B.A. in English and history. Soon after, he won the Asiatic Society Scholarship to attend the University of Montpellier in France. While in France, he studied under the literary historian Louis Gazamian, published in the periodical *Jaya Karnatak,* and researched the Indian influence on Irish literature. In Montpellier, he met Camille Mouly, a professor of French, who became his wife in 1937.

Rao was a member of the editorial board of *Mercure de France* of Paris from 1932 to 1937. He published a series of short stories in European periodicals between 1933 and 1938. During this period, he also came under the influence of socialist thought.

He published his first novel *Kanthapura* in 1938. The same year, he published his short story *The Cow of the Barricades* in *Asia.* In 1939, Rao returned to India when Europe was under the threat of Nazi Germany. From 1939 to 1948, he traveled and lived in India in search of a Guru. He was influenced greatly by Pandit Taranath because of his aesthetic theories. The master in Rao's short stories "Narsiga" and "The Cow of the Barricades" is modeled after Taranth. Rao's quest was fulfilled in 1943 when he met Sri Atmananda Guru in Trivandrum. Atmananda had a great spiritual influence on Rao: the epigraphs for both *The Serpent and the Rope* and *The Cat and Shakespeare* are believed to be taken from Atmananda's work on Vedanta; and the narrator in *The Serpent and the Rope* eventually finds his Guru in Trivandrum.

Other than his literary work, Rao was also committed to the cause of national independence. He joined Gandhi's Quit India Movement in 1942 and participated in underground socialist activities. In 1946, he joined the cultural organization Chetna (awakening). He returned to France in 1948 and visited the United States in 1950. In 1958, he traveled to India again. In 1965, he accepted an invitation from the University of Texas to teach philosophy and held the position until his retirement as professor emeritus in 1980. In 1965, he married his second wife, a young American stage actress, Catherine Jones. They have a son Christopher Rama. Two decades later, Rao parted from his second wife and later married another American woman.

Rao's major works include *The Serpent and the Rope,* published in London in 1960. The previous year, "The Cat" was published in the *Chelsea Review* in New York. *The Policeman and the Rose* was published in 1963, along with the American editions of *The Serpent and the Rope* and *Kathapura.* In 1964, *The Serpent and the Rope* won the prestigious Sahitya Akademi Award from the government of India. In 1965, he published *The Cat and Shakespeare: A Tale of Modern India,* a short novel of great artistic merits. The same year, he published the French version of *Comrade Kirillov.* In 1972, he was made fellow of Woodrow Wilson International Center, Washington, D.C. In 1976, his novel *Comrade Kirillov* was published in English. In 1984, the Modern Language Association elected him Honorary Fellow. In 1988, he published "*The Chessmaster and His Moves*" in New Delhi and was awarded the Tenth Neustadt International Prize for Literature by the University of Oklahoma. In 1989, he published *On the Ganga Ghat,* a collection of short stories set in New Delhi.

Rao's work mirrors his deepest concern for humanity. His characters echo the human sufferings under social injustice caused by centuries of social stratification and British colonization. Such humanistic concern led to an unrelenting quest for spiritual and cultural identity of the self. For Rao "what comes to weigh is a philosophical preoccupation with the nature of human identity in more than one sense" (Jha 30). His characters such as Ramaswamy, Nair, and Sivaraman, confronting social, political, and cultural actions in the world outside them, are on the quest of finding their lost selves.

Faith in God is another theme in his work. In spite of their miserable lives, his characters all hold on to their faith. Rao's work is his diagnosis of his people that "religion and traditions are still hidden springs in the desert of contemporary changes for the majority of his characters" (Khair 77). Furthermore, they remain effective antidotes to secular modernization. As such, his characters are mostly solitary: for instance, the young Bholanath, who has lost his family and retires to a life of devotion to his Guru; and Sudha, a young girl who renounces the world and thinks that men are all awkward and evil, but at the same time spends hours every day repeating the name of the Lord.

As a writer in English, Rao's work is the product of the encounter between the East and the West and bears the characteristics of a diasporic consciousness. His 1960 novel *The Serpent and the Rope* strikes a theme of an Indian's quest for truth in his encounter with modern Western culture. His main characters, Ramaswamy and his French wife, Madeleine, are metaphysical embodiments of the East-West encounter, which naturally does not survive the spiritual quest for Indianness. It is worth mentioning that Rao's work often reflects his own life. Ramaswamy, for instance, left India to study in France and later married a French woman, visited India, divorced his French wife, and eventually found peace in his Guru.

Rao is perhaps the most read and quoted Indian writer. The amount of books, articles, and reviews of Rao's works exceeds that of most other Indian writers. In 1988, after Rao received the Neustadt Award for Literature, *World Literature Today* dedicated an entire issue (Volume 62.4) to the scholarship on his work.

Holly Shi

Further Reading

Harris, Wilson. "Raja Rao's Inimitable Style and Art of Fiction." *World Literature Today* 62.4 (1988): 587–90.

Jha, Ashok K. "Identity and Its Quest in Raja Rao's Later Fiction." *Language Forum: A Half-Yearly Journal of Language and Literature* 18.1–2 (1992): 29–37.

Khair, Tabish. "Rajo Rao and Alien Universality." *Journal of Commonwealth Literature* 33.1 (1998): 75–84.

Maini. D. S. "Raja Rao's Vision, Values and Aesthetic." *Commonwealth Literature: Problems of Response.* Ed. C. D. Narasimhaiah. Madras: Macmillan, 1981. 64–89.

Naik, M. K. *Rao Raja.* Madras: Blackie and Son, 1982.

Rao, Ranga

Born Vadrew Panduranga Rao, in 1936, in Bhimavaram, a small town in South India, Ranga Rao is a self-educated and self-made man who struggled against many odds to make his mark. He earned a Ph.D., registering under the noted pioneering critic, K. R. Srinivasa Iyengar, to work on R. K. Narayan, the first time an Indian author was made the focus of doctoral research. Thereafter, from 1964 onward, he served as a teacher in a premier Indian university until he retired in 2001.

His first foray into the art of writing fiction was in his native Telegu. While he was at school, he wrote a mocking life sketch of a serving teacher, which greatly ruffled the school authorities. It was only much later, as a teacher of English literature, that he started using the English language as a medium of fictional creation. Although his profession naturally brought him to a wide variety of authors, his overall favorite has been the Russian writer, Anton Chekhov, whose short stories and sharp satirical humor captivated him and motivated him to begin writing.

It is worth noting that his long stay in the cosmopolitan capital of Delhi and his long innings as a teacher of English literature did not sever his links with his provincial origins. Therefore, significantly, his first two books, *Fowl-Filcher* and *Indian Idyll and Other Stories,* as well as his latest novel, *Land of Regrets,* are set in his home state of Andhra Pradesh.

The rigors that he went through trying to find a publisher for his early short stories replicated to some extent the problems that the legendary R. K. Narayan had been subjected to. One suspects that it was a prejudice against the provincial subject and his choice of the unpopular short-story form that worked against him. He has recorded his trials in his article, "Publication of Fowl-Filcher: A Case Study in Literary Obstetrics" (1990). Khushwant Singh was one of his earliest admirers, giving a couple of his stories, "The President's Teacher's Tale" and "The Apprentice," a berth in *The Illustrated Weekly of India,* of which he was the editor. The rest of his stories could not find a publisher until after he had published his first novel.

Even his first novel, *Fowl-Filcher,* had to do the rounds of publishers and languish on their shelves for several years before finally being chosen to herald the publishing operations of Penguin India in 1987. Much lauded, this novel has been variously singled out for the "stylistic virtuosity" it displays (K. R. Srinivasa Iyengar) and for its "Chaucerian" (Gopal Gandhi) vitality. In microcosmic detail, the novel concentrates on the political imbroglio in south India around the time of independence through the bizarre experiences of its ill-fated protagonist, Hunter Kotayya's son, cuttingly nicknamed Fowl Filcher for a chicken steal that he did not perpetrate.

The stories in *Indian Idyll and Other Stories* (1989) are characterized by their faithful depiction of small-town life in south India. Most of them have a touch of the R. K. Narayan brand of humor, a feature common to all of Ranga Rao's writing.

The Drunk Tantra (1994), his much underrated campus novel, gives voice to his idealistic beliefs and hopes regarding the teaching profession, typified in his lecturer-heroine Mohana and the humane Daash, the senior teacher who falls victim to the dirty campus politics of sycophancy and nepotism. This latter pillar of moral integrity is outsmarted by the wheeler-dealer, Hari Kishen, a.k.a Hairy, whose moral turpitude is marked by his lopsided desires to rule the teaching community by hook or by crook and to also seduce 108 women. The humor turns murky and dark with his sordid efforts to pep up his sexual urge by clandestine visits to a roadside quack selling herbal Viagra. This stimulus results in a comical permanent erection, the soreness of which is relieved only by the administration of a counter drug, which, in turn, produces impotence. Written lucidly, the narrative gains depth from a subtle and powerful symbolism that resides primarily in the creation of the elusive, idealistic space of Begumpuram.

His latest novel *Land of Regrets* (2000) is quite unlike his earlier writing both in style and subject. This historical novel, set in the days of the East India Company, the Jaan Kumpini (John Company) of the early decades of the nineteenth century, is evidence of the combination of an in-depth historical research and an acutely felt love for present-day Telengana. Interestingly poised chapters on the locals and the white man are alternated to give a sense of variety and multiple perspectives.

Ranga Rao is highly respected for his translation prowess as evidenced in his *Classic Telugu Short Stories* (1995). He is also well respected for his creative approach to criticism as well as his individualistic approach to contemporary authors such as Vikram Seth and Arundhati Roy.

Meenakshi Bharat

Further Reading

Narayan, Shyamala A. "The Higher Education of Geetika Mehendiratta and Other Campus Novels." *The Postmodern Indian English Novel.* Ed. Viney Kirpal. New Delhi: Allied, 1996. 153–62.

Raja, P. Rev. of *Fowl-Filcher* by Ranga Rao. *Literature Alive* 1:4 (Mar. 1988): 67–69.

Rao, R. Raj. "The Survival of the Fittest: *Fowl-Filcher* as a Picaresque Novel." *The New Indian Novel in English: A Study of the 1980s.* Ed. Viney Kirpal. New Delhi: Allied, 1990. 179–85.

Ratnam, A. S. "Fowl-Filcher: An Analysis." *Chiaroscuro: Critical Essays on Indian Writing in English.* Ed. A. S. Ratnam. Parbhani, India: Dnyanopasak Prakashan, 1991. 115–19.

Rothfork, John. "Freud and Postcolonialism in Ranga Rao's *Fowl-Filcher.*" *Journal of Indian Writing in English* 18:2 (July 1990): 66–78.

Red Earth and Pouring Rain by Vikram Chandra

Red Earth and Pouring Rain is the debut novel by Vikram Chandra. Born in Delhi in 1961, Chandra was raised by his father Navin, a company president, and his mother Kamna, a screenwriter and playwright. Chandra attended school at St. Xavier's College in Mumbai (formerly Bombay), then obtained degrees from Pomona College (B.A.), Johns Hopkins University (M.A.), and the University of Houston (M.F.A.); he also attended film school at Columbia University before pursuing a career as a writer. In addition to *Red Earth and Pouring Rain,* Chandra has published a collection of short stories, *Love and Longing in Bombay* (1997); authored the popular Indian television series *City of Gold* (1996); and coscripted a film, *Mission Kashmir* (2000), directed by his brother-in-law, Vidhu Vinod Chopra. He teaches creative writing at George Washington University and divides his time between Washington and Mumbai.

The plot of *Red Earth and Pouring Rain* is complex. Set in Bombay, the story begins when Abhay Misra, a college student recently returned from the United States, shoots and wounds a monkey that has stolen his jeans. The shock of the attack seems to reawaken the monkey's consciousness of its previous life, as a human poet named Sanjay. Sanjay finds that, though he cannot speak, he is able to communicate via typewriter. With this discovery, the Hindu god of death Yama appears, accusing Sanjay of failing to fulfill his monkey dharma (right actions) and preparing to transport him to a lesser incarnation. Sanjay strikes a bargain with Yama: as long as he can entertain at least half his audience with a story, which must last two hours per day, he will be permitted to live in his current state. Sanjay is assisted by the monkey-god Hanuman and the elephant-god Ganesh—who represent the protector of poets and the remover of obstacles, respectively—as he begins his tale. Since Sanjay's paws are ill suited to type for long periods of time, Abhay agrees to supplement the monkey's tales with some of his own. The novel as a whole comprises these two alternating narratives.

Sanjay's epic tale involves his links to the historical figure Colonel James "Sikander" Skinner, an Anglo-Indian who founded the near-legendary "Skinner's Horse," the nineteenth-century British Irregular Cavalry Corps regiment that later evolved into the 1st Bengal Lancers. In the library at Columbia University, Chandra had run across Skinner's autobiography, which had been translated from the original Persian, and he subsequently became very interested in the implications of Skinner's narrative. In particular, Chandra creates a detailed story for Skinner's mother, a Rajput (warrior) princess, Janvi, who committed *sati* rather than let her daughters be educated by Skinner's British father, Hercules. After a couple of short tales involving Benoit de Boigne and George Thomas, two other figures from India's colonial past, Sanjay tells the story of his supernatural connection to Sikander, and indeed Sikander's increasing fame as a warrior parallels Sanjay's efforts to become a poet.

Each is conflicted about his relationship to the colonizing British, as Sikander's allegiances become muddled and Sanjay's near-mystical affinity for the English language affects his writing politically and aesthetically. In one key passage, Sanjay uses his job as a typesetter of English-language books to plant anticolonial messages, in slightly different fonts, within the texts. To hide the evidence of his crime, Sanjay swallows the metal letters of the type, thereby metaphorically assimilating the English language so much that it becomes a part of him, at no small cost to himself. This emphasis on speaking

in another tongue emerges again when Sanjay tears out his own tongue to convince Yama to grant him immortality. Thus, Sanjay's part of the story foregrounds the collision between English and regional Indian languages and between oral and written forms of communication. In the end, Sanjay ends up opposed to Sikander, who has offered his allegiance to the British; after a climactic battle, Sanjay goes (at Yama's behest) to London to track down his archenemy, Dr. Paul Sarthey, the son of a bigoted minister who precipitates Sikander's mother's suicide. Driven mad by his torments at public school, Sarthey becomes Jack the Ripper, in a move that connects the violence of imperialism to the desire for purity. After he kills Sarthey, Sanjay surrenders his human self to Yama, asking that he not be reincarnated as a human being.

Interspersed within this main narrative are Abhay's series of stories, which begin in the somewhat desultory setting of his California college and proceed through another exchange of stories among his companions during a cross-country road trip. Abhay relates his roommate Tom's tale of high-school "mad love," Kyrie's description of how her mother's obsession with purity and control led to her own career as a pornographic film star; and his own cricket-match encounter with his girlfriend's father, William James, who has an odd nostalgia for colonial India. At the end of the novel, the listening crowd, which has been growing steadily throughout, erupts in violence, but Abhay has come to recognize the potential value in all fiction— the possibility that the act of storytelling can supply, however provisionally, the sense of community often lost in the modern world.

Receiving general critical acclaim upon its publication, in 1996 *Red Earth and Pouring Rain* won the David Higham Prize for Fiction and the Commonwealth Writers Prize for Best First Published

Book. Book reviewers generally hailed the evocative language and complex plotting of the novel, though a few critics found the writing style unnecessarily showy and bordering on kitsch. Critics have noted Chandra's influence by other texts, especially *One Thousand and One Arabian Nights,* and the exuberance with which he dramatizes and explores various narrative conventions. In his *Contemporary Authors* entry, Chandra himself has remarked that he now views the novel as an "attempt to hold all that is new, to contain all that is thrown up by the churning of time, to swallow it whole, and to connect it to the very old. Perhaps that is what is Indian about it."

Scott D. Walker

Further Reading

"Chandra, Vikram 1961– ." *Contemporary Authors.* Galenet. 9 July 2002 <http://web3.infotrac.galenet.com>.

Rollason, Christopher. "Vikram Chandra's *Red Earth and Pouring Rain:* Entwining Narratives and Intertextuality." *IndiaStar: A Literary-Art Magazine.* 9 July 2002 <http://www.indiastar.com/rollason.html>.

Salvador, Dora Sales. "Vikram Chandra's Transcultural Narrative: *Red Earth and Pouring Rain,* Much More than a Novel." *Beyond Borders: Re-defining Generic and Ontological Boundaries.* Eds. Ramon Alastrue and Maria Jesus Martinez-Alfonso. Heidelberg, Germany: Carl Winter Universitatsverlag, 2002. 175–84.

Riot: A Love Story by Shashi Tharoor

The genesis of the book may be traced to the simmering Hindu-Muslim discontent of the 1980s, culminating in the Babri Masjid violence at Ayodhya. In particular, Shashi Tharoor has in mind the description of a riot that actually broke out in 1989 in Khargone, Madhya Pradesh. Simultaneously, came the report of the death of an American woman in a different part of the world: in South Africa, a social worker, who had gone there to help the cause of

the blacks, was ironically killed by a black youth. In *Riot,* the two incidents coalesce into a single event: the death of Priscilla Hart, a volunteer from the United States working for a population-control awareness program, killed in a communal riot that breaks out in a small Indian town. This central event merges into a larger network of ideas with other related issues, all of which are worked into the narrative of *Riot.* The background is the Hindu-Muslim riots over the Ram Shila Pujan but, unlike *The Great Indian Novel,* Tharoor here chooses to work on a small canvas, a small, dusty town called Zalilgarh. At the same time, the story reaches out across narrow confines, taking into its purview two antipodal, culturally disparate continents, individuals and situations.

Tharoor is concerned with innovative forms of narration: conspicuous by its absence is the conventional "once upon a time" story, the "dear reader . . ." approach, or the omniscient narrator. "Down with the omniscient narrator. It's time for the omniscient reader," says a character in the novel (136), making Tharoor's attempt a self-conscious exploration of narratology, drawing the reader into the act of decoding of the story. *Riot* is not a conventionally structured novel: there is no formal beginning or end, no linearity or narrative or plot or formal constructions of the genre. It is more of a collage that brings together many different fragments of a jigsaw puzzle that the reader must put together to form a coherent whole. The pieces comprise an astonishing variety—there are diary entries, letters, memoirs, excerpts from scrapbooks and journals, transcripts of interviews, conversations overheard, entries in notebooks, journalistic reports, a handful of poems, even a birthday card and a cable. All the various pieces of the collage are different takes on a central event—the death of Priscilla Hart. How did she die and what were the circumstances? The reader is faced with the task of groping through the evidence and unraveling the story. At times, one has the uneasy feeling of being a voyeur peeping into a private chamber, reading another's personal diaries or letters, or eavesdropping into somebody else's very special, very intimate encounters. But the embarrassment is not allowed to linger, as almost immediately, there is a swing toward the impersonal, an interview conducted by an objective reporter, the official voice of police personnel in charge, or simply, a shift of perspective. All this is part of the narratological strategy. The story is not *told* to us, but it is *shown* through the pieces of the collage.

At the same time, what *Riot* seeks to present is not simply a whodunit tale or the story of the poignant death of a visiting American. It goes beyond mere statistics, beyond the factual details of the tragedy, to reconstruct the emotional life of the woman sketched vividly in a scrapbook that she maintains: the idealism that brought her to that remote spot, the passion for her job, the love interest in her life, the secret rendezvous from time to time, the uncertainty and the agony of entering into a doomed love affair. Her paramour, Lakshman, a local Indian administrator, who is married but finds himself involved in a relationship with the American, is also a writer of sorts and keeps his own journal. So there are two different perspectives on the relationship. The clash of cultures, the divergent viewpoints, the inability to understand the working of the other's mind, the imminent end of the relationship—all this comes across through the personal journals of the main characters of the novel. Despite the passion and the love, social pressures are far too strong for a lasting relationship. And then violence erupts, causing Priscilla's death and putting an abrupt end to the possibilities of the love story.

One of the main concerns of the novel is history as it is lived in a particular space and time. And history is nothing but truth. In an epigraph to *Riot* taken from Cervantes, Tharoor tells us: "History is a kind of sacred writing, because truth is essential to it, and where truth is, there god himself is," thus bringing the three together—history, truth, and god. Are they synonymous or is there simply a close kinship between the trinity? The novel lays bare a very personal concept of truth/history/god, presumably based on the author's private belief—that human life being a complex amalgam of paradoxes, human relationships are no less complex, and there are no certitudes, no finalities, no absolutes, no fixed beliefs, nothing good, and nothing bad. It is all a matter of perspectives.

What is truth, asks Tharoor, and where is it to be found? Whose truth is it? Truth is a readerly text, open to interpretation. *Riot* is about the ownership of truth and history. It presents about a dozen versions of a given situation, no single one being privileged over the other. If the story is told (or presented) from Lakshman's and Priscilla's points of view, it is also presented from the varying points of view of the other characters: the staunch Hindutva supporter, the Muslim activist, the police official, the grieving parents of the riot victim, the wronged wife, *et. al.* Their separate stories contribute toward the various pieces of the jigsaw puzzle called *truth* or *history*—the puzzle that Tharoor presents as *Riot.* Tharoor seems to suggest that history is not a web woven by innocent hands. The different pieces of the collage in his novel are often divergent, often contradictory accounts of the same event. Yet each has its validity, its own truth, and its own beauty.

Manju Jaidka

Further Reading

Chhabra, Aseem. "The Parallel Lives of Shashi Tharoor," Rediff U.S. Special. 15 Mar. 2001. 28 Nov. 2002 <http://www.rediff.com/news/2001/mar/15usspec.htm>.

"Running Riot," *Times News Network* 1 Sept. 2001. 28 Nov. 2002 <http://timesofindia.indiatimes. com/articleshow.asp?art_id=1288446596>.

The Romantics by Pankaj Mishra

The Romantics (2000), Pankaj Mishra's first novel, is narrated in the first person by a shy and reclusive north Indian youth. As the novel opens, Samar has arrived in Benaras to attend the Allahabad University and has taken up accommodation in a room rented out by Panditji in a "crumbling riverside house." In spite of himself, he finds himself developing a friendship with Miss West, who rents the room next door, and at a party organized by her, Samar meets the American and European expatriates in Benaras—Sarah, Debbie, Mark, Catherine, and her Indian musician lover, Anand. At first, Samar is taken up with them, intrigued by their sense of adventure and their journeying into another world, and he willingly accepts Miss West as a guide and interpreter of this world.

Samar begins with precise enumerating description and ends with uncertainty about his reading of the situation; this uncertainty is the essential problematic of the novel and is inseparably linked to its style and form. It allows the reader to infer the irony from the situation. Amit Chaudhuri in his introduction to Mishra's memoir "Edmund Wilson in Benaras" (1998) claims that when compared with Mishra's nonfiction, *Romantics* strikes an altogether different note because "[it] has little of the measured belligerence of his criticism, but is an exploration, instead, of uncertainty and a deep sense of inadequacy, of the desire to belong and the inability to do so" (355). Certainly, the reader finds here not only a submerged ideological rhetoric but also a muted literary style, an irony in which there is pain and uncertainty. While Samar is the chief instrument of irony, he is also the generator of ironic situations; and is himself alive to them. He is aware,

for instance, of the basic misconception around which others, particularly Miss West and Catherine, build their perception of him—the idea of him as an "autodidact," "a scholar," an "intellectual," and a "serious student." While these descriptions are superficially true, he is aware of Miss West's patronizing attitude when she introduces him to her friends as a "tireless autodidact," just as he is aware that "in trying to correct their notions of India, he has become false to himself" and has "turned into a performer, one eye and ear always open for Catherine" (91). But Samar is also aware that "the substitution of books for friendships has worked less and less," and that this has been standing in the way of any real involvement with people. This shuttling back and forth between text and awareness is represented at a larger level through Samar's journeying into the opposed and competing worlds of Catherine and Rajesh. Catherine's friends have traveled to India armed with "grubby backpacks, empty Perrier bottles, bundles of laundry, old copies of *Le Figaro,* and *L' Express,* and *Newsweek* in Air France folders" (88) in search of adventure; and these forays, Samar later realizes, are in the nature of "safe adventures." But it is Samar who makes a journey when he opens himself to a friendship with a fellow student, Rajesh, who has grown up in a world of stark poverty. If Samar feels the incongruity of Catherine's life with Anand and wants to understand "the peculiar chemistry of her relationship with Anand," (49) he feels with equal intensity the incongruity of Rajesh "lying face down on the cot, reciting in a low somber voice lines from Iqbal's poem, while a sack of pistols sits in the corner of the room" (26–27). He accepts Rajesh's invitation to visit his small town birthplace and finds himself unsettled by the poverty and the squalor, "shocked by what Rajesh's mother tells him about his childhood spent in maize fields and carpet factories." But Samar's confusion is not a result of indecisiveness, but rather of a deeper ambivalence. We see Samar puzzling things out, generating hypotheses, recognizing, and rereading with a fierce earnestness not only books—Flaubert's *Sentimental Education* and Edmund Wilson's commentary—but also people and landscape. In this sense Samar reminds the reader of the narrator in Naipaul's *Enigma of Arrival,* who is making sense of the local Wiltshire landscape and society by constant revision of his preconceptions and constant formation of new hypotheses.

That is why it does not seem odd that Samar's growing love of Catherine parallels his growing realization of the shallowness of the expatriate world that Catherine inhabits. Samar's infatuation with Catherine and his quiet suffering is something that the novel catches hauntingly. But the most striking aspect of the novel is Samar's encounter with the starkness and the pessimism of Rajesh's world, an aspect of the novel that has been ignored by all the reviews. Samar is made uneasy when he finds Rajesh seeking him out at the library, showing concern, or asking questions about Edmund Wilson. To fend him off, Samar lends Rajesh his copy of Flaubert's *Sentimental Education* and a photocopy of Edmund Wilson's essay; fairly certain that Rajesh will not read it or cannot read it. Meanwhile, Samar puts the pieces together: Rajesh's proclamations of revolution, his warnings about violence, his popularity among the students, his sudden mysterious disappearances and equally mysterious emergence from "green seedy Ambassador cars with tinted windows," (243) the student strikes, the police beating of students, and the police-student violence that had become common at the university.

At the end of the novel, it is Rajesh's reading of Edmund Wilson that becomes the instrument of illumination for Samar, who has now fled to the Himalayas to teach at a school in Dharmasala and is in danger of drowning himself in a placid

life, "his old striving" and his "contradictory hopes" all dried up. Samar's reading of Rajesh's notations on the Edmund Wilson essay open up Samar's time in Benaras in a new throbbing light. It allows him to see that "he had understood very little and misunderstood much during his time in Benaras." He is now aware that "the small, unnoticed tragedies of thwarted hopes and ideals Flaubert wrote about in *Sentimental Education* were all around us" and can now see that "this awareness had been Rajesh's private key to the book" (250). The end of the novel takes us into the timespace of the demolition of the Babri-Masjid and the violence and killings in Ayodhya in 1992. This is how history enters the novel, through the primal scene of Samar's struggle—his near failure—to read the unleashed violence of Rajesh's reading of Edmund Wilson.

The Romantics bears the marks of Mishra's essay anthologized in the *Picador Book of Modern Indian Literature,* "Edmund Wilson in Benaras" (1998), and has to be seen in that context. In this essay Mishra uses his autobiographical persona to explore a subject: his accidental discovery of Edmund Wilson's work while idly browsing the stacks at the library in Benaras Hindu University. For him, the experience of finding Edmund Wilson's books on "the overloaded, dusty shelves" is in the nature of a magnificent gift. He finds it extraordinary that they are all there albeit "dust-laden, termite-infested, but beautifully, miraculously present" and speak of an "old, and now vanished impulse, the desire among the Hindu reformists in the freedom movement to create indigenous centers of education and culture" (358). In this essay we see the full force of Mishra's attachment to Edmund Wilson—the critic, journalist, reporter, political thinker, and historian—who "showed the sources and effects of literature in the overlap between individual states of mind and specific historical realities" (370). In pursuing the subject of Wilson's voice and his lucid vigorous style, Mishra is also pursuing self-definition and self-representation. *Romantics* crosses this essay in multiple ways and this blurring of genres between essay and novel is illuminating because it dramatizes the reading, experiencing self.

The Romantics needs to be set in the context of Mishra's essays because such juxtaposition shows the emotional logic and the conceptual processes that run through both his journalism and his fiction. Mishra's multifarious activities, as a novelist, journalist, and thinker can be seen as parts of an organic whole whose impulse is indicated in the title of the novel—romantic. Here *romantic,* refers not just to the illusions that the characters in the novel believe in, but also specifically to Schlegel's use of the term to indicate the cataclysmic changes of his age—early nineteenth-century England—the landscape of feeling created by the changes and the power of literature to name this reality, to offer an account of reality that is multivoiced, more subtle and fuller than any other account. The popularity of *Romantics,* indicated by the number of favorable reviews it has received, makes us wonder to what degree Mishra's admiration of Edmund Wilson point to Mishra's own ambitions, to what he himself would like his readers to see in him—a journalist novelist with a wide readership who brings to his writing the concreteness of journalism and the insight of literature.

Padmaja Challakere

Further Reading

Bayley, John. "The Heart of the Matter." *The New York Review of Books* 47 (24 Feb. 2000): 8.

Chaudhuri, Amit, ed. *The Picador Book of Modern Indian Literature.* London: Picador, 2001. 356–72.

Chew, Shirley. Rev. of *The Romantics* by Pankaj Mishra. *Times Literary Supplement* 5053 (4 Feb. 2000): 21.

Kumar, Amitava. "Passages to India." *The Nation* (24 Apr. 2000): 36–38.

Sabin, Margery. "Pankaj Mishra and Postcolonial Cosmopolitanism." *Raritan: A Quarterly Review* 21:4 (2002): 198–219.

Sharrad, Paul. Rev. of *The Romantics,* by Pankaj Mishra. *World Literature Today* 74.3 (Summer 2000): 584.

Roy, Arundhati

Suzanna Arundhati Roy, who shot into the limelight in 1997 with her debut novel, *The God of Small Things,* was born in 1961. The daughter of divorced parents, she was brought up by her mother, Mary Roy, a well-known social activist who ran a school in Ayamanam (Kerala) and whose court case changed the inheritance laws in favor of women. A rebel right from her early years, Arundhati left home at the age of 16 to live in a squatter's camp in a small hut with a tin roof in Delhi's Feroze Shah Kotla. She trained as an architect from Delhi School of Architecture but her interests lay elsewhere. An early, brief marriage to a fellow student, Gerard Da Cunha, was followed by a few months spent with flower children on the beaches of Goa, after which Roy returned to Delhi and found a modest job. At this point she met Pradeep Krishen, the film director, for

Arundhati Roy. Courtesy of Paroma Basu.

whom she wrote some screenplays and whom she later married.

While Shekhar Kapur's *Bandit Queen* on Phoolan Devi was making waves, Arundhati Roy wrote a scathing criticism of the film, which led to controversy, culminating in a court case. Subsequently she withdrew from the public arena and concentrated on her writing, which ultimately went into the making of her novel. When *The God of Small Things* came out she was working as a freelance writer and part-time aerobics instructor. Even before the book hit the market there was unprecedented hype regarding the extraordinary monetary advance of half a million pounds that the author had received. Favorable reviews followed its publication and Roy's reputation as a writer was firmly established.

Prior to the publication of *The God of Small Things,* Roy began her career as a small-time actress and scriptwriter. She appeared in a minor role in Pradeep Krishen's *Massey Saab* (1985) and, in 1992, she wrote the screenplay for his film *Electric Moon,* which failed to attract attention despite a talented cast that included Nasiruddin Shah and Roshan Seth. She also wrote and starred in a television film, *In Which Annie Gives It Those Ones* (1989), for the Doordarshan.

The God of Small Things is Roy's major contribution to literature. It depends heavily on autobiography and traces the fortunes of a Syrian-Christian family in Kerala, focusing on a woman who tries to escape from the clutches of the orthodox setup by marrying out of caste. Fate rules otherwise, and she is forced to return home as a single parent with two children to face a life that is considered lived with nothing to look forward to. At this point, a low-caste "untouchable" whom she has known as a child reenters her life, leading to a relationship branded as "illicit" by social convention. Doomed from the very start, it drags into its tragic mess the innocent world of her children and claims the life of a third child, their half-English cousin.

The novel stands out for its invocation of childhood, which is reminiscent of the works of poets such as Blake, Wordsworth, and Dylan Thomas. The manner in which the narrative glides back and forth in time, in and out of her characters' inner consciousness, is close to the method of James Joyce. In the way she plays with language, in her ingenuity of phrase and style, in the use of Indian figures of speech, and in her transgression of all formal rules and regulations of the language, Roy has been called one of "Rushdie's children." She does not work on an ambitious scale; instead, she creates a small world with ordinary people in commonplace situations, easily recognized and understood.

After her debut novel Arundhati Roy has not produced any creative writing; instead she has shifted her focus to political journalism and has published several nonfictional prose pieces, many of which have been controversial. Convinced that a writer has a social function to perform, she has taken on the role of a social activist, with a deep involvement in burning issues like the Narmada Bachao Andolan (against the construction of the Sardar Sarovar Dam on River Narmada). *The Cost of Living* (1999) includes the two essays "The End of Imagination" and "The Greater Common Good." "The End of Imagination," written in response to the nuclear tests conducted by India and Pakistan in 1998, was the first essay she published after her Booker Prize. Here she criticizes India's nuclear policy, arguing vehemently against the race for arms. "The Greater Common Good," a well-researched and analytical piece, is a personal and emotional response to the tampering of ecology in the name of progress. It makes an inventory of 3,600 dams in India that have played havoc with the lives of 50 million people without fulfilling the advantages promised.

Roy is also critical of American foreign policy, particularly against Afghanistan. *The Algebra of Infinite Justice,* written soon after the attacks on the World Trade Center, warns against America's declaration of war on Afghanistan. This essay is included in her book *Power Politics* (2001) which comprises four other pieces that focus on varied issues: the construction of dams in India at the cost of human life and environmental hazards, the common man's reaction to nuclear war as opposed to the opinion of the experts, the privatization of power in India by Enron, and the various power games played in politics at different levels.

While her fiction writing created unprecedented hype in the literary world, her political involvements have produced mixed reactions. Salman Rushdie has described *The Cost of Living* as "brilliant reportage with a passionate, no-holds-barred commentary," but not all critics have been kind.

Arundhati Roy has invariably been at the center of controversy, beginning with the storm over *Bandit Queen*. Her Booker Prize, too, received its share of criticism, with some critics pronouncing her book an "execrable" one that should not have been shortlisted. In India there was a court case against her, alleging that her book was obscene and likely to corrupt the minds of young readers. She also drew the ire of the Kerala Communists whose leader, E. M. S. Namboodiripad, is caricatured in her novel. Namboodiripad is of the opinion that sexual anarchy is the leitmotif of the Booker novel.

Assuming the role of spokesperson for the Third World, Roy often gets carried away by the sweep of her own poetic language. Her point of view is generally considered more emotional than intellectual, or even practical. She is sometimes accused of attention-grabbing gimmickry: at a time when it is fashionable to be anti-American or antiwhite, she has been vociferous in her criticism of America's foreign policies and America's intervention in Afghanistan.

In the agitation against the Narmada Dam, Roy was arrested and had to appear in court for " antigovernment" activities. When she reacted by accusing the court of trying to "silence criticism and muzzle dissent," she was charged with contempt of court, awarded a one-day "symbolic imprisonment," and ordered to pay a monetary fine. While this kind of publicity draws a great deal of media attention to the Narmada agitation, it also serves to keep Arundhati Roy in the limelight.

Manju Jaidka

Further Reading

Arundhati Roy's Unofficial Web site. <http://website.lineone.net/~jon.simmons/roy/>.

Bose, Brinda. "In Desire and in Death: Eroticism as Politics in Arundhati Roy's *The God of Small Things*." *ARIEL* 29.2 (Apr. 1998): 59–73.

Dhawan, R. K. *Arundhati Roy: The Novelist Extraordinary.* Columbia: South Asia Books, 1999.

Dugger, Celia. "An Indian Novelist Turns Her Wrath on the U.S." *New York Times* 3 Nov. 2001. 28 Nov. 2002 <http://www.nytimes.com/2001/11/03/international/asia/03ROY.html>

Rothstein, Mervyn. "India's Post-Rushdie Generation." *New York Times* 9 July 2000: E1.

Roy, Arundhati. *War Talk.* Cambridge: South End, 2003.

Rushdie, Salman

Known primarily as a novelist, Salman Rushdie's work extends to essays, film, short stories, and most recently, drama. In 1981, he achieved literary prominence in England when his second novel, *Midnight's Children,* won the prestigious Booker Prize. In 1989, he achieved international notoriety when his fourth novel, *The Satanic Verses,* became the target of massive protests by Muslims and prompted Ayatollah Ruhollah Khomeini of Iran to issue a *fatwa* sentencing him to death. These two events have cemented Rushdie's reputation as a postcolonial literary icon, international cause célèbre, and marked man, all of which draw attention to, and often overshadow, the complex politics of cultural identification that he foregrounds in his work. While it is tempting to draw Rushdie's life into his fiction, it may be more accurate to think of him as using the often contradictory realities of his own subject position to document rapidly shifting senses of cultural allegiance, national identity, and communal history in an era of globalization.

Salman Rushdie was born in Bombay to Anis Ahmed and Negin Rushdie on June 19, 1947, two months before India's Independence and Partition. The eldest child of four in a wealthy Muslim family, Rushdie grew up in a house called Windsor Villa, later to be satirized in *Midnight's Children,* and at age 13, he left for England to attend Rugby, site of the kipper incident in *The Satanic Verses* (Hamilton 94). In 1964, Rushdie gained a third homeland when his family moved to Karachi, Pakistan, which he left one year later to begin reading history at Cambridge. Rushdie received his degree in 1968, but after his return to Pakistan he found himself creatively confounded: "In Pakistan, he discovered, censorship was 'everywhere, inescapable, permitting no appeal.' There was 'no room to breathe' " (Hamilton 97). On his return to England, Rushdie worked as an actor and an ad copywriter before finally publishing *Grimus,* his first novel, in 1975.

Grimus stands out as Rushdie's most atypical work, suggesting an author in the process of finding a voice and subject matter. *Grimus* is essentially a quest narrative, the story of Flapping Eagle, a Native American youth who, on his seven-centuries quest to find his sister, Bird-Dog, enters another dimension and does battle with Calf Island's magician-ruler Grimus. On revisiting the novel in light of Rushdie's later success, critics remark that *Grimus* stands out as a pronounced failure at the start of a distinguished literary career, an opinion shared by Rushdie. Hamilton points out a lack of affinity between author

and text that extended to the form of *Grimus* itself: "[D]espite its flamboyant self-display, 'Grimus' was a forbiddingly anonymous affair: one could deduce from it almost nothing about the author's background. 'I must try and write something from much closer to my own knowledge of the world,' Rushdie decided after [visiting] India. 'Something where I know what's happening and where I know the place and time' " (Hamilton 101). If *Grimus* represents Rushdie's initial failure as a fabulist, it also represents his first efforts to work with a narrative format that bucks realism; it reads as a polyvocal collection of mythologies compressed into a narrative of exile, heterogeneity, and indeterminate perceptions of space. However, *Grimus* had no firm ground on which to stand in its lack of a chronotope, and correcting this omission would become such a key structuring principle for his next novel, *Midnight's Children.*

Rushdie's fortunes took an emphatic upswing with the publication of *Midnight's Children* (1981) that in addition to the Booker Prize won the Booker of Bookers in 1993 for the best novel of the Prize's first 25 years. The work for which he is most highly acclaimed, *Midnight's Children* is an intense exploration of Indian history from the last three decades of the British Raj to the Emergency of 1975. Its narrator Saleem Sinai has been granted mystical powers due to his birth at the auspicious moment of India's Independence, midnight on August 15, 1947, and because of this coincidence, his life and the lives of those born at the same hour (the eponymous Midnight's Children) are mysteriously linked to the new Indian nation. *Midnight's Children* demonstrates Rushdie's signature style, featuring a hyperactivity of language and historical reimagination; it also establishes a common trope of his fiction, the use of a self-conscious, self-questioning, and often self-censoring narrator. Through his own magical connection with India, Saleem's narrative explores ways in which the lives of individuals and nations are intertwined within and limited by the destructive power of the state. Rushdie's extreme skepticism toward exercises of state authority extends beyond India to England and Pakistan, as we see in *The Satanic Verses* and his next novel, *Shame.*

Although Indira Gandhi won a libel suit against Rushdie over a passage in *Midnight's Children* (Saleem describes Sanjay Gandhi's resentment over the death of Indira's husband in a line that was stricken from later editions), he rarely shied away from negatively depicting people in power; nowhere is this more apparent than in *Shame,* which reads like a *roman à clef* of Pakistani history. Focusing on the regimes of Zulfiqar Ali Bhutto and Mohammed Zia ul-Haq, *Shame* (1983) is a blistering commentary on how despotism coexists with and takes advantage of gendered codes of repression. In a narrative filled with lengthy asides, the novel describes the rise and fall from power of the patrician Iskander Harappa, and then the Islamicist soldier turned ruler Raza Hyder. However, the brooding and violent center of the novel is Sufiya Zinobia Hyder, the living embodiment of shame who absorbs the outrageous behaviors of those around her until she explodes in waves of violence that eventually destroys not only her father Raza's power, but also her husband (antihero Omar Khayyam Shakil) and the narrative itself in an apocalyptic finale.

In *Shame,* Rushdie continues his imaginative reconstruction of the history of the subcontinent, explicitly addressing his appropriations of history into the fictional realm. The story and its landscape are, the narrator asserts, a palimpsest set over an original map and cast of characters, but slightly offset by a few degrees from reality. By foregrounding the uneasiness of its narrative project, *Shame* proceeds dialogically as a conversation between official histories of Pakistan and a slant history of women and migrants. *Shame* is much more cynical in its politics than *Midnight's Children;* it is sharply critical of Bhutto, his daughter Benazir, and Zia, the outright villain of the novel. Zia's presumptive military despotism went hand in hand with what Rushdie saw as a brutal Islamization program, leaving Rushdie with very little hope about Pakistan's future as a democratic, secular state. However, in the context of this despair, Rushdie develops a new mode of discourse that privileges the subjectivity of the migrant. Celebrating the ability of the migrant to figuratively defy gravity, Rushdie conjures the theme of translation in terms of language and space to evoke the radical reorientation that can occur when texts and people transcend borders. In this sense, *Shame* prefigures the central drama of *The Satanic Verses.*

The time gap between *Shame* and *The Satanic Verses* (1988) featured several beginnings and endings in Rushdie's personal life: he parted ways with his first wife, Clarissa Luard (with whom he had a son, Zafar); he became involved for two years with author Robyn Davidson, and married another author, Marianne Wiggins; and in 1987, he lost his father, whose deathbed reconciliation with Rushdie is invoked at the ending of *The Satanic Verses* (Hamilton 108). During this time, he remained creatively active, publishing *The Jaguar Smile,* a travel narrative and reflection on the Sandinista government in Nicaragua, and producing *The Riddle of Midnight,* a film documentary that reexamined India in its 40th year after Independence.

After the publication of *The Satanic Verses,* Rushdie was propelled into the international spotlight when his novel became the target of Muslim protest. While what is known today as the Rushdie Affair began in earnest on February 14, 1989, the day the Ayatollah Khomeini dictated in a *fatwa,* a sentence of death against the author and publishers, the controversy had already been brewing for several months. *The Satanic Verses* first caused a stir in India, where it was banned as the result of efforts of Muslim pressure on a weakening Congress Party. As the turmoil developed into censorship, book-burning, and rioting, the content of the novel began to matter much less than what it and its author symbolized: a former Muslim aligned with the West who wrote a critical, even condemnatory, revisionist history of Islam; a private citizen who became the target of an execution order from a foreign government and the cause of an international political/diplomatic furor; and an artist whose freedom of expression, individual liberty, and personal safety was attacked by a politically motivated religious fundamentalist who had not even read the book he condemned. As a result of Khomeini's *fatwa,* Rushdie was placed under police protection and went into hiding; his divorce from Marianne Wiggins followed soon afterward (he would marry again in 1997 to Elizabeth West, with whom he had his second child, Milan). So began his life in exile, which continued with the yearly renewal of the *fatwa* by the Iranian government, despite Khomeini's death in 1989. While certain restrictions on his movements have eased, at the time of this writing the specter of the *fatwa* remains. In 1998, the Iranian government finally disassociated itself from the *fatwa,* but militant groups like Iran's Revolutionary Guard still continue the call for Rushdie's death.

The Satanic Verses represents a further conceptual step from Rushdie's earlier work, as he explores the theme of migration through the parallel lives of two characters, Gibreel Farishta and Saladin Chamcha, who survive a fall from a hijacked airplane, land on England's shores, and undergo a series of bodily transformations that turns Gibreel into his angelic namesake and Saladin into a goat-legged satanic figure. The two episodes of the novel that feature "the satanic verses" incident (in which the Prophet Muhammad first allows for the acceptance of three goddesses and then retracts them—a story that appears in the writing of Islamic historian al-Tabari) and its aftermath take place within Gibreel's feverish dreams, in which he reimagines the founding of Islam. While it is quite clear that Rushdie carefully frames his controversial retelling of the history of Islam in this way, his use of names and events from the Quran suggest that no amount of literary framing devices would have made the novel acceptable to those who would read the text as caricaturing Muhammad, his wives, and his followers. However, while Islam is a major theme of the novel, it is oriented primarily around a Bombay-London axis, and as such features a strong critique of Thatcher's England, the mounting oppression and outrage of black Britain, and the Anglophilic Saladin Chamcha's reconciliation with his father and with India as his home.

During his first years in exile, Rushdie continued publishing: the fantasy novel *Haroun and the Sea of Stories* (1990), in which the forces of speech and stories win out over the forces of silence; the collection of essays *Imaginary Homelands* (1991), which contains literary analyses and political journalism about England, India, and Pakistan; and *East, West* (1994), a collection of short stories. The latter two are primarily compilations of previous work, and thus they serve as a means of taking stock of the literary career that preceded them. *Imaginary Homelands* is a collection of Rushdie's nonfiction, and while the vast majority of the pieces included consist of literary criticism or book reviews, Rushdie devotes the critical mass of his intellectual energy to the politics of his own work and to the governments of India, Pakistan, and England. In these essays, Rushdie shows himself to be an outspoken and eloquent opponent against what he sees as abuses of state power: in England, the racism of law enforcement and the passage of the Nationality Bill; in Pakistan, the tyranny of General Zia ul-Haq's Islamization program and the myopia of Benazir Bhutto toward her father's (Zulfiqar Ali Bhutto) own tyrannies; in India, the autocratic rule of Indira Gandhi and the dynastic rule of the Nehru family. Rushdie's cultural commentary is an outgrowth of these concerns, as his essays on England's Raj Revival and his own works *Midnight's Children* and *The Satanic Verses* suggest.

In contrast, the stories of *East, West* are considerably tamer. Divided into three sections—"East," "West," and "East, West"—*East, West* demonstrates the multiple themes, interests, and influences that are explored at greater length in Rushdie's novels. "Yorick" and "At the Auction of the Ruby Slippers," both featured in the "West" section, are linked to *Tristram Shandy* and *The Wizard of Oz,* two of Rushdie's significant Western influences. The stories of the "East" section feature a purposefully failed attempt to emigrate to England, a rickshaw driver who voluntarily undergoes a vasectomy during the Emergency, and the theft of a holy relic of Islam (a hair from the Prophet Muhammad), all of which come into play either literally or thematically in Rushdie's later work. The final section highlights the displacement of characters from the East relocating in the West, a theme Rushdie continues to explore in his work to date.

Rushdie's first major post-*fatwa* novel, *The Moor's Last Sigh* (1995), a reencountering of the Islamic world (linking the Moorish presence in Spain to Jewish and Muslim minorities in India), marks a return to his earlier narrative tactics of examining the fluidity of history and cultural drift. However, the novel also presents what amounts to a literary farewell to Bombay. Departing from the nostalgia of *Midnight's Children,* the Bombay of *The Moor's Last Sigh* is a communalist and crime-ridden city, much of which is blown to bits by the catastrophic and apocalyptic explosions near the novel's end. His next work, *The Ground Beneath Her Feet,* rapidly quits India in favor of a much broader internationalist scope.

Whereas *The Moor's Last Sigh* focuses on the visual arts, *The Ground Beneath Her Feet* (1999) explores the boundary-crossing potential of music. A retelling of the Orpheus and Eurydice myth set to modern music—largely Anglo-American pop and rock—*The Ground Beneath Her Feet* and its successor *Fury* (2001) both thematize creativity against a background of pop culture. The saturation of references to contemporary media figures signals a new trope of Rushdie's fiction: the emotional and cultural turmoil of globalization. Migrancy is more of a given in these texts than a condition of existential doubt and liberation, and gone is the urgency of reclaiming a past history or a present homeland. Instead, the narrative urgency stems from an increasing isolation. In *The Ground Beneath Her Feet,* the narrator Umeed Rai is forced to remain a passive witness to the all-consuming and ultimately destructive love affair between superstars Vina Apsara and Ormus Cama; in *Fury,* Malik Solanka is alienated from his wife and son, having abandoned them in fear of finally succumbing to his obliterating inner rage. The tight focus on a single character in one primary milieu, New York City, is new for Rushdie's fiction, but in his most recent essay collection, *Step Across this Line* (2002), he once more demonstrates his outward reach to world affairs.

Salman Rushdie and in particular *Midnight's Children* have been credited for having put Indian literature on the world literary map, a highly reductive contention that illustrates the central problematic of his reception in the West. While he has drawn a great deal of attention to anglophone Indian literature, he is often viewed to the exclusion of those working in Indian vernaculars, or as the sole literary progenitor of authors such as Arundhati Roy and Romesh Gunesekera. His reception in the Anglo-American academy has been more complex: Rushdie began to articulate some of the themes of postcolonial theory just as it was coming to the fore as part of an academic mainstream, and under these auspices he entered into canonical status. This canonical enshrinement has been, according to Brennan, indicative of a larger political dynamic surrounding Third World cosmopolitans:

> By "cosmopolitans" I meant those writers Western reviewers seemed to be choosing as the interpreters and authentic public voices of the Third World writers who, in a sense, allowed a flirtation with change that ensured continuity, a familiar strangeness, a trauma by inches. Alien to the public that read them because they were black, spoke with accents or were not citizens, they were also like that public in tastes, training, repertoire of anecdotes, current habitation. (viii–ix)

Thus, in addition to what many recognize as his considerable talent, Rushdie's prestige in the Western literary world may also reflect the Anglo-American canon's fetishizing of certain nonthreatening, non-Western writers—in other words, halting the search for the "real India" not in the Marabar Caves but in the pages of *Midnight's Children*. This privilege extends in some degree to his reception in India, where he remains a figure of some controversy and great public interest, both for his literary stature and his personal life. However, India has a greater hold over Rushdie than his celebrity or notoriety: its tradition of epic, unapologetically digressive, and all-encompassing literary works find a modern analogue in the sheer breadth and dynamism of Rushdie's storytelling. In this sense, though he has more often been compared with non-Indian authors—Günter Grass, Laurence Sterne, and Gabriel García Márquez, for example—the author and his fiction are firmly rooted in the subcontinent.

Jason Howard Mezey

Further Reading

Appignanesi, Lisa, and Sara Maitland, eds. *The Rushdie File.* Syracuse: Syracuse UP, 1990.

Brennan, Timothy. *Salman Rushdie and the Third World: Myths of the Nation.* New York: St. Martin's, 1989.

Chauhan, P. S., ed. *Salman Rushdie Interviews: A Source Book of His Ideas.* Westport: Greenwood, 2001.

Hamilton, Ian. "The First Life of Salman Rushdie." *The New Yorker* 25 Dec. 1995: 90–113.

Kuortti, Joel. *The Salman Rushdie Bibliography: A Bibliography of Salman Rushdie's Work and Rushdie Criticism.* New York: Lang, 1997.

Reder, Michael, ed. *Conversations with Salman Rushdie.* Jackson: UP of Mississippi, 2000.

Sanga, Jaina. *Salman Rushdie's Postcolonial Metaphors: Migration, Translation, Hybridity, Blasphemy, and Globalization.* Westport: Greenwood, 2001.

S

Sahgal, Nayantara

Nayantara Sahgal was born on May 10, 1927, in Allahabad, India, the second of three daughters to Vijayalakshmi and Ranjit Pandit. Of her generation Sahgal writes, "we are truly the children of Gandhi's India, born at a time when India was being reborn from an incarnation of darkness into one of light. Our growing up was India's growing up into political maturity" (*Prison and Chocolate Cake* 32). Sahgal's childhood was characterized by Kashmiri cultural traditions, Hinduism, political fervor, progressive thinking about women's status, and familial wealth—a privilege partially mitigated by her parents' involvement in the Swadeshi movement and Gandhi's jail-going program. Sahgal's father died in 1944 due to an illness contracted in prison. After his death, Sahgal's mother, Jawaharlal Nehru's sister, became a diplomat, first leading the Indian delegation to the first session of the United Nations in October 1946, and subsequently acting as Indian ambassador to Russia and the United States. As a child, Sahgal attended missionary schools. Sent to America in 1943 to attend college, Sahgal completed a B.A. in history at Wellesley in 1947, after which she returned to Delhi to live with her uncle, the new prime minister. This portion of her autobiography is related in *Prison and Chocolate Cake* (1954). In 1949, she married Gautam Sahgal, a businessman, and eventually gave birth to three children, Nonika, Ranjit, and Gita.

Her early married life is depicted in her second autobiography, *From Fear Set Free* (1962). She divorced Gautam Sahgal in 1967 and married E. N. Mangat Rai in 1979.

A political journalist and historian, Sahgal has written numerous articles and several historical texts, including *The Freedom Movement in India* (1970), *A Voice of Freedom* (1977), and *Indira Gandhi's Emergence and Style* (revised and published in the United States as *Indira Gandhi: Her Road to Power* in 1982). More recently, she has collected a selection of public addresses and published articles in *Point of View: A Personal Response to Life, Literature and Politics* (1997) and has edited a volume of letters from Nehru to her mother entitled *Before Freedom: Nehru's Letters to his Sister* (2000). The foremost concern of Sahgal's journalistic work is the preservation of freedom as an inalienable human right and a cultural value. She views communism as inappropriate for India and advocates instead for liberal democracy. She has been particularly critical of her cousin Indira Gandhi's authoritarian style of leadership, for its lack of moral integrity.

As a novelist, Sahgal has written poignantly and critically about what she knows—middle-class intellectuals—in her eight novels: *A Time to Be Happy* (1958), *This Time of Morning* (1965), *Storm in Chandigarh* (1969), *The Day in Shadow* (1971), *A Situation in New Delhi* (1977),

Rich Like Us (1985), *Plans for Departure* (1986), and *Mistaken Identity* (1988). Several themes emerge from these works. The most prominent, perhaps, is the imperative of social duty accomplished through the Gandhian philosophy of nonviolence. This theme of duty, service, or social reform is reiterated in many of her novels. For instance, *A Time to Be Happy,* set during the 15 years prior to Independence, depicts the contrast between Indians who aspire to "Englishness" and Indian nationalists. The narrative focuses on the maturation of the protagonist, Sanad, into a man who rejects Anglicization in order to "discover" his country. Midway through the story, the narrator (not Sanad) tells an English friend, "*Karma* merely means living your life and doing your duty to the best of your ability in whichever capacity you happen to have been born in. True, your present condition is the result of your past life and actions, but then it is equally true that what you do in this life will create the conditions for your next one. In other words, it rests wholly with you to better your status" (165). In *A Situation in New Delhi,* set in the period immediately following the death of Nehru, conflicting interpretations of social duty are presented as generational differences. The "freedom generation" advocates a nonviolent approach to reform, while the post-independence generation practices violent attempts at revolution. This younger generation is represented by Rishad, member of a disorganized Naxalite group whose modus operandi is the "systematic creation of panic" to generate a new social order (58). Rishad appropriates the lesson of the *Gita:* "If you had to kill, you killed without involvement, without personal passion or anger. You did it as a duty" (100). In contrast, the "freedom generation" is represented by Rishad's mother Devi, the widowed Minister of Education. Devi conceives of duty as continuing the freedom-seeking legacy of her dead brother Shivraj

(a portrait of Nehru), and she follows this conception of duty by working for educational reform and battling the corruption of the complacent post-Shivraj Cabinet. Devi explains her adherence to duty to a former lover: "It is a big word—for us. It is not something chilly and punishing. It's almost religion. Without it, my life would have no meaning" (54–55). In *Rich Like Us,* a meditation on the revisioning of history during the "bogus" Emergency (1975–77), the concept of duty is more ambivalently interrogated. This novel intertwines the narratives of Rose, the English second wife of an Indian entrepreneur, and Sonali, an unconventional civil servant newly dismissed from the Ministry of Industry for challenging its disregard for economic policies. Rose saves her husband's first wife, Mona, from self-immolation, and explains her selflessness as "ordinary duty" to her esteeming father-in-law, who mistakes her intentions as Dharma, or Duty with a capital D. While one critic has called Sonali a model of liberal feminism, in this narrative, Rose becomes a model practitioner of the social duty of secular humanism: she effects small changes in the abjected lives around her, like obtaining artificial hands for a beggar.

In addition to social duty, another persistent theme is the need for women to achieve self-realization, within or without the confines of marriage. Sahgal favors marriages of choice rather than arranged unions—a character in *A Situation in New Delhi* refers to these as "girl-disposal"— and depicts the ideal marriage as a reciprocal partnership. She suggests repeatedly that women should be seen as equal partners rather than possessions or pawns. Indeed, several of her early female protagonists manage to escape empty, nonreciprocal marriages: in *This Time of Morning,* Rashmi leaves her unfulfilling marriage; pregnant Saroj, in *Storm in Chandigarh,* finds the courage to leave her jealously volatile husband, taking her two children with her. The theme of women's emancipation is particularly developed in *The Day in Shadow,* which features recently divorced Simrit who, in the course of the novel, finds motivation to fight a devastatingly unfair divorce settlement. Later female protagonists—Devi in *A Situation in New Delhi* and Sonali in *Rich Like Us*—choose to remain unattached in order to better pursue their goals. In all Sahgal's novels, honest communication seals the bond between man and woman. Similarly, sexuality is unapologetically portrayed as a means by which women express and empower themselves. Sahgal's female characters tend to pursue meaningful sexual relationships both in and beyond marital relationships. However, divorce or extramarital sexuality, as Jasbir Jain points out, does not diminish the relevance of marriage; rather, "[w]hat concerns Nayantara most is the need for a mature approach to marriage, the need to nurture it with love and care and candour. She wants communication not perfection, for men and women have their own limitations" (60–61).

Early critics hesitated to consider Sahgal a political novelist and produced assessments of her fiction that relied too heavily on autobiographical information. Now, however, Sahgal is acclaimed as an important post-Independence political novelist. A. V. Krishna Rao's and Jain's early book-length studies emphasize that Sahgal does not neatly fit at either end of the tradition/modernity binarism; she occupies the middle ground. Critics have also commented on the limitations of Sahgal's focus on the urban educated elite. For example, Joya Uraizee argues that this focus effectively remarginalizes subaltern or peasant characters. Uraizee asserts, "Sahgal is severely limited in her social criticism because her elite status keeps her removed from the daily contact with economic hardship and exploitation" (46). Fi-

nally, several critics have too eagerly assigned Western conceptions of liberal feminism to Sahgal's work. Teresa Hubel problematizes this critical move, arguing that in *Rich Like Us,* Rose provides a valuable reminder that liberal feminist individualism is a "middle-class construct suited only to middle-class lives and woefully insufficient as an ideology that can honourably encounter and respect the divergence from the middle-class norm that those displaced from power represent" (94).

Kellie Holzer

Further Reading

Hubel, Teresa. "The Politics of the Poor and the Limits of Feminist Individualism in Nayantara Sahgal's *Rich Like Us.*" *Nayantara Sahgal's India: Passion, Politics, and History.* Ed. Ralph Crane. New Delhi: Sterling, 1998. 78–96.

Jain, Jasbir. *Nayantara Sahgal.* New Delhi: Heinemann, 1978.

Rao, A. V. Krishna. *Nayantara Sahgal: A Study of Her Fiction and Non-Fiction.* Madras: M. Seshachalam, 1976.

Uraizee, Joya. *This Is No Place for a Woman: Nadine Gordimer, Buchi Emecheta, Nayantara Sahgal, and the Politics of Gender.* Trenton: Africa World Press, 2000.

Sahitya Akademi

The Sahitya Akademi, the National Academy of Letters, is a cultural-literary organization established by the government of India in 1954. It is an autonomous institution, which elects its own body of members. The Akademi was formed to enable the mutual exchange between all the regional Indian languages, acknowledging the fact that the new Indian state, formed in 1947, could not urge for a monolithic concept of Indian literature, as it was nonexistent. Cultural exchange and the creation of a multilingual Indian community were considered as means of nation building. Involved in tracing an Indian literary genealogy, the Akademi accepts the fact that Indian literature comprises all the numerous regional languages with their own literary traditions and histories.

The Akademi publishes in 22 Indian languages that are recognized by the Constitution of India. The literary culture, as defined by the Akademi, also includes oral literatures. The Tribal Oral Literature Program, for example, is involved in recording oral narratives and tribal cultures, thus recuperating a vanishing folk tradition. The Akademi holds seminars, workshops and conferences, book releases and other literary activities, both at the national and international levels—programs not only designed to heighten awareness in the common readers, but also to allow for critical engagement with literary and aesthetic issues. Its publications include books, journals, monographs, encyclopedias, and anthologies on ancient, medieval, and modern Indian literatures. Two bimonthly journals are published, one in English *(Indian Literature),* and the other in Hindi *(Samakaleen Bharatiya Sahitya).* Though the emphasis is on contemporary Indian literature and issues of translation, writings in the journal include materials from minority, folk, and tribal languages, which do not have constitutional recognition, and also on the literatures of the world and new literary movements.

The role of the Akademi is to ensure that a constant exchange—through translations—occurs between different literary traditions. It also has a Cultural Exchange Program where world classics are translated and made accessible to the Indian readers. Thus, literary culture, as defined here, transcends borders, and the impetus is on making accessible to the Indian readers an awareness of world literatures. Translation comprises an important aspect of the Akademi's work, and most of the Indian writings are published in English. For the reader in English, the Akademi's publications are an important source to learning about Indian literary history, and the contemporary literary work being done in the regional languages. The Akademi performs an important function of publish-

ing texts independent of market demands, as it can disregard the tastes of the reading public—factors which publishing houses have to consider. The Akademi, housed in New Delhi at the Tagore Bhawan, has a library, which scholars and researches interested in any aspect of Indian literature and critical theory can use. Regional offices are also present in Mumbai, Calcutta, and Bangalore.

Tapati Bharadwaj

Further Reading

Datta, Amaresh, ed. *Encyclopaedia of Indian literature.* 6 vols. New Delhi: Sahitya Akademi, 1987.

Sahitya Akademi. Home page. 29 Nov. 2002 <http://www.sahitya-akademi.org/sahitya-akademi/home.htm>.

The Sandglass by Romesh Gunesekera

Born in Sri Lanka in 1954, Romesh Gunesekera was educated briefly in Colombo before moving to the Philippines with his parents. He settled down in London in 1972. Gunesekera's first book, *Monkfish Moon* (Granta 1992), was a New York Times Notable Book of the Year, while his first novel Reef, (Granta, 1994), was short listed for the Booker Prize. His other novels include *The Sandglass* (Viking, 1998) and *Heavens Edge* (Bloomsbury, 2002).

The Sandglass plots the lives of two families, the Ducals and the Vatunas, over three generations. The crucial event that complicates the story is Jason's mysterious death in "Arcadia," the home he had created in Sri Lanka. His wife Pearl flees to England soon after and is eventually joined by her children Anoja, Prins, and Ravi. The narrator, who is privy to Pearl's account of the Ducal/Vatunas feud in Sri Lanka and witnesses the lives of the Ducals in England is Chip, another Sri Lankan expatriate and a family friend. The first generation immigrants try to reconcile their existence in England with what they have left behind in Sri Lanka. With his brother Ravi committing suicide and mother dying of natural causes, Jason, dissatisfied with England, returns to Sri Lanka to solve the mystery surrounding his father's death, to succeed in business and to make a positive contribution to his homeland. His ambitions are not realized, however. He is no match for Dino who is now the head of the Vatunas dynasty, and his life becomes complicated and placed in jeopardy when he falls in love with Dino's sister Lola. Jason eventually disappears without trace (presumably killed by Dino) in a Sri Lanka that has become increasingly violent because of graft, greed and political machinations. Rendered distraught by the loss of his dearest friends and by his inability to properly piece together a complex tale, Chip's only hope is that "Dawn," Pearl's great granddaughter who is born just before the story ends, will "spin us forward from this hurt world to a somehow better world" (278).

The Sandglass provides a very convincing account of expatriate living, with several characters managing their lot in different ways. Pearl, who is unable to return to Sri Lanka, lives in the past, or in a world of "make believe." Ravi experiences latent and manifest forms of racism in the West and eventually commits suicide. Prins rejects the fetters of expatriation and determines to succeed in the corporate world in Sri Lanka. Mira tries to handle her situation by leading a hedonistic, bohemian existence. Chip who constantly agonizes about his expatriate identity initially finds a therapeutic value in writing. Finally, Anoja and her daughter Naomie choose to assimilate by marrying non–Sri Lankans in England. The thrust of the novel seems to suggest that expatriates will only settle if they effectively forget their homeland and totally embrace the mores and culture of their land of adoption. However, Gunesekera's portrayal of Sri Lanka is slightly problematic. All that has tran-

spired in "paradise" during the 50 years after independence is the emergence of a set of individuals who are merely interested in securing commercial success and political power. The means adopted are usually violent and dubious. It is a country in which "the rich are scheming and the rest are reeling" (70) so much so that, as Penelope Fitzgerald claims, "time is running out for Gunesekera's Sri Lanka" (14).

In addition to providing a characterization of expatriate living, this novel also chronicles the history of twentieth century Sri Lanka in a manner that is entertaining but not always accurate. Gunasekera is justified in situating the high point of the Ducal/Vatunas feud in 1956, the year that S.W.R.D. Bandaraniake gathered the support of Left Wing parties and the working/rural masses to sweep the largely upper-middle-class government out of power. The fact that the "respectable" Ducals are out maneuvered by the Vatunas who belong to a "lower" stock, therefore, has an important metaphorical reference. What is puzzling, however, is the author's insistence that the Ducals are in some way morally superior to the Vatunas, despite showing that both Jason Ducal and Esra Vatunas try to corner the market for alcohol, while a generation later, Jason's son, the initially idealistic Prins, works for the ruthless Dino Vatunas.

It is not a coincidence that Pearl knits while she recounts her family's history to Chip. *The Sandglass* is indubitably about the problems of knitting a story to make it organic; in fact, as Carmen *Wickramagamage* observes, "The Sandglass, at one level, is about the (im)possibility of story making" (112). If at a very elementary level the novel adopts the whodunit formula but frustrates the expectations of that formula by concluding that Jason's murderer will always be unknown, it shows at a deeper level that the histories of individuals and nations are opaque and can never be resolved.

British critics have praised the novel for its unflinching, honest assessment of conditions in Sri Lanka, while those in Sri Lanka have been more cautious. Perera feels that it is precisely Gunesekera's characterization of Sri Lanka that has rendered the novel problematic, while *Wickramagamage,* whose review is generally favorable, adds that "Gunesekera's disappointment at the trajectory traced by post-independent Ceylon/Sri Lanka prevents him from offering an objective and serious analysis of its socio-economic misfortunes" (116).

S. W. Perera

Further Reading

Binding, Paul. "A Tear-Shaped Homeland: *The Sandglass* by Romesh Gunesekera." Rev. of *The Sandglass* by Romesh Gunesekera. *The Independent on Sunday Review: Books* (22 Feb. 1998): 29.

Fitzgerald, Penelope. "A Sarong for Europe" Rev. of *The Sandglass* by Romesh Gunesekera. *The Observer Review: Books.* (22 Feb. 1998): 14.

Perera, Walter. "The Perils of Expatriation and a 'Heartless Paradise': Romesh Gunesekera's *The Sandglass.*" *Commonwealth: Essays and Studies* 29 (2000): 93–106.

Wickramagamage, Carmen. "Many Questions, Few Answers: Romesh Gunesekera's *The Sandglass.*" *Navasilu* 15–16 (1998): 112–17.

The Satanic Verses by Salman Rushdie

To speak of *The Satanic Verses* (1988) by Salman Rushdie as a transgressive work of postcolonial imagination is by no means original. Known internationally as the book whose publication launched and continues to propel contemporary debates surrounding artistic license, the right of free speech, and the role of art in political culture, *The Satanic Verses* is perhaps one of the most recognized, discussed, celebrated, and in contrast, vilified works of twentieth-century literature. It has established for Rushdie, in several quarters, the reputation of malicious anti-Islamic demagogue intent upon creating and spreading propaganda and tribal hatred, knowingly exciting unwarranted turmoil ending in bloodshed. Sadly, the book has been clouded by religious rhetoric, misappropriated as solely "a deeply Islamic book" (Suleri 191) and dismissed as a gross error in judgment on its author's part. The result has been the near ruin of a critically important and valuable text whose true element of transgressiveness lies in its espousal of newness, border experiences, transculturation or the "leaking" of one culture into another, and the possibility of historical, cultural, communal, and personal reinscription and rebirth. *The Satanic Verses* is a quintessential example of literature that seeks to disrupt the continuum of history and expose the excessive possibilities of the arrival of newness in the world.

In the wake of the Ayatollah Khomeini's 1989 pronouncement of the *fatwa,* or edict, to end Rushdie's life for the crime of offering, in fictional form, his vision of the world, scholar Gayatri Chakravorty Spivak famously pointed to the impossibility of a "mere reading" of *The Satanic Verses* (219). Many critics, including Rushdie himself, have vehemently insisted that the original intentions of the book have been severely misunderstood or entirely lost within the context of the so-called Rushdie affair. Since the text's publication in 1988, the political, cultural, and religious furor surrounding its controversial and, some consider, blasphemous content regarding the birth of Islam and the writing of the Qur'an, has, in subsequent examinations of the text, frequently obscured or obviated the intended message of the need for a secular humanism that challenges fundamentalism in all its avatars and recognizes the inevitable postmodern and postcolonial condition of cultural hybridity or mélange. Far from engineering an outright attack on Islam, Rushdie believed that he was writing a book about "migration, metamorphosis,

Thousands of Moslems kneeling during Friday prayers at the Badshahi Mosque in Lahore, Pakistan. © TRIP/ Ask Images.

divided selves, love, death, London and Bombay" ("My Book Speaks" A39). *The Satanic Verses* is above all a poetics of postmodern migration; that is, an exploration of the experiences of the dislocated individual in chosen exile, moving freely through the world in search of a sense of self and an alternative understanding of what constitutes as "home."

Desirous of enunciating his own experiences as a "translated man," born Indian but residing elsewhere, Rushdie shifted his literary focus from the modern nation-states of India and Pakistan as explored in his earlier novels, *Midnight's Children* (1981) and *Shame* (1985), to examine, on a global and transnational scale, the migrant condition at the convergence of East and West. In relating the story of two Indian immigrants, Saladin Chamcha and Gibreel Farishta, who migrate westward from Bombay to London, Rushdie articulates a radical and positive view of migrancy in *The Satanic Verses* in which

he addresses not as much the question of what may be lost in translation, as what might be gained by and learned from the culturally displaced person who accepts change, incorporates the new, and willingly adopts a more hybrid, cosmopolitan understanding of belonging and citizenship.

As the novel opens, the jumbo jet *Bostan* Flight 420 explodes over Ellowen Deeowen, the capital city of the "fabled country of Vilayet" (*Satanic* 36), Rushdie's fictional version of London, England. Saladin and Gibreel are explosively launched from the womb of the aircraft as the sole survivors to be reborn into the expanse of air and to enunciate their presence in the world. While Rushdie's primary concern is the internal effects of migration upon the migrant, the importance of *The Satanic Verses* as a crucial political discourse on the postcolonial phenomenon of the "margin" speaking, writing, and traveling back to the "centre" cannot be denied. The arrival of newness and the introduction of difference into the post-colonial Western world create an interstitial space and intermediary moment between fixed identifications, subverting European univocal discourses of authenticity, authority and binarism.

As Saladin and Gibreel descend from the heavens over the English Channel the horizons of their selves expand and they begin to acquire fantastical physical and psychic characteristics—for Saladin, horns and hoofs, for Gibreel, intensified dreams and encroaching madness. Both men strive to make sense of their new selves and surroundings and to meet the challenges of migrating from one culture to another; however, only Saladin is able to successfully reinvent himself and consolidate his fractured multiple selves into a new eclectic form. Initially optimistic about his unusual arrival and rebirth in Vilayet, and seemingly willing to embrace a multiplicity of cultural identifications, Gibreel is ultimately unable to contend with the changes brought upon him by migration. He chooses to remain "at bottom, an untranslated man" (*Satanic* 441–42), and succumbs eventually to a state of paranoid schizophrenia. Tormented by dreams that fracture his weakened sense of self, Gibreel finds that he no longer recognizes the distinction between the waking and the dreaming state, and it is his dream sequences in which he assumes the guise of the Archangel Gabriel, counseling the Prophet on the creation of the new religion of Islam and watching over the progress of a pilgrimage to Mecca, that form the basis for the novel's controversial chapters on the writing and subsequent removal of the so-called satanic verses in the Qur'an. In his retreat into fundamentalism and his rejection of a more hybrid, cosmopolitan understanding of the world, Gibreel's inner demons finally overtake him and his inability to accept the conditions of his transmutation prompts him to commit suicide upon his return to Bombay.

The task of embracing the metamorphosed self and contending with the "incompatible realities" (*Satanic* 325) of the postmodern world falls to Saladin, and it is through this character's experiences as a newly "translated man" that Rushdie explores questions of identity, the state of the soul in transformation, and the fate of the once-colonized Other in the metropole. Upon waking on the shores of Vilayet, Saladin is effectively transformed, in a feat of magic realism, into a "Goatman" complete with horns and cloven hoofs. He is subsequently forced to endure a scene of classic Althusserian subject interpellation that demonstrates the demonization and dehumanization of the Other and offers a biting commentary on British multiculturalism and immigration policies during the Thatcher era. Saladin's greatest challenge is to reject his interpellated self and his role as colonized victim at the mercy of the dominant culture's narrative of alterity, for Rushdie implies that as long as Saladin views himself as exclusively the victim of British multicultural racism, he will continue to exhibit goatlike characteristics as a manifestation of his own self-hatred and subjectivity. Saladin, prior to and following his radical transfiguration, is capable only of interpreting the world in binary terms: East/West, self/other, colonizer/colonized. Attempting to escape what he perceives as the weakness and inferiority of his Indian heritage, he opts to assimilate into the colonizer's culture and adopt a British persona, acquiring a split identity, as Jaina Sanga says, from "the desire to be English and the fact of being Indian" (83).

Eventually, with the help of a host of significant minor characters, including Muhammed Sufyan of the Shaandaar Café and love-interest Zeeny Vakil, Saladin begins to realize that in order to achieve physical, mental, and emotional wholeness he must reconcile himself with his essential Indian self and graft together his multiple identities into a new and more resilient hybrid form. Saladin, returned to his normal physical self, survives his migratory ordeal and his return to Bombay at the end of the novel to reunite with his father and pursue a life with Zeeny signifies that his global experiences have compelled him to reevaluate and revitalize his local and personal affiliations and connections, and inspired him to recuperate his Indian heritage while maintaining a sense of his position as a global citizen and agent of newness.

Dana Hansen

Further Reading

Rushdie, Salman. "My Book Speaks for Itself." *The New York Times* 17 Feb. 1989: A39.

Sanga, Jaina C. *Salman Rushdie's Postcolonial Metaphors: Migration, Translation, Hybridity, Blasphemy, and Globalization.* Westport: Greenwood, 2001.

Spivak, Gayatri Chakravorty. "Reading the Satanic Verses." *Outside in the Teaching Machine.* New York: Routledge, 1993. 217–42.

Suleri, Sara. *The Rhetoric of English India.* Chicago: U of Chicago P, 1992.

Sealy, I. Allan

I. Allan Sealy was born in 1951 into a Christian family and grew up in small towns in northern India. He attended La Martinere school in Lucknow, and went on to study at St. Stephen's College, Delhi. While still a young man Sealy earned a scholarship and a master's degree at Western Michigan University. He earned a doctorate at the British Columbia University, writing his dissertation on the Caribbean novelist Wilson Harris. Sealy lived for a while in New Zealand and Australia before he moved back to India. He currently lives in Dehradun, and is working on a new novel.

Sealy has often been labeled an Anglo-Indian writer, a category that is made to seem separate from that of the Indian writer. Sealy writes "Anglo-Indian is simply one of many possible versions whether regional or sectarian which together constitute Indian writing in English. . . . I don't think myself as an Anglo-Indian writer, though I have written an Anglo-Indian novel and am myself an Anglo-Indian. . . . My sensibilities are those of any Westernized urban Indian: a pride in things Indian that merit pride and a consciousness"(*The Trotter* 2). Thus, Sealy's work must be examined in the context of other Indian writing and not as a separate strain of Indian writing labeled Anglo-Indian.

One of Sealy's major themes is a character's search for identity. Sealy's first novel, *The Trotter Nama,* is set in the city of Nakhlau (Lucknow) and is the story of seven generations of Trotters living in Sans Souci. Justine Trotter, the first of the Trotters, wonders about his identity, "Fate having cast my lot in three separate lands of Europe, America and Asia and brought me at last to this place which I have come to consider my very home" (*The Trotter* 178). For succeeding generations of the Trotters, identity becomes a more complex issue. Their mixed parentage, depicted symbolically in their grey skin, forces them to question whether they are more Anglo than Indian or whether the opposite is true. Judith Plotz in writing about *The Trotter Nama* creates a perfect metaphor for these characters, that of the hijda or hermaphrodite. In *The Everest Hotel,* Ritu, a young nun, grapples with her own identity as she questions the doctrine of complete obedience that the sisterhood requires. However her most troubled tryst with identity is when she finds herself attracted to Brij, an attraction that goes against the grain of her calling and, therefore, leads her to question her very *raison d'etre.*

Another important motif that surfaces in Sealy's work is that of the miniature. *The Trotter Nama* makes explicit reference to this art form in which every detail is equally important: "With big canvases you're trying to match the world. With miniatures you're past imitation" (277). The chronicle of the Trotters is in itself a miniaturized version of Indian history, where characters interact with events of history in a way unique to the community of Anglo-Indians, who are "past imitation." This brings us to the third level of miniaturization —the Anglo-Indian community, which represents a tiny but unique facet of Indian culture. The idea of miniaturization is echoed in *Hero* as well, but less overtly. The lives and interactions between Hero, Zero, and Nero could perhaps be seen as a miniature version of those present in the Bombay film industry. Similarly the political events of Drummodganj could be seen as a miniature version of the tensions within India at the time.

The local flavor of each novel brings us to another motif present in Sealy's work—the exaltation of the ordinary and mundane. In *The Trotter Nama,* this theme is formulated in terms of the various recipes given, terms explained and advice meted out to the reader. While a recipe of "Mango Phool" does not play an essential role in the narrative, its presence (along with the presence of several other more forbidding recipes) is a testament to the existence of the everyday even within the lives of these extraordinary characters. In *Hero,* U. D.'s name in its very intonations represents the ordinary, for this is the popular pronunciation of "Eau de" in India. *The Everest Hotel* is the story of ordinary people, and their "ordinariness" in this novel is symbolized by their identification with grassroot movements.

Although Sealy's *The Trotter Nama* did not, on the whole, receive favorable reports abroad, some critics did praise the novel. For instance, Cryer, in his discussion of the novel directs our attention to the Anglo-Indians, a marginalized section of the Indian population: "Sealy deserves credit for calling attention to the Anglo-Indians, all too often despised by English and Indian alike" (9). The racially hybrid

Anglo-Indians are a metaphor for the hybrid genres that Sealy uses in *The Everest Hotel.* "His latest work *[The Everest Hotel]* re-establishes this sense of appropriation and creative reworking on the level of the evoked moods or potential emotional states which underlie Sanskrit dhvani-rasa aesthetics. . . . *The Everest Hotel* the thwarted love affair between Ritu and the idealistic political activist Brij, can be read as another gesture toward this earlier poetic mode (the baramasih)" (Tickell, 297).

Krupa Shandilya

Further Reading

Conrad, Linda. "I. Allan Sealy" *Writers of the Indian Diaspora.* Ed. Emmanuel Nelson. Westport: Greenwood, 1993.

Cryer, Dan. "Vast Land, Big Family, Sprawling Saga." *Newsday* 29 Feb. 1988: 9.

Mukherjee, Bharati. "An Anglo-Indian Family Caught between Two Worlds." *The Washington Post* 3 Apr. 1988.

Plotz, Judith. "Rushdie's Pickle and the New Indian Historical Novel." *World Literature Written in English* 35.2 (1995): 24–48.

Tickell, Alex. *SOAS Literary Review* (2). London: Transworld/Anchor, 1999. 297.

Selvadurai, Shyam

Shyam Selvadurai was born in Colombo, Sri Lanka, in 1965 and left the island for Canada with his parents at the age of 19 after the riots of 1983. He holds a B.F.A. from York University and has contributed extensively to television and journals. His first book, *Funny Boy,* won the W.H. Smith/Books in Canada First Novel Award and, in the United States, the Lambda Literary Award for Best Gay Men's Fiction. His second novel, *Cinnamon Gardens,* was published in 1998. He lives and works in Toronto.

Selvadurai's *Funny Boy* was the first novel written in a Sri Lankan context to foreground a palpably gay theme. The young Arjie finds boys' pursuits inimical to his personality and drifts toward the companionship of girls, with whom he participates in a game in which he plays the role of the bride. Although Mr. Chelvaratnam debars him from continuing with this game because he does not want his son turning out to be "funny," this early chapter prefigures the theme that eventually becomes the novel's major focus of attention.

It is only when he goes to school and meets Shehan who is gay that Arjie discovers his sexual orientation. Like Arjie, Shehan is an outsider living in a world that seeks to circumscribe and control. His relationship with Shehan is conveyed with delicacy. Arjie is neither "triumphalistic" in his sexual assertion nor insistent on placing homosexual love and heterosexual love in binary opposition. The author shows, however, that such relationships could be fulfilling for some.

Funny Boy is emphatically a novel that focuses on several kinds of victimization. Radha aunty is forced by her family to end her relationship with a Sinhala boy and marry a Tamil; Jegan, whose father was Mr. Chelvaratnam's best friend, makes a success of his life in Colombo but is forced to return to Jaffna because he is wrongfully accused of being a Tamil terrorist; and Darryl, a journalist and Mrs Chelvaratnam's former lover, comes to Sri Lanka to investigate human rights violations by the military/police and is (presumably) killed by them. In his description of the riots toward the end of the novel, Selvadurai shows how an entire community is victimized. Ultimately, the consequence for the Chelvaratmans is immigration to Canada.

Ironically, the only person who resists the forces of orthodoxy and achieves a measure of success is the weakest individual, Arjie: his relationship with Shehan is a subversive move against the patriarchy that his father represents, while his deliberately distorting the lines of a poem he was asked to recite on Prize Day is a blow against the neocolonial postures adopted by the principal, who had severely punished Shehan.

Drawn on a much broader canvas, *Cinnamon Gardens* is situated in the late 1920s when the Donoughmore Commissioners were in Ceylon to observe all aspects of life in the Crown Colony and to make recommendations for its future. The chief characters in this novel are Annalukshmi and her uncle, Balendran, who belong to the upper crust of the Tamil world in Sri Lanka. Balendran's father is a mudaliyar, one of the highest posts a Ceylonese could hold during British occupation, and a member of the National Congress. Despite their privileged backgrounds, however, Annalukshmi and Balendran find it difficult to achieve selfhood on account of the strictures imposed by society. Annalukshmi's ambitions are placed in jeopardy because a woman with her background is supposed to consent to an arranged marriage, and Balendran is forced to give up his homosexual inclinations and marry a cousin to maintain the family line and prevent scandal. Annalukshmi achieves a measure of independence at the end by resisting others' attempts to get her married and by becoming a successful teacher, while Balendran, though unable to pursue his homosexual affairs in the open, comes to respect and rely on his wife who is in many ways more liberated than he is.

Besides examining the careers of these two characters, Selvadurai also shows the irresponsibility and selfish motives of the upper class, which (according to Selvadurai) opposed the extension of the franchise to preserve the status quo. He also charts the origins of the women's movement in Sri Lanka, demonstrates how the divisions between the Sinhalese and the Tamils emerged during this stage of the country's history, and also assesses the contributions of labor leaders to electoral reform.

Himself a gay rights activist, Raj Rao argues in a controversial article on *Funny Boy* that the novel posits a binary with patriarchy, the Sri Lankan military and the government on one side; and women, the Tamil Tigers, and gays on the other. To Chelva Kanaganayakam, who takes a more conservative approach, one of the "salient aspects that contributed to the popularity of the novel was its translucent surface, its unadorned style and its conversational tone, totally unlike the narratives of other contemporary Sri Lankan writers"(1). Carmen Wickramagamage's review of *Cinnamon Gardens* uses the options open to Annalukshmi as a metaphor for the choices available to women at the time, while Perera's article disputes some of the criticisms made of the Sri Lankan elite in the same novel.

S. W. Perera

Further Reading

Kanaganayakam, Chelva. "Remembering Ceylon: A Reading of *Funny Boy.*" *Navasilu: Journal of the English Association of Sri Lanka* 15–16 (1998): 1–7.

Perera, S.W. "In Pursuit of Political Correctness: Shyam Selvadurai's *Cinnamon Gardens.*" *The Sri Lanka Journal of the Humanities* 24–25: 1, 2, 87–111.

Rao, Raj. "Because People Marry Their Own Kind." *Ariel: A Review of International English Literature* 28.1 (1997): 117–28.

Santiago, José Fernández Vázques. "The Quest for Personal and National Identity in Shyam Selvadurai's *Funny Boy.*" *Commonwealth: Essays and Studies* 24. 1 (2001): 103–15.

Wickramagamage, Carmen. " 'A Fish without a Bicycle'?: Annalukshmi's Choice in Selvadurai's *Cinnamon Gardens.*" *CRNLE JOURNAL: Sri Lankan and Indian Diasporic Writing* (2000): 130–40.

Seth, Vikram

Elusive, seductive, versatile, and genius are words that have been used to describe world-renowned Indian author, Vikram Seth. A man whose creativity is governed and shaped by bouts of obsession, Seth has spawned a plethora of masterpieces from musical scores, to travel dialogues, to poetry, to in-depth novels dealing with social histories, each reflecting his deep, multi-faceted talent and wide-ranging, diasporic experiences. And the high caliber of his work has received high praise from critics globally. "I have little doubt that . . . Vikram Seth is already the best writer of this generation," notes Eugene Robinson of the *Washington Post.* As if that were not enough, Seth's talent has been compared to writers such as Leo Tolstoy and Johann Goethe.

Interestingly, Seth's allure extends beyond the edges of his professional life into the depths of his phantomlike persona. "Vikram Seth is the rarest of creatures. . . . In the flesh he is small and has huge saucer eyes, a combination which lends him the sensitive and endearing appearance of a nocturnal creature," describes Cressida Connolly of *The Sunday Telegraph.* Michele Field of *Publisher's Weekly* writes: "Seth has such a seductive personality that one can hardly remember the disarray with which he dresses or his receding hairline; instead, what lingers on the mind are eyes as deep as a dolphin's, and the wholly ironic inflection in his answers."

Although Seth has provided a multitude of in-person interviews and despite the existence of an unquantifiable amount of reviews and essays concerning his work, all seem unable to grasp the core essence of this author. The public's interest in Seth is further fueled by its continued inability to pierce the veil that shields his reclusive and extremely private life. Virtually nothing is known about his personal relationships, and, to date, at age 50, Seth remains unmarried. He never resides in any one place at a given time but is rumored to split his life between England and India or wherever his current research takes him. It is said that he shies away from giving interviews in his own home and, instead, prefers alternate, decoy locations. Seth's mythical status is further magnified by his rumored dislike of cell phones and E-mail, lending weight to the perception that he is always mysteriously out of reach. "Oh yes. Yes. A gregarious recluse. I like that very much," he notes in an interview for the *Sunday Telegraph,* "My own coinage is that I'm cyclical obsessive. But gregarious recluse . . . Yes. That's me." Yet, despite his seemingly intangible nature, Seth does materialize for some very real, public activities, such as swimming outdoors *all* year round in the Serpentine with the Serpentine Swimming Club in England. He even claims to have swum the entire length of the Ganges.

Born in Calcutta in 1952, five years after India's Independence, Seth is the eldest of three children (he has a younger brother and sister) in an upper-class Hindu family. His father, Prem Seth, the executive of a shoe company, and his mother, Laila Seth, the first appointed female high-court judge in India, encouraged and steered their eldest son along traditional educational and professional paths, sending him to English schools in India, and, eventually, abroad to Corpus Christi College in Oxford University, where he earned a bachelor's degree in philosophy, economics, and politics (1971–75). Although in 1975 Seth pursued a demanding curriculum for the Ph.D. in economics at Stanford University, California, he still found time to nurture his personal interest in creative writing as a Wallace Stagner Fellow (1977–78). Eventually, the building tension between the two disparate callings came to a head when Seth happened upon a copy of verses by the Chinese poet Wang Wei (701–761 A.D.). Heavily influenced by Wei, in 1980 Seth "concocted" a dissertation focused on Chinese economic demography in order to travel abroad to China, where he studied classical Chinese poetry at Nanjing University in Eastern China (1980–82), eventually abandoning his Ph.D. "I was drawn first to be an economist of all things. I spent many years of my life as an economist and demographer," Seth notes in an interview for *BoldType,* "I was finally distracted by writ-

ing my novels and poetry. I am enormously happy that was the case. I feel that with writing I have found my metier."

Since 1980, Seth has published six books of poetry, three novels, a libretto, and a travelogue. In his first publication, *Mappings* (Writer's Workshop Books), Seth offers translations of poetry from a variety of authors worldwide, including Suryakant Tripathi Nirala (Hindi) and Heinrich Heine (German). *Mappings* was soon followed by his 1985 poetic collection, *The Humble Administrator's Garden* (Carcanet Press), winner of Britain's 1985 *Commonwealth Poetry Prize* (Asia). Through the verses of *All You Who Sleep Tonight: Poems* (1990, Knopf), Seth explores various levels of love, inviting top praise: "Certainly not since Byron has anyone been more elegantly and literally amusing in verse," notes the *Philadelphia Daily News.* In 1993, Seth released *Three Chinese Poets: Translations of Poems by Wang Wei, Li Bai, and Du Fu* (1993, HarperCollins), a composite translation of three Chinese poets of the Tang Dynasty (618–907 A.D.).

In 1983, Seth published his first prose work, *From Heaven Gate: Travel through Sinkiang and Tibet* (Chatto and Windus) in the form of a travelogue. Recounting Seth's adventures while hitchhiking through western China and Tibet during his stay at Nanjing University, the text's merit lies in its transnational viewpoint: the narrative is recounted in English by an Indian traveling through China. Glen E. Cox observes in *First Impressions.* "Seth isn't afraid to put some dangerous questions to his hosts and fellow travelers—questions about the Cultural Revolution and Red Guard, how life is now under the communists compared with before, could Tibet be a separate country once more?" Winner of the Thomas Cook Travel Book Award in 1983, the high caliber of *From Heaven Gate* is further reinforced by the fact that it was the only text to be published by Chatto and Windus in more than 11 years.

Moved by a translated version of Pushkin's *Eugene Onegin,* Seth returned to his first love, poetry, in 1986 with the publication of *The Golden Gate* (Vintage Books), only this time he experimented with verse in the novel format. The result was his first novel, a 300-page story related entirely in verse (690 tetrameter, rhyming sonnets, verse, accompanied by an acknowledgements, a dedication, and an author biography, all in verse), which the writer Gore Vidal noted as "The Great California Novel." Selling more than 150,000 copies, a standard remarkable for a work in verse, the satirical romance engages in dialogues concerning the love lives of yuppies during the 1980s in San Francisco.

But it was in 1993 that Seth made his mark on the world with the publication of *A Suitable Boy* (Harper Perennial), deemed the longest novel written in the English language after Samuel Richardson's 1747 novel, *Clarissa.* A daunting 3.5 pounds and 1,349 pages (cut down from the original of over 2,000 pages), Seth's *A Suitable Boy* was developed over the course of an eight-year stay in India from where he had been absent for approximately 14 years. Intermingling a multilayered plot of social history and romance in 1950s post-Partition India, at its heart, *A Suitable Boy* centers on the tale of a Hindu mother who searches for an appropriate husband for her daughter. True to issues of that time, *A Suitable Boy* revisits controversial topics concerning land rights, interreligious marriages, and politics integral to that chaotic period of Indian history and which still purport to intersectional identity crises endemic in modern-day India. The rights for *A Suitable Boy* claimed the highest price of any debut novel sold in Great Britain to date, eventually selling more than one million copies. The text also won high literary recognition, including Britain's The Com-

monwealth Writer's Prize for Best Book (1994), Britain's W. H. Smith Literary Prize (1994), and Britain's Connect Award in 1993, but fell short of a Booker Prize nomination in 1993. Seth's masterpiece has been praised widely not only by critics, but by fellow Indian literary peers, such as world-renowned author, Anita Desai: "Awe is what Seth's labor inspires in the reader. At the end it is as if one had listened to a raag played by a musician with skill, dexterity, and charm" *(New York Review of Books).*

Although Seth's 1999 text, *An Equal Music* (Broadway Books), the title of which was derived from a sermon of John Donne's describing life after death, proved to be more conventional in its structure (only 400 pages and fully prose), it was, nevertheless, a departure from his earlier material. A non-Indian-based love story between two musicians, the idea for *An Equal Music* was conceived in the midst of a walk with a friend in Kensington Gardens, London, during which Seth encountered a lone male figure. "Dressed against the weather, he was staring fixedly at the Serpentine at the water. The image fascinated me. And it seemed quite important to what might have been germinating in my head for a novel," Seth notes in an interview for *BoldType.* (The chance encounter led Seth to formulate the character and plot for *An Equal Music* while researching in Vienna and Austria, and, eventually, to an 80,000-pound publicity campaign and a series of book tours.

An avid singer of classical Indian music and a fan of Schubert, it is not surprising that Seth's multifaceted talent is also manifested in musical scores, namely, the 1994 libretto, *Arion and Dolphin: A Libretto,* commissioned by England's National Opera for the opening of its opera by the same name. Depicting the ancient tale of a Corinthian poet/musician, Arion, and his friendship with a dolphin, the opera blends Seth's words with the music of British composer Alec Roth. The success of the opera spawned a picture book by the same name (Dutton Books) in which, once again, Seth's words were brought to life by the illustrations of famed artist, Jane Ray, and, eventually, also a 25-minute animated piece. Seth further contributed to children's imaginations in his 1992 release of *Beastly Tales from Here and There* (Phoenix Books), a compilation of 10 traditional fables in verse from India, China, Greece, and the Ukraine.

Seth's track record of consistently exciting and solid work marks him as a leading literary figure not only of the recent wave of Indian literature that has dominated the global market in the late twentieth century, but of literature in general.

V. G. Julie Rajan

Further Reading

BoldType. "An Interview with Vikram Seth." <http://www.randomhouse.com/boldtype/0599/seth/interview.html>.

Connolly, Cressida. "A Secret Man." *The Sunday Telegraph Magazine* (London). 28 Mar. 1999: 32–34.

Cox, Glen E. *First Impressions.* Installment 4, Apr. 1993. <http://www.sfsite.com/fi/004.htm>.

Curry, Jay, and Michele Denis. *January Magazine* June 1999. <http://www.januarymagazine.com/profiles/vseth.html>.

Field, Michelle. "Vikram Seth." *Publisher's Weekly Interviews* 10 May 1993. <http://www.salon.com/audio/2001/10>.

Robinson, Eugene. "A Tolstoy—On His First Try." *The Washington Post Foreign Service.* 1 May 1993. <http://www.emory.edu/ENGLISH/Bahri/seth.html>.

The Shadow Lines by Amitav Ghosh

In Amitav Ghosh's *The Shadow Lines,* the narrator, a young boy, starts out by telling the story of Tridib, his uncle, and the various events of his life. This slowly spirals into a narrative of many people and places—Tha'mma Ila, Nick, May, London, Calcutta, Dhaka, to name a few. Though it is set in a fixed historical time—between 1939 and 1979—the novel is not a chronological narrative; rather, it glides effortlessly from one time period to the other and from one space to another. This heightens the reader's awareness of the contingency of time and place, and at the same time it gives the narrative a sense of immediacy, so that the reader travels through many different spaces in the 200-odd pages of the book.

The narrator allows the narrative of the other characters to flow through his own, so that the version we get is one that is filtered through his consciousness. As a young boy at the beginning of the novel, the narrator is fascinated with his elusive and exotic cousin, Ila, whom he becomes obsessed with in his adulthood. Ila, as a result of having traveled around the world, is unable and unwilling to identify with anything "Indian," and she roots her identity in Nick Price, who represents to her all things English. Ila's identity is inextricably tied up with a desire to be European—she joins Marxist organizations in London and marries Nick, hoping thereby to marry into a culture. Nick, however, disregards her completely; theirs is a failed love story. Geography and time thwart all love stories in this novel, as Tridib and May's love story is also doomed by the riots in which Tridib dies.

The novel then is also about history—not the public history of textbooks, but a public history made personal by memory and invention. Tridib's death is vivid in the narrator's memory, but when he searches in archived newspapers for mention of the riots of '64, the narrator sees only a small article, hidden in the corner of the front page, impersonally announcing "Twenty Dead." The narrator, in an attempt to rescue the memory of those fateful riots from the metanarrative of history, sets out to write of all the events associated with that time, personalizing history through memory and a process of reinvention.

It is not only public history that is reinvented as personal history, but personal history is also constantly revised and changed by characters, as they try to make sense of their reality. Tha'mma, a strong believer in reality, is as susceptible to invention as any of the other characters. As a young girl she invented the story of the upside-down house as a way to scare Mayadebi, but most importantly as a means to confront the unknown reality that lurked behind the partition of her father's house. In later years the fiction becomes more compelling than reality, as both women begin to imagine the house as upside down, even though they know otherwise.

The story of the upside down house becomes a graphic literalization of the partition of the country, which brings to bear notions of nation and identity. The partition creates an artificial line between Bengal (West Bengal) and Bangladesh (East Bengal), which impels people on both sides to see the other side as different—even though there are no cultural differences. As the narrator observes when looking at a map of Dhaka and Calcutta, "each city was the inverted image of the other, locked into an irreversible symmetry by the line that was to set us free—our looking-glass border" (228). Ideas of nation and identity are confusing for Tha'amma for whom home will always be Dhaka, though India is her country: "She had not been able to quite understand how her place of birth had come to be so messily at odds with her nationality" (149). In her confusion, Tha'mma interchanges the words "coming" and "going," which become important paradigms in the novel, as the wandering characters define "home" by whether they are "Coming Home" or "Going Away."

The Shadow Lines was hailed as a great Indian classic by magazines and newspapers across India when it was first published. In an interview with Amitav Ghosh, Aldama states: "Ghosh writes outside the box, mixing a gritty realism with a surrealist flair to map the brutal consequences of cultural and political structures

that restrict identity and the imagination" (85). Most writers from the subcontinent are fascinated with the novel's unique manner of representing history: "Amitav Ghosh's *The Shadow Lines* is a manifestation of the desire to validate the postcolonial experience and to attempt a reconstruction of 'public' history through a reconstruction of the 'private' or personal history" (Bagchi 187).

Amitav Ghosh was born on July 11, 1956, in Calcutta. He studied history at St. Stephen's College, Delhi University, and went on to pursue his doctorate in social anthropology at Oxford University. He did an ethnographic study in the fellaheen village of Lataifa while at the University of Alexandria. He has taught sociology at the Delhi School of Economics, and has been teaching comparative literature at Queen's College, City University of New York since 1999.

Krupa Shandilya

Further Reading

Aldama, Frederick Luis. "An Interview with Amitav Ghosh." *World Literature Today* 76.2 (Spring 2002): 84–90.

Bagchi, Nivedita. "The Process of Validation in Relation to Materiality and Historical Reconstruction in Amitav Ghosh's *The Shadow Lines.*" *Modern Fiction Studies* 39.1 (Winter 1993): 187–202.

Chowdhary, Arvind, ed. *Amitav Ghosh's "The Shadow Lines": Critical Essays.* New Delhi: Atlantic, 2002.

Ghosh, Amitav. *The Shadow Lines.* London: Penguin, 1990. References to the text are to this edition.

Kapadia, Novy. "Imagination and Politics in Amitav Ghosh's The Shadow Lines." *The New Indian Novel in English: A Study of the 1980's.* Ed. Viney Kirpal. New Delhi: Allied, 1990. 201–12.

Mukherjee, Meenakshi. "Maps and Mirrors: Coordinates of Meaning in *The Shadow Lines.*" The Shadow Lines, Ghosh Educational ed. New Delhi: Oxford UP, 255–67.

Sundar Rajan, Rajeswari. "The Division of Experience in *The Shadow Lines.*" Ghosh Educational ed. 287–98.

Shame by Salman Rushdie

Shame (1983) is the third novel by Salman Rushdie, the follow-up to his critical and popular success, *Midnight's Children* (1981). Though a shorter work than its predecessor, *Shame* is no less ambitious; attempting to do for Pakistan what *Midnight's Children* had done for India, namely, using the narrative strategies of postmodernism to present a symbolic history of the country. *Shame* was generally well received by Western critics: it was nominated for the Booker Prize and won the French Prix du Meilleur Livre Etranger. The novel was banned in Pakistan. Any controversy associated with the novel was overshadowed, however, by the storm over Rushdie's fourth novel, *The Satanic Verses* (1988). As a result, *Shame* has stood somewhat in the later novel's shadow. This is unfortunate, for it is a rewarding novel that offers the reader unfamiliar with Rushdie an ideal gateway into his work.

Salman Rushdie was born in Bombay, India, on June 19, 1947, the child of liberal Muslim parents. When he was 14, Rushdie left home to attend Rugby School in England. Although he would return to visit his family—by then moved to Karachi, Pakistan—for all intents and purposes this move marked his immigration to England. Following his graduation from Cambridge, Rushdie worked as an actor before taking a job as a freelance advertising copywriter in 1970. He held this job for the next decade, during which he published his first novel, the science-fictional *Grimus* (1975), which failed to make much impact. Rushdie's literary fortunes changed considerably in 1981, when he published *Midnight's Children,* which won the Booker Award and propelled him to the forefront of English-language writers. *Shame* solidified his reputation, while *The Satanic Verses* made him the center of intense controversy for its provocative examination of religious faith, particularly Islam. This furor reached its apex when Iran's Ayatollah Khomeini pronounced a death sentence on Rushdie for blasphemy and urged all dutiful Muslims to seek the writer's end. Although forced by the decree into hiding, Rushdie continued to write. To this date, he has produced a children's novel, *Haroun and the Sea of Stories* (1990); two collections of essays, *Imaginary Homelands* (1991) and *Step across This Line* (2002); a collection of stories, *East, West* (1994); and three more novels, *The Moor's Last Sigh* (1995), *The Ground beneath Her Feet* (1999), and *Fury* (2001). Rushdie has won numerous awards, including the Booker of Bookers in 1993 for *Midnight's Children.* In 1998, the government of Iran declared that it was no longer pursuing Rushdie's death, and he was been able to return to a more normal life. In recent years, Rushdie has immigrated again, this time to New York City, where he currently resides and continues to write.

Rushdie's work displays the influences of such diverse writers and works as Lawrence Sterne, James Joyce, Desani's *All about H. Hatterr,* Grass's *The Tin Drum,* and Garcia Marquez's *One Hundred Years of Solitude. Shame* is no exception to this rule. It is a playful, inventive, fantastic, albeit complex examination of the central role that shame has played in the lives of Pakistan's people. To allow himself sufficient authorial freedom, Rushdie is careful to tell us that "the country in this story is not Pakistan, or not quite" (23), but the novel's concern with Pakistan's history is clear, as the narrator recounts, in detail, not only the geographic spaces that actually exist, but also the various people and political happenings of the past several years. On one level, the novel can be read as a national allegory in which the gruesome politics of Pakistan's contemporary events take center stage. The oppressive and brutal regimes of Zulfikar Ali Bhutto and Zia ul-Haq, are chronicled in the novel with accuracy, and although the narration takes great pains to couch this reality under the rubrics of fantasy, and suggests, continuously, that this is not a realistic novel, it becomes apparent that this is in fact a version of the history of Pakistan. The narrator keeps insisting that if it were a realistic novel, he would be forced to write about a whole range of things. He then compiles a list of all the nefarious political activities of the government that he would have to include. Of course, in so doing, he immediately draws attention to what is purposefully being left out. As Sanga explains: "By self-consciously trying to avoid the recounting of history that would include the list of inappropriate subjects, the narrator, in fact, effectively rehearses that very history" (59–60).

Shame is divided into five parts. The first section recounts the story of the birth and early life of Omar Khayyam Shakil. The child of three mothers (the sisters Chhunni, Munnee, and Bunny Shakil, none of whom reveals whose child Omar in fact is), Omar is a prodigious autodidact. He grows to maturity in the large house his mothers share, demonstrating an intelligence that leads him to master hypnosis. The first section concludes with Omar, grown as fat as he is intelligent, departing his hometown of Q. for medical school. Needless to say, he is not a typical hero.

Also in the opening pages of the novel, Rushdie the narrator addresses the audience directly, reflecting on his story. This technique, direct authorial intervention in the narrative, is one that Rushdie has used only twice: in *Shame* and in *The Satanic Verses;* in his other novels, the author is always one of the characters in the story. This narrative strategy makes *Shame* one of Rushdie's most personal works.

With *Shame*'s second section, Omar's story takes a back seat to the narrative that is at the novel's core: the intertwined lives of Iskander Harappa and General Raza Hyder and their respective families. These men are Rushdie's versions of Pakistan's President Zulfikar Ali Bhutto and the man who deposed him, General Mohammed Zia ul-Haq. Rushdie spends the remainder of the novel presenting Hyder and Harappa's rises and falls, beginning with the marriages to two cousins that will make them relatives. As is the case with Rushdie's major works, this story focuses on family.

Both marriages produce daughters: Iskander's to Rani Humayun results in Arjumand Harappa, the "Virgin Ironpants" (paralleled to Benazir Bhutto) who eventually carries on her father's political legacy and wreaks vengeance on the forces that deposed and executed him; while Raza's to Bilquis Kemal produces Sufiya Zenobia, a child of little intelligence but fearsome strength. Sufiya is married to Omar Khayyam Shakil, by this time a famous doctor who becomes fascinated by Sufiya when he tries hypnosis to help her out of her lifelong silence. Omar's efforts prove futile, and eventually Sufiya escapes her husband to roam the country, murdering men with her bare hands, literally pulling their heads from their bodies. At once fearsome and pathetic, Sufiya is a walking symbol for the inarticulate violence that Rushdie contends inevitably accompanies a surfeit of shame. As Sanga writes:

> Sufiya represents an extremity of the destructive power of violence that erupts under the intolerable burden of shame. She blushes from the moment of her birth, to register, first, her own shame of being born female and then to expose the nation's shame. She thus becomes a repository of the people's unfelt shame. Her metamorphosis is the enactment of supernatural processes . . . and she becomes the locus of exposition of the nation's cultural and political repression. (62)

At the novel's apocalyptic end, after Raza, who overthrew Iskander and has been overthrown by Arjumand Harappa in turn, Raza and Omar flee together back to the house of Omar's mothers. There, Raza meets his end in a machine originally designed to protect the house from thieves. Omar, in turn, is confronted by Sufiya, who brings the novel to a close by killing the character whose birth had begun it. Rushdie concludes with a vision of the house, engulfed by fire, brooded over by the blood-streaked Sufiya, the emblem of shame.

While *Shame* has been overshadowed by Rushdie's other work, there are good critical introductions to it in Cundy and Harrison. Kuortti and Sanga's works offer more complex, though rewarding, analyses of the novel. While some of its links are out of date, the Web site at <http://www.trill.hom.com/rushdie.html> has a good overview of Rushdie-related materials online.

John Langan

Kamila Shamsie. Courtesy of Mark Pringle.

Further Reading

Cundy, Catherine. *Salman Rushdie.* Manchester and New York: Manchester UP, 1996.

Harrsion, James. *Salman Rushdie.* New York: Twayne, 1991.

Kuortti, Joel. *Fictions to Live In: Narration as an Argument for Fiction in Salman Rushdie's Novels.* New York: Peter Lang, 1998.

Rushdie, Salman. *Imaginary Homelands: Essays and Criticism 1981–1991.* London: Granta, 1991.

Sanga, Jaina C. *Salman Rushdie's Postcolonial Metaphors: Migration, Translation, Hybridity, Blasphemy, and Globalization.* Westport: Greenwood, 2001.

Shamsie, Kamila

Kamila Shamsie was born in Karachi, Pakistan, on August 13, 1973, and comes from a long line of women writers in her family. Shamsie's mother Muneeza Shamsie is also a writer and has edited "A Dragonfly in the Sun," Pakistan's response to the Rushdie-edited "Mirrorwork," an anthology of post-Partition Pakistani writing.

Her great aunt Attia Hosain, one of the first women writers of South Asia, wrote *Sunlight on the Broken Column.* Unfortunately, Attia Hosain died a month before Shamsie's first novel was published. Shamsie's grandmother Jahanara Habibullah has written a memoir of life in Rampur that will be published by Oxford University Press.

An avid reader since childhood, Shamsie decided to be a writer when she was nine years old and cowrote her first book with her best friend when she was 11. Now the author of three novels, she has already received international acclaim as a writer of repute. She makes her home both in Karachi and in London where she spends a few months every year while she writes and does some journalism. Journalism for Shamsie is an occasional sideline. She has published in *Guardian, Prospect, New Statesman, Index on Censorship,* and in Karachi for *Newsline* and *DAWN.* She is currently an adjunct professor at Hamilton College in New York.

All her three novels originated from short stories. Talking about her writing process Shamsie said that a novel usually takes shape from an occasional quote or a line that she might think up (Tripathi). Shamsie's first book was published when Alexandra Pringle, a friend who later became her agent, helped her sell it to Granta. *In the City by the Sea* began as a short story that she wrote for her undergraduate class at Hamilton College and which later became her master thesis in creative writing. Shona Ramaya, her thesis adviser at the University of Massachusetts, Amherst, had advised Shamsie to take her novel to an agent. The same agent had also had her aunt's book published from Virago. *In the City by the Sea* won the 1999 Prime Minister's Award for Literature in Pakistan and was also short listed for the John Llewellyn Rhys/Mail on Sunday award in Britain.

The novel describes a town divided, oppressed and humiliated. Karachi is a town where the only thing free is imagination and the only thing that can bring sanity to life is imagination. The country is driven by ethnic violence that pervades everything and makes normal life dangerous. It is defined by corruption of the powerful, which makes the entire concept of greatness illegitimate. It is oppressed by a military dictatorship, which is entirely arbitrary, protective of the corrupt and dangerous, and against anyone who says that the government should not function only for the greater well being of the rulers. And it is ruled by a sunken-eyed general who takes pleasure in house-arresting and killing his critics. In this country, in the city by the sea, lives 11-year-old Hasan.

Hasan comes from a close-knit family. His mother is an artist who also runs an art gallery. His father is an enlightened and modern man, allowing his sons and wives to think for themselves. His uncle is a political leader who heads a party that stands against corruption prevalent in the country. His neighbor is the beautiful Zehra for whom Hasan harbors feelings. Zehra on her part thinks Hasan to be too young, even though caring. Hasan has a suspicion that she prefers his cousin Najam whose only plus point is that he has hair growing on his chest.

Hasan's quiet life is filled with guilt at not having done anything to save the boy next door who fell down from the roof while flying a kite. Hasan suspects that the boy was trying to impress him by getting the kite to fly higher and therefore did not pay attention to where he was stepping. Had Hasan not been there to impress, the boy would not have tried to get the kite to go higher, and he would have watched his step and not fallen from the roof. Such are the serious problems with which a young man has to cope.

Living in the city by the sea, however, yields more problems. The one that comes to dominate Hasan's life is the house arrest of his uncle and the restrictions on the freedom of the family. Hasan sees how his uncle, father, neighbors, and others are helpless in the face of oppression by the government. The government also forces the closure of his mother's art gallery. Shamsie delves deep into young Hasan's mind and takes the reader back and forth from the reality of the world as it exists to the boy's very own private world of fantasy. Hasan's imagination houses his friends from another realm—goblins, knights, dragons, and what not. They help him out of his predicaments, clear his dilemmas, and provide him with the much-needed elements of fun and adventure in a world gone dangerous.

And Hasan knows why the dangers are there. Here, even a young boy is exposed to political currents, to the critiques of the government in which the elders participate. He also learns how to cock a snook at the oppressive regime without necessarily being too blatant. In a hilarious piece we have Hasan listening on to a telephonic conversation between Uncle Farooq who is on the other end of the line and his own beloved uncle Salman who is being detained. Farooq simply wants to know how Salman is doing. Salman is warned by his wife to be careful of what is said since Farooq is known to be close to the government. Having informed Farooq that all is well, and that he is enjoying the detention, Salman launches into a long description of how he spends his time growing, braiding, and maintaining his armpit hair.

Shamsie's second novel, *Salt and Saffron,* was published in the United States, England, Pakistan, and Italy. In 2000 she was listed as one of the Orange Futures Winners (21 great talents for the twenty-first century). The novel takes shape from the short story "Unspeakable Hunger." Set in London, Karachi, and the imagined region of Dard-e-Dil before Partition, Shamsie addresses issues that are parts of not just a Pakistani, but a South Asian diasporic reality. The questions that attract a reader's attention focus on the construction of one's own identity. Does leaving our country allow us to forget the constraints that we used to find ourselves bound in? Or do we seek to construct a new reality that partakes from both worlds?

Asking these questions in the center of the story is Aliya, 21, who has just finished the final semester at a university in the United States. En route to her annual summer holiday in Pakistan, she meets a young man, Khaleel, from "the wrong side of the city." As she slowly finds herself falling in love with him, the budding romance is quickly troubled by one word: *Liaquatabad,* the poor Karachi neighborhood where Khaleel's family lives. The disquieting divisions of class become even noisier as Aliya's inability to forget Khaleel, no matter how much her high-born family encourages it, prompts her to find the pieces of another love story troubled by the seemingly insurmountable class differences in Pakistani culture. Aliya starts to question her family history and begins a quest to find out what really happened to her "Not Quite Twin" Mariam Apa, who had run away with the family cook Masood.

The element of the myth of the "Not Quite Twins" brings another interesting angle to the story. With a genealogical chart that boasts of family members such as the Hairless Nawab and the Starched Aunts at the beginning of the book, the myth of the "Not Quite Twins," long descriptions of family histories that date back centuries as well as family histories affected by the partition, there are some obvious parallels to the writings of Salman Rushdie. However, where Rushdie belongs to that school of magical realism, Shamsie is strongly grounded in realism. Moreover, Aliya reveals at the beginning of the novel that she belongs to a family of storytellers and the entire novel unfolds in a series of stories periodically invoking the notion of storytelling, so much so that the narrative voice addressing the reader brings up the concept of orality, a strong part of the South Asian tradition.

It is also interesting to note the way in which Shamsie brings about a delightful amalgam of English and Urdu as well as witty wordplay that draws attention to itself. By infusing English with a Pakistani sensibility, Shamsie not only raises the important question of language but also manages to infect the novel with a definite sense of humor in sentences such as: "Racy desi viciously and vigorously checking you out. Sitting next to purple-haired woman." In addition, she paints pictures with her words, allowing us to glimpse bits and pieces of Lahore, its people, its culture, and (since one of the main characters is a cook) its food. Shamsie provides description of food that not only evokes gustatory pleasures but revives our imagination as well: "Curly shaped *jalai-*

bees, hot and gooey, that trickled sweet syrup down your chin when you bit into them; diced potatoes drowned in yogurt, sprinkled in spices; triangles of fried *samosas,* the smaller ones filled with mincemeat, the larger ones filled with potatoes and green chilies."

In *Kartography,* Karim and Raheen, now both in their early twenties, grow up together in the upper-middle-class enclaves of Karachi. Seeing each other's parents being good friends, these two were destined to be soul mates —as babies they sometimes even shared a crib. By 13, they enjoyed a coltishly close, taken-for-granted relationship. "Can angels lie spine to spine?" Raheen now wonders to herself "If not, how they must envy us humans." This self-consciously lyrical comment from the book's narrator sets the tone for the whole piece. This is a novel about Pakistan, about political violence, about growing up rich and comfortable in a land that is always on the edge of riot and despair. But it is also about a friendship that is predestined to turn into love.

Through a series of flashbacks to their 1970s childhood, bolstered by extracts from letters and phone conversations, Shamsie makes sure we focus on the ever-fluctuating relationship between these two young protagonists. But it's not that simple. Before either was born, Raheen's father was engaged to Karim's mother, Karim's father to Raheen's mother. It is common knowledge around Karachi that at some point and for some mysterious reason they swapped lovers. Slowly it dawns on Raheen that everyone except her knows, and also that something in her father's past behavior is stopping the morally serious, politically aware Karim from allowing himself to love her. Always restless, Karim leaves Karachi and travels to London, where he makes maps of his home city (Karachi is apparently to this day an unmapped city) that symbolizes his longing for both his home and for his childhood friend. Raheen meanwhile stays and waits and hopes for his eventual return.

Asked about her forthcoming novel, Shamsie conceded that it is set in present day Karachi and there is a mother-daughter relationship at the heart of it, with a little bit of mystery thrown in as well. Similar to her previous novels, this too will be set in the upper middle classes. Apart from fiction, Shamsie has also written essays, mostly on cultural and social issues—Partition and the effects of the bloody separation, religious intolerance, and political anarchy—subjects that she treats in her novels as well.

Rebecca Sultana

Further Reading

Hagestadt, Emma, and Boyd Tonkin. Rev. of *Kartography* by Kamila Shamsie. *The Independent* 12 Oct. 2002. 25 Nov. 2002 <http://www.tribuneindia.com/2002/20020526/spectrum/book3.htm>.

Kelapure, Pratibha. Rev. of *Salt and Saffron* by Kamila Shamsie. *South Asian Women's Forum* 25 Dec. 2000. 25 Dec. 2002 <http://www.sawf.org/newedit/edit12252000/bookrev.asp>.

Myerson, Julie. "Will They, Won't They . . . Who Cares?" Rev. of *Kartography* by Kamila Shamsie. *The Guardian* 3 Aug. 2002. 30 Nov. 2002 <http://www.books.guardian.co.uk/reviews/generalfiction/0,6121,768198,00.html>.

Raina, M. L. "Family Memories and Star Crossed Lovers." Rev. of *Salt and Saffron* by Kamila Shamsie. *The Tribune* 26 May 2002. 29 Nov. 2002 <http://www.tribuneindia.com/2002/20020526/spectrum/book3.htm>.

Shamsie, Muneeza. "They Made Their Mark." *The Dawn. Dawn Special Report: South Asia Century* 2000. 27 Dec. 2002 <http://www.dawn.com/events/century/culture.htm>.

Soni-Sharma, Kavita. "Political Tales from a Pak City." Rev. of *In the City by the Sea. The Tribune* 7 Mar. 1999. 26 Oct. 2002 <http://www.tribuneindia.com/2003/20030307/>.

Tripathi, Salil. Interview. "Karachi is the Only City I Want to Write About." *Tehelka.com* 30 Jan. 2001. <http://www.tehelka.com/channels/literary/2001/jan/29/printable/lr012901kamila1pr.htm> (22 Dec. 2002).

Short-Story Tradition

The search for a comprehensive generic definition of the short story often leads to more questions than conclusive answers about how accommodating it can be without becoming all-inclusive. However, Saros Cowasjee and Shiv K. Kumar write that the problem is not one of definition or agreement. It lies in "arriving at a criterion by which this sophisticated art form can be evaluated and enjoyed" (vii). They quote Eudora Welty who, writing in the *Atlantic Monthly* of February-March 1949, suggested that to begin with every good story has "mystery of allurement," which we eventually return to. "As we understand the story better, it is likely that the mystery does not necessarily decrease; rather it simply grows more beautiful" (viii).

Though the short story came into being in Indian literatures through Western contact, the oral tradition of ancient India has made a significant contribution to its historical development. The Panchatantra fables, some of which date back to 1500–500 B.C. spread through Europe in the Middle Ages through translation and have been assimilated into various cultures of traditional storytelling.

The first collection of short stories in English written by an Indian was Shoshee Chunder Dutt's "Realities of Indian Life: Stories collected from the Criminal Reports of India," published in London, in 1885. However the first prolific writer of short works was Cornelia Sorabji with the publication of *Love and Life behind the Purdah* (1901). Her four volumes of miscellaneous short fiction, sympathetic in overtone with an undercurrent of social reform, are studies of mostly Hindu and occasionally Parsi life in both princely and plebian circles (Naik 110). "The Doll Festival" in her second volume, *Sunbabies: Studies in the Childlife of India* (London, 1904), for instance, is a sensitive rendition of little Piyari's bafflement at civilized practices, like the ritual of burning away one's dolls by 12-year-old girls to purge their evils and moralizing lessons in school.

The writings in this genre in the 1920s and 1930s were done to "arouse national consciousness, to effect social reforms or to have moral and philosophical broodings" (Dwivedi 12). The writers of this period including K. S. Venkatramani, K. Nagarajan, and A. S. P. Ayyer mostly came from South India, the best known being T. L. Natesan, writing under the pseudonym Shankar Ram. His collections, *The Children from Kaveri* (1926) and *Creatures All* (1933), focus on the rustic life in Tamil Nadu. The tales of S. K. Chettur writing around the same time, while employing a variety of narrative modes, dealt with themes as varied as village feuds, murders, and the supernatural (Naik 177).

In the mid-30s, Mulk Raj Anand's *The Lost Child and Other Stories* ushered in a truly universal dimension to the short story. The consistent thread through Anand's prolific output, diverse in theme and style, is his overwhelming love for a cross-section of humanity. The urchins Gopal and Krishan and their relentless search for shelter in the title story, "Things Have a Way of Working Out," is documented with visual honesty and ends on a dramatically ironic note. In the title story of *A Pair of Mustachios and Other Stories* Anand takes a light-hearted look at people vainly clinging on to their ruinous past. The feathery creatures in his "Five Short Fables" from "Things Have a Way of Working Out and Other Stories" embody human passions of love, sacrifice and envy. Anand shows remarkable sensitivity in portraying his female protagonists, like Savitri and Lajwanti groaning under the yoke of patriarchy, or the sexually repressed Shrimati Sarojini Sharma, with the most adept use of psychological realism.

Nearly a decade later followed R. K. Narayan's first volume of short stories,

Malgudi Days (1941). Narayan's ironic treatment of life, rendered in lucid prose, results in a constant interplay between the serious and the trivial, with crises never unsettling the reader. The loveable postman Thanappa in "The Missing Mail," the gentle criminal Sidda in "Leela's friend" and the fraudulent Ramu in "A Career" are all readily accommodated in Narayan's Malgudi. In "Another Community" that appears in *Under the Banayan Tree and Other Stories* (1985) and "Martyr's Corner" from *Lawley Road and Other Stories* (1956), one finds a tone of regret rather than bitter criticism of mob fury. "A Hero," "Dodu," "Crime and Punishment," and "Sweets for Angels" betray the writer's keen understanding of a child's point of view at once carefree and impertinent.

The third of the Anand, Narayan, Rao triumvirate, Raja Rao grapples with Metaphysics, nationalism and social realism. The title story of the publication *The Cow of the Barricades* (1947) is a unique combination of symbolism and reality with the master probably a self-realized soul like Mahatma Gandhi (Srivastava 159). In "The True Story of Kanakpala, Protector of Gold" and "Javni," religious symbols and norms spill into people's lives often subduing them into submission. In *The Policeman and the Rose* (1978) Rao's overriding concerns are metaphysical. His latest volume, *On the Ganga Ghat* (1993) is set in a Banares checkered with taxi drivers, coolies, eccentric but endearing firewood sellers and collective memories.

A writer who has practically gone out of print but is nonetheless significant is Manjeri Isvaran. He has published 10 anthologies, the first being *The Naked Shingles* (1941). His stories are marked by a variety in characterization, situation, narrative strategies, and a concern with the supernatural.

Two major names associated with this genre during the early years of independent India are Khushwant Singh and Ruth Prawer Jhabvala. The late 1940s and subsequent decades also saw writers like Khwaja Ahmed Abbas, Ruskin Bond, Manoj Das, G. D. Khosla, and Manohar Malgaonkar make their debut. The reputations of Bhabani Bhattacharya, Anita Desai, Attia Hosain, Arun Joshi, Chaman Nahal, and Bunny Reuben as short-story writers, though formidable rest on a single anthology.

Khushwant Singh's stories, published in four volumes, thrive largely on the idiosyncrasies of the Sikh community seen among other stories in "Mr. Singh and the Color Bar" and "Abroad and Not-So-Innocent," published in *A Bride for the Sahib and Other Stories* (1967). In the title story that ends on a tragic note the quirks of other Indian communities are pointed out. "Man How the Government of India Run" that looks at the inactivity of our government offices, embodies the racy dialogue of his prose. The earlier "The Voice of God and Other Stories" (1957) is definitely more satiric in tone. The title story and "The Riot" are remarkably contemporary in their exposure of power politics and the utter thoughtlessness and bestiality of mob fury respectively. In "The Mark of Vishnu" old values and beliefs prove so costly that they result in their most ardent believer Gunga Ram's death.

Ruth Prawer Jhabvala has published five works of short fiction, the first entitled *Like Birds, Like Fishes and Other Stories* (1956). Her tales explore the often-thwarted expectations of her lonely characters negotiating different worlds. In " A Bad Woman" from *An Experience of India* (1972), Chameli is indebted to a much older Sethji for delivering her from an unhappy marriage. Her subsequent lonely existence is alleviated by a younger boy, Ravi, who soon turns abusive. "A Course of English Studies" is a sensitively portrayed, failed romance between a young student and an older professor with a fair share of lighter moments. In the recently published *East unto Upper East: Plain Tales from New York and New Delhi* (1998), Jhabvala's characters are not easy to condemn, though they fly in the face of societal mores, as in "Expiation."

Khwaja Ahmed Abbas launches a scathing attack on social structures plagued with poverty, ignorance, inefficiency, hypocrisy, selfishness, and unemployment in works such as *Rice and Other Stories* and *Thousand Nights on a Bed of Stones and Other Stories.* His two volumes, *Blood and Stones and Other Stories* and *Cages of Freedom and Other Stories,* betray his concerns with political problems like those of partition, bloodshed, and refugee influx (Dwivedi, 18).

Ruskin Bond basks in the sights and sounds closest to him in his representative collection *The Night Train at Deoli and Other Stories.* The beauty of the mystery of his favorite "Night Train at Deoli" lies in its not being unraveled. "The Woman on Platform 8" is truly moving for the things it says as much as for the things that it hints at. "The Boy Who Broke the Bank" deliberately uses exaggeration to comment on the human propensity for rumor, and "His Neighbor's Wife" has a rather dramatic ending. "The Leopard," narrated in a leisurely manner is about the tranquility of "green pastures" being rudely shattered by encroaching men.

Manoj Das's stories, spanning seven collections, are imbued with social realism, satire, psychological revelation, and human contact with supra or infrahuman elements, as seen in "The Crocodile's Lady" (Raja 118). His most widely anthologized story, "The Submerged Valley" reveals a unique act of humanity and consequently a surprising unearthing of character in the face of inevitable social change. "The Tree" is the repository of ritual, myth, life, death, and reincarnation, elements that are inextricably linked in the Indian psyche. Das's all-pervasive humor

stems from exploring the idiosyncrasies of the loveable Bhola-Grandpa, Shri Moharana, Babu Virkishore, and Binu "the murderer," within highly incongruous situations often told from a child's point of view.

Manohar Malgaonkar laces his fast-paced narratives in *A Toast in Warm Wine* (1974) with delightful intrigues. Name-dropping, flaunting of imaginary wealth, and role-playing make "A Pinch of Snuff" an entertaining read. "Cargo From Singapore" and "Bachcha Lieutentant" betray a reportorial style of narration. "Bachcha Lieutenant" from *Bombay Beware* (1975) is drawn from his experiences in World War II and contains slices of irony, examining the human stories that make up wartime tragedies. In the stories that he tries to replicate instances of Indian history and fortunes of families, he is believed to be less successful.

The title story of Anita Desai's maiden collection written in poetic prose, "Games At Twilight" (1978) is a fine rendition of the magnified impressions of a child's untutored mind. In "Studies in the Park" the disillusioned protagonist Suno unwittingly embarks on a process of discovery, triggered off by the sight of a beautiful face of a dying woman. "Sale" becomes progressively more tragic and the artist is reduced to a helpless salesman who cannot let his own moods dictate his sales pitch, for that is the very source of his and his family's livelihood.

Arun Joshi's volume, *The Survivor* (1975), has been noted for its technical finesse, variety of subject matter, its crystallizing of the abstract in concrete imagery, and its pan-Indian consciousness (Rao 45). His protagonists are disillusioned individuals who achieve insight by outgrowing their trappings that leave them gasping for breath. Mr. Kewal Kapoor, in the title story, and Mr. Lele, in "A Trip for Mr. Lele" are both redeemed by relating themselves to their daughters. In the more cryptic vision of "The Boy with the Flute," Mr. Sethi's redemption is delivered by an angelic boy who is presented almost as an apparition.

The last two decades have seen the arrival of writers like Rohinton Mistry, R. Raj Rao, Dina Mehta, and Anita Mehta on the short-story scene. Novelists such as Kiran Nagarkar, Upamanyu Chatterjee, Shashi Tharoor, and renowned poets like Keki Daruwalla and Shiv K. Kumar have also published a work or two of short fiction. Though their output is relatively limited, they all share with their predecessors, in varying degrees, the creative urge to show rather than tell, confronting the reader each time with a mystery that can only become more beautiful.

Bapsi Sidhwa.

Suhaan Mehta

Further Reading

Cowasjee, Saros, and Shiv K. Kumar. Introduction. *Modern Indian Short Stories*. Eds. Saros Cowasjee and Shiv K. Kumar. New Delhi: Oxford UP, 1982. vii–x.

Dwivedi, Amar Nath. Introduction. *Studies in Contemporary Indian English Short Story*. Ed. Amar Nath Dwivedi. New Delhi: B. R. Publishing, 1991. 9–21.

Naik, M. K. *A History of Indian English Literature*. New Delhi: Sahitya Akademi, 1982.

Raja, P. " Manoj Das." *Studies in Contemporary Indian English Short Story*. Ed. Amar Nath Dwivedi. New Delhi: B. R. Publishing, 1991. 117–23.

Rao, Krishna A. V. "Arun Joshi." *Studies in Contemporary Indian English Short Story*. Ed. Amar Nath Dwivedi. New Delhi: B. R. Publishing, 1991. 45–61.

Srivastava, Narsingh. "Raja Rao." Studies in Contemporary Indian English Short Story. Ed. Amar Nath Dwivedi. New Delhi: B. R. Publishing, 1991. 147–67.

Sidhwa, Bapsi

Bapsi Sidhwa, a leading Pakastani writer, was born on August 11, 1938, in Karachi, and then moved to Lahore with her family who belong to the Parsi minority group. As a child, she contracted polio and spent much of her early life as an invalid, reading voraciously. Growing up in Lahore she witnessed the human devastation caused by the political and religious conflicts and persecution associated with the 1947 partition of the South Asian continent that ultimately created Pakistan. In 1956, she earned her B.A. from Kinnaird College for Women, and after an early marriage to Gustad Kermani (deceased), she married Noshir R. Sidhwa in 1963. Much of her early adult life was spent as an upper-class Pakistani wife and mother of three children. Inspired by a story she heard on a family vacation about a young woman who was forced into a marriage and, when she tried to escape, was hunted down and killed, Sidhwa began to write her first novel, *The Bride,* followed by three more novels and various short stories and essays. Since moving to the United States in 1983 and becoming a citizen in 1992, Sidhwa has taught at St. Thomas University in Houston, the University of Houston, Columbia University, and Mount Holyoke College; in addition, she continues her writing career, giving frequent readings and conducting writing workshops, along with making regular visits back to Pakistan.

Over the past two decades, Sidhwa has published four novels: *The Crow Eaters*

(Jonathan Cape, 1980; St. Martin's, 1981); *The Bride* (Jonathan Cape, 1983; St. Martin's, 1983)*; Ice-Candy Man* (William Heinemann, 1988; Penguin, 1989), published in the United States as *Cracking India* (Milkweed, 1991); and *An American Brat* (Milkweed, 1993).

Since Bapsi Sidhwa began publishing fiction in 1980, she has received numerous literary awards, including the Pakistan National honors of the Patras Bokhri award for *The Bride* in 1985; a National Endowment of the Arts grant in 1986 and 1987 to support the completion of *Cracking India;* the Literaturepreis from Germany for *Ice-Candy Man* in 1991; the Sitara-i-Imtaiz, National Honor in the Arts, Pakistan in 1991; a nomination for Notable Book of the Year from the American Library Association in 1991 for *Cracking India;* and the Lila Wallace–Readers' Digest Writer's Award in 1993. Her works have now been translated into Russian, French, German, and Urdu; and in 1999, Deepa Mehta completed a film adaptation of *Cracking India,* entitled *Earth.* In addition to writing, Sidhwa has been active in social causes, including representing Pakistan at the Asian Women's Congress in 1975, helping to establish the Destitute Women's and Children's Home in Lahore, and organizing the Houston chapter of the Asia Society.

Ambreen Hai describes Sidhwa as a postcolonial feminist writer who confronts "a variety of historic constraints" and is "situated between polarized oppositions of gender, ethnicities, and ideology"—"a complicated and crucial endeavor" (382). In exploring these "borders" in all of her novels, Sidhwa examines the theme of injustice: the injustice toward women, who must struggle to overcome repressive social situations that deny them individuality and independence; the injustice toward religious intolerance, particularly toward the Parsi minority, but also toward Hindus, Sikhs, and Muslims; the injustice toward political unrest, especially in the historical context of the partitioning of Pakistan; and the injustice toward cultural prejudice experienced by minorities in Pakistan and immigrants in the United States. Sidhwa claims that she is driven to uncover injustices, the "lies so hard at the core of man's nature that neither education nor civilizing influence has so far tempered" (Dhawan and Kapadia 31).

Although her themes are serious, Sidhwa often employs humor, marked by irony, satire, caricature, or buffoonery, in an effort to make her writing entertaining and educational. Generally, her novels employ a linear, realist narrative structure, focusing heavily on character development. One of her great contributions has been her handling of language. Although her first language is Gujarati, Urdu her second, and English her third, Sidhwa has chosen to write in English, a language she feels is rich and flexible. By incorporating the rhythms and idioms of Gujarati into her English, she feels her language achieves a freshness and objectivity caused by twisting English to change its "inner structure to suit [her] new expressions" (Jussawalla 214–15).

Bapsi Sidhwa's first published novel, *The Crow Eaters* (her second novel), provides a rare glimpse into the Parsi community, a marginalized ethnic group in South Asia. It is an account of the Junglewallas, a Parsi-Zoroastrian family that emigrates during the time of the British Raj from Central India to Lahore, Pakistan, in order to gain greater economic status. Using unscrupulous business practices and manipulative tactics with the ruling British officials, Faredoon "Freddy" Junglewalla and his family manage to prosper; although he presents a philanthropic façade, his actions, including arson and bribery, reveal his hypocrisy. The novel involves the lively interaction of the various family members, as they expand their business; in the process, as K. Nirupa Rani suggests, they are often caught in the comic struggle to adapt to "a changing social milieu and identity crisis" (Dhawan and Kapadia, 128), along with dealing with generational conflicts. Putli, Freddy's wife and member of the older Parsi generation, is scandalized when her daughter Yamin walks ahead of her husband, when her daughter-in-law Tanya wears a revealing sari, when her son Billy shows preference for British customs; or when Yazdi, her poet-escapist son, announces that he wants to marry an Anglo-Indian woman of questionable respectability.

When *The Crow Eaters* was first published, the Parsi community in India and Pakistan criticized what they perceived to be a negative depiction of Parsi life and values. However, many critics praise the humorous handling of the characters and the Parsi community. Novy Kapadia, concludes that, although the characterization of Yazdi, which is left vague, is a structural flaw, the range of family figures, all fully developed and treated with "tolerance and mild corrective irony" are not "types" (Dhawan and Kapadia 133–35). In addition, Alamgir Hashmi suggests that, while the plot at times lags, the characters are "atypical" and memorable because Bapsi Sidhwa looks at her characters, not as an outsider, but "as a member of the Parsi minority . . . who knows her people's secrets, real strengths, and foibles" (Dhawan and Kapadia 139).

The Bride, Sidhwa's second published novel, is set in the Himalayas and Karakorams and focuses on issues of women and marriage. It is the story of a Muslim Punjabi girl, Zaitoon, who is orphaned by the Partition conflict and is adopted by a Kohistani tribesman, Qasim, who has also lost his family. Rescuing Zaitoon, Qasim escapes to Lahore, but, in an effort to re-establish his ties with his people, he arranges a marriage for Zaitoon to a mountain tribesman. Fearing for her life, Zaitoon decides to flee from her abusive husband, Sakhi, but is hunted by the tribe until she narrowly escapes. Interwoven with Zaitoon's story is that of Carol, an American woman who is married to Farukh, works in Pakistan, and faces various cultural and personal conflicts.

Fawzia Afzal-Khan concludes that, in creating a character like Zaitoon, who refuses to submit to societal expectations, Sidhwa "challenges the patriarchal culture and values of Indian-Pakistani society" so that her "ideological stance functions simultaneously as a strategy for challenging 'the system' dominated by men and a strategy of 'liberation' for the female self that remains marginalized within that system" (272). Furrukh Khan argues that Sidhwa uses the setting of the Partition as a recurring motif of "dis-location," including the displacement of Zaitoon as a woman in a male-dominated society; the displacement of Carol, who is " 'partition-ed' from her home and culture" (Dhawan and Kapadia 144); the displacement of Qasim, who has "lost connection with his past and his people" (145). He criticizes the novel as overly pedantic but concludes that Sidhwa "is able to formulate a poignant tale of a woman's struggle to fight and survive in contemporary society" (150). On the other hand, Indira Bhatt, argues that the strength of the novel is Sidhwa's ability to depict the narrator's inner journey from fantasy to reality and her ability to bring "to life and light" a "barbaric world of uncivilized people" (Dhawan and Kapadia 157).

Bapsi Sidhwa's third novel, *Cracking India (Ice-Candy Man),* relying on some autobiographical elements, is the story told by a young Parsi girl crippled by polio who witnesses the ethnic and religious atrocities associated with the Partition as it unfolds in Lahore, Pakistan. The novel begins with a description of the family and domestic characters, particularly Ayah, Lenny's sensuous, Hindu nursemaid, who protects her but also introduces Lenny to the world of male-female relationships.

Through various conversations and events, Lenny is exposed to the prejudices and growing conflict between Hindus, Muslims, Sikhs, Christians, and Parsis as they operate in her small world but then expand beyond to the larger horrors that culminate in the Partition, the "cracking of India." The climax occurs for Lenny when a gang of Muslim men, led by the Ice-Candy Man (a character who has been one of Ayah's admirers), enters her parents' home and abducts Ayah after Lenny, trusting the Ice-Candy M, exposes her whereabouts. When the family eventually discovers that the Ice-Candy Man has married Ayah and has turned her into a prostitute, Lenny's Godmother (aunt) initiates the rescue of Ayah, who in the end refuses to be a victim.

Critics have focused on various thematic and narrative elements of *Cracking India*. A few reviewers have pointed out the inconsistencies in the narrative voice, which at times shifts into that of an adult; however, other critics, such as Robert L. Ross points out that although the shift at times seems odd, the "narrator is not a child after all, but the child in the adult" (Dhawan and Kapadia 185). Jussawalla suggests that the use of the child-narrator effectively presents the loss of innocence but empowering experience of a character that gains "both knowledge of her body as well as knowledge of politics and otherness" (203). In addition, many critics have focused on the feminist perspective that derives from the characterization and central role of Ayah, who, according to Fawzia Afzal-Khan "symbolizes the anti-victim stance that Sidhwa advocates for women"; in the novel she "presents female bonding and feminine empathy as antidotes to the violence and corruption wrought by centuries of male dominance in religion and politics" (280). Ambreen Hai explores the "border feminism" of *Cracking India* and praises the novel's depiction of the "restorative work performed by women of the Parsee community, border women who

seek to heal the painful cracks in this partitioned Indian land-as-body" (407), but objects to the way that Sidhwa depicts the "violation of Ayah as exclusively the province of a rabid lower class maleness. It fails to acknowledge its own complicated fascination for and repudiation of that figure—the very figure that it seeks to ally itself with but needs to differentiate from" (416).

An American Brat is set primarily in the United States and explores issues of intercultural conflict and the difficulties of maintaining a sense of one's community in the new global context, particularly in intercultural marriages. The story focuses on Feroza Ginwalla, a young Parsi woman who grows up in Lahore, Pakistan, during the dictatorship of General Zia ul-Haq. Fearing for her in the climate of religious intolerance and political unrest, Feroza's family sends her to the United States to attend college in Idaho. There she is exposed to American friends and culture. Through the process of cultural exposure and self-discovery, she gains an appreciation of her Parsi culture, but also comes to appreciate her new independence, and chooses, in the end, to live on her own in the United States.

In this novel, Bapsi Sidhwa approaches the new subject of differences between the Eastern culture of her childhood in which a rebel is "finished off by the society for rebelling" (Montenegro 47) and the American culture of her more recent adulthood in which independence is valued. Although most American critics praise *An American Brat* for its exploration of the immigrant's encounter with American culture, other critics like Niaz Zaman argue that Sidhwa is at her best in this novel when she is describing her Parsi community (Dhawan and Kapadia 207). Although some critics like Novy Kapadia applaud this novel for its blend of humor and social realism, and Sidhwa's uses of irony, parody, and slang to create humor

(191), some critics feel she tends to "over-write" and project some discomfort with her American subject. Geoffrey Kain praises *An American Brat* as "a tale of continuity" that explores "the archetypal America of independence, individualism, open vistas, and energetic improvisation" and as "a tale of rupture" in which Feroza "is almost altogether lost to extended family, to her religion, to modes of traditional behavior, to native place and culture as she is 'swallowed' by the seductive giant of America" (245).

Although Sidhwa initially struggled to get her novels published, her reputation has grown and the critical reception of Sidhwa's four novels has continued to be enthusiastic. Because of her life experiences, Bapsi Sidhwa "insists on seeing herself as a Pakastani writer with an awareness of a Western audience," making her part of a unique group of writers whose broad, global vision is shaped by the "double migration" (Dhawan and Kapadia 9–10).

Ruth Forsythe

Further Reading

Afzal-Khan, Fawzia. "Bapsi Sidhwa." *International Literature in English: Essays on the Major Writers*. Ed. Robert L. Ross. New York: Garland, 1991. 271–81.

Dhawan, R. K., and Novey Kapadia, eds. *The Novels of Bapsi Sidhwa*. New Dehli: Prestige, 1996.

Hai, Ambreen. "Border Work, Border Trouble: Postcolonial Feminism and the Ayah in Bapsi Sidhwa's *Cracking India*." *Modern Fiction Studies* 46.2 (2000): 379–426.

Jussawalla, Feroza. "Interview with Bapsi Sidhwa." *Interviews with Writers of the Post-Colonial World*. Eds. Feroza Jussawalla and Reed Way Dasenbrock. Jackson: UP of Mississippi, 1992. 198–221.

Kain, Geoffrey. "Rupture as Continuity: Migrant Identity and 'Unsettled' Perspective in Bapsi Sidhwa's *American Brat*." *Asian American Literature in the International Context: Readings on Fiction, Poetry, and Performance*. Eds. Rocio G. Davis and Sami Ludwig. New Brunswick: Transaction, 2002. 237–46.

Montenegro, David. "Bapsi Sidhwa." *Points of Departure: International Writers on Writing and Politics*. Ann Arbor: U of Michigan P, 1991. 26–61.

Sister of My Heart by Chitra Banerjee Divakaruni

The novel, by Chitra Banerjee Divakaruni, is developed from a short story, "The Ultrasound" *(Arranged Marriage)*. Divakaruni was born in India and educated in India and the United States. After using magical realism in her first novel, *Mistress of Spices* (1997), she writes a realistic novel with melodramatic touches, but interweaves magic through references to stories told by some of her characters in *Sister of My Heart* (1999). The novel is set primarily in Calcutta, hometown of Divakaruni's own preimmigrant life; though it later moves to other settings such as another Indian town, Bardhaman, and to California.

The plot of *Sister of My Heart* revolves around the lives of two women who are distant cousins biologically; but destined to be born in the same house on the same night, they grow up together as inseparable sisters. Anju is heir to the illustrious Chatterjee family, but Sudha's family lineage is shrouded in mystery. Long before the girls were born, Sudha's father, Gopal, presented himself at the doorstep of Anju's father, Bijoy Chatterjee, and declared that he was the son of Bijoy's runaway uncle, who had made his home in East Bengal. His father was dead and his home lost due to the partition of India. Fleeing from his erstwhile hometown, he now seeks his cousin's help to build a new life in Calcutta. Bijoy opens his heart and his home to his cousin and his newlywed wife. Bijoy's wife and widowed sister also embrace the couple. For some time, they live harmoniously in the old ancestral Calcutta mansion. But Bijoy's family fortune is dwindling, and Gopal presents a fantastic scheme of traveling to a cave of rubies in the dense Sundarban jungles, which will change their fortunes. Leaving pregnant wives behind, Bijoy and Gopal go on this perilous quest, but never return.

Sudha and Anju are born the night their family receives the news of their fathers' deaths. They are brought up by three mothers without any male guardian. The intimacies between the two sisters, both everyday and profound; the old mythical stories their widowed aunt "pishi" tells, Sudha retells, and Anju questions; their juvenile adventures; resistance to repressive traditions; Sudha's unexpected romance with a man she meets in a cinema hall; Anju and Sudha's arranged marriages; and their different postmarriage experiences move the story at a fast pace. Through it all, one feels the deep love one sister has for another and the sacrifices each is willing to make. Sudha gives up her romantic plan of eloping with Ashok so that Anju's impending marriage with Sunil is not hampered by the taint of her elopement. The mystery of her father's relationship to the Chatterjee family, and his role in leading Anju's father to his death prompt Sudha to make her sacrifice as a payback for her father's wrongs. But when Sudha decides to abandon her marriage to save her unborn daughter from the punishment of abortion that her husband's family has decreed for the girl child, a pregnant Anju works tirelessly to buy Sudha's plane ticket to America. While the girl Dayita (Beloved) is born to Sudha, Anju has a miscarriage. Through all these troubles, the two sisters' love for each other grows stronger; and they are reunited as Sudha joins Anju in America in search of a new life.

Sister of My Heart is told in the alternate voices of Sudha and Anju, each one being the narrator of alternate chapters. The beautiful Sudha is gentle and quiet. She wants to be a good daughter in a traditional sense and is more amenable to the parameters set by the mothers. She is a believer of Hindu myths and tales and weaves them into her narration to interpret life's realities; while Anju is rebellious, always questioning the old tales that Sudha reveres. She takes the role of prince to Sudha's distressed princess in their childhood games; yet when Sudha is put to the test, she walks the boldest path. The novel is divided into two sections: "The Princess in the Palace of Snakes" and "The Queen of Swords"; it is Sudha who is transformed into the queen of swords from a princess imprisoned in the palace of snakes. This novel portrays two beautiful and strong protagonists, taking readers into the core of their hearts' desires as well as bringing through their voices fiery criticism of society's injustices against women. Its language is metaphoric and sensuous. Although some aspects of the plot are melodramatic and some characters appear formulaic, the sisters can make their way into most readers' hearts.

The reviews of *Sister of My Heart* have been mixed. Jamison in *People* magazine calls it an enchanting novel that presents conflicts with "deliciously operatic heights," yet creates "characters that come alive as real, modern women." Jamison admires how Divakaruni makes the smells and colors of Calcutta come to life with her "palpable" descriptions (41–42). But Anderson Tepper in *The New York Times Book Review* writes that in spite of the book's colorful surface qualities, its story lacks a believable heart (21). Williams in *Library Journal* writes that the plot is "contrived," but the novel is "still an engaging read, filled with moving, tender moments" (147). Published only at the end of the twentieth century, this novel has yet to receive in-depth critical explorations.

Husne Jahan

Further Reading

Curtis, Sarah. "Dreams Come True." Rev. of *Sister of My Heart* by Chitra Banerjee Divakaruni. *Times Literary Supplement* 5045 (10 Dec. 1999): 21.

Jamison, Laura. Rev. of *Sister of My Heart* by Chitra Banerjee Divakaruni. *People* 51.6 (15 Feb. 1999): 41–42.

Nazareth, Peter. Rev. of *Sister of My Heart* by Chitra Banerjee Divakaruni. *World Literature Today* 73.4 (Autumn 1999): 819.

Tepper, Anderson. Rev. of *Sister of My Heart* by Chitra Banerjee Divakaruni. *New York Times Book Review* 104.16 (18 Apr. 1999): 21.

Williams, Wilda. Rev. of *Sister of My Heart* by Chitra Banerjee Divakaruni. *Library Journal* 124.1 (Jan. 1999): 147.

Spivak, Gayatri Chakravorty

Gayatri Chakravorty Spivak is one of the world's leading literary and cultural theorists. She is widely known and greatly respected for her groundbreaking work in feminist and postcolonial theory. Currently, Spivak is Avalon Foundation Professor of the Humanities at Columbia University. She was born in Calcutta on February 24, 1942, into a middle-class urban family and obtained her undergraduate degree from the University of Calcutta in 1959. Spivak completed her graduate studies at Cornell University in 1967 under the directorship of renowned theorist, Paul de Man. Her dissertation on Irish poet W. B. Yeats was published as *Myself I Must Remake: The Life and Poetry of W. B. Yeats* (1974). Two years later, Spivak's translation of Jacques Derrida's *De la grammatologie* was published under the title, *Of Grammatology* (1976). The book was accompanied by a lengthy, erudite "Translator's Preface" that would secure Spivak a permanent place in poststructural theory and criticism. To some, this preface remains one of the key works published on poststructural theory since its zenith in the late 1960s. To date, she has published five books and a vast number of influential essays (Landry and Maclean).

Since the publication of *Of Grammatology,* Spivak has written numerous theoretical works that engage multiple philosophical models and fields of study. This has resulted in the development of a distinctively eclectic *oeuvre.* Spivak's work navigates poststructuralism, feminism, Marxism, psychoanalysis, pedagogy, and postcolonial studies. Although she is probably best known as a postcolonial critic—occupying one-third of the distinguished postcolonial triad with Edward Said and Homi Bhabha—in truth it is difficult to pinpoint which of these theoretical engagements is most important for her. Each one infuses all she writes in different ways. Her feminist theorizations are inseparable from the work she has done engineering postcolonial and cultural studies; likewise, her Marxism cannot be detached from her feminist or postcolonial concerns. The absence of a palpable leading allegiance is not all that surprising considering her position as a deconstructive critic. In fact, the methodological apparatus of deconstruction may constitute her only uninterrupted critical commitment.

In the recent documentary film, *Derrida,* Jacques Derrida states that a fundamental goal of deconstruction is to engender a "thinking mother," to undo the long-standing patriarchal bias of Western philosophy, the rigid historical reality of the "philosopher *king.*" Perhaps Spivak's lasting influence as a contemporary thinker makes her an example of the manifestation of this goal. Her work is some of the most provocative and resonant scholarship produced in recent decades; and in this regard, she has only a handful of rivals. As the colleague, friend, and strenuous critic, Terry Eagleton notes, Spivak "has probably done more long-term political good, in pioneering feminist and post-colonial studies within global academia than almost any of her theoretical colleagues" (Smith). With the publication of key works—"Three Women's Texts and a Critique of Imperialism" (1985), "Can the Subaltern Speak" (1988), and *The Postcolonial Critic: Interviews, Strategies, Dialogues* (1990)—we have in play the operation of a variety of ideas of consequence for the academy.

Spivak's work on colonial discourse theory has been valuable to many academics. Colonial discourse theory analyzes the various strategies by which colonized natives and colonial territories are constructed within imperial discourse, including "worlding" (her coinage) and "othering." "Worlding" refers to the way colonized terrains are brought into colonial discourse ("worlded") *as* colonial territories. They are designated "European" since defined in Eurocentric terms, for example, as individuals and areas are presided over, mapped or named by British representatives. Crucial to Spivak's work in this area are processes of "othering" and "Othering" (capitalized). The first usage involves the debasement of native populations. As Spivak has shown, this is exemplified in the character construction of the Creole woman in Charlotte Brontë's *Jane Eyre,* Bertha Mason, who is described in terms suggesting she is "not yet human"—she "groveled" and "snatched," she had a "grizzled" "mane" of hair, she "growled like some strange wild animal" ("Three Women's Texts" 899). Conversely, *Jane Eyre* also embodies the second usage—Othering—through its creation of Jane as a subject. She is constituted in opposition to Bertha, through her difference from this 'inferior' being, and thus represents the "soul-making" force—the colonizer—that will cultivate the native population and bring them *into* humanness ("Three Women's Texts" 900). The 1985 essay, "Three Women's Texts and a Critique of Imperialism," is a model work of postcolonial feminist criticism illustrating both uses of the term. Additionally, Spivak has written volumes on matters of postcolonial subjectivity. Her speculations on catachresis—Spivak's word for appropriation in the context of colonization (Ashcroft et al. 34)—and subaltern agency and voice have been widely discussed and debated. The subaltern is a figure of inferior rank that, for Spivak, is defined centrally by its *difference* from the privileged, enfranchised elite; by definition, then, the subaltern is a disenfranchised individual lacking social agency and "voice" (Landry and Maclean). In response to critiques of the essay in which these ideas were first articulated, "Can the Subaltern Speak?" Spivak devised the idea of "strategic essentialism," which has been one of her most controversial theories since, as a rule, essentialism runs counter to principles of deconstruction and contradicts a number of her earlier assertions. Finally, the fusion of feminist and postcolonial theory has been significant throughout Spivak's career. She can easily be credited with giving rise to this important conjunction in which "third world" women are brought *into* feminist discourse. As Columbia University colleague Edward Said states, Spivak "pioneered the study in literary theory of non-Western women" (Smith).

With the publication of her 1999 book, *A Critique of Postcolonial Reason: Toward a History of the Vanishing Present,* she endeavored either to distance herself from postcolonial theory or to remake it. Even though Spivak's work as a postcolonial critic has been largely influential, she insists that her singular classification along these lines is incorrect. In this text, she is concerned about the way postcolonial theory might pose certain hazards to its own areas of concern. For instance, this body of work risks functioning as a prop for neocolonial initiatives by erroneously constructing colonization as a thing of the past. Additionally, despite its absolute necessity as a discipline, Spivak fears that postcolonial studies "is becoming a substantial subdisciplinary ghetto" (*A Critique of Postcolonial Reason* 1). Ultimately, the book is an attempt to recreate the character and purpose of postcolonial criticism, in part to save postcolonial studies from academic ghettoization. Thus, the book is best viewed as an internal critique rather than a distancing maneuver.

There is a way in which, despite the variety of speculative fields traversed, Spivak's work has always revolved around a consistent grouping of linked issues. Her *oeuvre* constitutes a series of commentaries on transnational globalization that view its effects through specific, consistent lenses: economic (her Marxism: the colonized subject, the subaltern), gender (her feminism: female subjectivity and subjectification), and the conjunctions of the subject (her "native informant") with philosophy (deconstruction) and literature (criticism). And it is in this text that such concerns emerge as the nexus of Spivak's thought. *A Critique of Postcolonial Reason* is the masterwork in which all of her earlier thinking culminates. On the one hand, this book is a response to earlier collections, like *The Postcolonial Critic* and *In Other Worlds,* but it also includes reworkings of two influential and widely anthologized essays. Chapter Two, "Literature," expands and revises "Three Women's Texts and a Critique of Imperialism," and Chapter Three, "History," includes a rewrite of "Can the Subaltern Speak?" Like the poet Yeats, a deconstructive cultural theorist *remakes* herself by fashioning a self-critique. This makes it a tangible display of deconstructive principles. The primary supposition of all deconstructive criticism—that texts deconstruct themselves—is brought to light by the critic in the context of her own work. Thus, she is *devotedly* deconstructive, which makes Spivak exceptional in the academic world and signifies her development as one of philosophy's "thinking mothers."

The fact that Spivak was educated in the West and has been heavily influenced by Western philosophy has been a point of criticism, of both Spivak and postcolonial theory generally. Additionally, most of her critical writing has centered on works of Western literature. As she insists, "I am a Europeanist" (Smith). Other critics have complained of the Western bias inherent in Spivak and Bhabha's writings, citing postcolonial theory as a form of neocolonialism. Another area of contention, and probably her harshest criticism to date, regards Spivak's writing style. Friends and foes alike define her writing in disparaging terms, like "preposterous" or "pretentiously opaque" (Smith). Despite such complaints, Spivak's work is widely read and taught and has been deeply influential in the academic world.

Maureen E. Ruprecht Fadem

Further Reading

Ashcroft, Bill, Gareth Griffiths, and Helen Tiffin, eds. *Post-Colonial Studies: The Key Concepts.* New York: Routledge, 2000.

Childs, Peter, and Patrick Williams, eds. "Spivak and the Subaltern." *An Introduction to Post-Colonial Theory.* Essex, England: Prentice Hall, 1997. 157–184.

Landry, Donna, and Gerald Maclean, eds. *The Spivak Reader.* New York: Routledge, 1996.

Smith, Dinita. "Creating a Stir Wherever She Goes." *The New York Times* 2 Feb. 2002. <http://query.nytimes.com/search/articlepage.html?res=9F07E3D9153CF93AA35751C0A9649C8B63>.

Spivak, Gayatri. *A Critique of Postcolonial Reason: Toward a History of the Vanishing Present.* Cambridge: Harvard UP, 1999.

———. "Three Women's Texts and a Critique of Imperialism." *Feminisms: An Anthology of Literary Theory and Criticism.* 2nd ed. Eds. Robyn Warhol and Diane Price Herndl. New Brunswick: Rutgers UP, 1997.

Sri Lankan Literature in English

Sri Lankan writing in English came of age only in the 1980s. There were a number of reasons for this phenomenon, which marks a qualitatively different experience from that of other countries in the Commonwealth. It was particularly odd too, inasmuch as English is still a very dominant language in Sri Lanka, and it achieved this status long before independence in 1948. However, for a long time it was seen as markedly a language of the elite, and therefore, the experiences delineated by writing in English were considered to be outside the indigenous experiences deemed typical of the country.

Thus what might be termed the literary elite, cultivating an almost artificial nationalism, was highly critical of writing in English. An English professor claimed a Sri Lankan would surely write in Sinhala or Tamil if he could; if he does not it is because he cannot, while the poet Lakdasa Wikkramasinha vowed to stop writing in the language of colonial masters he deplored. In the period immediately after independence then, there was a downgrading of those few who had in fact written in English in the early years of the century. They were seen as being antinational. Hence, both the aping of English writers and also a sometimes-subtle critique of the anglicized elite, in the work of pioneers such as S. J. Crowther, were ignored, in favor of what were termed as more authentic writings in the indigenous languages.

A result of this downgrading (though it could be argued that it was a reason for it) is that there is really just the one writer in the first 20 years after 1948 who repays study. This is the poet Patrick Fernando, but since he made clear the inspiration he derived from his Christian religion and his classical education, he epitomized the alienation that critics assumed marked anyone who wrote in English.

A change began in the 1960s with the commitment of two writers of fiction, Punyakante Wijenaike and James Goonewardene, who explored a range of Lankan experiences in the English language. Though initially it was their presentation of rural life that won plaudits, from an elite anxious to affirm its indigenous roots, in time it was recognized that their analysis of the class from which they themselves sprang was infinitely more illuminating. Goonewardene's bitter account, in "The Awakening of Dr. Kirthi," of the downward spiral of public services through relentless politicization deserves particular commendation in this regard.

Fortunately by the late 1970s, English writing had become more respectable. Apart from these two writers, Fernando continued to produce innovative and exciting work that, albeit still through his Western cultural framework, explored more distinctively Sri Lankan themes. Lakdasa Wikkramasinha meanwhile, though continuing his attacks on colonialism, with imagery based on his intimate knowledge of European cultural traditions, also used English to produce brilliant vignettes of the decadent aristocratic community to which he belonged. And perhaps more important than all these in ensuring that English writing was taken seriously were two university academics. One was Ediriweera Sarachchandra, professor of Sinhalese and generally accepted even now as the most influential Sri Lankan writer since independence. Better known as a dramatist, he also experimented with novels, the most famous of which was written after the 1971 insurgency in which many university students were killed. His anguished, largely autobiographical account of a professor torn by conscience, published as *Curfew and a Full Moon* in his own translation into English, helped to restore writing in English to respectability. And his next novel, based on his experiences as an ambassador in France, was written in English straight away.

The other important influence was also an academic from Peradeniya University, the poet and critic, Yasmine Gooneratne, who began *New Ceylon Writing* to showcase material she felt deserved greater attention. Though Gooneratne immigrated to Australia in the '70s, the work she began was continued in the *New Lankan Review,* and also in later editions of *Navasilu,* the journal of the English Association of Sri Lanka that, at its inception, had been more concerned with writing in Sinhala and Tamil.

These developments came in time for writing in English to flower during the 1980s, though the main reason for this was not especially pleasant. The ethnic problems of that period inspired very dynamic writing that, perhaps more objectively than writing in Sinhala or Tamil, made clear the intensity of the divisions that political manipulations since independence had produced. The poetry of Jean Arasanayagam and Richard de Zoysa in particular brought home the anguish of a nation driven by chauvinistic language policies as much as anything else. Meanwhile Punyakante Wijenaike brought to exploration of the psyche of rural communities traumatized by violence and war the same incisive subtlety she had shown with regard to the sexual and financial embarrassments of an elite unbalanced by social change.

The pioneering work of the 1980s, however, has now yielded pride of place to a recent phenomenon, namely the publication of books about the country by expatriates. Rienzie Crusz, a poet now in Canada, even though he dealt with Sri Lanka in his work was not for instance seen in this country as belonging to it in any distinctive sense. However, with Michael Ondaatje's *Running in the Family* the situation changed. Though Ondaatje had lived abroad for all his working life, and his initial work owed nothing to Sri Lanka, he was clearly moved by the visits he made to Sri Lanka as an adult. Much poetry came out of this, and most remarkably the memoir that was soon recognized as a brilliant evocation of the now lost lifestyle of an earlier generation. The success of that book marked the acceptability of Sri Lanka as a subject, while events in the country added to its attraction in this respect. It was much easier in the years that followed for writers, even if settled abroad, to deal with current Sri Lankan experience, since the dramatic political developments in the country lent themselves to exposition even from outside on the basis of what could seem universal concerns—ethnicity and violence.

Most prominent amongst these expatriates were Shyam Selvadurai and Romesh Gunesekera. The former, now in Canada, explored in *Funny Boy,* the racial tensions that developed over a decade and culminated into the riots of 1983. He depicted this in juxtaposition with the growing self-awareness of a homosexual in a society that demands conformity. The intertwining of themes that deal critically with questions of tolerance and individuality was brilliantly done for a first novel. Selvadurai's second, *Cinnamon Gardens,* which explores similar themes in a less fraught colonial period, had a quieter reception but also shows involvement with what seems still his home country.

Romesh Gunesekera on the other hand clearly sees himself as a British writer and deals mainly with immigrant perceptions. His work has been less well received amongst Sri Lankan critics who see it as "orientalization" of a classic sort. That, however, is due to his publicists who claim he portrays the anguish of a fractured land. Though what he describes, both in *Reef* and his very strange second novel *The Sandglass,* is not easily recognizable by Sri Lankans, the presentation of expatriate outlooks cannot be faulted. His work then raises questions of what constitutes postcolonialism in a context in which the discourse is still dominated by the colonial power.

Of the writers resident in Sri Lanka, the most prominent now, apart from Wijenaike, are Carl Muller and Jean Arasanayagam. The former writes about the Burgher community in a manner that has irritated its more socially prominent members. The Burghers saw themselves as descendants of Europeans, and therefore, more civilized than Sinhalese or Tamils, but Muller presents a working-class element that has absorbed all aspects of Sri Lankan culture with great gusto. He also deals with sexuality in a very direct but also very humorous manner that has appealed to many readers.

A more searching account of multiculturalism occurs in the work of Jean Arasanayagam, also Burgher, but married to a Tamil and so caught up as a victim of race riots during the 1980s. Her poetry, anodyne before, moved into a strident political phase and has since explored various aspects of identity that have been fractured by recent problems. Her work is the best example today of Sri Lankan writing engaging at a profound level with the hybridity the politicians cannot deal with. More recently she has also emerged as a writer of fiction, and a few collections of short stories have been published in India to general acclaim.

At the risk of seeming parochial, I should also mention my own work, since it is the first by a Sri Lankan still resident within this county to be published in Europe, in translation in Italy. *Servants,* which explores social changes in the country over the last century through the shifting relationships between different classes, was short listed for the Premio Nonino. Other novels such as *Acts of Faith,* initially published in India, deal more directly with the political dimensions of the ethnic conflict, and the influence of India.

Meanwhile, in the last decade, several young writers have begun to deal in English with a range of Sri Lankan experiences with a confidence that the earlier generation could not command. Madhbhashini Ratnayake and Neil Fernandopulle seem the most committed of these, while the field of drama, comparatively neglected before, has seen extremely innovative work by Ruwanthi de Chickera. Previously, apart from the expatriate Ernest MacIntyre, and the somewhat cerebral Regi Siriwardena, drama in English was almost nonexistent.

It would seem then that Sri Lankan writing in English will develop over the next few years to achieve a similar status to that which such writing has in other former colonies. The relative paucity of critical attention however, and the shrinking readership, in a context in which English medium education was banned for several decades, may countermand the results of what are essentially individual efforts by several writers.

Rajiva Wijesinha

Further Reading

De Mel, Neloufer, ed. *Essays on Sri Lankan Poetry in English.* Colombo: English Association of Sri Lanka, 1995.

De Mel, Neloufer, and Minoli Samarakkody, eds. *Writing and Inheritance: Women's Writing in Sri Lanka 1860–1948.* Colombo: Women's Education and Research Centre, 2002.

Gooneratne, Yasmine, ed. *Celebrating Sri Lankan Women's English Writing: 1948–2000.* Colombo: Women's Education and Research Centre, 2002.

Wijesinha, Rajiva, ed. *An Anthology of Contemporary Sri Lankan Poetry in English.* Colombo: English Association of Sri Lanka, 2000.

———. *Breaking Bounds: Essays on Sri Lankan Writers in English.* Belihuloya, Sri Lanka: Sabaragamuwa UP, 1997.

Sri Lankan Poetry in English

English poetry in Sri Lanka appeared in the wake of the introduction of English education to the country in the nineteenth century after its subjugation by the British in 1815. The quality of the English poetry produced by Lankans (and British expatriates) in the nineteenth century, however, as Yasmine Gooneratne has pointed out in *English Literature in Ceylon: 1815–1878* (187–214), was by and large inferior; it merely tended to mimic ineptly some of the attitudes and styles of nineteenth-century British poetry, and indeed even of the British poetry of the previous century. The nineteenth century did not produce any significant Sri Lankan English language poets or even poems.

The first Lankan poet of any stature is George Keyt, better known for his painting, who published three collections of English poetry in the 1930s—*Poems* (1936), *The Darkness Disrobed* (1937), and *Image in Absence* (1937). Keyt's poetry is sometimes obscure and even pretentious (lines like, for example, "More is concealed in contemplation than the foliage and clouds reported in wrinkled display" *Collected,* 43), yet the accents and sensibility of twentieth-century modernist poetry emerge in Sri Lankan English poetry for the first time in his work. The characteristic idiom and sentiments of this poetry can be seen in such lines as: "I await in terror the awakening of the wind of distraction" (80) or "Feet wander among broken passages which seem to be long and lead nowhere" (76). Keyt's diction is largely free of the self-consciously poetic, flowery effects of earlier Sri Lankan English poetry, while in subject matter, he constantly turns to the familiar modernist themes of alienation, breakdown in communication, spiritual disorientation, and *angst*. Ashley Halpé observes that "Keyt's verse gives us Lanka's first authentically modern poetic voice" (19); he was also Sri Lanka's first—and possibly only—modernist writer. Keyt did not publish much English poetry after the 1930s, though, and the possibilities and directions revealed in his work were not, unfortunately, taken up by others.

Hardly any significant English language poets appeared in Sri Lanka in the period before independence, for example, 1948, apart from Keyt. There are some poems of Sunetha Wickremesinhe (whose *Poems* was posthumously published in 1941) that express themes related to spirituality, particularly spiritual yearning, with sincerity, considerable poignancy as well as reasonable technical competence, but her outlook and temperament are often immature; and her diction labors under the languorous, stylized, "late-Victorian" effects favored by Sri Lankan poets of the pre-Keyt era, as in: "In the dusk the shy-eyed *manels* faintly murmur o'er the meads" (*Poems,* 30) or "in the dusk the milky pigeons croon a haunting melody" (30). Wickremesinhe's poetry has obvious limitations; yet there is evidence in it that suggest that she may have matured into an important lyric poet if she had not died in 1941 at the age of eighteen.

Like Sri Lankan English fiction, the Sri Lankan poetry entered a phase of rapid growth, quantitatively and qualitatively, after the country got its independence from Britain. Ironically this growth developed in a post-Independence nationalist, sociocultural, and linguistic environment that was in general hostile to the development of the English language and literature in Sri Lanka. The factors that led to this paradoxical efflorescence have still not been satisfactorily investigated and established, although M. I. Kuruvilla claims in his essay "Modern Sri Lankan English Poetry" that the impetus may have come from the vibrant English department of the newly established University of Ceylon (in which many of the older post-Independence English language poets studied) is plausible. Be that as it may, the half century or so after Independence produced a number of outstanding Sri Lankan English poets whose work collectively laid the foundations for a tradition of distinctively Sri Lankan English poetry in style, language, imagery, and thematic concerns. Patrick Fernando, Lakdasa Wikkramasinha, Yasmine Gooneratne, Jean Arasanayagam, Ashley Halpé, Anne Ranasinghe, and Gamini Seneviratne, the more senior of these poets, were already established and receiving critical attention by the end of the 1970s, while poets such as Kamala Wijeratne, Richard de Zoysa, and Malinda Seneviratne began to publish from the 1980s onward.

Of the older post-Independence Sri Lankan English poets, Patrick Fernando,

Lakdasa Wikkramasinha, Yasmine Goo-neratne, and Jean Arasanayagam are the most significant, although Halpé, Rana-singhe, and Seneviratne, too, have pub-lished a substantial amount of first-rate poetry: for example Halpé's "Four Atten-uations," "April 1971," and "The Dream"; Ranasinghe's "At What Dark Point," "Auschwitz from Colombo," and "Secre-tariat"; and Seneviratne's "Song for the New Era," "Home," and "A Cure." Many of these poets had studied at the University of Ceylon, and belong(ed) to Sri Lanka's Anglicised, English-speaking class. Though they may be considered pre-dominantly Western in intellectual and cultural orientation, they have been recep-tive, too, to the cultural and literary tradi-tions of the indigenous environment that they inhabit as Sri Lankans, regardless of their ethnicity. This postcolonial cultural and literary plurality permeates the work of many of these writers.

Patrick Fernando was the earliest of these poets to bring out a collection, *The Return of Ulysses,* published in England in 1955, which was the only collection of his published in his lifetime. His second col-lection, *Selected Poems,* was brought out posthumously in 1984; apart from the po-ems included in these collections, Fer-nando has published poems in journals and anthologies as well. Fernando (a Catholic who studied the classics at the University of Ceylon) has written on classical and Catholic themes; satirical poems on hu-man folly and weakness; and others on such themes as death, aging, and the ero-sion of time in human relationships. His best poetry—"The Return of Ulysses," "The Late Sir Henry," and "The Way of the Adjutant Stork," for example—is finely crafted, urbane, witty, and often de-tached and ironic in its outlook on people, events, and experiences. Fernando rarely addresses specific social, political, and cultural issues; nor has he shown an inter-est, like some postcolonial writers, in cre-ating a recognizably indigenous style and diction. Fernando is an instance of a post-colonial writer who is not particularly con-cerned with either postcolonial issues or literary styles, but has still succeeded in producing poetry of considerable distinc-tion—written mostly in standard English, in conventional rhymes and metres, on topics of general or universal import.

Some of Fernando's poetic strengths are found also in the work of Yasmine Gooneratne, who published her first col-lection, *Word, Bird, Motif,* in 1971, a sec-ond collection, *The Lizard's Cry and Other Poems,* in 1972, and migrated to Australia the same year. Of Sri Lanka's English po-ets, Gooneratne is perhaps the most tech-nically accomplished; her work is often ironic, and except in a few satirical pieces, feeling and sentiment in her poetry tend to be carefully controlled and lucidly and precisely rendered. This is a classical vir-tue that she shares with Patrick Fernando. Gooneratne's range, though, is broader than Fernando's, and her style more ex-perimental and distinctive; at times it re-flects the kind of plurality and hybridity that is now almost synonymous with post-colonial literature. Poems like "Rocks on Marine Drive" and "Words to a Daughter" delicately examine subtleties of personal relationships, while in other poems, for ex-ample "The Peace-Game," The Big Match 1983," and "This Language, This Woman: A Lover's Reply," Gooneratne goes be-yond the personal domain and explores political and sociocultural issues, includ-ing the politics of the English language in Sri Lanka, and the race-related violence that has disfigured the country's post-Independence history.

Gooneratne is also a very effective sa-tirical poet. "The Lizard's Cry," is a tren-chant denunciation of the disorder and decay that she sees everywhere in Sri Lanka: "this haven of the second-rate," "ravaged, looted Kingdom," in which "light dies," and "breath recedes." "The

Lizard's Cry" has a composite (and complex) structure; conventions of traditional Sinhala poetry on the one hand and those of Augustan verse satire and Modernist poetry on the other, mingle and interact in this poem, enriching its structure and meaning. In formal terms, "The Lizard's Cry" is perhaps the most innovative and ambitious English poem to have appeared in Sri Lanka to date. Since migrating to Australia, however, Gooneratne has concentrated mainly on fiction, and published only one collection of poetry, *6,000 Ft Death Dive,* in 1981.

Although Lakdasa Wikkramasinha once declared (in a note to his first collection, *Lustre Poems*) that in writing in English he was "using the language of the most despicable and loathsome people on earth," and that for him, "writing in English is a form of cultural treason" (51), Wikkramasinha went on to become arguably Sri Lanka's most original and distinguished English poet. He is also possibly the only Sri Lankan English poet to have published poetry (two collections) in his mother tongue (Sinhala) as well.

Some of Wikkramasinha's best poetry is concerned with the predicament of the socially and economically disadvantaged in Sri Lanka. "The Death of Ashanti," for example, is a powerful indictment of the abuse of female domestic servants in Sri Lanka; the poem narrates the sexual abuse of Ashanti, a young domestic servant working in a presumably aristocratic household, who commits suicide by drinking acid when she is seven months pregnant. "Nossa Senhora Dos Chingalas" evokes the hardships undergone by Sri Lankan female laborers, and at the same time pays homage to their fortitude and dignity; the women are elevated to a Christlike status by their labor, suffering, and capacity for endurance: "Any one of them is our senhora," says the poet, "In the shadow of whose husked feet" "the men" may "recline" (*Nossa,* 10). Suffering of

another kind, inflicted on colonized peoples by colonizers, is the theme of "Don't Talk to Me about Matisse." This poem establishes vividly the violence of colonialism (where native "mud-huts were splattered with gunfire"), and simultaneously implies a nexus between European high culture and its colonies; it hints that the exploitation of the colonies had contributed to the creation of the conditions that enabled the emergence of this culture. Wikkramasinha has also written intense, brooding poems on such themes as the decay of feudal culture ("Stones of Akuratiye Walauwe"), traumatic personal relationships ("Wedding Night"), and the atrophy that he perceives in Sri Lankan culture and society ("The Waters").

"To My Friend Aldred," a lighthearted poem on the seduction of a servant maid by her master, discloses another side of Wikkramasinha's sensibility. The narrator of this witty, flippant piece (mimicking the suave speaker of the Horatian ode to Xanthias) tells his friend Aldred (to whom the poem is addressed), that "there is no shame" in sleeping with his "servant maid" since "the same passion moved others too [i.e., Achilles and Agamemnon] famous in time" (*Fifteen,* 10). The speaker then reinforces his argument by reminding Aldred that Lankans, "being classical in our traditions," are "not to such titillations immune." Part of the ironic and comic effect of this poem is achieved by juxtaposing European (Horatian, Homeric) and Sri Lankan literary traditions.

The Sri Lankan ethnic conflict is a major concern of Jean Arasanayagam's poetry. A Lankan Burgher married to a Tamil, Arasanayagam has personally known the insecurity and fear experienced by the Tamil community during attacks on Tamils that repeatedly occurred in the island in the post-Independence period. This violence and its consequences are the theme of several of her best poems: for example, "1958 . . '71 . . '77 . . '81 . .

'83," "In the Month of July," and "Refugees—Old Man, Old Woman." In other poems, Arasanayagam brings out the impact of the civil war on the country's North. In "Nallar 1982," for example, she writes, "the gods are blinded by the rain of bullets . . . the land is empty now" (*Apocalypse,* 2); and in "Remembering Nallur," "Nallur is now a battlefield," and that "all bear arms."

Issues and problems of identity and self-definition are another key theme in Arasanayagam's poetry. As a member of an English-speaking Burgher minority, a descendent of the Dutch colonizers of the country, Arasanayagam is uneasy and feels marginalized in contemporary Sri Lanka, incongruous and unable to arrive at a stable and valid sense of identity. Thus in "Roots" she states that she realizes the importance of roots "when it is too late and earth eroded"; while in "A Colonial Inheritance" Arasanayagam remarks that all that "history" has given her is "a name I do not want" (*Colonial,* 15). Arasanayagam's uncertainty about her identity is compounded when her Tamil husband's conservative Hindu family (represented by her mother-in-law) shuns her—a Burger Christian—after her marriage: "the locked doors," she says, "did not open however much I knocked."

Fernando, Gooneratne, Wikkramasinha, and Arasanayagam are the leading English language poets of Sri Lanka in the post-Independence period. Anne Ranasinghe, Gamini Seneviratne, and Ashley Halpé, roughly of the same generation, have also produced high-quality work, but not as consistently as Fernando and the other three. Of the younger post-Independence poets, Richard de Zoysa, who was murdered in 1990 for political reasons, was the most talented and technically accomplished. "Apocalypse Soon," "Gajagavannama," "Animal Crackers," "Rites of Passage," and "Birds, Beasts and Relatives" comment incisively (and wittily) on the intolerance and violence that Zoysa perceived in Sri Lankan politics of the 1980s. Zoysa's control over poetic technique and form can be seen in all these works. Zoysa wrote equally compellingly on private experiences too; "Oh, Boy . . . ," "Corporation Love Song (1)," "Corporation Love Song (2)," and "Song," are poems on personal relations in which feeling, sentiment, passion, and reflection are finely balanced and integrated. Had he not died at 30, Zoysa may well have developed into one of Sri Lanka's finest English-language poets.

A substantial amount of English poetry is being published in Sri Lanka at present, much of it by younger writers. While writers like Malinda Seneviratne have shown considerable promise, the younger generation of Sri Lanka's English poets is yet to produce writers of a stature comparable to that of Fernando, Gooneratne, Wikkramasinha, and Arasanayagam. Whether this is only a temporary dearth or the prelude to the (long anticipated) demise of English poetry in Sri Lanka is too early to say. It can be said, though, that the English poetry produced in Sri Lanka, particularly since Independence, is remarkable for a small nation in which English (spoken by a very small minority of the population) is only a second language—and one that was neglected and even derided in the immediate aftermath of Independence.

Nihal Fernando

Further Reading

Arasanayagam, Jean. *Apocalypse '83: Poems.*
———. *A Colonial Inheritance and Other Poems.* Kancy: n.p., 1985.
De Mel, Neloufer, ed. *Essays in Sri Lankan Poetry in English.* Colombo: English Association of Sri Lanka, 1995.
Gooneratne, Yasmine. *English Literature in Ceylon: 1815–1878.* Dehiwala: Tisara Prakasakayo, 1968.
———. "The English Poetry of Sri Lanka." *Diverse Inheritance: A Personal Perspective on Commonwealth Literature.* Ed. Yasmine Goone-

ratne. Adelaide: Centre for the New Literatures in English, 1980.

Goonetilleke, D.C.R.A. "Sri Lankan Poetry in English: Getting beyond the Colonial Heritage." *From Colonial to Post-Colonial.* Ed. Anna Rutherford. Sydney: Dangaroo, 1992.

Halpé, Ashley. "Introduction." *George Keyt: Collected Poems.* Ed. H. A. I. Goonetileke. Colombo: The George Keyt Foundation, 1991.

Keyt, George. *Collected Poems.* Ed. H. A. I. Goonetileke. Colombo: The George Keyt Foundation, 1991.

Kuruvilla, M. I. "Modern Sri Lankan Poetry." *Studies in World Literature.* Ed. M. I. Kuruvilla. New Delhi: Sterling, 1984.

Wickremesinhe, Sunetha. *Poems.* Mount Lavinia: The Ola Book Company, 1941.

Wikkramasinha, Lakdasa. *Lustre Poems.* Kandy: Ariya, 1965.

———. *Nassa Senhara Dos Chungalas: Poems 1965–1970.* Maradana: Praja Publishers, 1973.

———. *Fifteen Poems 1967–'68.* Kandy: Kandy Printers Limited, 1970.

A Strange and Sublime Address by Amit Chaudhuri

A Strange and Sublime Address, published in 1991, is Amit Chaudhuri's first book. The first 14 chapters of the book give an account of a young boy holidaying with his relatives in Calcutta. Sandeep is a 10-year-old living with his parents in Bombay, but Calcutta is their original family home. Sandeep makes two visits to Calcutta over a period of 18 months. His uncle (Chotomama), aunt (Mamima) and young cousins, Abhijit and Bablu, are the main characters in this section. The section closes with the gradual recovery and return to good health of Sandeep's uncle, who had been hospitalized with a heart ailment.

From the fifteenth chapter on, the narrative diverges. There is a sequence of seemingly unrelated and some plausibly related accounts of a young man (perhaps Sandeep?), alternately in Calcutta in his parents' house and in London as a visiting student from Oxford; and a middle-aged couple and their servants, who live in Calcutta. Tangentially, through hints, and the appearance of the same characters in multiple chapters, it appears that the middle-aged couple in one chapter is probably the same as the young man's parents (or perhaps the author does not mean his readers to go haring after this further).

The section of the book dealing with Sandeep and his cousins contains minutely observed details of daily life as seen by a young boy. Interspersed with these descriptions are sharp, tongue-in-cheek observations on such things as the nature of the world, what qualities one needs to acquire to get a job at 21, the nature of poverty ("displacement as well as lack"), and austerity ("being poor in a rooted way, within a culture of tradition"). Occasionally (as in the later book, *A Freedom Song*"), characters voice radical opinions, as for example when Chotomama describes Gandhi as a "sham yogi." In the latter sections of the book, the writing takes on a wry, mildly sad tone, as in the protagonist's encounter with a bookseller on Calcutta's College Street. Overall the result is a powerful evocation of contemporary Bengali culture and attitudes and life in Calcutta in the 1970s and 1980s.

A Strange and Sublime Address won the Betty Trask Award and the Commonwealth Eurasian regional prize. Critics were enthusiastic in their acclaim for the book, calling its prose "lyrical" and "raptly luminous."

Born in 1962 in Calcutta, Amit Chaudhuri was raised in Bombay and graduated from University College, London. He did his doctorate from Balliol College, Oxford. Chaudhuri lives in Calcutta with his wife and daughter. He has published four novels and a short-story collection, and he has written for several well-known publications such as *The Guardian* and the *London Review of Books.* He has been the recipient of several other awards for his writing, including the Commonwealth Writer's Prize for Eurasia and the LA

Times Award. Chaudhuri is also the editor of *The Picador Book of Modern Indian Literature* (2001).

Padma Chandrasekaran

Further Reading

Dey, Esha. "The Instant Made Eternity: Amit Choudhuri's *A Strange and Sublime Address.*" *Indian Literature Today.* Ed. R. K. Dhawan. Vol. 1. New Delhi: Prestige, 1994. 103–9.

Holmstrom, Lakshmi. "Writing of Childhood—Without Whimsy." *Indian Review of Books* 2.6 (16 Mar. 15–Apr. 1993): 25–26.

Paranjape, Makarand. "Give Us Style." Rev. of *A Strange and Sublime Address* by Amit Chaudhuri. *Indian Review of Books* 1.3 (Dec. 1991): 26.

Sengupta, C. "Amit Choudhuri's *A Strange and Sublime Address:* An Analysis." *Recent Indian Fiction.* Ed. R. S. Pathak. New Delhi: Prestige, 1994. 219–34.

Wormald, Mark. "Bengal Myths and Mores." Rev. of *A Strange and Sublime Address* by Amit Chaudhuri. *The Times Literary Supplement* (23 Aug. 1991): 21.

Such a Long Journey by Rohinton Mistry, film by Sturla Gunnarsson

Such a Long Journey (1998) is Canadian Icelander Sturla Gunnarsson's film adaptation of Canadian Indian writer Rohinton Mistry's award-winning 1991 novel of the same name. Bombay-based screenwriter Sooni Taraporevala *(Salaam Bombay, Mississippi Masala)* adapted the novel for the big screen. British and Canadian companies, Amy International Artists and The Filmworks respectively, produced the film. It received more critical than commercial success. In Canada, it garnered 12 Genie nominations and won three awards for Best Performance by an Actor in a Lead Role, Best Achievement in Editing, and Sound Editing. At the 1998 Vancouver International Film Festival, the film won the Most Popular Canadian Film award.

Set during the turbulent political times of 1971, on the brink of the third Indo-Pak war, *Such a Long Journey* is a story about Gustad Noble, a Parsi everyman, played with deep sympathy by Roshan Seth. Once a part of the Parsi upper classes, as a child Gustad sees his father's fortunes crumble. Now in his late 40s, he struggles through life in Bombay trying to do right by his family, friends, and his conscience in an increasingly hostile environment full of poverty, ill health, death threats, and corruption. Married to Dilnavaz (Soni Razdan) and a father of three children, Gustad earns his living as a clerk in a recently nationalized bank. Resisting and buckling under the pressures of middle-class urban life in Bombay (space, electricity, water, and the rising cost of living), Gustad puts all his hopes in his eldest son's future. Sorab (Vrajesh Hirjec), who yearns to choose a life in the arts, finds his father's ambitions for him to attend the Indian Institute of Technology to get a career as an engineer stifling. So after a series of arguments, Sorab walks out of his parents' house. Gustad and Dilnavaz snap at each other at the smallest instance, not for lack of love, but in frustration with the grind of daily life. A wall that divides their compound from the main road is being used as a public urinal and has become the breeding ground for mosquitoes. The municipal commissioner threatens to widen the main road cutting into the compound of the Khodadad Building, an old dilapidated chawl-type housing complex in which Gustad rents a flat. Living in such close proximity with equally put-upon neighbors has its own set of complications. But nothing hurts Gustad more than the sudden disappearance of his best friend and neighbor, Major Jimmy Bilimoria (Naseeruddin Shah), with whom he spent many an evening drinking rum and sharing their deepest secrets. Within the first few minutes of the film, Gustad receives a letter from Jimmy informing him that he has become a RAW (Research and Analysis Wing) agent for the Indian government, helping the guerilla movement in East Pakistan achieve its goal of an independent Bangladesh. Gustad is impressed with Jimmy's commitment and chides himself for doubting Jimmy's reasons for his absence in the first place. Jimmy asks Gustad to pick up a parcel for him and await further instructions. Gustad is torn between his desire, on the one hand, to do the right thing by his friend and vicariously participate in a worthy political cause, and on the other, his anxieties about endangering his family's security. Gustad follows his conscience and helps Jimmy out. Unbeknownst to him, the favor is far more complicated, and the next thing he knows he, along with Jimmy, is embroiled in a national plot of intrigue and corruption. When the film begins Gustad is cynical about friendships but optimistic about the government. By the end of Gustad's personal journey of revelation, he becomes cynical about the government and the future of his city, but grateful for the friends he has had, even though both his friends are now dead. He is also thankful for his family despite the misunderstandings and altercations.

The problems of adapting a 400-page novel like *Such a Long Journey* to screen are not easily solvable. The novel spans over a year, with 18 characters, and four plotlines. Mistry's worldview and style of narrative organization do not easily fit the dramatic principles of "rising stakes" nor clearly follow the "arc of the central protagonist" that are the prerequisites for conventional three-act feature films. The "dramatic" events in this tumultuous year in the life of Gustad Noble do not stack up neatly with the kind of causality demanded of most film narratives. Neither can these events be prioritized in terms of their narrative significance. No plotline in the novel is inherently more important than the other. For instance, when the book devotes several pages to Gustad's relationship with his friend Dinshawji's illness, all else is forgotten. That particular plotline takes precedence over others, not because it is more important than Jimmmy's betrayal or Roshan's illness, but because real life does not demand to be curtailed by the Aristotelian principle of unity of action in the way screen stories are limited. As Dinshawji often says, "thasuk thasuk my cart rumbles along," so does the narrative of the novel, *Such a Long Journey.* When translated to film, the rumbling of life's cart has little rhythm. Events seem episodic, and often disembodied from their context. For example, Gustad's sudden bursts of anger seem unmotivated, and Dilnavaz's faith in black magic is neither desperate nor comical.

Some critics of the film have attributed the weakness of its main plotline to the novel itself. But somehow one finds that weakness more apparent in the film, since we do not have the reflections of various characters and the texture of their lives to provide a "thick description" of lower middle-class Parsi life in Bombay. The audience is not invited to participate in the lives of the inhabitants of the Khodadad building. Mistry positions the reader in the midst of the domestic maelstrom of the Noble family. Gunnarsson renders the viewer compassionate but a more detached observer of events. Mistry grew up as a Parsi in Bombay. Though writing from the distance of diaspora in Canada, the book claims the world as his own. He writes with passion and possession. Gunnarsson handles the same material with gentle reverence and admiration. His fascinated but ultimately detached point of view is what we receive in the film. As summarized by one reviewer, "the cinematography seemed distant and cerebral—more like a bystander than a participant—a tourist taking pictures of India" (Yee).

In *Adaptations,* Deborah Cartmell suggests, "instead of worrying about whether a film is 'faithful' to the original literary text (founded in the logocentric belief that there is a single meaning), we read adaptations for their general plurality of meanings" (28). However, in its well-meaning attempt to remain faithful to its literary source, the film version of *Such a Long Journey* is ultimately little more than a competent paraphrase of the book. It remains true to the novel's spirit of human dignity against all odds, but devoid of the book's intimacy and claustrophobia, irony and humor. Adept at combining tragedy, comedy, action, and melodrama, Mistry's writing is often said to possess a Dickensian generosity. The tragic-comic tone that informs the novel splits into tragic and comic scenes in the film. The comic scenes are awkward when juxtaposed with the serious tone of the film.

The film also does not succeed in translating memory from litcrary to audiovisual text. The novel is rife with nostalgic ruminations about Gustad's childhood, his adult friendship with Jimmy Bilimoria, and his relationship with his son Sorab when he was a little boy. The novel takes detours and long pauses into the various nooks and crannies of individual memory. The film's golden-hued flashbacks adhere to events in the novel, but do little to explain or add to our understanding of Gustad's moral ambiguities. The closure in the personal scape of the novel is charged with more optimism in the film. Sorab returns home. Jimmy clears his name before he dies. Dinshawji proves he is more friend than fool before his death. And daughter Roshan's malaria is cured. But Mistry's novel avoids false closure in the political realm. The corruption does not stop, the government is not exposed, the wall that represents secularism in India is broken down despite protests from the people, and the artist who has transformed its edifice moves on to create other places of temporary significance. The Gustad of the novel seems less elated than the Gustad of the film. The metaphor of "the journey of the protagonist" seems more prescriptive in film. The protagonist must end up transformed, affected by small and large life

lessons along the way. At the very end, the film reveals a more hopeful Gustad as he tears the brown paper that has blocked natural sunlight into the apartment for years; whereas the Gustad of the novel only pulls at the paper covering the ventilators. In the film, the shaft of sunlight that bathes the room as the music rises provides a far more uplifting ending than the frightened moth that circles the room in the last sentence of the novel.

Shuchi Kothari

Further Reading

Cartmell, Deborah, and Imelda Whelehan, eds. *Adaptations: From Text to Screen, Screen to Text.* London: Routledge, 1999.

Yee, Nelson. *Such a Long Journey, Tone Standard: Word, Sound, Light, Colour.* <http://www.tonestandard.com/archives/>.

A Suitable Boy by Vikram Seth

On the primary level, Vikram Seth's *A Suitable Boy,* is about the search for a proper husband for Lata Mehra, the fourth child and only daughter of the widowed matriarch, Mrs. Rupa Mehra. From this perspective, Seth's novel is a chatty and much-extended drawing room melodrama of relationships, scandals, revealing conversations, and opportunities lost and found. From the larger perspective, *A Suitable Boy* reveals the political climate of the recent postcolonial India, in the first years of independence from the British Raj that began at midnight on August 15, 1947. Seth's realistic and affectionately created characters face the storms of partition, land wars, and Hindu-Moslem conflict. While the Mehras look for Lata's mate, Seth gives his readers a guided tour of the details and concerns of private lives set against the political turmoil of the newly emerging nation.

A Suitable Boy becomes a fictionalized chronicle of the early years of nation building, and Seth's focus upon the individuals who make up the new nation suggests another fundamental book about the formation and security of an Indian state. *The Mahabharata,* a core Hindu text dating broadly from between 2000 and 600 B.C.E., is the story of ruling family conflict, fortuitous marriage, war, tragedy, and eventual triumph and consolidation of a new nation state. Seth discreetly places himself in the position of Vyasa, grandfather to the heroes of *The Mahabharata* and teller of the story itself. In *A Suitable Boy,* Mrs. Rupa Mehra's father is Dr. Kishen Chand Seth. As grandfather Vyasa is a progenitor who narrates *The Mahabharata,* a character named Seth becomes the grandfather to the very suitable Lata, and Vikram Seth indeed is the storyteller. Central to the successful outcome of *The Mahabharata* epic is the marriage of Draupadi, a woman born with the mandate to help set the most deserving branch of the dynastic family in charge of the new nation. Draupadi marries five heroic and virtuous brothers who combine the best qualities for leadership. Lata has three worthy and gifted suitors but marries only one, the hardworking, self-made model man of new India, Haresh Khanna. Mrs. Rupa Mehra becomes the widowed queen who orchestrates her clan's continuation as does widowed queen Kunti of *The Mahabharata.* As Kunti's primary effort is to ensure the solidarity of the line of the Kurus through devious and concerted means, so Mrs. Mehra makes a career of marrying her offspring. As Seth's Contents page poem asserts for chapter nine: "A desperate mother ventures to deploy/Fair means or foul to net a suitable boy." Always attentive to the smallest, realistic detail, Seth places Mrs. Mehra as the protector of the newlyweds' wedding night as she thwarts a would-be prankster from doing any mischief with the union she has come to approve.

The great departure from the several, significant parallels with *The Mahabharata* that Seth achieves in *A Suitable Boy* is the rejection of caste and clan separatism that is the hallmark stamp of the Brahamanical contribution to the epic. Lata is courted by a Muslim intellectual, an indigent poet from a wealthy and influential Hindu family, and by Haresh Khanna. Haresh is a rising star, a practical dreamer and planner who has high standards for himself and his work. In choosing Haresh, Lata marries socially beneath herself to a man who is an entrepreneur in the shoe business. Like Draupadi in *The Mahabharata,* Lata makes her own choice in a much-extended *svayamvara,* and he, although not a high caste aristocrat, is the best man, the most suitable personality for the emerging India of the 1950s. Haresh is a hard-working, handcraft industrialist who makes no distinction between the ranks of either caste or status.

Another link to the *The Mahabharata* emerges in Seth's style. Seth glibly falls into alliterative verse that boldly employs both internal and end rhyme in the contents page and throughout the text. *The Mahabharata* is a very long poem composed of *sloka* stanzas that employ alliteration and end rhyme. In *A Suitable Boy,* the poetic sections, while indeed light poetry, give the virtuosic effect of the epic style, and that style is itself in turn often belied by the simple circumstances in the text which inspires the verses.

Although it is clearly not intended as an autobiography, *A Suitable Boy* is set to begin in the year Vikram Seth was born, 1952. There are other elements that reveal the author's close identification with the storyline. Seth's father was himself in the shoe business like the fictional Haresh. Seth's mother became a judge.

Women's education, employment, and empowerment are running themes. The virtuous female characters are certainly accomplished. Lata is a college student. Her sister Savita is an educated, young mother who prepares to study law when husband Pran is debilitated with heart trouble. In this segment of the novel, Seth recalls the Hindu myth of Savitri, one of the most admired mythical women, who goes into arbitration with Yama, God of Death, to restore her husband and family fortunes. Seth's accomplished Muslim courtesan Saeeda Bai is both an artist and a person of great soul, adding to the lineage of meritorious courtesans from Indian texts such as Vasantasena of the Sanskrit play "The Toy Cart" (c. 1st cent. A.D.) and Chandramukhi of Sharatchandra Chatterjee's *Devdas* (1901). The Begum Abida Khan comes out of *purdah* to advocate in the parliament for the nonrepression of the Urdu language in a Hindu majority state whose politicians are pushing for the instatement of Hindi as the official language.

Another important theme in *A Suitable Boy* is Hindu-Muslim relations. Lata's first boyfriend is the Muslim, Kabir Durrani, Seth's obvious reference to the poet Kabir (1398–1518) whose hagiography focuses upon his outspoken rejection of Hindu-Muslim separatism. When the character Firoz Khan urbanely observes, " 'Well, there are many possibilities for riots . . . Shias with Shias, Shias with Sunnis, Hindus with Muslims," he is supported by Maan Kapoor adding "And Hindus with Hindus" (1035). Seth brings Islam and Hinduism into conflict during the celebration of Moharram, the sober Muslim New Year that begins with mourning the death of the faithful Imam Husain who defended Islam against the usurper Yazid. Simultaneously, a fundamentalist Hindu group celebrates the triumph of Rama against Sita's demonic abductor Ravana. Through Seth's well-written juxtapositions, Rama becomes Yazid, and Husain becomes Ravana. Later in the novel, Firoz will stab his beloved Maan in a stupid, blind jealousy. Thus, in the macro and the microcosm Seth makes his point about the counter productivity and waste of religious separatism for India.

Seth's intimate portrait of credible Indian lives does not shy away from uncomfortable possibilities. The author addresses the tragedy and dysfunction of child molestation with the insightful creation of a slimy and yet believable uncle from Lucknow and his intimidated wife and daughter. Maan and Firoz are bisexual lovers and their tragic, shifting loyalties are handled with sensitivity. The comfort and security Mrs. Mehra strives to assure is undermined by the self-absorbed, unfaithful daughter-in-law Meenakshi, named wryly in reference to the mythical temptress nymph Menaka.

With a superficial title that suggests the topic of almost every Hindi movie of the recent two decades, Vikram Seth's *A Suitable Boy* overtakes and surpasses the scope of the American popular novel *Gone With the Wind* by Margaret Mitchell. There is also the suggestion of a theatrical production, such as the 1985 musical adaptation of Victor Hugo's *Les Miserables* that sets a personal romance against the backdrop of revolutionary history. But Seth's novel is one that will stand the test of time far better than Mitchell's outdated classic. His history is sound and his characters subtle. Unlike the musical production, Seth's text strikes a perfect balance between the procuring of a husband and other private and relatively small matters and the growing pains of a new nation. Time will decide if Seth's novel can become the subcontinental *A Tale of Two Cities* or *Anna Karenina,* if it will ever play as popularly as the movie version of *Doctor Zhivago* or if it will be accepted as the modern period's *Mahabharat* of national struggle post-Independence.

Helen Asquine Fazio

Further Reading

Agarwalla, Shyam S. *Vikram Seth's "A Suitable Boy": Search for an Indian Identity.* New Delhi: Prestige, 1995.

Desai, Anita. "Sitting Pretty." Rev. of *A Suitable Boy* by Vikram Seth. *New York Review* (27 May 1993): 23.

Mehta, Nina. Rev. of *A Suitable Boy* by Vikram Seth. *Christian Science Monitor* (19 July 1993): 13.

Mohapatra, Himansu S. "Riches of India: Reading Vikram Seth's *A Suitable Boy*." *The Postmodern Indian English Novel: Interrogating the 1980s and 1990s.* Ed. Viney Kirpal. Bombay: Allied, 1996. 41–48.

Myers, David. "Vikram Seth's Epic Renunciation of the Passions: Deconstructing Moral Codes in *A Suitable Boy*." *The Commonwealth Review* 5.1 (1993–94): 79–102.

Pandurang, Mala. "Multiple Readings of *A Suitable Boy:* Authorial Intention, Social Realism, Gender and the 'Family.' " *Vikram Seth: Multiple Locations, Multiple Affiliations.* Jaipur: Rawat, 2001. 103–49.

Rorty, Richard. "Towards a Liberal Utopia." Rev. of *A Suitable Boy* by Vikram Seth. *Times Literary Supplement* (24 June 1994): 14.

Suri, Manil

Manil Suri, author of the best-selling novel, *The Death of Vishnu,* was born in Bombay, India, in 1959, to Prem and Ram Lal Suri, both of Rawalpindi, now in Pakistan; the family migrated to Bombay after the partition. Prem, a triple graduate, was for a while personal secretary to Indira Gandhi, before Mrs. Gandhi became prime minister of India. In Bombay, Prem taught high school English and history and also became a social worker. Ram Lal served as assistant music director in the Indian film industry.

Manil Suri's path to literature came by a roundabout route. Had the extended family had its way, young Manil would have followed in his grandfather's footsteps and become a doctor. Instead, after graduating from Campion High School he chose chemistry as a major in college. When organic chemistry turned him off, he switched to physics. At the end of his third year, one of his professors, finding that he excelled in abstract algebra, persuaded him to switch to mathematics, and urged him to go to the United States for further studies. Suri did precisely that, enrolling at Carnegie Mellon University in Pittsburgh in 1979. On obtaining his Ph.D., he joined the University of Maryland in Baltimore County, where he is now a full professor of applied mathematics.

Although Manil Suri had written several book reviews for the Campion High School magazine and joined a succession of short-lived writing groups in Maryland, he says he felt little call to become a writer until events drove him to it. That happened in 1994, when he was visiting his parents in Bombay. A man named Vishnu, whom Manil had known as a child, died as he had lived for years—on the staircase of the building where the Suris had an apartment. Manil was disturbed to such an extent that he felt compelled to write Vishnu's story; however, he had to invent every bit of it, since he had very few factual details to go on. What he did know was that Vishnu functioned as a sort of caretaker of the building, and also saw to the tenants' personal needs. Vishnu was also rarely sober.

Manil Suri began writing the novel in 1995 as a short story and was very quick to set down the beginning and the end. The middle section bothered him; there were so many details to fill in, so many questions waiting to be answered, that the end kept receding. Also, he had to dream up the other residents. The short story he had started was now turning into a novel, to which he had the beginning and the end, and very little else.

Never one to turn down guidance, Manil took a fiction-writing workshop with Jane Bradley at the Bethesda Writers Center, and later a semester-long workshop with Vikram Chandra at George Washington University. Both these established writers praised his work and encouraged him to persevere. Manil then wrote the second chapter to the novel, but was not satisfied with the result. He developed writer's block.

Dropping the novel, he sent three short stories to a variety of magazines, harvesting a total of forty rejection slips. "I remember at times being quite despondent," he freely admits. Jane Bradley then urged him to take a fiction-writing workshop with Michael Cunningham, Pulitzer Prize-winning novelist, and now fiction editor at *The Atlantic Monthly.* Manil set himself a challenge: he would write a third chapter to the novel and submit it as his entry. Michael Cunningham loved it. He also suggested that Manil focus on developing the characters.

Following the workshop, writing came more easily and doors began to open. He was accepted at prestigious writers' colonies, including the Virginia Center for the Creative Arts and the world-famous MacDowell Colony in New Hampshire.

Once the manuscript for *The Death of Vishnu* was completed, Manil found that 10 top publishers were competing for it, a pleasant change from the 40 rejection slips he had received for his short stories. W. W. Norton finally won the bidding war, and the report gave rise to wild speculation. One report pegged the advance at five million dollars; this was based on a misreading of a source that claimed the advance was $500,000. Eventually Manil Suri revealed that the amount was $350,000, not for the one novel, but for a trilogy, of which the two other novels—*The Life of Shiva* and *The Birth of Brahma*—are yet to be written.

The Death of Vishnu has been widely translated into other languages and is now available in the vernacular in countries including Brazil, Denmark, Finland, France, Germany, Greece, Holland, Italy, Portugal, Spain, and Sweden. In India it has been published by Penguin Books. It has received wide critical acclaim throughout the world, and in the United States from such varied publications as *The New York Times, Time Magazine,* and other media. An extensive review by Pankaj Mishra appeared in *The New York Review of Books.*

Vishnu is not so much the hero as the all-pervasive presence in this novel, in which wit and satire and fond remembrance abound. Vishnu is a ne'er-do-well who lives, courtesy of the tenants, on a landing of a building at Kemp's Corner in Bombay; it is on that landing that we meet him, dying, as the novel opens. For the next 300 pages, we are not sure whether he is still alive and sentient, comatose, or actually dead. All we know is that he is now involved in an out-of-body experience that is always heightened, sometimes intense, sometimes morbid, and often pleasurable; thanks to Manil Suri's masterful deftness with words we are able to share in it.

Also unsure as to his status among the living and the dead are the tenants of the building on whose stairs his inert body lies sprawled. Mrs. Asrani continues to bring him tea; her erstwhile friend and squabbling neighbor Mrs. Pathak brings him three-day-old chapattis. The Asrani's teen-age daughter Kavita, eloping in the dead of night with a Muslim youth, drapes Vishnu in her dupatta to keep him warm and tucks a hundred-rupee note under his head as she tiptoes past him; moments later, her boyfriend steals the money. In *The Death of Vishnu,* when sentimentality threatens to strike, venality often follows close behind; yet Manil Suri manages to keep our emotions in balance.

While Vishnu's body lies still and inert, his inner being reacts to the sights and sounds that surround him. His life passes before his eyes in a series of vignettes, sometimes in fast forward mode, sometimes in rapid rewind. Poignant are the scenes where he seeks the love and companionship of Padmini, a prostitute. Often he sees himself as a child, feels his mother cradling him in her arms, hearing her soothing voice. "Vishnu of the ten avatars," his mother tells him at one time, tending to a wound his father had inflicted in a bhang-induced bout of mischief, "Rama and Krishna are part of you."

"You are Vishnu," his mother tells him, shortly thereafter, "keeper of the universe, keeper of the sun. What would the world be without you?" (21)

"I am Vishnu," he replies, "keeper of the universe, keeper of the sun. There is only darkness without me."

In time, his mother's message becomes near-reality. Vishnu becomes possessed with the need to know: is he the man, or is he the god, the preserver of order in the universe? The reader, too, finds himself caught up in the riddle: which of the two, man or god, will Vishnu turn out to be?

Suri delays in revealing the solution until the very end. In between, he provides us with profound insights into human nature. Even as we empathize with some of his characters, and laugh at the foibles of others, he leads us to realize that they are perhaps mirror images of ourselves; that their hopes and aspirations are equally ours, as are their prejudices. We are led to see how prejudice divides followers of different religions and how within the same religion, it divides one caste or social class from another; and within the wider society, how prejudice divides the rich and the richer from the poor and the poorest.

Yet, again like each one of us, these prejudiced souls in Suri's novel share a yearning for the spiritual side of life; in two of Vishnu's neighbors—Mrs. Asrani and Mrs. Pathak—the yearning manifests itself through acts of dubious charity; in a Muslim neighbor, father of the youth Kavita elopes with, this same thirst, this eagerness to reach, Akbar-like, across religious boundaries, leads to tragedy and perhaps redemption, and brings the novel to its dramatic climax.

Manil Suri himself was raised as a Hindu until the age of 13. He then went into a period of disbelief, but now is an agnostic. He does, however, hold up the Bhagavad Gita as an ideal.

Victor Rangel-Ribeiro

Further Reading

Agarwal, Ramlal. Rev. of *The Death of Vishnu* by Manil Suri. *World Literature Today* 75.3–4 (Summer-Autumn 2001): 135–36.

Mishra, Pankaj. "Dreaming of Mangoes." Rev. of *The Death of Vishnu* by Manil Suri. *The New York Review of Books* 48.9 (31 May 2001): 20–22.

Sarna, Navtej. "A God on the Landing." Rev. of *The Death of Vishnu* by Manil Suri. *The Times Literary Supplement* No.5110 (9 Mar. 2001): 22.

Wood, Michael. "Freedom to Tango." Rev. of *Babu Fictions: Alienation in Contemporary Indian English Novels* by Tabish Khair, *An Obedient Father* by Akhil Sharma, *The Death of Vishnu* by Manil Suri, and *The Glass Palace* by Amitav Ghosh. *London Review of Books* 23.8, (19 Apr. 2001): 28–29.

Syal, Meera

Meera Syal's creative oeuvre traverses the diverse genres of theater, film, television, and fiction. She was born and raised in Wolverhampton, England, in a Punjabi immigrant family. She studied English and drama at Manchester University, where she won the National Student Drama Award for her play *One of Us*. Among her early credits are the screenplays for *One of Us* and the widely acclaimed *Bhaji on the Beach*. She has gone on to produce and star in BBC shows such as *Goodness Gracious Me* and *All about Me*, while also publishing the novels *Anita and Me* (1996) and *Life Isn't All Ha Ha Hee Hee* (2001).

In spite of the forewarning in the title of her second novel, Syal's gift from her early work has indeed been her flair for comedy. While delving into serious issues like immigration, interracial relationships, cultural and generational conflicts, domestic violence, and custodial battles, Syal's method has been the comic, embodying an optimistic belief in the possibility of positive change.

In *Bhaji on the Beach,* Syal portrays the confrontation between two generations of South Asian women—the aunties and their daughters. Syal satirizes the aunties, as women who are caught in a time warp, upholding the values of a traditional Indian society they have left behind, in an absolute and uncritical way. They reject individual self-expression or sexual openness. The clash of the generations reaches a climax over the scandal of a young girl's unwed pregnancy, resulting from a relationship with a black man. Syal, however, also offers the possibility for introspection and change in at least some women of the older generation, resulting from a dawning awareness of the realities of gender and racial oppressions which confront young South Asian women.

The theme of generational conflict is also the focus of Syal's autobiographical novel *Anita and Me.* It is set in the distinctive milieu of a British mining village in the 1960s. Written from the point of view of a 10-year-old Punjabi girl, Meena, who is the only nonwhite girl in her village, the novel is a powerful rendition in its unfolding of the consciousness of race for Meena. Meena internalizes the everyday insults and slights and develops a profound crisis of identity. Rejecting her parents' ideal of the good Indian girl, Meena befriends the older white girl Anita, her partner in rebellion. Her parents are dismayed at their failure to discipline her. As the summer goes by, it brings Meena to an intimate knowledge of racial prejudice. The quiet acts of everyday violence reach a climax at the village fair, where Sam Lowbridge, the local ruffian, uses derogatory words like "wogs" and "darkies" in front of Meena and her father. This verbal abuse expands into physical violence, with the brutal beating of a Punjabi man at the Tollington bus station. When Meena realizes Anita and Sam's complicity in the crime, she is filled with revulsion and self-loathing. A nearly fatal riding accident follows, and at the hospital, Meena undergoes a maturing process, which culminates in the family's departure from Tollington, with Meena shedding the pain and betrayal of her first friendship with Anita.

The theme of female friendship is revisited in *Life Isn't All Ha Ha Hee Hee,* this time between three South Asian women—Tania, Sunita, and Chila. Tania is a documentary filmmaker struggling to change media stereotypes about the South Asian British community. The television industry is indifferent to her various interesting proposals and permit her to make only a film on marriage within the South

Kim Vithana and Mo Sesay in *Bhaji on the Beach.* Courtesy of Photofest.

Asian community. Tania films her friends' marriages, deliberately exploiting Chila's naiveté for the purposes of comic ridicule, and taping Sunita and her husband Akash without their permission. Syal weaves a self-reflexive critique of the postcolonial female artist in Tania's exploitation of the weaknesses of her community for the purpose of solitary fame. Chila's marriage to Deepak is doomed from the beginning, as it is entered under the shadow of mutual illusions. Soon after his marriage, Deepak renews his former intimacy with Tania, which fractures the bond between the three friends. However, when Deepak plans to kidnap Chila's son, born on the verge of their separation, Tania destroys his passport, preempting such a crime. This act reiterates the solidarity of the three women against structures of patriarchal domination.

Syal has won many awards including an MBE in 1997 and a Media Personality of the Year in 2000. *Anita and Me* won the Betty Trask award in 1996 and was shortlisted for the *Guardian* fiction award. Syal is already recognized as a pioneering artist in her thought-provoking representations of South Asians in the British media and in the sphere of fiction.

Lopamudra Basu

Further Reading

Davis, Rocio G. "India in Britain: Myths of Childhood in Meera Syal's *Anita and Me.*" *On Writing Race in Contemporary Britain.* Ed. Fernando Galvan and Mercedes Bengoechea. Alcala de Henares. Spain: Universidad de Alcala, 1999. 139–46.

Schoene-Harwood, Berthold. "Beyond (T)Race: *Bildung* and *Proprioception* in Meera Syal's *Anita and Me.*" *Journal of Commonwealth Literature* 34.1 (1999): 159–68.

T

Tagore, Rabindranath

Rabindranath Tagore (1861–1941), the youngest son of Maharshi Debendranath Tagore, was born in Calcutta (then, the capital of British India) at a time when Bengal was at the crossroads of numerous political, sociocultural shifts. The Tagore family played a central role in ushering in these changes. Tagore received his early education at home and was sent to England at the age of 17. Always rebelling against institutional systems of education, he returned home without completing his education and was married in 1883. As a member of a land-owning family, Tagore was put in charge of the family estates in 1890, thus spending a large amount of time in rural East Bengal (now Bangladesh) throughout his life. Tagore suffered tremendous personal losses between 1902 and 1907.

With the partition of Bengal in 1905 (the viceroy of India, Lord Curzon had introduced the policy of diving Bengal into two regions), Tagore became involved in the nationalist movement. *Gitanjali (Song Offerings)* was published in 1910, and Tagore himself did an English translation of the poems that came out in 1912. He won the Nobel Prize for English in 1913 and instantly became an international figure. In 1915, he was knighted by the queen of England, but returned his knighthood after the Jallianwala Bagh massacre in 1919 (when General Dyer of the British police indiscriminately shot innocent protesters in Amritsar, Punjab). Disillusioned by the way the nationalist movement was growing, with its insistence on noncooperation with the British government and rejection of the West, Tagore detached himself from the Swaraj (Freedom) movement by 1921. This same year also saw the inauguration of his university in Shantiniketan (meaning "Abode of Peace"), 80 miles from Calcutta, and he spent a large amount of time involved in literary and nonliterary engagements, traveling around the world and raising money for the university. It is important to remember that Tagore was an artist and also an educator. The latter part of his life was spent in traveling—as he was an international figure—and his global sojourns included meetings with Einstein, Romain Rolland, and H. G. Wells, amongst other personalities.

Though Tagore wrote successfully in all literary genres, he was primarily a lyric poet. Best known among his approximately 50 volumes of poetry are *Manasi (The Ideal One)* (1890), *Sonar Tari (The Golden Boat)* (1894), *Gitanjali (Song Offerings)* (1910), and *Balaka (Flight of Cranes)* (1916). The English translations do not usually correspond to any particular collection in the original Bengali, and *Gitanjali: Song Offerings* (1912), the best known of his poems, contains selections from other works besides its namesake. Central to his poetry is the theme of constant movement and restlessness that re-

Rabindranath Tagore. © The Nobel Foundation.

flects a religiometaphysical concern; an underlying theme in his poems is the "play of the universe, of a process at work in Nature and man that involves ceaseless change through time" but is also in tune with an "underlying and unchanging harmony" (Radice 21). He was also a modern, conscious of his times and always striving to break away from literary conventions; thus, Tagore has to be seen as an innovator, creating new forms in his poetry and altering the Bengali language.

Tagore was committed to the short story in the decade of the 1890s, mostly because he was writing for Bengali periodicals at that time and because the readership for those periodicals demanded this form. At this time he was a landlord, with his main address in East Bengal (Bangladesh), and this rural landscape was crucial to his literary sensibility. Certain themes recur in his short stories: pantheism, involvement with rural economic development, dislike for the city, calls for Hindu-Muslim unity, and an interest in folk music. Tagore also addressed issues that dealt with urban society and the nouveau riche of Calcutta. With the publication of *Binodini* in 1903 and *Naukadubi* in 1906, Tagore returned to writing novels. These novels dealt with contemporary Bengali society, especially the urban society. With the publication of *Gora* (serialized between 1907–10), Tagore ushered in a new phase in the Bengali novel, quite distinct from that of Bankimchandra Chatterjee—the writer who introduced the novel into Bengali literature. *Gora* focuses on the idea of institutionalized Indian/ Hindu tradition versus a more pluralistic perspective on religion, which Tagore refers to as the "religion of man." The novels written after this period—*Chaturanga* and *Ghare-Baire (The Home and the World)*— deal with issues of the nationalistic movement, women's liberation, and changing societal values. *The Home and the World* has been made into a film by world-renowned filmmaker, Satyajit Ray.

Tagore also wrote numerous plays, dance dramas, essays of all types, travel diaries, and two autobiographies. Despite the diversity of his works, an underlying theme unifies all of them: a sense that he is at the "mercy of a life-deity, a personality higher than his own, guiding him from outside" (Radice 35).

Although Tagore's works have been translated into English before (most notably by Edward Thompson), it was within the last decade or so that his writings began being introduced in Euro-American disciplinary studies. The recent interest in Tagore by the Euro-American academia can be partially explained by the present dominance and influence of postcolonial studies. One main aim of postcolonial theorists has been to broaden the nature of what comprises literary studies; and the point in including Tagore's works in translation is to subvert the hegemony of Euro-American texts. Moreover, of particular concern to these scholars is Tagore's notion of nationalism. As historians, social scientists and literary scholars engage with issues of postcolonial nationalisms, Tagore's writings and essays are seen as articulating an alternative perspective to Western models of the nation, where the artist critiques the fact that the emerging Indian state would have the "imperialistic features" he so deplored in the West (Radice 20). What is of interest to postcolonial scholars is that Tagore's writings problematize the postcolonial nation at the moment of its inception.

Tapati Bharadwaj

Further Reading

Dutta, Krishna, and Andrew Robinson. *Rabindranath Tagore. The Myriad-Minded Man.* New York: St. Martin's, 1996.

Nandy, Ashis. *The Illegitimacy of Nationalism.* New Delhi: Oxford UP, 1994.

Radice, William. "Introduction." *Rabindranath Tagore: Selected Poems.* Trans. William Radice. London: Penguin, 1985. 17–39.

Tagore, Rabindranath. *Nationalism.* New York: Macmillan, 1917.

Tharoor, Shashi

One of the leading Indian writers in English today, Shashi Tharoor was born in London in 1956, brought up in India (Mumbai, Kolkata, and Delhi), and went for further studies to the United States. By 1978 he had completed a Ph.D. at the Fletcher School of Law and Diplomacy at Tufts University, where he also earned two master's degrees. In the same year, Tharoor joined the staff of the United Nations (UN). Since then he has served the UN in several high-profile jobs. Since October 1989, he has been a senior official at the UN headquarters in New York. In June 2002, he was confirmed as the undersecretary-general for Communications and Public Information of the United Nations.

Perhaps not many people could boast of such a meteoric career. With a Ph.D. by the age of 22, a plush job in one of the world's most prestigious institutions, and

the recognition and awards he has received for his creative writing, one may say that Tharoor seems to have been born under a lucky star. However, under the brilliant sheen of his success lies a continual effort to successfully juggle the demands of two vastly different professions—the obligations of a diplomat functioning in the international arena and the inner compulsions of a creative writer. Because of these contradictory pressures, Tharoor has led a split life: in public obliged to be suave and diplomatic, justifying and defending the policies of the United Nations, no matter how controversial; and in his private hours following his vocation as a writer, pegging away at his computer, giving expression to the creative urges within him. The two careers are deliberately kept apart and not allowed to mingle.

Tharoor's ancestral home is in Mundarath, in Palakkad, Kerala, in the southern peninsula of India. He lives in New York but makes frequent visits to India, and he believes that he does not suffer the angst or alienation that diasporic writers often experience. With his high-status job and his elitist educational background, he is sometimes seen as belonging to an earlier, colonial period. However, he thinks of himself as mainstream Indian and describes his upbringing as middle class. Most of his major writing is about India. The subjects of his two forthcoming books are also Indian: one with M. F. Husain on Kerala and the other a biography of Jawaharlal Nehru.

Believing that the very nature of a novel obliges a novelist to try out something new and original in each of his works, Tharoor tries continually to experiment, not only with the stories he narrates but also with the mode of narration. His aim is to provoke people to think and to interrogate themselves. The author of numerous articles, short stories, and commentaries in Indian and Western publications, Tharoor is the winner of several journalism and literary awards, including the Commonwealth Writers Prize. His books include *Reasons of State* (1982); *The Great Indian Novel* (1989); *The Five-Dollar Smile and Other Stories* (1990); *Show Business* (1992); and *India: From Midnight to the Millennium* (1997), published on the fiftieth anniversary of India's independence. In 2001 he published his latest novel, *Riot: A Love Story* (published outside the United States as *Riot: A Novel*).

Even though he has led a nomadic life, Tharoor is emphatic that his idea of home is India and calls his books "explorations of Indianness." He is, self-consciously, an *Indian* writer, with a mission to uphold Indianness in his works even though his profession necessitates that he should live in New York. Straddling two worlds, he strikes a balance between them. He is aware that the two cultures he bridges are very different and do not necessarily mix, but he is confident that they can complement each other. From his Manhattan apartment, or wherever his job takes him, he uses memory and imagination to transport him back to India and recreate the reality of the subcontinent, its sights and smells, its heat, dust, and earthiness. Thus, he makes a conscious effort to reclaim stories for the Indian people, a discipline that he feels is the duty of every Indian writer—to hold up a mirror to India.

His books are strongly committed to this idea of Indianness, each in a different way, beginning with the first novel that catapulted him into the limelight. *The Great Indian Novel* is engaged in the conscious evocation of the *Mahabharata*, albeit in a parodic form. This ambitious novel dexterously retells a 2,000-year-old tale in contemporary terms, replacing legendary characters with recognizable twentieth-century ones from the Indian political scenario. More like a jigsaw puzzle, the novel presents a game that can best be played by the initiated reader, fully intelligible only to those who have read and understood the ancient Indian epic. It is comparable with *Ulysses* in the sense that James Joyce in the latter was doing with the Homeric epic what Shashi Tharoor does with Vyas's: drawing a parallel between contemporaneity and antiquity. Tharoor's work gives evidence of the writer's fascination with the great Indian epic in the manner that he plays with it, twists and reshapes it in the retelling.

Show Business: A Novel (1991) is again satirical in tone but has a much narrower focus: the ambition, greed, and deception of the film world. It is the story of a critically ill Bollywood superstar, Ashok Banjara, as he lies suspended between life and death in the intensive care unit of a plush Bombay hospital. He sees a recap of his life's struggles, from its humble beginnings, past the various milestones, to the zenith of power and popularity. In a manner resembling the celluloid fantasies of the hero's screen life, *Show Business* blends levity and seriousness. Written on an epic scale with many stories within the overarching tale, the novel is not just a spoof of Bombay cinema but also a story about the art of narration. Simultaneously, it explores the dividing line between illusion and reality: which of the two is authentic and how much credence should one give to it? Tharoor seems to suggest that the two are interdependent and must be found together. Incidentally, Ashok Banjara is a pseudonym Tharoor used when he wrote as a university student even though the author does not consider Banjara as his alter ego. The novel was made into a motion picture entitled *Bollywood*. Although the book is about mass entertainment, and Tharoor knows fully well that his novels are not meant for the masses, he packages his ideas in an intellectual format, presenting them in the novel form, showing that it is possible to revitalize and reinvent popular forms of culture.

India: From Midnight to Millennium sums up the challenges the country has faced over the last 50 years and attempts to visualize the future that lies ahead. There are chapters devoted to diverse topics like the partition of 1947, the caste system that still lingers in the country, the democratic setup, and the role Indira Gandhi has played in shaping the present state of affairs. He takes into cognizance the problem of illiteracy, of corruption in high circles, and of the violence that mars the political and social scene from time to time. Yet despite these depressing subjects, Shashi Tharoor remains optimistic about the future of the country and is confident that the country will find solutions for its problems. It seems as though he is deliberately trying to demolish negative stereotypes about India and present it as a successful independent nation. In doing so, his book renders a contrasting alternative to the Western world that he inhabits, even though his perspective remains that of a privileged member of the upper class.

Riot: A Love Story is a departure from his previous works—less satirical and more of an exploration of religion, cultural differences, and, especially, human relationships. Summing it up in a single sentence, Tharoor says that the book is about love, hate, the clash of cultures, the ownership of history, and the impossibility of knowing the truth. Here, for the first time in his novels, he introduces an American character around whom the action will revolve—a woman who is killed in a communal riot at the beginning of the novel. The rest of the narrative provides different perspectives on this central event. To study the mechanics of a communal riot, Tharoor accessed a report written by a college friend who was a senior officer in the Indian Administrative Services during a similar riot in Madhya Pradesh. However, the novel is not a dry summary of statistics or impersonal data: on the contrary, it takes the episode from an intimate angle, focusing on a personal relationship that becomes entangled in a larger political imbroglio. At the same time, it experiments with various forms of narration: the narrative presents an assortment of fragments, bits and pieces of information, transcripts of interviews, newspaper reports, and other factual data: these pieces ultimately form a collage, all the fragments presenting different aspects of the central event—the death of a woman called Priscilla Hart. How did she die and what were the circumstances? The story is shown through the pieces in the collagelike canvas, the mode of narration being as unusual as the tale itself.

Although he is located in the Western world, Tharoor's frequent trips to India and his emotional attachments to his country ensure that he is at home in both these worlds that have awarded him unstinted recognition. While there is no denying that his is a formidable talent on the present literary scene, he has been more fortunate than most of his contemporaries in the awards his works have received, both in India and in the West. Tharoor is the winner of numerous journalism and literary awards, including a Commonwealth Writers Prize for a First Novel awarded to *The Great Indian Novel.* In 1998, he received the Excelsior Award for excellence in literature from the Association of Indians in America (AIA) and the Network of Indian Professionals (NetIP). In May 2000 he was awarded the honorary degree of Doctor of Letters in International Affairs from the University of Puget Sound.

Manju Jaidka

Further Reading

Dhar, T. N. "Entering History through the Backdoor with Tharoor and Vijayan." *History-Fiction Interface in the Indian English Novel.* Ed. T. N. Dhar. New Delhi: Prestige, 1999. 207–48.

Field, Michele. "The Double Life of Shashi Tharoor," *ABC Radio Magazine* Oct. 1994. 28 Nov. 2002 <http://shashitharoor.com/profile/doublelife.htm>.

Mathew, Lukose. "The Elegant Satirist." *The Week Magazine* 6 July 1998. 28 Nov. 2002 <http://www.the-week.com/98jul26/life2.htm>.

Official Web site of Shashi Tharoor: <http://www.shashitharoor.com/>.

Shrikandath, Sivaram. "Back to Roots: Interview." *The Week Magazine* 22 Sept. 2002. 28 Nov. 2002 <http://www.the-week.com/22sep22/life9.htm>.

"The World Is His Oyster: Indians Abroad Who Make Us Proud." *Gentleman* Mar. 1999. 28 Nov. 2002 <http://shashitharoor.com/profile/worldishisoyster.htm>.

Third World

After World War II the Euro-American bloc of states together came to be called the First World, while the communist-socialist states including the Soviet Union, China, North Korea, North Vietnam, and until recently, Eastern Europe, were collectively termed as the Second World. The term *Third World* (Tiers Monde) itself, was first coined by French demographer Alfred Sauvy in 1952, to refer to a possible Third Estate or Third Way before and during the French Revolution. However, the term Third World soon began to be deployed to refer to the newly decolonized states of Africa, Asia, Latin America, and the Middle East. The Third World soon came to acquire both political and economic dimensions. Politically, the Third World emerged at the Bandung Conference of 1955, which led to the establishment of the Non-Aligned Movement—a result of the desire of the newly independent states to find a middle path between the conflicting and opposed ideologies of the First and the Second Worlds. The political coming together of the Third World countries led to the realization of their common economic disadvantages. The NAM countries started what came to be known as the Group of 77, in order to assert themselves and bring to the attention of the developed countries the linkages between factors such as social welfare, war, debt traps, and poverty. They strove to form a negotiating bloc, the aim of which was to bring about a fairer distribution of global income through agreed structural changes to the world economy. Thus, while the newly decolonized countries adopted the term *Third World* to generate and represent a new sense of common identity and a growing unity of purpose, the term also came to be used by others for the most diverse purposes and meanings. The term *Third World* is not universally accepted. Some prefer other terms such as the South, nonindustrialized countries, underdeveloped countries, undeveloped countries, maldeveloped countries, and emerging nations. The term Third World is probably the one most widely used in the media today.

With the changes in the political map of the world since the late 1980s, the relevance of the term Third World has been questioned on several grounds. The disintegration of the Soviet Union and consequently of the Second World and the simultaneous dominance of U.S. capitalism has made the term meaningless. Secondly, the new developments in the global order are also seen as contributing to the deterioration and relative disuse of the expression *Third World*. The term has increasingly acquired negative connotations, which paint a unidimensional picture that shows all the Third World countries as suffering from problems of economic dependency, neocolonialism and debt burdens, poverty, and high birth rates.

A third ground for criticism is the collective use of the term *Third World* to lump together all developing countries of Africa, Asia, Latin America, and the Middle East. The Third World is sharply differentiated, for it includes countries on various levels of economic development. And despite the living conditions of the rural poor and the urban slum dwellers, the ruling elites of most Third World countries are relatively quite wealthy. Sangari is critical of the way the term *Third World* is used by the West to indiscriminately lump together vastly different places. She argues that the term *Third World* is "a term that both signifies and blurs the functioning of an economic, political, and imaginary geography able to unite vast and vastly differentiated areas of the world into a single 'underdeveloped' terrain" (217). In response to this criticism, another category, the term *Fourth World,* has been instituted to include some of the poorest countries, especially in Africa. The introduction of new categories based on economic parameters serves to strengthen the argument that the term *Third World* has undergone radical redefinition from when it was first coined: from implying a third and alternative force, to the present day understanding of its being indicative of economic dependency and low living standards.

Sumati Nagrath

Victor Rangel-Ribeiro. Courtesy of Beck's Studio.

Further Reading

Miller, J. D. B. *The Politics of the Third World.* Oxford: Oxford UP, 1965.

Muni, S. D. "The Third World: Concept and Controversy" *Third World Quarterly* I [3] (1979): 119–28.

Sangari, Kumkum. "The Politics of the Possible." *The Nature and Context of Minority Discourse.* Eds. A. JanMohamed and D. Lloyd. New York: Oxford UP, 1990.

Worsley, P. *The Third World.* London: Weidenfeld and Nicolson, 1964.

Tivolem by Victor Rangel-Ribeiro

Victor Rangel-Ribeiro was past his seventieth birthday when *Tivolem* was published. Considering that he was born in Goa in 1925, migrated to Bombay in 1939, and has lived in the United States since 1956, it is surprising that he would choose, as the bucolic fictional setting of his novel, the tiny, nondescript village of Tivolem, in Portuguese India. But as Rangel-Ribeiro has himself admitted in an interview in *Goa Today,* "The pull of the mother country is very strong." Indeed for the author

it must be Herculean, for he has provided a map of the village "prepared by Fr. F.X.A.C. Pires, Curate of the Church of St. Cornelius the Contrite, March '33." This is the reader's first introduction to the created landscape of a spatial entity whose spectrum is far from tiny, for it encompasses the entire gamut of world affairs during the author's lifetime—Europe between the wars and the imminent collapse of global empires.

The action of the main plot begins, oddly enough, in "Spring 1933"—odd because in tropical Goa, the seasons are hardly noted by divisions that prevail in the world's temperate zones. Be that as it may, the novel's young heroine, Marie-Santana, stands aboard the *Lilavati,* a ship that negotiates the Mandovi River on its final passage from the Portuguese colony of Mozambique in Africa where she has lived for the past 23 years. This crossing of the river becomes a frequent motif in the novel symbolizing many transitions—from one religion (Roman Catholicism dominates) to the next (Hinduism's presence in the village is duly noted, though very minor); from Westernization (lovers serenade each other to the compositions of Beethoven and Bach) to indigenous coastal Konkan culture; from European languages (the major characters communicate in English and Portuguese) to vernacular ones (Marathi and Konkani, not to mention "the elegant Hindi of the north" are often uttered in this multilingual world). River and sea crossings with their attendant sirens remind the characters "of oceans ever to be crossed, of events beyond our control."

It is clear that Marie-Santana's return to her roots is motivated by an escape of some sort, a flight toward maternal comfort afforded by her grandmother's home. Slowly, it becomes evident that this woman, no spring chicken herself—in fact, clearly an old maid if the standards of her own times be applied, for she is in her mid-thirties, is fleeing an unhappy love affair, the sudden loss of a fortune and dealing with the residual grief from having recently become orphaned.

Before long, Marie-Santana finds herself embroiled in the affairs of the village whose *dramatis personae* include Father Jose Mascarenhas, vicar of the church and pastor of Tivolem; the local justice of the peace, Gustavo Tellis; principal of the local English high school, Prakash Tendulkar; the postmaster, Cajetan Braganza; Eusebio Pinto, back from the Persian Gulf; Senhor Teosodio Rodrigues, back from Africa; the local gossip Josephine Aunty; the village thief, Lazarinh'; Angelinh' Granny; Forttu, Atmaram, Dona Elena, and Dona Esmeralda, among others. But, most important of all, she makes the acquaintance of her earnest young neighbor, Simon Fernandes, a violin-wielding immigre, also returning to his roots after a long time spent overseas. It is not merely their disconnectedness from the culture around them, connecting this unlikely couple in a romantic bond that becomes the

talk of Tivolem, but the whiff of scandal that surrounds them both—the source of which the reader must then attempt to dig out and forgive.

Life in Tivolem is quiet, punctuated only by the excitement of events in the world outside its rice fields. Gathered around a short-wave radio, the sole one in the village and a status symbol of the community's wealthy landowner, Tivolem's intelligentsia tries to make sense and predictions about Hitler's advances on Allied soil, and the rise of Nazism. While closer to home, in British India, Mahatma Gandhi's rebellion against imperialism through the efforts of the Congress Party is minutely documented and dissected. Dialogue between the characters is consistently piquant, rife with the peculiar idiom that only small-town living can bestow upon its inhabitants' tongues, and hence always just on the verge of amusement. Noteworthy, too, is the novelist's wit, his pervasive sense of humor, and the tolerance with which he looks upon the village scoundrels, all of whom, of course, are lovable crooks. What is most fascinating is the interiority of the characters themselves who remain blissfully oblivious to the fact that they are a source of great comic effects. Only the chief protagonists, the outsiders as it were, Marie-Santana and Simon, who maintain a balcony view of the proceedings, look upon the action as if it is being played out upon one of life's great cultural stages. This detachedness makes them bond with the reader while isolating them from the goings-on of the mainstream.

As in the case of much contemporary fiction, the structure of Rangel-Ribeiro's novel allows many chapters to coexist as separate entities, detached from the continuity of the main plot line. It was these subplots, in fact, that first inspired the novel's creation. It was a relatively minor character called Lazarinh', the local village rapscallion, who inspired the broad sweep that the novel eventually covered, for he had appeared, decades ago, in the guise of "The Miscreant," the title of a short story that was first published in the *Iowa Review.* Building steadily from that base, Rangel-Ribeiro then peopled his landscape with the kind of personages that lend themselves to facile stereotyping. Much in the form of a medieval morality play, many of the characters represent some vice or virtue of human nature. But the author has handled them with such skill that they never degenerate into cardboard conceptions of abstract qualities, rather, they are superbly fleshed out to become individuals about whose outcomes we do begin to care.

Following the tradition of several multiethnic U.S. writers who choose a locale and build individual stories around it (Gloria Naylor's *The Women of Brewster Place* and *Linden Hills* and Amy Tan's *The Joy Luck Club,* for instance, come to mind), Rangel-Ribeiro presents a series of vignettes, each portraying, in the manner of a fully flavored mango or cashew, a juicy slice of Goan life. The honest and appropriate renditions of tragic events that occur through the story allow the narrative to strike a sound balance between nostalgia for an idyllic village and the evolving lives and predicaments of its inhabitants. Rangel-Ribeiro is at his strongest when exploring issues of individual and collective identity and gently probing the characters' spiritual sensibilities.

Toward the end of the novel the fortunes of the main protagonists revert, in the manner of conservative Roman Catholic Indians in the 1930s, to an expected form of grief resolution. This might disappoint some readers, but it is the most authentic of the endings that Rangel-Ribeiro might have written. One reviewer has complained that "the trove of stories (naive fairy tales at best, facile mysticism at worst) . . . never quite justify the novel's conservative Catholic conclusion," but this denouement is most natural in the circum-stances, and hardly a reason to denounce the entire work. In fact, an unraveling of the mysteries that surround the former lives of the main protagonists helps us to see how they were connected long before they first met and teaches us, as one of the characters puts it, that "our lives themselves are like the crossings and re-crossings of a river" (329). This is the philosophy that lies beneath the affairs of the motley lot that make up the funny and fascinating world of Victor Rangel-Ribeiro's *Tivolem.*

Rochelle Almeida

Further Reading

Anonymous. "A Story to be Savored." Review of Tivolem. Kirkus Review. 15 May 1998. <www.powells.com>.

Dwarakanath, Kala. "Novel Explores A Search for Life in Goan Village." Rev. of *Tivolem* by Victor Rangel-Ribeiro. *India Abroad.*

Rangel-Ribeiro, Victor. Interview with Derek Alger. 1–3.. , <http://www.pifmagazine.com>.

"A Story to Be Savored." *Kirkus Review* 15 May 1998. <http://www.powells.com/biblio>.

Stuhr, Rebecca. *Library Journal Fiction Reviews* 1 Apr. 1998.

Tepper, Anderson. Rev. of *Tivolem* by Victor Rangel-Ribeiro. *The New York Times Book Reviews* 5 June 1998. <http://www.goa-world.net/books/village.htm>.

Travelogues of V. S. Naipaul

In a career spanning 45 years, Naipaul has produced 26 books. Of these, 13 or fully half the output, consist of nonfiction in the form of travelogues, essays, and at least one historical memoir. If Naipaul's fiction, particularly his early novels, did much to establish his literary credentials, his documentary output has generated controversy, animus, and sometimes admiration, without detracting from, and actually greatly enhancing, his stature as a writer.

His first nonfiction book, *Middle Passage,* part travelogue and part commentary about the Caribbean, was commissioned by the Trinidadian government (he received a travel grant for this purpose), and was written in 1962. *India: An Area of*

Darkness followed this in 1964, after an extended first visit to India. From the 1970s to 1990s, he traveled extensively. Out of these travels emerged a series of such books, which were set almost uniformly in parts of the world that were troubled, lesser developed and had formerly been under colonial domination. *Among the Believers,* a book on Islam was written after travels in Iran, Pakistan, Malaysia, and Indonesia in 1981. In 1998, after revisiting these countries, Naipaul wrote *Beyond Belief,* the second of his Islamic books. *India: A Wounded Civilization* and *India: A Million Mutinies Now* were written in 1977 (immediately after the Emergency) and 1990 respectively. *A Congo Diary,* written in 1980, is about sub-Saharan Africa. Other books recount journeys in South America, Mauritius, and the southern United States.

In these books, Naipaul purports to understand the peculiar dynamics of the country or culture he is exploring, against an unstated background of what he later came to label as the "universal civilization." (In his 1990 Wriston lecture at the Manhattan Institute for Policy Research, Naipaul described the universal civilization as one that gives people the freedom to pursue happiness. Implicitly he seems to equate this with Western values, ideals and civilization.) Typically, each book contains accounts of people and places he has met or visited in the country or region. Interspersed with these accounts he provides sharply critical commentary about the country's culture, history, society, and values, and reasons for its social, political, and economic "backwardness" as compared to Western countries. Sometimes his statements have been seen as politically incorrect, even provocative. For example, in *Among the Believers* he says, "Islam sanctified rage—rage about the faith, political rage: one could be like the other." There is a distinct darkness of perspective and tone in these books (relative to his four

previous novels); especially in the books from the *Middle Passage* to *Among the Believers,* something that is perhaps not coincidentally reflected in the fiction he produced during the same period.

Not surprisingly, many critics, and not just those with allegiances to the respective countries and cultures of the political left, have reacted negatively. Typical negative reactions fall into three categories: dismissal based on accusations of faulty or flawed analyses, outrage, and muted or direct charges of racism or class-based bias. Some critics have also charged Naipaul with being the "mouthpiece" of Western, formerly colonial powers, engaged in exonerating themselves. Nissim Ezekiel concluded that while at a detailed level many of Naipaul's observations on India in *India: An Area of Darkness* had relevance, his analysis and the overall picture he drew was false and one sided. Edward Said has accused Naipaul of "having stopped thinking and [having] become a mental suicide," and having had an "intellectual catastrophe." Selwyn Cudjoe says, "Naipaul has clearly aligned himself and his writing on the side of the dominant class."

Some literary critics have sidestepped the controversies and focused on Naipaul's own background and motivations, in terms of his search for, and understanding of, his identity as someone doubly displaced— first as a Hindu in Trinidad, then as a colonial in Britain. Dissanayake and Wickramagamage relate his writing to his efforts to attain "fuller comprehension of his own self-identity," while also charging him with adopting a "colonial gaze." Judith Levy speaks of Naipaul's "writing to create a self," meaning that he is constantly using his writing as an exploratory device to attain a sense of belonging or identity.

Many critics have admired Naipaul for his courage and ability to tell the truth as he sees it. Others have gone further and praised his clarity of vision. This has been the case particularly over the last 10 years, as Naipaul's own writing (fiction and non-fiction) has reacquired a more sympathetic tone, and as a fuller perspective on the large body of his work, taken collectively, emerges. Lillian Feder in her book, *Naipaul's Truth,* writes, "Naipaul's truth is the sum of continuous investigation in which his 'eye' becomes keener and his knowledge of the seeker himself deepens."

Vidiadhar Surajprasad Naipaul was born in Trinidad in 1932 into a Hindu family whose forebears emigrated from India two generations earlier. He went to England to attend the University College, Oxford, in 1950 and has stayed on since then, becoming a British citizen. Aside from a few part-time jobs as a BBC broadcaster for Caribbean voices and fiction reviewer for leading publications, Naipaul has always been a full-time author. His first book, a novel was published in 1957. Since then he has published 26 books, in both the literary fiction and nonfiction (travelogues, essays) genres. Exile, alienation and displacement, the effects of colonialism, and the chaos of postcolonialism in Third World societies are some of his major themes. Naipaul has been the recipient of several awards including the Booker Prize (for *A Free State* in 1971), the T. S. Eliot Award for Creative Writing, the David Cohen British Literature Prize for lifetime achievement in 1990, and the Nobel Prize for Literature in 2001. He was knighted by Queen Elizabeth in 1990.

Padma Chandrasekaran

Further Reading

Cudjoe, Selwyn. *V. S. Naipaul: A Materialist Reading.* Amherst: U of Massachusetts P, 1988.

Dissanayake, Wimal, and Carmen Wickramagamage. *Self and Colonial Desire: Travel Writings of V. S. Naipaul.* New York: Peter Lang, 1993.

Ezekiel, Nissim. "Naipaul's India and Mine." *New Writing in India.* Ed. Adil Jussawala. Harmondsworth, UK: Penguin, 1974.

Feder, Lillian. *Naipaul's Truth: The Making of a Writer.* New York: Rowman and Littlefield, 2000.

Levy, Judith. *V. S. Naipaul: Displacement and Autobiography.* New York: Garland, 1995.

Said, Edward. "An Intellectual Catastrophe." *Al Ahram Weekly* 389 (6–12 Aug. 1998).

U

Untouchable by Mulk Raj Anand

In 1930, Mulk Raj Anand began work on his first novel, *Untouchable,* whose source material was an amorphous mass of writing concerning his boyhood experiences. By 1932 the novel had been reworked, since in the interim period, Anand had come into contact with the teachings of Mahatma Gandhi and had become his disciple. Moreover, being a resident in colonial India, Anand had been subjected to racial discrimination by certain supercilious Englishmen. This compelled him to look afresh at *Untouchable*—which revolves around the travails of a sweeper boy, from the Hindu caste known as "untouchables"—with a sense of anger and despair. Yet, these feelings were tempered by the humility he learnt from Gandhi, and ultimately *Untouchable* emerged as a novel of rage and helplessness, but also of hope.

Untouchable handles a very conventional Hindu theme—ritual pollution—but examines it, and provides a solution that overtly echoes twentieth-century pragmatism. It follows the modernist credo of rejecting the approved public perspective on the selection and significance of themes, but injects into a discussion of those themes, instead, Anand's own socialist ethics. Thus it deliberately chooses the provocative topic of untouchability and observes its squalid preoccupation with dung and human excreta, and unflinchingly recounts the abuse by members of the higher castes toward the untouchables who clean this squalor.

Anand does not even pretend to know everything about Bakha, the sweeper boy. All he is concerned with are Bakha's thoughts and feelings for the 14 odd hours that he as the author chronicles in the novel. We know without much certainty that Bakha is about 19 years old. But we know more clearly that he is handsome, athletic, unusually sensitive, much abused, and overworked. His father is a *jemadar* (headman) of sweepers for the military regiment stationed in the northern Indian town of Bulashah, and Bakha himself is in charge of cleaning three rows of public latrines.

In the opening pages of the novel, Anand in a frenzy of description outlines his protagonist with thick brush strokes. The author realizes that even one day is too long a time to record in complete detail, as Bakha has much to see and learn during its length. Hence, the opening sets the fast pace of the novel, warning that the narration will be an assault on the senses, rendered awkward by the unusual associations it creates between people, places, and things. There are elements of the stream-of-consciousness mode of narration here, with Bakha as the center of consciousness; and yet each sentence is convincingly grounded in everyday reality.

The first lines of the book alone explain the physical place of all untouchables in Indian society: "The outcastes' colony was a group of mud-walled houses that clustered together in two rows, under the shadow of the town and cantonment, but outside their boundaries and separate from them" (9). The untouchable is an absolute outsider, lacking individuality and performing societies' vilest tasks in silence. But Anand, unlike Gandhi, refuses to romanticize this role. Thus, Anand reacts cautiously to Gandhi's comment during a speech to a huge gathering at Bulashah: "they [the untouchables] are cleaning Hindu society" (148). To this, Anand responds: "He [Bakha] felt like shouting to say that he, an Untouchable, was there, but he did not know what the Mahatma meant by 'cleaning Hindu society'" (148). Anand believes that Gandhi is the only means of achieving independence, and to openly criticize him for romanticizing the place of the untouchable will evoke the ire of the public; but he cannot pardon the romanticizing either, and so he steps into the mind of Bakha to document what an untouchable himself feels about this. Bakha knows that he cleans society in a very physical way—sweeping roads and cleaning latrines—and he is sensible enough to understand that the Mahatma's statement means more than just that. But exactly what more he cannot say, for he lacks the requisite education to understand its deeper significance. By this, Anand implies that Mahatma's message is yet to touch many Indians and that whenever it does, it raises several questions. Bakha has been told that his position is in no way inferior to that of any other Indian. But does the mere saying of this sweep away his troubles? Anand does not venture to answer this last question in any overt fashion, although he is aware that only a mod-

ern way of life will lead to an overall improvement in the lives of the outcastes. He makes his sentiments clear by including the antithetical characters of the Muslim poet, and the Oxford-educated barrister. Says the poet: "When the sweepers change their profession, they will no longer remain untouchables . . . [Indians must accept] the machine that clears dung without anyone having to handle it" (155). The barrister replies mockingly: "In fact, greater efficiency, better salesmanship, more mass-production, standardization, dictatorship of the sweepers" (155).

The poet has earlier confessed that though he loathes machines he will go against Gandhian doctrine and accept them. He then presents the best option to Bakha and his lot—the flush system. In contrast, the barrister imbued with Western materialism dismisses the entire notion of social upliftment and ridicules the concept of class equality. He cannot understand that the change that the poet and Gandhi advocate is one not based on mechanical progress alone but rather on organic change wherein every Indian finds courage and self-respect, fostered in the milieu of democracy.

When *Untouchable* was first published, it was greeted with a storm of criticism by British reviewers who failed to grasp its social-humanist concerns and deemed it "dirty," completely missing the way in which it attempted to sensitize the reader to an outrageous situation. However, it rapidly gained acceptance and esteem through the efforts of several British authors, notably E. M. Forster who prefaced the novel and described it as "indescribably clean" (v) and saw how the work explored the extents of human oppression and endurance and finally affirmed the possibility of self-respect and greatness in every human being.

Devapriyo Das

Further Reading

Anand, Mulk Raj. "The Story of My Experiment with a White Lie." *Indian Literature* 10.3 (1967): 28–43.

———. *Untouchable*. Harmondsworth, England: Penguin, 1986. References to the text are to this edition.

Dhawan, R. K. ed. *The Novels of Mulk Raj Anand.* New York: Prestige, 1992.

Fisher, Marlene. *The Wisdom of the Heart.* New Delhi: Sterling, 1985. 24–31.

George, C. J. *Mulk Raj Anand: His Art and Concerns.* New Delhi: Atlantic, 2000. 29–44, 198–99.

Niven, Alastair. *The Yoke of Pity.* New Delhi: Arnold-Heinemann, 1978. 46–55.

Pontes, Hilda. "A Select Checklist of Critical Responses to Mulk Raj Anand's *Untouchable.*" *The Journal of Commonwealth Literature* 23.1 (1988): 189–97.

Vijayasree, C. *Mulk Raj Anand: The Raj and the Writer.* Delhi: B. R. Publishing, 1998. 24–29.

V

Vakil, Ardashir

In *Beach Boy,* a novel published to high acclaim in Britain, author Ardarshir Vakil provides a glimpse into the typical adolescent experience of an upper-class urbanite in the cosmopolitan Indian city of Bombay. Joining the ranks of such classic novels as J. D. Salinger's *The Catcher in the Rye,* Thomas Wolf's *A Boy's Lif*e, and more recently, Nick Hornby's *About a Boy,* this semi-autobiographical novel recalls Vakil's youth during the 1970s in Bombay. Fitting perfectly within the parameters of contemporary adolescent literature, it explores the landscape of the mind of a precocious eight year old whose world revolves around the fascinations of Bollywood, the sexy sirens that comprise his neighbors, and the mouthwatering meals they offer. Something of a hedonist, even for his tender years, the protagonist Cyrus Readymoney, Parsi and privileged, ekes out his days sauntering from one apartment to the next in his high-rise building—that is, when he is not playing truant from school with a bunch of classmates who also suffer from similarly raging hormones.

Born in 1962 and now permanently based in Britain, where he works as a teacher in an inner city school, Vakil feels compelled to narrate stories about his growing years in a city that has provided a creative fodder for the likes of Salman Rushdie, whose early schooling experiences fill the first few pages of *Midnight's*

Children, and Vikram Chandra whose *Love and Longing in Bombay* also superbly exploits the scenic vignettes of the city. Cyrus' experiences as a student at St. Mary's School in Mazagoan, Bombay, have not even been disguised for the purposes of fiction. The vice principal of the school, then one Fr. Alban D'Mello, who was known for his sadistic streak, is openly portrayed as the kind of Jesuit tyrant that was every little boy's nightmare. Amazingly, easily recognizable characters from Byculla and Mazagoan populate these stories without even having their names changed: Horace Lillywhite, for instance, one of Cyrus Readymoney's bosom buddies in the novel, actually lived in Mazagoan in the 1970s and was schooled at St. Mary's. Not merely has he been mentioned by name, but his brother Neville and his mother—all of whom actually exist—feature in Readymoney's accounts. How the author could have added the standard disclaimer at the beginning of the book that neither the characters nor the episodes bear any resemblance to people in real life is quite perplexing. This is autobiography only very thinly clothed in the guise of fiction and, in major parts of the novel, no attempt has been made to camouflage anything that took place in Vakil's own childhood. Vakil admitted to Nonita Kahlra as most authors do of their first work of fiction, that much of the novel's substance is drawn from his own experiences and observations of growing up in Bombay, but he refused to agree that Cyrus Ready-money is indeed Ardarshir Vakil himself.

The backdrop for Readymoney's coming-of-age is the darkened Hindi cinema house where film hero Rajesh Khanna frolics with a herd of elephants in the blockbuster, *Haathi Mere Saathi.* As the strains of popular Hindi film music envelop the theater, Cyrus finds himself mouthing the lyrics and getting lost in the tinsel world of movie magic. Like most consumers of such unrealistic cinema, he is an escapist, seeking a release from the tension of his home and the perpetual conflict that engulfs his parents' marital relationship. It is not surprising to the reader that the Readymoneys do decide to divorce halfway through the novel, bringing Cyrus's carefree life to a screeching halt. Moving from his palatial bungalow on the Juhu shoreline, he relocates to a building in the heart of the city, where he becomes acquainted with a motley lot of eccentric neighbors, including the erstwhile Maharani of Bharatnagar. Shortly afterward, his father suffers a massive heart attack and seeks treatment in a ritzy hospital in Chicago from which he never returns. Cyrus's moorings are rudely snatched away from under his feet, and he undergoes the painful rites of passage that characterize all such awakenings into maturity. To the extent, then, that the chief protagonist makes his way laboriously from childhood to adulthood, the novel is timeless and defies location in any one social ethos. Its uniqueness lies in the specific cultural experiences that color Cyrus's domain and impact upon his youth. These include the peculiar combination of his Zoroastrian religious upbringing and his exposure to Roman Catholicism that comes from the priests at his school.

Readers are sucked willy-nilly into the breathless experiences of this boy's life. In the tantalizing descriptions he provides of fresh-caught *hilsa* and crispy *utthampams*

and *dosas* that he receives from charitable neighbors in whose homes he turns up exactly at mealtimes, Cyrus takes us into the realm of the varied appetites that make up one's childhood years. As he suffers the growing pains of being a teenager, he becomes aware of other appetites—carnal ones—that he satisfies vicariously by ogling the heaving bosoms of Hindi film heroines and the rapidly developing figures of the Maharani's adopted daughters next door. He finds new families and new homes in the all-encompassing affection that he is freely given. He takes a vacation in Kerala with the Krishnans, and goes to the movies with the Vermas, so that the adage, "It takes a village to raise a child," is proved poignantly true as he slowly struggles toward adolescence.

With praise coming from prestigious circles and with Salman Rushdie calling it "a highly original book, sharp, funny and fast" (Rushdie included an excerpt in his *Mirrorworks*), it is not surprisingly that the novel won the Betty Trask Award in England and was a finalist for the Whitbread Prize for first fiction. One of the most insightful reviews comes from Harald Leusman who states, "Vakil cleverly invents emotionally alternating hot and cold baths, into which he dunks his protagonist and which constitute a tough place of socialization. Cyrus's life is characterized by dichotomies: sensuality and severity, material abundance and disintegration, security and indifference."

While the rambunctious romp through the pages of the novel keeps the reader transfixed, its conclusion has been disappointing for most reviewers. Unable to bring his reminiscences to a credible conclusion, the novelist careens toward the end, leaving readers hanging over the fate of the vast portrait gallery of characters with whom they have made intimate acquaintance. The author hurriedly and abruptly ends Cyrus's saga, but not without assuring the reader that having made the journey from adolescence to adulthood, Cyrus and his affairs will settle acceptably.

Rochelle Almeida

Further Reading

Curtis, Sarah. "A Bombay Boyhood." Rev. of *Beach Boy* by Ardashir Vakil. *Times Literary Supplement* (30 May 1997): 23.

Hawley, John C. "Bombay Boys in Ardashir Vakil and Firdaus Kanga." *South Asian Review* 22 (2001): 40–56.

Kafka, Paul. "Eating Up and Growing Up in Bombay." *The Boston Globe* (2 Aug. 1998): F2.

Leusmann, Harald. "Growing Pains in Bombay." Rev. of *Beach Boy* by Ardashir Vakil. <http://www.social.chass.ncsu.edu/jouvert/v5i1/leusma.htm.

Lundegaard, Erik. Review of *Beach Boy*. Originally published in *The Seattle Times,* 1998. <http://www.home.earthlink.net/~elundegaard/beachboy/htm>.

Selected Bibliography

Anthologies

Anand, Mulk Raj, and Eleanor Zelliot, eds. *An Anthology of Dalit Literature*. New Delhi: Gyan, 1992.

Behl, Aditya, and David Nichols, eds. *The Penguin New Writing in India*. New Delhi: Penguin, 1994.

Bhalla, Alok, ed. *Stories about the Partition of India*. 3 vols. New Delhi: HarperCollins, 1994.

Bhushan, V. N. ed. *The Blazing Shrine: An Anthology of One-Act Plays in English by Indian Writers*. Bombay: Padma, 1941.

Butalia, Urvashi, and Ritu Mennon, eds. *In Other Words: New Writing by Indian Women*. New Delhi: Kali for Women, 1992.

Chatterjee, Debjani, ed. *The Redbeck Anthology of British South Asian Poetry*. Bradford, U.K.: Redbeck, 2000.

Chaudhuri, Amit, ed. *The Picador Book of Modern Indian Literature*. London: Picador, 2001.

Cowasjee, Saros, and Shiv K. Kumar, eds. *Modern Indian Short Stories*. New Delhi: Oxford UP, 1982.

Dharwadker, Vinay, and A. K. Ramanujan, eds. *The Oxford Anthology of Modern Indian Poetry*. New Delhi: Oxford UP, 1994.

Ezekiel, Nissim, and Meenakshi Mukherjee, eds. *Another India: An Anthology of Contemporary Indian Fiction and Poetry*. New Delhi: Penguin, 1990.

Farooqi, Nasir Ahmad, ed. *Under the Green Canopy: Selections from Contemporary Creative Writings of Pakistan*. Lahore: Afro-Asian Book Club, 1966.

Gooneratne, Yasmine, ed. *Stories from Sri Lanka*. Hong Kong: Heinemann Asia, 1979.

Goonetilleke, D.C.R.A., ed. *Modern Sri Lankan Stories: An Anthology*. New Delhi: Sri Satguru, 1986.

———, ed. *The Penguin New Writing in Sri Lanka*. New Delhi: Penguin, 1992.

———, ed. *The Penguin Book of Modern Sri Lankan Stories*. New Delhi: Penguin, 1996.

———, ed. *Sri Lankan Literature in English 1948–1998: A Golden Jubilee Anniversary Independence Anthology*. Colombo, Sri Lanka: Dept. of Cultural Affairs, 1998.

Hameed, Yasmin, and Asif Aslam Farrukhi, eds. *So That You Can Know Me: An Anthology of Pakistani Women Writers*. N. p.: Garnet World Fiction Series, 1999.

Haq, Kaiser, ed. *Contemporary Indian Poetry*. Columbus: Ohio State UP, 1990.

Hashmi, Alamgir, ed. *Pakistani Literature: The Contemporary English Writers*. Islamabad: Gulmohar, 1978.

Holmstrom, Lakshmi, ed. *The Inner Courtyard: Stories by Indian Women*. London: Virago, 1990.

Kaul, H. K. ed. *Poetry India: Voices in the Making*. Delhi: Arnold, 1989.

Khwaja, Waqas Ahmad, ed. *Cactus: An Anthology of Pakistani Literature*. Lahore: Writers Group Publications, 1985.

———. *Mornings in the Wilderness: Readings in Pakistani Literature*. Lahore: Sang-e-Meel, 1988.

———, ed. *Pakistani Short Stories*. New Delhi: UBS, 1992.

Mehrotra, Arvind Krishna, ed. *Oxford Anthology of Twelve Modern Indian Poets*. New Delhi: Oxford UP, 1992.

Obeyesekere, Ranjani, ed. *Anthology of Modern Writing from Sri Lanka.* Tucson: U of Arizona P, 1981.

Paniker, Ayyappa K. ed. *Modern Indian Poetry in English.* Delhi: Sahitya Akademi, 1991.

Paranjape, Makarand, ed. *Indian Poetry in English.* Madras: Macmillan, 1993.

Ratti, Rakesh, ed. *A Lotus of Another Color: An Unfolding of the South Asian Gay and Lesbian Experience.* Boston: Alyson, 1993.

Ray, David, and Amritjit Singh, eds. *India: An Anthology of Contemporary Writing.* Columbus: Ohio State UP, 1983.

Rushdie, Salman, and Elizabeth West, eds. *The Vintage Book of Indian Writing 1947–1997* [also titled, *Mirrorwork: Fifty Years of Indian Writing 1947–1997*]. New York: Henry Holt, 1997; London: Vintage, 1997.

Said, Yunus. *Ten Years of Vision.* Karachi, Pakistan: Vision, 1963.

Sarang, Vilas, ed. *Indian English Poetry Since 1950: An Anthology.* Hyderabad: Orient Longman, 1989.

Satchidanandan, K. ed. *Gestures: An Anthology of South Asian Poetry.* New Delhi: Sahitya Akademi, 1996.

Shamsie, Muneeza, ed. *A Dragonfly in the Sun.* Karachi: Oxford UP, 1998.

Souza, Eunice de, ed. *Nine Indian Women Poets: An Anthology.* New Delhi: Oxford UP, 1997.

Tharu, Susie, and K. Lalita, eds. *Women Writing in India: 600 B.C. to the Present.* 2 vols. New York: Feminist P, 1991, 1993.

Wijesinha, Rajiva, ed. *An Anthology of Contemporary Sri Lankan Poetry in English.* Colombo, Sri Lanka: English Association of Sri Lanka, 2000.

Zide, Arlene R. K., ed. *In Their Own Voice: The Penguin Anthology of Contemporary Indian Women Poets.* New Delhi: Penguin, 1993.

Secondary Sources

Afshar, Haleh. *Women and Politics in the Third World.* New York: Routledge, 1996.

Ahmad, Aijaz. *In Theory: Classes, Nations, Literatures.* London: Verso, 1992.

Ahmed, Leila. *Women and Gender in Islam.* New Haven: Yale UP, 1992.

Allen, Richard, and Harish Trivedi, eds. *Literature and Nation: Britain and India 1800–1990.* London: Routledge, 2000.

Bahri, Deepika, and Mary Vasudeva, eds. *Between the Lines: South Asians and Postcoloniality.* Philadelphia: Temple UP, 1996.

Benson, Eugene, and L. W. Conolly, eds. *Encyclopedia of Postcolonial Literatures in English.* London: Routledge, 1994.

Bhabha, Homi, ed. *Nation and Narration.* London: Routledge, 1990.

———. *The Location of Culture.* London: Routledge, 1994.

Bhadra, Gautam, Gyan Prakash, and Susie Tharu, eds. *Subaltern Studies X.* New Delhi: Oxford UP, 1999.

Bhatta, S. Krishna. *Indian English Drama: A Critical Study.* New Delhi: Sterling, 1987.

Breckenridge, Carol A., ed. *Consuming Modernity: Public Culture in South Asia.* Minneapolis: U of Minnesota P, 1995.

Brennan, Timothy. *At Home in the World: Cosmopolitanism Now.* Cambridge: Harvard UP, 1997.

Butalia, Urvashi. *The Other Side of Silence: Voices from the Partition of India.* Durham: Duke UP, 2000.

Chatterjee, Partha. *Nationalist Thought and the Colonial World: A Derivative Discourse.* Minneapolis: U of Minnesota P, 1986.

Chavan, Sunanda P. *The Fair Voice: A Study of Indian Women Poets in English.* New Delhi: Sterling, 1984.

Chew, Shirley, and Anna Rutherford, eds. *Unbecoming Daughters of the Empire.* Sydney, Australia: Dangaroo, 1993.

Dhareshwar, Vivek, P. Sudhir, and Tejaswini Niranjana. *Interrogating Modernity: Culture and Colonialism in India.* Calcutta: Seagull, 1993.

Dodiya, Jaydipsingh, ed. *Perspectives on Indian English Fiction.* New Delhi: Dominant, 2002.

Gandhi, Leela. *Postcolonial Theory: A Critical Introduction.* New York: Columbia UP, 1998.

Gooneratne, Yasmine. *English Literature in Ceylon: 1815–1878.* Dehiwala, Sri Lanka: Tisara Prakasakayo, 1968.

———, ed. *Celebrating Sri Lankan Women's English Writing: 1948–2000.* Colombo: Women's Education and Research Centre, 2002.

Guha, Ranajit, ed. *Subaltern Studies I–VI.* New Delhi: Oxford UP, 1982–1989.

Gupta, Dipankar. *Mistaken Modernity: India between Worlds.* New Delhi: HarperCollins, 2000.

Harrex, S. C. *The Fire and the Offering: The English Language Novel of India, 1935–1970,* Vols. I and II. Calcutta: Writers Workshop, 1977.

Hawley, John C., ed. *Encyclopedia of Postcolonial Studies.* Westport: Greenwood, 2001.

Hubel, Teresa. *Whose India? The Independence Struggle in British and Indian Fiction and History.* Durham: Duke UP, 1996.

JanMohamed, Abdul, and David Lloyd. *The Nature and Context of Minority Discourse.* New York: Oxford UP, 1990.

Joshi, Priya. *In Another Country: Colonialism, Culture, and the English Novel in India.* New York: Columbia UP, 2002.

Kachru, Braj. *The Indianization of English: The English Language in India.* New Delhi: Oxford UP, 1983.

Kirpal, Viney, ed. *The New Indian Novel in English: A Study of the 1980s.* New Delhi: Allied, 1990.

Knippling, Alpana Sharma. "R. K. Narayan, Raja Rao, and Modern English Discourse in Colonial India." *Modern Fiction Studies* 39:1 (Spring 1993): 169–86.

Krishna, Sankaran. *Postcolonial Insecurities: India, Sri Lanka, and the Question of Nationhood.* Minneapolis: U of Minnesota P, 1999.

Kumar, Gajendra. *Indian English Literature: A New Perspective.* New Delhi: Sarup, 2001.

Kuruvilla, M. I. "Modern Sri Lankan Poetry." *Studies in World Literature.* Ed. M. I. Kuruvilla New Delhi: Sterling, 1984.

Landry, Donna, and Gerald Maclean, eds. *The Spivak Reader.* London: Routledge, 1996.

McCutchion, David. *Indian Writing in English.* Calcutta: Writers Workshop, 1969.

Mehrotra, Arvind Krishna. *A History of Indian Literature in English.* New York: Columbia UP, 2003.

Mel, Neloufer de, ed. *Essays on Sri Lankan Poetry in English.* Colombo, Sri Lanka: English Association of Sri Lanka, 1995.

Mel, Neloufer de, and Minoli Samarakkody, eds. *Writing and Inheritance: Women's Writing in Sri Lanka 1860–1948.* Colombo: Women's Education and Research Centre, 2002.

Mittapalli, Rajeshwar, and Alessandro Monti, eds. *Post-Independence Indian English Fiction.* New Delhi: Atlantic, 2001.

Mohan, Ramesh, ed. *Indian Writing in English.* Bombay: Orient Longman, 1978.

Mukherjee, Meenakshi. *The Twice Born Fiction: Themes and Techniques of the Indian Novel in English.* New Delhi: Heinemann, 1971.

———. *Realism and Reality: The Novel and Society in India.* New Delhi: Oxford UP, 1988.

———. *The Perishable Empire: Essays on Indian Writing in English.* New Delhi: Oxford UP, 2000.

Mund, Shubhendu Kumar. *The Indian Novel in English: Its Birth and Development.* New Delhi: Prachi Prakashan, 1997.

Naik, M. K. *A History of Indian English Literature.* New Delhi: Sahitya Akademi, 1982.

———. *Dimensions of Indian English Literature.* New York: Apt Books, 1984.

———, and Shyamala A. Narayan. *Indian English Literature 1980–2000: A Critical Survey.* New Delhi: Pencraft International, 2001.

Nandy, Ashis. *The Intimate Enemy: Loss and Recovery of Self under Colonialism.* New Delhi: Oxford UP, 1983.

Narasimhaiah, C. D. *The Swan and the Eagle: Essays on Indian English Literature.* 1968. Simla: Indian Institute of Advanced Study, 1987.

Natarajan, Nalini, ed. *Handbook of Twentieth-Century Literatures of India.* Westport: Greenwood, 1996.

Nelson, Emmanuel, ed. *Writers of the Indian Diaspora: A Bio-Bibliographical Critical Sourcebook.* Westport: Greenwood, 1993.

The New Yorker (special fiction issue, India focus) 23–30, June 1997.

Niranjana, Tejaswini. *Siting Translation: History, Post-Structuralism and the Colonial Context.* Berkeley: U of California P, 1992.

O'Hanlon, Rosalind. "Recovering the Subject: *Subaltern Studies* and Histories of Resistance in Colonial South Asia." *Modern Asian Studies* 22.1 (1988): 189–224.

Pandey, Sudhakar, and Freya Barua, eds. *New Directions in Indian Drama.* New Delhi: Prestige, 1994.

Pollock, Sheldon, ed. *Literary Cultures in History: Reconstructions from South Asia.* Berkeley: U of California P, 2003.

Prasad, Amar Nath, ed. *Studies in Indian English Fiction.* New Delhi: Sarup, 2001.

Rahman, Tariq. *A History of Pakistani Literature in English.* Lahore: Vanguard, 1991.

Raizada, Harish. *The Lotus and the Rose: Indian Fiction in English (1850–1947).* Aligarh: Aligarh Muslim U, 1978.

Said, Edward. *Orientalism.* New York: Pantheon, 1978.

Said, Edward. *Culture and Imperialism.* New York: Alfred A. Knopf, 1993.

Sanga, Jaina C., ed. *South Asian Novelists in English: An A-to-Z Guide.* Westport: Greenwood, 2003.

Sarkar, Sumit. *Modern India: 1885–1947.* Madras: Macmillan, 1983.

Sarma, G. P. *Nationalism in Indo-Anglian Fiction.* New Delhi: Sterling, 1978.

Sharma, K. K. ed. *Indo-English Literature: A Collection of Critical Essays.* Ghaziabad: Vimal Prakashan, 1977.

Shirwadkar, Meena. *Image of Woman in the Indo-Anglian Novel.* New Delhi: Sterling, 1979.

Singh, Pramod Kumar. *Five Contemporary Indian Novelists: An Anthology of Critical Studies on Mulk Raj Anand, Raja Rao, R. K. Narayan, Kamala Markandaya, and Bhabani Bhattacharya.* Jaipur: Book Enclave, 2001.

Spivak, Gayatri Chakravorty. *In Other Worlds: Essays in Cultural Politics.* New York: Methuen, 1987.

———. *Outside in the Teaching Machine.* New York: Routledge, 1993.

———. *A Critique of Postcolonial Reason: Toward a History of the Vanishing Present.* Cambridge: Harvard UP, 1999.

———. *Other Asias.* Malden: Blackwell, 2003.

Sukthankar, Ashwini, ed. *Facing the Mirror: Lesbian Writing from India.* New Delhi: Penguin, 1999.

Suleri, Sara. *The Rhetoric of English India.* Chicago: U of Chicago P, 1992.

Sumbamurthy, V. Indira. *An Annotated Bibliography of Indian English Fiction.* 3 vols. Delhi: Atlantic P, 2001.

Tickell, Alex. "How Many Pakistans? Questions of Space and Identity in the Writing of Partition." *Ariel* 33.3 (2001):155–80.

Vanita, Ruth, ed. *Queering India: Same-Sex Love and Eroticism in Indian Culture and Society.* London: Routledge, 2002.

Verghese, C. Paul. *Problems of the Indian Creative Writer in English.* Bombay: Somaiya, 1971.

Verma, K. D. *The Indian Imagination: Critical Essays on Indian Writing in English.* New York: Palgrave, 2000.

Viswanathan, Gauri. *Masks of Conquest: Literary Study and British Rule in India.* New York: Columbia UP, 1989.

Wijesinha, Rajiva. *Breaking Bounds: Essays on Sri Lankan Writers in English.* Belihuloya, Sri Lanka: Sabaragamuwa UP, 1997.

Williams, H. M. *Indo-Anglian Literature 1800–1970: A Survey.* Columbia: South Asia Books, 1977.

Zaman, Niaz. *A Divided Legacy: The Partition in Selected Novels of India, Pakistan, and Bangladesh.* Dhaka, Bangladesh: n.p. 1999.

Periodicals

ARIEL (A Review of International English Literature)

Asian Studies Review

Biblio: A Review of Books (New Delhi)

Contemporary South Asia (British Association for South Asian Studies)

CRNLE Journal (Centre for Research in the New Literatures in English, Australia)

Indian Literature (Sahitya Akademi)

Indian Writing Today

Interventions: International Journal of Postcolonial Studies
Journal of Commonwealth and Postcolonial Studies
Journal of South Asia Women Studies
The Journal of Commonwealth Literature
The Journal of English Literary Club (U of Peshawar)
The Journal of Indian Writing in English
Kunapipi: Journal of Postcolonial Writing (Wollongong, Australia)
(Mahfil) Journal of South Asian Literature
Modern Asian Studies
Navasilu: Journal of the English Association of Sri Lanka
Phoenix: Sri Lanka Journal of English in the Commonwealth
South Asia: Journal of South Asian Studies (Armidale, Australia)
South Asian Popular Culture
South Asian Review
The Sri Lanka Journal of the Humanities
Wasafiri
World Literature Today

Index

About the Editor and Contributors

JAINA C. SANGA received her Ph.D. in English from Case Western Reserve University. She has published a number of articles and reviews in journals and books. She is the author of *Salman Rushdie's Postcolonial Metaphors: Migration, Translation, Hybridity, Blasphemy, Globalization* (Greenwood, 2001), and the editor of *South Asian Novelists in English: An A-to-Z Guide* (Greenwood, 2003).

TANYA AGATHOCLEOUS is assistant professor of English at Yale University. She teaches nineteenth- and twentieth-century British literature and culture and postcolonial literature and theory. She is the co-editor of *Teaching Literature: A Handbook* (2002), author of *George Orwell: Battling Big Brother* (2000), and has also published on Victorian cosmopolitanism.

RACHANA AGGARWAL is completing a graduate degree in English literature from Mumbai University.

HENA AHMAD is assistant professor of English at Truman State University. She has published articles on Anita Desai and Kamala Markandaya. She is currently working on a book-length project on postnational feminism in Third World women's literature.

ROCHELLE ALMEIDA received her Ph.D. in literature from the University of Bombay and a second doctorate in multiethnic studies from St. John's University, New York. She currently teaches South Asian studies at New York University and English at Fairfield University in Connecticut. She is the author of *Originality and Imitation: Indianness in the Novels of Kamala Markandaya* (2000). Her book, *The Politics of Mourning: Grief-Management in Contemporary Cross-Cultural Fiction,* is forthcoming.

PRATHIMA ANANDAN is a Ph.D. candidate in English at the University of Oxford, England. Her research focuses on postcolonial cultural studies, especially the overlap between trauma, history, gender, and childhood.

ANUPAMA ARORA is a doctoral candidate in English at Tufts University, where she is currently writing her dissertation on South Asian American life writing.

SARTAZ AZIZ is a lecturer in English at the California State University, Hayward. He has coauthored with Dr. Thomas Cleary, *Twilight Goddess: Spiritual Feminism & Feminine Spirituality* (2000).

LOPAMUDRA BASU is a Ph.D. candidate in English at the Graduate Center of the City University of New York. Her dissertation examines the novels of Salman Rushdie, Bapsi Sidhwa, Ngugi wa Thiong'o, and Buchi Emecheta. Her interview with Meena Alexander was published in *Social Text 72*. Basu is Secretary of the South Asian Literary Association.

KANIKA BATRA is a senior lecturer of English at Janki Devi Memorial College, University of Delhi, India. She is currently enrolled in the doctoral program at Loyola University, Chicago, where she is Crown Fellow in the Humanities.

TAPATI BHARADWAJ is a doctoral student in the Department of English at Loyola University, Chicago. She is studying postcolonial studies, feminist theories, and the literatures of the twentieth century. She has written book reviews for *Feminist Teacher* and *Jouvert: A Journal of Postcolonial Studies.*

MEENAKSHI BHARAT is a reader in English at Sri Venkateswara College, University of Delhi. She is a well-known translator, reviewer, and critic. She is the author of *The Ultimate Colony: The Child in Postcolonial Fiction* (2003).

NANDINI BHAUTOO-DEWNARAIN is a lecturer at the University of Mauritius where she has taught English literature for the past 10 years. Her areas of interest are postcolonialism, postmodernism, South Asia, and diasporic writing.

MAMTA BHERWAN has served as the vice principal of the MPB School of Journalism. She is a freelance writer and the author of *Essence of Vedas, Kena Upanishad.*

DONOVAN S. BRAUD received his M.A. in English from Loyola University, Chicago, where he serves as the director of Writing Centers. He has written for *Tribe* magazine.

TESS E. CHAKKALAKAL teaches English at Williams College, Williamstown, Massachusetts. She received her Ph.D. from York University in Toronto.

PADMAJA CHALLAKERE is assistant professor of English at University of St. Thomas. Her interests include British literature, Black British cinema, and urban renewal. She has published articles on the works of Mukul Kesavan, Salman Rushdie, and Hanif Kureishi. She is finishing a book manuscript titled, "Reconfiguring London: Urban Thematics in the Work of Hanif Kureishi and Zadie Smith."

PADMA CHANDRASEKARAN is a software technology executive and entrepreneur in Chennai, India. Her interests also include South Asian literature in English, philosophy, history, and Indian classical music.

MICHAEL W. COX is adjunct assistant professor of English and Writing at the University of Pittsburgh at Johnstown. His essays and short stories have appeared in *South Asian Review, New York Times Magazine, Best American Essays, New Letters, Columbia,* and other periodicals and literary quarterlies. He is currently completing a dissertation on subversive writing in modern American literature.

DEVAPRIYO DAS is a graduate student in English at the University of Mumbai. He has coedited *Ithaka,* the literary journal of the Department of English at St. Xavier's College in Mumbai, and he has published papers on Lewis Carroll, George Orwell, and children's literature. He was also a reporter with the *Times of India,* Mumbai, and has published poems in the *Bombay English Association Magazine.*

JIGNA DESAI is assistant professor in the Department of Women's Studies at the University of Minnesota. She is currently working on a book on the emergence and formation of a South Asian diasporic cinema in the United States, Canada, and England, forthcoming in 2003. She has also published essays in *Social Texts* and *South Asian Popular Culture.*

MAUREEN E. RUPRECHT FADEM is a teaching fellow in the English and Women's Studies Departments at Hunter College of the City University of New York. She has also taught at Baruch College, Fordham University, and the Borough of Manhattan Community College. She is pursuing a Ph.D. in English at the Graduate Center of CUNY.

HELEN ASQUINE FAZIO is a Ph.D. candidate at Rutgers University. Her dissertation focuses on classical Hindu mythology in the writings of Shashi Tharoor, Gita Mehta, Vikram Chandra, and Manil Suri, and in the paintings of Madhvi Parekh, Chitrovanu Mazumdar, and Vinod Dave. At Rutgers, she teaches in the Comparative Literature Program, as well as in the Department of Asian Languages and Cultures.

NIHAL FERNANDO is senior lecturer in English at the University of Peradeniya, Sri Lanka. He has published on R. K. Narayan, Punyakante Wijeniake, James Goonewardene, and Carl Muller.

RUTH FORSYTHE is chair of the Department of English and founder of the Global Studies Program at Winona State University in Minnesota, where she teaches courses in comparative literature and modern fiction. She has written articles on Hayashi Fumiko, Shusaku Endo, and Kazuo Ichiguro.

MICHAEL J. FRANKLIN teaches English at the University of Wales, Swansea. He has edited *Sir William Jones: Selected Poetical and Prose Works* (1995),

Representing India: Indian Culture and Imperial Control (2000), and *The European Discovery of India: Key Indological Sources of Romanticism* (2001). He has also written a critical biography on Sir William Jones (1995) and has authored a series of articles on the Hastings circle that forms the current focus of his research.

ANTHONY R. GUNERATNE is associate professor of communication at Florida Atlantic University and has published extensively in the fields of postcolonial literature and cinematic traditions. His most recent work is the edited anthology *Re-thinking Third Cinema* (2003).

DANA HANSEN recently completed her master's thesis on the writings of Salman Rushdie. She is currently teaching and working as a freelance writer and photographer in Toronto, Canada.

JOHN C. HAWLEY is associate professor of English at Santa Clara University. He has edited 10 books, most recently the *Encyclopedia of Postcolonial Studies* (Greenwood, 2001), *Postcolonial, Queer: Theoretical Intersections* (2001), and *Divine Aporia: Postmodern Conversations about the Other* (Bucknell UP, 2000).

KELLIE HOLZER is a doctoral student in English and Women's Studies at the University of Washington. Her research focuses on feminist and postcolonial theories, transnationalism, and South Asian diasporic literature.

HUSNE JAHAN has taught English at Rutgers University, Rider University, and Santa Clara University. She is the author of two television plays, a book *Life Stories: Case Studies in Poverty Alleviation,* several conference papers, and magazine articles. She received her B.A. and M.A. from the University of Dhaka and her Ph.D. from the University of Wales.

MANJU JAIDKA, professor and chair of the English Department at Panjab University, Chandigarh, India, is the author of six books and about 30 articles. Her books include, *T. S. Eliot's Use of Popular Sources* (1996), *From Slant to Straight: Recent Trends in Women's Poetry* (2000), and *Twentieth-Century English and American Poetry: An Annotated Anthology* (2002). She has been a Fulbright Fellow at Harvard and Yale Universities. She pioneered the India Chapter of MELUS (the Society for the Study of the Multi-Ethnic Literature of the United States) and organizes its annual international conferences.

FEROZA JUSSAWALLA is professor of English at the University of New Mexico. She is the editor of *Conversations with V.S. Naipaul* (1997) and *Interviews with Writers of the Postcolonial World* (1992). She is the author of *Family Quarrels: Towards a Criticism of Indian Writing in English* (1985) and *Chiffon Saris,* a collection of poetry (2003).

SUKESHI KAMRA is assistant professor in the Department of English at Carleton University. She is the author of *Bearing Witness: Partition, Indepen-*

dence, End of the Raj (2002) and has published articles on Salman Rushdie, Rohinton Mistry and partition literature. She is currently working on popular culture and the Indian nationalist movement.

SHUCHI KOTHARI is a lecturer in the Department of Film, Television, and Media Studies at the University of Auckland, New Zealand. She is also a screenplay writer and works in the film industries in New Zealand, India, and the United States.

JOHN LANGAN is a Ph.D. candidate in English at the CUNY Graduate Center. He is also an adjunct instructor at SUNY New Paltz. His nonfiction has appeared in *Lovecraft Studies, Fantasy Commentator,* and *South Asian Novelists in English.* His fiction has appeared in *The Magazine of Fantasy & Science Fiction.*

CAROL E. LEON teaches in the English department at the University of Malaya, Kuala Lumpur, Malaysia. Her research interests include postcolonial literature and eighteenth-century and contemporary travel writings. She has written "'Dwelling-in Travel': Spatial Representation in Michael Ondaatje's *Running in the Family*" in *Creative Communication.* (2000).

HARVEEN SACHDEVA MANN is associate professor of English at Loyola University, Chicago. She has published extensively on postcolonial literature and theory and is currently completing a book on feminism and nationalism in South Asian women's writing.

SUHAAN MEHTA is a graduate student in the Department of English at Mumbai University in India.

JASON HOWARD MEZEY received his Ph.D. at the University of Iowa. His research and teaching interests include the literature of partition, Bollywood film, and world Anglophone literature. He has published on James Joyce and Raja Rao. He has taught at the New College of Florida and Whitman College, and is a member of the English department at Saint Joseph's University.

NAYANIKA MOOKHERJEE is a research fellow in social anthropology at the University of Sussex, England. Her Ph.D. in anthropology is from the School of Oriental and African Studies, University of London. She has published articles in edited collections such as *South Asian Masculinities* (2003), and *Critical Reflections on Gender and the South Asian Diaspora* (2003).

MELANIE A. MURRAY received a B.A. and M.A in literature from the Open University. She is currently a doctoral student at University College Northampton, England, researching postcolonial literatures of Sri Lanka and the Caribbean.

SUMATI NAGRATH is a doctoral student at University College, Northampton, England. Her research focuses on the global flows of Bollywood-based fashion in a postcolonial context.

MASRUFA AYESHA NUSRAT is senior lecturer in English at East West University, Dhaka, Bangladesh. She received her M.A. in English literature from the University of Dhaka and an M.A. in English studies from the University of Nottingham, England.

PUSHPA N. PAREKH is associate professor in English and the director of the Honors Program at Spelman College, Atlanta, Georgia. She is the author of *Response to Failure: Poetry of Gerard Manley Hopkins, Francis Thompson, Lionel Johnson, and Dylan Thomas* (1998) and co-editor of *Postcolonial African Writers: A Bio-Bibliographical Critical Sourcebook* (Greenwood, 1998). She has also published chapters and articles on British, American, and postcolonial literature.

SUNEETA PATNAYAK is currently working on her dissertation on diasporic women writers in the United States. She teaches English in a local college in Chandigarh, India.

PREMILA PAUL is a reader in English at the American College, Madurai, India. She is the author of *The Novels of Mulk Raj Anand: A Thematic Study* (1983) and many articles on Indian literature and feminist literature.

S. W. PERERA is professor of English at the University of Peradeniya and editor of the *Sri Lanka Journal of the Humanities*. His research on postcolonial/expatriate/Sri Lankan writing has appeared in several journals. He is the bibliographical representative in Sri Lanka for *The Journal of Commonwealth Literature* and was chairperson of the Commonwealth Writers' Prize (Eurasia) in 2002/2003. He has been the recipient of several commonwealth and Fulbright awards.

N. POOVALINGAM is lecturer in English at Manonmaniam Sundaranar University in Tamilnadu, India.

JANET M. POWERS has been teaching South Asian literature and civilization at Gettysburg College since 1965. She has published a number of articles on the novels of Raja Rao and on South Asian women writers who write in English. She holds a Ph.D. from the University of Wisconsin–Madison, an M.A. from the University of Wisconsin–Madison, and an M.A. from the University of Michigan.

G. J. V. PRASAD teaches at the Centre of Linguistics and English, Jawaharlal Nehru University, New Delhi, India. He has written a novel, *A Clean Breast* (1993), a book of poems, *In Delhi without a Visa* (1996), and co-edited a book of short stories, *Imaging the Other* (1999). He is also the author of *Continuities in Indian English Poetry: Nation Language Form* (1999) and has published monographs on the Indian English dramatist, Mahesh Dattani, and the Australian, David Williamson. He is the current editor of *JSL: The Journal of the School of Language, Literature and Culture Studies*.

V. G. JULIE RAJAN is a Ph.D. candidate in comparative literature at Rutgers University, New Brunswick, where she is focusing on gender and religious representation in contemporary texts written by South Asian women in English. A freelance writer since 1996, Rajan has explored social issues relating to improving the status of women and minorities. She is on the editorial board for various Web sites including *Monsoon Magazine* and *Exit 9*.

ANURADHA RAMANUJAN is lecturer in English at Janaki Devi Memorial College, University of Delhi, India. She is currently pursuing a doctoral degree at the University of Florida where she is an alumni fellow in the Department of English. Her research interests focus on the intersections of gender, caste, and communalism in contemporary India.

VICTOR RANGEL-RIBEIRO is a fiction writer. His publications include a collection of short stories, *Loving Ayesha* (2003) and a novel, *Tivolem* (1998). He has also written *Damoreau: Classic Bel Canto Technique* (1997), *Chamber Music: An International Guide* (1991; coauthor, Robert Markel), and *Baroque Music: A Practical Guide for the Performer* (1980). He was awarded the NYFA Fiction Fellowship in 1990 and the Milkweed National Fiction Prize for his first novel in 1998. He is a member of the international online teaching faculty at Fairleigh-Dickinson University.

K. SUNEETHA RANI teaches English at the University of Hyderabad in India. Her Ph.D. is in the area of Australian aboriginal women's writing. She also translates literature from English to Telugu and Telugu to English.

PALLAVI RASTOGI is assistant professor of English at Utah State University. She is completing a book-length project entitled, "Indianizing England: Cosmopolitanism in Colonial and Post-Colonial Narratives of Travel."

T. RAVICHANDRAN is assistant professor of English at the Indian Institute of Technology, Kanpur, India. He has written many research articles and poems, as well as a book-length work, "Understanding Postmodern Identity through the Fictional Labyrinths of John Barth and Thomas Pynchon."

MALA RENGANATHAN teaches English at Assam University in Silchar, India. Her doctoral work is on Maria Irene Fornes, a Cuban American dramaturge. She was a Fulbright Fellow in the Long Island University's (New York) Theatre and Film Department. She was also a recipient of the ASIA Fellowship for 2000–01 for her postdoctoral project on Chinese theater.

DIPLI SAIKIA has worked as an editor in the area of translated literatures in New Delhi. She is currently a doctoral student in England working on Sri Lankan literature.

NITI SAMPAT-PATEL received her Ph.D. at New York University and now teaches English and film studies at St. Xavier's College, Mumbai. She has published articles in several books and journals and has served on the editorial board for this volume. She is the author of *Postcolonial Masquerades* (2000).

PURVI SHAH is completing her doctoral studies in poetry and Asian American literature at Rutgers University. She has published articles in reference encyclopedias as well as journals such as *Amerasia* and the *Minnesota Review.* She is the executive director of Sakhi for South Asian Women, an antiviolence organization.

KRUPA SHANDILYA is a graduate student at the University of Rochester, New York. Her research focuses on postcolonial literature and theory with an emphasis on postcolonial feminism.

LAVINA D. SHANKAR is the co-editor of the multidisciplinary essay collection *A Part, Yet Apart: South Asians in Asian America* (1998). She has published numerous essays in different journals and books. She teaches Asian American and postcolonial literatures at Bates College in Maine. She is working on a book manuscript on South Asian American women's literature.

HOLLY SHI is professor of English at Winona State University. She teaches courses in linguistics and literature.

REBECCA SULTANA received her Ph.D. in postcolonial theory and literature from Texas Christian University, and is now professor of English at East West University in Dhaka, Bangladesh. Her interests include South Asian English literature, diaspora studies, and immigration issues.

HARISH TRIVEDI is professor of English at the University of Delhi and has been visiting professor at the University of Chicago and the University of London. He is the author of *Colonial Transactions: English Literature and India* (1993, rpt.1995), co-editor of *Interrogating Postcolonialism* (1996), *Postcolonial Translation* (1999), and *Literature and Nation: Britain and India 1800–1990* (2000), and has contributed a chapter, "Hindi and the Nation" in Sheldon Pollock (ed.), *Literary Cultures in History: Reconstructions from South Asia* (2003).

ABID VALI is a doctoral student in English at Loyola University, Chicago.

SCOTT D. WALKER is visiting assistant professor at Wake Forest University in Winston-Salem, North Carolina. He has published articles and presented papers on Vikram Chandra, Rohinton Mistry, and Salman Rushdie.

RAJIVA WIJESINHA obtained his doctorate in English from Oxford, England. He is currently professor of Languages at Sabaragamuwa University in Sri Lanka, as well as president of the Liberal Party of Sri Lanka. His novel *Servants* was recently translated into Italian, and short-listed for the Premio Nonino, Italy's major prize for translations of fiction. He is on the board of the *Journal of Commonwealth Literature* and consultant editor for Sri Lanka for the *Annotated Bibliography of English Studies.*